Understanding
Documents
for Genealogy
& Local History

UNDERSTANDING
DOCUMENTS
FOR GENEALOGY
& LOCAL HISTORY

BRUCE DURIE

The
History
Press

Published 2013

The History Press
The Mill, Brimscombe Port
Stroud, Gloucestershire, GL5 2QG
www.thehistorypress.co.uk

British Library Cataloguing in Publication Data.
A catalogue record for this book is available from the British Library.

isbn 978 0 7524 6464 0

Typesetting and origination by The History Press
Printed in Great Britain

Contents

Introduction

This book emerged from courses taught at the universities of Edinburgh and Strathclyde in Scotland, Guelph in Canada and elsewhere, and talks given at family history societies, local heritage groups and professional genealogy conferences throughout the UK, Europe and North America. That isn't a boast – nor a travelogue – it's a testament (appropriate word) to the current interest there is in older documents and their comprehension.

There are various overlapping reasons for this:

i. most amateur genealogists and family historians are finding that they have now seen just about every birth, marriage, death and census record they ever will, and are starting to discover that the brick walls they face can be scaled by looking for different sorts of documents;

ii. for the same reasons, professional genealogists are increasingly being asked to find, and then interpret, explain, translate and/or transcribe, whole new classes of records, many in manuscript, that they may be unfamiliar with;

iii. historians and students of history need to understand older documents too – and yet the teaching of palaeography seems to be a dying art in most universities;

iv. Latin has dropped off the radar at most schools, even the private ones, over the last couple of decades – although there are encouraging signs of a renaissance in Latin teaching in Scotland, at least.

It is the intention of this book to go beyond the usual collections of handwriting samples, and the 'here are some reproduced documents, now you're on your own' style of books that usually present 'templates' or actual document examples without much examination of why a particular document was constructed in that specific way. Unless you know which law had just been passed, or was about to be enacted, it may be hard to understand why a certain will or property transaction was written as it was. Likewise, the historical and geographical context can determine the shape and nature of a document – apprenticeship indentures spring to mind. Equally, there are regional variations in documents intended to achieve the same thing – you will find land inheritance details in an English will, but not in a Scottish testament before the 1860s. And, of course, the law is and was different in the assorted parts of the United Kingdom. All of that has been uppermost in mind when constructing this book. (Readers will perhaps excuse any inadequacies in detailed understanding of the law: it has changed so often and has been so variously interpreted by judges that it is occasionally hard to keep up with.)

Essentially, this is intended to be a handbook-cum-reference-cum-textbook for those embarking on the study of documents, and those who want an occasional refresher. There are extensive glossaries of legal and occupational terms, personal and place names and Latin and Scots words commonly encountered – although there is no substitute for a decent dictionary and grammar guide.

Most Scottish record images, unless otherwise stated, are reproduced here by the kind permission of George Mackenzie, until recently Keeper of the Records of Scotland, and their English equivalents courtesy of The National Archives, Kew.

ACKNOWLEDGEMENTS

This book is, as ever, for those who watched it emerge, like some rough beast slouching towards Bethlehem to be born.

The National Records of Scotland, The National Archives, Kew, and the Lyon Office, Edinburgh, were ever unstintingly helpful.

Thanks are due in particular to erstwhile colleagues and continuing friends Alasdair MacDonald (partner in palaeographic crime), Dr David McOmish (Mediaeval Latinist *sans pareil*) and Adrian Ailes (whose enthusiasm for the unreadable knows no bounds). The many and various students over the years who offered up documents because they were interesting, puzzling or (in many cases) unintelligible were a constant inspiration.

Finally, Charles Burnett, Esq., Ross Herald Extraordinary at the Court of the Lord Lyon, gets a more than honourable mention for this overheard conversation at Edinburgh Castle:

> American tourist (to young soldier on guard), pointing at the Royal Standard above the gateway: 'Say, son, what does that *Nemo Me Impune Lacessit* thing mean?'
> Soldier (after a quick glance): 'I think it means "No 10-ton trucks over the drawbridge", Sur.'

If only that sojer had had some schooling in Latin, history and heraldry!

Dr Bruce Durie was, until 2011, Course Director of the much-praised Professional Postgraduate Genealogical Studies programme at the University of Strathclyde in Glasgow. He now teaches mainly for the Universities of Edinburgh and Dundee. He has written numerous books on genealogy and local history, mostly for The History Press, plus Victorian crime and other fiction, and is best known for the long-running BBC Radio series *Digging Up Your Roots*.

www.brucedurie.co.uk

PART I

READING THE DOCUMENTS

I

Transcription and Palaeography

TRANSCRIPTION

The aim of making a transcription is to ensure that you – and others – can read the transcript alongside the document and make sense of both. That means getting the 'navigation' right as well as the words. For that reason, it is best to transcribe documents using the same line-lengths ('lineation').

Making a transcript is not an editing process – the idea is to record exactly what the text in the manuscript says, with all its faults and imperfections retained. Here is a straightforward example:

– Number the lines on a COPY of your document;
– Transcribe line by line: it's easier in a Word table;

On board the Active at Spithead. May 28th 1758

1 My Dear Bell, Before I left London I took care to make a proper
2 disposition of my worldly Concerns, and in such a manner as
3 I hope you are satisfied with, but one thing remains which I
4 cannot now avoid mentioning as I am going upon service, and
5 for the concealement of which, I ask pardon of God and of yourself
6 and indeed my inducement for concealing it from you, was to
7 avoid giving you uneasiness of any kind, especially as
8 the case was without Remedy. Indeed at the time I was soli-
9 citing you to marry I ought then to have requainted you
10 with it; but my fears of loosing you, prevailed over reason,
11 and I was also advised by a friend of both, to conceal it,
12 which I listned to the sooner, as I did not entail any Charge
13 on you, having a little income from my Company, which

    – Translate (if necessary) line by line where possible, but don't worry about it too much. If it's Latin, for instance, the word order will be so different that a strict lineation is impossible (see Chapter 2);

    – Add footnotes if you need to.

On board the Active[1] at Spithead May 28th 1758
1. My Dear Bell, Before I left London I took care to make you a proper
2. disposition of my worldly Concerns, and in such a manner as
3. I hope you are satisfied with, but one thing remains which I
4. cannot now avoid mentioning as I am going upon Service, and
5. for the concealment of which, I ask pardon of God and of yourself,
6. and indeed my inducement for concealing it from you was to
7. avoid giving you **xxx**[2] uneasiness of any kind, especially as
8. the case was without Remedy. Indeed, at the time I was solli
9. :citing[3] you to marry I ought then to have acquainted you
10. with it; but my fears of losing you, prevailed over reason,
11. and I was advised by a friend of both, to conceal it,
12. which I listened to the sooner, as I did not entail any Charge
13. on you, having a little income from my Company,[4] (which

Notes: 1. 'Active': name of a ship.
          2. Word crossed out, possibly 'any'.
          3. Colon used as a hyphenation.
          4. 'Company' in the military sense.

This is known as a 'full diplomatic' transcription: every feature of the script has been captured, including unusual spellings ('solliciting') and capitalisations ('Remedy').

Semi-diplomatic transcription

This is a further stage in the process. The transcriber makes changes in the interests of understanding and expanding abbreviations for example (see below), and modernising spellings, names and so on. However, it is necessary to indicate what has been done, so that a later reader can check, and if necessary, correct it. There are some conventions for this:

– Keep the lineation.
– Replace ampersands or other abbreviations for 'and' with the appropriate word: 'and' in English, '*et*' in Latin.
– Lower any raised letters, expand contractions and italicise any letters added (wᵗ becomes w*ith*) or encase them in square brackets (umqˡ becomes umq[hi]l[e]).
– Expand terminal -*es*, -*is* or -*ys* graphs with their full forms.
– Replace 'fossil' letters (see p. 14) with their full modern forms.
– If there is any italic script in the document, show this by enclosing it in double slashes: '//…//'.
– If text has been deleted, show it as 'ᴛᴇxᴛ'.
– Text inserted by the writer between lines or in margins should be indicated by caret marks, for example: '^text^'.
– Put illegible text and missing or blank text in curly brackets: '{text}', '{…}'.
– Put any interpretative text added by the transcriber/editor in square brackets, for example: 'MDCCLXVI [1766]'.

PALAEOGRAPHY

What may at first sight be an unreadable manuscript can often turn out not to be as difficult as it first appears, especially as most official documents are written in a rather formulaic way. The majority of documents that family and local history researchers deal with will be wills and testaments, various deeds and charters, manorial records and court cases. These are normally in English or Scots but examples may be encountered in Latin up to the mid-1800s (see Chapters 5, 10, 16). Frankly, they would all be easy to read except for:

- Unusual (i.e. non-modern) letters.
- Idiosyncratic writing flourishes.
- Abbreviations.
- Unfamiliar words.

Hands

This book does not deal much with hands or documents much before the mid-1500s, so the main hands considered here are Court and Chancery hand in England, and Secretary hand in Scotland.

There are a number of forms of handwriting that you may come across when researching older documents. In rough chronological order, and somewhat simplified, these are:

Twelfth to fifteenth century

Book hands (also called Gothic or text hands). Formal writing, usually fairly readable, upright and angular, used in manuscript volumes and ecclesiastical works produced in scriptoria before the widespread availability of print. **Charter hand** was a development of this, with taller ascenders in some letters.

Court hands (also called Business hands). For business, government and literary purposes, more cursive than **Book** or **Charter hands** in order to cope with increased speed of writing. Some are quite stylised and particular to certain offices or professions, such as **Chancery hand** or **Exchequer hand**. They survived alongside **Secretary hand** (below).

Fifteenth to eighteenth century

Chancery hand. The official style used in the Royal Chancery at Westminster, and that continued to be used for the enrolment of Acts of Parliament until 1836. There were two forms, **Set** (or **Sett**) and **Fast**, which hardly differ.

Italic hand. Created in Italy around 1400, but derived from an older **Roman hand**, popular from the early 1500s and a major influence on **Secretary hand**.

Secretary hand. A development of the **Court hands** of the early sixteenth century and in general use for almost 200 years. It met the growing need for a universally intelligible script as the amount of business, legal and personal correspondence increased after the Renaissance. Another reason for its spread, strangely, was the arrival of printing at the end of the fifteenth century. There was less work for the medieval penman and the scriptoria, so they taught writing to the growing middle classes and took work as scriveners (document copyists).

There is a derivative called **Bastard hand**, which was in popular use.

Round hands. Gradually **Italic** overtook **Secretary** from the 1650s onwards, producing the **Italic hand** we use today.

See p. 20 for examples.

TRANSCRIPTION FOR REAL

Here is a strategy for deciphering a document.

If you can, find a document of the same type but written at a later date, when the handwriting is easier to read (there are examples of these throughout this book). Familiarise yourself with its structure, contents and vocabulary, then use the diplomatic of the later document to understand the older one.

Spend a few minutes just reading through your document, familiarising yourself with the hand, identifying where particular clauses start and making out any individual words that you can. Start by identifying typical words and phrases, names and places (likely to be in the index of where you found the document).

Go through the document, but not in too much detail, noting with a pencil where you can identify words or characters (see below). Start with the letters most similar to those of the modern day (see below).

Start constructing a letter list each time you come across a new letter form, especially for those letters likely to differ from our today's.

Go through the document a second time from the start and fill in the words and blanks.

If a phrase seems impenetrable, try entering it, as it, into a search engine: you never know, someone may have transcribed a very similar document.

Some letters are very similar to modern versions:

a, b, d, f, i/j, l, m, n, o, p, t, u/v/w, z

Some are very different in some hands:

c, e, g, h, k, q, r, s, x, y

Some are particular to a time and place: yogh (*gh* or *ngy*) and thorn (hard *th*), the ampersand &, the various forms of capital *D* in England.

Be especially careful with the letters that are likely to be confused:

b, s, u/v and *6*; *d* and *e*; *ll* and *w*; *sh*, *ch* and *th*; capital *M* and other three-minim characters (see below) or ligatures such as *in*, *w* and *iij*.

Abbreviations, brevigraphs and contractions

Presumably for reasons of speed and space, many writers of documents developed and used standard contractions for words or parts of words. We do the same today: the contraction etc. for the Latin 'et cetera', the brevigraphs ampersand & and what has come to be called the 'commercial at' or 'arroba', @. These and many more can be found in older documents. In some cases they are specific (see the versions in the list on p. 13) and some general (such as the 'suspension mark' indicating double letters).

First, some technical terms.

Minim. This is a single downstroke of the pen, forming *i* with one minim, *n* or *u* with two minims and *m* with three; in modern cursive writing, the *i* is dotted and the stroke joined up, so a *u* is different from an *n*; in old handwriting, they can be difficult to distinguish. See the Court hand example on p. 13, and consider how the word 'minimum' might look:

Diacritic. A mark added to a letter to indicate a particular phonetic value or stress, such as the c-cedilla in 'façade' or the accented final *é* of *neé*. It can also indicate an abbreviation (see below).

Jot and tittle. Ever wondered how this phrase (by which we mean 'every little detail') came about? It crops up in the 'Sermon on the Mount' (Matthew, 5: 17–18): 'Till heaven and earth pass, one jot or one tittle shall in no wise pass from the law'. That, of course, is an English translation: the original Greek said *iota* and *keraia* (κεραία), *iota* being the smallest letter of the Greek alphabet, but also coming to mean the dot above a letter *i* or some other diacritic; *keraia* meant a hook or serif, but came to mean a diacritic mark in printing or handwriting. The word 'tittle' derives from the Latin *title*, meaning superscription, but in medieval Latin, *titulus* was a diacritical mark, and it survives in the Spanish tilde used above, the letter *ñ* for example.

Suspension. This is a word in which the end has been cut off, as in *etc.* for *et cetera*, but sometimes down to a single letter, such as *AD* for *Anno Domini*.

Omission. A doubled *m* or *n* is represented by a tittle written over the preceding vowel or the remaining single letter, and an omitted *i* is similar, as in the word *cōmissōn* (commission) or *om~es* (*omnes*); similarly, *~t* is *et* (Latin 'and'). Some examples include: *antiqā* (*antiquam*), *hōiū* (*hominum*), *nō* (*non*), *quā* (*quam*).

Superscripts. Letters written above the line to indicate abbreviation, for examples: *exʳ* (executor), *pⁱmis* (*primis*), *qhlᵏ* (*quhilk*) (or 'which' (Scots)); *Mʳ* (Master), *nⁱ* (*nisi*), *sⁱ* (*sibi*), *uᶠ* (with), *uᶠʰ* (which).

Abbreviations and brevigraphs

ꝛ	and (&)
@	may be 'at', 'after', 'afore' or 'above', which should be obvious from the context: @*mentᵈ* could be 'aftermentioned' or 'abovementioned'. But it could stand for 'at', as when giving a price (three cows @ £1 each)
ꝵ	-er: *habꝵe* = *habere* (to have)
&̄	*etiam* (we have also)
÷	*est* (it is)
ꝛ	-cer-: *feꝛit* = *fecerit* (they did)
p / ꝑ / ꝓ	per-, par-, por-; as in person, parson, portioner pre- (as in presents) pro- (as in propose)
9	com- or con-: 9*tenta* = *contenta*; 9*peared* = *compeared*

ꝰ	-us = *huiꝰ* = *huius*, but can also be: -os or -ost = *pꝰ* or *ptꝰ* = *post*
3	-us at the end of dative or ablative plurals: *quib3* = *quibus*; -et: *hab3* = *habet* (he has)
ꬺ	-mer-: *aꬺciament* = *amerciament*; *ꬺcator* = *mercator*, merchant
ȝ	-ser-: *ȝervitor* = servant
ꝷ	-ter-: *et ceꝷa* = *et cetera*; *ꝷra* = *terra* (land)
ꭒ	-uer-: *pꭒ* = *puer* 'boy'; *f ꭒamus* = *fueramus* (we had)
ꝟ	-ver-: *ꝟitas* = *veritas* 'truth'; *vocaꝟis* = *vocaveris* (summon)
z	-tz: Fi**z** Gerald = FitzGerald; peasaun**z** = peasauntz (peasants)
ℯ	plural abbreviation for *es*, *is*, *ys*: as in Scott**ℯ** = Scottis, Scots(men) also signifies & or the letter *x*
ꝵ	-rum: *nostꝵ* = *nostrum* (our)
β	-ss (plural); *premiβa* = *premissa*, к alone = shillings (cf. German *scharfes*)
q̃ or q̗	-que 'and'; *at̃q* = *atque*
ꝑ, ħ, к, ₤	a line drawn through the head of a letter with an ascender can mean the addition of other letters, usually *is* or *e*, and can be confused with a double *tt*: *noꝱ* = *nobis*, *baꝱꝱs* = *ballius*; **h**eat = *habeat*; the capital form of barred-double L (for *Libris* 'pounds') has become our ₤ sign.
þ or y	this is not a *p* but a fossil letter known as *thorn*, imported from Runic script to denote the sound 'th' and usually looks like a *y*. This is what has led to the nonsense of 'ye olde tea shoppe', which no one ever said. The rule is: *yat* = *þat* = *that* (which is different from *ye* as an old form of *you*).
ȝ	This is the fossil letter known as *yogh* and is also Runic in origin, found mainly in Scots and indicating the sound 'ngy' as in the name Menzies, pronounced '*Ming-iss*', not '*Men-zeez*'.

Taken and adapted from *Court-hand restored, or, The student's assistant in reading old deeds, charters, records, etc.* by Andrew Wright of the Inner Temple, 9th edn (1879).

But for the moment, and without worrying about the letters too much, let's look at an actual document transcription from Scotland in 1613. Two tools were used to make the task easier:

    – A graphics program (paid-for, such as Adobe Photoshop or PaintShop Pro) or free (Gimp or Picasa) to make the document more readable by extracting relevant sections, changing the contrast or stretching it.

    – A free transcribing program, Transcript.exe, available from www.jacobboerema.nl/en/Freeware.htm

The point of stretching a document (changing the height but not the width) is to straighten out very slanted letters and also to introduce more space between the lines, both of which can help legibility.

The Transcript.exe program does not, let's be clear, do transcriptions, but it does display a graphic in one window and a text file in a separate window below, which removes the need to switch between, say, an image file and a Word document window on the desktop.

On pp. 17–18 is the document in question, showing the portion to be transcribed, how it looks after it has been cut out, and again after it has been stretched by 150 per cent and cropped slightly.

Contractions of the Court Hand.
The Syllables following are usually Abbreviated.

Armiger,		rus, rum.
ber, bus.		ter, tra, tur
cer, certum, cetera,		ver
di, do, dum.		ser sus.
ger, gra.		um.
mer mus.		fio, tio, cio.
ner		xer.
per, pra, pre, pro.		
quem, quam, que, quod	fra, gra, pra, tra.	

These Syllables following are usually contracted at the beginning and middle of words.

B	ber		Libertas, Gilbertus.
	cer		certus, liceret, doceri.
	gra		gratis, graviter. Rogerus.
	mer		mercator, meruit,
	ner		vulneravit. amerciamentum
	per		percussit, superius.
	pre		premissa, predictus.
	pro		prohibit, prout, prope.
	ter		terra, terrorum. mitteret
	fio & tio		proclamationem
	tra		transgressio, intravit, extra.
	ver		versus, diversas, verberavit.

Wright, A., *Court-hand restored, or, The student's assistant in reading old deeds, charters, records, etc.* (9th edn 1879).

This produces a Rich Text Format (.rtf) file that can be imported into Word or another text file and manipulated accordingly, including adding line numbers.

Full diplomatic transcription

1 ^Testamentum
2 testamentarum
3 Durie^
4 The testament testamentar and inventarie of þe gudes
5 geir and debtis of umq^{ll} Henrie Durie Mariner burgess of
6 Kirkaldie in the pareochin thereof and Shefdome of fyff þe
7 tyme of his deceis quha decessit in the moneth of {....} 1612
8 years ffaithfullie maid and gevin up be Agnes Maluill [=Melvill]
9 his relict spous executrix testamentar Nominat be him for
10 her self and in Name of agnes Issobell Margaret David
11 and ewpham Duries Law^{ll} bairnes to the said umq^{ll} Henrie
12 as executoris Nominat be him in his Latterwill efterspde
13 of þe dait the xiij day of may 1612 years
14 In the first the said umq^{ll} henrie þe tyme of his deceis foresaid
15 had the gudis and geir following towit the quarter of þe ship

Semi-diplomatic transcription

^Testamentum
testamentarum
Durie^
The testament testamentar and inventarie of the gudes
geir and debtis of umq[uhi]l[e] Henrie Durie Mariner burgess of
Kirkaldie w[ith]in the pareochin thereof and She[rif]fdome of fyff the
tyme of his deceis quha decessit in the moneth of {...} 1612
years ffaithfullie maid and gevin up be Agnes Maluill [=Melvill]
his relict spous executrix testamentar Nominat be him for
her self and in Name of agnes Issobell Margaret David
and ewpham Duries Law[fu]ll bairnes to the said umq[uhi]l[e] Henrie
as executoris Nominat be him in his Latterwill eftersp[ecifie]d
of the dait the xiij day of may 1612 years
In the first the said umq[uhi]l[e] henrie the tyme of his deceis foresaid
had the gudis and geir following towit the quarter of the ship

Modernised translation, punctuation added

Testament testamentar Durie
The testament testamentar and inventory of the goods,
gear and debts of the late Henry Durie, Mariner Burgess of
Kirkcaldy within the parish thereof and Sheriffdom of Fife, the
time of his decease who deceased the month of {blank} 1612
years. Faithfully made and given up by Agnes Melvill
his relict, spouse, executrix testamentar nominated by him for
herself and in name of Agnes, Issobell, Margaret, David

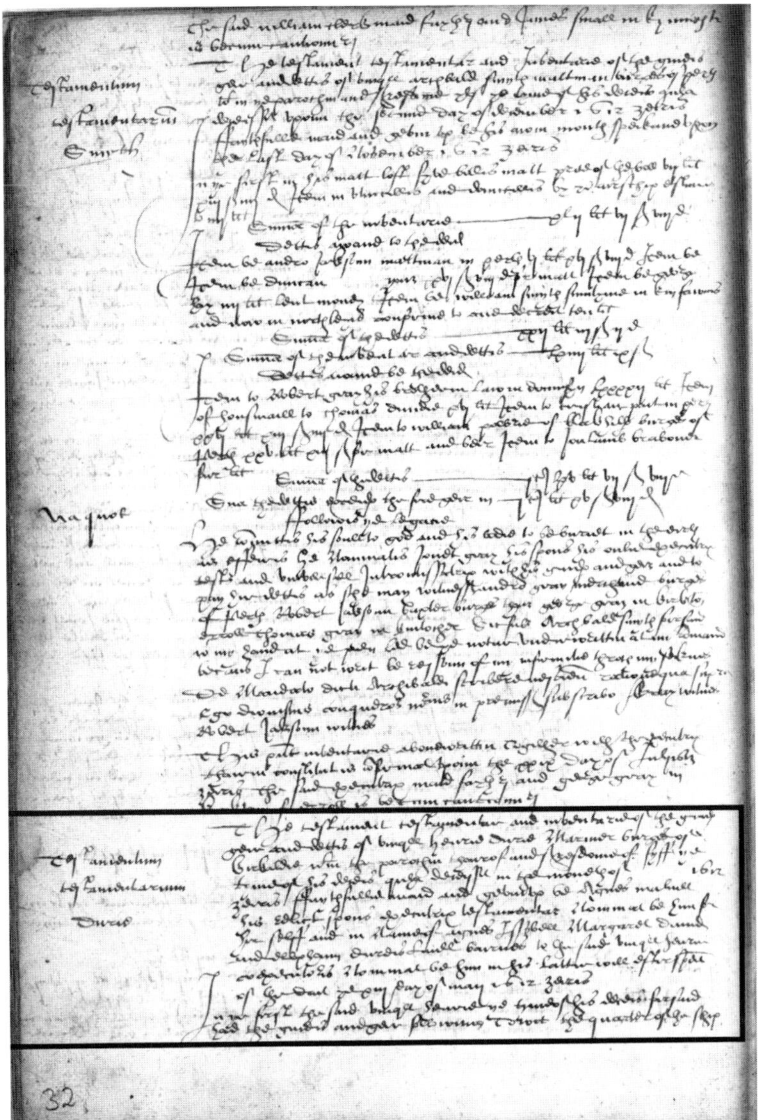

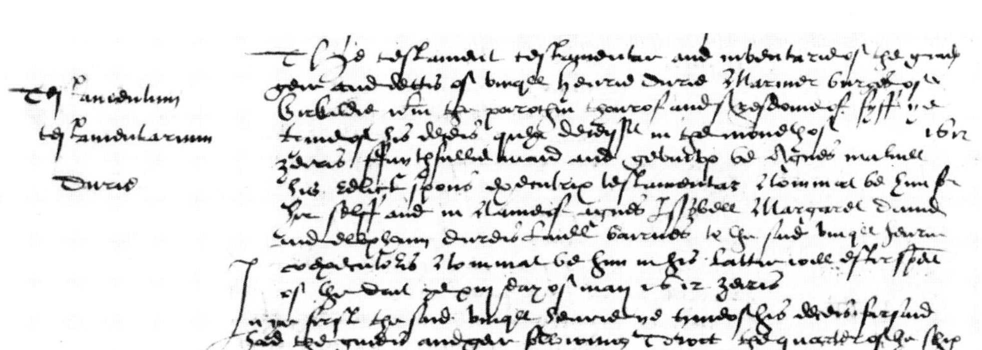

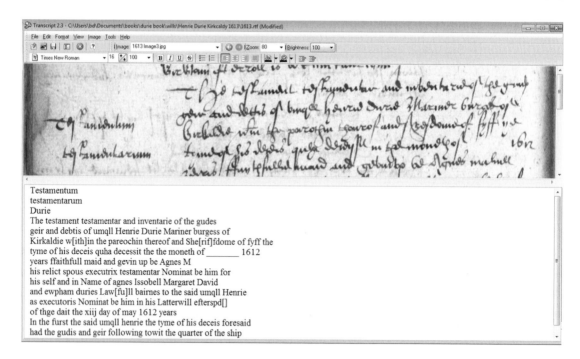

The image and text file displayed in the programme transcript.exe.

and Eupham Durie(s), Lawful children to the said late Henry,
as executors nominated by him in his Latterwill afterspecified
of the date the 13 May 1612.
In the first the said late Henrie the time of his decease foresaid
had the goods and gear following: towit, the quarter of the ship

Notice a number of things here:

– There are some unfamiliar Scots words (*umqhuill*) or legal terms ('faithfully made and given up') that will be covered in later chapters and in the Glossaries (Chpater 20).
– Punctuation is non-existent, so do not put it in to the diplomatic or semi-diplomatic versions (examples of when it does occur will appear later in the book).
– Plurals are irregular: for example '*executoris*', and the pluralised surname 'Duries' when more than one person called Durie is named.
– two forms *the* and *þe* are used indiscriminately (see line 13 for example).

Here's one to try. The transcription follows:

The will of John Muddock, proved 1 December 1791. *By kind permission of The National Archives*

John Muddock
In the Name of God Amen
I John Muddock of this Parish of Saint Mary White
Chapel virtualler & being in sound mind and memory
thanks be to God do make this my last will and
Testament in manner and form following *viz*: I give to

and bequeath unto my son James Muddock the sum
of fifty pounds principal money I give and bequeath
unto my son Emerson Muddock the sum of fifty
pounds principal money to be paid them by my
Executrix herewith named where they shall respectively
arrive at the age of eighteen years. I give and bequeath
unto Sarah Coward my wife's sister the sum of five
pounds to be paid out by my Executrix at the
expiration of Six months after decease All the rest
and residue I give and bequeath unto my dearly
beloved wife Susannah Muddock who I hereby make and
appoint my whole and sole Executrix of this my last
will and testament hereby revoking all former wills by
me made Dated this sixth day of November in the
year of our Lord One thousand seven hundred and
ninety one – John Muddock – Signed Sealed and
declared in the presence of us and in the presence of
the testator John Muddock and at his request we
have hereunto set our hands in the presence of each
other as witness to the same – George Foster –
John Muddock
This will was proved at London the first
day of December in the year of our Lord one thousand
seven hundred and ninety one before the worshipful
William Battine Doctor of Laws and Surrogate of the
Right Honourable Sir William Wynne Knight also Doctor
of Laws Master Keeper or Commissary of the prerogative
Count of Canterbury lawfully constituted by the oath of
Susannah otherwise Susanah Muddock widow the Relict
of the deceased and the sole executrix named in the
said will to whom administration was granted of all
and singular the goods chattels and credits of the
said deceased having been first sworn only to administer
[etc.]

LETTER FORMS OF HANDS AND EXAMPLES

Before embarking on more transcriptions, it is necessary to deal with the different letter forms used in the hands that may be encountered in older documents.

Court hand letter samples

On p. 21 is a particularly interesting example of a charter from the time of Edward III – largely because it is a forgery! It is not a modern fake but illustrates a fairly common practice in the fourteenth century, when the enrolment scribes of the Chancery were either careless or corruptible and would forge charters to be presented for royal confirmation, presumably where the original grants were missing (in this case, from the twelfth century).

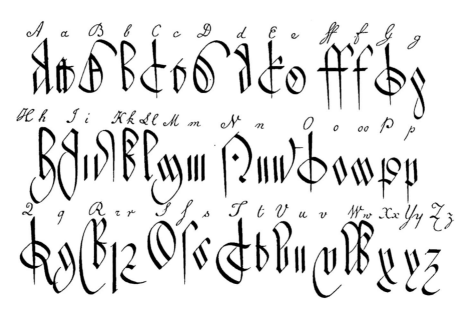

Small Court hand letter samples

Diplomatic

Humfrŭs Connyngtoñ nup de Londoñ armiger sum͠ fuit ad

responden Emanueli Somerby militi de pͧito q͠d

reddat ei centum ͠t quinq libras quas ei debet ͠t

injuste detinet ͠tc Et unde idem E. ͠t

Semi-diplomatic

Humfridus Connyngton nuper de London Armiger summonitus fuit ad

respondendum Emanueli Somerby Militi de placito quod

reddat ei centum et quinque libras quas ei debetet

injuste detinet etc. Et unde idem Emanuel etc.

Modernised translation

Humfrey Connyngton once of London, Armiger, was summoned by Emanuel Somerby, knight, to answer a plea that he return to him one hundred and fifty pounds which he owes and unjustly detains etc. And whence the same Emanuel etc.

A a	B b	C c	D d	E e	F f	G g	H h	I i
A a	B b	C c	D d	E e	F f	G g	H h	I i
J j	K k	L l	M m	N n	O o	P p	Q q	R r
J j	K k	L l	M m	N n	O o	P p	Q q	R r
S s	T t	U u	V v	W w	X x	Y y	Z z	&
S s	T t	U u	V v	W w	X x	Y y	Z z	&

Secretary hand letter samples

In the name of God Amen Know all

christian people by these presents to whom it may concern that I John Ducy

the fifth and youngest Soune of S[ir] Robert Ducy late P[??] and baronett and Alderman

of the citty of London In consideration of my owne mortality and the inevitability of my

owne naturall transitory condition that being now arrived to the age of one and twenty years
and one month, and so being capable of receiving the disposition of the whole
estate left mee by my S^{ir} Robert Ducie my father and Dame ~ ~
Elizabeth Ducy his wife my mother Do hereby ordaine, and order, constitute etc.

Notes:
− The writer uses the surname variants Ducy and Ducie interchangeably.
− Line endings are filled in by the writer (shown here as '~ ~') in order to prevent later additions.

Set Chancery hand letter samples, James VI & I

A a   B b   C c cc   D d   E e   F f   G g   H h   I i ij

K k   L l   M m   N n   O   O o   oo   P p   Q q q

R   r   S s   T t   t   tt   U V u v   X x   Y y   Z z

23

Diplomatic

Jacobus dei gͬa Anglie Scotie ffrancie
~t Hirɒnie Rex fidei defensor ~tc. Omiℨ
ad quos p̓sentes lr̃e Ρuerϑint saltm
Sciatis qd̄ nos de gͬa nr̃a spīali ac
octagin~t sex solid̄ ~t octo denar̃ ~tc.

Semi-diplomatic

Jacobus Dei gratia Angliae Scotiae Franciae
et Hiberniae Rex Fidei Defensor, etc. Omnibus
ad quos praesentes litterae pervenerint Salutem
Sciatis quod Nos de gratia nostra speciali ac
pro octaginta sex solidis et octo denariis, etc.

Modernised translation

James, by grace of God, King of England, Scotland France and Ireland, Defender of the Faith etc. To all to whom these present letters shall come, Greetings. Know ye that we of our special grace and for eighty-six shillings and eight pence, etc.

Later Chancery hand letter samples

Semi-diplomatic

1   *Sententia pro valore Testamenti Johannis Wood defuncti*
2   *In Dei Nomine Amen*
3   *Auditis visis et intellectis ac plenarie et mature discussis per*
4   *nos Ricardum Raines Militem et legum Doctorem Curia*
5   *Praerogativa Cantuariensis Magistrum Custodem sive*
6   *Comissarium legitime constitutum Meritis et Circumstancijs*
7   *cuiusdam negotij Probationis per Testes Testamentarij sive*
8   *ultima voluntatis in Scriptis Johannis Wood nuper Parochia*
9   *Sancti Salvatoris in Burgo de Southwark in Comitatu*
10 *Surria defuncti quod coram nobis in judicio inter Ricardum*
11 *Wood et Henricum Wood fihios et Executores in Testamento*
12 *praedicto nominatos partes agentes et quarelantes ex una et*
13 *Aliciam ffoster alias Wood (uxorem Gabrielis ffoster) filiam*
14 *dicti defuncti partibus ex altera nuper vertebatur et pendebat etc. …*

Translation from Latin

Sentence to confirm the testament of John Wood, deceased [1701]
In the Name of God Amen
Having heard, seen and understood and by complete and perfect examination by us Richard Raines Knight and Doctor of Laws Master Custodian or Commissary of the Prerogative Court of Canterbury lawfully constituted on the merits and circumstances of certain matters of probate by testament of witnesses or the last will in the hand of John Wood lately of the parish of San Salvator in the Burgh of Southwark in the County of Surrey deceased that in our presence in judgement between Richard Wood and Henry Wood sons and executors in the foresaid testament their nominates, parties agents and complainants on the one hand and Alica Foster alias Wood (wife of Gabriel Foster) daughter of the said deceased on the other hand recently being considered and pending etc. …

A a   B b   C c cc   D d   E e   F f   G g

H h   I i J j K k L l M m   N n nn   O o oo

P p   P pp   Q q   R r   S s s

T t tt U u V v W w X x Y y Z z

Numerals

Some numbers will be given in their Latin form, such as MDXXVI for 1526 (see Chapter 3), but from the twelfth century Arabic numerals rapidly became popular, along with the very useful zero (0).

Centuries

12th	13th	14th	15th	Modern
3	*3*	*2*	*1*	1
3	*2*	*3*	*2*	2
3	*3*	*3*	*3*	3
R	*1*	*R*	*T*	4
9	*8*	*9*	*5*	5
6	*6*	*6*	*6*	6
1	*7*	*A*	*7*	7
8	*8*	*8*	*8*	8
9	*2*	*9*	*9*	9
0	*o*	*0*	*o*	0

Comparison chart of hands

This is not a complete letter list of all possible variants of letter forms, but should help identify the hand and give clues to particular letters.

Modern Gothic	English Gothic	Set Chancery	Fast Chancery	Court hand	Secretary hand	Scottish Secretary hand
A						
B						
C						
D						
E						
F						
G						
H						
I						
K						
L						
M						
N						
O						
P						
Q						
R						
S						
T						
U						
W						
X						
Y						
Z						

Scots variants ſʒ = ss & = e yogh = ȝ thorn = y

Letter lists

It is a good idea to make a letter list for each document you come across, which includes all possible forms of each letter that you encounter. Letter lists will help with other documents of the same type, date and place. There is a blank list on p. 30 – feel free to copy and use it.

You can either cut and paste individual letters from a digitised document (as in the example below) or copy the letters by hand.

Modern	Lower case.	Upper case	Initial	Final	Notes
A					
B					word is 'be'
C					
D					

Further Reading

Online

For palaeography exercises, tutorials and information:
   www.nas.gov.uk/learning/publications.asp
   www.scottishhandwriting.com
   www.nationalarchives.gov.uk/palaeography
   http://medievalwriting.50megs.com/
   www.geocities.com/CollegePark/Library/2036/paleo.htm
   www.ualberta.ca/~sreimer/ms-course/course/pal-hist.htm
   http://paleo.anglo-norman.org/medfram.html (mediaeval English) and http://paleo.
   anglo-norman.org/empfram.html (early modern English)

For Scots legal and land terms, consult the Scotland's People website:
   http://www.scotlandspeople.gov.uk/content/help/index.aspx?r=551&431

For Scots words more generally, see the Scottish Language Dictionaries website:
   www.scotsdictionaries.org.uk/

Images of wills and testaments from 1513 to 1925 are available at:
   www.scottishdocuments.com and www.scotlandspeople.gov.uk

Books: English and general

Bishop, T.A.M. and Chaplais, P., *Facsimiles of English Royal Writs to AD 1100* (Oxford: Clarendon Press, 1957)
Denholm-Young, N., *Handwriting in England and Wales* (Cardiff: University of Wales Press, 1954)

Derolez, A., *The Palaeography of Gothic Manuscript Books* (New York Cambridge University Press, 2003)

Fairbank, A., *A Book of Scripts* (Harmondsworth: Penguin, 1952)

Grieve, H.E.P., *Examples of English Handwriting 1150–1750* (Essex Record Office Publications No. 21, 1954)

Hector, L.C., *The Handwriting of English Documents* (Dorking, Surrey: Kohler and Coombes, 1980 (reprint of 2nd edn, originally published 1966))

Jackson, D. *The Story of Writing* (London: Studio Vista, 1981)

Jenkinson, H., *The Later Court Hands in England from the Fifteenth to the Seventeenth Century* (Cambridge University Press and New York: Frederick Ungar Publishing Co., 1927 and 1969)

Johnson, C. and Jenkinson, H., *English Court Hand A.D. 1066 to 1500 Illustrated Chiefly from the Public Records,* 2 vols (Oxford: Clarendon Press, 1915, and New York: F. Ungar Publishing Co., 1967)

Ker, N.R., *English Manuscripts in the Century after the Norman Conquest* (Oxford: Clarendon Press, 1960)

Parkes, M.B., *English Cursive Book Hands 1250–1500* (Oxford: Clarendon Press, 1969)

Preston, J.F. and Yeandle, L., *English Handwriting 1400–1650: An Introductory Manual* (Binghampton, New York: Medieval and Renaissance Texts and Studies, 1992)

Roberts, J., *Guide to Scripts used in English Writings up to 1500* (London: The British Library, 2005)

Salter, H.E., *Facsimiles of Early Charters in Oxford Muniment Rooms* (Oxford University Press, 1929)

Warner, G.F. and Ellis, H.J. (eds), *Facsimiles of Royal and Other Charters in the British Museum, Vol. 1, William I–Richard I* (Oxford University Press, 1903)

Watson, A.G., *Catalogue of Dated and Datable Manuscripts c.700–1600 in the Department of Manuscripts, The British Library*, 2 vols, (London: British Museum Publications, 1979)

Wright, A., *Court-Hand Restored* (London: Reeves & Turner, 1879)

Wright, C.E., *English Vernacular Hands from the Twelfth to the Fifteenth Centuries* (Oxford: Clarendon Press, 1960)

Books: Scots

Gouldesbrough, P., *Formulary of old Scots legal documents* (Edinburgh: Stair Society, 1985)

Rosie, A., *Scottish Handwriting 1500–1700: A self-help pack* (Scottish Records Association and The National Archives of Scotland, 1998)

Simpson, G.G., *Scottish Handwriting, 1150–1650: an introduction to the reading of documents*, (East Linton: Tuckwell Press, 1998)

Specifically Latin

Bischoff, B., *Latin Palaeography: Antiquity and the Middle Ages* (Cambridge University Press, 1990)

Harrison Thomson, S., *Latin Book Hands of the Later Middle Ages 1100–1500* (Cambridge University Press, 1969)

Latham, R.E., *Revised Medieval Latin Word-List from British and Irish Sources* (Oxford University Press, 1965)

Palaeography: letter list

Modern	Lower case	Upper case	Initial	Final	Notes
A					
B					
C					
D					
E					
F					
G					
H					
I					
J					
K					
L					
M					
N					
O					
P					
Q					
R					
S					
T					
U					
V					
W					
X					
Y					
Z					
Yogh					
Thorn					
Numbers 1	2	3	4	5	
6	7	8	9	0	
Document source(s) and date(s):					

2

Latin

Latin's a dead language
As dead as dead can be
It killed the ancient Romans
And now it's killing me!

Schoolboy rhyme

Latin terms often crop up in genealogical and historical research, especially in church records, legal documents and on inscriptions. Therefore, the genealogist and the historian will need a working knowledge of the language.

This is not a Latin textbook as such, and learning Latin is probably not the aim of anyone reading this. Rather, the aim is to provide a basic understanding of the language and how it works, and the appropriate tools to get to grips with Latin as found in documents. The 'Further Reading' section at the end of this chapter provide background materials and information on how to take the study of the language further. Most readers will want to:

– Understand common words and phrases that genealogists need to be able to translate from documents.
– Know how to interpret ecclesiastical Latin such as inscriptions and dates on gravestones.
– Be able to extract genealogical and other information (such as land details) from such records.
– Be familiar with numbers, dates and money expressed in Latin.
– Know where to get help if necessary.

The Glossaries provided at the end of this book (Part III, p. 255) and the formularies of old documents that use Latin are not as complete as they would be in a proper dictionary, but should suffice for most purposes.

BUT IS IT THE RIGHT LATIN?

Those who took Latin at school may remember enough to make sense of documents, but there is one major complication with this: the classical Latin of Cicero and Caesar that we all learned is now 2,000 years old and is different from the late mediaeval/early modern Latin of Church and legal documents, even though those who wrote these documents had been brought up on the Renaissance revival of interest in Livy, Vergil, Horace and Ovid.

Over the centuries, the Church and the law had developed an enlarged Latin vocabulary that had made use of borrowings from other languages and resources. *The Vulgate* (St Jerome's late-fourth-century Latin translation of the Bible) contained a lot taken from Hebrew and Greek, precisely because clerical and secular writers needed a technical vocabulary that had not existed before Christianity. The Germanic tribes who supplanted the Roman Empire provided a vocabulary of law and rule. Other ordinary words were taken from local languages. So it shouldn't come as a surprise that there are differences between the Latin of the High Roman period and the working language of church and courts 1,600 years later.

It is also important to realise that when the Romans vacated Britain *c.* 450 CE they did not leave Latin as an everyday language, and that many of our 'Latinised' words were either imported via Norman French after 1066 or were 'scholarly borrowings': made-up words based on what the Greeks or Romans would have said if they had thought of it. For example, 'thermometer' was coined from the Greek *thermos* (hot) and *metron* (measure) about 1630 and *vox populi, vox Dei* (the voice of the people is the voice of God), were not seen until the 1540s.

It is in the nature of languages to change: the English in Chaucer's *Canterbury Tales* became the medium for Shakespeare and eventually the BBC and even *Eastenders*, but although different from current usage in vocabulary, syntax, grammar and pronunciation, these works are recognisably all examples of the same language we use today.

In the neo-Latin of documents, however, the pronunciational differences are minor and similar enough to modern English (and detailed syntactical and grammatical differences are not the province of this book). Anyone who remembers '*amo, amas, amat*' and '*mensa, mensam, mensae*' will cope just fine. Vocabulary is where the major differences are, and there's a very good reason for that: many words needed by churchmen, lawyers and legislators just didn't exist in Roman times, or had come to mean something different.

Differences between classical and early modern Latin

Take this example from a retour (see Chapter 13) of 1643. Some words, such as *haeres* (heir), *patris* (to his father) or *in terris de* (in the lands of) would make perfect sense to a Roman. But *decimis garbalibus* (of teind sheaves, a tithe or tenth of produce) and Scottish land-holding terms such as *in baronia, dominio* and *feudifirmae* would have been meaningless.

This isn't surprising. Language moves on: no one in England has said 'Thou gorbellied, clay-brained, swag-bellied malt-worm' since Elizabethan times, and hardly anyone in Scotland would now recognise the word *rexive* (in respect of). New words are coined, or borrowed from elsewhere, to express new concepts such as a barony, glebe or merk (the currency). Even in Latin

(1198)   Jul. 26. 1681.
HENRICUS MAY de Bonningtoune, *hæres* Roberti May de Bonningtoune, *patris,*—in terris de Brigtoune et Currieholl nunc vocatis Bonningtoune, cum communi pastura de Threapmure et Currieholl, et pastura de Bougans de Cults, cum decimis garbalibus, in baronia de Cults, dominio de Coulrose.—E. 4*l.* 18*s.* 8*d. feudi-firmæ.*   **xxxv. 270.**

this process is still happening, as Vatican linguists working on the *Lexicon Recentis Latinitatis* regularly produce 'new' Latin words for objects, such as *telephonium albo televisifico coniunctum* (videophone), or concepts such as *tempus maximae frequentiae* (rush hour).[1]

LATIN PRONUNCIATION

Consonants

There are twenty-four letters in the post-classical Latin alphabet: *a, b, c, d, e, f, g, h, i, j, l, m, n, o, p, q, r, s, t, u, v, x, y, z*.

There is no *k* or *w* in Latin: *u* was written as *v*. Therefore, *vxor* is the same as *uxor* (wife).

The consonants *i* and *j* are used interchangeably (*cuius* or *cujus*) and in numbers such as *iij* (three).

The letter *c* may be used for *qu* in manuscripts (*condam* for *quondam*). Mostly, consonants are pronounced exactly the same as today, except: *z* like '*dz*' (*baptizo* pronounced '*bahpteedzo*') and *qu* (usually like '*qw*' as in *quondam*). Whereas a *c* was always hard (like a *k*) in classical Latin (Caesar, pronounced like 'Kaiser', which is where the German word comes from) it became more like our current usage: soft before *i, e, ae, oe* (*cerebrum*, like 'cent'; *caeculum*, pronounced '*sigh-kyoolum*'; *coepi*, pronounced '*saypee*') but otherwise hard (*candida* like 'candidate', so-called because candidates for office wore a white toga, and *candida* translates as 'white').

A *g* is also softened when it precedes *i, e, ae* and *oe* as in *gelato* (ice cream).

The *t* before *ia* is softened as in *Scotia*, pronounced '*Scosihah*' and may even be replaced by a soft *c* as in *Scocia*.

Classically, *v* was pronounced as *w*, except before a consonant – *vita* (life) was pronounced '*weeta*' – but we can ignore that in more 'modern' Latin and say *veni* (I came) with a *v* as in 'vicar'.

Vowels

All vowels have long and short pronunciations:

a (short) = '*ah*' (as in 'bat'); *a* (long) = '*aah*' (as in 'bath');
e (short) = '*eh*' (as in 'pet'); *e* (long) = '*ey*' (as in 'honey');
i (short) = '*ih*' (as in 'pit'); *i* (long) = '*ee*' (as in 'Tahiti');
o (short) = (as in 'gong'); *o* (long) = '*oh*' (as in 'ago');
u (short) = '*oo*' (as in 'soot'); *o* (long) = '*yoo*' (as in 'suit').

Diphthongs

As in English, two vowels can combine in Latin to make a diphthong (think of 'pie' or 'head'). The four main diphthongs in Latin are: *ae, oe, au* (out), and *ui* (wi), and whereas in neo-Latin *au* and *ui* remain fully 'rounded' – *aurum* ('*ou-room*' (gold)), *cuius* ('*koo-ee-yus*' (of whom)) – the rounded *ae* and *oe* of classical Latin as in *Caesar* ('*kai-sar*'), *coepi* ('*koi-pee*' (beginning)) later 'collapsed' to be pronounced '*ay*', like a long *e*, so there is often a collapse in written form too:

e used for *ae* (æ) (*cecum* instead of *caecum* 'blind');
e used for *oe* (œ) (*celum* instead of *coelom* 'heaven').

1. The *Lexicon Recentis Latinitatis*, produced by the Opus Fundatum Latinitas, established in 1976 by Pope Paul VI; www.vatican.va/roman_curia/institutions_connected/latinitas/documents/index_en.htm

Stress

This usually falls on the last-but-one syllable in a long word, and the syllable before that in a shorter word, as with *in saeculo saeculorum* 'for ever and ever'.

WORD ORDER

In English, 'John loves Janet' is not the same as 'Janet loves John' and 'John gave Janet a dog' is not the same as 'John gave a dog Janet', or even 'a dog gave John Janet'. We make the distinction either through word order – John (subject) loves (verb) Janet (object) – or by changing the verb from active to passive – 'Janet is loved by John' – or by inserting prepositions – 'John gave a dog to Janet'.

Latin doesn't worry about word order so much, but the usual order is subject-object-verb. So, with the phrase 'John Janet loves': Latin sorts it out by 'inflecting' the subject and object (see below). For now, just accept that '*Johannis Janetam amat*' is not the same as '*Janeta Johannem amat*'.

GENDER, CASE AND NUMBER OF NOUNS: AN INTRODUCTION

Latin is inflected: nouns and adjectives have gender, case and number, indicated by the word endings. So for instance, *villa* (country house) is feminine gender, *annus* (year) is masculine and *testamentum* (covenant, will) is neuter. 'One house' is *una villa*, 'one year' is *unus annus* and 'one will' is *unum testamentum*.

The case matters, too: that is, whether the noun is the subject or object of the sentence or is referred to in some other way. In English phrases like 'year of death', 'Lord James' and 'in the year of our Lord', the words 'year' and 'lord' are the same regardless of case. In Latin, 'year' is *annus* but 'in the year' is *anno*, as with *anno domini*. 'Lord James' is *Dominus Jacobus* but 'of our Lord' is … *domini*; and where, say, land is given 'to John' (*Johannis*) this would be *ad Johannem* in Latin.

Number can be singular – *villa* (a/the house) *filius* (a/the son); or plural – *villae* (houses), *filii* (sons).

In fact, we do still have this in English to some extent: there is a difference between mouse, mouse's (belonging to the mouse), mice (plural) and mice's (of more than one mouse). There will be more detail on this later.

PERSON, NUMBER AND TENSE OF VERBS: THE BASICS

In the same way as nouns, verbs are inflected according to person, number and tense. We also do this in English to a degree, particularly with irregular verbs.

Consider a regular verb: 'to walk'. We have three persons singular (I, you, he/she/it), three plural (we, you, they) and a choice of tenses (present, past, future etc.):

To walk	Present tense		Past tense		Future tense	
	singular	plural	singular	plural	singular	plural
First person	I walk	we walk	I walked	we walked	I will walk	we will walk
Second person	you walk (thou walkest)	you walk	you walked	you walked	you will walk	you will walk
Third person	he/she/it walks (walketh)	they walk	he/she/it walked	they walked	he/she/it will walk	they will walk
	Present participle	walking	**Past participle**	walked		

Notice that the only inflection is in 'he/she/it walks', ignoring the antique versions 'walkest' and 'walketh'.

Irregular verbs (which are often the most commonly used) are different, as with 'to be' and 'to go':

To be	Present tense		Past tense		Future tense	
	singular	plural	singular	plural	singular	plural
First person	I am	we are	I was	we were	I will be	we will be
Second person	you are (thou art)	you are	you were (thou wert)	you were	you will be	you will be
Third person	he/she/it is	they are	he/she/it was	they were	he/she/it will be	they will be
	Present participle	being	**Past participle**	was/were		

To go	Present tense		Past tense		Future tense	
	singular	plural	singular	plural	singular	plural
First person	I go	we go	I went	we went	I will go	we will go
Second person	you go (thou goest)	you go	you went	you went	you will go	you will go
Third person	he/she/it goes (goeth)	they go	he/she/it went	they went	he/she/it will go	they will go
	Present participle	going	**Past participle**	went		

Latin does the same. Taking the present tense only for a regular verb such as *amare* (to love) and an irregular verb *esse* (to be):

amare	Present tense	
	singular	plural
First person	*amo* (I love)	*amamus* (we love)
Second person	*amas* (you love)	*amatis* (you love)
Third person	*amat* (he loves)	*amant* (they love)
	Present participle	*amans*

esse	Present tense	
	singular	plural
First person	*sum* (I am)	*sumus* (we are)
Second person	*es* (you are)	*estis* (you are)
Third person	*est* (he is)	*sunt* (they are)
	Present participle	*esse*

Now we can construct 'John loves Janet' (*Johannis Janetam amat*) and 'Janet loves John' (*Janeta Johannem amat*). *Johannis* is the subject of the verb in the first example, and *Janetam* is the object, but in the second example, it's the other way round. Notice the use of the third person singular *amat* (so it's literally 'John, he loves').

NUMBERS, DATES, DAYS OF THE WEEK, MONTHS, ROMAN CALENDAR

Roman numerals

It's a mystery how the Romans ever managed arithmetic with their littoral numerals and no concept of zero. This system was fine for tallying sheep or goats by carving notches on a stick, but not much use for sums. However, Roman numerals persist in genealogy (and clock faces) even today and certainly V is easier to carve on a tombstone than 5. The letters can be capitals (XIV) or lower-case (xiv).

The basic numbers:	These can be combined:
I = 1	VII: 5+2 = 7
V = 5	IX: 1 before 10 = 10-1 = 9
X = 10	XL: 10 before 50 = 40
L = 50	LXX: 50 +10 +10 = 70
C = 100	MDCCII: 100+500+200+2 = 1702
D = 500	MCMLXXIV: 1000 + (1000-100) + (50+10+10) + (5-1) = 1974
M = 1000	MMIII = 2003

D is sometimes represented by the symbol I⊃ and *M* by the symbol CI⊃ or as *Jaj* (which is actually a stylised *IM* = 1000).

Common Roman numerals				
1 = I	10 = X	20 = XX	100 = C	1000 = M
2 = II	11 = XI	21 = XXI	101 = CI	1400 = MCD
3 = III	14 = XIV	30 = XXX	110 = CX	1600 = MDC
4 = IV	15 = XV	40 = XL	150 = CL	1700 = MDCC
5 = V	16 = XVI	41 = XLI	160 = CLX	1742 = MDCCXLII
6 = VI	19 = XIX	50 = L	200 = CC	1800 = MDCCC
7 = VII		60 = LX	400 = CD	1900 = MCM
8 = VIII		70 = LXX	500 = D	2000 = MM
9 = IX		80 = LXXX	600 = DC	2003 = MMIII
		90 = XC	900 = CM	2013 = *MMXIII*

The number 4 can be IV or IIII, especially on clocks and in some documents. The year 1999 should be written as MIM, but just before the last millennium it was often given as MDCCCCLXXXIX, which is just plain daft.

Days, dates and time

Days	
English	**Latin**
Sunday	*dies dominica, dominica, dominicus, dies Solis, feria prima*
Monday	*dies Lunae, lune, feria seconda*
Tuesday	*dies Martis, martis, feria tertia*
Wednesday	*dies Mercurii, mercurii, mercurinus, mercoris, feria quarta*
Thursday	*dies Jovis, jovis, feria qunta*
Friday	*dies Verenis, verneris, feria sexta*
Saturday	*dies Saturni, dies sabbatinus, sabbatum, sabbati, feria septima*

Months	
English	**Latin**
January	*Januarius, Januarij*
February	*Februarius, Februarij*
March	*Martius, Marcij*
April	*Aprilis, Aprilij*
May	*Maius, Maij*
June	*Junius, Junij*
July	*Julius, Julij*
August	*Augustus, Augustij*
September	*Septembris, September, 7ber, VIIber*
October	*Octobris, October, 8ber, VIIIber*
November	*Novembris, November, 9ber, IXber*
December	*Decembris, December, 10ber, Xber*

Because *i* and *j* are interchangeable, and a final *i* is usually written as *j*, *Julii*, *Julij* and *Iulii* all mean 'July'.

Numbers

There are cardinal numbers (one, two, three etc.) and ordinal (first, second, third etc.). One, two and three take gender (e.g. masculine *unus*, feminine *una*, neuter *unum*), as do all of the ordinals, which act as if they were adjectives. Church and legal records often end the ordinal with an *o* (*tertio* for 'third', *tricesimo* for 'the 30th'). Notice that seventeen is the sensible *septendecim* ('seven-ten') but eighteen is *duodeviginti* ('two-less-than-twenty') and nineteen is *undeviginti*. As for 28th, it seems that the Romans couldn't make up their minds between *vicesimo octavo* or *duodetricesimo* ('two-less-than-thirty').

Cardinal		Ordinal		Dates/Fractions
1	*unus una unum*	1st	*primus prima primum*	*primo*
2	*duo duae duo*	2nd	*secundus/a/um*	*secundo*
3	*tres, tria*	3rd	*tertius/a/um*	*tertio*
4	*quattuor*	4th	*quatrus or quartus/a/um*	*quarto*
5	*quinque*	5th	*quintus/a/um*	*quinto*
6	*sex*	6th	*sextus/a/um*	*sexto*
7	*septem*	7th	*septimus/a/um*	*septimo*
8	*octo*	8th	*octavus/a/um*	*octavo*

Cardinal		Ordinal		Dates/Fractions
9	*novem*	9th	*nonus/a/um*	*nono*
10	*decem*	10th	*decimus/a/um*	*decimo*
11	*undecim*	11th	*undecimus/a/um*	*undecimo*
12	*duodecim*	12th	*duodecimus/a/um*	*duodecimo*
13	*tredecim*	13th	*tertius/a/um decimus/a/um*	*tertio decimo*
14	*quattordecim* or *quattuordecim*	14th	*quartus/a/um decimus/a/um*	*quarto decimo*
15	*qundecim*	15th	*quntius/a/um decimus/a/um*	*quinto decimo*
16	*sedecim*	16th	*sextus/a/um decimus/a/um*	*sexto decimo*
17	*septendecim*	17th	*septimus/a/um decimus/a/um*	*septimo decimo*
18	*duodeviginti*	18th	*duodevicesmus/a/um*	*duodevicesimo*
19	*undeviginti*	19th	*undeviceimus/a/um*	*unodevicesimo*
20	*viginti*	20th	*vicesimus/a/um* or *vigesimus/a/um*	*vicesimo*
21	*viginti unus/a/um*	21st	*viceimus/a/um primus/a/um*	*vicesimo primo*
22	*viginti duo/duae*	22nd	*vicesimus/a/um secundus/a/um*	*vicesimo secundo*
23	*viginti tre*	23rd	*vicesimus/a/um tertius/a/um*	*vicesimo tertio*
24	*viginti quattuor*	24th	*viceimus/a/um quatrus/a/um*	*vicesimo quarto*
25	*viginti quinque*	25th	*vicesimus/a/um quintus/a/um*	*vicesimo quinto*
26	*viginti sex*	26th	*vicesimus/a/um sextus/a/um*	*vicesmo sexto*
27	*viginti septem*	27th	*vicesimus/a/um septimus/a/um*	*vicesmo septimo*
28	*viginti octo*	28th	*vicesimus/a/um octavus/a/um* or *duodetricesimus/a/um*	*vicesimo octavo* or *duodetricesimo*
29	*viginti novem*	29th	*vicesimus/a/um nonus/a/um* or *undetericemimus/a/um*	*undetericesimo*
30	*trigenta*	30th	*tricesimus/a/um*	*tricesimo*
31	*triginta unus/a/um* or *unus/a/um et triginta*	31st	*triceimus/a/um primus/a/um* or *unus/a/um et tricesimus/a/um*	*tricesimo primo*
40	*quadraginta*	40th	*quadragesimus/a/um*	*quadragesimo*
50	*quinquaginta*	50th	*quinquagesimus/a/um*	*quinquagesimo*
100	*centum*	100th	*centesimus*	*centesimo*
500	*quingenti*	500th	*quingentensimus* or *quinquecentesimus*	*quingentensimo* or *quinquecentesimo*
1000	*mille*	1000th	*millesimus*	*millesimo*

Examples of the use of numbers in fractions can be found in retours and sasines (Chapters 12, 13). For example, *decimis garbalibus* (of teind sheaves) was a tithe or tenth of produce; *in quarta parte* was in a fourth part, or a quarter, but 'a half' would be *dimidia pars*.

Latin records often write dates out in full, and numbers usually end with *o*:

Anno Domini millesimo quinquecentesimo tricesimo quarto et die vicesimo secundo mensis Aprilij.

In the year of (our) Lord one thousand five hundred and thirty-four, and the twenty-second day of the month of April.

The Roman calendar

Here is an inscription taken from a monument in Haddington, East Lothian:

Hic denique jacet Joannes Sleich, artium magister, hujus filius, illius vero nepos, majoribus haud degener ; qui, prætura fungens, in medio vitæ curriculo, abreptus est 6 kal. April. Ætatis 35.

Hic denique jacet Joannes Sleich, artium magister,
hujus filius, illius vero nepos, majoribus haud degener;
qui, praetura fungens, in medio vitae curriculo, abreptus
est 6 kal. April. Aetatis 35.

Lastly, here lies John Sleich, Master of Arts, son to the last, grandson to the former, by no means inferior to his ancestors, who, exercising the duty of a Baillie, was carried away in the middle race of life, 27 March and aged 35.

Not worrying about the rest of the inscription for the moment, notice the date. It says '*6 kal. April*', but this translates as a date in late March. How so?

Particularly on tombstones and memorials, and especially when showing off, the educated, landed and noble would often give dates in the Roman style, not only using Latin numerals, but also counting backwards from three important days in each month: the *Kalends*, *Nones* and *Ides*.

This works by starting at the next of these days (see the table overleaf) then counting back, including the day itself. Thus six days back from 1 April will be (1st, 31st, 30th, 29th, 28th, 27th) 27 March.

Some more examples:

1 August	*Kalends Augusti*;
31 May	*a.d.* [*ante diem* = the day before] *Kal. Junii*;
27 February	*III Kal. Martii* [count 1 March, 28 Feb, 27 Feb to get 3, but in a leap year it would be *IV Kal. Martii*, because of counting in the 29th];
4 October	*IV Nones Septembris* [7th, 6th, 5th, 4th hence 4];
10 May	*VI Ides Maii* [six back from the 15th inclusive].

Yes, it's silly, but *non immittet angelus* (don't shoot the messenger)!

Month	Day	Kalends	Nones	Ides	Examples	
January	31	I	5	13	4 Jan	a.d. *Nones* Jan
February	28 or 29	I	5	13	5 Feb	*Nones* Feb
March	31	I	7	15	6 Mar	a.d. *Nones* Mar
April	30	I	5	13	7 Apr	vii *Ides* Apr
May	31	I	7	15	8 May	viij *Ides* Mai
June	30	I	5	13	9 Jun	v *Ides* Jun
July	31	I	7	15	10 Jul	vi *Ides* Jul
August	31	I	5	13	11 Aug	iii *Ides* Avg
September	30	I	5	13	12 Sept	a.d. *Ides* Sept
October	31	I	7	15	13 Oct	iii *Ides* Oct
November	30	I	5	13	14 Nov	xviij *Kal.* Dec
December	31	I	5	13	15 Dec	xviij *Kal* Jan

Two mnemonics that may help: '30 days hath September, April June and November' and 'In March, October, July and May, *Ides* is on the fifteenth day'. Incidentally, *Ides* is pronounced '*ee-daze*', not rhyming with 'hides' as in 'Beware the Ides of March'. For more on (non-Roman) calendars and dates, see Chapter 3.

You may like to try these exercises (answers on p. 94):

1)   iij Kalends Martii 1800
2)   Ides Februarij 1600 (in Scotland)
3)   Ides Februarij 1600 (in England)
4)   viij Jun MDCxviij
5)   Lammas Day 41 Jac VI
6)   Michaelmas 5 Jac I (be careful here!)

Handwritten numbers and 'long' dates

The palaeographic aspects of this are dealt with in more detail in Chapter 1, but here are some basics. You will see, in some documents, dates expressed as either '*xj Aprilis Jaj vC Dxxxv*' or '*Jaj vC fourscore and fifteen*'. The answer is the same: 11 April 1595.

'*xi° mensis october 1598*' is 11 October 1598.

Notice how similar the *x* is to the final *r* in 'October' and the use of the superscript *o* to indicate *undecimo*.

Die xvij° maii 1599: the day 17 of May 1599.

Roman numerals in sums of money

The pound sterling is the world's oldest currency still in use, and the pre-decimal notation will be everywhere in documents (see Chapter 4 for UK money pre-1971), with the added complication of being expressed in Roman numerals.

(1759)
Summa inventarij [the sum of the inventory] *is L lib viij ss 1d [£50 8s 1d] Sterling which in*
Scots money is viCiv lib xvij ss [£604 17s] salvo justo calculo ['without prejudice to the calculator', meaning 'don't blame me if I got that wrong'].

(1743)
Summa of the debts owing to the dead} viCvi lib xj ss viiij d [£606 11s 8d]

Incidentally, a *calculus* was originally a pebble used for counting, hence the noun above and the verb *calculare* 'to count'. Anyone who has suffered from kidney stones may have heard them referred to as 'renal calculi'.

Notice a few things here:

– Do not confuse *L* ('50') for the pound sterling sign £. The indicator for pounds here is *lib*, from *libra* (plural *librae*) Latin for 'pound' but also for 'scales' or 'balance', as that's how a pound of silver (or anything else for that matter) would be weighed. The £ sign is, of course, a stylised *L*, showing its derivation from *libra*.
– The *v* ('5') can look like a *b* if it has a long leading stroke, especially in earlier hands.
– The capital *C* ('100') looks like an ampersand (&).
– The *x* ('10') is written as *c*.
– The symbol for shillings (*ss*, abbreviation indicating *solidi*, the plural of *solidus*) is similar to a German *scharfe* (ß), a double-s formed from a long *s* and a smaller one (*fs*).
– The penny is *d* for the Latin *denarius* (plural *denarii*).

COMMON WORDS AND PHRASES

There is a more extensive Latin glossary starting at p. 255 that will help with the Latin examples in this chapter. Common abbreviations are given in brackets, e.g. *ibidem* (*ib.*, *ibid.*), as are genitives: *index* (*indicis*). Some phrases commonly encountered in documents are listed by first word: *ex hac mortali ad immortalem vitam* (from this mortality to immortal life). Some male and female forms are given: *neosponsus, neosponsa* (newlywed) but not all. Numbers are largely not included, see p. 38 for those.

HERE COMES THE LATIN GRAMMAR

Now the whole thing again, but in more detail.

Cases of nouns

As we have seen, a noun is a naming word: the name of a person, place, thing or quality. Take this short sentence: 'James likes the dog.'

'James' is the subject of the verb 'to like' and 'dog' is the object. In English, it's obvious who is doing the liking (James) and what is liked (dog) because of the word order. But imagine the verb had to come at the end and the order of the nouns didn't matter, as happens in Latin:

> James the dog likes.
> the dog James likes.

Now what is the subject, and what is the object? Latin and other inflected languages solve this by having different word endings to indicate case:

> *Jacobus canem amat.*

If you wanted to say 'the dog likes James', it would be:

> *canis Jacobum amat.*

Notice that Latin has no words for articles and does not distinguish between the definite article (the) and the indefinite (a).

Jacobus is the subject of the verb in the first example, and *canis* is the object, so it is used in the accusative case. In the second example, it's the other way round.

Here are the endings and cases for a feminine proper noun of the first declension (we'll get to what that means later):

English	Latin [plural]	Case
girl (just naming her)	*puella [puellae]*	Nominative: used when the noun is the subject.
hey, girl	*(o) puella [puellae]*	Vocative: when addressing the subject.
to a/the girl (object)	*(ad) puellam [puellas]*	Accusative: when the noun is the object.
of a/the girl	*(de) puellae [puellarum]*	Genitive: indicating possession by the noun.
about/to a/the girl	*(in re) puellae [puellis]*	Dative: concerning the noun.
by/with/from a/the girl	*(per, cum, ab) puella [puellis]*	Ablative: when the action is 'away' from the noun.
English uses prepositions (of, from etc.) but no case endings	Latin uses case-specific endings as well as prepositions	

Prepositions are words such as to, of, about, by, with and from.

Here is the same thing for two masculine nouns of the second declension (*Dominus*) and third declension (*pater*):

Second declension		Third declension	
English	**Latin [plural]**	**English**	**Latin [plural]**
Lord (just naming him)	*Dominus*	father	*pater [patres]*
O, Lord	*(O) Domine*	O, father	*patre [patres]*
to the Lord (*object*)	*(ad) Dominum*	To father (*object*)	*patrem [patres]*
of the Lord	*(de) Domini*	Of father	*patris [patrum]*
about/to the Lord	*(in re) Domino*	About father	*patri [patribus]*
by, with or from the Lord	*(per, cum, ab) Domino*	By, with or from father	*patre [patribus]*

Congratulations. You've just declined your first two nouns. Now let's add a verb, and an extra case.

> The girl gives a table to the Lord.
> *Puella mensam Domino donat.*

The girl (*puella*) is the subject (nominative case) of the verb *donare* (to give), *mensa* (a table) is the object (and so takes the accusative case *mensam*) and *Domino* (Lord) takes the dative because it is the indirect object: the person given to, not the thing given.

Gender of nouns

We have largely lost this in English, but nouns can be thought of as having gender: masculine, feminine, neuter or common. Boy is obviously masculine, as would be son, man and bull. Woman is clearly feminine, likewise daughter, girl, and cow. Words such as table, field, war or burden are neuter (no gender). Those that could refer to male or female – such as dog, fish, person, citizen, name, thing – are common.

This doesn't matter for most purposes in English, except in deciding whether to use the pronoun he, she or it; in the plural, everything becomes 'they'. But in Latin, every noun has a gender, and some of them are a surprise. Obviously, *vir* (man), *puer* (boy) and *taurus* (bull) are masculine. But so are *ager* (field) and *civis* (citizen). Clearly, *femina* (woman), *puella* (girl) and *vacca* (cow) are feminine. Yet so are *res* (thing), *mensa* (table) and some surprising examples such as *barba* (beard) and *legio* (legion), while *agricola* (farmer) and *nauta* (sailor) are obviously masculine yet are declined as feminine nouns. *Pater* (father) is masculine while *mater* (mother) is feminine, but they are declined exactly the same. *Bellum* (war) is neuter as are *cubile* (bed), *corpus* (body) and *onus* (burden). Common nouns are not so common (as it were) in Latin, but an example would be *bos* (ox or cow).

Anyone who knows some French, Spanish or other romance languages will be used to the idea of noun gender, which is often illogical and just has to be learned. In French, *la table* (table) is feminine while *le cahier* (notebook) is masculine for no apparent reason – that's just the way it is.

Number of nouns

A noun can indicate one of something, but also two or more. We do indicate number in English, but simply by sticking a plural ending onto the singular – house/houses, cat/cats – but also with irregular forms such as man/men, child/children, mouse/mice and sheep/sheep. Latin has the full set of cases in the plural. *Mensa* (table) is first declension feminine, and declined like this:

Case	Singular		Plural	
Nominative	*mensa*	a table (subject)	*mensae*	tables (subject)
Vocative	*mensa*	O table!	*mensae*	O tables!
Accusative	*mensam*	table (object)	*mensas*	tables (object)
Genitive	*mensae*	of a table	*mensarum*	of tables
Dative	*mensae*	for a table	*mensis*	to/for tables
Ablative	*mensa*	by/with/from a table	*mensis*	by/with/from tables

Why bother?

There are three main reasons this matters in Latin:

1. As we've seen, you can't always work out the subject and object from word order.
2. Certain prepositions govern certain cases.
3. Adjectives have to agree with nouns, in case, gender and number.

There will be more (MUCH more) on adjectives later, but for now just accept that a word such as *bonus* (good) has three forms: *bonus* (m.), *bona* (f.) and *bonum* (nt.). So you could say: *vir bonus* (a good man); *femina bona* (a good woman); *corpus bonum* (a good body).

Just in passing, notice that the adjective's ending goes by the case, and while that is usually clear from the noun ending (-*us* masculine, -*a* feminine), it isn't always so (as with *corpus*, which is third declension neuter).

Adjectives also agree in case and number:

Case	Masculine		Feminine		Neuter	
	Singular	Plural	Singular	Plural	Singular	Plural
Nominative	*bonus*	*boni*	*bona*	*bonae*	*bonum*	*bona*
Vocative	*bone*	*boni*	*bona*	*bonae*	*bonum*	*bona*
Accusative	*bonum*	*bonos*	*bonam*	*bonas*	*bonum*	*bona*
Genitive	*boni*	*bonorum*	*bonae*	*bonarum*	*boni*	*bonorum*
Dative	*bono*	*bonis*	*bonae*	*bonis*	*bono*	*bonis*
Ablative	*bono*	*bonis*	*bona*	*bonis*	*bono*	*bonis*

Examples: *de vires bonorum* (of good men); *ad bonas feminas* (to good women); *pro bono nomini* (for a good name: dative case).

I'm afraid the only way to learn these declensions is to lie in bed chanting them. It's better than *computatis oves* (counting sheep).

CASE, NUMBER AND GENDER IN ENGLISH

Actually, we do use these, but only really in pronouns. Consider the verb 'to love' plus some personal pronouns and demonstrative pronouns (p. 70):

I love her   we love this
you love him   you love these
he/she/it loves them they love those

There is a distinction between the subject and object forms of I/me, he/him, she/her, we/us, they/them, but not for you or it.

I, he, she, we and they are the nominative case (used as the subject) while me, him, her, us and them are the other cases. There is an obvious gender difference between 'he/him/his' (m.), 'she/her/hers' (f.) and 'it/it/its' (nt.). You is the same in all cases, gender and number (except in Glasgow and Liverpool where, for a plural, they use 'youse'!).

The difference between subject and object with pronouns and prepositions can be seen in English sentences like: 'I gave it <u>to</u> her'; 'she took it <u>from</u> me'; 'you and I will eat lunch'; 'he gave it <u>to</u> you and me'; 'there's no difference <u>between</u> you and me'.

Please do not let anyone tell you that 'he gave it to you and I', or 'between you and I' are somehow more proper, correct or indicative of good breeding: they are just plain wrong grammatically.

There is some verb inflection in English, such as 'I once loved', where the ending -ed indicates a past action.

A BIT MORE GRAMMAR

Sadly, not all sentences are as simple as 'John loves Janet' (subject, verb, object) or 'Julius likes the dog' (subject, verb, object).

The simplest sentence is subject, verb, object. More complicated sentences may have subject, verb, predicate: 'John hit the noisy sailor with sticks frequently.'

John	hit	the	noisy	sailor	with	sticks	frequently
noun subject	verb	article	adjective	noun object	preposition	noun	adverb
							predicate

Sentences can be analysed into subject, predicate, object, verb, adverb, adjective, pronoun and preposition. The subject (John, or 'he' if using a pronoun) is the one doing the action indicated by the verb (hit) on the object (sailor). All the rest is colour and extra information. In Latin, the adjective (noisy) would have to agree with the object (sailor), both taking the accusative case. The plural noun (sticks) is after the preposition (with) and so would take the ablative case. We'll get to adverbs later on, but take heart from knowing that they don't behave in a complicated way like adjectives. No case, number or gender, promise!

SUMMARY

Nouns

- A noun is the name of a person, place, thing or quality: *Julius* (Julius), *Britannica* (Britain), *mensa* (table), *virtus* (courage).
- Nouns are either proper (names of persons or places such as *Julius*, *Britannica*, which are capitalised), or common *pes* (foot), but don't confuse that with common gender.
- Nouns are either concrete (a thing) or abstract (a concept).
- Concrete nouns indicate objects *mons* (mountain), *manus* (hand), *dies* (day) or collections *legio* (legion).
- Abstract nouns are qualities *fides* (trust).
- Nouns have case, number and gender in Latin. English has mainly lost this, except for plural endings.
- Latin has no articles: definite article (the) or indefinite (a). So *agricola* could mean either 'a farmer' or 'the farmer'.

More on gender

Latin nouns have gender: masculine (m.), feminine (f.) or neuter (nt.). In some cases, this is obvious. Names of people, for example, (proper nouns) will be masculine (*Julius*) or feminine (*Olivia*). So will most common nouns, including animals, which are clearly one or the other:

Masculine		Feminine	
cervus	stag	*cerva*	hind
filius	son	*filia*	daughter
maritus	husband	*sponsa*	wife
pater	father	*mater*	mother
vir	man	*femina*	woman
puer	boy	*puella*	girl
rex	king	*regina*	queen
aries	ram	*ovis*	ewe

Corinthus (Corinth), *Rhodus* (Rhodes) and other towns and islands ending in *-us* are feminine. Other names of towns and islands follow the gender of their endings: *Caledonia* (Scotland) is feminine, *Londinium* (London) is neuter, *Albion* (Britain) and *Alba* (Scotland) are both feminine.

Remember too that a lot of masculine nouns end in *-us* and feminine in *-a*, but this is not always so. Many neuter nouns end in *-um* but not all, by any means (*corpus*). And why is beard (*barba*) considered feminine? Some nouns can have a gender regardless of the gender of whom they refer to: *poeta* (poet), *nauta* (sailor) and *agricola* (farmer) are feminine in declension even if the poet, sailor or farmer in question is male, which they typically were in Roman times.

Some nouns exist in two or three forms according to gender:

Masculine (m.)	Feminine (f.)	Neuter (nt.)	
neosponsus	*neosponsa*		newlywed
unus	*una*	*unum*	one

Other nouns have a gender that is more or less unpredictable and is determined by the word ending (or declension, as we will see later):

Masculine (m.)		Feminine (f.)	
Sequana	River Seine (and all rivers)	*mensa*	table
Eurus	east wind (and all winds)	*sapientia*	wisdom
Ianuarius, Aprilis	January, April (and all months)	*malus, quercus*	apple tree, oak tree (and all trees)
pilus	hair	*urna*	urn
autumnus	autumn	*aestas*	summer
inquisitor	investigator	*barba*	beard
anser	goose or gander	*vulpes*	fox or vixen

Note that one form takes in both genders of the animal, as with goose or fox. But there is a gender difference between *taurus* (m.: 'bull'), *vacca* (f.: 'cow') and *bos* (c.: 'ox', 'cow').

Neuter (nt.)		Common (c.)	
malum	apple	Nouns that can be (m.) or (f.)	
pilum	javelin	civis	citizen
gaudium	joy	parens	parent
mare	sea	sacerdos	priest or priestess
ver	spring	This matters when we come to adjectives, as they have to agree with the noun, e.g. bona civis (good (female) citizen); bonus parens (good (male) parent); bona parens (good (female) parent).	
nefas	wrong		
nihil	nothing		
And all other indeclinable nouns.			

DECLENSION

Now we come to the difficult stuff. However, it is meant mostly for reference rather than to be absorbed. Nouns are usually listed by the nominative and genitive cases (explained later) as this indicates the declension, and sometimes just by indicating the stem and genitive ending, so *mensa, mensae* or *mensa, -ae.*

The declension is an indication as to all the possible word endings in the various cases, which is why they are grouped together that way.

	Declension										
	First (D1)		Second (D2)			Third (D3)		Fourth (D4)		Fifth (D5)	
	table	girl	son	boy	war	king	name	hand	house	day	thing
Singular	f.	f.	m.	m.	nt.	m.	nt.	f.	f.	m.	f.
Nom.	mensa	filia	filius	puer	bellum	rex	nomen	manus	domus	dies	res
Voc.	mensa	filia	fili	puer★	bellum	rex	nomen	manus	domus	dies	res
Acc.	mensam	filiam	filium	puerum	bellum	regem	nomen	manum	domum	diem	rem
Gen.	mensae	filiae	filii	pueri	belli	regis	moninis	manus	domus	diei	rei
Dat.	mensae	filiae	filio	puero	bello	regi	nomini	manui	domui	diei	rei
Abl.	mensa	filia	filio	puero	bello	rege	nomine	manu	domo	die	re
Plural											
Nom.	mensae	filiae	filii	pueri	bella	reges	nomina	manus	domus	dies	res
Voc.	mensae	filiae	filii	pueri	bella	reges	nomina	manus	domus	dies	res
Ac.	mensas	filias	filios	pueros	bella	reges	nomina	manus	domus	dies	res
Gen.	mensarum	filiarum	filiorum	puerorum	bellorum	regum	nominum	manuum	domuum	dierum	rerum
Dat.	mensis	filiabus	filiis	pueris	bellis	regibus	nominibus	manibus	domibus	diebus	rebus
Abl.	mensis	filiabus	filiis	pueris	bellis	regibus	nominibus	manibus	domibus	diebus	rebus
	★See note 5 p. 48		★See note 5 p. 48								

Some Nouns Declined

First declension (D1)

Singular	gate, door	woman	table	land	girl	goddess	Mary
Nom.	*porta*	*femina*	*mensa*	*terra*	*filia*	*dea*	*Maria*
Voc.	*porta*	*femina*	*mensa*	*terra*	*filia*	*dea*	*Maria*
Acc.	*portam*	*feminam*	*mensam*	*terram*	*filiam*	*deam*	*Mariam*
Gen.	*portae*	*feminae*	*mensae*	*terrae*	*filiae*	*deae*	*Mariae*
Dat.	*portae*	*feminae*	*mensae*	*terrae*	*filiae*	*deae*	*Mariae*
Abl.	*porta*	*femina*	*mensa*	*terra*	*filia*	*dea*	*Maria*
Plural							
Nom.	*portae*	*feminae*	*mensae*	*terrae*	*filiae*	*deae*	See notes
Voc.	*portae*	*feminae*	*mensae*	*terrae*	*filiae*	*deae*	below
Acc.	*portas*	*feminas*	*mensas*	*terras*	*filias*	*deas*	
Gen.	*portarum*	*feminarum*	*mensarum*	*terrarum*	*filiarum*	*dearum*	
Dat.	*portis*	*feminis*	*mensis*	*terris*	*filiabus*	*deabus*	
Abl.	*portis*	*feminis*	*mensis*	*terris*	*filiabus*	*deabus*	

Notes:

– Almost all D1 nouns are feminine (except where they refer to a male: *agricola*, *nauta* etc.).

– All D1 nouns end in –a in the nominative singular and –ae in the genitive singular.

– But *dea* (goddess) and *filia* (girl) take *-abus* rather than *–is* in the dative and ablative plurals, probably to avoid confusion with *filiis* (dative and ablative plurals of *filius* 'son') and *deis* (dative and ablative plurals of *deus* 'god'). There are a few others: *libertabus* (from *liberta* 'freedwoman') to avoid confusion with *libertis* (from *libertus* 'freedman'); *equabus* (mares); and *equis* (from *equus* 'horse').

– You will see an older form of the genitive singular (*-as* instead of *-ae*) in the combinations *pater familias* (father of the family); *mater familias*, *filius familias*, *filia familias* as well the regular form (*pater familiae*).

– There is an occasional locative singular case ending in *-ae* as in *Romae* (at Rome) and *Edimburgae* (at Edinburgh). (We haven't dealt with the locative case, and it won't be mentioned again. But it's obvious from this description what it's for: 'at' a location or place.)

– Of course, there are normally no plurals with proper names, but you could invent them, if you had to, for example, *quattuor Mariae* ('the four Marys').

– You do get the occasional male proper name behaving like a first declension female noun (*Aeneas*, *Aenea*, *Aeneam*, *Aeneae*, *Aeneae*, *Aenea*, and Dido didn't have any complaints).

Second declension (D2)

	Masculine								Neuter		
	Master	Horse	God	Boy	Field	Man	Son	Julius	Age	War	Talent
Singular											
Nom.	dominus	equus	deus	puer	ager	vir	filius	Julius	aevum	bellum	ingenium
Voc.	domine	eque	deus	puer	ager	vir	fili	Juli	aevum	bellum	ingenium
Acc.	dominum	equum	deum	puerum	agrum	virum	filium	Julium	aevum	bellum	ingenium
Gen.	domini	equi	dei	pueri	agri	viri	filii	Julii	aevi	belli	ingenii
Dat.	domino	equo	deo	puero	agro	viro	filio	Julio	aevo	bello	ingenio
Abl.	domino	equo	deo	puero	agro	viro	filio	Julio	aevo	bello	ingenio
Plural											
Nom.	domini	equi	dei or di	pueri	agri	viri	filii		aevi	bella	ingenia
Voc.	domini	equi	dei or di	pueri	agri	viri	filii		aevi	bella	ingenia
Acc.	dominos	equos	deos	pueros	agros	viros	filios		aevos	bella	ingenia
Gen.	dominorum	equorum	deorum	puerorum	agrorum	virorum	filiorum		aevorum	bellorum	ingeniorum
Dat.	dominis	equis	deis or dis	pueris	agris	viris	filiis		aevis	bellis	ingeniis
Abl.	dominis	equis	deis or dis	pueris	agris	viris	filiis		aevis	bellis	ingeniis

Notes:
– Almost all of these nouns are masculine and many end in *-us* except a few ending in *-r* or *-er*.
– Feminine examples of D2 nouns ending in *-us* are names of some towns (*Corinthus*), islands (*Rhodus*), some countries (*Aegyptus* 'Egypt') and trees (*quercus* 'oak'). Other examples include *alvus* (belly), *carbasus* (flax), *colus* (distaff), *humus* (ground), *vannus* (winnowing fan) and some words imported from Greek such as *atomus* (atom), but see below for *malus*.
– There are a few neuter examples, ending in *-um*: *bellum* (war), *ingenium* (talent).
– There are even some neuter nouns ending in *-us*: *pelagus* ('sea'), *virus* ('poison'), *vulgus* ('crowd'). *Puer* and *deus* have unusual vocative singulars.
– Proper names ending with *-ius* (*Julius, Lucius*) behave like *filius* and have an unusual vocative singular (*fili, Juli, Luci*).
– The three genders form of *malus* have different meanings: *malus, -i* (m.) 'mast or beam'; *malus, -i* (f.) 'apple tree'; *malum, -i* (nt.) 'apple', 'lemon', 'quince' or fruit generally, but also 'evil', 'mischief', 'disaster', 'misfortune', 'calamity', 'plague', 'punishment', 'harm' or 'hurt'; it is also an adjective meaning 'bad', 'evil', 'wicked', 'ugly' or 'unlucky'.

Third declension (D3)

	king (m.)	body (n.)	law (f.)	legion (f.)	citizen (m.)	praise (f.)	custom (m.)	father (m.)	old man (m.)	force (f.)	age (f.)	name (nt.)	burden (nt.)	work (nt.)
Singular														
Nom.	rex	corpus	lex	legio	civis	laus	mos	pater	senex	vis	aetas	nomen	onus	opus
Voc.	rex	corpus	lex	legio	civis	laus	mos	pater	senex		aetas	nomen	onus	opus
Acc.	regem	corpus	legem	legionem	civem	laudem	morem	patrem	senem	vim	aetatem	nomen	onus	opus
Gen.	regis	corporis	legis	legionis	civis	laudis	moris	patris	senis		aetatis	nominis	oneris	operis
Dat.	regi	corpori	legi	legioni	civi	laudi	mori	patri	seni		aetati	nomini	oneri	operi
Abl.	rege	corpore	lege	legione	cive	laude	more	patre	sene	vi	aetate	nomine	onere	opere
Plural						character (m.)			strength (f.)					
Nom.	reges	corpora	leges	legiones	cives	laudes	mores	patres	senes	vires	aetates	nomina	onera	opera
Voc.	reges	corpora	leges	legiones	cives	laudes	mores	patres	senes	vires	aetates	nomina	onera	opera
Acc.	reges	corpora	leges	legiones	cives	laudes	mores	patres	senes	vires	aetates	nomina	onera	opera
Gen.	regum	corporum	legum	legionum	civium	laud(i)um	morum	patrum	senum	virium	aetat(i)um	nominum	onerum	operum
Dat.	regibus	corporibus	legibus	legionibus	civibus	laudibus	moribus	patribus	senibus	viribus	aetatibus	nominibus	oneribus	operibus
Abl.	regibus	corporibus	legibus	legionibus	civibus	laudibus	moribus	patribus	senibus	viribus	aetatibus	nominibus	oneribus	operibus

Notes:

– This declension is a grab bag of irregular nouns of all genders.

– Quite often they change their stems (*rex*, *regem*; *legio*, *legionis*; *nomen*, *nominis*; *senex*, *senis* etc.).

– Notice that *mos* and *vis* change their meanings in the plurals.

– Don't confuse *vis* (D3 (f.) 'force') with *vir* (D2 (m.) 'man') and the plural of *vis* (*vires*), which means strength or power.

– The genitive plural of *aetas* can be *aetatum* or *aetatium*, and likewise with *laus*.

– Neuter nouns in D3 can be strange: the first three cases in the singular are the same (also with *flumen* (nt.) 'river'). The ablative singulars of *mare* ((nt.) 'sea') and *animal* are the same as the dative (*mari*, *animali*).

– *Honor* ((m.) 'honour') and *color* ((m.) 'colour') and a few others started linguistic life as *honos*, *colos* but the *-r* of the stem has crept into the nominative and vocative singulars. Otherwise, they behave like *mos*.

– When the stem is one syllable (as with *urbs* and *vis*) the genitive plural usually ends in *-ium* (e.g. *mos* and *bos*, which is unusual anyway). And *laus* pleases itself, as does *aetas*.

– Remember that *vis* is (f.) whereas *amor* is (m.).

	city (f.)	citadel (f.)	race, family (f.)	mountain (m.)	praise (f.)	night (m.)	bridge (m.)		ox, cow (c.)	Jupiter (m.)	city walls (nt.)	love (m.)	descent, family (nt.)
Singular													
Nom.	urbs	arx	gens	mons	laus	nox	pons		bos	Iuppiter		amor	genus
Voc.	urbs	arx	gens	mons	laus	nox	pons		bos	Iuppiter		amor	genus
Acc.	urbem	arcem	gentem	montem	laudem	noctem	pontem		bovem	Iovem		amorem	genus
Gen.	urbis	arcis	genis	montis	laudis	noctis	pontis	and	bovis	Iovis		amoris	generis
Dat.	urbi	arci	geni	monti	laudi	nocti	ponti	some	bovi	Iovi		amori	generi
Abl.	urbe	arce	gene	monte	laude	nocte	ponte	irregular	bove	Iove	only plural	amore	genere
Plural								ones		no plural			
Nom.	urbes	arces	genes	montes	laudes	noctes	pontes		boves		moenia	amores	genera
Voc.	urbes	arces	genes	montes	laudes	noctes	pontes		boves		moenia	amores	genera
Acc.	urbes	arces	genes	montes	laudes	noctes	pontes		boves		moenia	amores	genera
Gen.	urbium	arcium	genium	montium	laud(i)um	noctium	pontium		boum		moenium	amorum	generum
Dat.	urbibus	arcibus	genibus	montibus	laudibus	noctibus	pontibus		bobus		moenibus	amoribus	generibus
Abl.	urbibus	arcibus	genibus	montibus	laudibus	noctibus	pontibus		bobus		moenibus	amoribus	generibus

Fourth declension (D4)

	Most are masculine		A few neuter (end in –*u*)		A very few feminine			
	army (m.)	**harbour** (m.)	**horn** (nt.)	**knee** (nt.)	**hand** (f.)	**Ides** (f.)	**house** (f.)	
Singular								
Nom.	*exercitus*	*portus*	*cornu*	*genu*	*manus*		*domus*	
Voc.	*exercitus*	*portus*	*cornu*	*genu*	*manus*		*domus*	
Locative							*domi*	= at home
Acc.	*exercitum*	*portum*	*cornu*	*genu*	*manum*		*domum*	
Gen.	*exercitus*	*portus*	*cornus*	*genus*	*manus*		*domus*	
Dat.	*exercitui*	*portui*	*cornu*	*genu*	*manui*		*domui*	
Abl.	*exercitu*	*portu*	*cornu*	*genu*	*manu*		*domo*	
Plural			*cornu*			plural only		
Nom.	*exercitus*	*portus*	*cornua*	*genua*	*manus*	*Idus*	*domus*	
Voc.	*exercitus*	*portus*	*cornua*	*genua*	*manus*	*Idus*	*domus*	
Acc.	*exercitus*	*portus*	*cornua*	*genua*	*manus*	*Idus*	*domus*, *domos*	
Gen.	*exercituum*	*portuum*	*cornuum*	*genuum*	*manuum*	*Iduum*	*domuum*, *domorum*	
Dat.	*exercitibus*	*portibus*, *portubus*	*cornibus*	*genibus*, *genubus*	*manibus*	*Idibus*	*domibus*	
Abl.	*exercitibus*	*portibus*, *portubus*	*cornibus*	*genibus*, *genubus*	*manibus*	*Idibus*	*domibus*	

Notes:
– Most D4 nouns are masculine and many end in -*us*.
– Don't confuse *genu* (D4 (nt.) 'knee') with *genus* (D3 (nt.) 'descent' or 'family') or *gens* (D3 (f.) 'tribe' or 'family'). The difference between *gen* and *genus* is that you will see *gens* meaning a tribe, clan or ethnic group, while *genus* indicates a bloodline or immediate family.
– The only neuters of this declension commonly used are: *cornu* (horn), *genu* (knee) and *veru* (spit).
– The D4 feminine nouns ending in -*us* often confuse, because they look like they might be D2 masculine: examples are *domus* (house), *manus* (hand) and *Idus* (ides, used only in the plural) as we've seen. Others include *acus* (needle), *porticus* (colonnade) and *tribus* (tribe). Recall that the names of some trees and islands ending in –*us* are D2 feminine: *quercus* (oak), *Corinthus* (Corinth) and *Rhodus* (Rhodes).

Fifth declension (D5)

At last, an easy one. There are only a few, they all end in -es and most are feminine except *dies* (day) and, therefore, not surprisingly, *meridies* (midday, noon).

	thing	**trust**	**people**	**point**	**hope**	**row**	**sight, appearance**	**day**	**midday**
	f.	f.	f.	f.	f.	f.	f.	m.★	m★.
Singular									
Nom.	*res*	*fides*	*plebes*	*acies*	*spes*	*series*	*species*	*dies*	*meridies*
Voc.	*res*	*fides*	*plebes*	*acies*	*spes*	*series*	*species*	*dies*	*meridies*
Acc.	*rem*	*fidem*	*plebem*	*aciem*	*spem*	*seriem*	*speciem*	*diem*	*meridiem*
Gen.	*rei*	*fidei*	*plebi★*	*acie★*	*spei*	*seriei*	*speciei*	*diei*	*meridiei*
Dat.	*rei*	*fidei*	*plebei*	*acie★*	*spei*	*seriei*	*speciei*	*diei*	*meridiei*
Abl.	*re*	*fide*	*plebe*	*acie*	*spe*	*serie*	*specie*	*die*	*meridie*
Plural									
Nom.	*res*			*acies*	*spes*	*series*	*species*	*dies*	*meridies*
Voc.	*res*	Not usually used in the plural: **plebes** and **fides**, although singular, are used as if they were plurals already						*dies*	*meridies*
Acc.	*res*			*acies*	*spes*	*series*	*species*	*dies*	*meridies*
Gen.	*rerum*							*dierum*	*meridierum*
Dat.	*rebus*							*diebus*	*meridiebus*
Abl.	*rebus*							*diebus*	*meridiebus*
			★unusual					★unusual	

Notes:
– *Fides* can mean a variety of things: trust, faith, honour, trustworthiness, loyalty, truth, promise, guarantee, protection, credit or good faith.
– Most D5 nouns are not declined in the plural. Exceptions are: *dies* and *res; acies, series, species, spes* and a few others are used only in the nominative and accusative plural.
– *Acies* means a sharp point or blade edge, but also has the same connotation as 'sharp eye' or 'sharp mind' in English. It can also mean a battle order of troops. Notice the unusual genitive and dative singular.
– The English word specie, meaning 'coin' or 'cash money', is derived from the ablative phrase *in specie* (in real or actual form) and indicates money in the form of coins as opposed to 'unreal' paper.
– Just to confuse matters, *dies*, usually masculine, is sometimes used as a feminine noun, as in *statuta dies* (the appointed day). '*Cum statuta venerit dies*': when the appointed day has come.

The five declensions: a summary

These are distinguished by the final letter of the stem, and the ending of the genitive singular:

Declension	Typical nominative singular ending	Genitive ending	Final letter of stem	Examples	
First	-a	-ae	a	*mensa, mensae*	table
Second	-us, -r, -er	-i		*servus, servi*	slave
Third	various	-is	i/a consonant	*legio, legionis*	legion
Fourth	-us	-us		*fructus, fructus*	fruit
Fifth	-es	-ei / -ei	e	*dies, diei*	deie

Some 'False Friends': don't be taken in by them!

	Man	Force
Singular	D2 (m.)	D3 (f.)
Nom.	*vir*	*vis*
Voc.	*vir*	
Acc.	*virum*	*vim*
Gen.	*viri*	
Dat.	*viro*	
Abl.	*viro*	*vi*
Plural		Strength
Nom.	*viri*	*vires*
Voc.	*viri*	*vires*
Acc.	*viros*	*vires*
Gen.	*virorum*	*virium*
Dat.	*viris*	*viribus*
Abl.	*viris*	*viribus*

CASES AND PREPOSITIONS

Prepositions governing the accusative			
ad	to towards	*ad hominem* *ad Londiniam*	to the man to London
adversus, adversum	opposite against	*adversus me* *adversum bellum*	opposite (facing) me against the war
ante	before (place and time)	*ante meridiem* *ante portam*	morning before the door
apud	at (places, persons) before in (the works of)	*apud Striveling* *apud regem* *apud Baconem*	(written) at Stirlin before the king in Bacon's books
circum, circa (pl.)	around (place, people)	*circum puerum* *circa mille centum*	around the boy around 1100
contra	against, opposite	*contra Anglicas* *contra domum*	against the English facing the house
extra	outside beyond	*extra muros* *extra vires*	outside the walls beyond (his) powers
inter	among between during	*inter senes* *inter pares* *inter hos dies*	amongst the old men between parties during these days
intra	within (time and place)	*inter moenia* *inter tres horas*	within the city walls within three hours
iuxta	close to, next to right after according to	*iuxta agrum* *iuxta patrem nostrum* *iuxta judem*	next to the field after (our) father according to a judge
ob	because of	*ob vim* *quam ob rem*	due to the strength (of) therefore
per	through by	*per diem* *per aetatem (obiit)*	through the day (he died) of old age
post	after (time and place)	*post urbem conditam* *post hoc*	after the foundation of the city after this
praeter	beyond except for	*praeter mentem* *praeter te*	beyond reason except for (besides) yourself
prope	near	*prope naves*	near the ships
propter	because of	*propter morbum*	on account of illness
secundum	along, behind (place) right after (time) next to (rank) according to	*secundum Thamesem* *secundum prandium* *secundum princepem* *secundum morem*	along the Thames after breakfast after the chief (or prince) according to custom
trans	across (time, measure etc.)	*trans Alpes*	across the Alps
ultra	beyond	*ultra vires* *ultra fines*	beyond (one's) powers beyond the limits

Prepositions governing the ablative

a, ab	from by	a sinistra ab urbi ab domino dat	from the left from the city (given) by the master
coram	in the presence of	coram reginam	in the Queen's presence
cum	with	magnaa cum laude sum nota	with great praise with a mark
de	from about during, at (time)	de caelo de minimis non curat lex de die	from heaven (the law is not concerned) with trifles by (during) daytime
e ex	out of, from from (made) from	e domo ex puero ex auro	out of the house after boyhood from gold
f pro	for on behalf of in front of	pro patria pro bono publico pro senato	for (one's) country for the public good before the Senate
sine	without	sine prole	without issue (children)

Prepositions governing both the accusative and ablative

in	acc.	into until concerning	in urbem in meridiem in rem	into the city until noon regarding a thing
in	abl.	in on within (time) in (condition or quality)	in domo in capite in hic anno in utero	in the house on (his) head during this year unborn
sub	acc.	beneath below (with motion) before (time)	sub arcem sub terram (ire) sub quietam	beneath the citadel (to go) below ground before sleep
sub	abl.	under (place, authority)	sub collibus sub rosa	under the hills beneath the rose (i.e. secret)
super	acc.	over (place) in addition to	super astra super officiium	above the stars (i.e. heaven) above and beyond the call of duty
super	abl.	about (concerning)	super his civibus	about these citizens

Prepositions, conjunctions and adverbs using prepositions

ac (conj.)	and
ad huc/adhuc	thus far, as yet, still, in addition, in the future
ad modum (adv.)	very, quite; fully; + non. = at all
aliquam	in some degree
aliquando	at times, sometimes; once, formerly
aliqui/qua/quod	some, any
aliquis/qua/quid	someone, something; some, any

aliquotiens	several times, at different times
at (form of *ad* = in addition to)	but (introducing changes)
atque	and as well, even, together with, in all
atque … atque	both … and
atqui	rather, however, but at any rate, but for all that
aut	or, at least, or else
aut … aut	either … or
autem	but, on the other hand, however
coram (adv.) and (prep.)	in the presence of, before
dehinc (adv.)	while, from here, from now, henceforth; then, next
deinde (adv.)	from there; then, afterwards; secondly, next (in order), in second (next) place
demum (adv.)	at last, finally, not till then; precisely, exactly, just, in fact, certainly, to be sure
denique (adv.)	finally
donec	while, as long as, until
dum (conj.)	while, now; so long as, provided that, if only; until
enim (conj.)	namely, indeed, certainly, in fact, for, because
eo quod	because
etenim (conj.)	and indeed, for, as a matter of fact
etiam	also, besides; even, actually; (time) still
etsi (conj.))	though, although, and yet
fas (*est*)	(it is) right, proper
huc	here, to this place; so far, for this purpose
ibi	there, then, therein, on that occasion
idcirco	for that reason, on that account, therefore
ideo	therefore, for this reason
illuc (adv.)	(to) there; to that; to him/her
immo (adv.)	or rather; indeed; no, yes (emphasis)
in quantum	to what extent
inde	from there, from that source, then, after; from then
interdum	occasionally, sometimes, now and then
ita	thus, so, in this way
ita … quomodo	just as
ita … ut	just as, so … that
iuxta (adv.)	nearby, alike, equally
iuxta (prep.)	close to, right after, near to, beside, according to
iuxta aliquid	to some extent
licet	all right; (with dative + infinitive) it is right to
licet (conj.)	although, even if
modo	only, just now

modo demum	only now, just now
necnon	also, moreover, certainly, besides
nempe	to be sure, of course
non numquam	sometimes
nondum	not yet
nonnullus/a/um	some, several
nuper	recently, lately
nusquam	nowhere
ob (prep.)	before, in front of; on account of, because of; for the sake of; instead of; in proportion to
ob rem	to the purpose, usefully
olim	once; of old; one day
postea	afterwards
postmodum	afterwards; presently
praeterea	besides, moreover; hereafter
procul	far off
proinde (adv.)	consequently, therefore; just as
propterea	for that reason, therefore
prorsus/um (adv.))	forwards; absolutely; in short
prout (conj.)	according as
qua (adv.)	where, as far as, how; qua ... qua
qualibit	anywhere, any way, as you please
qualis -e	what sort of, what kind of, such as, as
qualiter (adv.)	how, as, just as
quam (adv.)	how, how much; as, very
quam ob rem	wherefore, accordingly
quamdiu	as long as; while; inasmuch as
quamquam	although
quamvis (adv.)	however
quamvis (conj.)	although
quando	when (after *nisi, ne*) ever;
quando (conj.)	when, since, because
quandoque (adv.)	at some time
quandoque (conj.)	whenever, as often as, since
quanto	for how much
quantum (adv.)	as much as, as far as, so much as, to what extent
quantum ad	in terms of, as far as x is concerned, with respect to
quantus	how great, how much
quapropter	wherefore
quare	by what means, how; why, wherefore

quasi	as if, as though
quatenus (adv.)	(interrog.) how far, how long? (rel.) as far as, in so far as, since
quemadmodum (adv.)	in what way, how
quemadmodum (conj.)	as, just as
quicquam	anything
quicumque/quae-/quod-	whoever, whatever; all that, any whatever
quidam/quae-/quid-	a certain one, someone, a kind of
quidem	indeed, in fact
quippe (adv.)	certainly, of course
quippe (conj.)	(explaining) for in fact, because, since
quisquam quid-	anyone, anything
quisque quidque	each, each one, every
quisquis/quisquid	whoever, whatever; all
quo	where, what for, to what end
quoad	as to, with respect to
quocumque	how so ever; wither so ever
quod (conj.)	because, as far as, in so far as, as for the fact that, in that, that
quod si	but if
quodamodo	in a way
quomodo	how, in what way; (rel.) as, just as
quondam	once, sometimes, formerly
quoniam	because, since, seeing that, now that
quoque	also, too
quot	how many; (conj.) as many
quotiens	how often (rel.) as often as
recte	rightly, correctly
rursum	again
rursus	again, in turn
sane	reasonably, sensibly; certainly, doubtless, truly; of course
scilicet (adv.)	evidently, naturally, of course
scilicet (as explanatory)	namely, that is to say, in other words
semel	once
seu	and (= et)
simul	at the same time; together; likewise
sin	but if
sivi (conj.)	or, or if, whether … or
siquidem	if in fact; if only, if indeed; since indeed, since that
talis/-e (adj.).	such, of such a kind, the following
taliter	in such a manner, so
tam	so, so greatly

tam ... quam	so ... as, much ... as, as well as
tamen	yet, nevertheless, still
tamquam	as, just as; (conj.) as if, just as if
tandem	at last, finally
tantum (adv.)	so much, so greatly; to such a degree; so far; only
tantus/-a/-um (adj.)	of such (a size); so great, so much
tot	as many, so many
tunc (adv.)	then, just the; thereupon, accordingly, consequently
ubicumque	wherever, everywhere
unde	whence, from where; wherefore; this being the case
usque	as far as, all the way, continually, straight on, up to; until
ut ... ita	while ... nevertheless
uterque/-raque/-rumque	both, each (of two)
utinam	would that, if only
utique	anyhow, at least, at any rate
utpote	as, in as much as
utrum (conj.)	either, whether
velut	as, just as, as it were, as though
vero (conj.)	but, truly
verumtamen	but yet, nevertheless
videlicet	clearly, evidently; namely

A STRATEGY FOR TRANSLATION

Translating from Latin can be tricky, especially since it doesn't 'read' like English, thanks to the word order: putting adjectives after nouns and the verb at the end etc. But there are some basic rules:

- Find the verb (usually at the end of a sentence but not always). This tells you what is being done, who is doing it and to whom.
- Look at the ending of the verb and work out which person it is (I, you, he/she/it, etc.) ...
- ... and whether it is singular or plural.
- Which tense (present, past, future, etc.)?
- Voice and mood: active or passive, indicative or subjunctive etc.

- Find the subject: a noun or nouns in the nominative case.
- If the verb is singular (I, you, he, she or it), the noun will be nominative singular.
- If the verb is plural (we, you, they) the noun will be nominative plural or there will be two or more nouns in the nominative case joined by 'and' (*et* or *-que*).

- Find the object: a noun or nouns in the accusative case.
- Don't translate the object before the verb.
- Analyse the sentence by writing *V* over a verb, *S* over the subject and *O* over the object. If the subject is 'in the verb', write *V+S* over the verb. The endings, not the word order, tell you whether a noun is the subject or object.

	S	O	V	both mean 'the girl loves the farmer'.
e.g.	*puella*	*agricolam*	*amat*	
	O	S	V	
and	*agricolam*	*puella*	*amat*	

At this point we could do no better than to quote directly from Brian's Latin lesson in *Monty Python's Life of Brian* (1979):

> Brian is writing a slogan on a wall, oblivious to the Roman patrol approaching from behind. The slogan is 'ROMANES EUNT DOMUS'.

Centurion:	What's this thing? 'ROMANES EUNT DOMUS'? 'People called Romanes they go the house?'
Brian:	It … it says 'Romans go home.'
Centurion:	No it doesn't. What's Latin for 'Roman'?
	Brian hesitates.
Centurion:	Come on, come on!
Brian:	(*uncertain*) 'ROMANUS'.
Centurion:	Goes like?
Brian:	'-ANUS'.
Centurion:	Vocative plural of '-ANUS' is?
Brian:	'-ANI'.
Centurion:	(*Takes paintbrush from Brian and paints over*) 'RO-MA-NI'. 'EUNT'? What is 'EUNT'?
Brian:	'Go'.
Centurion:	Conjugate the verb 'to go'!
Brian:	'IRE'. 'EO', 'IS', 'IT', 'IMUS', 'ITIS', 'EUNT'.
Centurion:	So 'EUNT' is … ?
Brian:	Third person plural present indicative, 'they go'.
Centurion:	But 'Romans, go home!' is an order, so you must use the … ?
	He lifts Brian by his short hairs
Brian:	The … imperative.
Centurion:	Which is?
Brian:	Um, oh, oh, 'I', 'I'!
Centurion:	How many Romans? (*pulls harder*)
Brian:	Plural, plural! 'ITE'.
	Centurion strikes over 'EUNT' and paints 'ITE' on the wall.
Centurion:	'I-TE'. 'DOMUS'? Nominative? 'Go home', this is motion towards, isn't it, boy?
Brian:	(*Very anxious*) Dative?
	Centurion draws his sword and holds it to Brian's throat.
Brian:	Ahh! No, ablative, ablative, sir. No, the, accusative, accusative, ah, 'DOMUM', sir.
Centurion:	Except that 'DOMUS' takes the … ?
Brian:	… the locative, sir!
Centurion:	Which is?
Brian:	'DOMUM'.
Centurion:	(*Satisfied*) 'DOMUM'.
	He strikes out 'DOMUS' and writes 'DOMUM'.
Centurian:	'-MUM'. Understand?
Brian:	Yes sir.
Centurion:	Now write it down a hundred times.

… except that the locative of *domus* is actually *domi*. Anyway, it should be *domum* (homewards, to one's home) or more likely the plural *domos* (homewards, to their homes). Sorry, Mr Cleese.

ADJECTIVES

An adjective 'qualifies' a noun. A *good* ship; a *tender* woman; a *bold* man; a *huge* city; a *brave* dog; a *keen* soldier; an *old* wall; a *rich* king; a *poor* queen. In Latin, the adjective usually follows the noun (a good ship: *navis bona*) but may precede it when special emphasis is needed.

Adjectives must 'agree' with (have the same gender, case and number as) the nouns they qualify.

Gender. For instance, because *filia* (girl) is feminine and *filius* (son) is masculine, 'a good daughter' is *puella bona* and 'a good son' is *filius bonus*. There is also a neuter form: 'a good war' (if there is such a thing) is *bellum bonum*.

Case. As we have seen, in English phrases like 'year of birth' and 'in the year of our Lord', the words 'year' and 'Lord' are the same regardless of case. In Latin, 'year' is the nominative *annus* but 'in the year' is the ablative *anno*, as in *Anno Domini*. So 'a good year' would be *annus bonus*; 'of a good year' *anni boni*; 'in a good year' *anno bono*. Adjectives take the same six cases as nouns.

Number. There are singular and plural forms too: 'good daughters' is *puellae bonae*; 'good sons' is *filii boni*; 'good wars' is *bella bona*.

Declensions. As you'd expect, adjectives are organised into declensions. But there are only three and two of those are sort of merged. In the third declension the masculine and feminine (and sometimes neuter) genders are much the same, which simplifies matters. Below are complete tables for a number of adjectives, by declension and type of ending.

Adjectives in the first and second declensions

	good m.	good f.	good nt.	free m.	free f.	free nt.	beautiful m.	beautiful f.	beautiful nt.	another m.	another f.	another nt.	one m.	one f.	one nt.
Singular															
Nom.	bonus	bona	bonum	liber	libera	liberum	pulcher	pulchra	pulchrum	alius	alia	aliud*	unus	una	unum
Voc.	bone	bona	bonum	liber	libera	liberum	pulcher	pulchra	pulchrum	*Gen. sing. alius*			*Gen. sing. unius*		
Acc.	bonum	bonam	bonum	liberum	liberam	liberum	pulchrum	pulchram	pulchrum	*Dat. sing. alii*			*Dat. sing. unii*		
Gen.	boni	bonae	boni	liberi	liberae	liberi	pulchri	pulchrae	pulchri	:			Same		
Dat.	bono	bonae	bono	libero	liberae	libero	pulchro	pulchrae	pulchro	one of two			no, none		
Abl.	bono	bona	bono	libero	libera	libero	pulchro	pulchra	pulchro	alter	altera	alterum	nullus	nulla	nullum
Singular															
Nom.	boni	bonae	bona	liberi	liberae	libera	pulchri	pulchrae	pulchra	*Gen. sing. alius*			any		
Voc.	boni	bonae	bona	liberi	liberae	libera	pulchri	pulchrae	pulchra	*Dat. sing. alii*			ullus	ulla	ullum
Acc.	bonos	bonas	bona	liberos	liberas	libera	pulchros	pulchras	pulchra	which of two?			alone, only		
Gen.	bonorum	bonarum	bonorum	liberorum	liberarum	liberorum	pulchrorum	pulchrarum	pulchrorum	uter	utra	utrum	solus	sola	solum
Dat.	bonis	bonis	bonis	liberis	liberis	liberis	pulchris	pulchris	pulchris	*Gen. sing. utrius*			whole		
Abl.	bonis	bonis	bonis	liberis	liberis	liberis	pulchris	pulchris	pulchris	*Dat. sing. utri*			totus	tota	totum

Notes

- Compare these with the nouns: *dominus* (D2 m.), *mensa* (D1 f.), *bellum* (D2 nt.).
- Compare *puer* (D2 m): retains the –er. Similarly declined: *miser* (unhappy), *tener* (tender).
- Compare *ager* (D2 m): –er becomes –r. Similarly declined: *aeger* (sick), *integer* (whole), *sacer* (sacred).
- Same; neither — *neuter*, *neutra*, *neutrum*.

Adjectives in the third declension

Case differences are underlined.

	powerful		loving		fierce		brave		sharp			old		rich	poor
Singular	m. & f.	nt.	m. & f.	nt.	m. & f.	nt.	m. & f.	nt.	m.	f.	nt.	m. & f.	nt.	m. & f.	m. & f.
Nom.	potens	*potens*	amans		ferox	ferox	fortis	forte	acer	acris	acre	vetus		dives	pauper
Voc.	potens	*potens*	amans		ferox	ferox	fortis	forte	acer	acris	acre	vetus		dives	pauper
Acc.	potentem	*potens*	amantem	*amans*	ferocem	ferox	fortem	forte	acrem	acrem	acre	veterem	vetus	divitem	pauperem
Gen.	potentis		amantis		ferocis		fortis		acris	acris		veteris		divitis	pauperis
Dat.	potenti		amanti		feroci		forti		acri	acri		veteri		diviti	pauperi
Abl.	potenti		amante★		feroci		forti		acri	acri		veteri		divite	paupere
			★(amanti when adjective)												
Plural															
Nom.	potentes	potentia	amantes	amantia	feroces	ferocia	fortes	fortiores	acres	acres	acria	veteres	vetera	divites	pauperes
Voc.	potentes	potentia	amantes	amantia	feroces	ferocia	fortes	fortiores	acres	acres	acria	veteres	vetera	divites	pauperes
Acc.	potentes	potentia	amantes	amantia	feroces	ferocia	fortes	fortiores	acres	acres	acria	veteres	vetera	divites	pauperes
Gen.	potentium		amantium		ferocium		fortium		acrium			veterum		divitum	pauperum
Dat.	potentibus		amantibus		ferocibus		fortibus		acribus			veteribus		divitibus	pauperibus
Abl.	potentibus		amantibus		ferocibus		fortibus		acribus			veteribus		divitibus	pauperibus

powerful	loving	fierce	brave	sharp	old	rich / poor
Same diligens (careful) frequens (frequent) innocens (innocent) ingens (huge) prudens (prudent)	This is really the present participle of *amare* (to love). All present participles are declined like *amans* (cf. *habens*)	Same: audax (bold), felix (lucky)	Same: brevis (brief) facilis (easy) gravis (heavy) levis (light) omnis (all), talis (of such) qualis (of which type) tristis (sad)	Same: alacer (lively) equester (mounted) Slightly different celer, celeris, celere (fast) keeps the second *e-* (celer, celer, celerem, celeris, celeri, celeri)	Note the *-um* in the gen. plural	No neuter. Note the *-um* in the gen. plural

Numbers

Latin treats numbers as adjectives (and there is no vocative case).

	one			two			three			quattuor (four) to centum (100)	ducenti (200) to nongenti (900)			milia (1,000)	ordinal numbers
	m.	f.	nt.	m.	f.	nt.	m.	f.	nt.		m. pl	f. pl	nt. pl	nt. pl	(*primus, secundus* etc.)
Nom.	*unus*	*una*	*unum*	*duo*	*duae*	*duo*	*tres*		*tria*	do not decline	*ducenti*	*ducentae*	*ducenta*	*milia*	declined like bonus, *–a, –um*
Acc.	*unum*	*unam*	*unum*	*duos*	*duas*	*duo*	*tres*		*tria*		*ducentos*	*ducentas*	*ducenta*	*milia*	
Gen.	*unius*			*duorum*	*duarum*	*duorum*	*trium*				*ducentum*			*milium*	
Dat.	*uni*			*duobus*	*duabus*	*duobus*	*tribus*				*ducentis*			*milibus*	
Abl.	*uno*			*duobus*	*duabus*	*duobus*	*tribus*				*ducentis*			*milibus*	

Good, better, best

Adjectives can have comparatives and superlatives. In English, most of these are formed by adding -er and -est to the simple form: hard, harder, hardest; fast, faster, fastest.

Some are irregular – good, better, best – while others, usually longer words, take 'more' and 'most': difficult, more difficult, most difficult.

Latin adds -ior to the stem (m. and f.) for the comparative and something ending in –imus, –ima, –imum for the superlative. Just be careful with what the stem is.

		Comparative	Superlative	
Most adjectives	**stem**	**–ior**	**–issumus**	**Others similar**
altus (high)	*alt-*	*altior*	*altissimus/a/um*	*fortis* (brave)
ferox (fierce)	*feroc-*	*ferocior*	*ferocissimus/a/um*	
audax (bold)	*audac-*	*audacior*	*audacissimus/a,–um*	*felix* (lucky)
potens (powerful)	*potent-*	*potentior*	*potentissimus/a/um*	*prudens* (prudent)
antiquus (old)	*antiqu-*	*antiquior*	*antiquissimus/a/um*	
Ending in **–dicus, –ficus** and **–volus**		**–ior**	**–issimus**	Note stems have **–ent**
maledicus (slanderous)	*maledicent-*	*maledicentior*	*maledicentissimus/a/um*	
magnificus (magnificent)	*magnificent-*	*magnificentior*	*magnificentissimus/a/um*	
benevolus (kindly)	*benevolent-*	*benevolentior*	*benevolentissimus/a/um*	
Ending in **–er**		**–ior**	**–rimus** (note the double r)	
liber (free)	*liber*	*liberior*	*liberrimus/a/um*	*celer* (fast), *asper* (rough)
pulcher (beautiful)	*pulchr–*	*pulchrior*	*pulcherrimus/a/-um*	*aeger* (sick)
integer (whole)				
Ending in –*is*		**–ior**	**–limus** (Note the double 'l')	
facilis (easy)	*facil-*	*facilior*	*facillimus/a/um*	*difficilis* (difficult), *dissimilis* (unlike), *similis* (like), *gracilis* (slender), *humilis* (humble). There are only six.
Participles				
doctus (learned)		*doctior*	*doctissimus/a/um*	
egens (needy)		*egentior*	*egentissimus/a/um*	

Just as English has 'good, better, best', Latin has these irregular comparisons:

	Comparative	Superlative
(1) Irregular forms		
bonus (good)	*melior* (better)	*optimus/a/um* (best)
malus (bad)	*peior* (worse)	*pessimus/a/um* (worst)
magnus (great)	*maior* (greater)	*maximus/a/um* (greatest)
parvus (small)	*minor* (smaller	*minimus/a/um* (smallest)

multus (much)	*plus* (more)	*plurimus/a/um* (most)
multi (many)	*plures* (more)	*plurimi/ae/a* (most)
frugi (thrifty)	frug**alior**	frug**alissimus/ae/a**
nequam (worthless)	nequ**ior**	nequ**issimus/ae/a**
(2) No simple form		
	magis (more)	*maxime* (most)
citra (this side of)	*citerior* (on this side)	*citimus* (near)
de (down)	*deterior* (inferior)	*deterrimus* (worst)
extra (below)		
exteri (foreigners)		
nationes exterae (foreign nations)	*exterior* (outer)	*extremus/ae/a*, *extimus* (outermost)
infra (below)		
inferi (gods of the underworld)		
Mare Inferum (Mediterranean)	*inferior* (lower)	*infimus/ae/a* or *imus/ae/a* (lowest)
intra (within)	*interior*, inner	*intimus*, inmost
post (after)		
postero dei (the day after)		
posteri (descendants)	*posterior* (later)	*postremus/ae/a* (latest, last)
postumus (late-born, posthumous)		
potis (possible)	*potior* (preferable)	*potissimus/ae/a* (chiefest)
prae (in front of)	*prior* (former)	*primus/ae/a* (first)
prope (near)	*propior* (nearer)	*proximus/ae/a* (nearest)
super (above)		
superi (gods above)		
Mare Superum (Adriatic Sea)	*superior* (upper)	*supremus/ae/a or summus/ae/a* (uppermost)
ultra (beyond)	*ulterior* (farther)	*ultimus/ae/a* (farthest)
(3) Like 'difficult, more difficult, most difficult' any adjective ending in *-us* after any vowel except *u* (see *antiquus*, above) takes the adverbs *magis* (more) and *maxime* (most).		
idoneus (suitable, adapted)	*magis idoneus*	*maxime idoneus*
dubius (doubtful)	*magis dubius*	*maxime dubius*
arduus (steep)	*magis arduus*	*maxime arduus*
necessarius (necessary)	*magis necessarius*	*maxime necessarius*
(4) No comparative		
vetus (old)		*veterrimus/ae/a*
fidus (faithful)		*fidissimus/ae/a*
novus (new)		*novissimus/ae/a (last)*
sacer (sacred)		*sacerrimus/ae/a*
falsus (false)		*falsissimus/ae/a*
(5) No superlative (also in many adjectives ending in **-alis, -ilis, -ilis, -bilis**)		
alacer (lively)	*alacrior*	

ingens (great)	*ingentior*	
salutaris (wholesome)	*salutarior*	
juvenis (young)	*junior*	
senex (old)	*senior*	
(6) No comparison at all		
hodiernus (of today)		
annuus (annual)		
mortalis (mortal)		

How comparisons decline

You are probably wondering about this. Relax, it's simple. The comparatives are like D3 adjectives (e.g. *fortior*) and the superlatives like D1/2 adjectives (e.g. *bonus*).

Comparative		Superlative		
m. & f.	nt.	m.	f.	nt.
braver			bravest	
fortior	*fortius*	*fortissimus*	*fortissima*	*fortissimum*
fortior	*fortius*	*fortissime*	*fortissima*	*fortissimum*
fortiorem	*fortius*	*fortissimum*	*fortissimam*	*fortissimum*
fortioris		*fortissimi*	*fortissimae*	*fortissimi*
fortiori		*fortissimo*	*fortissimae*	*fortissimo*
fortiore		*fortissimo*	*fortissima*	*fortissimo*
fortiores	*fortiora*	*fortissimi*	*fortissimae*	*fortissima*
fortiores	*fortiora*	*fortissimi*	*fortissimae*	*fortissima*
fortiores	*fortiora*	*fortissimos*	*fortissimas*	*fortissima*
fortiorum		*fortissimorum*	*fortissimarum*	*fortissimorum*
fortiorbus		*fortissimis*	*fortissimis*	*fortissimis*
fortiorbus		*fortissimis*	*fortissimis*	*fortissimis*

ADVERBS

Adverbs usually come before the verb, adjective or other adverb they modify, but often at the start of a sentence they modify:

a <u>verb</u>: he <u>ran</u> *quickly*
an <u>adjective</u>: he was *fairly* <u>quick</u>
another <u>adverb</u>: he ran *fairly quickly*
a <u>noun</u> : *twice* a <u>father</u>

In English, a lot of adverbs end in *-ly* but not all *-ly* words are adverbs: ugly, lovely, lucky etc. are adjectives. In Latin, most adverbs are formed from adjectives by simple rules (and hundreds of exceptions!).

Adjectives ending in -er change to -e			Adverb	Comparative Change -ior to –ius	Superlative Change –imus to –ime
celer (fast)	celerior (faster)	celerrimus (fastest)	celere (quickly)	celerius (more quickly)	celerrimue (most quickly)
pulcher (beautiful)	pulchrior	pulcherrimus	pulchre	pulchrius	pulcherrime
Adjectives ending in -us change the ending to -e					
altus (highly)	altior	altissimus	alte	altius	altissime
carus (dear)	carior	carissimus	care	carius	carissime
Exceptions: crebro (frequently); falso (falsely); continuo (immediately); subito (suddenly); raro (rarely); cito (quickly)					
Adjectives of the third declension add -ter or -iter					
sapiens (wise)	sapientior	sapientissime	sapienter	sapientius	sapientissime
audax (bold)	audacior	audacissimus	audacter	audactius	audactissime
brevis (short)	brevior	brevissimus	breviter	brevitius	brevitissime
But: facilis (easy)	facilior	facillimus	facile	facilius	facillime
Irregular adjectives and their adverbs					
bonus (good)	melior	optimus	bene (well)	melius	optime
malus (bad)	peior	pessimus	male (ill)	pejus	pessime
magnus (great)	maior	maximus	magnopere (greatly)	magis	maxime
multus (much)	plus	plurimus	multum (much)	plus	plurimum
			non multum, parum (little)	minus	minime
prope (near)	propior	proximus	prope (nearly)	propius	proxime
potis (possible)	potior	potissimus	——	potius (rather)	potissimum (especially)
prae (in front of)	prior	primus	——	prius (previously)	primum (first)
			diu (long)	diutius	diutissime
			nequiter (worthlessly)	nequius	nequissime
			nuper (recently)	——	nuperrime
			saepe (often)	saepius	saepissime
			mature (betimes)	maturius	maturrim, maturissime
			secus (otherwise)	setius (less)	

Some common adverbs

How?	aliter (otherwise); forte (by chance); firmus (firmly); ita (thus); sic (thus, so); iuste (justly); libere (freely); magnopere (greatly)
Where?	ubi (where), unde (where from), quo (where to); ibi (there), inde (from there), eo (to there) hic (here), hinc (from here), huc (to here); usquam (anywhere); nusquam (nowhere)

When?	*iam, nunc* (now); *antea* (before); *postea* (after, afterwards); *umquam* (ever); *numquam* (never) *primum* (first); *simul* (simultaneously); *iterum* (again); *diu* (for a long time); *mox* (soon); *interim* (meanwhile); *tum* (then); *tunc* (then, at that time); *saepe* (often) ; *cotidie* (everyday); *hodie* (today); *heri* (yesterday); *cras* (tomorrow); *postridie* (next day); *statim* (immediately); *nuper* (recently)
How much?	*etiam, quoque* (also); *multum* (much); *paulum, non multum, parum* (little); *nimium* (too much); *aliquantum* (somewhat); *ceterum* (for the rest)
Others	*consulto* (purposely); *fortasse* (perhaps); *quidem* (indeed); *scilicet* (no doubt)

PRONOUNS

There are the words used instead of nouns, such as I, me, she, my, mine, yours, this, that, who, what, which and so on. They are thought of in eight classes, but if you look at them carefully, you will see the relationships between (for example) I, my, mine etc.

Personal pronouns.
These correspond to the English I,
you, he, she, it, etc.

	I, we	you, thou	he	she	it, that
Singular					
Nom.	ego	tu	is	ea	id
Voc.	——	tu			
Acc.	me	te	eum	eam	id
Gen.	mei	tui	ejus	ejus	ejus
Dat.	mihi, mi	tibi	ei	ei	ei
Abl.	me	te	eo	ea	eo
Plural					
Nom.	nos, we	vos, you	ei, ii, i	eae	ea
Voc.	——	vos			
Acc.	nos	vos	eos	eas	ea
Gen.	nostrum, nostri	vestrum, vestri	eorum	earum	eorum
Dat.	nobis	vobis	eis, iis	eis, iis	eis, iis
Abl.	nobis	vobis	eis, iis	eis, iis	eis, iis
Emphatic	egomet, I myself	tibimet, to you yourself★			

★Also, tu has *tute* and *tutemet, tutimet*

Reflexive pronouns.
Used when referring to the subject of the sentence
('I hurt myself', 'They did it themselves.')

	myself	yourself	himself, herself, itself, themselves
Singular			
Voc.	——		
Acc.	me	te	se
Gen.	mei	tui	sui
Dat.	mihi	tibi	sibi
Abl.	me	te	se
Plural			
			Same as singular
Voc.	——		
Acc.	nos	vos	se
Gen.	nostrum, nostri	vestrum, vestri	sui
Dat.	nobis	vobis	sibi
Abl.	nobis	vobis	se

Notice the similarity to the personal pronouns

Unlike English, the personal pronouns aren't used as subjects, as the person of the verb does that: *amo*, rather than *ego amo* ('I love'). However, they can be used for emphasis (*ego sum, tu non es* 'I am, you are not').

Possessive pronouns

If you want to say 'my hand' or 'love of you', you don't use the genitive of the personal pronouns (*mei, tui*) but a special set of pronouns that behave like adjectives: 'my hand' (*manus meum*); 'of my hand' (*mani mei*); 'love of you' (*amor tuus*); 'few of us' (*pauci nostrum*). The possessives are declined like the adjective *bonus* (*–a, –um*).

Singular	my			your			his	her	its
	m.	f.	nt.	m.	f.	nt.		*eius* or	
Nom.	*meus*	*mea*	*meum*	*tuus*	*tua*	*tuum*	*suus*	*sua*	*suum*
Voc	*mei*★	*mea*	*meum*	*tue*	*tua*	*tuum*	*sue*	*sua*	*suum*
Acc.	*meum*	*meam*	*meum*	*tuum*	*tuam*	*tuum*	*suum*	*suam*	*suum*
Gen.	*mei*	*meae*	*mei*	*tui*	*tuae*	*tui*	*sui*	*suae*	*sui*
Dat.	*meo*	*meae*	*meo*	*tuo*	*tuae*	*tuo*	*suo*	*suae*	*suo*
Abl.	*meo*	*mea*	*meo*	*tuo*	*tua*	*tuo*	*suo*	*sua*	*suo*
Plural									
Nom.	*mei*	*meae*	*mea*	*tui*	*tuae*	*tua*	*sui*	*suae*	*sua*
Voc	*mei*	*meae*	*mea*	*tui*	*tuae*	*tua*	*sui*	*suae*	*sua*
Acc.	*meos*	*meas*	*mea*	*tuos*	*tuas*	*tua*	*suos*	*suas*	*sua*
Gen.	*meorum*	*mearum*	*meorum*	*tuorum*	*tuarum*	*tuorum*	*suorum*	*suarum*	*suorum*
Dat.	*meis*	*meis*	*meis*	*tuis*	*tuis*	*tuis*	*suis*	*suis*	*suis*
Abl.	*meis*	*meis*	*meis*	*tuis*	*tuis*	*tuis*	*suis*	*suis*	*suis*
	★ Not *mee*.								

	our			your			their		
							m.	f.	nt.
Nom.	*noster*	*nostra*	*nostrum*	*vester*	*vestra*	*vestrum*	*eorum*	*earum*	*eorum*
Voc	*noster*	*nostra*	*nostrum*	*vester*	*vestra*	*vestrum*			
Acc.	*nostrum*	*nostram*	*nostrum*	*vestrum*	*vestram*	*vestrum*			
Gen.	*nostri*	*nostrae*	*nostri*	*vestri*	*vestrae*	*vestri*			
Dat.	*nostro*	*nostrae*	*nostro*	*vestro*	*vestrae*	*vestro*			
Abl.	*nostro*	*nostra*	*nostro*	*vestro*	*vestra*	*vestro*			
Plural									
Nom.	*nostri*	*nostrae*	*nostra*	*vestri*	*vestrae*	*vestra*			
Voc	*nostri*	*nostrae*	*nostra*	*vestri*	*vestrae*	*vestra*			
Acc.	*nostros*	*nostras*	*nostra*	*vestros*	*vestras*	*vestra*			
Gen.	*nostrarum*	*nostrarum*	*nostrorum*	*vestrarum*	*vestrarum*	*vestrorum*			
Dat.	*nostris*	*nostris*	*nostris*	*vestris*	*vestris*	*vestris*			
Abl.	*nostris*	*nostris*	*nostris*	*vestris*	*vestris*	*vestris*			

Demonstrative pronouns

These point out an object as 'here' or 'there', or as previously mentioned. They are: *hic* 'this' (where I am); *iste* 'that' (where you are); *ille* 'that' (something distinct from the speaker); *is* 'that' (weaker than *ille*); *idem* 'the same'.

	Hic (this)			*Iste* (that, that of yours)			*Ille* (that, that one, he is)			*Idem* (the same)		
Singular	m.	f.	nt.	m.	f.	nt.	m.	f.	nt.	m.	f.	nt.
Nom.	hic	haec	hoc	iste	ista	istud	ille	illa	illud	idem	eadem	idem
Acc.	hunc	hanc	hoc	istum	istam	istud	illum	illam	illud	eundem	eandem	idem
Gen.	hujus	hujus	hujus	istius	istius	istius	illius	illius	illius	ejusdem	ejusdem	ejusdem
Dat.	huic	huic	huic	isti	isti	isti	illi	illi	illi	eidem	eidem	eidem
Abl.	hoc	hac	hoc	isto	ista	isto	illo	illa	illo	eodem	eadem	eodem
Plural	m.	f.	nt.	m.	f.	nt.	m.	f.	nt.			
Nom.	his	his	his	isti	istae	ista	illi	illae	illa	eidem, iidem	eaedem	eadem
Acc.	hi	hae	haec	istos	istas	ista	illos	illas	illa	eosdem	easdem	eadem
Gen.	horum	harum	horum	istorum	istarum	istorum	illorum	illarum	illorum	eorundem	earundem	eorundem
Dat.	hos	has	haec	istis	istis	istis	illis	illis	illis	eisdem	eisdem	eisdem
Abl.	his	his	his	istis	istis	istis	illis	illis	illis	eisdem	eisdem	eisdem

'is', 'he', 'this', 'that' could also be considered demonstrative

V. Intensive pronouns			VI. Relative pronouns			VII. Interrogative pronouns		
Ipse (self) is used for emphasis			*Qui* (who? which?)			*Quis* (who?), *Quid* (what?)		
Singular	m.	f.	nt.	m.	f.	nt.	m.	f.	nt.
Nom.	ipse	ipsa	ipsum	qui	quae	quod	quis	quis	quid
Acc.	ipsum	ipsam	ipsum	quem	quam	quod	quem	quam	quid
Gen.	ipsius	ipsius	ipsius	cuius	cuius	cuius	cuius	cuius	cuius
Dat.	ipsi	ipsi	ipsi	cui	cui	cui	cui	cui	cui
Abl.	ipso	ipsa	ipso	quo	qua	quo	quo	qua	quo
Plural	m.	f.	nt.	m.	f.	nt.	m.	f.	nt
Nom.	ipsi	ipsae	ipsa	qui	quae	quae	qui	quae	quae
Acc.	ipsos	ipsas	ipsa	quos	quas	quae	quos	quas	quae
Gen.	ipsorum	ipsarum	ipsorum	quorum	quarum	quorum	quorum	quarum	quorum
Dat.	ipsis	ipsis	ipsis	quibus	quibus	quibus	quibus	quibus	quibus
Abl.	ipsis	ipsis	ipsis	quibus	quibus	quibus	quibus	quibus	quibus

Quis and *qui* may be strengthened by adding *-nam*

Substantive:	*quisnam* (who, pray?) *quidnam* (what, pray?)
Adjective:	*quinam, quaenam, quodnam* (of what kind, pray?)

Indefinite pronouns

Substantive	m.	f.	nt.	Adjective	m.	f.	nt.
anyone, anything	quis		quid	any	qui	quae qua	quod
someone, something	aliquis		aliquid	any	aliqui	aliqua	aliquod
anyone, anything (no plural)	quisquam		quidquam, quicquab	any (rare)	quisquam	quisquam	quidquam, quicquam
anyone, anything	quispiam		quidpiam	any	quispiam	quaepiam	quodpiam
anyone?	ecquis		ecquid	any?	ecqui	ecqua	ecquod
each	quisque		quidque	each	quisque	quaeque	quodque
anyone (anything) you wish	quivis	quaevis	quidvis,	any you wish	quivis	quaevis	quodvis
	quilibet	quaelibet	quidlibet		quilibet	quaelibet	quodlibet
a certain person, thing	quidam	quaedam	quiddam	a certain	quidam	quaedam	quoddam
whoever, whatever	quicumque	quaecumque	quodumque	whoever, whatever	quicumque	quaecumque	quodumque
	quisquis	quidquid	quoquo	whatever	quisquis	quidquid	quoquo

1. Decline the pronominal part, e.g. *aliquis* genitive singular *alicujus* (of someone); *quilibet, cujuslibet* (of any you wish).
2. The nominative singular feminine and nominative and accusative plural neuter of *aliqui* are *aliqua* (*qui* has *qua* and *quae* in these cases).
3. *Quidam* accusative singular *quendam, quandam*; genitive plural *quorundam, quarundam*; the *m* changes to *n* before *d*.
4. Both *quis* or *qui* can be substantive with *ne, si, nisi, num -si quis, si qui* etc.

VERBS

At last, we get to the verb. There are lots of jokes about the complexity of Latin verb construction, most of them not very good and almost all poking fun at the tendency to use combinations such as 'having been about to be' and 'might have been about to be doing' and the like. But that's the complexity of English, not Latin, which can usually get all of that into one word.

Latin does this by having a whole skein of tense, number, person, voice and mood combinations, but it's all very logical.

Tense, person, number

The tense indicates whether the action is now (present), before (past) or to come (future). English only really has two cases – present and past – and builds everything else from them. Take a verb such as 'to jump' and the three persons, singular and plural in number (I, you, he/she/it, we, you, they):

	Present tense		Past tense		Future tense	
First person sing./plural	I jump	we jump	I jumped	we jumped	I will jump	we will jump
Second person sing./plural	you jump	you jump	you jumped	you jumped	you will jump	you will jump
Third person sing./plural	he/she/it jumps	they jump	he/she/it jumped	they jumped	he/she/it will jump	they will jump
	Present participle	jumping	Past participle	jumped		

Like many verbs, we make the past from the present by adding -ed, but use participles to form other tenses:

Tense	Example	Tense	Example	Uses	
Infinitive	To jump				
Present	(I/you/he etc.) jump(s)	Future	(We/they etc.) will jump		
Present continuous	(I am/you are/she is) jumping			Present participle	jumping
Past	(I/we/they etc.) jumped	Perfect	(I/he) have/has jumped	Past participle	jumped
Imperfect	(I/you/she etc.) was/were jumping	Future continuous	(We/they etc.) will be jumping	Present participle	jumping
Past perfect (pluperfect)	(I/you/she etc.) had jumped	Future perfect	(He/you/they etc.) will have jumped	Past participle	jumped
		Future pluperfect	(We/they etc.) will have been jumping	Present participle	jumping

Principal Parts				
Present indicative	Present infinitive	Perfect indicative	Perfect infinitive	Future participle
sum (I am)	*esse* (to be)	*fui* (I was)	*fuisse* (to have been)	*futurus* (going to be)
Present imperative			Future imperative	
es (be thou)		*este* (be ye)	*esto* (you shall be) *esto* (he shall be)	*estote* (you shall be) *sunto* (they shall be)

Indicative mood		Singular	Plural
Present		*sum* (I am)	*sumus* (we are)
		es (you are)	*estis* (you are)
		est (he is)	*sunt* (they are)
Imperfect		*eram* (I was)	*eramus* (we were)
		eras (you were)	*eratis* (you were)
		erat (he was)	*erant* (they were)

Future	ero (I shall be)	erimus (we shall be)
	eris (you will be)	eritis (you will be)
	erit (he will be)	erunt (they will be)
Perfect	fui (I have been, I was)	fuimus (we have been, we were)
	fuisti (you have been, you were)	fuistis (you have been, you were)
	fuit (he has been, he was)	fuerunt fuere (they have been, they were)
Pluperfect	fueram (I had been)	fueramus (we had been)
	fueras (you had been)	fueratis (you had been)
	fuerat (he had been)	fuerant (they had been)
Future perfect	fuero (I shall have been)	fuerimus (we shall have been)
	fueris (you will have been)	fueritis (you will have been)
	fuerit (he will have been)	fuerint (they will have been)

Subjunctive mood

	Singular	**Plural**
Present	sim (may I be)	simus (let us be)
	sis (mayst thou be)	sitis (may you be)
	sit (let him be, may he be)	sint (let them be)
Imperfect	essem (I should be)	essemus (we should be)
	esses (you would be)	essetis (you would be)
	esset (he would be)	essent (they would be)
Perfect	fuerim (I may have been)	fuerimus (we may have been)
	fueris (you may have been)	fueritis (you may have been)
	fuerit (he may have been)	fuerint (they may have been)
Pluperfect	fuissem (I should have been)	fuissemus (we should have been)
	fuisses (you would have been)	fuissetis (you would have been)
	fuisset (he would have been)	fuissent (they would have been)

In English we do sometimes have different variations of a verb in the tenses: 'I go' (present); 'they are going' (present continuous); 'you went' (past perfect); 'he has gone' (past imperfect) and so on. This has usually come about because two different words for the same concept have been welded together, in this case 'gang' and 'wend'. The verb 'go' comes from the Old English 'gan', similar to the German 'gehen', and survives in the Scots verb 'gang', meaning precisely 'to go'. The verb 'wend', which gives us 'went', the modern past tense of 'to go', comes from the past-tense form of Old English 'wendan' (to turn, depart) (this survives in modern English as 'wend our weary way' for instance), and similar to the modern German 'wenden', and the Scots legal construction 'to wend to the horne', meaning to be proclaimed an outlaw. You may occasionally see in Scots 'I have went' instead of 'I have gone'.

As usual, it's the most common verbs that tend to have irregular constructions:

To be: I am, you are, he is, they were, we shall be, you have been etc.
To do: I do, she did, you were doing, they have done etc.

But most simple verbs have simple constructions, like 'jump', above.

For once, when it comes to tenses, Latin is simpler than English. There are tenses formed for the present stem, and those from the perfect stem, to make six tenses in all.

Voice and mood

The two voices are active and passive. The difference is between 'I hit' (active) and 'I am hit' (passive). The moods are imperative ('I go', 'I love', 'I jump') and subjunctive ('I might go', 'I would love', 'I may jump').

Any grammar textbook will go into intense detail about present and perfect stems, the supine, the difference between a gerund and a gerundive and so forth. For our purposes, it is best just to present verb tables of the four conjugations, plus some common irregular verbs, starting with the most common of all: *esse* (to be).

First conjugation

Active voice: *amo* (I love)						
Principal Parts						
Present indicative	Present infinitive	Present imperative	Perfect indicative	Perfect infinitive	Future infinitive	Future imperative
amo (I love)	*amare* (to love)	*ama* (love!) (s.) *amate* (pl.)	*amavi* (I loved)	*amavisse* (to have loved)	*amaturus esse* (to be about to love)	*amato* (you shall love) (s.) *amatote* (pl.)
Present participle			Perfect passive participle		Future infinitive participle	
			amatus (loved, having been loved)		*amaturus* (about to love)	

Gerund		Gerundive	Supine	
Gen.	*amandi* (of loving)	*amandus* (to be loved deserving to be loved)		
Dat.	*amando* (for loving)			
Acc.	*amandum* (loving)		Acc.	*amatum* (to love)
Abl.	*amando* (by loving)		Abl.	*amatu* (to love, be loved)

Indicative mood		
	Singular	**Plural**
Present	*amo* (I love)	*amamus* (we love)
	amas (you love)	*amatis* (you love)
	amat (he loves)	*amant* (they love)
Imperfect	*amabam* (I was loving)	*amabamus* (we were loving)
	amabas (you were loving)	*amabatis* (you were loving)
	amabat (he was loving)	*amabant* (they were loving)
Future	*amabo* (I shall love)	*amabimus* (we shall love)
	amabis (you will love)	*amabitis* (you will love)
	amabit (he will love)	*amabunt* (they will love)

Perfect	*amavi* (I have loved, I loved)	*amavimus* (we have loved we loved)
	amavisti (you have loved, you love)	*amavistis* (you have loved, you loved)
	amavit (he has loved, he loved)	*amaverunt -ere* (they have loved, they loved)
Pluperfect	*amaveram* (I had loved)	*amaveramus* (we had loved)
	amaveras (you had loved)	*amaveratis* you had loved)
	amaverat (he had loved)	*amaverant* they had loved)
Future perfect	*amavero* (I shall have loved)	*amaverimus* (we shall have loved)
	amaveris (you will have loved)	*amaveritis* (you will have loved)
	amaverit (he will have loved)	*amaverint* (they will have loved)

Subjunctive mood		
Present	*amem* (may I love)	*amemus* (let us love)
	ames (may you love)	*ametis* (may you love)
	amet (let him love)	*ament* (let them love)
Imperfect	*amarem* (I should love)	*amaremus* (we should love)
	amares (you would love)	*amaretis* (you would love)
	amaret (he would love)	*amarent* (they would love)
Perfect	*amaverim* (I may have loved)	*amaverimus* (we may have loved)
	amaveris (you may have loved)	*amaveritis* (you may have loved)
	amaverit (he may have loved)	*amaverint* (they may have loved)
Pluperfect	*amavissem* (I should have loved)	*amavissemus* (we should have loved)
	amavisses (you would have loved)	*amavissetis* (you would have loved)
	amavisset (he would have loved)	*amavissent* (they would have loved)

Passive voice: *amor* (I am loved)						
Principal parts						
Present indicative	Present infinitive	Present imperative	Perfect indicative	Perfect infinitive	Future infinitive	Future imperative
amor (I am loved)	*amari* (to be loved)	*amare* (be loved) (s.) *amamini* (pl.)	*amatus sum* (I was loved)	*amatus esse* (to have been loved)	*amatum iri* (to be about to be loved)	*amator* (you/he shall be loved) *amantor* (they shall be loved)

Indicative mood		
	Singular	**Plural**
Present	*amor* (I am loved)	*amamur*
	amaris	*amamini*
	amatur	*amantur*
Imperfect	*amabar* (I was loved)	*amabamur*
	amabaris or *-re*	*amabamini*
	amabatur	*amabantur*

Future	amabor (I shall be loved)	amabimur
	amaberis or –re	amabimini
	amabitur	amabuntur
Perfect	amatus (–a –um) sum (I was/have been loved)	amati (–ae, –a) sumus
	amatus es	amati estis
	amatus est	amati sunt
Pluperfect	amatus eram (I had been loved)	amati eramus
	amatus eras	amati eratis
	amatus erat	amati erant
Future perfect	amatus ero (I shall have been loved)	amati erimus
	amatus eris	amati eritis
	amatus erit	amati erunt
Subjunctive mood		
Present	amer (may I be loved)	amemur
	ameris or –re (be loved)	amemini
	ametur (let him be loved)	amentur
Imperfect	amarer (I should be loved)	amaremur
	amareris or –re (you would be loved)	amaremini
	amaretur	amarentur
Perfect	amatus sim (I may have been loved)	amati simus
	amatus sis	amati sitis
	amatus sit	amati sint
Pluperfect	amatus essem (I should have been loved)	amati essemus
	amatus esses (you would have been loved)	amati essetis
	amatus esset	amati essent

Now that we have seen a full conjugation exploded, with English meanings, we can compare the four conjugations side by side, and see what the word endings are.

Active voice: amo (I love)						
Principal parts						
Present indicative	Present infinitive	Present imperative	Perfect indicative	Perfect infinitive	Future infinitive	Future imperative
amo (I love)	amare (to love)	ama (love!) (s.) amate (pl.)	amavi (I loved)	amavisse (to have loved)	amaturus esse (to be about to love)	amato (you shall love) (s.) amatote (pl.)
Present participle			Perfect passive participle		Future infinitive participle	
amans (loving) (Gen. amantis)			amatus (loved, having been loved)		amaturus (about to love)	

Gerund		Gerundive	Supine	
Gen.	*amandi* (of loving)	*amandus* (to be loved, deserving to be loved)		
Dat.	*amando* (for loving)			
Acc.	*amandum* (loving)		Acc.	*amatum* (to love)
Abl.	*amando* by (loving)		Abl.	*amatu* (to love, be loved)

Conjugation Infinitive	First	Second	Third		Fourth
	amare (to love)	*monere* (to advise)	*regere* (to rule)	*capere* (to capture)	*audere* (to hear)
Present stem	*ama-*	*mone-*	*reg-*	*capi-*	*audi-*
Indicative Mood					
Present e.g. I love	*amo*	*moneo*	*rego*	*capio*	*audio*
	amas	*mones*	*regis*	*capis*	*audis*
	amat	*monet*	*regit*	*capit*	*audit*
	amamus	*monemus*	*regimus*	*capimus*	*audimus*
	amatis	*monetis*	*regitis*	*capitis*	*auditis*
	amant	*monent*	*regunt*	*capiunt*	*audiunt*
Imperfect e.g. I was loving	*amabam*	*monebam*	*regebam*	*capiebam*	*audiebam*
	amabas	*monebas*	*regebas*	*capiebas*	*audiebas*
	amabat	*monebat*	*regebat*	*capiebat*	*audiebat*
	amabamus	*monebamus*	*regebamus*	*capiebamus*	*audiebamus*
	amabatis	*monebatis*	*regebatis*	*capiebatis*	*audiebatis*
	amabant	*monebant*	*regebant*	*capiebant*	*audiebant*
Future e.g. I will love	*amabo*	*monebo*	*regam*	*capiam*	*audiam*
	amabis	*monebis*	*reges*	*capies*	*audies*
	amabit	*monebit*	*reget*	*capiet*	*audiet*
	amabimus	*monebimus*	*regemus*	*capiemus*	*audiemus*
	amabitis	*monebitis*	*regetis*	*capietis*	*audietis*
	amabunt	*monebunt*	*regent*	*capient*	*audient*
Perfect e.g. I have loved/ I loved	*amavi*	*monui*	*rexi*	*cepi*	*audivi*
	amavisti	*monuisti*	*rexisti*	*cepisti*	*audivisti*
	amavit	*monuit*	*rexit*	*cepit*	*audivit*
	amavimus	*monuimus*	*reximus*	*cepimus*	*audivimus*
	amavistis	*monuistis*	*rexistis*	*cepistis*	*audivistis*
	amaverunt	*monuerunt*	*rexerunt*	*ceperunt*	*audiverunt*

Pluperfect e.g. I had loved	amaveram	monueram	rexeram	ceperam	audiveram
	amaveras	monueras	rexeras	ceperas	audiveras
	amaverat	monuerat	rexerat	ceperat	audiverat
	amaveramus	monueramus	rexeramus	ceperamus	audiveramus
	amaveratis	monueratis	rexeratis	ceperatis	audiveratis
	amaverant	monuerant	rexerant	ceperant	audiverant
Future perfect e.g. I shall have loved	amavero	monuero	rexero	cepero	audivero
	amaveris	monueris	rexeris	ceperis	audiveris
	amaverit	monuerit	rexerit	ceperit	audiverit
	amaverimus	monuerimus	rexerimus	ceperimus	audiverimus
	amaveritis	monueritis	rexeritis	ceperitis	audiveritis
	amaverint	monuerint	rexerint	ceperint	audiverint

Subjunctive mood

Present e.g. may I love	amem	moneam	regeam	capieam	audieam
	ames	moneas	regeas	capieas	audieas
	amet	moneat	regeat	capieat	audieat
	amemus	moneamus	regeamus	capieamus	audieamus
	ametis	moneatis	regeatis	capieatis	audieatis
	ament	moneant	regeant	capieant	audieant
Imperfect e.g. I should love	amarem	monerem	regerem	audivrem	audivrem
	amares	moneres	regeres	audivres	audivres
	amaret	moneret	regeret	audivret	audivret
	amaremus	moneremus	regeremus	audivremus	audivremus
	amaretis	moneretis	regeretis	audivretis	audivretis
	amarent	monerent	regerent	audivrent	audivrent
Perfect e.g. I may have loved	amaverim	monuerim	rexerim	ceperim	audiverim
	amaveris	monueris	rexeris	ceperis	audiveris
	amaverit	monuerit	rexerit	ceperit	audiverit
	amaverimus	monuerimus	rexerimus	ceperimus	audiverimus
	amaveritis	monueritis	rexeritis	ceperitis	audiveritis
	amaverint	monuerint	rexerint	ceperint	audiverint
Pluperfect e.g. I should have loved	amavissem	monuissem	rexissem	cepissem	audivissem
	amavisses	monuisses	rexisses	cepisses	audivisses
	amavisset	monuisset	rexisset	cepisset	audivisset
	amavissemus	monuissemus	rexissemus	cepissemus	audivissemus
	amavissetis	monuissetis	rexissetis	cepissetis	audivissetis
	amavissent	monuissent	rexissent	cepissent	audivissent

Passive voice: *amor* (I am loved)						
Principal parts						
Present indicative	Present infinitive	Present imperative	Perfect indicative	Perfect infinitive	Future infinitive	Future imperative
amor (I am loved)	*amari* (to be loved)	*amare* (be loved) (s.) *amamini.* (pl.)	*amatus sum* (I was loved)	*amatus esse* (to have been loved)	*amatum iri* (to be about to be loved)	*amator* (you/he shall be loved) *amantor* (they shall be loved)

Indicative mood	
Present I am loved	*amor*
	amaris
	amatur
	amamur
	amamini
	amantur
Imperfect I was loved	*amabar*
	amabaris or *–re*
	amabatur
	amabamur
	amabamini
	amabantur
Future I shall be loved	*amabor*
	amaberis or *–re*
	amabitur
	amabimur
	amabimini
	amabuntur
Perfect I was/have been loved	*amatus (–a –um) sum*
	amatus es
	amatus est
	amati (–ae –a) sumus
	amati estis
	amati sunt
Pluperfect I had been loved	*amatus eram*
	amatus eras
	amatus erat
	amati eramus
	amati eratis
	amati erant

Future perfect I shall have been loved	*amatus* **ero**
	amatus **eris**
	amatus **erit**
	amati **erimus**
	amati **eritis**
	amati **erunt**
Subjunctive mood	
Present	*amer* (may I be loved)
	ameris or **-re** (be loved)
	ametur (let him be loved)
	amemur
	amemini
	amentur
Imperfect	*amarer* (I should be loved)
	amareris or **-re** (you would be loved)
	amaretur
	amaremur
	amaremini
	amarentur
Perfect	*amatus* **sim** (I may have been loved)
	amatus **sis**
	amatus **sit**
	amati **simus**
	amati **sitis**
	amati **sint**
Pluperfect	*amatus* **essem** (I should have been loved)
	amatus **esses** (you would have been loved)
	amatus **esset**
	amati **essemus**
	amati **essetis**
	amati **essent**

AIDS TO LATIN TRANSLATION

Old Latin teachers never die;
They just decline
Schoolboy jibe

Want a Latin translation program? Go here: *http://users.erols.com/whitaker/words.htm.* It needs to be installed and runs in a DOS window, and only deals with one word at a time, but it does give full grammatical information.

Google Translate can also help with phrases: *http://translate.google.co.uk/?hl=en&tab=wT#la|en|*

It's not perfect by any means. Here's what it made of the Latin on p. 189. Pretty mangled, but quite good for short phrases:

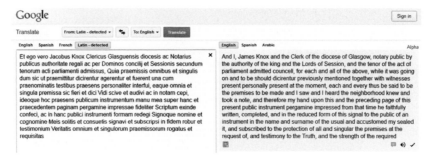

Someone out there in cyberspace may have translated a document like yours before. Try a Google search for a phrase, for example: '*quia praemissis omnibus et singulis dum sic ut praemittitur agerentur dicerentur et fierent una cum praenominatis testibus interfui.*'

Further Reading

Online

Notre Dame: http://archives.nd.edu/latgramm.htm

Palaeography: a limited resource for would-be palaeographers, but with some interesting information: www.jaydax.co.uk/genlinks/palaeography.html

Ductus: online palaeography course from the University of Melbourne, with handwriting from the medieval period (CD-ROM plus web-based tuition) www.medieval.unimelb.edu.au/ductus/

Dictionary of the Scottish Language: online Scots dictionary www.dsl.ac.uk/dsl/

Scottish Language Dictionaries: www.scotsdictionaries.org.uk

English handwriting: from Cambridge University, concentrates on English handwriting 1500–1700: http://www.english.cam.ac.uk/ceres/ehoc/

From Leicester University, contains sample images, tutorials and bibliographies for medieval and early modern handwriting: http://paleo.anglo-norman.org/

Books

Collins Latin Dictionary and Grammar (get the latest edition)

Latham, R.E., *Revised Medieval Latin Word-list: from British and Irish sources* (British Academy, 1973)

3

Dates and Calendars

Dates would seem to be a straightforward issue: after all, today is today, the day before was yesterday and next comes tomorrow. But it isn't that simple. Dates are complicated by a number of things:

– Calendar reform between the 1580s and 1750s.
– The peculiar way the Romans gave dates, which can be found repeated in quite modern Latin inscription (on gravestones, for example).
– The date of the New Year.
– Differences in ways of recording dates 'at the terms of Whitsun and Martinmas' for instance.
– Regnal years.

THE JULIAN AND GREGORIAN CALENDARS

In Julius Caesar's time, it was clear that the solar and calendar years were out of sync. Midsummer's day, for instance, was clearly not the day on the calendar that the sun was highest in the sky. This mattered because of its importance to agriculture, but also because of the religious observances that had to take place on stated days.

The astronomers of Rome knew that the error had been introduced because of a 365-day year, whereas the Sun takes 365¼ days (they reckoned) to go round the Earth, as they saw it. Hence, they introduced the Leap Day every four years and set things back to rights.

There is slightly more to it than that, of course. At first the Romans had ten named months – *Martius, Aprilis, Maius, Junius, Quintilis* (July), *Sextilis* (August), *September, October, November, December* – plus two unnamed months corresponding to our January and February. Note that March was the beginning of the year: this is a point we will return to. *Januarius* and *Februarius* were added around 700 BCE (roughly when Rome was just getting going) and New Year was moved to *Januarius.* Occasionally they added an 'intercalendar' month to cope with leap years, thereby turning *September* (literally 'seventh month') into the ninth month, and the same for *October, November* and *December,* which had been eight, nine and ten in the calendar, but from the point of view of a March year-start, were still in the right place. Later, in the time of Julius Caesar, they made the number of days in some months an odd 'lucky' number and gave February an extra day every fourth or 'leap' year. This gave us the so-called Julian calendar and the year-structure we now have – 'Thirty days hath September' etc. – although the names of the months *Quintilus* and *Sextilis* were eventually named after Julius and Augustus respectively.

(For the idiosyncratic way the Romans gave the days of the month, see Chapter 2. For the moment, just accept that it matters, as this style can be seen on gravestones and church inscriptions.)

This did not fix everything, however. The Earth's rotation around the sun (as we now think of it) is actually a bit slower than 365¼ days, so there was still an accumulated error of some eleven minutes and fourteen seconds each year. In 1582, the Vatican's astronomers faced up to this just as the Romans had some 1600 years before: the calendar was again some days ahead of the sun. Pope Gregory XIII reformed the Julian calendar to correspond to the solar year and took out ten days (5–14 October) and the rule for leap days was changed so that centenary years would not be leap, except when divisible by 400, which is why 1900 wasn't a leap year but 1600 and 2000 were.

Naturally, all the Catholic countries did what they were told, but Protestant northern Europe – including Scotland and England – were certainly not going to obey anything that came from Rome.

This led to 170 years of confusion that affected foreign trade and travel. To take two examples: first, it is often said that William Shakespeare and Miguel Cervantes died on the same day (23 April 1616), but that Cervantes, living in Catholic Spain, went to his reward ten days earlier than the Swan of Avon, who was in Protestant England; second, when William of Orange came to accept the English and Scottish crowns jointly with his wife Mary Stuart (the Glorious Revolution of 1698), they appear to have arrived in London a week before they left the Netherlands.

So how could a merchant trading to, say, France, rely on a contract with dates that could be interpreted in two ways?

Other countries adopted the Gregorian calendar piecemeal: Sweden, for instance, started in 1700 by removing leap days over forty years, but missed the boat twice and reverted back to the Julian. They adopted the Gregorian fully in 1753. Denmark, Norway and the German Protestant states adopted the solar portion of the calendar in 1700 but took another seventy-six years to adopt the lunar adjustments that determined, for example, Easter. This is summarised in the table on p. 87.

In Britain, calendrical reform became obviously necessary by 1750 when ruling the waves meant listening to the astronomers who were producing navigation tables and the like. The Calendar Act of that year, introduced by Lord Chesterfield, accounted for the (by then) eleven extra days by having Wednesday 2 September followed by Thursday 14 September. The Act recognised that the status quo was:

> attended with divers inconveniences, not only as it differs from the usage of neighbouring nations, but also from the legal method of computation in Scotland, and from the common usage throughout the whole kingdom, and thereby frequent mistakes are occasioned in the dates of deeds and other writings, and disputes arise therefrom …
>
> Calendar (New Style) Act 1750 c. 23 (Regnal. 24 Geo II)

Therefore, the year 1751 in England was 282 days long, running from 25 March to 31 December; 1752 began on 1 January. Parliament also adopted the better (Gregorian) rules for leap years and reckoning the date of Easter.

Contrary to popular retellings (and isn't that always the case!) there were no 'riots in the streets' by calendrical fundamentalists demanding back the days lost from their lives, although imagine how you would feel if your birthday had been on 3 September. On the other hand, there was widespread disquiet about the fiscal implications, stirred up by Tories to embarrass the Whig government in the lead-up to the 1754 elections. It was portrayed as 'Popish' and for some strange reason advantageous to 'foreign Jews'. There is a well-known 1755 Hogarth painting and engraved print in which the

Tory campaign slogan 'Give Us Our Eleven Days' appears written on a newspaper, that later led to apocryphal stories of widespread insurrection.

If you were paying an annual rent, think how you would react if you were told to pay for a full year, but eleven days earlier. And why should you pay a whole year's taxes on 354 days of economic activity? A fudge was introduced that moved the start of the financial year from 25 March (see 'Term days', on p. 88) to 5 and later 6 April (because of the non-leap year of 1800), which is what we still have today.

Old Style (OS) and New Style (NS) years

The year 1752 was also the start of reckoning the first day of the year as 1 January rather than 25 March (Lady Day, see below). Scotland had made that change in 1600, largely to give the Scots a Yule celebration that the Church couldn't disagree with (because being joyful at Christmas, for some reason, was seen as both pagan and also inappropriate on the day of the Birth of Our Lord). The Privy Council of Scotland passed an Act on 17 December 1599 (PC1/17) commanding all royal officials, clerks, judges, notaries, and others:

> … in all tyme heireftir date all thair decreittis infeftmentis charteris seasings letteris and writtis quhatsumeuir according to this p[rese]nt ordinance, Compting the first day of the yeir fra the first day of Januare yeirlie.

This entirely accounts for the reputation the Scots have for Hogmanay, whereas in England, 31 December/1 January didn't matter all that much.

So, for dates up to 1752 in England and up to 1600 in Scotland, 31 December 1565 (for example) was followed by 1 January 1565 and 24 March 1565 was followed by 25 March 1566. Dates between January and March are usually given as 1565/66 to make that clear. However, 1 January 1601 in Scotland would have been called 1 January 1600 in England, as the New Year wouldn't start south of the border until 25 March.

This is referred to as OS (Old Style) and NS (New Style). A well-known example is the execution of King Charles I, which took place on 30 January 1648 as recorded in English documents of the time, but we would now consider this to be 30 January 1649 NS, as the Scots did at the time. It all went away, thank goodness, in 1752, but please do not confuse the New Year issue with the change to the Gregorian calendar.

An example is given below where the change is explicitly mentioned in a parish register of marriages.

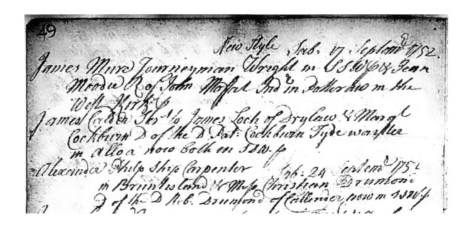

1582	Flanders, France (1564), Italy (some states), Lorraine, Luxembourg, Polish-Lithuanian Commonwealth, Portugal and its territories (1556), Savoy, Spain and its territories (1556), Spanish Netherlands (1556), Vatican, Venice (1522)	1875	Egypt
		1896	Korea
		1908	European Turkey
		1912	Albania, China (Republic)
1583	Austria, German states (1544), Catholic Switzerland	1914	Asian Turkey
1584	Bohemia and Moravia	1915	Latvia, Lithuania
1587	Hungary	1916	Bulgaria (part), Greece (part)
1605–1710	Nova Scotia (Julian 2 October 1710–12 September 1752) Gregorian since 14 September 1752	1918	Estonia, Latvia, Lithuania, Russia (1700)
1610	Prussia	1919	Croatia, Romania, Serbia, Slovenia, Yugoslavia
1648	Alsace	1920	Greece (remainder)
1682	Strasbourg	1922	USSR
1700	Denmark★ (early 1700s), Protestant Germany★ (1544), Prussia (1559), Protestant Netherlands (1583), Norway★, Sweden and (gradually) Switzerland ★ Solar only; lunar in 1776	1923	Ecumenical Patriarchate of Constantinople, Patriarchate of Alexandria, Patriarchate of Antioch, Orthodox Churches of America, Cyprus, Greece, Poland, Romania, Serbia
1750	Tuscany (1721)	1926	Turkey
1752	Scotland (1600), England and Wales (1752), Ireland, British territories (but see below for America)	1929	China (Nationalist government), Soviet states
1753	Finland (1559), Sweden (1559)	1949	Taiwan (People's Republic of China)
1760	Lorraine (when it passed from Hapsburg rule to France) (1579)	1963	Orthodox Church of Bulgaria
1811	Grisons (Swiss Canton)	Julian to 2008	Orthodox Churches of Georgia, Jerusalem, Russia, Serbia, Ukraine, Greek Old Calendarists
1846	Greece (civil)	Own calendar	Eastern non-Orthodox Churches: Armenian, Coptic, Ethiopic, Jacobite, Nestorian
1867	Alaska (sold by Russia to USA)		
1873	Japan		

Adoption of the Gregorian calendar in various jurisdictions, with the date (in brackets) when New Year became 1 January.

The 'American confusion'

Be careful with dates on American documents prior to 1752. British dates before then are usually given in the original OS, but dates of events in (then British) America prior to 1752 have usually been converted to NS. George Washington was born on 11 February OS, but his birthday is celebrated on 22 February NS, because as a 21-year-old surveyor he understood the point and changed it himself. Many American genealogists (and genealogical software programs) ignore this, and the OS/NS designation, so be careful.

Then there's Alaska. The Alaska Purchase from Russia in 1867 meant that Friday 6 October was followed by Friday 18 October, due to the US being on Gregorian time while Russia was still on the Julian calendar, and because the International Date Line was moved west of Alaska at the same time.

Nova Scotia, flipping from French to British control at various times, was Gregorian from 1605 to 1710, Julian from 2 October 1710 to 2 September 1752 and Gregorian since 14 September 1752.

The date of Easter

Easter is a moveable feast: the date changes every year. Easter Sunday can fall on any date from 21 March to 25 April. The reason for this is Easter's origins in pagan festivals dedicated to the fertility goddess Eoster, which the Christian Church incorporated with the Passion and Resurrection of Christ. The date is based on the lunar calendar and takes place (by the official Western definition) on the first Sunday after the first full moon on or after the vernal equinox (usually 20 or 21 March).

The Western Churches use the Gregorian calendar to calculate the date of Easter, and Eastern (Orthodox) Churches use the Julian calendar. So for example:

	2011	2012	2013
Shrove Tuesday (Mardi Gras)	8 March	21 February	12 February
Ash Wednesday (beginning of Lent)	9 March	22 February	13 February
Vernal equinox	21 March	20 March	20 March
Palm Sunday (beginning of Holy Week)	17 April	1 April	24 March
Good Friday	22 April	6 April	29 March
(Western) Easter Sunday	24 April	8 April	31 March
(Orthodox) Easter Sunday	24 April	15 April	5 May

Term days and quarter days

Why was New Year on 25 March in England (and elsewhere, but not Scotland) until this was changed in 1752? It's because of the importance of term days (Scotland) and quarter days (England).

There were four specific days in the year when rents were due, when church ministers' stipends were paid (at least in Scotland), when leases and other contracts would begin or end and when workers and servants were hired. In Scotland, they are still associated with legal 'terms' and in England some leasehold payments and business rents are still payable on quarter days.

The English quarter days fell on four important religious holidays about three months apart. The English cross-quarter days were holidays based on the old Celtic calendar, about halfway between quarter days, and approximate to the Scottish term days. For an example of the usage, see the 'Trust Disposition and Settlement of Walter Bannerman' on p. 168.

Of course, all of these dates started out as important pagan festivals that the Church wisely decided not to interfere with except to give them a new Christian spin (see the table on p. 89).

Lady Day (25 March) was also New Year's Day in Britain and the British Empire until 1752 (except Scotland, where it has been 1 January since 1600). The UK financial year and tax year starts on 'Old' Lady Day (25 March OS or 6 April NS/Gregorian). Candlemas was also known as the Feast of the Presentation of Jesus at the Temple, and the Feast of the Purification of the Virgin. Whitsun is also called Pentecost. Lammas Day (*Lughnasa*) is the festival of the first wheat harvest of the year, and was an important hiring day for farm workers. Some Scottish towns still have a Lammas Day Fair.

In Scotland, the new term days have been used since 1886 for the removal and hiring of servants in towns, and the Term and Quarter Days (Scotland) Act 1990 redefined these, at least in official usage, as 28 February, 28 May, 28 August and 28 November. The law courts also use these dates.

English terms (the dates on which courts sat) were complicated because they depended on the dates of Easter, and also because the ancient universities also used these for academic terms, but at different dates. Oxford had Hilary or Lent term (14 January to the Saturday before Palm Sunday), Easter term (ten days after Easter to the Thursday before Whit Sunday), Trinity Term (Wednesday after Trinity Sunday to whenever the university decided to rise) and Michaelmas term (10 October to 7 December). Cambridge had Lent term (13 January to the Friday before Palm Sunday), Easter term (Wednesday after Easter week to the week before Whit Sunday), Trinity Term (Wednesday after Trinity Sunday to the Friday after Commencement) and Michaelmas term (10 October to 16 December).

Other important dates, especially for the payment of rents etc. in early manorial custumals (p. 235) and an excuse for a party were:

– Hockday or Hocktide, the second Monday and Tuesday after Easter, and therefore likely to be about the end of April or early May, which was originally a Saxon festival held to celebrate either the massacre of the Danes on St Brice's Day (13 November 1002), or the death of Harthacanute (8 June 1042) and the subsequent expulsion of the Danes from England. Epiphany, the feast and holiday held on 6 January to commemorate the presentation of the divine nature of Christ to the Magi and also the day after Twelfth Night.
– *Natale* (Christmas).
– *Pascha* (Easter).
– St John's Day (24 June and also Midsummer).

	England & Wales quarter days, also observed in Ireland	English cross-quarter days	English term days	Scottish term days (old)	Scottish term days (now fixed by law)	Corresponding Celtic festival
February		Candlemas (2 Feb)	Hilary term (23 Jan–12 Feb)	Candlemas (2 Feb)	28 Feb	Imbolc
March	Lady Day (25 Mar)		Easter term (Wednesday two weeks after Easter Day to Monday after Ascension Day)			Ostara
May		May Day (1 May)		Whitsunday (fixed by law as 15 May)	28 May	Beltane
June	Midsummer Day (24 June)		Trinity term (Friday after Trinity Sunday to Wednesday two weeks later)			Midsummer
August		Lammas Day (1 Aug)		Lammas (1 Aug)	28 Aug	Lughnasadh
September	Michaelmas (29 Sept)					Mabon
November		All Hallows (1 Nov)	Michaelmas (6–28 Nov) (Ireland starts 13 Oct)	Martinmas (11 Nov)	28 Nov	Samhain
December	Christmas (25 Dec)					Yule (midwinter)

Trinity Sunday falls one week after Pentecost Sunday (Whit Sunday) and in 2012 was 3 June. Ascension Day is the fortieth day of Easter: for example, 17 May 2012.

Saints' days

There are often references to holy days, not least when law terms start and contracts etc. were issued (see p. 89). Saints' days may also be responsible for the Christian name of a child baptised that day, and in many old documents (including manor and court rolls) the day and even the month may not be mentioned, but given as 'the day after the feast of St Cecilia' for example. Remember Good King Wenceslas looking out 'on the feast of Stephen'? We may have forgotten most of these 'red letter days' but here they are for reference:

January

1   Circumcisio Domini
13 St Veronica
13 St Hilary
25 Conversion of St Paul

February

1   St Bride (Bridget)
2   Purification of the Virgin, Candlemas Day
24 St Matthias the Apostle

March

1   St David
2   St Chad
4   St Lucius
14 St Benet (Benedict)
18 St Edward
19 St Joseph
20 St Cuthbert
25 Annunciation, Lady-Day

April

23 St George
25 St Mark the Evangelist

May

1   St Philip and St James the Less
2   St Athanasius
3   Invention (or discovery) of the Holy Cross
5   St Hilary, Bishop of Aries
26 St Augustine

June

11 St Barnabas
13 St Anthony of Padua
22 St Alban
24 St John the Baptist, Midsummer
29 Sts Peter and Paul
30 St Paul

July

2   Visitation of the Blessed Virgin
15 St Swithin
22 St Mary Magdalen
25 St James the Great
25 St Christopher, Lammastide

August

1   St Peter ad Vincula
5   St Oswald
6   Transfiguration of our Lord
15 The Assumption of the Virgin
21 St Bernard
24 St Bartholomew
28 St Austin (Augustine)
29 Beheading of St John the Baptist

September

1   St Egidius (Giles)
8   Nativity of the Blessed Virgin
14 Exaltation of the Holy Cross
21 St Matthew
29 St Michael and All Angels, Michaelmas

October

4   St Francis of Assisi
9   St Denis (Dionysius) of Paris
17 St Audry (Etheldreda)
18 St Luke the Evangelist
21 St Ursula and 11,000 virgins
25 St Crispin
28 St Simon the Canaanite

November

1   All Saints' Day
2   All Souls' Day
11 St Martin, Martinmas
16 St Edmund
21 Presentation of the Blessed Virgin

22 St Cecilia

25 St Catherine

30 St Andrew

December

 6 St Nicholas

 8 The Conception of the Blessed Virgin

13 St Lucy

21 St Thomas

25 The Nativity of our Blessed Lord
    Christmas

26 St Stephen

27 St John, Evangelist and Apostle

28 The Holy Innocents

29 St Thomas à Becket

Regnal years

These are the years in which a particular monarch reigned. They matter because many documents are dated by the year of reign, such as: *Anno Domini* 1490, *Anno Regni* 3 Jac IV: indicating the third year of the reign of James (Latin, *Jacobus*) IV, which is 1490, as he came to the throne in 1488. The Married Women's Property Act, 1882 (45 & 46 Vic. Cap. 75) was passed in the session of Parliament that spanned the forty-fifth and forty-sixth years of Queen Victoria's reign (1880, in this case).

There is a distinction between Public Acts, which were given Arabic numerals, 1, 2, 3 etc. (e.g. 50 + 51 Vic c. xx) and Local Acts, which were given roman numerals, i, ii, iii etc. (50 + 51 Victoria c.20). In 1963 this was simplified to using just the calendar year and not the reign of monarchs or the session of Parliament (e.g. 1973 chapter 10 or just c.10), the tenth act passed in the year 1973.

There a number of things to watch out for – traps for the unwary!

The regnal year starts when the monarch accedes to the throne, not the date of coronation. For example, Queen Elizabeth II (b. 1926) became queen on 6 February 1952, when her father, George VI, died, but she was not crowned until 2 June 1953, by which time it was 2 E. II.

The regnal years start on the date of accession, so 1 January 1953 was still 1 E. II.

The count starts at 1, not 0; so 45 Vic. is 1837 + 44 = 1881, but will spill over into 1882 until 19 June that year.

The Stuart sovereigns from James VI and I to Anne were separately monarchs of Scotland and of England, and therefore James VI and I had two separate regnal years, counting from 24 July 1567 in Scotland (when Mary abdicated) but 24 March 1602/03 in England (when Elizabeth died). Therefore a date in 1615 after 24 March would be in 48 Jac. VI but 13 Jac. I. After that, the accession dates were the same in both countries.

The tables below give the birth, accession and death (or deposition) of monarchs of England and Scotland from about 1000 CE. There is a handy converter for English and Scottish regnal years to calendar years at: www.bsswebsite.me.uk/Daysanddates/regnal_year_converter.htm.

	Born	Succeeded	Died
House of Dunkeld, 1034–1286			
Duncan I		1034	1040
Macbeth		1040	1057
Lulach		1057	1058
Malcolm III		1058	1093
Donald III		1093	1097
Duncan II		1094	1094
Edgar		1097	1107
Alexander I		1107	1124
David I		1124	1153

Malcolm IV (Canmore)		1153	1165
William I (the Lion)		1165	1214
Alexander II		1214	1249
Alexander III		1249	1286
First interregnum (1290–92)			
House of Balliol (1292–96)			
John Balliol (Toom Tabard 'Empty Coat')	*c.* 1249	1292–96	1314
Second interregnum (1296–1306)			
House of Bruce (1306–71)			
Robert I (the Bruce)	1274	1306	1329
David II	1324	1329	1371
House of Stewart (1371–1567)			
Robert II (the Steward)	1316	1371	1390
Robert III	*c.* 1337	1390	1406
James I	1394	1406	1437
James II (Fiery Face)	1430	1437	1460
James III	1451	1460	1488
James IV	1473	1488	1513
James V	1512	1513	1542
Mary I	1542	1542–67	exec. 1587
House of Stuart (1567–1651)			
James VI	1566	1567	1625

England

	Born	Succeeded	Died
House of Wessex (Saxons)			
Edward the Confessor	1004	1042	1066
Harold II	1022	1066	1066
House of Normandy			
William I (the Conqueror)	1027	1066	1087
William II (Rufus)	1056	1087	1100
Henry I	1068	1100	1135
Stephen	1105	1135	1154
House of Plantagenet			
Henry II	1133	1154	1189
Richard I (Lionheart)	1157	1189	1199
John (Lackland)	1166	1199	1216
Henry III	1207	1216	1272
Edward I	1239	1272	1307

Edward II	1284	1307	1327
Edward III	1312	1327	1377
Richard II	1366	1377	dep. 1399 d. 1400
House of Lancaster			
Henry IV (Bolingbroke)	1367	1399	1413
Henry V	1387	1413	1422
Henry VI	1421	1422	dep. 1461
House of York			
Edward IV	1441	1461	1483
Edward V (one of the 'Princes in the Tower')	1470	1483	1483
Richard III	1452	1483	1485
House of Tudor			
Henry VII.	1457	1485	1509
Henry VIII	1491	1509	1547
Edward VI	1537	1547	1553
Jane (Reigned 14 days)		1553	1553
Mary I	1516	1553	1558
Elizabeth I	1533	1558	1603
House of Stuart			
James I (VI of Scotland)	1566	1603	1625
Charles I	1600	1625	exec. 1649
Commonwealth (declared 19 May 1649)			
Oliver Cromwell, Lord Protector	1599	1653	1658
Richard Cromwell, Lord Protector	1626	1658–59	d. 1712
Charles II	1630	1649 res. 1660	1685
James II (VII of Scotland)	1633	1685	dep. 1688 d. 1701
William III Mary II	1650 1662	1689	1702 1694
Anne	1665	1702	1714
House of Hanover			
George I	1660	1714	1727
George II	1683	1727	1760
George III	1738	1760	1820
George IV	1762	1820	1830
William IV	1765	1830	1837
Victoria	1819	1837	1901
House of Saxe-Coburg (House of Windsor from 1917)			
Edward VII	1841	1901	1910

George V	1865	1910	1936
Edward VIII (reigned eleven months)	1894	1936	abd. 1936 d. 1972
George VI	1895	1936	1952
Elizabeth II	1926	1952	

Abbreviations: exec., executed; dep., deposed; res., restored; d., died; abd., abdicated.

ISLAMIC DATES

The Islamic Hijri date (*Anno Hejira*) is based on the lunar calendar starting from the 'Hijrah', the year Mohammad moved from Mecca (Makkah or Yathrib) to Medina (Madinah) to avoid assassination. The year 1 AH corresponds to either 15 (astronomical) or 16 (civil) July 622 CE. Because the moon rises progressively later than the sun as you move west, western Muslim countries will celebrate a holy day one (Gregorian) day earlier than in the east. For instance, Isra and Mi'raj are Wednesday 29 June 2011.

JEWISH DATES

The Hebrew lunisolar calendar is based on the date of creation, worked out by Rabbi Yose Ben Halfta around the year 160 CE, which equates to the Gregorian year of 3761 BCE. Each Jewish lunar month starts with the new moon. There is a fixed lunar year, with twelve lunar months of twenty-nine or thirty days, plus an intercalary lunar month added seven times every nineteen years to synchronise the twelve lunar cycles to the slightly longer solar year. This means that the Hebrew year can have from 353 to 385 days, and New Year (Rosh Hashanah, falling on 1 and 2 Tishrei, the seventh month of the ecclesiastical year) falls on a variable date no earlier than 5 September and no later than 6 October: year 5772 was from sunset on 28 September to nightfall on 30 September 2011 and year 5773 is from sunset on 16 September to nightfall on 18 September 2012.

The major Jewish holidays (including New Year, Sukkot, Passover and Shavuot) correspond to important agricultural times of year such as the coming of rains, planting and harvesting, but also have religious significance. Shavuot, for example, day six to seven of the month of Sivan, fell on 26–28 May 2012 but in 2011 was 7–9 June.

Answers to calendrical exercises on p. 40

1. 27 February (1800 was not a leap year)
2. 13 February 1600
3. 13 February 1601 (New style)
4. 8 June 1618
5. 1 August 1606
6. 29 September 1410 (James I of Scotland)
   or 29 September 1607 (James I of England, VI of Scotland)

4

Money, Coinage, Weight and Measure

Britain has had a decimal system since 1970. One pound sterling (£1) consists of 100 pennies (100p). There are notes in various denominations (£1, £5, £10, £20, £50 etc.) and coins (1p, 2p, 5p, 10p, 50p, £1, £2) plus rare 'crowns' of face value £5 issued mainly to mark important occasions such as the Queen's Jubilee.

Before this, the monetary system was more complicated, with a confusing variety of coins of various values in circulation at various times. Add to this the fact that until 1707 (see examples on p. 96), Scotland had an entirely separate monetary system based on the pound Scots and the merk (mark) that continued to be used in documents well into the nineteenth century, and the additional complication that three banks in Scotland and four in Northern Ireland continue to issue their own notes, and you can see the potential for confusion. These are all sterling, and are identical in value, despite the problems that some Scottish and Northern Irish tourists have changing them abroad. The Republic of Ireland now uses the euro (€), in common with many other European Union countries, but not all (such as the UK). Sterling banknotes are also issued by British dependencies outside the UK: the Isle of Man, Jersey, Guernsey, Gibraltar, Saint Helena and the Falkland Islands. These are all for local use, but are exchangeable at par with the pound sterling and they circulate freely alongside English, Scottish and Northern Irish notes. Wales is not a nation, and has none.

Americans reading this and familiar with the standardised 'greenback' dollar bills might reflect that until almost the end of the Civil War (1863), notes were issued by over 1,600 state-chartered private banks of variable liquidity, and until 1935 by a network of licensed national banks, and not every dollar bill was considered to be worth the same – it depended on the bank.

BRITISH MONETARY SYSTEM (PRE-DECIMALISATION IN 1970)

Before 1970, money was calculated in pounds, shillings and pence (*L.s.d.*) with 1 pound = 20 shillings = 240 pence. The pound symbol in documents is either *l* (don't confuse it with a numeral), a stylised *L* (£) or *lb* or *lib*, all from the Latin *libra*, meaning a pound (originally, of silver).

One shilling is represented by */-* or *s* (for '*solidus*', a Roman coin) plural *ss*, and often written as *ß*, which is really a long *s* (*ſ*) followed by a small *s*. This will be familiar to anyone who knows German as the *scharfe* or double *s*. One shilling was equal to twelve pennies and the penny is represented by *d*, short for *denarius*, also a Roman coin. One halfpenny is written as ½*d* but also *ob*, short for *obolus*, yet another Roman coin. One farthing is written as ¼*d* and is represented by *qua*, short for *quadrans*, which is a quarter penny.

There was also a common coin called a groat, typically worth 4*d* in England, 6*d* or 1*s* in Scotland. Later we'll get to the bawbee, florin, lion, demi-lion, noble, half-crown, crown, sovereign, guinea, unicorn, Thistle half-dollar and the dollar.

4 farthings	=	1 penny (1*d*)
12 pence	=	1 shilling (1*s* or 1/-)
2 shillings	=	1 florin (2*s* or 2/-)
2 shillings and 6 pence	=	a half-crown (2/6*d*)
5 shillings	=	1 crown (5*s*)
20 shillings	=	1 pound (a sovereign, £1 or L1)
21 shillings	=	1 guinea (£1 1*s*)

There were 240 pennies (*d*) to the pound (£)
Thus one 'new penny' (p) = 2.4 'old pennies' (*d*) and 5p = 12*d* = 1*s*

The convention that £1 1*s* (21*s*, today £1.05) is called a guinea, although there has been no coin of that value issued since 1813, derives from the high-quality guinea gold used, which therefore made the coin worth more than the £1 value sovereign. The crown has not been a coin in general circulation since 1937, unlike the half-crown, which was. Americans who find this quaint or puzzling should remember that they call 25 cents 'two bits' although there is no coin equal to one 'bit': a reference to the *peso* (meaning 'weight') or 'piece of eight' into which a dollar could be divided.

Scotland had a silver dollar (or ryal) in the time of Mary, Queen of Scots and after, derived (as is the American version) from the thaler or joachimsthaler of central Europe and popularised by Dutch traders. Charles II had a different value dollar worth 4 merks, or 2 16*s* Scots. Incidentally, the dollar sign is said to be that of the Spanish peso (an *S* over a *p*) and two Scots immigrants – John Baine and Archibald Binney – can be thanked for first casting the dollar sign for use on coins in 1797; the spanish dollar was adopted as the standard currency by the United States in 1785.

SCOTTISH COINAGE WAS DIFFERENT FROM ENGLISH

Just as with Scottish weights and measures, Scottish denominations were similar to those in England, but could be of different values. Originally coins had an intrinsic value (they actually contained an amount of silver or gold equivalent to the value) but eventually became tokens of baser metal, valueless in themselves but signifying a value guaranteed by the Crown. The denominations that matter most in documents are the pound Scots, the merk and the dollar.

The merk (derived from the mark) was around in the late sixteenth and seventeenth centuries in Scotland, originally a mark of pure silver (20 sterling pennies) and equal to two-thirds of a pound (160*d* or 13*s* 4*d*). It was used mainly to value land.

There were a number of surprising coins around at various times, such as dollars, ryals, ducats, testoons, pistoles and unicorns, many of which were foreign (Dutch, German, French, Spanish etc.) but freely exchangeable largely because Scotland ran out of currency at various times, especially after the disaster of the Darien Scheme and the lead-up to union in the early 1700s. Scots did their accounts in pounds and valued their land in merks, but paid for high-value items with dollars, as many household and business tallies of the time show.

The most common coins in Scotland, with dates and composition, were:

Coin	Value	Dates	Composition
plack	one-twelfth *d*		
farthing	¼*d*	1279–1672	silver
		1672–1860	copper
		1860–1956	bronze
halfpenny	½*d*	1280–1672	silver
		1672–1859	copper
		1860–1970	bronze
penny	1*d*	1700s–*c.* 1797	silver
		1257	gold
		1797–1860	copper
		1860–1970	bronze
threepence	3*d*	1551–1944	silver
		1937–70	nickel-brass, twelve sided
groat	4*d*	1279–1662, 1838–55	silver
groat (Scots)	6*d*	1406–37	silver (Scotland)
groat (Scots)	12*d*	1437–88	silver (Scotland)
bawbee (Scots)	6*d* Scots	1538–	silver
sixpence	6*d*	1551–1920	silver
		1920–46	half silver
		1947–67	cupro-nickel
shilling	1*s*	1504–1919	silver
		1920–46	half silver
		1947–66	cupro-nickel
florin	2*s*	1344, 1526–1625	gold, value: 6*s.*, not 2*s.*
		1849–1919	silver
		1920–46	half silver
		1947–67	cupro-nickel
demi-lion	2*s* 6*d*	1390–1406	gold (Scotland)
half-crown	2*s* 6*d*	1470–1551	gold
		1551–1850, 1874–1919	silver
		1927–37	half silver
		1947–67	cupro-nickel
half noble	40*d*	1344–1634	gold
double florin	4*s*	1887–90	silver
half demy	4*s* 6*d*	1406–37	gold (Scotland)
crown	5*s*	1526–51	gold
		1551–1902	silver
		1927–37	half silver
		1951, 1953, 1960, 1965, 1981	cupro-nickel (commemorative)

half lion	5s Scots	1437–60	gold (Scotland)
half lion	6s 8d Scots	1488–1513	gold
lion	5s	1390–1406	gold (Scotland)
quarter guinea	5s	1718, 1762	gold
dollar	$1	1895–1934	silver (for trade with the East)
noble	80d	1344–1634	gold
demy	9s	1406–37	gold (Scotland)
third guinea	6s 8d	1797	gold
lion	10s Scots	1437–60	gold (Scotland)
lion	13s 4d Scots	1488–1513	gold
half sovereign	10s	1831–1915, 1980–present	gold
half guinea	10s 6d	1625–1760	gold
merk (mark)	160d = 13s 4d	until the eighteenth century	[value]
merk (thistle half dollar)	13s 4d	1580–1660	silver (there were also ½, 2 and 4 merk coins)
unicorn (Scots)	18s Scots	1460–1513	gold (Scotland)
	20s Scots	1513–42	gold (Scotland)
	22s Scots	1526–	gold (Scotland)
sovereign	£1	1489–1660, 1831–1925, 1957–present	gold
	20s	1642	silver
		1660–85	gold
pound	£1	1914–83	note
guinea	21s	1663–1799, 1813	gold, fixed at 21/- in 1717
two pound	£2	1831, 1887, 1893, 1902, 1911, 1937, 1980, 1982–83	gold
two guineas	£2 2s	1625–1760	gold
dollar	£3	1542–67	silver
	£1 10s	1567–1603	silver
	4 merks	1650–86	silver
ryal	£3	1542–67	gold
	£1 10s	1567–1603	silver
five pound	£5	1839, 1887, 1893, 1902, 1911, 1937, 1980–82, 1984–85, 1990	gold
five guineas	£5 5s	1625–1760	gold
pistole	£12 Scots		gold

Converting Scots to English

In 1707 Britain's monetary systems were unified, and both the pound Scots as a notion and all Scots coins disappeared. Before that, the pound (pund) Scots had been worth less than the English pound sterling, due largely to debasement of the currency. The rate was different at various times. A shorthand for the conversions rates is:

Up to 1355	equal	1476–1544 (all coinage)	1:4
1356–90	1:2	1545–60	1:5
1391–1451	1:2½	1561–65	1:6
1452–53	1:3	1566–79	1:8
1454–67	1:3½	1580–97	1:10
1468–75 (gold only)	1:4	1598–1601	1:12
		after 1603	1:12

There were various exchange rates during Cromwell's time, 1649–60.

Taken from Cochran, P., *Records of the Coinage of Scotland*, lxxvi.

Thus, after 1603, 1 Scots shilling equalled 1 English penny and 1 Scots merk was equal to 1 English shilling, approximately. If this is confusing, and if British *L*, *s* and *d* causes difficulties, there is a handy conversion spreadsheet at: www.scan.org.uk/researchrtools/converterpop.htm.

Examples

1. From the records of Culross Kirk Session, 1642:

> **1642, July 10.—Isobel Cursone a distressed woman from Yrland borne w'in this towne gave in a bill desyring some helpe to convoy hir to England w' her husband and bairns, where she may find hir calling, to receave 4 dollars.**

Given that 1 dollar (Scots) equalled 4 merks and 1 merk was equal to ⅔ of a pound Scots, how much was that in pounds sterling at the time? Four dollars equalled 16 merks, equal to 16 x ⅔ pound Scots, which equalled 20 x 16 x ⅔ Scots shillings or 213s 4d Scots. The correct conversion factor for Scots/English in 1642 was 12:1, so about 17s 9d in sterling. Something less than £1 sterling, in fact. (For what this would be worth today, see 'Relative values' on p. 100.)

Another way to look at it is that 1 dollar (Scots) equalled about 60s (Scots), which equalled 60d (sterling) or 5s (sterling).

2. Retour, 1554, showing land extent (annual value):

> **(26)**   **Aug. 11. 1554.**
> **JONETA DURIE,** *hæres* Roberti Durie de Eodem, *patris*,—in terris et baronia de Durie, viz. terris de Durie ;—terris de Balcurryquhy-Mekill ;—terris de Balcurryquhy-Litill ;—terris de Hauch, cum aliis terris in Perth unitis in baroniam de Durie.—A. E. 50*m*. N. E. 200*m*.—(Vide Perth.)   i. 76.

A.E. = 'Auld Extent'; N.E. = 'New Extent'. The term 'extent' refers to value, and therefore a reflection of both the size and the annual value in terms of either produce or rent, as good arable land is obviously worth more than hill scrub or moorland. This has nothing to do with equivalence to English currency, but was a recognition, around 1474, that the thirteenth-century valuations were out of date, given inflation. The Auld Extent was replaced by the New Extent often just by multiplying by four, five or six. Lands continued to be described in terms of extents long after the values had any meaning e.g. 'the ten-shilling land of John Smith of auld extent'. The New Extent is the relevant value here; 200 merks is equal to 133 6s 8d Scots or just over £11 2s sterling. (See 'Relative values', below.)

3. Summa of the Inventory of George Durie, Lord Rutherford, 1759.

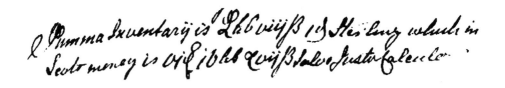

Summa Inventarii is L lib viij   1d Sterling which in Scots money is viC iv lib xvij   Salvo Justo Calculo

This is a good example of the persistence of Scots money in a notional sense even after the Union of 1707. The sterling value of Lord Rutherford's moveable estate was £50 7s 1d, which multiplied by twelve equals £604 17s Scots, and exactly what the document says. (See 'Relative values'.)

Relative values

Once you have a value in sterling and a year, it is possible to calculate the equivalent value today – possible, but not straightforward. Economists use a variety of measures to calculate equivalences over the ages, and they give wildly differing results. One method is to compare the price of something still for sale, such as a pint of beer, a chicken or a loaf of bread. But who is to say the costs of producing these haven't changed? Another is a working man's wage, or a week's rent. But has labour got cheaper or more expensive compared to housing? A third is a per-head evaluation of a nation's total Gross Domestic Product (GDP) but this is perhaps the least relevant as Britain was once a far richer country in international terms than it is today, and at times has been poorer. Yet another is the price of gold or silver, but currencies are no longer tied to these precious metals.

There is far more detail on this, plus calculators, at the Economic History Services website http://www.measuringworth.com/calculators/ppoweruk/, which also has converters from sterling to US dollars. If the value £100 is entered and the year 1830 and it is set to derive 2009 values, we get the following results:

– £7,550.00 using the retail price index
– £9,450.00 using the GDP deflator
– £82,900.00 using the average earnings
– £111,000.00 using the per capita GDP
– £289,000.00 using the share of GDP

That's a discrepancy of almost forty-fold across the five measures. Here is a 'realistic' table worked out from prices and wages:

Year	Value	Year	Value	Year	Value
1600	233	1750	205	1955	25
1620	221	1800	77	1965	19
1640	194	1850	126	1970	16
1660	156	1900	114	1980	3.5
1680	187	1914	107	1990	1.75
1700	158	1919	47	2011	1
1720	168	1939	60		
1740	166	1946	39		

To use the table, look up any year. In that year £1 would have the purchasing power equivalent to the value against that year. For instance, if something cost £2 in 1800, it should cost 2 x 77 = £154 in 2011. To reverse that, £1 in 1750 would be worth £205 now.

Even this apparently simple method yields surprises. For instance, in 1600 a bottle of French wine cost 2s (about £38 now), a chicken cost 1p (£1), a tankard of ale ½p (50p) and a pair of boots £4 (£931). Present-day tax on beer makes the current cost nearer £3, and the boots look expensive, but the wine (if it's really good) and chicken are about right.

On the other hand, this is not a dependable index to wages. The weekly wage of a carpenter in the early 1600s was about 5s (£100 per week or £5,000 per annum now) and a typical wage for a head footman in 1761 was £7 per year (£1,430 now). Try getting anyone to work for those salaries today!

Our three examples above work out as follows:

– £1 in 1642: perhaps £190 today, which would be enough to get a family on a train to England.
– £11 in 1554: maybe 11 x 250 or £2,750, not much of an annual income to live on, but the calculator referred to above also gives £2,600 using the retail price index and £41,600 using average earnings, which is more like it.
– £50 in 1759: possibly 50 x 200 or £10,000, which isn't much for a man's total worth (excluding land and 'real' property).

In 1815 a newspaper cost 7d (mostly taxes on the newspaper, on the paper used to print it and on advertisements), which should equate to about £2.25 today, but a craftsman's daily wage was 6s (£23) and therefore a daily paper cost about a tenth of a day's pay; the average industrial wage now is about £100 per day, so a paper would cost, in relative terms, £10. (Newsprint got a lot cheaper when the various taxes were dropped in the 1850s and the 'penny paper' was born, which is more akin to the prices we pay today, relatively speaking.)

So, monetary conversion across the ages is not an exact science, but for a rule-of-thumb calculation, use 200x for 1600–1800 and 100x for 1800–1900.

WEIGHT, VOLUME AND DISTANCE

Scottish measurements fell into line with the English (Imperial) measures in 1707, although Scots merchants continued to use both for purposes of trade. Scottish weights and measures disappeared slowly and only after the Imperial Weights and Measures Act of 1824. Therefore, take care when reading quantities and measures in documents from the eighteenth and early nineteenth centuries as they may refer to Scots or English measures. In both Scotland and England, references may be to the 'old' measures such as the ell, the reel, the boll and the firlot.

In England, weights and measures were standardised. In Scotland, they were regulated locally, mainly by burghs, which would have a public weighing machine or tron (from the French *troneau*, meaning 'balance'), which was also in many cases the main place for public meetings and punishment, and incorporated into the tollbooth. Glasgow still has a Trongate ('gate' in this context meaning 'street', from the Old Norse *gata*). From 1661, particular burghs in Scotland were made responsible for standard weights and measures: Stirling had the pint for liquid measure; Edinburgh had the ell for length; Linlithgow kept the firlot for dry measure (cereals etc.) and Lanark was the keeper of the troy stone for weight.

Weight

The Scots troy pound was slightly heavier than the English pound avoirdupois (about 496 *v.* 454 grams).

16 draps (drops)	=	1 ounce
16 ounces	=	1 pound (496 grams)
16 pounds	=	1 stone (almost 8 kilograms)
English (Imperial) 14 pounds	=	1 stone

The pound is often abbreviated as lb, which can be confused with the monetary pound, *lib.*

Length and area

Scots inches, feet, chains and miles were slightly longer than the Imperial equivalents by a factor of about 1.12. The ell was 42 Scots inches but 37 Imperial inches and was supposed to measure the distance between the end of the nose and the fingertips.

12 inches	=	1 foot
3 feet	=	1 ell
6 ells	=	fall (or fa)
4 falls	=	1 chain
10 chains	=	1 furlong
8 furlongs	=	1 mile = 80 chains
1 Scots mile	=	.52 Imperial yards, 5929.56 Imperial feet

Square measure

The ell was also a square measure used for cloth, slightly larger than an Imperial square yard and slightly smaller than a square metre.

36 sq. ells	=	1 square fall
40 sq. falls	=	1 rood
4 roods	=	1 acre (1.257 Imperial acres)
12–13 acres	=	1 oxgang (literally 'where the oxen go')
8 oxgangs	=	1 ploughgate, about 100 acres
4 ploughgates	=	1 davach, roughly 400 acres, 162 hectares or 5/8 of a square mile

In England, the rood or rod is also called the pole or perch.

Dry measure

The basic measure was the firlot, equal to about 36 litres of wheat, peas, beans and meal, or about 53 litres of barley, oats and malt. A smaller unit, the lippie or forpet, was ¹/₁₆ of a firlot and thus around 2.25 or 3.3 litres. It was equivalent to the Imperial (English) half-gallon or 4 pints. Prices were usually expressed by the boll (4 firlots or 2 Imperial gallons).

There was also the leispund, lesh pund or lispund, a weight equal to 18 pounds Scots; it was mainly used for butter, wool and oil. Its value was often different from other parts of Scotland in, say, Shetland.

```
 4 lippies or 4 forpets = 1 peck
16 lippies = 4 pecks = 1 firlot (2214.3 cubic inches or 8 Imperial gallons for wheat etc. 3230.3 cubic
inches or 11.65 Imperial gallons for barley etc.)
64 lippies = 16 pecks = 4 firlots = 1 boll
16 firlots = 4 bolls = 1 quarter (equivalent to an English bushel)
64 firlots = 16 bolls = 4 quarters = 1 chalder
31 Scots pints = 1 barley firlot
```

Liquid measure

Originally, the Scots pint was equal to about 2.75 Imperial pints (1.56 litres), later standardised at 104.2034 cubic inches, or 3.01 Imperial pints (1.7 litres). Thus the Scots gallon was 3 Imperial gallons (13.7 litres) and a barrel was equivalent to about 41 litres. Remember that a US gallon is 0.833 Imperial (UK) gallons. This was standardised by the Stirling Jug, said to have been established in 1457 by Stirling Burgh Council to regulate liquid measures, but mentioned in Acts of Parliament as being in the town before the reign of James II in 1437. It was the yardstick by which all other Scottish quantities were standardised and was not superseded until Imperial measures were introduced in 1707. The actual jug itself can be seen in the Smith Art Gallery and Museum in Stirling (along with the world's oldest football).

The gill is an interesting unit, as it is still used informally in whisky measures today. The standard measure of a glass of spirits in England is ¹/₆ of a gill, whereas in Scotland it is ¹/₅ (the 'nip') or in the better pubs, ¼ of a gill. There are therefore 80 nips in an old Scots pint, and about 26 in an Imperial pint. You may hear Scotsmen ask for a 'half and half', which is a half-gill (a double measure) of whisky and a half-pint of beer to wash it down.

```
 4 gills  =  1 mutchkin
 8 gills  =  2 mutchkins  =  1 chopin
16 gills  =  2 chopins    =  1 pint (in Scotland, sometimes called the 'joug') = 2.75 imperial pints
 8 pints  =  1 gallon
64 pints  =  8 gallons    =  1 barrel
```

Example

1. It may help to review Chapter 10 on Scottish Testaments:

> *Testament Dative and Inventar of the goodis gere Dettis + articles pertaining to umquhile Johne Chissolme of Kinneries within the parochin of Kiltare Littil the tyme of his decease wha deceasit intestat the twentie twa day off maij Jaj vj + threttie yeiris [1603] faitufullie gevin up be Margarat Grant relict of the defunct upon hir sworne aith [oath] as follows.*

John Chisholm of Kinerries, 22 May 1603

In the first it is gevin up the said umqll Johne Chissolme to have had the tyme of his decease forsaid the goodis + gere underwr<it>tin of the avail and pryces after spe<cifie>t viz Ten great Ky p<ry>ce of the peice xiij lib vj   viijd [£13 6/8*d*] Inde jCxxxiij lib vj   viijd [£133 6/8*d*].

Item nyne yield ky pr<y>ce of the piece x lib [£10] Inde iiij*xx* x lib [£90].

Item twa ky p<ry>ce of the piece v lib [£5] Inde x lib [£10].

Item twa stirks p*ce* [price] of the piece iij lib vj   viijd [£3 6/8*d*] Inde vj lib xiij   iijd [£6 13/6*d*]

Item twa horse p*ce* of the piece xiij lib vj   viijd [£13 6/8*d*]. Inde xxvj lib xiij   iiijd [£26 13/4*d*]. Item ane mear and foill p*ce* xiij lib vj

vjijd [£13 6/8*d*]. Item twentie gayt [goats] p*ce* of the piece xx [20/-] Inde xxlib [£20]

Item sawin in Kinerres sixteen bollis estimat to the third corne Inde xLviij [48] bollis aitts p*ce* of the boll L   [50/-] Inde jCxx lib [£120]

Item sawin thair twa bollis bere [barley] estimate to the fore corne Inde aucht [8] bollis p*ce* of the boll v lib [£5] Inde xl lib [£40]

Item sawin in Knockfine aucht bollis aitts estimate to the third corne Inde xxiiij [24] bollis aitts p*ce* of the boll L   [50/-] Inde iij*xx* lib [£60]

Item sawin thair sevin for beare estimat to the fore corne Inde sevin bolls beare p*ce* foresaid Inde xxxb lib [£35]

Item the Domicilies estimat to xxlib [£20]

Summa of the Inventar vCiij*xx*xv lib [£575]

Dettis award be the dead

In the first restand to Alex*r* Chissolme of Comer for the dewtye of the towne and landis of Knockfine xxxiij lib vj   viij d [£33 6/8*d*]

Item of tenands fees vj lib [£6]

    Summa of the dettis xxxix lib vj   viijd [£39 6/8*d*]

    Summa of the inventar the dettis deductit

                                    – vCxxv lib xiij   iiijd [£525 13/4*d*]

    To be devydet in twa p,air.tis

    The deadis pairt – iiC iij*xx*ij lib xvj   viijd [£262 16/8*d*]

Key to some terms:

aith: oath	*d*: pence	lib: Scots pounds
aitts: oats	fore corne: four harvests	mear and foill: mare and foal
aucht: 8	gayt: goats	sawin: sowings of cereals
award: owing	*iij*^{xx} = 3 x 20 = 60	: ss, shillings stirks: steers, bullocks
be: by	Inde: subtotal	third corne: three harvests
bere: barley	Junij: Juneky: cows	yield ky: milk cows

The third corn and ferd, fore or fourth corn were estimates of the value of grain sown, multiplied by the amount sown to calculate the worth of the eventual yield after three or four crops.

Further Reading

Online

Economic History Net: http://eh.net/hmit/

Current Value of Old Money: www.ex.ac.uk/~RDavies/arian/current/howmuch.html

Consumer Price Inflation Since 1750: www.statistics.gov.uk/cci/article.asp?ID=726

Books

Zupko, R.E., *A Dictionary of Weights and Measures for the British Isles: the middle ages to the twentieth century* (Philadelphia: American Philosophical Society, 1985)

5

Inscriptions and Gravestones

Burial and lair records are dealt with alongside death records in Chapter 8, along with the Latin found in baptism and marriage records. This chapter has some examples of monumental inscriptions (MIs) and memorials, as exercises for translation, using the Glossaries (Chapter 20).

The two main complicating factors encountered in reading MIs are: the use of abbreviations and Latin. It also doesn't help when there are abbreviations in Latin!

Examples

1. Monument of PENELOPE BOOTHBY in Ashborne church, Derbyshire:

I was not in safety, neither had I rest, and the trouble came.
To PENELOPE,
Only Child of Sir BROOKE and Dame SUSANNA BOOTHBY, Born April 11th, 1785, died March 13th, 1791.
She was in form and intellect most exquisite. The unfortunate parents ventured their all on this frail Bark, and the wreck was total.
Omnia tecum una perierunt gaudia nostra.
Tu vero felix Et beata Penelope mea,
Quae tot Tantisque Miseriis una
Morte perfuncta es.

(All our joys are perished with thee alone.
But thou art happy and blessed, my dear Penelope,
who, by one touch of Death,
hast escaped so many and so great miseries.)

2. New Burial Ground, Calcutta:

Hic Sepultus Jacet HIPPOLOTUS POIGNARD
Natus die 29 Augusti, Anno Domini 1761,
Obiit die 10 Maii, 1805

Ad lenitatem quam erga uxorem,
Ad amorem quem erga liberos,
Ad libertalitatem quam erga socios,
Ad urbanitatem quam erga omnes
Ille habuit, nihil potest accedere.
Hoc marmor multum moerens
Posuit die Junii 9 Anno Domini 1805

(Here lies buried HIPPOLOTUS POIGNARD

Born 29 August, the year of our Lord 1761,

Died 10 May, 1805

To the gentleness towards his wife,

To the love for his children,

To the generosity to his companions,

To good manners toward all

That he had, nothing can approach.

This marble mourns much

Was laid 9 June the year of our Lord 1805)

3. Hereford Cathedral:

Jocosa Aubrey, 1638.

Infra jacet quantum.

Mortale fuit Jocosæ Aubrey, uxoris Samuelis Aubrey, Militis, filiæ et cohæredis Gulielmi Rudhall, de Rudhall, Armig. quæ obiit duodecimo die Julii, Anno Dom. 1638.

Could dull words speak what buried here doth lie,
'Twould raise both Envy and Idolatry.
'Twas an Exchequer, throng'd with so much good,
The age that lost it, never understood.
Just heaven finding 'twas but envied here,
Left us the Casket, fix'd the Jewel there.

Juxta charissimæ sponsæ cineres depositum est corpus Samuelis Aubrey, Militis, filii Morgani Aubrey, Armig. qui obiit decimo nono die Maii, Anno Domini, 1645.

He who did never lodge within his breast
Dishonour, Baseness or selfe Interest,
The just man's Friend, the poor man's Treasury,
The oppress'd Man's Patron in extremity,
Lies here (Reader) if now thou grudge a Tear,
Find some more worthy object, spend it there.

On a small black marble slab in 1st bay of B. C., formerly on W. wall of N.T., Dingley CLXXVIII. and CLXXXI. gives these inscriptions with the following addition—"Vita et Morte Concordes Conjuges Samuelis et Jocosa Aubrey hic jacent."
R., 18. D., 573. The inscribed stone formerly in the pavement is lost. See Lane's G.P., No. 3.

4. Hedenham St Peter, Norfolk:

C004 – Slate monument on South wall of nave

Sacrum memoriae Phillipi BEDINGFELD de Ditchingham armiger

qui obiit 25 die Augusti anno domini 1696

aetatis suae 42

necnoni Elizabethae uxoris ejus (filiae

et cohaeredis Gulielmi STRODE de Newhouse

in comitatu Somersetiae, armigeri)

quae obiit 28 die February anno domini 1723\4

aetatis suae 69

Ac etiam STRODE alias BEDINGFELD. Generosi

dicti Phillipi BEDINGFELD

natu quinti qui obiit 18 die maii anno domini 1725

Johannes Jacobus Carolus et Thomas

filii superstites hoc posuerunt

Sacred to the memory of Philip of Ditchingham BEDINGFELD, Esquire, who died 25 day of August in the year 1696 at the age of 42 and also of Elizabeth his wife (daughter and co-heir of William Strode of Newhouse in the county of Somerset, Esquire) who died on 28 February in the year 1723/4 at the age of 69 And also STRODE alias BEDINGFELD. Of the noble family of the said Philip BEDINGFELD, fifth-born who died on May 18 1725. John, James, Charles and Thomas his surviving sons set this.

C006 Ledger in floor of choir

Hic tumulo requieseunt
exuviae Mariae BEDINGFIELD
filiae natu minimae Philippi BEDINGFIELD de Ditchingham
in Comitati Norfolciae armigeri et Elizabethae uxoris
ejus quae obiit vigesimo
die Maii Anno Domini 1716 aetatis suae 22

In this tomb rest the remains of Mary BEDINGFIELD youngest daughter of Philip BEDINGFIELD of Ditchingham in Norfolk, Esquire, and of his wife Elizabeth, who died on the twentieth day of May AD 1716 at the age of 22

5. Holyrood House churchyard, Edinburgh:

NICOL PATERSON'S Monument
Hic habentur reliquiae Nicolai Patersoni, nobilissimi Joanni, inclyto Rothusiae comiti, clarissimo Scotorum proregi, a secretioribus ministris. Obiit postridie iduum Decemb. 1665.

Here are lodged the remains of Nicol Paterson, secretary to the most noble and excellent John Earl of Rothes, most famous viceroy of Scotland. He died 14 December 1665.

JOHN PATERSON'S Monument
Memoriae dilectissimi conjugis Joannis Patersoni qui, cum suavissimo matrimonij vinculo, 35 plus minus annos transegisset; & aliquoties Balivi munere, in vicecanonicori functus esset, obijt anno Christi 1663 April 23, aetatis 63.
Amoris & officij ergo, monumentum hoc dicavit Agneta Lyell, quae haec ipsa obijt, 1664 April 23, aetatis
Ecce Patersoni, mortis secura secundae,
Mens peregrinantes quae peragenda monet

To the memory of her most beloved husband John Paterson who after he had lived about 35 years in the sweet bond of marriage, and several times had discharged the office of a baillie in the Canongate, died in the year of Christ 1663, April 23, aged 63.
In token of her love and duty Agnes Lyell dedicates this monument who herself died in April 1664.
Lo, Paterson's kind ghost, redeem'd from hell,
To sojourners their duty clear doth tell.

Here is one with a couple of (so-called) puns in Latin. Revd Joshua Durie (son of a much more famous and more turbulent cleric) was the incumbent at Inverkeillor Parish church, Angus, from 1613 to 1631.

QVOD DVRVM EST
FRACTVM NEC PLVS.
DVRARE VIDETVR
DVREVS AT DVRAT.
CLARAQVE FAMA VIGET

(That which is Durable
is broken, nor appears
any longer to endure
but Durie still endures,
and flourishes with bright renown)

The rest of the inscription gives the date (3 September 1631) and the initials of Joshua as MID (Master Joshua Durie, using 'I' for 'J') and his wife as DEM (Dame Eupham McKane or Maklene). Incidentally, the coat of arms is wrong, and not Joshua's to display in any case.

ABBREVIATIONS AND OMISSIONS

Consult the section on brevigraphs (p. 12) but be aware that inscriptions and epitaphs often have common abbreviations, with or without a full stop, including:

– Names: *Jac.* for *Jacobus* (James), *Joh.* or *Jno.* for *Johannes* (John).
– Titles: *Esq.* for Esquire, *arm.* for armiger (which could mean either 'has arms' or Bailie), *Dom* for *Dominus* (Sir, Lord or a clerical title, depending on context).
– Word endings: *-q* indicating *-que* (and as in *atq.* for *atque*), *–m* or *-u* instead of *–um* (as in *dominu* or *dominm* for *dominum*).

Sometimes this was just about fitting a word into a line.

Further Reading

Online

Jervise, A. *et al.*, *Epitaphs & inscriptions from burial grounds & old buildings in the north-east of Scotland, with historical, biographical, genealogical, and antiquarian notes, also, an appendix of illustrative papers* (1875). Available at: http://archive.org/details/epitaphsinscriptoojerv

Books

Parker, J., *Reading Latin Epitaphs: a handbook for beginners*, 4th edn (University of Exeter Press, 2008)

6

Heraldic Documents and Artefacts

A knowledge of heraldry is an important club in the bag of any historian or genealogist. This isn't the place for a disquisition on coats of arms, and even a glossary of heraldic terms would be a book in itself (see 'Further Reading' p. 117). However, there are references to printed and online sources for anyone interested in this area.

This chapter contains a brief description of the rules and vocabulary used when blazoning (describing) arms, plus the assignments of planets and precious stones to the tinctures, and the *Petra Sancta* system for rendering the tinctures in engravings or stone carvings, plus various documents and artefacts concerned with or concerning heraldry:

– Grant of arms (England)
– Results of an Heraldic Visitation (English and Welsh)
– An example of Letters Patent (Scottish)
– A page from the Public Register of All Arms (Scottish)
– A page from an Ordinary of Arms (Scottish)
– A page from an armorial
– Armorial seals and bookplates

THE LAW OF ARMS

All coats of arms are the individual, heritable property of one person. There is no such thing (in Britain at least), as a 'family coat of arms' and anyone in someone else's arms could find themselves subject to a Civil Law suit in England or statutory penalties in Scotland. However, in Scotland only the senior line can have the undifferenced arms, while in England all heirs may, leading to considerable confusion over cadet branches.

Heraldic practice is more or less the same in England and Scotland and arms are granted by the appropriate heraldic authorities. In England and Wales this is the College of Arms. The English heralds have been operating in an organised way since at least 1420, and were granted a charter of incorporation plus premises by Richard III in 1484. They currently operate under a charter of Mary Tudor from 1555. There are three Kings of Arms – Garter Principal, Clarenceux and Norroy, and Ulster – plus six heralds and four pursuivants. Garter receives an annual salary of £49.07

(no, that isn't a misprint) and the rest of the income of the College comes from granting and confirming arms, and professional fees for private practice in heraldry and genealogy.

In theory, and even to this day, every property owner in Scotland is supposed, by law, to have armorial bearings, so it is not in any way restricted to the great and the noble. The Lord Lyon King of Arms has statutory jurisdiction and a position in the hierarchy of the Scottish government that the English heralds can only dream of. The Lyon Court deals with all matters relating to Scottish heraldry and coats of arms and the associated Lyon Office maintains the Public Register of All Arms and Bearings and the Public Register of Genealogies and Birthbrieves. Lord Lyon is a judge in his own court, a minister of state and the officer responsible for state ceremonial in Scotland. His Procurator-Fiscal has considerable powers to prosecute over the improper use of arms, up to and including fines and imprisonment, and does exercise them – the Lyon bites!

TINCTURES, RULES, *PETRA SANCTA* AND 'TRICK'

There are nine 'tinctures' used in heraldry: actually, two metals and seven colours, of which only four are common. These are named in the table below, along with heavenly bodies and stones associated with them, more of which later. The basic rule in heraldry is that there cannot be a metal on a metal – no Or (gold) on Argent (silver/white) or vice versa – and no colour on a colour. There is no problem showing the colours on a painted or colour-printed page, in enamelwork, on stained glass etc., but because of the difficulty of displaying the tinctures on carvings, engravings, metal casts and black-and-white print (as here) a system of hatchings was developed in the 1630s. This is named after the Jesuit heraldist Silvester Petra Sancta but may have been the creation of Marcus Vulson de la Colombière, a French heraldist and poet, and was possibly based on an earlier method of the Flemish engraver, publisher and typographer Johannes Baptista Zangrius, or an even earlier schema dating from soon after 1555.

Heraldic tinctures

Heraldic term	Colour	Heavenly body	Precious stone	Abbreviation	Notes
Metals					
Or	gold	sun	thopasis	Or	a peridot
Argent	silver/white	moon	pearl	Arg.	
Colours					
Azure	blue	Jupiter	sapphire	B. as A3.	
Gules	red	Mars	ruby	Gu.	
Sable	black	Saturn	diamond	Sa.	
Vert	green	Venus	emerald	Vt.	
Purpure	purple	Mercury	amethyst	Pur.	rare
Stains					
Tenné	tawny/orange		cassidony	so rare as to have no planet or abbreviation	rare
Murrey	mulberry		sardonyx		rare

Notice that the names and their abbreviations are capitalised, largely to avoid ambiguity between Or (gold) and 'or' (the conjunction), that Azure is often abbreviated B. (blue) because of potential confusion with Argent, and Argent is usually depicted as white or the colour of the background paper rather than any kind of light grey. There are also furs, including ermine, vair and others.

The origins of the tinctures are rather prosaic, in that knights on a battlefield had to be distinguishable at a distance by bold designs in contrasting colours, made from plant and mineral dyes available in the twelfth century, when heraldry as we know it started. The rather fanciful association with stones and planets, and the addition of the 'stains' were mediaeval conceits based on there being nine orders of angels (apparently) but sadly only seven heavenly bodies (excluding the Earth, of course) were known at the time.

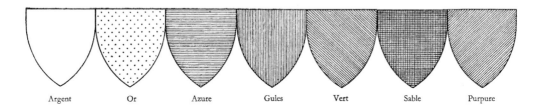

| Argent | Or | Azure | Gules | Vert | Sable | Purpure |

The *Petra Sancta* system

Example of *Petra Sancta* in an engraving on silver (left); the Lowe of Bromsgrove arms as they would be in *Petra Sancta* (middle) and Trick (right):

BLAZONING

The apparently obscure language of heraldry is in fact an extremely precise way of describing a shield in such a way that another herald could draw and paint it accurately. The important points on a shield are shown here: 'dexter' (literally 'right') is indeed right, from the point of view of the person holding the shield, and 'sinister' is left. Heraldists never refer to 'left' or 'right'.

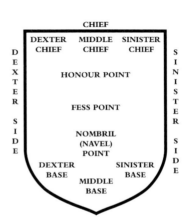

Grant of Arms (England)

This is a transcription of a Grant of Arms from 1657. The spellings and capitalisations have been left as in the original. Notice the references to the Kings of Arms, Garter Principal and Clarenceaux

> Lowe. [Vol. 16, p. 149]
> Grant of Arms to Humphrey Lowe of Bromsgrove,
> To all an singular as well noblemen as gentlemen to whome theis presents
> shall come Edward bishe esq. garter principall King of Armes of Englishmen
> sendeth greeting Whereas it hath beene an Antiente custome of long
> continuance that men of antient decents have been in all ages distinguished by
> certaine signes & toakens called armes being noe other then outward
> demonstrations of worth & valor acheived either in war or by virtuous endeavours
> in time of peice & wheras humfrey Lowe of Bromsgrave in ye county of
> Worcester esq. high sherife of ye said county is decended of a good family of
> gentry & yet is uncertaine what armes he may duly beare by his perticular
> disent and wheras Micaell Lowe gentleman deceased who was of ye same family
> and obteyned an exemplification of armes vizt. arg. on a bend betwene two
> cotices azure thre lions heads erazed of ye first from Robert Cooke clarenceiux
> King of armes hath left noe issue male of his bodie nowe living nowe I ye said
> Ed: Bishe Garter principall King of armes of Englishmen in consideration of
> the premises have Assigned unto ye said humfry lowe the said armes thus
> differenced vizt. or on a bend betwixt two cottices sables thre lions heads
> erased or And for ye creast on a helmett & wreath of his colors a demy
> griffin segeant erazed or mantled gules doubled argent as in ye margent more
> lively is depicted which armes & creast I ye said Edward bishe by vertue of
> my office doe assigne Ratifie & conferme unto ye said humfrey Lowe and his
> heires & Posterity lawfully begotten for ever to be by him & them borne with
> theire due differences according to the lawes & customes of armes in witness
> whereof I have caused theis presents to be registered in ye office of armes
> & have hereunto subscribed my name & sealed ye same with ye scale of my
> office dated ye eight day of february in ye yeare of our Lord god 1657.
> Edward Bisshe, Garter
> Principall King of Armes
> of Englishmen.

British Museum, Stowe MSS., 677, folio 61

Heraldic visitations (English and Welsh)

These were tours of inspection made by Kings of Arms and heralds in England and Wales between 1530 and 1688 (and also in Ireland) for the purpose of registering existing arms and recording pedigrees. The idea was to bring some order and regulation to the arms used by nobility, gentry and the boroughs. The records of visitations, especially the recorded pedigrees, are an important source for genealogists, heraldists and historians. (See 'Further Reading' on p. 117.)

While the original records of the visiting heralds have not been kept by the College of Arms, it does have an extensive library of manuscript copies, but most are in the British Library. Some have been published by the Harleian Society (http://harleian.org.uk, which was founded for that purpose), others by county record societies and so on, and many were printed privately. Possibly the most complete accessible set is the multi-volume *Visitation of England and Wales* edited by Frederick

Arthur Crisp (1851–1922) and Joseph Jackson Howard (1827–1902) and privately printed in the early 1900s. These should all be available, including individual files, at www.archive.org. But take care, the published versions often differ substantially from the official records at the College of Arms.

Pedigree, taken from a visitation

This shows the first page, below, of the pedigree relating to the family of Humphrey Lowe, whose Grant of Arms is shown, copied from volume 12 of Crisp's *Visitations* (see below):

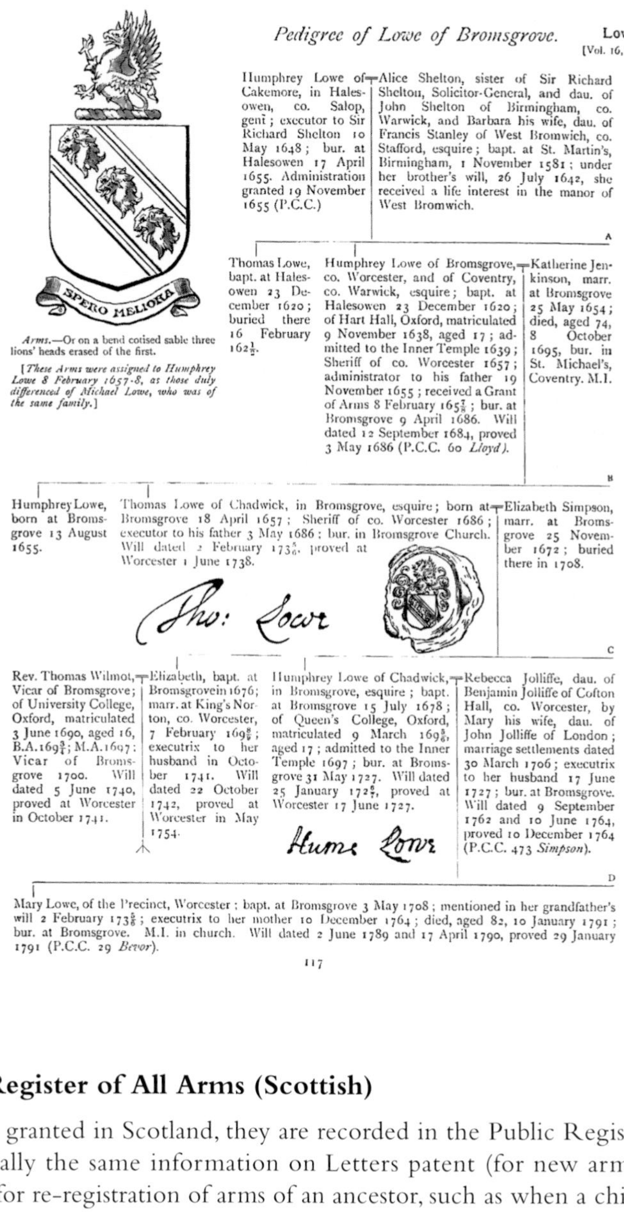

Pedigree of Lowe of Bromsgrove. **Lowe.** [Vol. 16, p. 149.]

Arms.—Or on a bend cotised sable three lions' heads erased of the first.

[*These Arms were assigned to Humphrey Lowe 8 February 1657-8, as those duly differenced of Michael Lowe, who was of the same family.*]

Humphrey Lowe of Cakemore, in Halesowen, co. Salop, gent; executor to Sir Richard Shelton 10 May 1648; bur. at Halesowen 17 April 1655. Administration granted 19 November 1655 (P.C.C.) = Alice Shelton, sister of Sir Richard Shelton, Solicitor-General, and dau. of John Shelton of Birmingham, co. Warwick, and Barbara his wife, dau. of Francis Stanley of West Bromwich, co. Stafford, esquire; bapt. at St. Martin's, Birmingham, 1 November 1581; under her brother's will, 26 July 1642, she received a life interest in the manor of West Bromwich.

A

Thomas Lowe, bapt. at Halesowen 23 December 1620; buried there 16 February $162\frac{1}{2}$.

Humphrey Lowe of Bromsgrove, co. Worcester, and of Coventry, co. Warwick, esquire; bapt. at Halesowen 23 December 1620; of Hart Hall, Oxford, matriculated 9 November 1638, aged 17; admitted to the Inner Temple 1639; Sheriff of co. Worcester 1657; administrator to his father 19 November 1655; received a Grant of Arms 8 February $165\frac{7}{8}$; bur. at Bromsgrove 9 April 1686. Will dated 12 September 1684, proved 3 May 1686 (P.C.C. 60 *Lloyd*). = Katherine Jenkinson, marr. at Bromsgrove 25 May 1654; died, aged 74, 8 October 1695, bur. in St. Michael's, Coventry. M.I.

B

Humphrey Lowe, born at Bromsgrove 13 August 1655.

Thomas Lowe of Chadwick, in Bromsgrove, esquire; born at Bromsgrove 18 April 1657; Sheriff of co. Worcester 1686; executor to his father 3 May 1686; bur. in Bromsgrove Church. Will dated 2 February $173\frac{5}{6}$, proved at Worcester 1 June 1738. = Elizabeth Simpson, marr. at Bromsgrove 25 November 1672; buried there in 1708.

C

Rev. Thomas Wilmot, Vicar of Bromsgrove; of University College, Oxford, matriculated 3 June 1690, aged 16, B.A. $169\frac{3}{4}$; M.A. 1697; Vicar of Bromsgrove 1700. Will dated 5 June 1740, proved at Worcester in October 1741. = Elizabeth, bapt. at Bromsgrove in 1676; marr. at King's Norton, co. Worcester, 7 February $169\frac{8}{9}$; executrix to her husband in October 1741. Will dated 22 October 1742, proved at Worcester in May 1754.

Humphrey Lowe of Chadwick, in Bromsgrove, esquire; bapt. at Bromsgrove 15 July 1678; of Queen's College, Oxford, matriculated 9 March $169\frac{5}{6}$, aged 17; admitted to the Inner Temple 1697; bur. at Bromsgrove 31 May 1727. Will dated 25 January $172\frac{6}{7}$, proved at Worcester 17 June 1727. = Rebecca Jolliffe, dau. of Benjamin Jolliffe of Cofton Hall, co. Worcester, by Mary his wife, dau. of John Jolliffe of London; marriage settlements dated 30 March 1706; executrix to her husband 17 June 1727; bur. at Bromsgrove. Will dated 9 September 1762 and 10 June 1764, proved 10 December 1764 (P.C.C. 473 *Simpson*).

D

Mary Lowe, of the Precinct, Worcester; bapt. at Bromsgrove 3 May 1708; mentioned in her grandfather's will 2 February $173\frac{5}{8}$; executrix to her mother 10 December 1764; died, aged 82, 10 January 1791; bur. at Bromsgrove. M.I. in church. Will dated 2 June 1789 and 17 April 1790, proved 29 January 1791 (P.C.C. 29 *Bevor*).

117

The Public Register of All Arms (Scottish)

When arms are granted in Scotland, they are recorded in the Public Register and the armiger receives essentially the same information on Letters patent (for new arms) or an Extract of Matriculation (for re-registration of arms of an ancestor, such as when a child inherits the arms

From *The Public Register of All Arms and Bearings in Scotland*, Vol. 3, p. 10 (1824). *With the kind permission of Lyon Clerk*

from his or her parent. An example from the Public Register is shown opposite. Arms granted up to 1908 can be searched for free and the actual page images can be downloaded at a cost of £10 from www.scotlandspeople.gov.uk (click on 'Coats of Arms').

The example is the record of arms granted to James Tytler of Woodhouselee, a lawyer and Lyon Depute. Notice that it recites his genealogy, gives details of land holdings and how these were acquired and lists his professional accomplishments. See also p. 116 for related armorial carvings.

Scottish heraldry, unlike in England, is part of the general law, and justiciable in the ordinary courts. Strictly speaking, owners of heritage in Scotland are required by law to have armorial bearings. For the record, the relevant statutes are:

– The Officers of Arms Act 1587 cap. 46
– The Lyon King of Arms Act 1592 Jac. VI cap. 125; fol. edit cap. 29
– The Lyon King of Arms Act 1662 Car. II cap. 53
– The Lyon King of Arms Act 1663 Car. II cap. 15
– The Lyon King of Arms Act 1672 Car. II cap. 21; fol. edit., cap. 47
– The Lord Lyon Act 1867 30 & 31 Vict. Cap. 17

These laws can be read at: www.heraldica.org/topics/britain/lyondocs.htm. See Chapter 3 for the dating of laws by regnal years.

Letters patent (English)

The illustration on p. 115 shows the letters patent of Jane Nickels. Her husband, John Tunesi of Liongam, has a separate grant of arms in Scotland.

Ordinary of arms (Scottish)

To find out what arms are borne by whom, or just to identify a coat of arms, the publications to consult are *An Ordinary of Arms* by Sir James Balfour Paul, which lists all Scottish arms in the Public Register up to the 1890s (first edition) or 1901 (second edition), and a successor volume that brings it more up to date (see 'Further Reading'). This is organised by charge (the main element on the shield) but also indexed by name. For example, Tytler of Woodhouselee appears on a number of pages because of the complicated arms.

An appropriate place to start looking up English and Welsh arms is Fox-Davies (see 'Further Reading').

Az. a bend engrailed between three cinquefoils arg. (1st and 4th quarters of 3rd grand quarter), all within a bordure erm. TYTLER OF WOODHOUSELEE (1824).

Gu. three antique crowns or (2nd and 3rd quarters of 3rd grand quarter), all within a bordure erm. TYTLER OF WOODEHOUSELEE (2nd matric. 1824).

Erminois, on a fess parted per fess embattled gu. and az. three crescents arg. (2nd quarter for *Craig of Dalnair*), all within a bordure erm. TYTLER OF WOODEHOUSELEE (2nd matric. 1824).

Gu. a lion's head erased arg. between three crescents or, within a bordure of the last. TYTLER OF WOODHOUSELEE (1st matric. 1768).

Gu. a lion's head erased arg. between three crescents or within a bordure of the last (1st and 4th quarters), all within a bordure erm. TYTLER OF WOODHOUSELEE (2nd matric. 1824).

Quarterly: 1st and 4th, Gules, a lion's head erased Argent between three crescents Or within a bordure of the last [the last colour mentioned = Or]; 2nd, Erminois on a fess parted per fess embattled Gules and Azure three crescents Argent (for Craig of Dalmuir); 3rd (1st and 4th quarters of 3rd grand quarter) Azure a bend engrailed between three cinquefoils Argent, (2nd and 3rd quarter of 3rd grand quarter) Gules, three antique crowns Or, all within a bordure ermine.

Armorials

These are collections of arms brought together for private collections. In the *Armorial de Gelré*, a fourteenth-century Flemish armorial there are three folios of Scottish knights and nobles. The names are given in mediaeval Flemish, e.g. 'gr[a]f de Karric' (Earl of Carrick); 'gr[a]f a straderen' (Earl of Strathearn).

Armorial seals, castings and bookplates

Seals often have details of the bearer's position and status. For example, the seal of George Durie, last Abbot of Dunfermline, has his coat of arms at the foot, below figures of St Andrew (dexter), Mary and Jesus (centre) and St Margaret (sinister) and the legend 'S GEORGII ABBATIS DE DUMFERLING ARCH S ANDR' (Seal of George Abbot of Dunfermline Archdeacon of St Andrews). The date is *c.* 1550.

The next two illustrations are English armorial bookplates: the first, from a knight of the garter and the next from a book owned by the 2nd Earl Spencer. The final illustration is taken from a menu of Viceregal Lodge, dated 1873, and this plus the garter collar, the demi-wyvern crest and the badge of St Patrick (replacing the knight-on-horseback garter badge) identify it as referring to John, 5th Earl Spencer KG, PC (1835–1910), great-great-grandfather of Diana, Princess of Wales, twice Lord Lieutenant of Ireland (1868–74 and again in 1882–85).

Armorial carvings

This illustration shows the arms of Tytler carved at the parish church and parochine of Glencorse, now called Woodhouselee, over which Tytler had the rights of patronage.

The one on p. 107 refers to Joshua Durie, minister at Inverkeilor parish. What's special about it is:

1. the arms are wrong (three crescents but no chevron);
2. the inscription displays more puns than you might think the average Presbyterian minister was capable of. It says:

MEMENTO MORI / 3 SEPT 1631 / MID [Master Joshua Durie]
QVOD DVRVM EST / FRACTVM NEC PLVS DVRARE VIDETUR / DVREVS AT DVRAT CLARAQVE FAMA VIGET
That which is durable is broken, nor appears any longer to endure;
but Durie still endures, and flourishes with bright renown.

Further Reading

Online

College of Arms (England): http://college-of-arms.gov.uk
The Lyon Court (Scotland): www.lyon-court.com
Heraldry Society of Scotland: www.heraldry-scotland.co.uk
Heraldry Online: www.heraldry-online.org.uk
Heraldica: www.heraldica.org
For a list of heraldic authorities worldwide, see: http://en.wikipedia.org/wiki/Heraldic_authority

Books

Siddons, M.P., *Visitations by the Heralds in Wales* (London: The Harleian Society, 1996)
Crisp, F.A. and Howard, J.J. (eds), *Visitation of England and Wales*. Multiple volumes available at www.archive.org
Dennis, M., *Scottish Heraldry* (Edinburgh, 1999). Available from the Heraldry Society of Scotland (see below)
Durie, B. (ed.), *Heraldry in Scotland*, by J.H. Stevenson (new edition, 2012, www.brucedurie.co.uk/books)
Fox-Davies, A., *Armorial Families* (various editions up to 1929)
Balfour P.J., *An Ordinary of Arms* (1893 and 1903, available at www.archive.org and from the Genealogical Publishing Co., Baltimore)
Reid, D. and Wilson, V., *An Ordinary of Arms Volume II (1902–1973)*, (Lyon Office, 1977)

The matriculation of arms of Lord MacDonald of MacDonald in 1947. The peerage barony is in the Peerage of Ireland, but he also had a Scottish feudal barony, and bears a chiefly coronet. Notice the inheritance of the titles from his grandfather, as his uncle died unmarried and *sine prole* (without issue). *From The Public Register of All Arms and Bearings in Scotland, used here with the kind permission of Lyon Clerk*

7

Gaelic Words in Scots and English

Present-day inhabitants of Scotland are (linguistically, at least) an admixture of *Scotii* who arrived from Ireland to mingle with Picto-Celts living around present-day Fife and the north-east and British Celts (speaking a language like Welsh, sometimes called 'Cambric') in Strathclyde and the area around Edinburgh, jumbled up with the Danes who arrived from Northumbria, Scandinavian Vikings in the north and west, and later the Anglo-Normans, who came to live mainly in the Lowlands. The Highlanders' language evolved into Gaelic, but lowlanders have long spoken Scots, the distinctive Germanic language that developed alongside English. However, there are many Gaelic words and names in Scottish history and geography and it helps to know them. Also, there are many Gaelic inclusions in present-day language – some quite surprising.

English, like Scots, is a late Germanic language and has borrowed heavily from older languages. It therefore has more Celtic words than is commonly realised, including those that came indirectly by way of Gaulish into French and then English. Many of those Gaulish words are close to the older Goidelic (Gaelic) Celtic language spoken in Ireland in pre-Christian times. There are also Brythonic (British or Welsh) sources as well as continental Celtic and Indo-European roots.

Scots contains a great many Gaelic words unfamiliar outside Scotland, for example dule or dool, meaning grief or distress, comes from the Gaelic *doilgheas* (sorrow, affliction) and *duilich* (difficult, sorry, grievous). The Latin-derived words dolour, doleful and dolorous have the same meanings. But many are universally recognisable by English speakers everywhere: keelie (a self-assured young man) and gillie (an attendant on a Highland estate) both derive from *gille* (a young man or servant).

A number of widely known words may come from either Scots or Irish Gaelic (whisky or whiskey would be a good example) and it will surprise many Americans to realise that cowboy, cracker and redneck are actually Scottish words in origin. Some words (ceilidh, grotty) entered directly into English, without necessarily first becoming widely used in Lowland Scotland, and although some are old – pet or caddie for instance – many of these are twentieth-century borrowings. Examples would be 'smashing' (Gaelic *'s math sin*) meaning 'excellent' and *sporran*.

Then there are the many cognate words, sufficiently similar, that exist because they either entered Gaelic from English or have the same influences (Latin, French, Indo-European roots etc.). They look like straight imports from one language to another but are actually parallel developments from common origins: Gaelic *baist* (baptise) and English baste (moisten) are examples.

Scots/English	Irish	Scots	Meaning
airt	*aird*	*aird*	point of the compass
bannock	*bonnach*	*bonnach*	bread cake
banshee	*bean-sidhe*	*bean-sidhe*	wailing spirit, woman of the *sidhe* (pronounced 'shee') meaning 'fairyland'
bard	*bàrd*	*bàrd*	poet, singer
Beltane	*Bealltainn*	*Bealltainn*	spring festival
blather	*bladar*	*bladar*	nonsense or gossip
bog	*bogach*	*bogach*	soft ground, bog
bog	*bog*	*bog*	soft
bonnyclabber	*bainne-clàbar*	*bainne-clàbar*	curdled milk
booley	*buaile*	*buaile*	fold or pen for livestock
bothy	*bothan*	*bothan*	small hut
brae	*bràighe*	*bràighe*	hill
brat	*brat*	*brat*	unruly boy
braw	*brèagha*	*brèagha*	nice, fine, beautiful
breeks	*briogais*	*briogais*	trousers, pants
brisk	*brisg/briosc*	*brisg/briosc*	fast, bracing
brogue	*bròg*	*bròg*	shoe
brogue	*bròg*	*bròg*	accent (especially Irish)
brogue	*bróg*	*bròg*	shoe, boot
bun	*bun*	*bun*	base, bottom, posterior
burn	*bùrn*	*bùrn*	small river
caber	*cabar*	*cabar*	as in 'tossing the caber'
caber	*cabar*	*cabar*	pole, rafter
caddie	*cadaidh*	*cadaidh*	porter, golfclub carrier
cairn	*carn*	*càrn*	heap, pile
carrageen	*cairgein*	*cairgein*	moss
carrageenan	*carraigín*	*carraigean*	Irish moss seaweed
cateran	*ceatharn*	*ceathairne, ceatharn*	peasantry, freebooter
ceilidh	*céilidh*	*céilidh*	dance, party
clan	*clann*	*clann*	family
clarsach	*clàrsach*	*clàrsach*	a musical instrument
cleave	*claidheamh*	*claidheamh*	sword
claymore	*claíomh mór*	*claidheamh mór*	great sword
coleen	*cailín*	*caileag*	girl
cowboy	*cowhuby*		cattle drover
curragh	*currach*	*currach*	coracle
corrie	*coire*	*coire*	rocky valley
crag, craig	*creig*	*creag*	rocky outcrop

Scots/English	Irish	Scots	Meaning
crannog	*crannag*	*crannag*	fortified lake-dwelling
creel	*criol*	*criol*	lobster trap
cross	*cros*	*cros*	cross
dig, twig	*tuig*	*tuig*	understand
dochandoris	*deoch-an-dorus*	*deoch-an-dorus*	a little drink
dour	*dùr*	*dùr*	gloomy
down	*dún*	*dún*	dune, hill
dulse	*duileasc*	*duileasg*	edible seaweed
dun	*dun*	*dun*	brown-coloured
gab	*gobgab*	*gobgab*	talk, jabber
Gael	*Gaedheal*	*Gàidheal*	a Gaelic speaker
Gaeltacht	*Gaidhealtachd*	*Gaidhealtachd*	the community of Gaelic speakers
galore	*go leor*	*gu leòr*	plenty, enough
gillie	*giolla*	*gille*	lad, servant
glen	*gleann*	*gleann*	valley
gloamin	*glòmainn*	*glòmainn*	dusk, twilight
glom	*glám*	*glam*	grab, clutch
grotty	*grod*	*grod*	dirty
hooligan	*uilligán*	*uilligán*	rowdy person
ingle	*aingeal*	*aingeal*	fireplace
inch (island)	*innis*	*innis*	island
island	*innis*	*innis*	island
gob	*gob*	*gob*	mouth
jabber	*gobgab*	*gobgab*	talk
kail	*càl*	*càl*	cabbage-like vegetable
keech	*cac*	*cac*	ordure, dung
keen	*caoin*	*caoin*	weep, lament
kibosh	*caidhp báis*		cap of death
knock	*cnoc*	*cnoc*	knock
kyles	*caolas*	*caolas*	headland
leprechaun	*leipreachán*	*leipreachán*	Irish imp
linn	*linn*	*linn*	pool
loch	*loch*	*lough*	lake
machar	*machair*	*machair*	poet (literally 'maker')
oxter	*achlais*	*achlais*	armpit
pet	*peata*	*peata*	favourite
philabeg	*feileadh-beag*	*feileadh-beag*	short kilt
phony	*fáinne*	*fàinne*	ring (from a gilt brass ring)
pibroch	*piobaireachd*	*piobaireachd*	style of pipe music

Scots/English	Irish	Scots	Meaning
pillion	*pillín*	*pillean*	small pad, cushion
plaid	*pluid*	*plaide*	blanket
pony	*pónai*	*pónai*	pony
poteen	*poitín*	*poitín*	distilled spirit
puss	*pus*	*pus*	face
reel	*righil*	*righil*	dance
ross	*ros*	*ros*	promontary
Sassenach		*Sasunnach*	English person (possibly from 'Saxon')
shabeen, shebeen	*síbín*	*siopín*	illicit drinking den
shamrock	*seamróg*	*seamrag*	shamrock
shanty	*seantigh*	*seann taigh*	old house
shennachie	*seanachaidh*	*seanachaidh*	bard and genealogist to a chief
shillelagh	*sail éille*		cudgel (also a village in Co. Wicklow)
shoo	*siuthad*	*siuthad*	chase away
skean	*sgian*	*sgian*	dagger
skiff	*sgiobhag*	*sgiobhag*	snow
slew	*slua*	*sluagh*	host, multitude
slob	*slaba*		mud, slovenly person
slogan	*sluagh ghairm*	*sluggh-ghairm*	call to the multitude
slug	*sluig*	*sluig*	swig
smashing	*is math sin*	*'s-math-sin*	literally 'it is great'
smidgen	*smidin*	*smidin*	small piece
smithereens	*smidiríní*	*smidiríní*	small pieces
sneck	*sneag*	*sneag*	latch
soutar	*sutair*	*sutair*	travelling tinker
sporran	*sparán*	*sporan*	purse
spunk	*spong*	*spong*	courage
strath	*srath*	*srath*	land around a river
strontium		*Strontian*	from Strontian, a village in Argyllshire
swap	*suaip*	*suaip*	exchange
tack	*tac*	*tac*	leased farm
Tory	*tórai*	*tòraiche*	pursuer; robber; bandit
trouser	*triús*	*triubhas*	trews; pants
twig	*tuig*	*tuig*	understand
weem	*uamh*	*uamh*	cave (as in Wemyss, Pittenweem)
whisky	*uisge beatha*	*uisge beatha*	water of life
winnock	*uinneag*	*uinneag*	window

GAELIC PRONUNCIATION

There are eighteen letters in the Gaelic alphabet:

 – Thirteen consonants: b, p, f, m, c, g, l, n, r, t, d, s, h.
 – Five vowels. Broad vowels: a, o, u. Slender vowels: e, i.
 – H is aspirate. After the consonants b, p, f, m, c, g, d, t, s, it forms the aspirates, bh, ph, fh, mh, ch, gh, dh, th, sh. At the beginning of a word it is written h-; as na h-uain; and has a strong aspiration (breathy sound, properly called 'lenition').
 – The letters sg, sm, sp and st have no aspirated form.

Consonant sounds

Consonants fall into two categories: broad and slender.

 – Broad consonants are surrounded by a, o, u.
 – Slender consonants are surrounded by i, e.
 – The consonants p, t and k are preaspirated – preceded by a voiceless h – in the middle and ends of words.
 – There are three different kinds each of l, n and r that are almost impossible to understand. You have to be there.
 – Almost every consonant is different depending on whether it comes at the beginning, middle or end of a word. But not always. Not only that, but many are silent, sometimes. For instance, the Gaelic for 'Gaelic' is Ghàidhlig, pronounced 'gay-lik'.

Confused? You will be.

		Example 'Translation' Pronounced
B	like the English b in 'bag' at the beginning of words, elsewhere sounds like the p in 'hop'.	
Bh	mostly, this is pronounced v; sometimes in the middle and at the end of certain words it is like u, and sometimes it is silent.	Tahpuh leeve
F	like f in English.	
Fh	silent, except in the three words fhéin, fhuair, fhathast, when it has the sound of h.	
M	like m in English.	Tha gu math 'I'm fine' Ha goo mah
Mh	like v, and more nasal than bh; silent in the middle and end of some words, and gives a nasal sound to the vowel; in some areas it has the sound of u; as, samhradh, pronounced 'sow-rah', 'sow' as in 'how'.	Glè mhath 'Very well' glay vah
P	like p in English 'pin'.	Tapadh leibh 'Thank you' Tahpuh leeve
Ph	like f in English 'prophet'.	

C	always hard, like 'cat'; before *a, o, u*, it has the sound of *c* in 'can'; after *a, o, u*, it has the same sound in some districts. As *cnoc*, like *ck* in 'lock'; but more often like '*chk*'. Before *e, i* and after *i*, like *c* in 'cane'.	ciamar a tha thu? 'How are you?' *kemuhr a ha oo*
Ch	before or after *a, o, u*, it is a gutteral sound as in 'loch'; in contact with *e* or *i*, it has a more slender sound.	
Chd	has the sound of '*chk*'; as *luchd*, pronounced '*luchk*'.	
G	more or less like English; before and after *a, o, u*, it is like *g* in 'got'; in contact with *e, i*, it sounds like *g* in 'get'.	
Gh	before and after *e, i*, it has the sound of *y* in English 'yet'; in contact with *a, o, u*, it has a broader sound like *g* in 'get'. In the middle and end of certain words it is silent.	
T	before or after *a, o, u*, the sound is like '*th*' in 'than'; in contact with *e, i*, it has the sound of '*ch*' in 'chin'.	Tapadh leibh 'Thank you' *Tahpuh leeve*
Th	beginning a word has the sound of '*h*'; silent in the pronoun '*thu*' (pronounced '*oo*') and in certain tenses of irregular verbs when preceded by *d*; in the middle of some words it has a slight aspiration, in others it is silent.	Glè mhath 'Very well' *glay vah*
D	initially, like English *d*, elsewhere like English *t*, but at the end, it can be like *ch* or *j*.	
Dh	same as 'Gh'.	
S	in contact with *a, o, u*, is like *s* in English; before or after *e, i*, like '*sh*'; after *t-* (with hyphen) it is silent.	Sidhe 'fairy land' *shee*
Sh	has the sound of '*h*'.	
L	before or after *a, o, u*, and *ll* after *a, o, u*, have a flatter sound than *l* in English, with the point of the tongue against the teeth; in contact with *e, i*, the sound is like *ll* in 'million'. It has a simple sound after *i*, and when aspirated it is like *l* in English 'hill'.	
N	in conjunction with *a, o, u*, is like *n* in English 'new'; with *e, i*, it has a slender sound like '*n*' in *pinion*; '*n*' aspirated has the sound of '*n*' in English 'pin'; after *c, g, m, t*, it resembles the sound of '*r*'.	
R	rolled, like *r* in English 'burrow'.	
	Monosyllables ending in -*lb*, -*lbh*, -*lg*, -*lm*, -*nm*, -*rg*, -*rb*, -*rbh*, -*rm*, are sounded as two syllables; thus, *fearg* ('*fearug*'), *dealbh* ('*dealuv*'), *marbh* ('*maruv*').	
	The letters *l, n*, have an aspirated sound, though the aspirate letter is not used. So also has *r*, though much slighter.	

Vowel sounds

Vowels may have a duration accent mark over them:

– Short-sound vowels *a, o, u, e, i* – no accent.
– Long-sound vowels *à, ò, ù, è, ì* (Gaelic vowels have a grave accent – *à* – but traditional texts may use the acute accent on *á, é* and *ó*).
– Two and three vowels coming together, with the sound of the one passing into the other, are called diphthongs and triphthongs:

uan;
uaigh.

– *ao* is pronounced like the beginning of the French *oeuvre*.
– Some have one simple sound, e.g. gaol ('*gal*'), *ceum* ('*kem*').

Short sounds	Gaelic example	English equivalent	Long sounds	Gaelic example	English equivalent
a	bas	cat	à	bàs	far
a	bata	sofa	à	làdhran	far
o	mol	hot	ò	òl	lord
o	bog	smoke	ó	mór	more
u	cur	put	ù	cù	moor
u	solus	but			
e	fear	net	è	nèamh	where
e	fead	rate	é	fhéin	fain
e	gile	whet			
i	mil	milk	ì	trì	tree

Further Reading

Online

MacBain, A., *An Etymological Dictionary of the Gaelic Language*. Available online, along with other resources, at www.ceantar.org/Dicts
For pronunciations, listen to examples here from the BBC: www.bbc.co.uk/alba/foghlam/beag_air_bheag/sounds/page2/index.shtml

8

Scotland, England and Wales: Old Parish Registers

In England and Wales, statutory (civil registration) started in 1837; in Scotland it started in 1855. The earliest UK-wide census with genealogically useful information was that of 1841. Therefore, to get back before the start of Queen Victoria's reign, the obvious source is the documents variously called Old Parish Registers or Old Parish Records (OPRs) or sometimes known as the Parish Chest. These are often referred to as BMD (Birth, Marriage, Death) records, but in the main they record baptisms, proclamations ('banns') of marriage and burials, although on occasion the actual date of birth, marriage and death may also be given.

ENGLAND AND WALES

In 1538, following Henry VIII's split with Rome, his vicar general, Thomas Cromwell, decreed that clergy in England and Wales should be instructed to keep weekly records of baptisms, marriages and burials, kept in a 'sure coffer' with two locks (one for the vicar, one for the churchwardens). It was not a great success, for a number of reasons. First, where records were kept at all, they were usually on paper, and were sometimes loose sheets, so were prone to deterioration and loss. Second, there was a fine of 3s 4d for failure to comply, which many parishes considered to be the thin end of a taxation wedge, so they just ignored it. To allay their fears on this score, the order was issued again in 1547 making it clear that the fine, if any, should to go to the poor relief fund.

The Roman Catholic Church finally got round to issuing a general order to keep baptismal and marriage records in 1563.

Back in the Church of England, Henry's daughter Elizabeth I had another try at getting parish registers to be kept in 1598. Clergy were instructed to use parchment registers (more likely to last than paper) into which they were to copy the old records, although many were unreadable even by that time. A reasonable number of the new parchment registers contained records from 1538, but many more began in 1558, which was the first year of Elizabeth's reign. The 1598 order also required that transcripts of the registers should be sent to the diocesan registry annually: these are known as 'bishop's transcripts'. Furthermore, the books were to be kept in a chest this time with three locks, and the entries for the week were to be read out after each Sunday evening service. And how to pay for this? The dreaded tax finally arrived. The cost of what were called 'great decent books of parchment' would be met by the parish by charging a fee per entry. Again, this met opposition and was not really enforced until five years later in 1603 when James VI of Scotland also became James I of England and Wales.

For the brief but turbulent duration of the Commonwealth or Cromwellian period, after Charles I was deposed and beheaded, registration became a matter for the State rather than the Church, and from 1653 a new post of parish register (rather than 'registrar') was created. Elected by the ratepayers in the parish, the parish register's job was to keep the registers of births, baptisms, deaths and burials. In addition, in 1654, civil marriage was introduced, solemnised by a justice of the peace. For records kept during this period, the date of birth as well as baptism is usually recorded. This system only lasted for a short period, until the Restoration of King Charles II in 1660, at which point the registers were handed back to the parishes.

In 1678, Charles II came up with a great wheeze to cheer up the wool trade, and made it compulsory for all burials to be in a woollen shroud, with an affidavit made to that effect and recorded as such in the parish register. (Coffins were only for the rich, although the corpse was usually taken to the graveside in a rented parish coffin, then removed for burial in the shroud alone.)

In 1694 the cost of registration was increased dramatically: from 4d to 2s for a baptism entry, 1s to 2s 6d for a marriage and 4d to 4s for a burial, plus (in 1696) a tax of 6d for any birth not reported within five days, and a fine imposed on the vicar of £2 for failing to record it. Given that a vicar might be living on £30–£100 per annum, that was at least a week's earnings. It would be nice to think that this was occasioned by a desire to sort out a decent registration system, but the motivation was actually so that James VII & II could raise cash for the ruinously expensive war against France. The whole idea was abandoned in 1706, amid genuine fears that it would drive many clergymen to financial ruin.

However, there was an attempt to regulate the state of affairs in the keeping of registers in 1711, during the last days of Anne (d. 1714) and with a new Tory-dominated Parliament under Robert Harley, 1st Earl of Oxford, which indulged the queen's patronage of the Church.

There was an order that the registers pages should be ruled and numbered, although few were, in fact. In 1733, the government of George II declared that all entries should be in English rather than Latin.

Hardwicke's Marriage Act of 1753 made it compulsory for all marriages, except Jewish and Quaker, to be registered in the Church of England. There was a stamp duty of 3d on entries from 1783 to 1794 with an exemption for the poor. The Act also required marriage registers to be kept in a standard format and volumes containing printed forms were at last produced for the purpose. Up to that point, the information recorded is usually fairly basic: baptisms give the name of the child, the date of baptism, the name of the father and sometimes, but not always, the name of the mother; the mother's maiden name is hardly ever stated.

Dade and Barrington registers

At this point, two well-meaning men of the cloth decided to enter the fray and sort things out.

The Revd William Dade was a Yorkshire clergyman who might have been invented to cheer up future genealogists. He even referred to 'the researches of posterity'. Dade saw the value of recording as much information as possible in parish register entries and in 1777 persuaded Archbishop William Markham to introduce his format in his archdiocese of York. Known as Dade Registers, the baptism entries include the child's name, date of birth and baptism, position in the family (e.g. first daughter, third son), the father's name and profession, place of residence and – glory be! – genealogical details (names, occupation and residences of the father's and mother's parents). Burial records may have the age of the deceased, occupation, cause of death, names of parents and the name of a married woman's husband. Anyone who finds a Dade Register will wonder why they aren't all like that.

Take care though: the term Dade Register has come to be used for any record that has more detail than might be expected, and, to be frank, the Dade system was not uniformly applied even in the York archdiocese. In addition to that, a number of vicars, especially in larger towns, found it all too much like hard work, so it didn't last long. They may have had a point, as they still also had to produce the bishops' transcripts, which was regarded by many as a duplication of effort. The newspapers in Yorkshire at the time have many letters for the equivalent of 'Disgusted of Murgatroyd' complaining about this, and when the archbishop caved in to the extent of failing to impose any penalty on clergy who wouldn't comply, the death knell for Dade's scheme was sounded.

Example of the information in a Dade Register for baptism in the parish of Thorganby, Yorkshire:

Name:	Joseph Allison
Gender:	Male
Birth Date:	29 May 1796
Christening Date:	12 Jun 1796
Christening Place:	Thorganby, Yorkshire, England
Age at Christening:	0
Father's Name:	William Allison
Mother's Name:	Mary
Paternal Grandfather's Name:	John Allison
Paternal Grandmother's Name:	Mary
Maternal Grandfather's Name:	Robert Johnson
Maternal Grandmother's Name:	Frances

However, around the same time (actually, from 1783 or so) the Revd Shute Barrington, then Bishop of Salisbury, put in place a similar, if less unwieldy, system than Dade's, and imposed it on Northumberland and Durham when he became Bishop of Durham in 1797–98. Shute was a keen amateur genealogist, and it shows in the detail of the registers he inspired.

The 1812 Rose Act

But it was, ultimately, all for naught. In 1812, an Act proposed by George Rose, a Scot by birth but member of parliament for Christchurch, and Richard Brinsley Sheridan's successor as treasurer of the navy, resulted in registers with printed forms and stipulated entry fields for baptisms, burials and marriages. (An Act for the better regulating and preserving Parish and other Registers of Births, Baptisms, Marriages, and Burials, in England, Cap.146, 28 July 1812.) A handful of parishes continued to keep registers in the Dade or Barrington format after this date, and some kept both, for example the parish of Whickham in Co. Durham from 1813–19, after which only the Barrington format was adhered to.

Rose's Act meant that from 1813 there were pre-printed forms for:

− Baptisms: mother's name, father's occupation and place of abode.
− Marriages: names of the couple and date (from 1754) printed forms; condition (bachelor, spinster, widow or widower), parish of residence, occupation, whether the marriage was by banns or licence, names of witnesses (which often included relatives).
− Burials: name of the deceased, date of burial, sometimes age (more likely if a young child, and then often with the name of the father), age and abode.

The marriages are the most complete records, followed by burials and then baptisms.

Finding and using parish registers

Unlike the situation in Scotland (see below), parish registers for England and Wales are mainly held in the county record offices or archives (which have generally subsumed the old diocesan archives). Actual images of register pages are otherwise hard to come by, although they may be available alongside the widely available transcripts and indexes. Many are published by Phillimore and by local family history societies, and large libraries as well as the Society of Genealogists in London will have collections.

Apart from that, check:

FreeReg (www.freereg.org.uk).

Ancestry (www.ancestry.co.uk).

The Borthwick Institute for Archives, previously the Borthwick Institute for Historical Research in York (www.york.ac.uk/library/borthwick/).

The International Genealogical Index or IGI: not comprehensive, generally does not include burials and in many cases has entries submitted by members of the LDS Church, which may or may not be accurate and are uncheckable because there is no source information (www.familysearch.org).

The National burial index for England and Wales, now searchable by county on the Family History Online Web of the Federation of Family History Societies (www.ffhs.org.uk), which has now joined up with FindMyPast (www.findmypast.com).

Bishops' Transcripts for Northumberland and Durham are held at the University of Durham (www.dur.ac.uk/library/asc/).

Other indexes

These include:

'Boyd's Marriage Index', covering English parishes from 1538 to 1840, compiled originally from parish registers, bishops' transcripts and marriage licences and covering perhaps 12–15 per cent of the marriages in England but 95 per cent of parishes in East Anglia (see next entry).

'Boyd's London Burials Index 1538–1872', which, with 243,000 records, indexes a few of the London burials (see next entry); City of London Burials 1742–1904 but mostly 1788–1855 (www.findmypast.co.uk/content/sog/misc-series.html).

'Pallot's Marriage Index': over 1.5 million entries from 1780–1837, and although smaller than 'Boyd's Index', good for London and the Home Counties, as it covers all but two of the 103 parishes in the City of London and has some information from other counties (www.ancestry.co.uk).

In all of these, the information is sparse, as the examples on p. 131 show.

Marriage banns, allegations, licences and bonds

The two main methods by which a couple could marry were through publication of banns, and by licence, both of which are merely documentary proof that a wedding was intended, not that it actually took place.

Banns of marriage: Scotland, England and Wales

Banns are a declaration of intended marriage read in the relevant parish church or churches of the bride and groom on the three successive Sundays. By their very nature, banns are public but were not always written down until the Hardwicke Marriage Act (see p. 136) made this compulsory in

England, except for Quakers and Jews, from 1754 to 1812. Banns dating from before and after this are often found in parish registers, as in the examples on the pages following.

Marriage licences

Anyone wishing to avoid the reading of banns for whatever reason (privacy, keeping it quiet from the families, one or both of the couple away from his or her own parish, or just not prepared to wait three weeks) could apply for a licence to marry. Licences were the preferred route of the gentry and nobility who felt the whole public banns exercise a touch too 'common'. It also cost money. Few of these documents have survived as they outlived their usefulness once they were presented to the conducting vicar, but the best place to look for them is in the records of the issuing body, usually the diocese in which the groom, bride or both lived. In addition, a marriage licence was dependent on two other documents that were usually retained for record – bonds and allegations – which are more likely to have survived.

Marriage allegations

This worked as follows: the groom (usually) visited the diocesan registry (in England) or some other approved issuing body (such as a Sheriff Court in Scotland) and made an 'allegation' (a sworn statement) that Church law had been complied with, that there was no known impediment to the marriage taking place and so on. If one of the parties was not 'of full age' (21 or over), written consent of parents or legal guardians was required. Allegations usually give the names, ages and home parishes of the intended couple and the church where the wedding was licensed to be solemnised.

Bonds ('cautions' in Scotland, pronounced 'kay-shun')

A marriage bond was a contract by the groom or someone acting on his behalf (called a 'cautioner' in Scotland, see p. 130), with payment of the surety. Then, if any statement sworn in the marriage allegation proved to be untrue and/or there was some impediment to the marriage, the bonded party would forfeit the sum stipulated. These were not required in England after 1823.

The bond documents themselves are interesting. They were in two parts: an obligation (written in Latin until 1733 in England) giving the names and parishes of those bound (which may or may not have included the groom) and the bond or penalty; and a second part, always in English, laying out the terms under which the penalty would have to be paid, and naming the bride-to-be.

Occasionally such documents still turn up: the Surrey Commissary Court Licences were discovered archived with wills in about 1900. Printed examples of the form and bond used in Surrey in the 1700s are on p. 134.

Post-1837

Statutory registration in England and Wales in 1837 and in Scotland in 1855 swept away such records, although churches did not stop keeping them. These civil registrations are not dealt with in this book, and in any case they can only really be accessed in England and Wales by paying for a copy extract of an actual individual certificate, although the register page images are available in Scotland.

SCOTLAND

The situation for pre-1855 church registers north of the border is much more straightforward, as all pre-1855 OPRs (Old Parish Registers) are kept in one place, and are available online (www.scotlandspeople.gov.uk) although indexes and transcripts are available at Ancestry, FamilySearch and elsewhere (see 'Finding and using parish registers' on p. 128).

All 900 or so Church of Scotland parishes kept registers of baptisms and/or births; banns/proclamations of marriages and/or the marriage date; burials and mortcloth rentals and sometimes deaths. However, there are caveats (see below):

1. We only have the records of the Church of Scotland – after 1560 or so, Presbyterianism was the predominant denomination of the population, but there were still Catholics, Episcopalians and those of other minority faiths such as Judaism.
2. There is no absolute starting date for these records: the earliest is from 1553, which predates the Reformation, but not many date so far back and the majority started in the seventeenth or even the eighteenth centuries. Some are even later and some parishes have no records at all.
3. There was no standard format, so individual ministers or session clerks decided how to keep them and many have no death or burial registers.
4. Not everyone chose to register a birth, marriage or death, as it generally cost money, especially during the imposition from 1783 to 1794 of a 3d stamp duty on each registration.
5. Some registers have just become lost or damaged beyond recovery.
6. There were considerable splinterings of the Established Church, not least the two major secessions in the 1700s and the great Disruption of 1843, and unless these churches came back into the Church of Scotland – which many did, especially in 1929, but not all – their records may simply not be readily available.

If this sounds a rather haphazard system, it was. However, it is always worth inspecting the OPRs, not least because they are very accessible and searchable online at www.scotlandspeople.gov.uk, or on microfilm at many libraries and LDS Family History centres; they are also indexed or transcribed at www.familysearch.org, www.ancestry.co.uk and elsewhere.

The caveats are:

1. The amount of information in OPRs is often restricted to: (in the case of baptisms) the name of the child, date, parish and father's name, but the mother's names, the place of residence and father's occupation, and even the baptised child's sex, may not be given (usually indexed as U for 'unknown' in the index).
2. A baptism record may or may not give a date of birth.
3. What appear to be double entries may be due to the proud parents being from different parishes and wishing to have the baby registered at both.
4. Records of the proclamation of banns might be made in two parishes (that of the bride and that of the groom), and one may give more details than the other, but typically you will find the names of the parties to be wed, their places (or often just parishes) of residence and the date of the proclamation, sometimes with a statement that the marriage took place (which it may not have) and there may be names of witnesses but not necessarily the names of the couple's parents.
5. Burial records often have no more detail than the name of the deceased and the date of interment, but often a child's age is given, along with 'lair' information (exactly where the grave was) plus mortcloth rental costs.
6. Some parishes chose to record other information such as the mother's maiden name in a baptismal entry, a cause of death or a fee paid in caution (pronounced 'kay-shun', essentially a bond or surety), whether a child was legitimate or not and the relationships of witnesses or godparents to the married couple or child. Ages are rarely recorded, except in the case of child burials, but a surviving spouse might be mentioned.

All of this makes the OPRs ripe for overenthusiastic identification, especially in parishes where there are a number of individuals with the same name and of a similar age – cousins, for instance, all christened with the grandfather's first name – who married others with common or locally predominant names.

It is also possible to assume that the same person is two or more different individuals, if the occupation is listed differently in the births of his children, or if his wife's name is subject to variants, as with Margaret, Meg, Peggy or Isabel, Isabella, Isa, Bel and so on.

Examples of OPRs and other registers

Because these are so inconsistent, it is impossible to give illustrations of all variants. However, the main challenge in reading them is palaeographic, and in understanding abbreviations and conventions. Therefore, a number of exemplars are given in the following pages, from the 1500s to the early 1800s.

Bishops' transcripts, Kent, 1672/73 OS

The New Year started on 25 March (see Chapter 3) so today we would consider these entries to be in January, February and March 1673.

Baptized 1672
December the 12th – William Burton the sonne of John Burton and Anne his wife
January the 16th – Elizabeth Grey the daughter of William Gray and Margaret his wife

Buried 1672
December the 12th – Ann Westbeech the wife of John Westbeech
June the 16th – Bennett Weeks the daughter of James Weekes

Married 1672
June the 24 – Jacob Walrane and Mary Hill
December the 29 – Abraham Estes and Ann Burton Widdow

Baptismal register, Kippax St Mary, West Yorkshire, 1672

The third entry says:

Sep 8th William [notice the correction] Burton ye son of John and Hester Burton of North Dighton.

Courtesy of West Yorkshire Archive Service

Marriage register, Heptonstall St Thomas, West Yorkshire, 1749

This particular clearly written register gives residence and occupation of the groom.

[April 25] Stephenson James Stansfield Webster [= weaver] and Lancaster Mary Ditto Spinster
[August 22] Barritt Jonathan Stansfield Mason and Brooks Mary Do. Spin.

But compare these registers to the printed forms in use after 1753:

Parish Marriage Register of Ealing St Mary, Middlesex, 1781, p. 52

The top two entries are transcribed as follows:

> No. 204 William Smithson of this Parish Bachelor
> and Esther Allen of this Parish Spinster were
> Married in this Church by Banns publish'd Aug[us]t 26th Sept 2nd, 9th
> this twentieth Day of September in the Year One Thousand seven Hundred
> and eighty one By me Rich[ar]d Shury
> This Marriage was solemnized between us { William Smithson Esther Allen
> In the Presence of { Tho[mas] Oliver Rich[ar]d Atlee
> No. 205 William Mandy of the Parish of Ealing
> in the County of Middlesex Batchelor and Mitchell Cleverly of the Parish of Chiswick in the same
>   County Spinster were
> Married in this Church by Licence
> this twenty fifth Day of September in the Year One Thousand seven Hundred
> and eighty one By me Charles Sturges Vicar
> This Marriage was solemnized between us { William Mandy Mitchell Cleverly
> In the Presence of { Rich[ar]d Atlee William Atlee

Notice a number of things:

– The use of a standard form, which sometimes made the written information quite cramped.

- The distinction between marriage by three publications of banns and marriage by licence.
- The multiple appearances of Richard and William Atlee as witnesses for those couples who didn't bring their own, such as No. 209 (Alexander Dury and Lucy Bowles).

The Atlees were most likely employees of the church and were prepared to stand in as witnesses for a small cash consideration. We know from a completely different record (Old Bailey Proceedings, 4 February 1850, Ref t18500204-451) that a Richard William Atlee was parish clerk of Ealing in 1845, and that the Middlesex Sessions Book 516 for October 1694 lists William Atlee, churchwarden of Ealing Parish, so unless this William lived to at least 180 years old, the church was obviously being run by a dynasty!

Printed examples of the form and bond used for a marriage allegation in Surrey in the 1700s.

FORM USED IN 1766-68.

Commiffary }
of Surry }

Appeared perfonally
and made Oath that he is of

and intendeth to marry with

and that he knoweth of no lawful Impediment, by reafon of any Pre-contract entered into before the twenty-fifth Day of *March*, one Thoufand feven Hundred and Fifty-four, Confanguinity, Affinity, or any other lawful Means whatfoever, to hinder the faid intended Marriage, and prayed a Licence to folemnize the fame in

and further made Oath, that the ufual Place of Abode of

hath been in the faid Parifh of

for the Space of four Weeks laft paft.

Sworn before me

BOND (1737) IMPRESSED WITH 3 SIXPENNY STAMPS.

KNOW all Men by these Prefents That we *Joseph Nost of the Parish of Streatham in the County of Surrey yeoman;* and *Edward Kempton of the Parish of Tooting in the County of Surrey Gardiner* are holden and firmly bound to the Right Reverend Father in God Benjamin by Divine permifsion Bishop of Winchester in the fum of Two hundred pounds of lawful Money of GREAT BRITAIN to be paid to the faid Right Rever⁴ Father or his certain Attorney, his Executors, Adminiftrators, or Affigns : To which Payment, well and truly to be made, we bind ourfelves, and each of us by himfelf for the whole, our Heirs, Executors, and Adminiftrators, firmly by these Prefents. Sealed with our Seals, Dated the *Seaventh* Day of *January* in the Year of our Lord One Thoufand Seven Hundred and *Thirty Seven.* . . . . . .

THE Condition of this Obligation is fuch, That if hereafter there shall not appear any lawful Let or Impediment, by reafon of any Pre-contract, Confanguinity, Affinity, or any other lawful Means whatfoever ; but that *Joseph Nost, Widower, and Mary Warner, Widow,* may lawfully solemnize Marriage together, and in the fame afterwards lawfully remain and continue for Man and Wife, according to the Laws in that behalf provided : And moreover, if there be not at this prefent time any Action, Suit, Plaint, Quarrel, or Demand, moved or depending before any Judge Ecclefiaftical or Temporal, for or concerning any such lawful Impediment between the faid Parties : Nor that either of them be of any better Eftate or Degree, than to the Judge at granting of the Licenfe is fuggefted,

And laftly, if the fame Marriage fhall be openly folemnized in the Church, in the Licenfe fpecified, between the Hours appointed in the Conftitutions Ecclefiaftical confirmed, and according to the Form of the Book of Common Prayer, now by Law eftablifhed, then this Obligation to be void, or else to ftand in full Force and Virtue.

Joseph Nost. (SEAL)

Sealed and Delivered
in the Presence of
N. Brady.

Edward Kempton. (SEAL)

From Bax, A.R. (ed.), *Allegations for marriage licences issued between 1673–1770* (Surrey Commissary Court, 1907).

Pallot's Marriage Register and Baptism Register

Durie David. w
= ann Heston ʷˢ his
ˢ·SAYR SOUTHWARK 1684 *63*

Durie David. w
= ann Heston ʷˢ his
ˢ·SAYR SOUTHWARK 1684 *63*

This is all the information usually found in the early paper slips of marriages.

The first Pallot's entry merely tells us that David Durie was a widower and Ann Heiton was a widow, married at St Saviour's, Southwark, London, 1789.

The baptism entry of William Dury is scarcely more informative, except that it took place in Teddington, Middlesex in 1808 and the parents were Wm (William) and Eliz (but is it Elizabeth or Eliza?)

Burials Register of Bradford St Peter (Bradford Cathedral), 1749

Parish Burials Register of Guiseley and Horsforth, Yorkshire, 1750

The paucity of information in the above registers show that the whole registration system needed reform.

Gretna Green marriage registers

Between the 1754 Hardwicke Act in England, Wales and Ireland (which tightened up the existing ecclesiastical marriage rules in England and Wales with statutory legislation to require a formal ceremony, a licence or banns etc.) and Brougham's 1856 Act in Scotland (which attempted to do much the same) there was no three-week residency requirement, no need for parental consent for a groom over 14 and a bride over 12 and no real need for a church. Irregular marriage in Scotland was valid, even if at times illegal. It therefore became popular for English couples to head for one of the

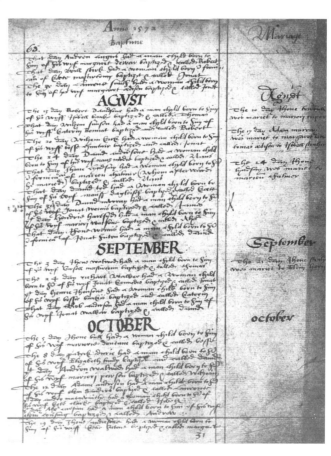

Borders towns, such as Gretna Green or Lamberton Toll, to tie the knot. Among those willing to oblige were father and son team David and Simon Lang, who performed over 10,000 such marriages in Gretna Green between 1794 and 1828, possibly half of all the nuptials in the town during this period. This was known, somewhat scathingly, in England, as the 'Scotch Form of Marriage', but there was no going back from it.

This page from 1820 happens to show a number of couples from the north of England, but although Gretna was handy for them, they weren't the only customers – people came from other parts of Scotland too.

It starts with a record of an unpaid debt, then records the marriage on 29 February 1820 of John Hamilton from Arthuret and Elizabeth Cuthbertson of Camerton, both in Cumberland, about 5 miles apart and some 35 miles from Gretna.

Early Scottish parish register

This is an example of a combined register of baptisms and marriage banns for Dunfermline in 1572. The first baptism entry, which refers to a date in July, says:

> That Day Androu Angus had a man chyld born to him of his wyf Margaret Dewar baptized & called Robert.

The second marriage entry for August 1572 says:

> The 17 Day Adam Murray was mariet to Margaret Law
> Tomas aedison [Edison?] to Isobel Stenhus

Scottish parish register: Fordyce Baptisms 1701 (p. 137)

What makes this register so interesting is the inclusion of symbols for heavenly bodies to express days of the week. This appears to be a peculiarity of this one parish – Fordyce in Banffshire – but the practice stretches over records during the period 1665 to about 1742/43, and is written in

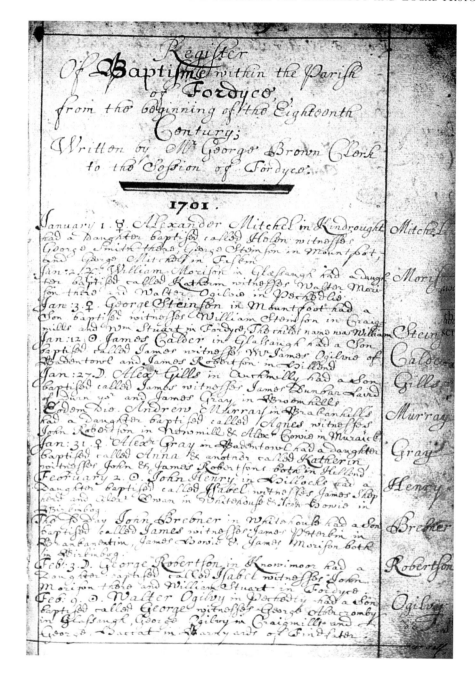

the hands of successive session clerks. It would appear to have been a common practice. It must have started with a minister or clerk who had an interest in astronomy. Notice that only seven bodies were known at that time. Uranus was the first planet discovered with a telescope, in 1781; Ceres and the other largest inner asteroids were all first seen between 1801 and 1807; Neptune followed in 1846; Pluto was not discovered and named until 1930.

Anyone familiar with Latin or French days of the week (p. 138) will immediately spot the correspondence of days of the week to planets, as follows:

Day	Planet	Symbol	Latin	French
Sunday	Sun	☉	*Solis dies*	*Dimanche*
Monday	Moon	☾	*Lunae dies*	*Lundi*
Tuesday	Mars	♂	*Martis dies*	*Mardi*
Wednesday	Mercury	☿	*Mercurii dies*	*Mercredi*
Thursday	Jupiter (Jove)	♃	*Jovis dies*	*Jeudi*
Friday	Venus	♀	*Veneris dies*	*Vendredi*
Saturday	Saturn	♄	*Saturni dies*	*Samedi*

Transcription of the first few entries:

> Register
> of Baptisms within the Parish
> of Fordyce
> from the beginning of the Eighteenth
> Century;
> Written by Mr George Brown Clerk
> to the Session of Fordyce
> 1701
> January 1 ☿ [Wednesday] Alexander Mitchell in Kindrought   Mitchell
> had a daughter baptised called Helen witnesses
> George Smith there George Steinson in Mountfort,
> and George Mitchell in Faskin
> Jan 2 ♃ [Thursday] William Morison in Glashaugh had a   Morison
> daughter baptised called Katherin witnesses Walter
> Morison there and Walter Ogilvie in Pechedlie
> Jan 3 ♀ [Friday] George Steinson in Mountfoot had a   Steins[on]
> son baptised [no name] witnesses William Steinson in Craig

Incidentally, place names were confirmed (where possible) by consulting the appropriate gazetteer. Genuki (www.genuki.org.uk) is generally a good place to start for county, local and parish information in the UK, and in this particular case see: www.abdnet.co.uk/genuki/BAN/Fordyce/locations.html.

Parish Marriage Register, St Cuthbert's (Edinburgh) 1807 (p. 139)

This extract of marriage banns from 17 June 1807 (St Cuthbert's Edinburgh Midlothian 685/02 0180 0226) names the father of the bride, but not the groom. The third entry says:

> Moubray   John Moubray Writer to the Signet [= lawyer] and
>   Patricia Hodge daug[hte]r of the late …….. Hodge
>   residing in the New Town gave up their names
>   for proclamation of Banns Matrimonial

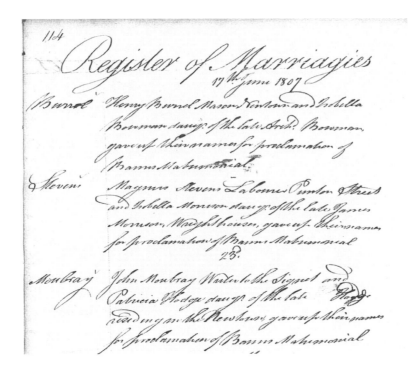

Parish Burial Register, Edinburgh, 1750 (685/01 0094) (p. 139)

This lair record shows the burial places of the deceased, plus other details. For example, the first few entries give:

No. of			Persons' names	Designations	Buried the		Place of interment
Men	Women	Children			month	day	
I I			T	William Tod	poor	October	I	West Laigh
2		I	M	a child of	James Mack j[ourneyma]n mason		2	W[est of] the Blew Stone S. Al[le]y
3		2	R	a child of	James Rutherford poor		2	S. the well
4		3	C	a child of	John Cunningham	D[itt]o	2	3 DPW Beaton's tomb
5		5	H	a child of	William Hill	D[itt]o	3	N. the Well
6	I		R	Marg[ate]t Kerss	sp. to … [above] … mason	D[itt]o	3	West Laigh

Monumental inscriptions, headstones and other records of interment are dealt with in Chapter 5.

Latin in birth and baptism records

Often, the record is given in Latin, but using a restricted vocabulary. Examples of this include:

Jacobus filius Roberti Tod et Maria uxor ejus baptizatus fuit (date) Anno Domini 1728.
James son of Robert Tod and Mary his wife was baptised etc.

Johanna filia Roberti Tod et Maria sponsa ejus baptizata fuit (date) Anno Pdo.
Joanna son of Robert Tod and Mary his wife was baptised etc.

Thomas naturalius puer Thomae Bremner et Francesca Wallace natus fuit (date) Ano. D. 1744. Nominatus (date) AD 1745 et in Eccle. receptus (date) Anno Dni (date) 1745.
Thomas, natural (i.e., illegitimate) boy to Thomas Bremner and Frances Wallace was born (date), named (date) and received into the church [= baptised, and notice the abbreviation for Ecclesiam] (date) 1745.

– The words for 'son' (*filius*) and 'daughter' (*filia*) might be replaced by *puer* (boy) or *puella* (girl). They might be abbreviated *fil*. and *fil*.
– Notice the two words used for wife: *uxor* and *sponsa* (*sponsus* is husband). The gender of the child is indicated by the infelction of *baptizatus* (male) and *baptizata* (female).
– The verb *fuit* strictly speaking means 'has been' rather than 'was' (*erat*).
– *Anno Domini* might be abbreviated *Anno Dni, Anno. D.* or AD.
– *Anno P* (followed by other letters) might stand for: *Anno pto.* ('in the current (present) year') or *Anno pdo., predit., praedicto* ('in the foresaid year'). Sometimes *Anno* was written *Año* with a tilde or stroke over the *n* indicating a double letter.

Latin in marriage records

There are various formulations for marriage in Latin and a number of relevant verbs for the act, including:

– *In matrimonium ducere* (literally, 'to lead in marriage') but watch the conjugation of *duco, ducere, duxi, ductus* – *in matrimonium duxit* means 'he has married'.

– *matrimonium solemnizat fuit inter* 'marriage has been solemnised between'.
– *In matrimonio conjuncti sunt* 'they were joined in marriage'.

Examples of marriage entries:

Jacobus Tod in matrimonium duxit Juliam Smith (date)
James Tod married Julia Smith

Henricus Brown duxit Carolinam Becket uxor ejus (date)
Henry Brown married Carolin Becket his wife (rather obviously!)

Johannes White viduus de eadem parochiae duxit Lydiam Green vidua de Ketil (date)
John White widower of this parish married Lydia Green widow of Ketil

Matrimonio conjuncti sunt inter: Ricardus Black coelebis et Margaretham Grey coeleba de eadem vicarium (date)
Marriage was joined between: Richard Black, bachelor (literally, 'celibate', indicating 'single') and Margareth Grey spinster of this parish (notice the alternative word, *vicarium*)

Other formulations might include *connubia juncti* (connubially joined) and *solutam … nupta* (free to marry or freely married) (from the verb *nubo, nubere, nupsi, nuptus* (to marry), but *nupta* can also be the noun 'bride').

Alternatives to 'single' include *innuptus/innupta* (unmarried).

The female name is in the accusative as the man is doing the marrying, and it is being done to the woman.

Other information might be:

– An occupation (e.g. *fabri ferarii* 'metal worker' or *agricola* 'farmer'), status (*Gent.* 'gentleman' or *armiger* indicating someone entitled to bear arms and thus addressed as 'Esquire', but be careful of this as in legal records it could indicate 'bailie', 'magistrate' or 'mace bearer').
– Education (magister (master), signifying an MA degree).
– Proclamations (*notificationes matrimonii in utra paroecia antea notae erant* 'banns were previously read in both parishes').

Latin in death and burial records

The usual formula uses the verb *sepelio, sepelire, sepelivi, sepultus, sepultus* (to bury) usually in the passive form: *sepultus/sepulta est/fuit* or *humatus*:

Sarah Overton vid. sepulta fuit decimo quarto Iulii 1674.
Sarah Overton, widow, was buried 14 July 1674.

Johnes. Wright sepultus fuit 23 August? 1675. A. ptdo.
John Wright was buried 23 August 1675.

Alicia Lusher coelebs sepulta fuit tricesimo Die Novemr. 1675 A. pdo.
Alicia Lusher, singlewoman, was buried 30 November 1675.

Rather than write out each one individually, one recorder wrote: '*Sepulti sunt:*' (the burials are:) then listed names and dates:

Debora uxoris Henrici Negus … (Deborah wife of Henry Negus …)

Alina ux. Johnes Tilles … (Alina wife of John Tills …)

Henrici Negus, Ar. … (Henry Negus, Esquire …)

Sarah Davis puella (Sarah Davis, girl …)

John Wollmanns jnr. (John Wollmanns, Junior …)

See Monumental inscriptions, headstones and other records of interment in Chapter 5. For Kirk Session and other parish records, see Chapter 15.

9

Scotland, England and Wales: Entails

Imagine this scenario: Mr Bennet has the estate of Longbourn in Hertfordshire, England, but only in life interest, and has entailed so that it can only be passed on to a male heir; he has five daughters and no son, so it will pass to his nearest male relative, his cousin, the unlikeable Revd William Collins. If at least one of the Bennet daughters cannot make a good marriage, they will all be destitute, but fortunately, the second eldest, Elizabeth, meets and finally gets to like the extremely wealthy and gratifyingly good-looking Mr Darcy.

Now consider this: it is 1745, and when Bonnie Prince Charlie raises the Jacobite standard, the Laird of Durrisdeer decides that his elder son James Durie should join the rebels while his younger son Henry Durie takes sides with the Hanoverians, thereby hedging his bets so as to preserve the estate. James is reported dead, but in fact has been a spy for the Loyalists, and returns to claim a share of his inheritance in cash. However, the Durie fortunes are much depleted by the '45 Rebellion and the only solution is for the laird to alienate (sell off) part of the estate, which he is not strictly entitled to do because of a condition requiring that it should stay in the family; but as there is no-one else to inherit except James, Henry and Henry's son Alexander, there is no legal problem.

Recognise these? The first is of course the plot of *Pride and Prejudice* by Jane Austen and the second of Robert Louis Stevenson's *The Master of Ballantrae*. Both are fictional (sadly for the current author, Durrisdeer exists but no Durie ever owned it) but they show how important the legal concept of an entail can be. The reason the entail figures so frequently in fiction written or set in the eighteenth and nineteenth centuries (compare *Middlemarch* by George Eliot, *The Adventure of the Priory School* by Arthur Conan Doyle or, more recently, *Downton Abbey* by Julian Fellowes) is that many families were land rich but cash poor and – more to the point – were unable to sell off their land assets to raise capital because the property was held by each generation on the condition that it must pass to the next, or to a male heir only, or some similar proviso.

And that's an entail or, in England and Wales, a fee tail: a condition in the inheritance of 'real' property (see Chapters 9, 10, 16) such that it cannot be sold, devised in a will, or alienated in any other way except to the landholder's heirs. The purpose was usually sensible when conceived: it was designed to keep the estate intact within the family and ideally in the main line of succession, and could not pass to, say, a daughter (whose husband would then own it, until the Married Women's Property Acts of 1870 and 1882), to an illegitimate child, or to a third party just because the current landholder needed the cash. However, the law of unintended consequences often meant that generations or centuries later, this had become unreasonable or undesirable.

Other examples of entailments are that the property could only be inherited by someone of the same surname – in which case a maternal cousin, who was the rightful heir, might have to change his name to get it – or that the inheritor must matriculate and bear the coat of arms of the deceased, and so on.

An entail might be in the original charter granting the land, in a will or testament, enshrined in a trust deed (see Chapter 11) or might arise from a marriage contract or settlement.

What marks the fee tail or entail apart from the fee simple was a phrase such as 'to X and the heirs of his body' rather than 'to X and his heirs' or 'to X, his heirs, assigns and successors'. In that case, the heirs 'in tail' must be the biological children of the landowner: not an adopted child for example. It may also be that the property was entailed in 'fee tail male' (only sons could inherit), or 'fee tail female' (only daughters) or 'to X and the heirs of his body lawfully procreated' (which ruled out illegitimate children), or some other 'fee tail special'.

The origin of the term is from the mediaeval Latin *feodum talliatum*, which means 'fee cut short'. In Scotland the equivalent of fee tail is called tailzie (pronounced 'tail-ye') and an heir in tailzie could not dispose of the property unless to the feu superior and holder of the *dominium directum* if any.

Today, this has largely fallen by the wayside. English law evolved a complex set of legal flummeries and fictions called 'common recovery' (see below) to get around the fee tail and the Fines and Recoveries Act of 1833 c. 74 3 and 4 Will IV made it even simpler. It has not been possible to create new fee tails since the Trusts of Land and Appointment of Trustees Act 1996 c. 47.

In Scotland, the Rutherford or Entail Amendment Act 1848 and an amendment in 1875 enabled an heir in tailzie to apply to the Court of Session to remove the deed of tailzie and take possession of the property in fee simple. There had been complaints, repeated in Parliament, that:

> … the restrictions under the Scotch Entail Act of 1685 had become so rife and so great that, as Lord Rutherfurd had said, a nobleman could not alter the inscription on a button worn by his livery servant. That state of things was to some extent remedied by the Rutherfurd Act of 1848, and it was not proposed by the present Bill to affect or alter the Law of Entails in Scotland, which were analogous to English entails with one exception. In England, as their Lordships knew, the tenant for life and the tenant in tail in remainder might, since 1848, by consent with each other break the entail, and the tenant in tail might do that as soon as he reached 21 years of age. In Scotland a tenant in tail could not give his consent until the age of 25.

The Abolition of Feudal Tenure etc. (Scotland) Act 2000 (enacted in 2004) disentailed all land and required the keeper of the registers of Scotland to close the Register of Entails (and also finally abolished feudalism), although it is still not possible to will a certain share of property away from children (*legitim*) or a surviving partner (*jus relictae*) see Chapter 10.

There is a well-known example of an entail in Scotland based on the case of the 12th Duke of Hamilton, whose fourth cousin became the 13th Duke in 1895 and got the land, rather than it going to his daughter, Lady Mary, despite the 12th Duke's best efforts to get the two of them married. On the downside, the 13th Duke didn't get everything (it wasn't all entailed) but was saddled with £1 million of debt to go with Hamilton Palace, later pulled down.

For the record, in Ireland the Land and Conveyancing Law Reform Act 2009 removed fee tail and converted all existing entails to fee simple. In America, it either never existed in many states, or now hardly exists at all, except in a restricted way and only in Delaware, Maine, Massachusetts and Rhode Island.

So, although the whole concept of entail does not have much currency today, it is of intense importance to family and social historians.

Examples of Scottish entails (tailzies)

Stirling of Ardoch

Sir Henry Stirling, 1st Baronet of Ardoch (referred to on p. 155ff in relation to the testament of Jonet Hempseid or Faichney). His father had conveyed Ardoch to him in 1635 and he was created a Baronet of Nova Scotia by patent dated 2 May 1666, and containing a limitation of this dignity to the heirs male of his body. He married Isobel, daughter of Sir John Haldane of Gleneagles and died in February 1669, leaving the baronetcy to his son, who became Sir William Stirling, 2nd Baronet, and to his son, 3rd Baronet. However, the 4th Baronet had only daughters, so on his death the baronetcy went to his brother, who became Sir Thomas Stirling, 5th Baronet, and when he died unmarried in 1808 all his brothers had predeceased him, so the Ardoch baronetcy became extinct.

On the other hand, the estates of Ardoch were not so entailed, and at the death of the 4th Baronet, Sir William, they went to his daughter, Anne Stirling, who married Col. Charles Moray of Abercairny. Their son died, so Christian Moray was the heiress to the Ardoch lands, and by her husband Henry Home-Drummond she had George, succeeded by his son, who changed his name to George Stirling-Home-Drummond of Blair Drummond and Ardoch and, despite two marriages, died without issue.

Durie of Durie and the Craigluscar Duries

On p. 148 the main Durie lines are shown from John Durie of Durie to his eldest son, Robert Durie of Durie, Andrew (Bishop of Galloway, who had no heirs) and George, last Abbot of Dunfermline. Robert had a daughter, Jonet, his heiress. In about 1532 she was 'persuaded' to marry a companion of James V, Henry Kemp of Thomastoun, who changed his name to Durie to preserve the entail that allowed their son, David, and grandson, Robert, to be Durie of Durie. (In the event, that Robert sold the estate and barony in 1614, but had descendants.)

In the other line, George had four sons (not bad going for a Benedictine abbot) including Henry, who held the estate of Craigluscar. This descended in an almost unbroken line (George, captain in Louis XIV Scots Guards, was served heir by his brother, John, when he died in 1682) until Charles Durie, 10th of Craigluscar, who had Robert and Eliza. Robert died young and unmarried in 1868, leaving Eliza, 12th of Craigluscar. She married a local doctor, Andrew Dewar, who changed his name to Dewar-Durie, again to preserve the entail on Craigluscar, which they sold anyway in 1909. But the entail also covered the 'Name and Arms', and in time their grandson, Raymond Varley Dewar-Durie became 14th of Craigluscar *de jure*, and chief of the Arms and Name of Durie. The title is held today by his grandson, Andrew Durie, 16th of Craigluscar.

The implication for DNA testing is interesting: descendants of Robert Durie of Durie presumably have the Kemp Y-chromosome and will appear to be completely unrelated to the Craigluscar Duries with their Dewar Y-chromosome, and also to any Duries who descended in cadet branches from before either of those entailment name changes.

Chisholm

On p. 149 is one page from the 1813 Retour (see Chapter 13) of James Chisholme of Chisholme, in favour of Charles Chisholme, referring back to a number of previous documents, including a deed of tailzie. This document will provide practice in Latin and in the palaeography of the early nineteenth century, so a full transcript of the page is given:

Page 2

[Qui jurati di]cunt magno sacramento interveniente quod	[who being sworn] by their great oath that
quondam Jacobus Chisholme Armiger	the late James Chisholme Esquire
ultimus de Chisholme obijt ad fidem	last of Chisholme died in the faith
et pacem S.D.N Regis Georgij tertij nunc	and peace of our sovereign lord King George III
regnantis. Et quod Carolus Chisholme nu:	then reigning. And that Charles Chisholme
per scriba in servitio Honorabilis Socie:	recently a clerk in the service of the Honorable
tatis mercatorum in India orientali	Society of Merchants in East India
apud Calcutta in Bengal nunc resi:	at Calcutta in Bengal now resident
dens Londini filius Guilielmi Chisholme	in London, brother of William Chisholme
Armigeri olim de Chisholme nunc	Esquire once of Chisholme now
demortui est legitimus et propunquior	deceased is the legitimate and nearest
haeres talliae et provisionis dict demortui	heir of entail and provision of the said deceased
Jacobi Chisholme virtute Dispositionis	James Chisholme by virtue of disposition
et syngraphiae talliae per eum concess.	and deed of entail by him granted
per quam dedit concessit et disponit	by which he gave, granted and disponed
ad et in favorem sui ipsius et haeredum	to and in favor of him himself and the heirs
masculorum ex ejus corpore ^in feodo Quibus	male of his body [added] in fee whom
deficien dict Caroli Chisholm latoris	failing the said Charles Chisholm bearer
presentium haeredumque masculorum	of these presents and heirs male
vel foemellarum ex ejus corpore Quibus	or female of his body whom
deficien Gulielmi Chisholm Scott	failing William Chisholme Scott
filii secundi demortui Roberti Scot	second son of the deceased Robert Scott
de Coldhouse sororis filii dict demor:	of Coldhouse, sister-son of the said deceased
tui Jacboi Chisholme et heredum mas:	James Chisholme and the heirs male
culorum ex ejus corpore – Quibus deficien	of his body – whom failing
Thomae Chisholme Scot natu maximi filij	Thomas Chisholme Scott firstborn son
dict demortui Roberti Scott haeredumq[ue]	of the said deceased Robert Scott and the heirs
masculorum ex ejus corpore Quibus deficien	male of his body whom failing
Roberti Scot filij quinti dict demortui	Robert Scott, fifth son of the said deceased
Roberti Scot haeredumque masculorum	Robert Scott and the heirs male
ex ejus corpore Quibus deficien Alexandri	of his body whom failing Alexander
Scott filij sexti dict demortui Roberti	Scott sixth son of the said deceased Robert
Scot haeredumque masculorum ex ejus	Scott and the heirs male of his
corpore	body

It goes on to say:

whom failing the second legitimate son of Mary Agnes Chisholme daughter of the said James Chisholme now wife to the most honourable Charles Lord Sinclair and the heirs male of the body of the said second legitimate son. Whom failing other younger legitimate sons born or to be born of the body of the said Mary Agnes Chisholme in their order and the heirs male of their bodies Whom failing whichever person or persons are nominated by the said James Chisholme in any nominations or elsewhere written by him granted after the date of the said deed of entail and in the absence of any such nomination or persons so nominated at that time, of his nearest heirs whomsoever and of their assigns firstborn female heirs and descendants of his body excluding heirs portioners and firstborn female heirs succeeding always without division for all lines of female succession all and whole of the lands of Chisholme (etc.)

Work your way through that, and you'll see the lengths Chisholme was prepared to go to in order to determine the succession. It ends by saying:

> … provided that the heirs male succeeding to the said lands and hereditary honours by the foresaid Dispositions and deeds of entail will be obliged held and bound to be called and designated [themselves] by the name of Chisholme to such a degree and to bear and use the arms and insignias of honour of the family of Chisholme as their particular names, arms, titles and designations. – And also providing in the same way thereafter specifically provided that if it happens that succession to the said lands and heritable honours of the said entail by lack of heirs male devolves to the heirs female then and in that case the said heirs female such as succeed will be obliged, held and bound to marry nobles [meaning here 'of good stock'] of the name of Chisholme or which of their heirs who continue to succeed to the said lands and heritable honours of the said entail shall assume the name and shall bear and use arms and family insignias of the said family of Chisholme as their proper arms, name, title and designation. the heirs male succeeding to the said lands and hereditary honours by the foresaid Dispositions …

In the event, Charles – a lowly clerk at the time – was the nearest heir. Some present-day Chisholmes dispute this.

Common recoveries (England and Wales)

These were legal fictions prosecuted in England and Wales up until 1833 in order to convert an entailed estate into fee simple or freehold. They are dealt with (as were Fines and Recoveries) in Chapter 17:

Finding Entails

Such documents can be found in the following places:

– For documents in public archives, the National Records of Scotland (NRS) (the new name for the National Archives of Scotland) and the National Register of Archives in Scotland (www.nas.gov.uk/onlineCatalogue/).
– For documents in private hands, the Scottish Archive Network, SCAN (www.scan.org.uk/catalogue/).
– For English and Welsh documents, using the wider search capabilities of AccessToArchives (A2A) via The National Archives in Kew, London, which has online catalogues describing archives held locally in England and Wales from the eighth century to the present day (www.nationalarchives.gov.uk/A2A/).

Here is just one example, searching using the keywords 'Durie' and 'tailzie OR entail' at NRS:

GD7/2/335
Letters of general charge at the instance of David Weymes of Foodie against Euphemia and Elizabeth Weymes, daughters of deceased Mr. Patrick Weymes of Gladney by his first marriage [with Elizabeth Hamiltoun, see GD7/2/338], Janet Weymes, only daughter of said deceased's second marriage [with Janet Durie, see GD7/2/338], and Mr. James Weymes, principal of St. Leonard's College, heir of tailzie and provision of said deceased, his brother, to enter as heirs of said deceased Mr. Patrick Weymes. Also execution of above letters, dated 18 March 1669.

Further Reading

Maitland, F.W., *Forms of Action at Common Law* (1909). Available at Medieval Sourcebook (www.fordham.edu/halsall/basis/maitland-formsofaction.asp)

Biancalana, Joseph, *The Fee Tail and the Common Recovery in Medieval England 1176–1502* (Cambridge University Press, 2001)

Descendants of John DURIE

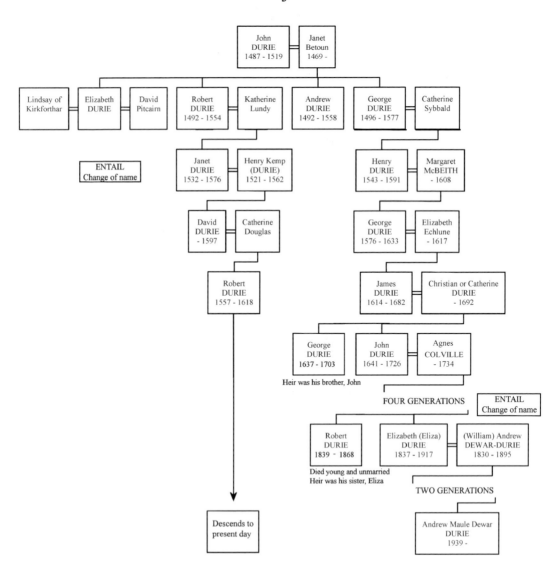

curit magno sacramento interveniente quod
quondam Jacobus Chisholme Armiger
ultimus de Chisholme obijt ad fidem   448
et pacem S.D.N. Regis Georgij tertij nunc
regnantis. Et quod Carolus Chisholme nu:
per scriba in servitio Honorabilis Socie:
tatis mercatorum in India orientali
apud Calcutta in Bengal nunc resi:
dens Londini filius Gulielmi Chisholme
Armigeri olim de Chisholme nunc
demortui est legitimus et Propinquior
haeres talliae et Provisionis dict demortui
Jacobi Chisholme virtute Dispositionis
et Syngraphae talliae per eum concess.
per quam dedit concessit et disposuit
ad et in favorem sui ipsius et haeredum
Masculorum ex ejus corpore X— Quibus X in feodo
deficien dict Caroli Chisholm latoris
Praesentium haeredumque masculorum
vel foemellarum ex ejus corpore Quibus
deficien Gulielmi Chisholme Scott
filii secundi demortui Roberti Scot
de Coldhouse sororis filii dict demor:
tui Jacobi Chisholme et haeredum mas:
culorum ex ejus corpore.— Quibus deficien
Thomae Chisholme Scot natu maximi filij
dict demortui Roberti Scott haeredumque
masculorum ex ejus corpore Quibus deficien
Roberti Scot filij quinti dict demortui
Roberti Scot haeredumque masculorum
ex ejus corpore Quibus Deficien alexandri
Scott filij sexti dict demortui Roberti
Scot haeredumque masculorum ex ejus
                                        corpore—

Courtesy of The National Records of Scotland

10

Scotland: Wills and Testaments

Scottish testamentary documents are often a disappointment for genealogists and historians for a number of reasons. First, up until 1868, they were concerned only with moveable estate (goods, money, jewellery, investments, bank accounts, books, furniture, tools, animals, farm crops and produce etc.). Second (and as a consequence) there is rarely any mention of land, houses or other 'real' (immoveable) property, which could only be passed on by the system of retours (Chapter 11) or by a trust disposition and settlement (Chapter 13). Third, they often do not have the names of any children or relatives, for the following reasons:

– The eldest son inherited everything heritable (immoveable property, land and buildings) by the principle of primogeniture, which still applied from 1868 until 1964.
– All other children had an equal share of moveables, regardless of order of birth.
– The 'relict' (widow or widower) also had a share.
– The relict may be named if he or she is the executor or executrix, and there may a 'cautioner' (pronounced 'kay-shunner') made responsible by surety or guarantee that the stipulations were carried out and the estate distributed as directed.

Fourth, although there was provision for leaving a will or legacie (the wishes of the testator) this was often not expressed. Finally, there was no legal requirement to make a will and few did. There was also no legal requirement to use a court procedure and in most cases the deceased's affairs were settled without a testament, so there is no documentary trace today.

THE SCOTTISH TESTAMENT

With all that in mind, let's start again at the beginning. Strictly speaking, inheritance of moveables, is managed by a testament. A will or legacie is one clause of a testamentary document. Heritable (immoveable) property was land and buildings as well as any minerals, mining rights, heritable titles and offices etc. and was passed to the eldest son (or to daughters if there was no son).

Moveable property is referred to in testaments as 'goods, gear, sums of money and debts' and was divided into three parts at most: the widow's part or *jus relictae*; the bairns' part or *legitim* (all children, not including the eldest, having an equal share); and the deid's part (in other words, the dead person could dispose of it according to his or her 'will').

Scotland had a system of confirmation, rather than probate, administered by commissary courts (see 'The courts', p. 152). The simplest case is of a man leaving a surviving wife, children and an expression of his will, where one-third went to the widow, one-third was divided equally amongst the children (or all to an only child), and the remaining one-third was disposed of according to any instructions the deceased gave in his will. The widow's and bairns' parts went automatically to the wife and children without any need for these parts to be given up by the executor to the commissary court for confirmation. However, if there were a will or legacie, the deid's part required the court's confirmation if not stipulated in a will. In the absence of any disposition this share was taken up by the deceased's next of kin by confirmation.

However, where there was 'heritage' (immoveable or 'real' property), which went to the eldest son, that son would automatically be barred from receiving a share of the *legitim* but would inherit the 'heirship moveables' (the 'best' of the goods, furniture, farming animals and implements etc.) so that the house and land were not inherited empty.

If there were no surviving wife, the moveables were divided into two equal parts, one half to the children and the other to any persons named in the will.

If survived by a widow and no children, the division was in two halves: the widow's part and the deid's part (if a will existed). In the absence of any surviving wife or children, the whole of the moveables were the deid's part, bequeathed as per any will, pre-existing marriage contract, bonds of provision for children of a marriage etc. In the absence of a will, the next nearest of kin were his surviving brothers and sisters and the estate would be distributed equally between them.

The moveable estate of a widow was divided into two parts, *legitim* and the deid's part. The document may say 'Na division', which may mean that there is no survivor to inherit, but may indicate that family members are *forisfamiliat* (disinherited, or simply not living with the family for some reason). Do not take this as evidence that there were no children.

On death, an executor would be appointed to dispose of moveable property. The executor may have been named in a will, or if not, would be appointed by the court. If there were no will and the deceased intestate, there may still be a testamentary document, because the executor had to report to the court about the disposition of assets. The record of this process would either be:

– If the deceased left a will: a testament testamentar and inventar (TTI).
– If the deceased left no will: a testament dative and inventar (TDI).

Where wills exist (in a testament testamentar), these can be a rich source of genealogical information as they may give the names of heirs, grandchildren, other relatives, friends and so on.

However, most people did not leave a will, as most had very little to dispose of and it was clear what the widow and children would inherit. In this case there was absolutely no need to name the widow/widower, the eldest son, or any other children.

Confirmation

To settle affairs before death, it was possible to draw up a testament giving instructions about the disposal of moveables, and naming an executor to administer the estate. The executor had to be confirmed by a court and a document was drawn up by the court for this purpose.

A testament testamentar is the equivalent of English probate. It typically had four sections:

– An introductory clause (who died, where, when and 'given up' by whom).
– An inventory of the moveable estate and any debts owing or owed.
– A copy of the deceased's will or legacie, with his or her wishes as to disposal of the estate and naming an executor (usually close family); if the will clause is not included in the testament,

because it was contained in a separate document, there will be a reference to where it was recorded (most likely in the court's registers of deeds) but often a recitation of its main provisions.
- A confirmation clause, giving the names of executor, cautioner, the '*Notar Publick*' and the commissar.

A testament dative is the equivalent of the English letters of administration. The deceased had died intestate (no will), the testament was drawn up by the court and an executor was appointed on the court's behalf (but quite often the relict). It had three parts:

- Introductory clause.
- Inventory of possessions.
- Confirmation clause.

This is identical to the testament testamentar, except for the will clause.

The executor might be a family member, but if there were considerable debts, the court might appoint a creditor as executor. The testament will list the debts and creditors and allow their discharge to be authorised.

Inventar or inventory

This is usually of great interest to social historians as it shows the possessions, income and debts of the deceased, and may indicate business and other relationships. There will be a list of all the moveable property belonging to the deceased at the time of death, money owed (to creditors) and due (from debtors), expected income after death from rents, crops already sown, bonds and so on. Sometimes it only gives a short, total valuation, but in some testaments it can be very detailed, with every item listed and valued. Where the estate was to be liquidated by roup (a public auction) there would be a 'roup roll' itemising each lot, the amounts paid and in some cases the creditors' and buyers' names.

Bear in mind too that a testament dative may record the estate as being in debt (*debita excedunt bona*) even though there was heritable property: land rich but cash poor was a not-uncommon scenario.

There are examples of inventories in this chapter (below) and in Chapter 4.

The courts

Before the 1560s wills were church records (and remained so in England until the mid-1800s, see Chapter 16) administered by diocese. After 1564, a system of civil commissary courts was established, but based on the same 'footprint' as the old diocesan courts – note that these are not by county.

Up to 1823 testaments were recorded in the local commissary court, which had jurisdiction over the deceased's parish. There were twenty-two of these, but the Edinburgh court had jurisdiction over all Scotland and those dying abroad. The commissariot jurisdictions bear more relation to the pre-Reformation medieval dioceses (St Andrews, Edinburgh, Dunkeld etc.) than county boundaries. Edinburgh Commissary Court was superior and could confirm testaments where the deceased had moveable property in more than one commissariat, across commissariot boundaries and where a Scot had died 'abroad' (including England). There was no absolute requirement to use the commissariot overseeing the parish of the deceased: it might have been more convenient for someone living in the south of Fife to use the Edinburgh court and someone in the north-west of Fife to use Dunkeld (in Perthshire) rather than St Andrews.

Testaments may also be registered in the Commissary Court of Edinburgh, and will be referenced CC8, if the *'frie geir exceedeth L lib'* (more than £50). Therefore, it is worth checking Edinburgh as well as all the local court records.

From 1 January 1824 commissary courts ceased to exist and sheriff courts took over confirmation of testaments, but there was some overlap during the handover, into the late 1820s.

After 1868

Eventually, the inability to direct the inheritance of immoveable property in a will was removed, and in any case, those who wanted to were using the legal machinery of the trust disposition and settlement to get round the restrictions. The elaborate procedures of testaments and services of heirs fell away and individuals could pass on heritable property (including land and buildings) through a will.

It sometimes became necessary for a court to be involved years after the death – where a dispute arose over inheritance, for example – so a testament may exist but might be recorded at a later date.

Finding testaments

Larger libraries will have bound indexes to commissariot records up to 1800, but often only for their local area. These were printed for the Scottish Record Society in the 1900s and many are available for download as PDFs from www.archive.org (see the example on p. 154).

All testaments and inventories (except Orkney and Shetland) are with the NRS and over 600,000 have been indexed and digitised, dating from 1513 to 1925. These can be downloaded from www.scotlandspeople.gov.uk for 10 Credits per document regardless of length. An index search is free after registration, and viewing the digitised document is free at the ScotlandsPeople Centre at New Register House in Edinburgh (although you will have paid for the half-day or day to be there and it does cost to make a print). Go up to the Historical Search Room and there is no day fee.

Although the index entry is usually enough to identify the person concerned, there is no way of knowing if it is the correct person until it has been paid for and read. Below is a search for John Thomson, 1800–20, using the keyword 'Glasgow'. Is this the same person? Or is it a coincidence?

Also note that a surname is not necessary for a ScotlandsPeople search. Use the keyword field and enter a place name or an occupation, for example. It is possible to restrict the search to certain dates and to particular records (Aberdeen Sheriff Court wills 1824–1901, for instance).

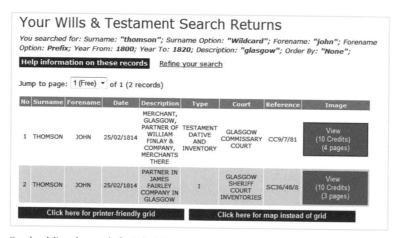

ScotlandsPeople search for John Thomson, 1800–20, using the keyword 'Glasgow'.

Dunkesoune, Henrie   26 Oct. 1583
Dunmuir, Mr. Alexander, minister at Kilspindy   12 June 1588
Dunress, David, in Mirriehaltoun of Struther.   *See* **Morris**, Effie.
    „   Euphaim, spouse to David Gray, in Pitgarvy, par. of Aberluthnot
                                                                            18 Feb. 1614
    „   Janet, spouse to Andrew Moncreiffe, in Easter Rind, par. of Rind
                                                                            26 Apr. 1620
    „   Margaret, in Sounshill, par. of Dun   16 June 1618
Dunsire, Andrew, feuar in Ceres   29 July 1778
Dures, Elspet, widow in Balkellie, par. of Inchebreak   29 June 1620
Durie, Alexander, in Slateford, par. of Edzell   24 Apr. 1777
    „   Andrew, of Wester Newtoun.   *See* **Cockburn**, Barbara.
    „   Christian, relict of George Gledstanes, Archibishop of St. Andrews
                                                                            17 June 1618
    „   David, sometime Dean of Guild of Kirkcaldy   5 Dec. 1681
    „   David, custumer, citiner in St. Andrews   11 Mar. 1691
    „   David, of Duryhill, par. of Edzell   3 June 1751
    „   David, merchant, burges of Kirkcaldy.   *See* **Hutcheoun**, Margaret.
    „   David, sklaitter in Aberbrothok.   *See* **Liddell**, Elspet.
    „   David, sometime maltman in St. Andrews.   *See* **Murray**, Christian.
    „   David, in Monthryve.   *See* **Pryde**, Margaret.
    „   David, in Cottoun of Durie.   *See* **Wilson**, Elspet.
    „   Elspet, spouse to William Littilljohn, in Auld Durie-mylne,
                    par. of Markinch   17 June 1635
    „   Euffame, spouse to George Gray, in the Burns, par. of Kennoquhy
                                                                            14 July 1595

Part of a page from the *Commissariot Record of St Andrews, Register of Testaments, 1549–1800* (1902).

Check for both testaments and inventories, plus any accessory document such as an eik (an amendment to the inventory, pronounced '*eek*'). Remember too that the same person might not have identical names or spellings for different documents: Margaret Brown in one but Mgt Broun in another, say.

Wills after 1925

To find a will or other document of executry for most of the twentieth century (and also the will and/or inventory of someone Scottish who died elsewhere) it is necessary to know:

– The name.
– Where the deceased lived.
– The date of death.

At the Historical Search Room in Register House in Edinburgh, there is an annual index of testaments called the Calendar of Confirmations in printed or typed volumes from 1901–59, from 1960 on microfiche cards and from 1985–96 in a computerised index. (The Mitchell Library, Glasgow, has the printed calendar up to 1936.) This calendar covers the whole of Scotland and gives details of the deceased, place and date of death, and details of when and where the testament is recorded. For any death in the last ten years, it is necessary to contact the Commissary Department, Edinburgh Sheriff Court, 27 Chambers Street, Edinburgh, EH1 1LB.

Probates resealed

Before 1858, someone who died owning moveable property in Scotland but who normally lived in England, Ireland or Wales (or, indeed, anywhere else) would have all executry dealt with by the Commissary Court of Edinburgh. From 1858 there was a system of 'probates resealed' whereby inheritance of the moveable property in Scotland could be handled by the English, Welsh or Irish courts who then sent a copy of the grant of probate or letters of administration to Edinburgh. These records up to the early 1900s are available via the ScotlandsPeople website, and in the Calendar of Confirmations from 1902 onwards.

Examples of testaments

The form of testamentary documents, with typical or formulaic phrases, remained more or less the same for centuries, so knowing the 'diplomatic' (structure) of a document that is easier to read will help identify difficult words and phrases in a later one. Get to know and recognise the words and phrases you will find in each clause, regardless of careless writing or abbreviations. Examples are:

cautioner	faithfully made and given up	Sherriffdom
citation	by	*summa inventarij*
commissariot	foresaid	testament
confirmed	goods, gear & debts	testamentar
dated	*imprimis*	the time of his decease
dative	inventory	*umqll* (*umquhile*, deceased)
decreet	moveables	underwritten
defunct (deceased)	parochyn (parish)	*viz* (*videlicet*)
estimate and valued	pertaining and belonging to	
executor/executrix	relict	

The testament testamentar and inventory of Jonet Hempseid, 1611

The handwriting in testaments is usually fairly easy to interpret back to about 1700, but before that date it requires practice. This is covered in Chapter 1. However, the structure of the earlier wills is the same and similar phrases crop up. A full transcription of this is given below and the actual document is on p. 160, so it can also be used for palaeography practice.

Jonet Hempseid
1. The Testament testamentar
2. latter will & Inventar of the guids & geir debtis
3. and utheris perteining to androw faichenay in
4. nether ardoche the tyme of the deceis of umquhile
5. Jonat hempseid his spous quhilk was in the moneth
6. of february 1611 yeireis maid and geawin up be the said
7. andro executor dative nominat To and decernit to hir
8. according to hir nominatione to that effect of
9. the dait the xiiij of Januar the yeir of god foirsaid
10. In the first the said andro grantit and confessit him to haue the tyme
11. of hir deceis foirsaid the guids and geir wndirwritten of the valour &
12. estimatione following To witt four meiris quherof ane gray meir of xiiij yeir
13. auld pryce x lib ane broun meir of xij yeir auld pryce x lib ane uthir

14. gray meir of xj yeir auld pryce xij lib ane uthir blak crukit mair
15. of four yeir auld pryce xiij lib vj s viij d Item tua tua yeir auld
16. staigis pryce of the peice vj lib xiij s iiij d inde xiij lib vj s viij d Item
17. v newcalfitt ky quherof three ky pryce of the peice overhead xij lib Inde
18. xxxvjlib And the uthir twa ky of aucht yeir auld is pryce of the
19. peice xiij lib vj s viij d Inde xxvj lib xiij s iiij d Item thrie yeld ky
20. Quherof ane auld kow of xv yeir auld without milk or calff price x lib ane
21. uthir in Jon Malcumis possession in ganzeochin price x lib Item the
22. uther yeld kow in the possession of Jon gentilman in Raharnis pryce
23. x lib Item twa quoyis the ane ther of foir yeir auld the uther thrie yeir
24. pryce of the peice overheid vj lib xiij s iiij d Inde xiij lib vj s viij d
25. Item in the possessiounr of Jon Neilson in over ardoch three quoyis the
26. ane of four yeir auld the uther tua thrie yeir auld is pryce of the
27. peice overhead vj lib xiij s iiij d Inde xx lib Item tua drawin oxin
28. the ane xij yeir auld pryce x lib the uther viij yeir auld pryce xiij
29. lib vj s viij d Item ane Lytill stott of twa yeir auld owtgane
30. pryce vj lib xiij s iiij d Item ten yowis with nyne lambis pryce of
31. the peice with the lambis xL s Inde xx lib Item vj auld hoggis
32. pryce of the peice xx s Inde vj lib Item in the barne & barne
33. yaird the tyme of hir deceis foirsaid thrie rukkis of small aits
34. ilk ruk estimat to v bolls aittis with the foddir inde xv bolls aitis
35. with the foddir pryce of the boll with the foddir xL s inde xxx lib Item
36. ane Lytill ruk of beir estmat onlie to twa bolls beir pryce
37. of the boll with the fodir v lib Inde x lib Item the insicht & plein
38. ishing of the hous estimat to x lib
39. Summa of the Inventar ij ᶜ iiij ˣˣ xj lib 13s 4d
40. Na debtis awand to the defunct
41. Followis the dettis awand be the said
42. Andro the tyme foirsaid
43. Item in the first to henrie struiling of ardoch his master of _____
44. plennishing seid resavit upon the ground of thair occupatione ij cha
45. lder seid aitis pryce of the boll xxxvj s viij d Inde Lviij lib 13s 4d
46. Item ane boll seid beir pryce vj s upra v lib Item awand
47. to him of plennishing oxen being four drawin oxen pryce of the
48. peice xx lib inde iiij ˣˣ lib Item twa pleuch hors pryce of
49. the peice xxxiij lib vj s viij d inde iij ˣˣ vj lib xiij s iiij d Item
50. pleuch and pleuch irins awand to them pryce viij lib Item awand
51. to Andro tailzeor in rathine ij bolls seid beir cost fra him at beltane
52. Last pryce of the boll v lib vj s viij d inde x lib xiijs iiij d Item
53. to Jon gentilman in Raharnis for the vintering of v young heid
54. of quoyis & stottis vj lib xiij s iiij d Item to donald hempseid
55. servand for his fie viij lib Item to helener dow of fie xL s Item
56. to thomas andersone of fie iiij lib
57. Summa of the dettis ij ᶜ xLix lib xiij s iiij d
58. Summa of the frie geir debtis being
59. deducit extendis to ij ˣˣ ij lib
60. Quhich being devydit in twa pairts
61. Deadis pairt is xxj lib

Quota xxj s

62. Legacie
63. At Ardoch the xiiij of January 1611 Befoir thir witnesses andro
64. tailzeor in Raterine henrie tailzeor his sone Thomas Cambell in
65. Dunblaine Alex gallowa in Ardoche Jon Malcum in gannachane
66. Jonat hempseid spous to andro faichney seik in body nominatis the said
67. andro hir husband hir onlie executor & intromettor with hir guids & geir
68. With power to him to giff inventar therof als weill of debtis awand
69. to hir as be hir to utheris Item scho leavis hir saull to god and hir
70. body to be bureit in the buriall plaice of the parochiners of muthill
71. Item scho leavis to Issobell neilsone hir half sister hir haill abulze
72. mentis of hir body mair to hir ane rigit quoy Item scho leavis to
73. Jon Neilsone hir half brother ane spangit blak quoy To Jonat Neil
74. hir sisters dochter ane yow and ane lamb with ane quhyit skuring
75. velicoit and the rest of hir haill geir to hir husband Hir debtis
76. being payit Seing thair is na bairins & secluding all utheris heaw
77. eand entres therto Sic Subscribitur N Neven N.P.in premissis
78. Alex galloway witnes Thomas Cambell witnes
79. Confirmatio
80. I Johne Sinclair Commissar of Dunblane Be the tennor heirof
81. Ratifies approwes and confermis this present testament testamentar
82. latter will and Inventar in sa far as the samyn is Justlie maid and
83. geavin wp And als confermes the said andro faichnay husband to
84. the said defunct hir onlie executor testamentar with power to him to intromett with hir guids &
geir To
85. outredd debtis to creditors and to do haunt use and excerce all
86. thingis theranent quhatsumeurer perteinis to executoris testamentaris to
87. do in the lyk caiss Provyding he rander compt of his intromiss
88. ione as efferis and hes maid faith on the said Inventar &
89. debts ar leallalie and trewlie geavin up na thing omittit
90. furth of the samyn nor sett within the just availl therin contenit
91. and hes fundin henrie striuiling of ardoch cautioner that the sa
92. myn salbe furthcumand to all pairties haweand entres therto
93. as law will In:Att Dunblane the second day of July 1611

Cautioner   Henrie Striuiling of Ardoche

Translation

1–9 [*Introductory clause*] Andrew Faichney in Nether Ardoche is spouse to Jonat Hempseid who died in February 1611, with Andrew nominated executor dative 14 January that year

10–38 [*Inventar*] Andrew has the goods and gear of the values given:
Item one – four mares: one gray mare of 14 years £10, one brown mare of 12 years £10 one other gray mare of 15 years £12 one other black crooked mare of four years £13 6s 8d
Item – two year-old staigs [colts] each £6 13s 4d inde [together] £13 6s 8d
Item – five newly-calfed ky [cows] whereof three ky at Overhead [average] £12 Inde £36 and the other two ky of eight years old each £13 6s 8d Inde £26 13s 4d
Item – three yeld ky [barren or non-pregnant cows] whereof one old cow of 15 years without milk or calf £10; one other in John Malcum's possession in Ganyeochin price £10; Item the other yeld cow in the possession of John Gentleman in Raharnis price £10

Item – two quoys [heifers] one of four years the other three years each £6 13s 4d Inde £13 6s 8d

Item – in the possession of Jon Neilson in Over Ardoch three quoys one of four years the other two three years old each £6 13s 4d Inde £20

Item – two drawing oxen one 12 years old price £10 the other eight years old pryce £13 6s 8d

Item – one little stott [bullock or young ox] of two years auld owtgane [past] price £6 13s 4d

Item – ten yowis [ewes] with nine lambs price each with the lambs 40s Inde £20

Item – six old hogs each 20s Inde £6

Item – in the barn & barn yard the time of her decease foresaid three rukkis [ricks] of small aits [oats] each ruk estimate to five bolls oats with the fodder inde 15 bolls oats with the fodder price of the boll with the fodder 40s inde £30

Item – one little ruk of beir [barley] estmate only to two bolls beir price of the boll with the fodder £5 Inde £10

Item – the insight & plenishing [furnishings] of the house estimate to £10

39 Summa of the Inventar £291 13s 4d

40 No debts owing to the defunct [deceased]

41–56 Follows the debts owing by the said Andrew the time foresaid

Item – in the first to Henry Stirling of Ardoch his Master of _____ plenishing seed received upon the ground of their occupation two chalders [1 chalder = 16 bolls] seed oats price of the boll 36s 8d Inde £58 13s 4d

Item – one boll seed beir price 6s upra [updraw, value when harvested] £5

Item – owing to him of plenishing oxen being four drawing oxen price each £20 inde £80

Item two pleuch [plough] horse price each £33 6s 8d inde £66 lib 13s 4d

Item – pleuch and pleuch irons owing to them price £8

Item owing Andrew Tailyeor [Taylor] in Rathine two bolls seed beir cost from him at Beltane [1st May, the beginning of the summer pastoral season] last price per boll £5 6s 8d inde £10 13s 4d

Item – to John Gentleman in Raharnis for the wintering of five young head of quoys & stotts £6 13s 4d

Item – to Donald Hempseid servand for his fee [in other words, a hired agricultural labourer] £8

Item – to Helen Dow fee 40s

Item – to Thomas Anderson fee £4

57 Summa of the debts £249 13s 4d

58 Summa of the free gear debts being

59 deducted extends to £42

60 Which being divided in two parts

61 Dead's part is £21 [this is what Jonet could will]

Quotta 21s

62–78 Legacie [the will clause]

At Ardoch the 14 of January 1611 Before these witnesses Andrew Taylor in Raterine, Henry Taylor his son, Thomas Cambpell in Dunblane, Alex Galloway in Ardoch, Jon Malcolm in Gannachane,

Jonet Hempseid spouse to Andrew Faichney sick in body nominates the said Andrew her husband her only executor & intromettor with her goods & gear With power to him to give inventar thereof as well of debts owing to her as by her to others

Item – she leaves her soul to god and her body to be buried in the burial place of the parishioners of Muthill

Item – she leaves to Isobell Neilson her half sister her whole abulyementis of her body [personal possessions] more to her one rigit quoy [has a coloured streak on its back]

Item – she leaves to John Neilson her half brother one spangit black quoy [literally, 'spangled', presumably meaning spotted]; To Jonat Neil her sister's daughter one ewe and one lamb with one white

skuring velicoit [cleaning coat] and the rest of her whole gear to her husband Her debts being payed
Seeing there are no children & excluding all others having interest thereto
Sic Subscribitur [here subscribed] N Neven N.P. [Notary Public] in premises [in the sense of things mentioned before]
Alex Galloway witness Thomas Campbell witness

79–93 Confirmation [*final clause*]
I John Sinclair Commissar of Dunblane By the tenor hereof ratifies approves and confirms this present testament testamentar latter will and Inventar in so far as the same is Justly made and given up And also confirms the said Andrew Faichney husband to the said defunct her only executor testamentar with power to him to intromett [deal] with her goods & gear To outredd [settle] debts to creditors and to do haunt use and exercise all things theranent [about these] whatsoever pertains to executors testamentars to do in the like case Providing he render compt [provides accounts] of his intromission as effeirs [concerns] and has made faith on the said Inventar & debts are leallalie [loyally, faithfully] and truly given up nothing omitted furth [left out] of the same nor set within the just availl [value] theerin contained and has found Henry Stirling of Ardoch cautioner [guarantor] that the same shall be forthcoming to all parties having interest thertoe as law will In: At Dunblane the second day of July 1611
Cautioner   Henry Stirling of Ardoch

Notes:
- L. 39, 48: note the use of 'score' counting (iiij ^{xx} = 4 x 20 = 80 etc.). See Chapter 4 for more detail on numbers and money.
- Place names: Ardoch is a civil parish in Perth, nowadays Perth and Kinross, and the others (Rathine, Raterine, Gannachane, Muthill etc.) are place names or names of farms.
- Names have been modernised (Andrew, Henry, John, Campbell, Faichney, Gentleman, Malcolm, Taylor) and 'Striuiling' is given in its modern form: Stirling.
- Notice that most of the people named are 'in' a place (i.e. tenants) whereas Henry Stirling 'of' Ardoch has heritable possession and is 'Master' (feudal superior, loosely 'landlord'). This is Sir Henry Stirling, Baronet, and a major landholder in the area. (See Chapter 13, Retours, for more detail).
- This document is more of a genealogist's dream than most of this type. Jonet Hempseid is married to Andrew Faichney, has a half sister Isobell Neilson, half brother John Neilson, a niece (her sister's daughter) Jonat Neil and no children. We also get the name of at least one other likely relative (hired hand Donald Hempseid).
- Jonet and Andrew had at least 4 mares, 2 colts, 8 cows, 5 heifers, 2 drawing oxen, 1 bullock, 10 ewes, 9 lambs, 6 hogs, 2 plough-horses and crops and other possessions worth £10. The total value of her goods and gear was £291 13s 4d but debts of £249 13s 4d leaving £42 of which Andrew has a claim to half as the *jus relicti* and he will end up the rest (the 'deid's pairt') less the items Jonet has willed to others.

Transfer of heritage (land and buildings)

As mentioned above, before 1868, wills could only transfer moveable property. Land and buildings could be inherited by the separate process of Retours of Services of Heirs (Chapter 13) or by a trust disposition and settlement (Chapter 11). From 1868 to 1964 both moveable and heritable property could be transferred by a will. Always check both testamentary records and retours. From 1964, most property was inherited through wills.

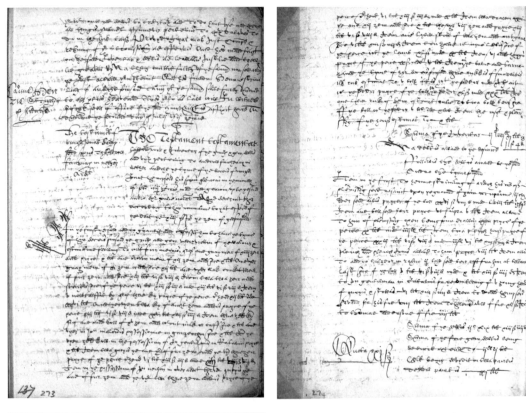

Testament testementar and inventar of Jonet Hempseid, 1611, spouse to Andrew Faichenay. Nether Ardoch, Dunblane Commissary Court (CC6/5/3). *Reproduced by kind permission of The National Records of Scotland*

Trust dispositions and settlements

See Chapter 11 for more detail. The trust disposition let an individual specify the transfer of landed property to his named heirs. In effect, the ownership of the property was transferred to a group of named trustees by a deed of trust disposition. The granter retained certain powers and the more or less complete use of and control over the property. Normally the deed was recorded only after the death of the granter and often included a settlement of succession to the granter's moveables. As these documents did not have to be registered to have validity, and could be registered in a number of places, they can be hard to track down. A major landowner would probably use the register of deeds of the Court of Session in Edinburgh and most others would record the disposition in the register of deeds of the local commissary court (up to 1809), the local sheriff court or the appropriate royal burgh. After 1868 inheritance was by conventional will.

Unclaimed estates and chancery

England has a Chancery system where unclaimed estates can be held until claimed. There is no Scottish Chancery system of that kind: if the beneficiary of a will cannot be found, the property is reported as *bona vacantia* to the king's (or queen's) and the lord treasurer's remembrancer (nowadays, the Crown Office), and is sold off and the cash held until a claimant appears.

If an individual dies intestate and without known heirs, the property falls to the Crown as *ultimus haeres* ('the last heir'), and is advertised and sold. After a decent interval it becomes 'the Crown's share'. There are records of *bona vacantia* and *ultimus haeres* in the series of exchequer records at the NRS, and these are dealt with by the Crown Office in Edinburgh. Newer unclaimed estates (*Bona Vacantia*, *Ultimus Haeres* and Treasure Trove) are advertised every three months, and there is a dedicated National Ultimus Haeres Unit based in Glasgow (see www.qltr.gov.uk).

Further Reading

Durie, B., *Scottish Genealogy*, 3rd edn (The History Press, 2012)

11

Scotland: Trust Dispositions and Settlements

As discussed in Chapters 10 and 13, immoveable property was conveyed by means of a retour and moveable property by a testament (with or without a will or 'legacie' clause). Because of the rules regarding disposition (heritage to the eldest son by primogeniture, or to heirs portioners, moveables divided in a certain way) it was often impossible to determine succession. For instance, the testator may have wanted to give the land to a second son and carve up all of the moveable estate equally between grandchildren, bypassing everyone else.

The only way not to have property distributed as the law directed was not to own anything at the point of death, and the way to ensure that was to put everything in trust. At its simplest, the trustor (sometimes also called the creator, granter, donor or settlor) draws up a deed that transfers ownership of the land (or the whole estate) to a group of named individuals (trustees), who then have certain rights and responsibilities. Among these might be the right to run the farm, business etc. for the benefit of the survivors, who may themselves be the trustees, or to distribute it after the testator's death in a particular way (a portion to John, a portion to Janet, nothing to James until he behaves etc.) or to sell it all and divide up the proceeds in a certain way.

However, that leaves the trustor with nothing of his or her own before death – or does it? The granter could, for example, retain the 'liferent' of property (the right to live in the house, spend the income and in all ways enjoy the benefits of the property as if still in full ownership) until death. The trust deed might also give liferent to the eventual widow, or to an unmarried daughter until her marriage, or to two younger children equally or some other formula. This had the effect that the granter was still in complete control until called to his or her reward.

That's the trust element. It may have been recorded (in the Register of Deeds, for instance) before death but quite commonly was not registered until after the death of the granter. This registration would then include the details of the settlement of the succession to the moveable property. Together, the document would then be known as a trust disposition and settlement (TD&S or TDS).

A TDS might also lay down rules about the inheritance of name and arms, including an entail so that only someone bearing the family surname could inherit, requiring anyone who married an heiress to take the name, compelling direct heirs to matriculate and use the coat of arms and so forth.

FAMILY TRUSTS AND SEDERUNT BOOKS

Family trusts might be in place because of a sequestration or bankruptcy, a marriage contract or an entail, or from the need to have an estate administered while the granter was overseas, subject to some incapacity (such as minority), too young to inherit fully, or suffered from mental incapacity or long-term illness. Most commonly, these (almost 90 per cent) arise from executry as described above, and are intended to direct the disposition and settlement of assets after death and sometimes down through the succeeding generations.

These would almost certainly be administered by a solicitor, and recorded in individual minute books, also called sederunt books. They can be an absolute gold mine for genealogists and local historians, as the trust may have run for a number of generations and will usually contain handwritten minutes of trust meetings, copies of accounts, letters and other legal documents (such as challenges to aspects of the trust in court). It is a welcome feature of Scottish legal practice that quite often every detail and document was transcribed into sequential bound volumes and indexed, rather than consisting of a chaotic bundle of documents tied up with the familiar red tape. Long-established legal firms may still hold a great many of these sederunt books, but not always: they may have been destroyed after the trust was wound up, passed back to the family or – in the best-case scenario from the researcher's perspective – lodged with an archive. Quite often though, because of the merging of solicitors into large firms, the collective memory of the individual component firms has been lost and it can be a detective job in its own right to find the successor firm and discover whether it has even kept the original archives or, if not, where they have gone. Approaching law firms with a request to look for such items may result in a 'what's in it for us' response, especially if the trust is wound up.

A sederunt book usually begins with a recitation by transcript of the original trust disposition and settlement. This will encapsulate the wishes of the trust's creator, in terms of which members of his family and friends will be the trustees and executors and, if necessary, the tutors or curators of any minors. It will lay out their powers and responsibilities and conveyance to the trust the property, both heritable and moveable, to take effect from death. If the purpose of the trust is to provide income for the widow/widower and any children, especially unmarried daughters, sons under 21, maiden sisters and aunts, this will be laid out in detail.

The trust document will probably end with a general power to the granter to revoke any disposition at any time during the remainder of life, to alter it by codicil and to retain the liferent. Any amendments will be transcribed into the sederunt book. Added to this, in time, will be a note of death (possibly with a certificate or its transcript) and the trustees' agreements to act as directed. There will be a full inventory and valuation of the estate (which will often be a separate document, as required for confirmation and executry) and may contain a very detailed listing of abulyements (p. 158), house contents (including pictures and books), bank accounts, shares held, rented property, crops growing in fields for later harvest and so on.

From thereon in, the books will largely consist of minutes of trustees' meetings, accounts, copies of correspondence and any other legal documents generated (such as legal challenges to the trust or some aspect of the settlement) and the eventual winding-up. Trusts may be short term – wound up after all children are 21, the youngest daughter marries, the relict dies or simply after a stated period of so many years – but they can roll on for up to a century and involve the children of the children of the children, not to mention a much later generation of lawyers and accountants.

Value to historians

Contrary to expectation, not only the great, the good and the landed left TDSs. For genealogists, biographers, historians of place, time and professions, and even architecture and fine arts researchers, they offer a fascinating microscope down which to examine the middle classes of the Victorian period, when so many self-made businesspersons and entrepreneurs came into their own.

Small businesses and shopkeepers figure, particularly when they wanted to ensure that their shop remained and was run by the one child who showed an interest (rather than sold to provide a distributed settlement), or that it would guarantee a home and income for their wife. These give details of their assets, perhaps including their businesses, if they were still in business when they died; the inventories are of interest for the material culture of their homes and daily lives.

Especially valued by social historians, trusts were often set up by unmarried and childless women who owned property in their own right and wanted to make sure it was inherited in a certain way: by nieces only, used for an endowment, distributed to certain charities and so on.

Where to find TDSs and sederunt books

Sadly, these were not always registered or recorded – they did not need to be in order to be valid – and could be held in a number of places, including simply with a lawyer (see p. 167). This makes finding such documents problematic. Large estates (such as those of a large landowner, a wealthy individual or a business owner) may well be recorded in the Register of Deeds of the Court of Session. Otherwise, the documents may be in the Register of Deeds of the local sheriff court, of the local commissary court (up to about the period from 1809 to the early 1820s) or the local royal burgh. All will require checking.

Sederunt books are mostly found in the 100 years after 1820, as changes in the law of executry eventually made the TDS mechanism unnecessary. They may still be in the records of old family-law firms, but may have been deposited in archives, in which case they will be calendered and possibly indexed, very likely online. The National Records of Scotland and the Glasgow City Archives are the largest of these, but do not ignore county, sheriff court and burgh records. Occasionally, they are bequeathed to a university or specialist private archive, particularly when the creator was a person of some note, made a major bequest to an organisation such as a library or operated in a particular business sector.

Online

Start at ScotlandsPeople (SP), where they are treated along with wills and testaments, and do not forget to look for accessory documents such as an inventory or an *eik* (a kind of inventory codicil giving the executor or trustees title to additional estate, such as when an extra bank account is discovered).

For example, searching online at ScotlandsPeople under 'Wills & Testaments' – without surname, and putting 'DISPOSITION' in the 'Description' box – gives a number of returns, including this one: at forty-nine pages, this will be a good bedtime read:

No	Surname	Forename	Date	Description	Type	Court	Reference	Image
1	BELL	ALEXANDER	23/02/1844	ESQ, OF NORTH NEWTON, RESIDING IN FALKIRK, SPOUSE OF ISABELLA CAMPBELL	INVENTORY; 2ND EXTRACT TRUST DISPOSITION AND SETTLEMENT; EXTRACT CONTRACT OF	STIRLING SHERIFF COURT	SC67/36/23	View (10 Credits) (49 pages)

NAS/NRS: a search at http://www.nas.gov.uk/onlineCatalogue/ using the keywords TRUST DISPOSITION SETTLEMENT produced almost 3,000 hits. I refined it by adding DURIE, which reduced it to two.

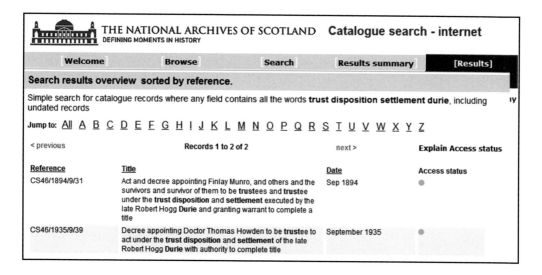

This looks very interesting, as a trust established in the 1890s was clearly still going strong in 1935. The Reference CS shows it is a Court of Session record (in fact, Warrants of Register of Acts and Decreets). One of the earliest TDSs on record is by William Govan of Spitle of Balturick in favour of John and Archibald, his sons, dated 13 February 1727 (GD47/271) and there is a trust sederunt book, 1741–51, relating to Robert Bull, merchant, Edinburgh and a trust set up for behoof of various creditors, also all Edinburgh merchants.

NRAS: a similar search at the National Register of Archives for Scotland (www.nas.gov.uk/nras), but starting the search at www.nas.gov.uk/onlineRegister shows, for example, that Glasgow Archives has the records of Newlands and Walker, Solicitors, Glasgow, from 1714–1956, including 'Sederunt and other books of trust etc. for clients, 1843–1956' (NRAS396/162).

SCAN: www.scan.org.uk/catalogue shows, for example, that the University of Aberdeen Special Libraries and Archives holds miscellaneous local trust minute books and one solicitor's registry index (GB231/MS 3765).

NLS: the 'Guide to Manuscripts' contains details of the collections, the Named Manuscripts index (http://www.nls.uk/catalogues/online/cnmi/index.cfm) and details of collections of solicitors' papers are available online as downloadable PDF files. These are not the documents themselves: it will be necessary to order a copy of the actual document, or visit to view (see below).

Local courts and local archives: for example, a search for the keywords '+SEDERUNT +TRUST' at Falkirk Council Museum and Archive (http://collections.falkirk.gov.uk) came up with twelve results, the first few of which are shown on p. 166. Most refer to trusts. The database tells us that the Alexander Bell Trust was set up in 1835, enacted after his death in 1842, with trustees Revd William Welsh, (minister Falkirk Relief church), James McLaren (merchant, Edinburgh), James Russel and Henry Aitken.

Sometimes indexes have been transcribed and published as booklets by local family-history societies or online. One example would be the Sheriff Court of Fife Deeds, 1715–1809 at www.fifefhs.org/Records/Court/fife.htm (Deed Registers, SC20/33) one of which reads:

ADIE, JOHN snr: merchant in Dunfermline; Bond in life-rent in favour of spouse, Ann Walker, dau of dec Robert Walker, late Bailie of Dunfermline, 27 Aug 1778; also Assig to dau, Ann Adie (whom failing to son, David Adie, yst dau, Mgt Adie, & 2nd dau, Catherine Adie), + Declaration of Trust, + Disp in favour of only son, David Adie, all 27 Sep 1778 [SC20/36/13]

And that may be all the researcher needs to know.

Gazettes: it is worth checking the London, Edinburgh and Belfast gazettes (start at www. london-gazette.co.uk) for notices of trusts. For example:

MARGERY YAPP WINNALL, Deceased.

Pursuant to the Act 22nd and 23rd of Victoria, cap. 35, intituled "An Act to further amend the Law of Property and to relieve Trustees."

NOTICE is hereby given, that the creditors and all persons having any claims against the estate of Margery Yapp Winnall, late of Burton, in the parish of Linton, in the county of Hereford, Widow, deceased (who died on the 2nd day of June, 1860, and whose will was proved on the 31st day of August, 1860, by William Stallard, of the parish of Brockhampton, in the said county of Hereford, Gentleman, the sole executor therein named), are hereby required to send to the said William Stallard, or to me, as his Solicitor, on or before the 2nd day of December next, their claims against the estate of the said Margery Yapp Winnall, deceased, and that at the expiration of such last-mentioned time, the said William Stallard will proceed to distribute the assets of the said Margery Yapp Winnall, deceased, amongst the parties entitled thereto, having regard to the claims of which he shall then have had notice, and that he will not be liable for any claim of which notice shall not have been given.—Dated this 10th day of October, 1860.

London Gazette, Issue 22436, 19 October 1860, p. 24.

TNA (England): The National Archives has many Scottish-related documents. A search brought up 'Mss Eur F206/69 1832–61, Copy and Abstract Trust Disposition and Settlement by Macnabb 1832, 1842, 1848; copy of Marriage Settlement of Sophia Adelaide Macnabb and Henry Hugh Macneile 1859; executry papers of James Munro Macnabb' (actually held at the British Library, Asia, Pacific and Africa Collections).

In person

Glasgow: the Glasgow Archives are searchable by surname in the computerised catalogue database and the Search Room card file index.

NAS/NRS: because the catalogues to collections of lawyers' papers have not all been added to the searchable database (either online or in the database on-site) it may be necessary to ask the helpful Search-Room staff.

Some examples from the NRS database

GD139/78

1. 1768, February –.
Scroll trust disposition and settlement by Janet Sutherland [relict of George Sinclair, 3rd of Brabster] in favour of her grandchildren Alexandrina and George Sutherland, children of Capt. Robert Sutherland of Langwall and Brabster and Ann Sinclair, daughter of Janet.

2. 1768, March 11.
Trust disposition and settlement (cancelled) by Jannet Sutherland in favour of Capt. Robert Sutherland, whom failing Mrs Ann Sinclair.

3. 1772, January 25.
Disposition and settlement (cancelled) by Mrs Janet Sutherland in favour of Anna Sinclair, her only surviving child, exclusive of Robert Sutherland and his *jus mariti*.

5. 774, July 28.
Disposition and settlement (cancelled) by Mrs Jannet Sutherland in favour of Anna Sinclair, exclusive of Robert Sutherland and his *jus mariti*.

NLS: check the 'Guide to Manuscripts' at the National Library of Scotland website first, then visit. It may be necessary to consult the published *Catalogue of Manuscripts Acquired Since 1925*, vols I–VIII.

Tracking down lawyers: three bodies may be able to help identify lawyers and their successors. The Society of Writers to Her Majesty's Signet (WS Society) was established in 1594 and maintains the Signet Library (www.thewssociety.co.uk). The Royal Faculty of Procurators in Glasgow (www.rfpg.org) dates from some time before 1668. The Law Society of Scotland has been in existence since 1949 (www.lawscot.org.uk).

Did it work?

Of course, all of this put a considerable amount of power in the hands of the trustor: it was a good idea to keep Great-Uncle Willie sweet in case you were dropped from the settlement. But if Great-Uncle Willie's intention was to simplify matters on his demise, it often didn't: legal challenges over last-minute changes, accusations of unsoundness of mind, late marriages to a much younger spouse, the appearance of a previously unacknowledged child or a long-lost brother, unhappiness with the way trustees were conducting the business: all of these are the stuff of detective novels and movies, but they certainly happened in real life. The Bannerman TDS is a good example.

The Bannerman case

Walter Bannerman (1806–79) was a wealthy Glasgow businessman – he is usually described as a 'wright' (carpenter) but he made a fortune out of property development and ownership – and was a city councillor, an important member of various Incorporated Trades of Glasgow (essentially social and charitable organisations by this time) and a philanthropist. There are two relevant documents of executry relating to his death and property:

Inventory of Walter Bannerman, Wright and Builder, Glasgow, who died 7 August 1879, in the Glasgow Sheriff Court Inventories, dated 13 January 1880 (SC36/48/90).
Trust Disposition and Settlement (but indexed as a will) of the same Walter Bannerman, also dated 13 January 1880 at Glasgow, Glasgow Sheriff Court (SC36/51/78).

The handwriting in these documents is not challenging as the small sample shows, so this isn't a palaeographic exercise. A transcription of the TDS is given below.

This document has been transcribed exactly as written, without punctuation and using the original capitalisations and lines, except that line-end hyphenations have been concatenated and the occasional missed word inserted. Insertions and expansions are in [square brackets]. The page numbers are those of the folios in the original sederunt book. Explanatory notes are referenced in brackets, e.g. (a) because of the infuriating Scottish practice of naming children after their parents, aunts and uncles, and of marrying people with the same first names as their relatives, it will help to refer to the Bannerman family tree on p. 178.

[page 742]

1st January 1880
I Walter Bannerman residing at Cawder House Bishopbriggs do hereby
in order to regulate the succession to my means and estate after my death
Give Assign and Dispone to and in favour of Robert Bannerman my son
residing at number Nineteen Newton Street Glasgow Walter Bannerman
junior my son residing with me Jesse Bannerman my daughter residing
with me *(a)* Robert Robinson Partick Saw Mills Partick John Hunter
residing at number thirty Elmbank Crescent Glasgow William Miller of
Eastwoodhill by Thornliebank George Munsie Yarn Merchant Glasgow
and David Bannerman Grain Merchant there and such other person or
persons as may hereafter be nominated by me or as may be assumed

*(a) There is a
Bannerman family tree
(p. 178) and a discussion
of its implications below.*

[page 743]

into the trust hereby created and the acceptors and acceptor and survivors
and survivor of them the major number of those who accept and survive
and are resident in Great Britain from time to time being a quorum and
the heir of the last survivor as Trustees and Trustee for the ends uses and
purposes after written the whole means and estate heritable and moveable
real and personal wherever situated that shall belong to at my death
with the writs and vouchers thereof and I appoint my Trustees to be my
Executors and Executor But these presents are granted in Trust always for
the ends uses and purposes following viz^{li} [*videlicet*] First For payment of
all my just and lawful debts Second I direct my Trustees to allow to my
daughter Jessie the liferent *(b)* use of my whole household furniture and
plenishing including therein silver plate bed and table linen books and
pictures so long as she remains unmarried with power to her to give or
to bequeath such part or parts thereof to my said Sons or either of them
as their absolute property as she may think proper & upon her death or
marriage whichever event may first happen my Trustees shall divide and
apportion the remainder of said furniture (including as aforesaid) among
my whole children equally or the survivors or survivor of them according
to a valuation to be put thereon by a neutral party to be appointed by my
Trustees Third I direct my Trustees to allow my daughter the use of my
house in Jane Street Blythswood Square

*(b) Liferent is the
right to live in and/
or enjoy the fruits of a
property but short of
actual ownership and
without using up its
substance.*

[page 744]

so long as she remains unmarried and so long as my Trustees may retain the
property unsold and that at a rent of Ninety pounds per annum payable
half yearly as usual Fourth I direct my Trustees to pay and fulfil any legacies
or instructions which I may specify in any Codicil hereto or in any separate
writing under my hand although such Codicil or Writing may not be
formally executed Fifth I direct my Trustees to pay to my Sister Many
Bannerman residing at Garscadden Street Glasgow an annuity of Thirty

five pounds Sterling during her life and to my Sister in law Margaret Gow
residing at Greatdovehill Gallowgate an annuity of Twenty pounds Sterling
during her life both of said annuities being free of Government Duty and
being payable quarterly at the terms of Candlemas Whitsunday Lammas
and Martinmas in each year *(c)* the first payment being made at the first
of these terms which shall occur after my death for the period preceding
My Trustees shall also allow the said Mary Bannerman to occupy during
her life free of rent the house occupied by her at present Sixth I direct
my Trustees to make payment to Miss Janet Miller residing at Springhill
Cottage Bishopbriggs for behoof of Jessie Ure her aunt residing there an
annuity of Fifteen pounds a year during the life of the said Jessie Ure and
free of legacy duty And to be paid half yearly commencing at the first term
of Whitsunday or Martinmas after my death for the period thereto from
the date of my death Seventh

(c) For terms etc. see Chapter 3.

[page 745]

I recommend my trustees to retain my farm properties in their hands for a
period of twenty years after my death but if they should decide upon selling
said properties or any of them I should like sons or either of them to have
the option of purchasing the same at the price or prices which may be
offered by others therefor Eighth I direct my Trustees to divide and pay the
free annual produce and rents at the time of my Estate to and among my
children during their respective lives in the following proportions namely
three eighth parts of such produce and rents to my Son Robert Bannerman
three eighth parts thereof to my Son Walter Bannerman junior and the
remaining two eighth parts to my daughter Jessie Bannerman and that at
such terms in each year as my Trustees may think proper Ninth I direct my
Trustees to pay and convey to and for behoof of the issue of each of my
said children the fee *(d)* of the respective shares of my Estate directed to be
liferented by their parents respectively and that in such proportions at such
time or times and subject to such conditions as my children respectively may
redirect by a Writing under his or her hand and failing such writing in the
case of any of my children then my Trustees shall pay and convey the fee of
the share of such child equally to and among his or her issue or the survivors
of them upon their respectively completing the age of twenty five years until
which period the Trustees shall apply the annual income of such shares for

(d) Fee: the right to an interest in a heritable property (essentially, ownership) which may be held separate to the liferent (see above).

[page 746]

the general maintenance and education of such issue Tenth in the event of
one of my children dying (whether before or after my death) without leaving
issue who survive the term of payment of their shares I direct my Trustees
to hold pay and convey the share before provided to such child deceasing
and his or her issue in two equal parts and to pay the annual income of one
of such parts to each of my other two children if in life and the fee thereof
to his or her issue in the same manner and subject to the same conditions in

all respects as is before provided in regard to the shares originally destined to my children and their issue Eleventh In the event of two of my children dying (whether before or after my death) without leaving issue who survive the term of payment of their shares I direct my Trustees to hold pay and convey the whole residue of my Estate to and for behoof *(e)* of my other child (if he or she be then surviving) in liferent and to his or her issue in fee in the same manner and subject same conditions in all respects as is before provided with regard to the shares of my Estate originally destined to my children and their issue respectively Twelfth Should the survivor of my children die without leaving issue who survive the term of payment of their shares (but survived by issue of my other children or one of them) my Trustees shall pay and convey one half of the fee of the portion of my Estate liferented by such survivor to and among the issue of my other child or children in such way and manner and in such

(e) Behoof (advantage, benefit).

[page 747]

proportions and subject to such conditions as such survivor may have directed by any Deed or Writing under his or her hand and failing such Writing then equally between the families of my other children (the share of each family in such case being divided equally among the members thereof) or if one only shall leave issue then to such issue equally among them And with regard to the other half of the fee liferented by the survivor I hereby declare that he or she shall have full power by any Mortis causa *(f)* Deed or Writing by him or her to dispose of the same and direct the succession thereto in favour either of Religious or Charitable Institutions one or more conducted according to Protestant Principles or of any person or persons whom such survivor may appoint or partly in favor of such Institution or Institutions and partly in favor *(g)* of such person or persons all in such terms & subject to such conditions and directions as such survivor may think proper But should the survivor not exercise the foregoing power of disposal then the said one half of the fee or any portion thereof not disposed of in virtue of the foregoing power shall be divided equally among the issue of my other children by families Thirteenth Notwithstanding what is before written I hereby declare that should any of my children leave a husband or wife surviving her or him it shall be in the power of such child to direct my Trustees to pay such husband or wife subject to such limitations and conditions as

(f) Mortis causa – literally 'in contemplation of death', such as a will or bequest.
(g) Notice the Scottish spelling of the word 'favor'.

[page 748]

he or she may think right any portion not exceeding one fourth part of the annual income of the share originally liferented by such deceasing child or children and I direct Trustees to give effect to any such instructions by any of my children Fourteenth I hereby direct and provide that in the event of the decease of all my direct descendents before the arrival of the period of payment of their shares my Trustees shall pay and convey the residue of my Estate (subject to all rights of liferent destinations directions burdens and restrictions which may have been imposed thereon in virtue of the powers conferred by me) in such a way and manner and to such person or persons as the last survivor of my said children may have directed by any mortis causa Deed or Writing which may have been executed by him or her And I hereby confer on such survivors power of disposal of said Residue to take effect in the event above provided And failing such Deed or Writing then after giving effect to any disposal of one half of the Estate liferented by the survivor or part thereof under the power before conferred my Trustees shall pay and convey said Residue to and equally among the families of my brothers (the share of each family being divided equally among the members thereof) And I hereby declare that in the event of any of the beneficiaries under these presents presumptively entitled to any share of the fee of my Estate predeceasing the term of payment of their shares and leaving issue such issue shall succeed equally among them to the share which their

[page 749]

parent would have taken had he or she survived and I declare that all powers of disposal direction and division herein contained may be exercised by the parties entitled to exercise the same either by special Deeds or Writings or by General Disposition and Settlement or partly by both ways And I explain that any sums which I may have already paid to my son Robert and my daughter Jessie were so paid in terms of an arrangement made between my late wife Mary Miller and me considering that my son Walter was to succeed to her Estate And such payments so made by me to my said son Robert and my daughter Jessie shall therefore not be reckoned or imputed to account of the provisions hereby made in their favor but as in addition thereto And I hereby declare that all provisions which under these presents or under any Codicil hereto are conceived in favor of or may descend to females shall be exclusive of the jus mariti *(h)* and right of administration of any husband to whom they then are or may be subsequently married and that all provisions out of income shall be held to be purely alimentary and not assignable by nor liable for the debts or deeds of the respective recipients and I further declare that the foregoing provisions to my children shall be held and taken as in full satisfaction to them of their legitim *(i)* and of all claims legally competent to them on my Estate at my death And in addition to all powers privileges and immunities conferred

(h) jus mariti: the right of a husband, in this case the right to absolutely own the property of his wife; see p. 143.

(i) legitim: the inheritance among all children of a share in the moveable property.

[page 750]

and to be conferred on gratuitous Trustees by statute and at Common Law I hereby empower my Trustees if they see fit to sell the whole or any part of the Trust Estate by public Roup *(j)* or private bargain at such price or prices as they may fix &on such conditions as they may consider expedient to borrow money on the Security of the Trust Estate and grant

(j) A roup is an auction.

in favor of the Creditors Bonds and Dispositions or Assignations in Security
containing powers of sale or such other Deeds Writings or Securities as
they may consider proper to invest the Trust funds in the purchase or on the
Security of Lands Buildings Feuduties Ground annuals or other heritable
property and to realize and change the said investments from time to time
as they may consider expedient Declaring always that purchasers lenders
and all other parties contracting with or paying money to my Trustees shall
be in no ways concerned with the application thereof but shall be fully
exonerated by the receipts and discharges of my Trustees And I further
empower my Trustees to settle and pay out the amount of my shares of
the beneficiaries entitled to the fee of the residue of my Estate as such
provisions become payable either by payment in money or by conveyance
of part or parts of my Estate or party in each way as to my Trustees shall
seem expedient and upon such valuation of the amount and value of my
means and Estate or any part or parts thereof as to my Trustees shall seem
right whether made by themselves or by any other party With power

[page 751]

also to them to appoint a Law Agent Factor or Manager one or more (who
may be of their own number) with suitable remuneration for trouble for
which Factors or Managers my Trustees shall be no further liable than that
such Factors or Managers were [by] habit and repute responsible at the
time of appointment And I dispense with delivery hereof And I reserve
my own liferent and full power to alter or revoke these presents at pleasure
(k) And I consent to registration hereof for preservation In Witness
Whereof these presents written on this and the five preceeding pages by
Alexander Robertson Clerk to Robert Stewart Writer in Glasgow the
syllables "Banner" at the end of the thirty first line of page second hereof
being partly written on an erasure are subscribed by me the said Walter
Bannerman now residing at number Thirteen Jane Street Blythswood
Square Glasgow At Glasgow the fourth day of May eighteen hundred
and seventy seven years before these Witnesses William John Ellison and
James Steven both Clerks to me the said Walter Bannerman (signed) Walter
Bannerman W J Ellison Witness James Steven Witness (l) We Robert
Bannerman Walter Bannerman Jessie Bannerman Robert Robinson
John Hunter and David Bannerman all designed in the foregoing Trust
Disposition and Settlement of the late Walter Bannerman sometime
residing at Cawder House Bishopbriggs thereafter at number Thirteen
James Street Blythswood

*(k) This is an example
of the trustor retaining
effective control and
use of the properties
before death, and the
right to change the
conditions of the trust.*

*(l) The acceptance
by the nominated
trustees.*

[page 752]

Square Glasgow hereby accept the office of Trustee and Executor conferred
upon us by the said Trust Disposition and Settlement In Witness Whereof
this Minute written by Colin Brown Clerk to McGrigor Donald and
Company Writers in Glasgow is subscribed as follows <u>videlicet</u> by us the said

Robert Bannerman Walter Bannerman Jessie Bannerman Robert Robinson
& John Hunter all at Glasgow on the twenty seventh day of August
eighteen hundred & seventy nine before these Witnesses John Baird Smith
Writer in Glasgow and the said Colin Brown and by me the said David
Bannerman at Glasgow on the twenty fourth day of September in the year
last mentioned before these Witnesses the said Colin Brown and William
Storrie Clerk to me the said David Bannerman (signed) Jessie Bannerman
Robert Bannerman Walter Bannerman John Hunter Robert Robinson
D. Bannerman J Baird Smith Witness Colin Brown Witness Colin Brown
Witness Will Storrie Witness Extracted from the Register of Deeds &c in
the Books of Council & Session on this and the twenty three preceding
pages by me Assistant Keeper of said Register holding Commission to
that effect from the Lord Clerk Register of Scotland (signed) Geo. Young
Glasgow 27th Decr. 1879. This is the Extract Trust Disposition & Settlement
by the within named & designed Walter Bannerman referred to in my
Disposition of this date relative to the Inventory of his Personal Estate
(signed) Walter Bannerman William McEwen J.P. (Over)

[page 753]

[margin Letter of Directions] *(m)* To the Trustees under my Trust Disposition
and Settlement I Walter Bannerman residing at Thirteen Jane Street
Blythswood Square Glasgow do hereby Leave and Bequeath (First) to Jess or
Jessie Ure residing with her neice Miss Miller at Bishopbriggs a free yearly
annuity of Fifteen pounds Sterling during all the days & years of her life from
and after the first term of Whitsunday or Martinmas after my death payable
half yearly in advance the first halfyearly payment being made at the first of
said terms of Whitsunday or Martinmas occurring after my death and that
in addition to the sum of Fifteen pounds per annum already provided to her
by my said Settlement and (Second) to Katherine Miller presently residing in
family with me a free yearly annuity of Twelve pounds Sterling payable half
yearly in advance the first half yearly payment being made at the first term of
Whitsunday or Martinmas occurring after my death And I direct my Trustees
to make payment of said annuitiues free of legacy duty And I direct my said
Trustees to make payment of (the) said annuities out of the Estate conveyed
to them In Witness Whereof these presents written by David Wilson Writer
in Glasgow are subscribed by me at Glasgow on the thirteenth day of May
in the year eighteen hundred seventy eight before these Witnesses Matthew
Wallace Writer in Glasgow and the said David Wilson (signed) Walter
Bannerman M Wallace Witness David Wilson Witness [margin Codicil] *(n)*
I Walter Bannerman within designed Considering

[page 754]

that Janet Miller residing at Springwell Cottage Bishopbriggs recently lost
her whole means through the failure of the City of Glasgow Bank and that
Jess or Jessie Ure her aunt who resides with her will in the event of her

*(m) Walter adds
additional elements to
the trust, as a codicil.*

*(n) There is a further
codicil making up the
loss sustained by Janet
Miller. The failure of
the City of Glasgow
Bank in 1878 is
reminiscent of the more
recent bank failures: in
this case the shortfall in*

surviving her said niece not be so well provided for as she would otherwise have been do hereby Leave and Bequeath to the said Jess or Jessie Ure in the event of her surviving the said Janet Miller a further annuity of Twenty pounds Sterling from and after the said Janet Miller's death in addition to the annuity of Thirty pounds provided to her by the foregoing Codicil and my Trust Disposition and Settlement making in all an annuity of Fifty pounds Sterling in the event of her surviving her said niece which additional annuity shall be payable in the same way as provided with regard to the said annuity of Thirty pounds And I consent to registration hereof along with the foregoing Codicil and my said Trust Disposition and Settlement In Witness Whereof this Codicil written by David Wilson Writer in Glasgow is subscribed by me at Glasgow on the twenty fifth day of March eighteen hundred and seventy nine before these Witnesses Matthew Wallace Writer in Glasgow and the said David Wilson (signed) Walter Bannerman M Wallace Witness David Wilson Witness Glasgow 27th Decr 1879 This is the Separate Letter of Directions and Codicil thereto by the within named and designed Walter Bannerman referred to in my Disposition of this date relative to the Inventory of his Personal Estate space

capital was over £5 million, a staggering figure at the time, possible £600 million at 2012 prices. The bank had been supporting its apparently high share value by secretly buying its own stock and the directors were arrested and imprisoned. At that point it had 133 branches and over 1,200 shareholders, whose liability was absolute and unlimited. All but 254 of them were ruined.

(signed) Walter Bannerman William McEwen JP
       [Justice of the Peace]

At the point of death, the estate of Walter(1) was worth the following (rounded to nearest whole pounds):

1.	Cash	127
2.	Household furniture etc.	554
3.	Assurance policies	1,372
4.	Debts due	3,997
4B.	Arrears of Ground Annuals due	658
5.	Book debts, including Disputed and doubtful debts considered recoverable	94
6.	Ground Annuals due to date of death	27
7.	Rents of Heritage due	1,252
7.*	Sums due under Bonds and Dispositions on Security	13,883
	Total of personal estate	21,965

* (The repeat of item number 7 is obviously a mistake.)

Walter(1) owned and rented out a considerable number of properties in and around Glasgow, including Bath Street and Newton Street (twenty-nine tenants, including his son Robert(1) Bannerman); Sauchiehall Street (including the post office); Garscadden Street (sixteen tenants including a Miss Bannerman); Cowcaddens Street (four tenants); Richmond Street (two tenants); Stockwell Street (nine tenants); Argyle Street (one tenant); Jane Street (Miller & Bannerman); Rutherglen Road (nine tenants); Commercial Road (seven tenants); and three farms at Davidston, Dalshannon and Gartcoulter, for which he was receiving rents and feuduties.

These are all in addition to his own properties (the house at 13 Jane Street; Cawder House in Bishopbriggs and a farm), which form part of his heritage rather than moveables listed in the inventory. His real property was worth possibly £80,000: as much as £10 million in today's terms. Cawder House is an impressive A-listed pile, designed by prolific Glasgow architect David Hamilton around 1815 for Charles Stirling, and the land included stables, dovecot, three lodges and an icehouse. It is now the clubhouse for Cawder Golf Club and can be seen at www.cawdergolfclub.com.

Walter(1) had also lent money or given mortgages to the tune of almost £14,000, notably in favour of Janet Miller and Janet Ure, invested in the Glasgow Working Men's Investment Building Society and various builders. he had also put money into the firm of Miller and Bannerman.

Walter(1) had married twice: Jeanie Gow bore him Jessie(1) and Robert(1) as well as four other children who died young, and after her death in 1843, aged 37, he had three more by his second wife, Mary Miller, but only Walter(2) survived childhood.

So, by the time of his death on 7 August 1879, Walter(1) has three living children, an unmarried sister (Mary Bannerman, who would only live until 27 August 1880 and had no offspring but collected an annuity of £35 plus free rent), a sister-in-law (Margaret Gow, who got £20 yearly) and his wife's sisters (Janet and Katherine Miller) plus their aunt (Jessie Ure).

Walter(1) was clearly in business with the Miller family, and that may have been the cause of his demise.

There are two relevant entries in the *Edinburgh Gazette*: one six years before his death and one immediately after it:

THE EDINBURGH GAZETTE, SEPTEMBER 16, 1873. 569

NOTICE.

The Subscriber Walter Bannerman on 7th October 1872 transferred the Business previously carried on by him under the Firm of MILLER & BANNERMAN, Wrights in Glasgow, to the other Subscribers Robert Bannerman and John Shearer, who will continue to carry on the same under the same Firm, for their own behoof, as sole Partners.

The Subscriber Walter Bannerman continues to carry on business at 85 Hope Street as a Land and Property Valuator, and he will collect the debts due to him as sole Partner of the said Firm prior to 7th October 1872.

WALTER BANNERMAN.
ROBERT BANNERMAN.
JOHN SHEARER.
WM. J. ELLISON, Witness.
ROBERT DUNLOP, Witness.
Glasgow, 15th September 1873.

Walter(1) had transferred his interest in the business to Robert(1) who, for whatever reason, went bankrupt in August 1879 and had his goods sequestrated on the 12th of that month. As Walter(1) died of what his death certificate merely gives as 'cerebral', it's tempting to speculate that his elder son's bankruptcy brought on a stroke.

However, what of his various legacies? It is possible that he left everything in trust to keep it out of the hands of Robert(1) or to prevent family squabbles. If so, he failed. Other documents in NRS tell the rest of the tale.

842 THE EDINBURGH GAZETTE, AUGUST 15, 1879.

THE Estates of MILLER & BANNERMAN, Wrights and Packing Box Makers in Glasgow, and Robert Bannerman, Wright and Packing Box Maker there, an Individual Partner of that Company, as such Partner, and as an Individual, were Sequestrated on the 12th day of August 1879, by the Sheriff of the County of Lanark.

The first Deliverance is dated 29th July 1879.

The Meeting to elect the Trustee and Commissioners is to be held at twelve o'clock noon, on Monday the 25th day of August 1879, within the Faculty Hall, Saint George's Place, Glasgow.

A Composition may be offered at this Meeting ; and to entitle Creditors to the first Dividend, their oaths and grounds of debt must be lodged on or before the 12th day of December 1879.

A Warrant of Protection has been granted to the Bankrupt, Robert Bannerman, till the Meeting for election of Trustee.

All future Advertisements relating to this Sequestration will be published in the Edinburgh Gazette alone.

GORDON-SMITH & LUCAS, Writers, Glasgow, Agents.

Daughter Jessie(1) had liferent on the large house in Blythswood Square so long as she remained unmarried, and she must have preferred that to any gentleman caller as she died still a spinster, leaving £8,000 between her one niece and three nephews (Jessie(2), Robert(3), Walter(3) and Stanley).

Robert(2) becomes the Factor for the trustees (he probably needed the job and the money) but almost immediately there was trouble. He brings in accounts in 1886, late and unverified, so the trust decides to see an annual account. He still has not submitted these by 1889 and Walter(2) sends them for audit. Robert(2) recovers some £1,700 from a loan but does not credit it to the trust and is told to pay it back. He also claims £945 for management 1879–88 (£105 per annum) but this is denied as the trust has already paid for his clerk, the rent of his office, and all property repairs 'paid for by him at his own rates'. There are further financial shenanigans, culminating in an audit (December 1890) dating back to 1879, which concludes that 'there are considerable errors charged to capital in the accounts for repairs on the trust properties' and that 'debits are warranted by the nature of the repairs'. Walter says that they are being rooked by Robert carrying out repairs and charging over the usual rates for them, despite being a trustee, and Robert replies that he was saving them money. A new Factor is appointed.

When Jessie(1) died in 1896, her share of the trust must have devolved on the half-brothers Robert(1) – by now on his third wife and with a child, Stanley – and Walter(2) – married but with no children. As both Jessie(1) and Walter(2) died without issue, under the ninth condition of the TDS everything would eventually have ended up in the hands of the children of Robert(1), namely: Jessie(2), Robert(2) and Walter(3). But when Robert(1) dies in 1902, and Walter(2) dies in 1903, more legal difficulties arise. Walter(3), the surviving child, had issues and outlived the other two until 1903, but before he died (in 1894, in fact) Walter(2) had executed a Deed of Direction in 1894, saying that everything he had was to go equally to his wife, Mary Ramsay, and his niece Jessie(2), daughter of his half-brother Robert(1), who also had Robert(2) and Walter(3) by his first wife, and Stanley by his third wife Mary Woods.

In 1905, Mary, wife of Walter(2), takes direct action against the trustees for what she reckons is the share 'of the estate to which she has absolute right' and makes that to be ¹/₁₆. Meanwhile, Robert(2) goes bankrupt the same year, and not for the last time, suggesting a like-father-like-son approach to financial management.

By 1912, Walter(3) is in Gartnavel Hospital, where he dies from 'organic brain disease'. In 1913 'Mrs Mary Woods or Bannerman and others (Walter Bannerman's trustees)' sue 'Mrs Jessie Bannerman or Brodie and others'. Mary Woods and Robert(2) obviously felt left out, sueing Jessie(2) and Mary Ramsay for a share, but this was thrown out. Mary Woods had had her late husband's share, so there was nothing to Robert(2), his wife Isabella or their children. By this time, everyone had received everything they were going to get, as lump sums.

In 1916–17 Robert(2) goes bankrupt again, and even gets sued by his lawyer, which is a neat trick by any standards.

So, anything that could be inherited is now with Mary Ramsay – who had no children – and Jessie(2), who in 1909 had married a merchant in Calcutta called William Gibson Brodie. When Jessie(2) died in 1925, she was widowed, back from Calcutta, and left everything to her daughter by the deceased Mr Brodie, who was living in England.

When Mary Ramsay died in 1928, she gave at least some property in Holland Street to the Education Board of Glasgow (where the old Glasgow High School was; the building is still there).

The trust itself rumbled on until about 1946–47 (there is evidence of sales of the remaining properties) and there were small proceeds to descendants: Robert, son of Walter(3) recalls getting something about then (personal communication by his daughter) but that the majority had ended up with 'that woman in England': an obvious reference to the daughter of Jessie(2) and Mr Brodie.

So, as usual in these cases, there is no money, no land, and almost everyone felt cheated at some point. Yet it all started when a good and prudent man tried to ensure a measure of fairness.

Those who were alive to inherit have their surnames capitalised in the tree on p. 178.

Descendants of David Bannerman

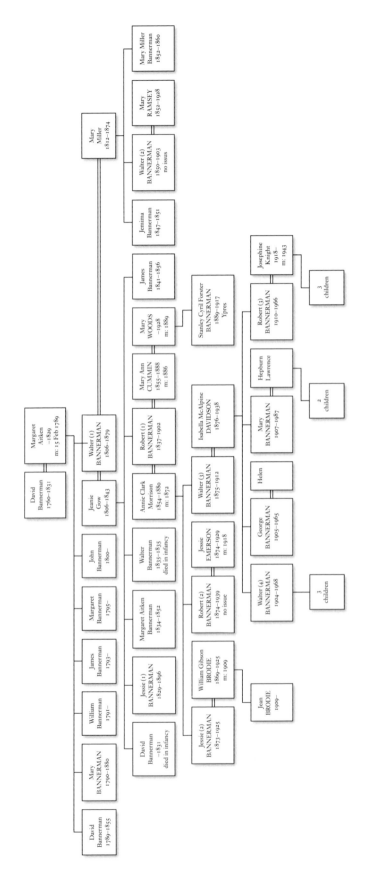

12

Scotland: Sasines

REGISTER OF SASINES AND NOTARY PUBLIC RECORDS

The word sasine is pronounced '*say-zin*', not '*sass-een*', '*sass-yne*', '*say-zyne*' or any other such monstrosity. The word is related to 'seize': a landholder was 'seized of' land, which implies physical holding, and indeed this is what happened. On a sale and purchase, the two parties would call out the notary public to witness the new owner physically holding a token piece of the land, usually a stone or a clod of earth (see below). A notary would write an instrument of sasine (see below) in his protocol book. Some of these still exist. But just before 1600, Scotland decided to record all property transfers, loans against security and mortgages (called *wadsets*), largely as a guard against fraud, multiple mortgaging and the like.

There was an early and incomplete attempt at a the Register of Sasines from 1599 to 1609, but it was not a success and the system started again in 1617. However, the registers are nothing like complete until about 1660. The registers are a large series of records – held at General Register House, Edinburgh – recording (in theory) every change in ownership of property in Scotland. This system lasted until 6 April 1981 when it was gradually replaced by Registration of Title, county by county, (held by Registers of Scotland, a different organisation). This means that the Scottish Sasine Register is one of the oldest continuous records of land transfers in Europe.

Not all Registers of Sasines are indexed, but such indexes as exist are organised by location and date as follows:

– Secretary's Register: 1599–1609, incomplete, by counties.
– General Register: 1617–1720 and 1781–1868 for all of Scotland, except East Lothian (previously called Haddingtonshire), Midlothian (Edinburghshire) and West Lothian (Linlithgowshire), and for properties that sat across county boundaries.
– Royal Burgh Registers: there are sixty-six, some indexed from about 1809, although those for Glasgow, Aberdeen and Dundee pre-1809 are kept locally.
– County Registers: 1617–1780, 1781–1868 and 1869 onwards.

Although the General Register is indexed from 1617 to 1735 the indexes to sasines are incomplete before 1781: the Clackmannan, Peebles, Renfrew, Roxburgh, Selkirk, Stirling and Wigtown indexes are missing. Many of the existing indexes are published and available in libraries although there are hardly any published indexes for burgh registers until the 1900s when they became amalgamated with the county registers, and those that do exist are in manuscript or (later) typescript form and are only available at the NRS. Otherwise, it is possible to consult minute books, which were compiled daily by the clerks writing the sasines into the register and therefore are in chronological order, with a short summary of each and the date of registration from which the full document can be found in the register.

The register is public, and while the NRS charges for consulting the register for legal reasons, there is no charge when doing so for family history or historical purposes.

Sasine abridgements

From 1781 the indexes are good and there are printed abridgements for every record, arranged in county volumes and covering both general and particular registers. The index identifies people and/or property names, gives the number of the abridgement, and so leads the original document if needed (but often the abridgement has enough information). There is a full set of abridgements at the NRS (General Register House, Edinburgh) and some local authority archives have local sets. Check the Scottish Archive Network (SCAN) website for details.

Another useful starting point and short cut are the search sheets for properties in Scotland from 1876, which give the volume and page numbers of all the sasines and deeds for a building or piece of land, available at modest cost from Registers of Scotland.

The sasine register also records secured debts, such as mortgages ('*wadsets*'), which often give financial relationships between landowners, merchants, lenders etc. and genealogical information, but need time and patience.

Instrument of sasine

The instrument is the document that records the transfer of ownership of land or a building by sale or inheritance. The original document will have details of purchase, sale or handing down, with dates and names of the parties, the land referred to, the exact time and the names of witnesses. These have being digitised and are available on computer at NRS, but are not yet online.

It was (and still is) legally required to record a sasine or equivalent title deed within a few days of it being drawn up. However, if a person was already resident in the inherited property with undisputed possession (say, a sole son on his father's death) there would be no need to incur the cost of having a sasine executed, unless possession was later disputed or the property was sold.

Two examples of sasines are given and transcribed below. The first is from 1785, in English, and the second is from about 1695 and is entirely in Latin. These will provide transcription and palaeographic practice in typical hands of the day, and also show that the form of the sasine was basically unchanged over the years. If the original writing looks cramped, it's because in the early years clerks had to buy the blank sasine volumes themselves and so tried to get as much on each page as they could.

First, it is important to understand how the sasine was constructed.

Structure of the instrument of sasine

The form of this dates back to about the year 1430, in the reign of James I, and carried on until recently. The nature of it, the process it referred to and the terms used are explained below.

Precept of sasine

The first step was to appoint a baillie (representative) who would actually deliver sasine. The precept – essentially authority to proceed – was a separate document until 1672, after which they were engrossed towards the end of a charter or deed, as in the example below. Take the case of a subject superior, called A.A. (the disponer) conveying property to a vassal, B.B. (the disponee). For feudal law and landholding see p. 238. The superior 'commands' his baillie to infeft the vassal of the subjects contained in the 'dispositive' or disponing clause of the charter, by the delivery of symbols of possession (described below).

> Moreover I hereby desire and require you and each of you my baillies in that part hereby specially constituted That on sight hereof ye pass to the ground of the said lands and others and there give and deliver to the said B.B. or his foresaids heritable state and sasine with real actual and corporal possession of all and whole the lands teinds and others particularly above specified with the pertinents lying and described as aforesaid and here held as repeated *brevitatis causa* [in the interests of brevity] to be holden in manner foresaid and for payment of the feu (or blench) duties before specified and that by delivering to the said B. or his foresaids or to his or their attorney in his or their names bearers hereof of earth and stone of the ground of the said lands and a handful of grass and corn for the said teinds with all other symbols usual and necessary and this in no ways ye leave undone Which to do I commit to you and each of you my full power by this my precept of sasine directed to you for that effect.

If the land is held of the 'Crown and Prince' (the sovereign), the precept of sasine will be addressed to the sheriff of the shire in which the lands are situated, usually including the clause '*dilectis nostris et vestrum cuilibet conjunctim et divisim vicecomitibus nostris in hac parte specialiter constitut*' (our well-beloved, together and separately and to each of you, our sheriffs specially appointed in that part).

Clauses of the instrument of sasine

The ceremony of infeftment (see below) is expressed in the instrument of sasine, which contains the following clauses, given in the style used in Queen Victoria's time, which will vary in earlier documents:

1. The invocation:

   > In the Name of God, Amen …

2. The date necessary for fixing the time within which the instrument must be registered:

   > Know all men by this present public instrument, That upon the day of XXX in the year of our Lord YYYY, and of the reign of her Majesty, Victoria the First, by the Grace of God, of the United Kingdom of Great Britain and Ireland Queen, Defender of the Faith, the ZZ year …

3. The 'appearance on the ground' (turning up for the ceremony), the names and designations of the procurator or attorney for the vassal, and of the superior's baillie:

   > In presence of me notary-public, and of the witnesses herein after named and designed, and hereto with me subscribing, and upon the ground of the lands and others after described, compeared [appeared] personally D.D. as procurator and attorney for B.B., whose power of attorney was sufficiently known to me notary-public as also compeared C.C., baillie in that part, specially constituted, by virtue of the precept of sasine herein after transcribed, contained in the charter after narrated …

4. The narrative: this clause of the instrument narrates the warrant on which the ceremony proceeds, and if sasine is given to an heir or assignee, the retour (see Chapter 13) or assignation likewise must be described (the legal term is 'deduced') in the instrument, and the writs that the attorney produces should be so described as to admit of complete identification, which is best secured by specifying their dates, and the names and designations of the grantors and disponees:

> … the said D. D. having and holding in his hands the said charter, of the date under written, made and granted by A. A., heritable proprietor of the lands and others after described, to and in favour of the said B. B., whereby the said A. A., for the causes therein specified, sold, alienated, and in feu (or blench) ferme disponed from him, his heirs and successors, to and in favour of the said B. B., his heirs and assignees whomsoever, heritably and irredeemably, all and whole (*the lands, with restrictions, etc. as in the dispositive clause of the charter*) to be holden of and under the said A. A. and his foresaids in feu (or blench) ferme, fee and heritage for ever, for payment of the feu (or blench) duty, and other prestations [payments] specified in the said charter; as the same, containing clause of absolute warrandice, the precept of sasine herein after transcribed, and other usual clauses, more fully bears …

5. The vassal's requisition to his baillie: this clause describes the exhibition and production to the baillie of the warrant of infeftment, and the requisition of the vassal or his attorney that he should proceed to execute the office committed to him:

> … which feu (or blench) charter, the said D.D. as procurator and attorney foresaid, exhibited and produced to the said baillie, desiring and requiring him to proceed to the execution of the office of bailliary thereby committed to him …

6. The baillie's acceptance of the warrant, and delivery of it to the notary for publication to the witnesses:

> … which desire the said baillie finding to be reasonable, he received the said charter into his hands, and delivered the same to me, notary public subscribing, to be read and published to the witnesses present …

7. The publication of the charter by the reading and explanation of the terms by the notary to the witnesses, and including the precept of sasine, the testing clause and subscriptions:

> … which I did, and of which precept of sasine the tenor follows in these words (precept of sasine inserted verbatim, plus the testing clause, and the subscriptions of the granter of the charter and the witnesses to his subscription, precisely as appearing on the deed) …

8. The delivery of sasine: this records the giving of 'state and sasine', or symbolical possession (see below), to the vassal or disponee in a ceremony held on the land itself; before the introduction of the sasine registers, this formal procedure was important to make public the transfer of real property to the neighbours and anyone else interested:

> … after reading and publishing of which feu (or blench) charter, containing the said precept of sasine, the said baillie received the same again info his hands, and by virtue thereof, and of the office of bailliary thereby committed to him, GAVE AND DELIVERED to the said B. heritable state and sasine, real, actual and corporal possession of All and Whole the lands and others particularly before specified, with their pertinents, lying and described as aforesaid, and here held as repeated, *brevitatis causa* …

9. The taking of instruments: the asking of instruments was at one time deemed necessary in order to retain the notary by a payment in part:

> … whereupon, and upon all and sundry the premises, the said procurator and attorney asked and took instruments in the hands of me, notary-public, subscribing …

10. The summary of the *res gesta* and description of the witnesses: this states that the ceremony was performed upon the ground, or in respect of each separate premises contained in the charter; if these were discontiguous or each a separate tenement, each would require distinct infeftment, achieved by using the words 'respectively and successively' or equivalent terms, referring to the subjects described in a former clause of the instrument:

> … these things were so done upon the ground of the said lands and others [*respectively and successively* if legally discontiguous] betwixt the hours of___ and ___ of the day of the month in the year of our Lord and of the Queen's reign respectively above written before and in presence of E.E. and F.F. witnesses to the premises specially called and required and hereto with me subscribing …

11. The notary's certificate, or *doquet*, an old English term for a brief or summary of a longer writing, is an attestation by the notary of the facts contained in the instrument and at one time had to include the terms '*vidi, scivi et audivi*' (seen, known and heard) and the concluding words '*rogatus et requisitus*' (requested and required), because a notary can do no official act unless called on to perform it; this was usually verbatim an approved and well-tested form of words in Latin, so that it couldn't be called into question (see the examples at the end of the two transcripts following) but the odd slip didn't really matter, because of the legal principle that '*mala grammatica non vitiat chartam*' (bad grammar does not vitiate a writ).

The ceremony of infeftment

This was a recondite and, from the modern perspective, faintly laughable process that involved grown men standing in muddy fields handing things to each other and exchanging formal verbal statements (much more fun than sitting in a lawyer's office signing things). It worked like this:

- The vassal or his attorney appeared on the ground of the lands or other subject of the conveyance, with the superior or his baillie (clutching his precept of sasine) and attended by a notary and two witnesses.
- The vassal or his attorney began the ceremony by delivering the warrant to the baillie, who again gave it to the notary, who in turn explained ('published') the nature of the conveyance to the witnesses, and read the precept of sasine.
- The notary then redelivered the charter to the baillie.
- Now that the baillie had the warrant for infeftment in his hands, he gave the proper symbols of possession to the vassal's attorney.
- The attorney put a piece of money, usually silver, into the notary's hand, saying: 'I take instruments in your hands before these witnesses'.
- A note was taken of the hour and of the names and designations of the baillie, attorney and witnesses.
- Everyone went to the local tavern to toast the deal and to clean the mud off their boots (well, perhaps not, but they should have).

You can see how each of these steps was reflected in the various clauses of the instrument of sasine: it was essentially a recipe for getting the process right as well as a record of it happening. But it is important to realise that the instrument was *only* a record: the legal act was the exchange of symbols and payment, and the reading or publishing.

Symbols of delivery

If you buy a car from someone, you turn up at the appointed place, both parties sign the registration document for later dispatch to the appropriate vehicle registration body (but retaining a part of it each, as vendor and purchaser), the seller hands over the keys and you hand over the money. Then you drive away in the car, which is now yours.

But it's a bit more complicated with fixed property: you can't actually pick up an entire field or a house and hand it to someone. Therefore, symbolic possession was used. Traditionally, when selling a house, the vendor walked out of the door, and left the premises unoccupied so that the buyer could physically enter and take actual possession. But how do you do that with a field, or a whole estate, or some intangible right such as a multure (the right to receive teinds or tithes from cereals ground at a mill)? And what if you weren't actually going to live in the property yourself, or would move in at a later date? In many cultures, symbols were and are used to indicate the will of a disponer to divest himself of a property, by the delivery to the disponee or his representative of a rod or baton as the symbol of ownership. (We still see this, when a monarch is crowned and is handed the mace of state.) The symbols used in Scotland for the transfer of property and rights were:

– For lands and houses: earth and stone.
– For mills, when conveyed as separate tenements: clap and happer (seed-hopper).
– For teinds: a handful of grass and corn.
– For patronages and advowsons (the right to appoint the minister to a church living): a psalm book and the keys of the church (compare St Peter receiving 'the keys of the kingdom of heaven').
– For the investiture of an heir in houses held by the tenure of burgage (i.e. within a burgh): hasp and staple (of a lock).
– For annual rents: a piece of money, but if payable in victual, a handful of corn.
– For salmon fishings: net and cable.
– For jurisdictions: the book of the court.
– For a right of ferry: an oar and some water.

In practice, it was usual (and, it was felt, safer) to add, after the details of the particular symbols appropriate to the things conveyed, 'and all other symbols usual and requisite'.

The purchaser or vassal would then hand back a symbol of payment such as a silver penny or, if *blenche ferme*, some nominal symbol such as a peppercorn (hence 'peppercorn rent'), a pair of silver spurs, a snowball at midsummer, a mirror for larks. This reflects the *reddendo* (p. 354) expected for *blenche-ferme* tenure, often expressed as '*si petatur tantum*' (and then only if asked for).

Sasine of John Lindsay 1785

This documents the transfer of the heritable property of the Mason Lodge and Society of Free Operative Masons in Kilbride in the year 1785 to John Lindsay. This sasine follows the basic structure that identifies the buyer (the grantee) of the property and lands, John Lindsay, the writer (solicitor) James Telfor and the Baillie, John Riddel.

The sasine gives a detailed account of the property and adjoining land, such as that of John Craig and John Greenhills, and in this case the previous owners of the bordering land. It also clearly lays out the rights of passing and repassing through the land, specifically a yard in the property.

The last part explains some amendments to the dispensation document dated 10 and 14 January with some words to be inserted. The act of handing over the 'earth and stone' to John Lindsay gives the time of day between noon and 1 p.m.:

Granters/disponers – the Mason Lodge and Society of Free Operative Masons in Kilbride:

John Hamilton in Devonhil – Mason and present master (head of Lodge)

Matthew Bryce in Carmunnock – Mason and warden (one of the senior officials)

John Granger in Kittochside – Warden

Archibald Bryce in Carmunock – Trades master

Matthew Gilmour – Trades master

John Wilson in Gorbals – Boxmaster (Treasurer)

Robert Struthers in the Kirkton of Kilbride – Mason, Boxmaster & Grand Steward

John Tassie in Kittochside – Mason and coroner (more likely, 'crouner'?) of the Masons

John Lindsay in Platthorn – grantee/disponee (buyer)

James Telfor – Writer (solicitor) in Hamilton

John Riddel – Baillie [in that part]

Witnesses

Robert Hamilton

William Robertson

John Russel in Dikenook, Avendale

James Knox

John Wilson in Platthorn

John Hamilton

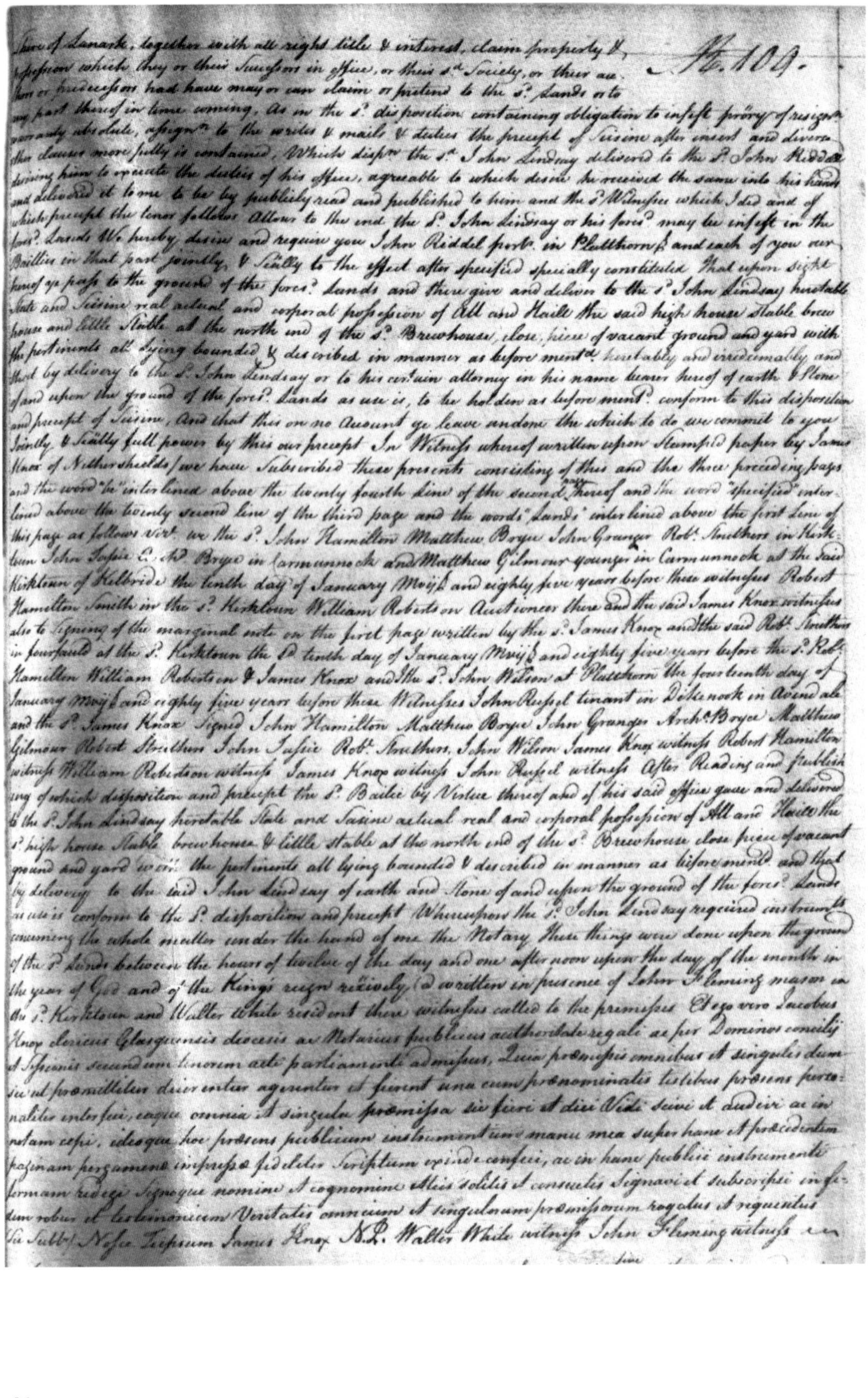

Shire of Lanark, together with all right title & interest, claim property & — No. 108.
possession which they or their Successors in office, or their sd. Society, or their au-
thors or predecessors had have may or can claim or pretend to the sd. Lands or to
any part thereof in time coming, As in the sd. disposition containing obligation to infeft procry. of resign.
warranty absolute, assignn. to the writes & mails & duties the precept of Seisine after insert and divers
other clauses more fully is contained, Which dispon. the sd. John Lindsay delivered to the sd. John Riddel
desiring him to execute the duties of his office, agreeable to which desire he received the same into his hands
and delivered it to me to be by publickly read and published to him and the sd. Witnesses which I did and of
which precept the tenor follows Allow to the end the sd. John Lindsay or his foresd. may be infeft in the
foresd. Lands We hereby desire and require you John Riddel prob. in Plotthorn & and each of you our
Baillies in that part jointly & Seally to the effect after specified specially constituted That upon sight
hereof ye pass to the ground of the foresd. Lands and there give and deliver to the sd. John Lindsay heritable
State and Seisine real actual and corporal possession of All and Haill the said high house Stable brew
house and little Stable at the north end of the sd. Brewhouse, close, piece of vacant ground and yard with
the pertinents all lying bounded & described in manner as before mentd. heritably and irredeemably and
that by delivery to the sd. John Lindsay or to his certain attorney in his name bearer hereof of earth & Stone
of and upon the ground of the foresd. Lands as use is, to be holden as before mentd. conform to this disposition
and precept of Seisine, And that this on no account ye leave undone the which to do we commit to you
Jointly & Seally full power by this our precept In Witness whereof written upon Stampd paper by James
Knox of Nethersheilds/we have Subscribed these presents consisting of this and the three preceding pages
and the word "he" interlined above the twenty fourth line of the second thereof and the word "specified" interlined above the twenty second line of the third page and the words "Lands" interlined above the first line of
this page as follows viz. we the sd. John Hamilton Matthew Bryce John Granger Robt. Struthers in Kirktown John Tassie & Archd. Bryce in Carmunnock and Matthew Gilmour younger in Carmunnock at the said
Kirktown of Kilbride the tenth day of January Mvijc and eighty five years before these witnesses Robert
Hamilton Smith in the sd. Kirktown William Robertson Auctioneer there and the said James Knox witnesses
also to Signing of the marginal note on the first page written by the sd. James Knox and the said Robt. Struthers
in fourfauld at the sd. Kirktown the sd. tenth day of January Mvijc and eighty five years before the sd. Robt.
Hamilton William Robertson & James Knox and the sd. John Wilson at Plotthorn the fourteenth day of
January Mvijc and eighty five years before these Witnesses John Russel tenant in Dikenook in Avondale
and the sd. James Knox Signed John Hamilton Matthew Bryce John Granger Archd. Bryce Matthew
Gilmour Robert Struthers John Tassie Robt. Struthers, John Wilson James Knox witness Robert Hamilton
witness William Robertson witness James Knox witness John Russel witness After Reading and publish
ing of which disposition and precept the sd. Bailie by Virtue thereof and of his said office gave and delivered
to the sd. John Lindsay heritable State and Sasine actual real and corporal possession of All and Haill the
sd. high house Stable brewhouse & little stable at the north end of the sd. Brewhouse close piece of vacant
ground and yard with the pertinents all lying bounded & described in manner as before mentd. and that
by delivery to the said John Lindsay of earth and Stone of and upon the ground of the foresd. Lands
as use is conform to the sd. disposition and precept Whereupon the sd. John Lindsay required instruments
one or more the whole matter under the hand of me the Notary These things were done upon the ground
of the sd. Lands between the hours of twelve of the day and one afternoon upon the day of the month in
the year of God and of the Kings reign resively (sd) written in presence of John Fleming mason in
the sd. Kirktown and Walter White resident there witnesses called to the premisses Et ego vero Jacobus
Knox clericus Glasguensis diocesis ac Notarius publicus authoritate regali ac per Dominos concilij
et Sessionis secundum tenorem acti parliamenti admissus, Quia premissis omnibus et singulis dum
sic ut premittitur dicerentur agerentur et fierent una cum prenominatis testibus presens perso-
naliter interfui, eaque omnia et singula premissa sic fieri et dici Vidi scivi et audivi ac in
notam cepi, ideoque hoc presens publicum instrumentum manu mea super hanc et precedentem
paginam pergamene impressa fideliter Scriptum exinde confeci, ac in hanc publici instrumenti
formam redegi Signoque nomine et cognomine Meis solitis et consuetis Signavi et subscripsi in fidem robur et testimonium Veritatis omnium et singulorum premissorum rogatus et requisitus
Sic Subt. Nosce Teipsum James Knox N.P. Walter White witness John Fleming witness

Transcription

Sas[ine]: John }

      Lindsay }

1. At Hamilton the twenty ninth day of April MvijC and eighty five years [1785] the sasine
2. underwritten was produced by James Telfer Writer in Hamilton and Registered said
3. day as follows.
4. In the name of God amen be it known that upon the Second day of March MviiC and eighty five
5. years and of the reign of our Sovereign Lord George the third, by the grace of God, King of Great Britain
6. France and Ireland defender of the faith the twenty fifth year in presence of me notary public and witnesses
7. Sub[scribed] compeared personally upon the ground of the houses and others afterment[ione]d John Lindsay resident in Plat
8. thorn together with John Riddel Por[tioner] then Baillie in that part by the precept of Sasine after specified con-
9. -tained in the disp[ositio]n afterment[ione]d specially consitituted and there the s[ai]d John Lindsay holding in his hands
10. the s[ai]d disp[ositio]n dated the tenth and fourteenth days of January last whereby for the houses therein said the
11. granters thereof John Hamilton mason in Devonhill present master, Matthew Bryce mason in Carmun-
12. -nock and John Granger in Kittochside present Wardens Arch[ibal]d Bryce in Carmunock and Matthew Gil-
13. -mour there present Trades masters, John Wilson in Gorbals and Rob[er]t Struthers mason in the Kirkton of
14. Kilbride present Boxmasters Rob[er]t Struthers in fourfaulds [possibly Fairfields, today] present Grand Steward and John Tassie mason
15. in Kittochside present Coroner of the mason Lodge and Society of free operative masons in the Kirktoun
16. of Kilbride in name and behalf, and for the use and behoof of the said Lodge and society sold & disponed
17. for themselves and in name & behalf of their s[ai]d Constituents heritably & irredeemably to and in favour
18. of the s[ai]d John Lindsay and his heirs and assigns whatsoever All and Haill that high house, stable,
19. Brewhouse, the close between the said high house stable and brewhouse, with the little stable at the
20. north end of the s[ai]d Brewhouse, and that piece of Vacant ground before the door of the said high house with the
21. North part of the yard as the same is pilled off straight from the Southwest corner of s[ai]d Stable westward to
22. the pitstones fixed a little northwest from the west gavil (= gable) of the houses of John & Robert Fleming, and from
23. the s[ai]d pitstones straight west to the hedge between John Craig's yard and the yard thereby disponed, bounded
24. by the other part of the yard belonging to John & Rob[er]t Fleming on the South, the yard of the s[ai]d John
25. Craig and Wanscroft on the west, the yard of John Greenhills formerly belonging to the deceased James

26. Dalgliesh & Jennet Dick in the north west and the houses and yards belonging sometime to William

27. Robertson & now to William Orr on the north, & the high way on the east, with liberty of passing and

28. repassing to and from the said yard by the southend of the s[ai]d stable down to the pitstones a[fore]mentioned

29. for a foot road outwith the said yard therein disponed as the same were sometime possessed by Matthew

30. Legat and presently by Hugh Riddel their tenant lying within the parish of Kilbride and

31. Shire

[Page 2]   No 109

32. Shire of Lanark, together with all rights title & interest claim property &

33. possession which they or their successors in office, or their s[ai]d Society, or their au

34. thors or predecessors had have may or can claim or pretend to the s[ai]d Lands or to

35. any part thereof in time coming, as in the s[ai]d disposition containing obligation to infeft pr[ocurato]ry of resign[ation]

36. warranty absolute, assign[atio]n to the writes & mails & duties the precept of Sasine after insert and diverse

37. other clauses more fully is contained, Which disp[ositio]n the s[ai]d John Lindsay delivered to the s[ai]d John Riddell

38. desiring him to execute the duties of his office, agreeable to which desire he received the same into his hands

39. and delivered it to me to be by publicly read and published to him and the s[ai]d Witnesses which I did and of

40. which precept the tenor follows Allows to this end the s[ai]d John Lindsay or his fores[ai]ds may be infeft in the

41. fore[sai]d Lands We hereby desire and require you John Riddell port[ioner] in Platthorn & each of you our

42. Baillies in that part jointly & Se[ver]ally to the effect after specified specially constituted that upon sight

43. hereof ye pass to the ground of the fores[ai]d Lands and there give and deliver to the s[ai]d John Lindsay heritable

44. State and Sasine real actual and corporal at possession of All and Haill the said high house stable brew

45. house and little stable at the north end of the s[ai]d brewhouse, close, piece of vacant ground and yard with

46. the pertinents all lying bounded & described in manner as before ment[ione]d heritably and irredeemably and

47. that by delivery to the s[ai]d John Lindsay or to his certain attorney in his name bearer hereof of earth & stone

48. of and upon the ground of the fore[mentione]d Lands as use is, to be holden as before ment[ione]d conform to this disposition

49. and precept of sasine, And that this on no account ye leave undone the which to do we commit to you

50. jointly & Se[ver]ally full power by this our precept In witness whereof written upon Stamped paper by James

51. Knox of Nethershields / we have subscribed these presents consisting of this and the three preceding pages

52. and the word 'be' interlined above the twenty fourth line of the second ^page^ hereof and the word 'specified' inter

53. lined above the twenty second line of the third page and the words "Lands" interlined above the first Line of

54. this page as follows viz. we the s[ai]d John Hamilton, Matthew Bryce, John Granger, Robt. Struthers in Kirk

55. toun, John Tasssie, Arch[ibal]d Bryce in Carmunock and Matthew Gilmour younger in Carmunnock at the said

56. Kirktoun of Kilbride the tenth day of January MvijC and eighty five years before these witnesses Robert

57. Hamilton Smith in the s[ai]d Kirktoun, William Robertson Auctioneer there and the said James Knox witnesses

58. also to signing of the marginal note on the first written by the s[ai]d James Knox and the said Robt. Struthers

59. in fourfauld at the s[ai]d Kirktoun the s[ai]d tenth day of January MvijC and eighty five years before the s[ai]d Robt.

60. Hamilton William Robertson & James Knox and I the s[ai]d John Wilson at Plathorn the fourteenth day of

61. January MvijC and eighty five years before these witnesses John Russel tenant in Dikenook in Avendale

62. and the s[ai]d James Knox signed John Hamilton, Matthew Bryce, John Grange, Arch[ibal]d Bryce, Matthew

63. Gilmour, Robert Struthers, John Tassie, Rob[er]t struthers, John Wilson, James Knox witness, Robert Hamilton

64. witness, William Robertson witness, James Knox witness, John Russel witness After reading and publish-

65. ing of which disposition and precept the s[ai]d Baillie by virtue thereof and of his said office gave and delivered

66. to the s[ai]d John Lindsay heritable State and Sasine actual real and corporal possession of All and Haill the

67. s[ai]d high house stable brewhouse & little stable at the north end of the s[ai]d brewhouse close piece of vacant

68. ground and yard with the pertinents all lying bounded & described in manner as before mentioned and that

69. by delivering to the said John Lindsay of earth and stone of and upon the ground of the fore[sai]d lands

70. as use is conform to the s[ai]d disposition and precept Whereupon the s[ai]d John Lindsay required instrum[en]ts

71. concerning the whole matter under the hand of me the notary These things were done upon the ground

72. of the s[ai]d Lands between the hours of twelve of the day and one afternoon upon the day of the month in

73. the year of God and of the King's reign rexively (= respectively) abovewritten in presence of John Fleming mason in

74. the s[ai]d Kirktoun and Walter White resident these witnesses called to the premises *Et ego vero Jacobus*

75. *Knox Clericus Glasguensis diocesis ac Notarius publicus authoritate regali ac per Dominos concilij*

76. *et Sessionis secundum tenorum acti parliamenti admissus, Quia praemissis omnibus et singulis dum*

77. *sic ut praemittitur dicirentur agerentur et fuerent una cum praenominatis testibus praesens perso*

78. *naliter interfui, eaque omnia et singula premissa sic fieri et dici Vidi scive et audivi ac in*

79. *notam cepi, ideoque hoc praesens publicum instrumentum manu mea super hanc et praecedentem*

80. *paginam pergamine impressae fideliter Scriptum exinde <u>confeci,</u> ac in hanc publici instrumenti*

81. *formam redegi Signoque nomine et cognomine Meis solitis et consuetis signavi et subscripsi in fi-*

82. *dem robur et testimonium Veritatis omnium et singulorum praemissorum rogatus et requisitas*

83. *(Sic Sub[scripe]) Nosse Teipsum* James Knox, Notary Public Walter White witness, John Fleming witness.

Lines 74–83 Latin translation

And I truly, James Knox, clerk of the diocese of Glasgow, notary public by royal authority and of the lords of council and session, and according to the tenor of the act of parliament was admitted, because all and sundry of the foregoing were so acted, spoken and done, were offered him and, together with the foresaid witnesses I was present in person and all and sundry these things so done and spoken I did see, know and hear and took note thereof from which this present public instrument with my hand over this and the preceding pages faithfully written and made from these, and I have made and rendered into this public instrumental form and have signed with my sign and usual name signed subscribed in faith and testimony trult all and singular the foregoing as called and required (so subscribed, know ye James Knox N[otary] P[ublic] Walter White, witness John Fleming)

Template 'Sasina' from the *Stylorum veterum ac recentiorum* compiled by William Grant, Younger of Creichie, *c.* 1695

Two pages are given, with Latin transcript and English translation of the first page.

Sasina

In de[i] no[min]e Amen per hoc presens
publicum instrumentum cunctis pateat evidenter et sit notum
quod Anno incarnationis dominice &c mensis vero &c die Regni[que]
Excellentissimi serenissimi principis Jacobi &c Magnae Britanniae
franciae et Hiberniae Regis fideiq[ue] defensoris § anno &c In mei
notarij publici Et testium sub[scriptorum] presentijs personali
ter comparuit ^&c honorabilis vir WG de &c In cujus favorem prae
ceptum sasinae infrascript[um] fact[um] et concessum est modo inframentionat
et accessit cum discreto et honorabili viro JK de &c viceco
mite vicecomitatus de &c rexive in hac parte infraspecificat spe
ciatiter constituto Ad maneriei locum de &c secundum tenorum in
feofementi infrascript[] et virtute unionis et dispensationis inibi
content Habens et in suis manibus tenens ejusdam precept[um]
sasinae e cancellario memoriali Sup: Dom: Nost: Regis sub testimonio
magni sigilli praenominato JK tanquam vicecomiti antedict direct ut
dict honorablum virum WG In totis et integris terris deci
mis maneriarum locis domibus aedificiis molendinis piscationibus
Aliisque inframentionat jacens pertinens et appretiat modo infras
cript[] Infeodaret QUODQU[I] DEM sasinae preceptum sub
insert dictus WG Exhibuit et presentavit praenominale JK tan
quam vicecomiti in hac parte per eundem legittime constituto
eundem Requirens Quatenus ad Executionem ejusdem sasinae pre
cept Et officii vicecomitatus in hac parte sibi comissi debite proc
ederet QUID QUIDEM vicecomes sciens et percipiens dictam

Reqisitionem et desiderium fere justum Rationique Consentan ne(?)
sasinae preceptum subinsertum omni qua debuit Reverentia
manibus suis accepit mihique notario publico subscribenti perle
gendum publicandum et astantibus Exponendum tradavit(?)
et deliberavit Cujus sasinae precepti tenor sequit[]ur
et est talis

Sasine

In the name of God Amen by this present public instrument be it clearly known and made manifest to all men that in the year of the Incarnation of the Lord &c the month of &c day and of the Reign of the most excellent and most serene Prince James &c King of Great Britain, France and Ireland defender of the faith the year &c In the presence of me, notary public and in the presence of witnesses underwritten, personally compeared ^&c an honorable man, WG of &c in whose favor the precept of seisin written below was made and conceded in the manner undermentioned, and along with the distinguished and honorable man JK of &c sheriff of the county of &c respectively in that part underspecified specially constituted to the manor place of &c according to the tenor in the infeftment underwritten and by the power of the unions and dispensations thereof holds, has and possesses in his own hands the these precepts of sasine of the private chancellor of our Supreme Lord the King: under the testimony of the Great Seal the aforementioned JK as the sheriff foresaid, direct that the said honorable man WG be infeft in all and whole the lands, tithes, manor places, houses, buildings, mills, fishings and others undermentioned lying pertaining and apprised in the manner described below THAT INDEED the precept of sasine inserted below the said WG has produced and presented to the aforenamed JK as to the sheriff lawfully constituted by requiring to seek the execution of the same precept of sasine and himself to duly go and execute the office of sheriff THAT SAID the sheriff knowing and understanding the said Request and desire for justice and reason consent the precept of sasine inserted below is all as it should be Respected, accepts with his hands and delivered and handed it over to me, notary public subscribed, to read publish and explain it to bystanders of which precept of sasine the tenor follows and it is in the following terms

(etc)

Further Reading

Durie, B., *Scottish Genealogy*, 3rd edn (The History Press, 2012)

13

Scotland: Retours

INTRODUCTION

Chapter 10 deals with wills and testaments in Scotland, but for now it is only necessary to remember that:

– Until 1868, wills (strictly speaking, testaments) could only transfer moveable property.
– 'Real' property (also called immoveable or heritable) – essentially land, buildings and heritable titles or offices – were inherited by the separate process of Retours of Services of Heirs.
– There was a way to subvert that, through the use of a Trust Disposition and Settlement ('deed of settlement', see Chapter 11).

Before examining these records, it is necessary to understand something of inheritance, and also the feudal system that governed landholding in Scotland. Most of Scotland's inhabitants were tenants rather than landowners or householders until well after the 1950s, and 100 years before that the majority were agricultural tenants or labourers, factory or mill workers, coal miners and so on. Records of land and property ownership will only be useful for tracking and identifying property owners rather than tenants or workers, but after 1858 it was possible, but not necessary, to register long leases on properties so renters might well appear in the Register of Sasines (Chapter 12).

INHERITANCE AND PROPERTY UNDER THE FEUDAL SYSTEM

Scotland had a feudal system until the Abolition of Feudal Tenure (Scotland) Act 2000, which came into force in 2004. In theory, all land belonged to the Crown, which passed heritable possession to immediate vassals ('subject superiors' or 'Crown tenants', also called 'feudal barons'), who in turn could pass heritable possession of parts of the property to their tenants and vassals, or alienate (dispose of, sell) the lot.

Just as in England, this began as a system of military duty in return for the land granted, but later this aspect was replaced by payment of teinds (tithes) of produce or money. If, for instance, the Crown had granted lands to an abbot or bishop, that churchman could then dispose of it in parcels to others, rent it or lease it etc. This ensured that abbeys, churches and other lands were maintained by an income and produce, and that the land was worked.

But it also meant that when a vassal died, it was not automatic that the property would be passed to his or her designated heir – that would depend on what the original grant said, and on the ability to prove inheritance.

Sale or transfer of ownership (or, properly, vassalage) in life was by means of sasines (Chapter 12) whereas inheritance was by 'service of heirs'.

Heritable immoveable property and retours of services of heirs

When a vassal died, his heir had to prove their right to inherit. In the case of a subject superior (a vassal directly of the Crown), a jury of fifteen local landholders or other 'upright and worthy men of the country' was given a brieve (warrant) to convene and hear pleas, consider any documents provided and decide who was the rightful heir. Their findings were sent as a retour (return) to the Royal Chancery to confirm inheritance. If approved, the Chancery would serve the individual as heir and the process could start to give full title to the property. Where these retours are especially important for family history purposes, is that they often help to clarify connections, such as when land was inherited by a grandson, brother, cousin or nephew.

There are a number of forms of retour:

– Special Retours dealt with lands of subject superiors, and unambiguously described the property in some detail.
– When it concerned their own vassals, subject superiors could confirm an heir's right to inherit by a Precept of *Clare Constat* (clearly shows) essentially authorising the grant of title to the heir. There is no central register of these, but they are within many collections of family papers at the NRS and elsewhere.
– Where a vassal may have had to prove to a subject superior the right to inherit, possibly because there was a dispute or because the superior did not know the heir personally, or was refusing to grant title for some reason, the vassal could use the Chancery to get a jury's opinion on the claim and use this, if beneficial, to get the superior's consent or to require him to consent, producing a General Retour (which did not give any great detail about the property itself, merely those involved in the transfer).
– There are also lists of valuations of land (*Inquisitionum Valorum* and *Inquisitionum de Possessione Quinquennali*) and enquiries into matters of Tutory (*Inquisitionum de Tutela*, looking after the interests of minors) and Curatory (looking after the infirm etc.).

All of these documents are available in the records of the Chancery (NRS Ref. C22 and C28), but there is rarely much need to consult them directly. They were indexed and calendared by the wholly wonderful Thomas Thomson, appointed to the new office of deputy clerk register in 1806. Between 1811 and 1816, Thomson produced his indices in two series: 1544–1699 (mostly in Latin except for 1652–59, but all with English indexes) and 1700–1859 (in English). The first series consisted of two volumes of printed summaries, *Inquisitionum ad Capellam Regis Retornatarum Abbreviatio* and a third volume carrying indices to the first series, arranged by county, of names (*Index nominum*) and places (*Index locorum*). The second series (1700–1859) is for all of Scotland, arranged by decades. Two CD-ROMs are available from the Scottish Genealogy Society, and they have also been printed (see 'Further Reading'). Usually the printed abridgement is all the information that is needed, but the documents themselves, particularly the Special Retours, usually contain important information about the property itself and any special conditions attached to it.

Understanding a retour

A retour begins with the date of the inquest, the names of the jury, the name of the deceased, the lands concerned (if a Special Retour), and the name of the legitimate heir. The extent (worth) of the land was sometimes given in Auld Extent (AE) and New Extent (NE), reflecting the change in value of the Scottish pound. Land values are often expressed in merks (1 merk = $^2/_3$ pound Scots, see Chapter 4).

(18)   Dec. 9. 1640.
ARCHIBALDUS STIRLING, *hæres* Archibaldi Stirling burgensis de Stirling, *patris*,—in annuo redditu 640m. de terris dominicalibus de Menstrie ;—terris de Westertoun et Middiltoun de Menstrie, in parochia de Logie ;—et de terris de Westertoun de Tulliecultrie, infra parochiam de Tulliecultrie :—E. 512m.—annuo redditu 508m. de prænominatis terris et baronia de Menstrie, extendentibus ad 20 libratas terrarum antiqui extentus, in parochia de Logie, et de firmis, &c. dictarum terrarum et baroniæ de Menstrie.—E. 406m. 5s. 4d.   xvi. 135.

(30)   Oct. 6. 1654.
ALEXANDER BRUCE, *heir* of Hendrie Bruce son to Sir Robert Bruce of Clakmanan knight, *his father*,—in ane annuelrent of 200m. furth of the barroney and lands of Clackmanan ;—ane uther annuelrent of 200m. furth of the said lands.   xxiii. 72.

Abridgements of two Special Retours from Clackmannanshire in the 1600s, one abridgement in Latin, one in Scots. The end references (xvi. 135 etc.) are to the actual Retours.

Translation

ARCHIBALD STIRLING, heir to Archibald Stirling Burgess of Stirling, his father, – in annual rent 640 merks of the demesne lands of Menstrie, in the parish of Logie; and of the lands of Westerton of Tillicoutry, under the parish of Tillicoutry: – Extent 512 merks – annual rent 508 merks of the aforesaid lands and barony of Menstrie, extending to 20 pounds (Scots) of land of Old Extent, in the parish of Logie, and of the forms etc of the said lands and barony od Menstrie – Extent 420 merks 5s 4d.

(50)   Oct. 16. 1600.
STEPHANUS LAW, *hæres* Alexandri Law notarii ac incolæ burgi de Edinburgh, *patris*.   ii. 67.

(51)   Oct. 18. 1600.
MAGISTER GEORGIUS BONYMAN, *hæres* Georgii Bonyman mercatoris ac burgensis de Edinburgh, *patris*.   ii. 64.

(52)   Oct. 31. 1600.
JOANNES GORDOUN, *hæres* Domini Joannis Gordoun de Pethurg militis, *patris*.   ii. 61.

(53)   Nov. 8. 1600.
MAGISTER JACOBUS DURHAME de Duntarvie, *hæres* Capitanei Alexandri Durhame de Houschgour in Denmark, *filii patrui*.   ii. 79.

Abridgements of some General Retours from the 1600s.

Translation

(50) STEPHEN LAW, heir to Alexander Law notary and resident of the town of Edinburgh, his father.

(51) MASTER GEORGE BONYMAN, heir to George Bonyman merchant and burgess of Edinburgh, his father.

(52) JOHN GORDON, heir to Sir John Gordon or Petlurg, knight, his father.

(53) MASTER JAMES DURHAM od Duntarvie, heir to Captain Alexander Durham of Houschgour in Denmark, his paternal uncle's son (*i.e. his cousin*).

Note that *Dominus* when followed by *militis* is 'Sir' and '*Magister* signifies a graduate (MA).

> **(38)**   **Oct. 4. 1603.**
> **MAGISTER THOMAS GAIRDYNE** de Blairtone, patruus
> **WALTERI, GILBERTI, MARIÆ, MARGARETÆ** et **ISA-**
> **BELLÆ GAIRDYNIS,** liberorum legitimorum quondam Magistri
> Gilberti Gairdyne de Boithis,—*propinquior agnatus,* id est con-
> sanguineus ex parte patris dictis liberis quondam Magistri Gilberti
> sui fratris germani.   **iii. 54,**

Retour of Tutory (care of minors):

Translation
MASTER THOMAS GAIRDYNE of Blairton, uncle of Walter, Gilbert, Mary Margaret and Isabella
Gairdyne, legitimate children of the deceased Master Gilbert Gairdyne of Boithis,– nearest relation
by blood on father's side of the said children of the deceased Master Gilbert his brother-german
(full brother).

Tailzie

An heir might be served as 'heir of tailzie', meaning that the property was 'entailed': essentially, its
further transfer was restricted to, say, the male line, for generations. This prevented the property
going out with the family and could, for instance, require the heir of tailzie to take the surname of
the entailer. Thus, an outsider marrying a sole heir daughter would take the daughter's family name.
(To see what this does to DNA tracking, see Chapter 13.)

Retours for counties and burghs from 1700

From 1700 to 1859 the printed *Indexes to the Services of Heirs in Scotland* are arranged as decennial
sections, after which they became annual. From the name of the heir in the index it is possible
to find the heir's designation, details about the ancestor (sometimes with the death date), the
type of heir, the names of lands (if a special retour) and the retour date. Original records before
15 November 1847 have the NRS reference prefix C22, and after that, C28.

Don't be confused by dates

There was no time limit for recording a retour, unlike with sasines (Chapter 12), so do not expect
to equate the retour date with death date. It could sometimes take years. Some heirs only bothered
to get a retour years later if, for example, the inheritance was challenged or if they wanted to sell the
property and required evidence of clear title.

Refer to the 'Retours of Services of Heirs' (see 'Further Reading'), the Register of the Great
Seal and the Register of Sasines (Chapter 12). If the original charter is lost an official extract can be
obtained from the Register of the Great Seal, which has the same legal status as the original charter.

The document is a general retour, concerning the inheritance of land:

> This inquest was made in the Burgh court
> of the Canongate 30 March 1812 AD
> in the presence of the honourable man George

Gordon Armiger one of the Bailies

of the said Burgh by these worthy and faithful

countrymen Viz. Alexander

Ross, William Howitson, John

Newlands, George Walker, George Carphin Jnr., John Alexander,

Henry Prager, John [?]Welch, and

John Mason writers [solicitors] in Edinburgh

Henry Martin upholsterer ibid. [at the same place]

Herry Watson merchant ibid.

Partick Main painter ibid. George

Swan merchant ibid. Robert …

[page 2]

Robert Henderson roof-shingler ibid. and

Andrew Paterson, resident in Canongate

which said jury having sworn [marginalia – Chisholm]

on oath that the late

Nigel [Neil] Stewart (Merchant in Edinburgh) uncle of Stewart Chisholm

only legitimate son of John Chisholm

merchant in Perth and the deceased Isabella

Stewart his wife who was sister

to the said late Neil Stewart who died in the faith

and peace of our sovereign lord the King and that the said

Stewart Chisholm the bearer of these presents

is the legitimate and nearest heir in

general to the said late Neil Stewart his

uncle and that he is of lawful age

In witness whereof the seals

of those who took part in the said inquest are

affixed with subscription [signature] of the clerks

of the said Burgh with the inclusion of the seal

of the said Bailie with the brieve of the King included

in the place, day, month and year aforesaid (as

underwritten) John MacKitchie (signed) 5th May 1812

Thus, Stewart Chisholm is the heir to Neil Stewart, brother of Isabella Stewart who married John Chisholm.

Notice, by the way, that fifteen jurors were involved, which is the origin of the phrase 'Fifteen men on a dead man's chest', the 'chest' being his document-chart or 'kist'.

Here is a copy of the extract of retour (and all other Chisholms in that decade):

Chisholm—Alexander William .	to his Father William Chisholm of Chisholm, who died 22d March 1817—Heir Male of Tail. and Prov. Spl., in Breckachy, Inverchannich, Comar, and Forests of Apharick and Breamsallich, and others-Inverness and Ross-shires-28th July 1817	1817, Aug. 27	31
Chisholm—Elizabeth—(or Emond)	Wife of James Chisholm, Weaver, Selkirk, to her Uncle William Emond, Weaver there—Heir Port. Genl.—21st Mar. 1810	1810, April 2	2
Chisholm— Elizabeth—(or Emond)	above designed, to her Uncle John Emond, Weaver in Selkirk—Heir Portioner General—dated 21st March 1810 .	1810, April 2	3
Chisholm—James . . .	Grainmeter, Leith, to his Aunt Isobel Hastie, Wife of Robert Tweedie, Cowfeeder, Edinburgh-Hr. Port. Gl.-18th Apr. 1810	1810, Apr. 24	31
Chisholm—Lilley—(or Nicolson) .	Wife of Archibald Chisholm, Dunse, to her Grandfather Patrick Nicolson, Weaver, Hayshaw-Hr. Port. Gl.-14th July 1814	1814, July 20	26
Chisholm—Stewart . . .	to his Uncle Neil Stewart, Merchant, Edinburgh—Heir in General—dated 30th March 1812	1812, May 5	8
Chisholm—William . . .	Merchant in Inverness, to his Father Hugh Chisholm, Merchant there, who died 12th February 1808—Heir Special, in Lands in Inverness-Inverness-shire—dated 24th May 1819	1819, July 26	44

Incidentally, Neil Stewart (Hardware Merchant in Edinburgh) died 19 February 1812 in Leith South (692/02 0126) and his inventory and trust disposition was confirmed on 20 November 1812 at Edinburgh Sheriff Court (Inventories SC70/1/6).

His inventory and trust disposition runs to twenty-five pages.

An earlier retour

(57)   Aug. 26. 1634.
THOMAS CHISSOLME filius legitimus secundo genitus Joannis Chissolme de Comer, *hæres masculus tallie et provisionis* Alexandri Chissolme de Kynneres filii legitimi quondam Joannis Chissolme de Kinneres, *filii patrui*,—in terris et villa et Kinneres extendentibus ad dimidium davatæ terrarum antiqui extentus, existentibus 17 solidatis 6 denariatis terrarum, cum multuris et potestate molendina ædificandi super aliqua parte earundem, infra baroniam de Bewfort et Drumchardony et vicecomitatum de Innernes.—A. E. 17s. 6d. N. E. 3l. 10s.   xiii. 250.

(57)   August 26 1634
Thomas Chissolme second born legitimate son of John
Chissolme of Comer, hair male of tailzie and provision[1] of
Alexander Chissolme of Kynneres [Kinneries] legitimate son of the deceased John
Chissolme of Kinneres, son of his father's brother – in the lands and town [of] Kinneres
extending to half a davach[2] of land of auld extent[3], extending
to 17 shillings and 6 pence of land, with the multures[4] and power
over the mill buildings over any parts of them under the
Barony of Bewfort and Drumchardony and the county of
Innerness [Inverness]. – A[uld] E[xtent] 17s. 6d. N[ew] E[xtent] 3l.10s ($£3$ 10s)[5]

Notes:
- Heir of tailzie: succeeding by virtue of an entail; provision: having right by settlement or will.
- Davach: about 32–48 acres of sown land, roughly the same as an English ploughgate, about the area that a single plough could turn over in a season.
- Auld Extent, New Extent: there was a revaluation of land values in the 1400s but a factor of four or five, but most people used both to avoid ambiguity. Think of this as the annual rent or produce realisable, so it's sort of a rateable value.
- Multure: the right to extract a tithe of grain etc. ground at the mill.
- This is in pounds Scots: the exchange rate at this date was 12:1, so $£3$ 10s = about 6s, or perhaps about $£100$ in today's terms – not much!

Two examples, for practice:

(862)   Aug. 16. 1628.
WILLIELMUS STRIVILING, *hæres* Henrici Striviling de Ardoch, *patris*,—in dimidietate terrarum de Rahalloch, in parochia
de Stragaith.—E. 5m. et 16s. 8d. in augmentationem. x. 111.

(804)   Mar. 10. 1670.
DOMINUS GULIELMUS STIRLING de Ardoche, *hæres*
Domini Henrici Stirling de Ardoche militis baronetti, *patris*,—in
6 mercatis terrarum de Ovir Ardoche cum crofta terræ vulgo
Wattersyid nuncupata seu Brewlandes;—altera crofta terræ nuncupata Raith alias Chappelland;—molendino de Ovir Ardothe
infra baroniam de Dumblane;—terris de Nathir Ardoche cum
privilegiis communitatis in mora de Ovir et Nathir Ardoches vo-
cata Kauhkymure, infra parochiam de Muthill:—A. E. ....
N. E. ....—terris de Garvock infra senescallatum de Stratherne:—A. E. ...., N. E. ....—terris de Bany et Kath-
kyne;—occidentali dimidietate terrarum de Eister Feddales exten-
dente ad 16 bovatas terrarum, infra regalitatem de Lindoires:—
A. E. ...., N. E. ....—terris de Dalclevan extendentibus
ad 10 mercatas terrarum antiqui extentus, infra baroniam de Keir
per unionem et incorporationem:—A. E. ...., N. E. ....—
terris de Blackfoord alias vocatis Blacksauche infra senescallatum
de Stratherne:—A. E. .... N. E. ....—terris de Eistir
Panhollia, Wester Panhollis et Midle Panhollis, infra senescallatum
de Stratherne:—A. E. .... N. E. ....—terris et baronia de
Bracco;—terris de Keirsbane;—terris de Gannochen;—3 quar-
teriis terrarum de Drummoquhence;—dimidietate terrarum de
Wester Drummoquhence;—villa et terris de Athrie;—terris de
Eistir Rochburne, Westir, Midle, cum decimis garbalibus in vice-
comitatibus de Perth et Stirling respective:—A. E. ....
N. E. ....—molendino de Cames alias molendino de Callentin
nuncupato, cum pecia terræ et Brae de terris de Callentine, infra
senescallatum de Monteith.—A. E. .... N. E. ....
(Vide Stirling.)   xxx. 124.

Further Reading

Durie, B., *Retours of Services of Heirs 1544–1859*, 3 vols (2012). See www.brucedurie.co.uk/books

'Retours of Services of Heirs' available on CD from the Scottish Genealogy Society, www.scotsgenealogy.com

Abolition of Feudal Tenure etc. (Scotland) Act 2000, www.hmso.gov.uk/legislation/scotland/acts2000/20000005.htm

'Report on Abolition of the Feudal System', www.scotland.gov.uk/deleted/library/documents-w10/afs1-00.htm

Gretton, G., 'The Law of Property in Scotland', in Reid, K.G.C. (ed.), *Butterworth's Edinburgh* (Law Society of Scotland, 1996), pp. 31–100

McNeill, P.G.B. and MacQueen, H.L. (eds), *Atlas of Scottish History to 1707* (University of Edinburgh, 1996)

14

Scotland: Tacks, Assedations and Maills

James V, like his father before him, often went about in disguise so as to interact with his subjects. He called himself the 'Guidman of Ballengeich' (which is the area around Stirling Castle) and 'guidman' or 'goodman' is another word for 'tacksman'. Nothing to do with 'tax', though.

A tack is essentially a form of lease on land, with associated contract documents. It predates the feu and the rental as the most common form of landholding and was a convenient middle ground between outright heritable possession and merely working the land. These categories can usually be distinguished by someone being called 'of' somewhere (heritable possession), 'in' (tack) and 'at' (residing there). However, a tack could itself be heritable and was often given for 'three lives' (the tacksman or leaseholder, his wife and his heir) thus ensuring some sort of security of tenure.

The document recording a tack usually contains a phrase like:

> hath set, and in tack let, as he hereby sets, and in tack and assedation sets, to the said A. B. and his heirs, secluding assignees and subtenants, legal or voluntary, without the express consent of the proprietor, all and whole the land of X lying in the parish of Y and county of Z.

It may describe actual land boundaries and will set out the conditions by which the land is tacked. The tacksman can therefore be considered a tenant farmer with a document to prove it, unlike a renter, who may leave no more trace than an entry in an estate rent book.

Often, the overlord had some responsibility for repairs of major structures – walls, watercourses and the like – but the tacksman also had a duty to use and maintain the land properly. This is rather like the modern-day situation where the landlord has the repair of a building but the occupier looks to the decoration and general upkeep.

Unfamiliar terms found in a tack may include:

– Assedation: a Norman word, derived ultimately from Latin, signifying a settlement for a defined period of time, so a tacksman may be described as an 'assedatarius'.
– Tack duty: the payments or dues, in cash or in kind (such as produce).
– Maills: often combined as 'maills and duties', maill means more or less the same as rent, whereas duties are the services due; by extension, 'blackmail' is rent extorted illegally.
– The phrase 'against all deadly' is Scottish legal parlance for 'against all mortal people'.

Originally, and especially on clan-held lands in the Highlands in the seventeenth and eighteenth centuries, tacksmen were very often cadet branches of the chiefly line. This was a way of keeping the majority of the lands within the extended family and still in the ultimate possession of the chief, but managed out. The tacksman might rent out parts of the land to rentallers (usually on a yearly basis without much security of tenure) or hire labourers to work parts of it. We think of the Highland Clearances as principally affecting crofters, but the tacksman system was more thoroughly disrupted than crofting. Many tacksmen then emigrated to Canada, America or the Caribbean, including, famously, Flora MacDonald who had helped Bonnie Prince Charlie escape from Hanoverian troops after the 1745 Jacobite Rebellion by dressing the Young Pretender in women's clothes. Flora's husband Allan MacDonald had held the tack of Kingsburgh from Macdonald of Sleat while Flora's father, Ranald, had the tack of Milton in South Uist from MacDonald, Chief of Clanranald. Flora and Allan emigrated to North Carolina in 1773, just in time to end up fighting on the Hanoverian side, strangely, in the Wars of Independence. She eventually returned to Skye.

A tack is often for nineteen years or for multiples of nineteen years. There is also some speculation in legal history circles that nineteen years was considered a 'life' (you got the land at 19 and were dead by 38) but in reality, tacks were often granted for multiples of nineteen years. This may seem a rather random number, but there were two reasons for it. First, there was an assumption in law, certainly from 1806, that a lease of twenty years or longer implied the ability to sublet, unless specifically ruled out, and that a shorter lease precluded subletting unless specifically allowed. Second, until 1762 any tack in excess of nineteen years was thought too much like an alienation of the land, or a liferent, which would require a sasine (Chapter 12). Why 1762? This was the year that the House of Lords accepted the validity of very long tacks (60 x 19 = 1,140 years in one case!) although there were many examples of tacks for longer than twenty years, and even liferent tacks set for the life of the lessee (or three lives as described above).

The document on pp. 204–5 is the liferent tack of 1751 on tenanted lands of Dirleton, East Lothian, between Jean Bennett, relict (widow) of William Nisbet, and her grandson, also William Nisbet, in respect of lands called Fenton and East Fenton along with some properties in Dirleton. Essentially, she's allowing her son to manage the lands left to her by her deceased husband, without giving up control and while receiving an income for life. Sensible woman!

The genealogy of this situation is complex. William Nisbet, (1666–1724), son of Alexander Nisbet of Craigtinnie, married two different women called Jean Bennet(t): the first (m.1688) was Jean, daughter of Sir William Bennet of Grubett; and the second (m.1710) was Jean, daughter of Robert Bennett, Dean of the Faculty of Advocates. His son William (1699–1733) succeeded and also married a Bennet. On his death, Dirleton passed to his son William, who died in 1783, leaving Dirleton to his son, yet another William.

There are various stipulations as to the income from farm produce at various 'crops' (harvests or season's yields) and to the term days of Candlemas, Whitsun, Lammas and Martinmas (p. 89).

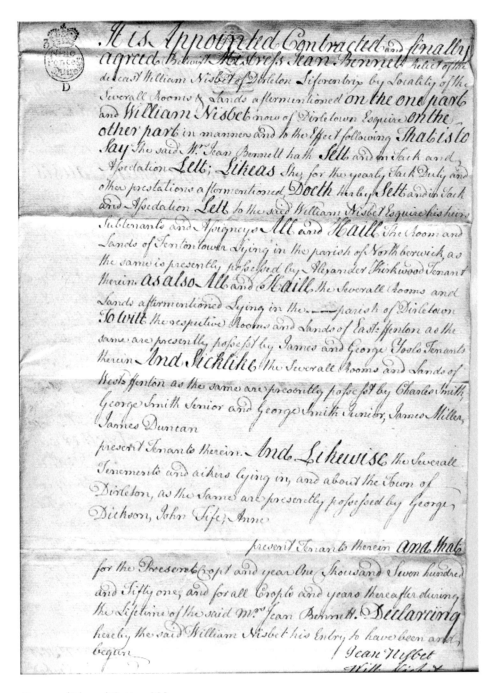

Courtesy of John and Catriona McInnes

begun as to the Houses and Grass at the Term of *Whitsunday* last and as to the arrable Land at the Seperation of the last Crop from the Ground *with full power* to the said William Nisbet and his foresaids to Out:pull and In:pull Tenants in the foresaid Lands and possessions at pleasure. *And* the said Mistress Jean Bennett doeth hereby Bind & oblige herself and her heirs and Executors to Warrand this Tack at all hands and against all Deadly. *For the which Causes* and on the other part The said William Nisbet hath become bound & obliged and doeth hereby Bind & oblige himself and his heirs Executors or Assigneys to Content and pay to the said Mrs Jean Bennett and her heirs Executors or Assigneys, in name of Tack: Duty Yearly during all the years & Terms of her Lifetime as aforesaid, The Rent which she the said Mrs Jean Bennet presently receives for the said Lands *Videlicet* Six pence Sterling money more than the Highest fiars of East Lothian for each Boll of the following Quantitys of Victuall *To witt* One hundred and fourty Nine Bolls and one firlot of Wheat, Two hundred and fifty two Bolls and one firlot and three Pecks of Barley and Two hundred and Thirty Eight Bolls and one firlot of Oats *Together* with Two hundred Hain Hens and Twenty four Hain Poultrie fowles, or in the said Mrs Jean Bennets option Seven pence Sterling for each Hen, and five pence Sterling for each hain poultrie fowle *And that* at four Terms in the year Candlemass Whitsunday Lambmass and Martinmass after each Cropt by equall portions *Beginning* the first Terms payment of the said Tack: Duty at the Term of Candlemass One Thousand Seven hundred and fifty two Years for the fourth part of the Rent of Cropt and year One Thousand

Jean Nisbet
Will: Nisbet

Courtesy of John and Catriona McInnes

Thousand Seven hundred and Fifty one And the remaining three payments for said Croft and year at the Term of Whitsunday Lambmass and Martinmass One Thousand Seven hundred and fifty two *and so furth* yearly & Termly thereafter during the lifetime of the said Mrs Jean Bennet *And* the said William Nisbet doeth hereby Bind & oblige himself and his heirs Executors and Assigneys or Subtenants whatever to pay all Cess Ministers Stipends Schoolmasters Sallarys and other Publick Burdens & Exactions of whatever Denomination either already Imposed or that shall be hereafter Imposed upon the said Liferented Lands Yearly during the Subsistance of this Lease, *and that over & above* the Tack duty stipulate to be paid by him to the said Mrs Jean Bennet which she is to have payment of free of all Deductions whatever yearly and Termly as aforesaid during this Tack.— *And Sicklike* the said William Nisbet hereby Binds and obliges him and his foresaids to uphold all the Houses and Biggings on the said Liferented Lands during the Continuance of this present Sett thereof. *And Lastly* Both Partys Bind & oblige them and their foresaids to perform and fulfill their Severall parts of this Tack to the other, and the party faillieing to pay to the Party performing or willing to perform their part of the premisses the Sum of Fifty pounds Sterling money of liquidate penalty by and attour performance *And they Consent* to the Registration hereof in the Books of Councill and Session that a Decreet of the Lords thereof may be Interponed hereto And that Letters of Horning on Six days Charge and all other Executorialls needfull pass

Jean Nisbet

Courtesy of John and Catriona McInnes

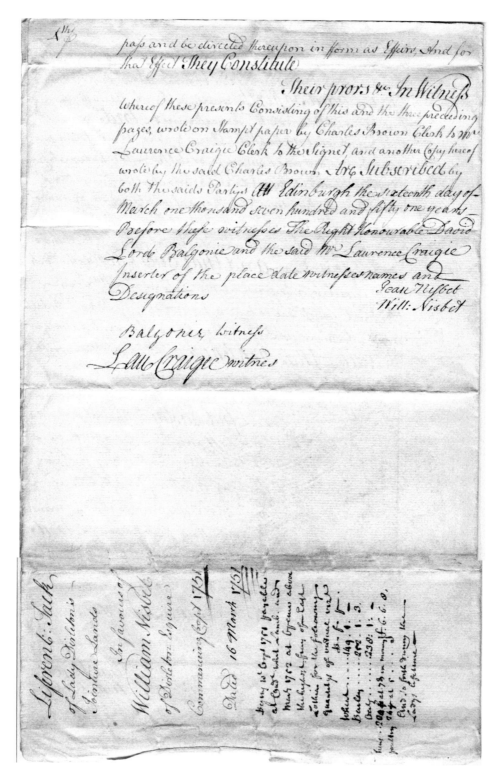

Courtesy of John and Catriona McInnes

15

Scotland: Kirk Sessions

KIRK SESSIONS (See also Chapter 8)

Since the Scottish Reformation, every congregation of the Church of Scotland has had a Kirk Session, essentially the lowest (and local) court of the Church of Scotland. It consisted of the minister(s) and senior elders and its main duties were to maintain order. When the congregation was effectively everyone in the parish, this was the unit of social control, and the Kirk Session could not help but to enquire into the moral status of the parishioners.

Kirk Session records are essentially the business records of a parish, and contain a vast amount of information valuable to the genealogist. If your ancestor was chastised for some reason (non-attendance, squabbling with a neighbour, misbehaving before marriage, having a child out of wedlock and even witchcraft) or was involved with the Kirk Session in some other way, it will likely be recorded here. The illegitimacy records in particular are a rich vein for genealogists unable to find an individual in other records. Kirk Session minutes (or separate accounts) might also include details of monies raised and disbursed, often with lists of recipients. These minutes survive from the late sixteenth century for some parishes, and are in unbroken runs for most parishes from the late seventeenth century. Many are in print or available on the Internet.

The Kirk Session and the heritors (local landowners) ran the parish and often had responsibility for the Poor Law, school, hospital, alms house and other parochial resources. The records, along with those of presbyteries, synods and the General Assembly of the Church of Scotland, are deposited at the National Records of Scotland (NRS) in Edinburgh and over 5 million pages covering the period from 1500 to 1901 have been digitised by a partnership between the NRS, the Church of Scotland and the Genealogical Society of Utah (GSU).

The timetable for their online availability is at www.scottishdocuments.com, but the plan is to have them available by the end of 2013. However some local presbyteries have access for testing, as do some local archives.

HERITORS' MINUTES

Heritors were landowners living in the parish who were bound by law to contribute to the maintenance of a church (capable of accommodating two-thirds of the population aged over 12), the stipend of the minister plus a manse and a glebe (garden, orchard or farmland), a school and the stipend of the 'Dominie' (schoolmaster) as well as other public works. Although there was a system in place for the formal assessment of heritors' payments towards poor relief, they often just made voluntary contributions to the parochial structure. They paid according to the size of their estates, so the largest landowners had the majority of the costs and also, therefore, the greatest influence. Since the same people were likely to be elders of the kirk, and also commissioners of supply as well as holding other burgh or county duties, they exercised considerable sway over the parish and area.

Extract from the Kirk Session minutes of 1639/40 of various parishes within the Presbytery of Kirkcaldy

Showing the degree to which the kirk elders took witchcraft seriously at the time, and acted as local court in such matters. It also shows what a rich source of names, offices, occupations and other genealogical information such a record can be.

Kirkcaldie, December 27

Mr Georg Gilespie Minister at Weyms, declaired to the brethern sundrie presumptiouns of witchcraft aganest ane Janet Durie in Weyms. The brethern desyres him first to try the saids presumptions befoir his sessioun and thairafter to bring them to the Presbytrie.
Dysert, Januarii 10
Janet Durie to be sowmonti to the nixt day.

Dysert, Januarii 17
Compeired Janet Durie in Weyms challenged of witchcraft: denyes all: sowmonit *apud acta* to compeir the nixt day in Dysert.

At Dysert, 24 day of Januarii, 1639
Compeired Janet Durie challangit anent sundrie poynts of witchcraft; denyed the same. Sundrie witnesses compeireand aganest hir being admittit and deiplie sworne deponed as follows:– *Imprimis* Adam Blaikwood Reider at Weyms deponed that he comeing to visit James Kedie in Weyms being sick the said James said to him that Janet Durie was the causs of his death he having stickit ane swine to the said Janet Durie befoir for whilk she had professit to causs him rewit.

Compeired John Walker who deponed that Robert Bennett he being sick and dead (as was thought) for he was streakit said that Janet Durie had the wyte of it.

Compeired Geills Thomson relict of Umqll James Keddie who deponit that hir husband

Kirkcaldy, December 27 1639

Mr George Gillespie Minister at Wemyss, declared to the brethren sundry presumptions of witchcraft against one Janet Durie in Wemyss. The brethren desire him first to try the said presumptions before his [Kirk] Session and thereafter to bring them to the Presbytery.
Dysart, January 10
Janet Durie to be summoned to the next day.

Dysart, January 17
Compeired [appeared in court] Janet Durie in Wemyss challenged of witchcraft: Denies all: summoned at the time of the proceedings to appear the next day in Dysart.

At Dysart, 24th day of January, 1639 [1640 by modern calendar]
Compeired Janet Durie challenged about various points of witchcraft; denied the same. Various witnesses appeared against her being admitted and truly sworn testified as follows:– In the first, Adam Blackwood Reader [Minister] at Wemyss testified that he coming to visit James Keddie in Wemyss being sick, the said James said to him that Janet Durie was the cause of his death, he having hit with a stick a pig [belonging] to the said Janet Durie before for which she had professed to cause him to rue it.

Compeired John Walker who testified that Robert Bennett, he being sick and dead (as was thought), for he was laid out [presumably unconscious], said that Janet Durie had knowledge of it.

Compeired Geills Thomson, relict of deceased James Keddie, who testified that her husband was sick of the disease whereof he died, hee said to Adam Blaikwood that Janet Durie was the causs of his death for when he stickit hir swine she said that she would causs him repent it. Compeired Kathren Courtier deponed that James Keddie being sick laid his death upon Janet Durie. The Presbytrie considering the things alledgit aganest hir thinks it is reason that she be wardit to abyd further tryell.

was sick of the disease whereof he died, he said to Adam Blackwood that Janet Durie was the cause of his death, for when he hit her pig she said that she would cause him [to] repent it. Compeired Kathren Courtier testified that James Keddie being sick laid his death upon Janet Durie. The Presbytery considering the things alleged against her thinks it is reason that she be held to wait further trial.

Although heritors had no responsibility for the religious, moral or pastoral care of the parishioners, they did share the duties of poor relief. They often held joint meetings with the Kirk Session and usually had their own meetings in the parish church. (The situation in burghs was different, and where the parish church was burghal (that is, wholly within the burgh) the magistrates were the heritors.)

After the 1845 Poor Law Act the new parochial boards did impose assessments on landowners and occupiers, and the place of heritors in the scheme of things dwindled away to nothing.

Example

The following is an extract from the Presbytery Book of Lanark (the presbytery is the level of church administration above parish and below synod). It concerns the big issue of the day – the Covenant – which was occupying the hearts and minds of everyone in 1638.

In 1637, Charles I and Archbishop Laud were keen to merge the Established Churches of Scotland and England, by introducing a new Book of Canons to replace John Knox's *Book of Discipline* as the handbook for the Kirk and a modified form of the English *Book of Common Prayer*, both without consultation. The Scottish Parliament and the General Assembly of the Kirk reacted with predictable outrage from Scots being told what to do in matters they considered their own business, and an Edinburgh lady called Jenny Geddes (it is said) flung her prayer stool at the Dean of St Giles when he read from the new prayer book on 23 July 1637. Then there was a riot, literally.

In February 1638, at Greyfriars Kirk in Edinburgh, many Scots nobles, landed gentry, clergy and burgesses signed the National Covenant, and this document, dedicated to preserving the purity of the Kirk, was circulated all through Scotland for signing. Popular support was immense, and any clergy who demurred were simply removed. By the end of May that year, the only resistance was in the furthest western Highlands and in Aberdeen and Banff, where the arch-royalist Marquis of Huntly held sway.

This document, dated 29 March 1638, shows the strength of local feeling and the moves taken:

March 29 1638
[etc.]
The Covenant
Forsameekle as the frequent supplicationes against the service booke, and booke of canones, presented befoir the Counsell, had gottin no answer nor sa-
-tisfaction, bot by the contrare, proclamation made discharging all the meetings of the subjectes for that earand, under the paine of treasone, and so encreasing the feares of the well affected of all degrees of people that the truthe of religion and puritie of the gospell wer now in extream hasert of a fearfull decay, It is thought good by the nobilitie and all degrees of supplicantes, that the old Confessione of Faith subscryved dyverse

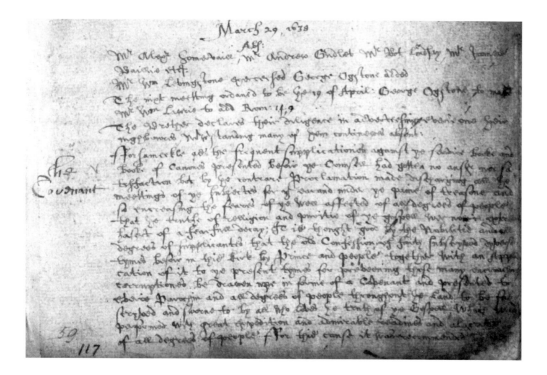

tymes befoir in this kirke, by prince and people, together with an appli-
-cation of it to the present tymes for preveening those many encroaching
corruptiones be drawen upe in forme of a covenant, and presented to
everie parochin, and all degrees of people throughout the land to be sub-
-scryved and sworne to by all who loves the truth of the gospell ; which was
performed with great expedition and admirable readines and alacritie
of all degrees of people. For this cause it was recommended
[next page, not shown here but transcription added for the sake of completeness]
by the commissioners of schyres that they sould take notice if their was any
kirkes within their boundes quherunto the couenant had not yet been
presented.
Heirfoir the brether efter tryall taken finds that thir wer 3 kirkes
within our presbyterie quher the covenant had not yet been red, viz. Doug-
-las, Carmichall, and Carstaires.

Further Reading

'Update on digitisation of church court records at the NRS', www.scottishdocuments.com/
opImages/ChurchRecordsOnline1203.pdf

16

England and Wales: Wills – Bequeathing and Devising

Wills in the English style are more straightforward than their Scottish equivalent, testaments. One main difference is that an English will could be used both to bequeath and to devise.

Scots law (as English law once did) made a distinction between 'real' (immoveable) heritable property, such as land, houses and titles on the one hand and moveable property (money, furniture, crops etc.) on the other. But in English law, unlike in Scotland, both could be included in a will. To 'devise' is to make a gift of real property by will (to a 'devisee') whereas to bequeath is to dispose by will of 'personal' property: that other than land, buildings etc. (such as money). A devise may be specific (such as 'I devise my manor or lordship of X to A.B. of Y'); general ('... all my real property whatsoever to C.D.') or residuary (that part not specifically devised to someone). A bequest is a gift by will of property other than land.

Gift of personalty (personal property) is a bequest. Strictly speaking, a will deals with real property and a testament deals with bequests of personalty, but a will and testament could be in the same document.

INHERITANCE IN ENGLAND

From 1066 real property fell automatically to the heir of the deceased, in accordance with Norman law. This was usually the eldest surviving son by the rule of primogeniture. However, there was also (in some parts of England):

– 'Borough English': the youngest son inherits.
– Gavelkind (in Kent, but also found in Wales and Ireland): all sons inherit equally.

Personal property (and later, leaseholds) could be disposed of at will, but Church law held that:

– $\frac{1}{3}$ went to the widow (as the 'widow's dower').
– $\frac{1}{3}$ went to children.
(Compare this to Scottish rules of inheritance, Chapter 10.)

The Statute of Distributions (1670) confirmed this but divided the rest equally among any children, otherwise to parents or (if dead) to siblings of the deceased. The Administration of Estates Act (1925) has similar provisions.

Important statutes

- Statute of Wills (1540): males from 14, females from 12 could inherit.
- Wills Act (1837): ages raised to 21 for both (but not traitors, heretics, lunatics, slaves or prisoners) and disallowed nuncupative wills.
- Before the Married Women's Property Act (1882), an unmarried woman (*femme sole*) could own and dispose of property but possessions of a married woman (*femme couvert*) other than paraphernalia, see below, were the property of the husband. Wills were only valid with a husband's permission. A woman had a right to retain her paraphernalia – essentially her 'bottom drawer': clothing, jewels, ornaments etc. – as her own property after her husband's death, even against creditors and although in his lifetime the husband might have sold or given them away, he could not bequeath them by his will.

Getting around the law

Some property owners avoided all this legal restriction by vesting property in trustees who acted according to deed or a will in disposing of property after death (compare Trust Disposition and Settlement in Scotland, Chapter 11). This was prohibited by the Statute of Uses (1535) but the Statute of Wills (1540) allowed real property to be devised (gifted to others rather than an heir) and this applied to all land from 1661.

Ecclesiastical courts

Another difference between Scots and English executry law is that in Scotland, all commissary functions were taken from the diocesan courts and given to new secular commissary courts. In England and Wales this remained the province of the Established Church right up to 1858.

The early Christian Church very quickly developed a set of rules for governing itself and administering its business, based either on what the Bible said, or what the Church said the Bible said, with full apostolic authority. This included the claim that anything to do with life or death was within its jurisdiction. This took in almost everything we would now call family law, including the proving ('probate') of wills, but also matrimonial causes such as divorce, annulment, judicial separation and questions of legitimacy.

In Saxon times, Christianity was so amalgamated with civil administration that bishops commonly held court during the local Hundred Court sessions. In 1072 William the Conqueror set up separate courts to deal with ecclesiastical matters, and these courts took this to mean the maintenance of spiritual discipline, so, exclusive jurisdiction over lay people in all criminal cases where a cleric was the defendant, offence against religion or morality, anything concerning consecrated land and buildings and – as we have seen – all matrimonial causes and the granting of probate.

There was a hierarchy of Church courts, from archdeaconry to prerogative (archiepiscopal), and the more important or complex the matter, the higher the court to deal with it would be. Essentially, it went like this:

- Parishes were grouped into archdeaconries.
- Archdeaconries were grouped into dioceses.

- Each diocese was administered by the bishop's consistory (commissary) or episcopal courts, held regularly, usually every two weeks, in the cathedral or main church of the diocese.
- The dioceses themselves were in two archiepiscopal provinces: York (north of the River Trent) and Canterbury (south of the River Trent), administered by the archiepiscopal or Prerogative courts.
- The Court of Chancery had ultimate jurisdiction.

What determined the court in which a will would be proved (which means 'approved') depended on where the deceased had lived and died, where the properties and goods were geographically, and (to an extent) the value of the estate. It went more or less as follows:

- Within one archdeaconry (even if in different parishes): archdeacon's court.
- In more than one archdeaconry but all in the same diocese: bishop's consistory court.
- Across more than one diocese: the appropriate archbishop's prerogative court.
- Value of the goods more than £5 (£10 in London): prerogative court.
- Value of the goods more than £5 (£10 in London) and spread across the two provinces: both prerogative courts, first York, then Canterbury.
- Property owner in England or Wales who died overseas (including soldiers and sailors): Prerogative Court of Canterbury (PCC), regardless of where their property was.

There was a predicable interruption in the functioning of the ecclesiastical courts during the Civil War and Interregnum. Oliver Cromwell suspended these courts from 1642 (1653 for the PCC) but they were reopened when the Episcopacy was reinstated at the Restoration of the Monarchy in 1660. Their power and influence was never quite the same and much of their jurisdiction ended up in secular courts.

Up to 1804, these records also contain sentences: judgements concerning disputed wills, which may not contain the same details as the disputed will itself.

Between 1836 and 1858 the Church courts gradually lost their authority over matrimonial causes, defamation, tithes and all matters of probate and though they still exist, they are limited to matters of Church property and ecclesiastical discipline. The Probate Act (1857) gave jurisdiction to Court of Probate and probate registries around the country, and has been merged into the Probate, Divorce and Admiralty division of the High Court of Justice since 1875.

For wills and other executry after 1858, it is necessary to deal with the Probate Service (www.justice.gov.uk/courts/probate) at the Principal Registry in High Holborn, London. There are eleven district probate registries and eighteen probate sub-registries situated throughout England and Wales.

PCC wills

This means that the Prerogative Court of Canterbury (PCC) was the most important of the church courts up to 1858. But it did not just deal with the wills of wealthy individuals in the south of England and most of Wales, but many common people too. This is fortunate, as the PCC wills are the easiest to get to online, via The National Archives (www.nationalarchives.gov.uk). The digitised images available are copies of original probates written into volumes by the Church Court clerks, and date from 1384 to 12 January 1858, after which the responsibility shifted to new probate courts. Wills proved before the archbishop's court between 1312 and 1384 are enrolled on registers held at Lambeth Palace Library.

County records offices also have wills, and if the executor or lawyer kept a copy (as most did) they may be in private archives or with family papers. Often it is enough to look at the extracts in the National Probate Calendar, which gives names of deceased, date of death, place and time of probate, date of letters of administration, value of estate and names of executors (with addresses and relationship from 1858 to 1892).

Structure and language of wills

What is loosely referred to as a will may be:

- A Grant of Probate: where the testator has left a will, which is then proved in the court.
- Letters of Administration: either where the deceased has died intestate and the estate has to be settled, or when the deceased left a valid will but administration is granted to someone other than an executor.
- Sometimes merely a codicil: amending a previous will, which may or may not exist.

The will may start with the word 'memoranda', indicating that the will was spoken and quite probably on the deathbed. This is not quite the same as 'nuncupative', which means given orally to witnesses rather than written.

Before 1733, the main body of the text of wills, as well as sentences (see below) and probate clauses were in Latin (except during the Interregnum, when they were in English). After this, most wills are written in English but the probate clause may be in Latin (example below).

The executor or executrix was appointed by the deceased, but the will/testament would have to be proved by persuading a court that it was valid and was 'final' or 'last', the process called probate.

A will or testament could be changed by substitution (a new will) or a codicil (addition and/or amendment). But if you see these words: 'I hereby revoke all wills and testamentary dispositions previously made by me and declare this to be my last will', it does not necessarily mean there was an earlier will – it's just lawyers being careful!

Examples of wills

Three are given just as transcripts and a fourth – Will of William Stevens, 1584 – in its full form with transcript, including a very typical Latin probate clause:

PCC 8 Alenger Register. TNA Catalogue reference PROB 11/28
Bookill, Robert,
Of Orford in the Diocese of Norwich dated 1st March 1539.
I give my body to be buried in the parish church of Orford by my wife.
I bequeath to the high altar there, for tithes negligently paid, 3s. 4d.
To the necessary reparations of the parish church, £3 6s. 8d.

I will have an honest priest to pray there for me and my friends for one whole year.
I give to Robert Jacobbe, my daughter's son, my tenement that I dwell in.
Sir William Osmond shall have 40s. to pray for me and my friends for one whole year.
John Jacobb, my daughter's son, shall have the tenement I purchased of my father; and Robert Cooke, my daughter's son, shall have my tenement at the church gate. All my said grandsons to enter the premises at their ages of 21. My son in law Robert Cooke shall have the profits thereof in the meantime, towards the bringing up of the said children.
All my household stuff shall be parted among Robert Jacobb, John Jacobb, and Robert Jacobb the younger, and Robert Pawling shall not meddle with my salt nor wood, nor with anything in my house that I dwelt in.
I give to Robert and John Jacobbe, Robert Cooke and Elizabeth Pawlyng a cow apiece.

To every of my godchildren, 12d.

To Robert Pawlyng, 20 of my best sheep in the chantry flock.

Robert Cooke shall have my part of the Freres houses, and tiles to repair the children's houses withal.

John Clobbard shall have the lease of my part in Wargate Marshe.

I give to the reparations of the bridge way, 6s 8d.

Sir George Goore shall have 10s in money, and am thackke [thick] tyle to his reparacions ward to praye for my soule.

I give to Margaret Cooke a cow.

To Robert Cooke, my scalbotte [sailboat], my best anchor and all things belonging thereto, and a spurlyng [young herring] boat.

To Robert Cooke and Robert Pawlyng, a havyn cocke.

To Robert Jacobbe, my other cocke.

My executors shall sell my marsh that I hold of Sir Anthony Wyngfeld, Kt., the residue of my neat [heifer], two great anckors and the residue of my sheep for the performance of my will; and I make Robert Cooke and Robert Pawlyng my executors.

Witnesses : Sir George Goore, chantry priest, John Clobbard,

Robart Partryche, Mathewe Ferror.

Proved, 3 July 1540, by the proctor of the executors named.

PCC Wingfield Quire Number 61.TNA reference PROB 11/116

Beversham, Susan.

Abstract of the nuncupative will of Susan Beversham, late wife of James Beversham of Orford, made *ca.* September 1609.

Being asked by Magdalen Darbye, a kinswoman of hers, if she wold bestowe something upon her, if it shoold please God to call the said Susan out of this world, she replied that all shee had she did give to her husband, meaning the said James Beversham.

Witnesses: Magdalen Darbye, Katheren Petley, Susan Wood.

22 June 1610. Commission issued to the abovenamed James

Beversham to administer the goods etc. of the said deceased.

PCC 167 Goare Register.TNA Catalogue reference PROB 11/21

Derehaugh, Robert.

Nuncupative will of Robert Derehaugh of Gedgrave, gent.

About Christmas 1615 'having a purpose then shortly to travell beyond the seas' said 'yf I do nob leave a will in writeing I give all my estate to my sister Sexie'. [Mary, widow of William Sexe, alias Saxey, Esqre., of St Martin's in the Fields]

15 December 1637. Commission granted to William Cardinall, husband of Mary Cardinall alias Sexie, deceased, to administer the goods of the said Robert Derehaugh, during the minority of William & Anne Cardinall, children of the said William & Mary Cardinall, no executor being named in the will.

Will of William Stevens, 1584

I   William Stevens

In the name of god amen. The nynetenth daye of

December in the yeare of our Lord god a thousand five hundred fourscore and seven [1587] I

William Stevins of Burton upon the hill in the countie of Glocester gent. being sicke

of bodye but of good and perfect memorye thankes be given unto god doe make this my last

will and testament in manner and forme following ffirst I bequeath my soule into the

handes of almightye god and I will my bodye to be buried in the churche of Burton ~ ~

115

aforesayd Item I bequeathe unto the poore people of Burton forty shillinges to be distri=
buted at the discretion of my executor and of Mr Bocke (?) parson of Burton within one
moneth next after my deathe Item I give unto my Sister Catharine one hundred poundes
over and above the hundred poundes that is already due unto her for that my will and
meaning is that my sayd Sister Catherine shall have payd her by my executor two hundred poundes
within six ~

monethes after my deceasse for that she shall acquit my sayd executor from any further demande of any parte

or parcell of my brother Rowlandes goods and from all other legacies left her by my father. Item I give unto

my brother James and his assignes one yearly annuitye of thirtie poundes by the year be taken out of Blocklye

parke during both the leasses by my sayd brother James his heires executors or assignes for that he shall also

acquit and discharge my executor of and from any further demande of any parte or parcell of my brother Rowlands goods or of any difte or legacye given or bequeathed him either by my father or mother or by any other

person. Item I give unto my servante John Braby for and in considerat[i]on of his true and faithfull service

to me done the full and inst some of tenne poundes and a nagge And I will that all other debtes due unto

him by my brother John or by me shable well and truly payd him The rest of all my goods landes and leases

my debtes being payd my legacyes performed and my funeralle discharged I give and bequeathe unto my

brother John Stevens whome I make and appointe my sole and onelye executor of this my last will and testament And doe ordeyne and appointe my well beloved uncles Mr Rowland Baugh and Robert Lyster over=

seers of my last will requesting them to see the same well and truly to be observed performed and kepte And

I give either of them for their paynes to be taken herein fortye shillinges a peece And I will that theie twoe or the longer liver of them shall have the ordering and ending of all sutes or controvercies that shall channce to fall betwene my executor or anyone to whome I have given any thing in this my sayd testa= ment or last will. Item I will that Richard Ducke (?) of Liviton [Leveton] nigh unto Exceter my olde good friend be

payd him his twentye poundes that I owe him and he to deliver a bande [bond] that is in his custodye for moneye

that one Richard Harding (?) oweth me Item I give and bequeath unto my well beloved uncle Roberte ~

Lyster the goeing pasturing and feeding of one horse in Blocklye Parke [Blockley Park] during his lief Item my further

will ^is^ and be it provided alwayes that yf my brother John Stevins shall refuse to prove this my will and testament or yf he shall fortune to prove the same and then doe not performe and execute the same according to my tone entent and meaning and paye such giftes and legacyes as I have geven and bequeathed in this my sayd will within one yeare next following after my decease and soe continew the true payment of my brother James his legacye of thirtie poundes by the yeare to him and his assignes during both the Leasses of Blockly Parke Then I will that my foresaid uncles Mr Roland ~ Baugh and Robert Lyster shalbe my executors and theie to paye my debtes and legacyes and theie to have all

my goods and chattells Leasses or my parte or parcell of the Leasses. ffurthermore because my desire is to have my debtes well and truly payd and this my last will performed I will and appointte and ordeyne

that my brother John Stevins shall not be my executor neither yet medle with anye parte or parcell of my goods or chattells after my deceasse untill he hath entred into a good and sufficient band of one thousand poundes unto my uncle Robert Lyster as well and truly to paye my debtes as also well and truly to pay all such giftes and legacyes as I have bequeathed and given by this my last will and testament And yf my sayd brother John shall refuse to enter into this sayd band or obligation Then my will is that my sayd Uncles Mr Roland Bough and Robert Lister shalbe my executors of this my sayd will and testament Item I give unto my honest friend Richard Porter in consideration of his paynes taken with me in the tyme of my sickness and for his good will and meaning to me alwayes fortye shillinges Item I doe give also unto Robert Winscombe my man one yearlye pension or annuity of twentye shillinges by the yeare to be taken during his lief out of Blocklye Park or the farme of Burton for and in conside= ration of his service done to me Item my will is that Phillip Paxford shall have holde and quietlie occupie that parte and parcell of the beeretithe during his lief as he is and hath bene in possession of ever since the deathe of my father

PROBATUM fuit Testamentum suprascriptum apud London coram venerabile viro Mr
Will[iel]mo Drury Legum Doctore Curiae Prerogativae Cantuar[iensis] mag[ist]ro Custodis sive Commissario
eadem septimo
die mensis ffebruarij Anno dni juxta cursum et computac[i]onem eccl[es]ie anglicane Millesimo quingentesimo ~
octogesimo septimo [7 Feb 1587] Juramento John Stevyns executoris in h[ujus]modi testamento nominat quibus Commissa
fuit adminisitracio omnium et de bono et fideliter administrando eadem Ad sancta dei evangelia jurat

This will was proved at London before the venerable man William Drury, Doctor of Law, Master Keeper Commissary of the Prerogative Court of Canterbury on the seventh day of the month of February in the year of our lord according to the course and calculation of the Church of England one thousand five hundred and eighty seven by the oath of John Stevens, executor named in the said will to whom administration was granted of all and singular goods he having sworn duly to administer on the holy Gospel

Notes:
- Variable spellings of the surname (line 2 'Stevins'; line 22 'Stevens'; line 55 'Stevyns').
- Line 19 'nagge': a nag, pony, small horse.
- Line 28 'Leveton': a small village or hamlet near Ilsington, on the eastern side of Dartmoor, some 17 miles south-west of Exeter.
- Line 50: probably 'beer tithe', either the right to brew beer, or receive the tithe (local tax) on beer brewed. Nice earner!
- Blockley Park is about 10 miles north of Bourton-on-the-Hill, but it's not clear what lands 'Burton' actually refers to.

… after the Reformation the stock seems to have been allowed to decline, though John Bell, Bishop of Worcester, in granting a lease of the park to Humphrey Talbot and Thomas Hungerford, made a condition that 100 deer should be inclosed. After the death of Talbot, Hungerford assigned his interest to John Stevens, who seems to have conveyed the unexpired term of the lease to Oliver Dawbney, retaining the under-tenancy for himself. John Stevens, however, while in possession of the lease, had failed to inclose the deer according to the terms of the agreement, and after the expiration of the year's notice, as provided in the lease, the bishop re-entered and granted a new lease to William Sheldon, which was confirmed by the dean and chapter. John Stevens was thereupon expelled by Richard Hecks, sub-lessee for five years under William Sheldon, and the park became the subject of proceedings in the Court of Chancery.

… John Stevens was still in possession of a moiety of Blockley Park in 1572; this was afterwards leased for thirty-five years to John Talbot, who conveyed his interest in the lease together with property in Bromsgrove to William Sebright for £200 in 1574.

... Leave to inclose a common leading from Blockley to Bourton-on-the-Hill was granted to Sir William Juxon, bart., in 1669, on condition that he made a road for travellers in his own grounds.

'Parishes: Blockley', in *A History of the County of Worcester: Volume 3* (1913), pp. 265–76.

In 1382 the land in Bourton was held by Edmund Stonor with his land in Condicote with which it descended until after 1565. This estate was often called the manor of Bourton-on-the Hill And Condicote ... Richard Palmer, who sold Condicote manor, was succeeded at Bourton by Thomas Palmer. In 1598 John Palmer of Compton Scorpion (Warws.) sold Bourton manor to Nicholas Overbury (d. 1643).

'Parishes: Bourton-on-the-Hill', in *A History of the County of Gloucester: Volume 6* (1965), pp. 197–206.

BOURTON-ON-THE-HILL, a parish in the upper divisions of the hundreds of Tewkesbury and Westminster, in the county of Gloucester, 4 miles to the S. of Chipping Campden. Moreton-in-the-Marsh is its post town. It is situated near the border of Warwickshire, in a hilly country, commanding much fine scenery. The living is a rectory in the diocese of Gloucester and Bristol, of the value with the perpetual curacy of Moreton annexed to it, of £675, in the patronage of Lord Redesdale. The church

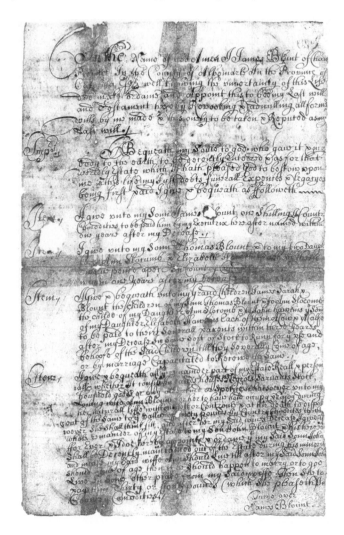

is dedicated to St. Lawrence. The National school has an endowment of £112 per annum. Bourton was the birthplace (1581) of Sir Thomas Overbury, who was imprisoned and poisoned in the Tower in the reign of James I., at the instigation of the favourite, Somerset.

The National Gazetteer of Great Britain and Ireland (1868).

Example

Here is an earlier will, that of William Blount, 1685. The palaeography is not too challenging:

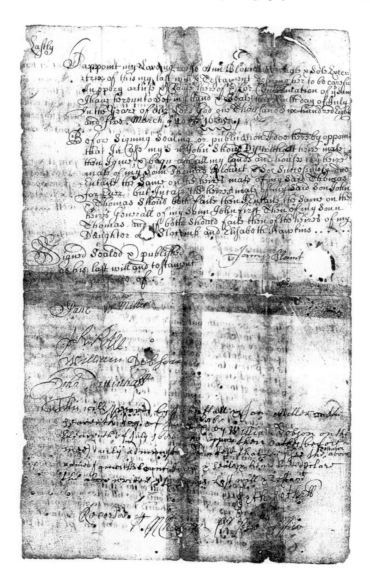

Further Reading

Grannum, K. and Taylor, N., *Wills and Probate Records* (The National Archives, 2009)

Arkell, T., Evans, N. and Goose, N., *When Death Do Us Part: Understanding and interpreting the probate records of early modern England* (Local Population Studies, 2000)

17

England and Wales: Fines, Recoveries and Final Concords

INTRODUCTION

Common Recoveries were convenient legal fictions used in England and Wales up until 1833 to convert an entailed estate into fee simple or freehold (see Entails, Chapter 9).

Feet of fines are another example of a legal fiction concerned with land transactions ('conveyances').

Common recoveries (England and Wales)

These were legal fictions (as were fines, see p. 222) prosecuted in England and Wales up until 1833. They were necessary because of the complicated nature of land law, especially when property was entailed and the landholder wished to convert it into a fee simple or freehold (see Entails, Chapter 9). This performance was also necessary because in medieval land law there was no provision for registration of title (which only became compulsory with the Land Registry Act of 1925) and at a time when lives were short and titles to property were not always secure, this contrivance meant that titles were on record at the Royal Courts.

It was a complex process, but at its simplest it worked like this:

- X, the landholder in tail conveys the title to Y (known as the 'tenant *in precipe*') but so that a third party Z ('the demandant') should then sue for it.
- Z issues a writ against Y, who goes to court and defends his right saying that he had acquired it from X, which indeed he had.
- X (who is now called the 'vouchee') is called to court to vouch that he had a right to the land in the first place.
- X says that he got it from V (known as the 'common vouchee') who in fact had nothing to do with it at all.
- V would then either fail to appear, or sometimes run from the court.

- If the rights of other persons P had to be barred – trustees, for example – X would allege that he had acquired it from P and P would claim it had been acquired from V. It was the same thing, just with an added step.

The judge (who of course saw through all this) had no option in law but to rule that Z should recover the property, and that V should compensate Y with property of equal value. But V was carefully chosen because he had no property (what the law called a 'man of straw') so the judgement was unenforceable. Therefore, Z had recovered land in fee simple, which X had owned in fee tail and so the entail was barred V (often a beggar chosen off the streets, or a lowly lawyer's clerk) was presumably rewarded.

Whoever thought all that up deserves either a medal or a hanging.

The substance of the common recovery will be determined by the last few lines in the conveyance, such as: 'to the use of John Smith and his heirs in fee simple'; (if in connection with a mortgage or other security) 'to the use of James Brown, but provided that if John Smith repays the principal and interest then it shall revert to John Smith and his heirs'; 'John Smith and his son Henry Smith may jointly dispose of the property as they wish'; or other details and conditions concerning future interests in the land (such as destination on marriage).

Sadly, the documentation from a common recovery is usually a disappointment. It never says what the purpose of the exercise was and mostly is merely a description of the land in terms of area, the number of buildings and the parish or town where it was situated.

After common recoveries were abolished in 1833, a disentailing deed would be enrolled in Chancery, but these have become redundant since the 1926 Act. These judgements were enrolled at court on the Plea Rolls until 1583 (CP 40 at TNA) then on the Recovery Rolls (CP 43) and the Court of Common Pleas Prothonotaries' Docket Rolls are indexed (CP 60 at TNA).

Prothonotaries were the chief clerks, with duties similar to the present masters of the High Court. There were three prothonotaries at the Court of Common Pleas, who each kept his own set of docket rolls until 1770 (probably as an accounting measure to calculate their fees), then up to 1838 kept a single collection for all three of them in common and after that date by their successors, the masters. There are quite a few missing, and no surviving documents from the years 1770–91.

Ejectments (England and Wales)

However, do not confuse a recovery with an ejectment: a civil action to recover the possession of and title to land, say from a defaulting tenant, usually the consequence of a real dispute, but dressed up in a fictitious form. The whole point was to get a court to decide who actually had rights in the land, and it went like this:

- X wants to get rid of Y from a piece of land.
- X grants a lease in the land concerned to a (real) friend Z and later to a fictitious friend (say, John Doe).
- An action is raised in the name of John Doe (who doesn't exist) against another fictitious person (say, Robert Roe) who, the equally fictitious Doe alleges, has evicted him.
- A letter is then sent in the name of John Doe to Y, inviting him to defend the case on behalf of his fictitious tenant, which establishes X's right to appear against Y on the basis of the fictitious lease (but which he could not deny).
- By this farrago, the rights of the true claimant and defendant got an airing in court and either X or Y was confirmed as having the rights. Of course, if Y genuinely had defaulted, he would not win.

Why was all of this nonsense necessary until 1833 and the Real Property Limitation Act 3 and 4 Will. IV, c. 27, sec. 36? Because the law of land title was so complicated that nobody could navigate it. Luckily, such dodges went away as new laws were enacted to provide proper remedies.

Feet of fines and final concords (England and Wales)

Another piece of legal invention, but a necessary one given the vicissitudes of English feudal land law, was the 'fine'. These extend over a period from the end of the twelfth century to the early nineteenth in an almost unchanged form, which rather suggests that they were useful legally, not least because they meant there was a lasting record (see Common Recoveries, p. 220). Apart from that, they are recognised as being of great importance to historians and genealogists and therefore many have been published as abstracts, usually by county and for particular reigns or years (see 'Further Reading'). Below are two examples of pages from such a publication, *An Index to Worcestershire Fines, 1649–1714* (Worcestershire Historical Society, 1896), showing the sort of information available. They also provide good practice in translating Latin from a restricted vocabulary.

426   INDEX TO THE FINES IN THE REIGN OF ANNE.

Year of
the Reign.

13th.   Trinity Term
continued.

Inter Casp. Fred. Heming armigerum et alios querentes et Ricardum Greaves armigerum et uxorem defendentes in Church Honyborne.

Inter Willelmum Somerscales querentem et Robertum Such et uxorem defendentes in Newbold et aliis.

Inter Georgium Pinches et alios querentes et Johannem Haughton Dewee et uxorem Gill defendentes in Churchill et aliis.

Inter Johannem Cookes generosum querentem et Phine. Dabtott generosum et uxorem defendentes in Bently et aliis.

Inter Ricardum Walker et alios querentes et Josephum Pearce Parsons et Beaufoy Ramell et uxorem defendentes in Evesham et aliis.

Inter Elizabetham Seaborne spinster querentem et Thomam Harris et Walterum Harris et uxorem defendentes in Shrawley.

Inter Johannem Hancox et alios querentes et Ricardum Baker et uxorem defendentes in Stourbridge.

Inter Caleb Tilt et alios querentes et Johannem Shaw et uxorem defendentes in Dudley.

Inter Thomam Cookes querentem et Willelmum Biggs et uxorem defendentes in Bromesgrove.

Inter Johannem Dean clericum querentem et Johannem Ingles et uxorem defendentes in Blockley et aliis.

Inter Willelmum Wheeler et alios querentes et Samuelem Lowbridge defendentes in Rushock.

Inter Isaa. Averill querentem et Willelmum Billy et uxorem defendentes in Broadway.

Inter Johannem Pope generosum et alios querentes et Samuelem Swift armigerum Jacobum Swift defendentes in Astwood et aliis.

Inter Thomam Haselwood militem querentem et Andreum Allen et uxorem defendentes in parochia Sancti Andree et aliis.

AN INDEX

TO

WORCESTERSHIRE FINES, 1649—1714.

INDEX OF PERSONS AND PLACES.

NAMES occurring more than once in a page, whether as names of persons or of places, are indexed only once.

Evident misspellings are indexed as rightly spelled. Names nearly certainly referring to the same family or place are grouped together. In cases where there is more doubt, and in some other instances, the spelling is given in the Index as it occurs in the text.

CLENT, *July*, 1897.   J. A.

Final concords can be recognised from the opening sentence: '*Hic est finalis concordia facta in curia Domini Regis*' 'This is the final agreement made in the court of the Lord King' until 1732, after which it became 'This is the final concord …', followed by the sovereign's name, the year, the names of the buyers and sellers and a 'terrier' (a description of the size, tenements etc. of the property concerned), a warrant of the whole for life to the buyer and the sum of money paid.

The 'fine' referred to is not as we understand it today – a penalty imposed by law, such as for a parking ticket – and not called that because money was paid to another party (even though it often was). It is used here in the Latin sense of *fine* meaning 'finished' because the agreement brought the dispute to an end by the parties coming to an agreement usually called a 'final concord'. It also put an end to any argument or ambiguity about ownership or imperfections as to title, and was therefore an absolute sale with all other claims made void. However, the 'dispute' in these cases was a completely invented one, and here's why.

Sale by fine is an ancient practice, possibly starting in pre-Norman times. When the system as we know it started to become popular, in the twelfth and thirteenth centuries, there were often genuine legal disputes over land, which had to be settled in court and a 'fine' agreed to. By the time of Edward III the process of subinfeudation (see Chapter 19) had all but gone, but the complexities of feudal land law remained. The apparently deceitful and clunky process of using an invented court action to have a pre-existing agreement upheld and recorded was a more effective device than the land law process, and enabled everyone to cut through the nonsense.

The idea was to provide incontestable evidence, recorded in court and by all parties concerned, that a transaction or conveyance had taken place and was legally binding. It was used, for example, to record land ownership, to define and protect reversionary interests (the rights a person has in property upon the termination of the preceding estate), to establish the rights of married women in a particular property, to direct the future succession (much like an entail) and to impede any claims others might make, within limits.

The reason for the term 'feet' is quite straightforward: when the final agreement was granted by the court it was written up (the legal term is 'engrossed') as a three-part document or 'chirograph'

(literally, 'written by hand') on a single membrane of parchment or vellum, one copy each on the right and left, head to head, and a third along the bottom, or side-to-side with a 'foot'. The three copies were then divided by cutting or tearing indented lines between the two halves and above the lower third. The saw-tooth nature of the division meant that the parts could, in theory, be brought together and matched up in the case of any dispute or alleged alteration, for example. This is how any agreement between parties torn that way has come to be called an 'indenture'. (The other sort, which only involved one party, such as a bond, was cut straight across or 'polled', hence a deed poll, see Chapter 19.) The two parties kept the right and left halves and the court retained the 'foot'.

The final concord ('final agreement' is a better term) is always written in Latin, right up to the mid-1800s.

Feet of fines are usually inscribed with words and figures not part of the actual agreement; often (as an added measure of security) the word 'chirograph' may be written along the indented (torn) line separating the three parts of the document.

Example

Like all documents that lawyers have found to do the job, fines follow a set model across the centuries, but there may be variations depending on circumstances. However, here is a typical formula:

> This is the final agreement made in the king's court at Westminster on the morrow of St Martin in the twenty-fifth year of the reign of Edward king of England, the Third from the Conquest, and the twelfth of the reign of the same king of France, before John de Stonore, Roger Hillary, Richard de Kelleshull, Richard de Wylughby, John de Stouford, and Thomas de Fencotes, justices, and others of the king's faithful subjects then there present, between Robert le Copener, plaintiff, and John Vyrly of Chaldrynton, deforciant, concerning one messuage and two virgates of land with their appurtenances in Chaldrynton, whereon a plea of covenant was summoned between them in the same court, that is to say that the aforesaid Robert has acknowledged the aforesaid tenements with their appurtenances to be the right of that John, as those which the same John has by gift of the aforesaid Robert, and for this acknowledgement, fine, and agreement the same John has granted the aforesaid Robert the aforesaid tenements with their appurtenances, and has rendered them to him in the same court, [to have and to hold to the same Robert and his heirs from the chief lords of that fee by the services which belong to the aforesaid …

A fine is dated by the 'return day', the writ stating that the action had to be returned with the parties making a nominal appearance in court at a specified time and date, usually given as the beginning of the week. Standard return days, at least in the Wiltshire fines of Edward III's reign, were these (see Chapter 3 for dates and term days):

— Four in Hilary term: the octave (or day a week after: thus 8 days) (20 January) and quindene (or day two weeks after: thus 15 days) (27 January) of St Hilary, the morrow (3 February) and octave (9 February) of the Purification.
— Four in Easter term: the quindene of Easter, three weeks from Easter, one month from Easter, and the morrow of Ascension.
— Four in Trinity term, from five possible days: the octave and quindene of Trinity, and the morrow (25 June), octave (1 July), and quindene (8 July) of the nativity of St John the Baptist.
— Eight in Michaelmas term: the octave (6 October) and quindene (13 October) of Michaelmas, three weeks (20 October) and one month (27 October) from Michaelmas, the morrow (3 November) of All Souls, and the morrow (12 November), octave (18 November) and quindene (25 November) of Martinmas.

Because Easter is a 'moveable feast' the return days in Easter term and the first two in Trinity are not fixed. Return days in Trinity term vary according to the date of Easter. There would be years where the quindene or octave of Trinity would extend beyond the morrow of St John the Baptist. A fine may be made on one day and granted or at least recorded on another, and so would bear a double date.

The parties are called the 'plaintiff' and the 'deforciant' or 'defendant' and in either case could be a number of people, such as a married couple, or a father and son. If one or more was represented in court by someone else, the document will say something like 'by M.N. in their place [or in W.'s place] for winning or losing'. Often, women were represented by another party, as were plaintiffs more so than deforciants. While parties are usually identified by forename and surname only, there are instances where a surname substitute is used, such as 'G. Bishop of H' or 'L. Earl of M', and it was sometimes necessary to distinguish between 'the elder' and 'the younger'.

The property conveyed or settled by fines had to be freehold, not held in villeinage, and in perpetuity or for life, nor for a term of so many years, which would be a lease (see pp. 242–4). Other land terms encountered are manors, messuages (houses), arable land (given in carucates, virgates, or acres), meadow, pasture, woodland and rents: in every case recorded as 'with appurtenances', and the advowson (the right to appoint the vicar) of one or more churches.

Identifying the actual location of the property can be tricky if it doesn't have a modern equivalent. Usually only the name of the containing manor or *vill* ('hamlet' or 'township') and the county are given, the last especially when the property concerned or the containing manor crossed a county boundary. After 1759, it was only necessary to give the county of the property.

Fines may include an acknowledgement by the deforciant of the plaintiff's right to the property, and will indicate this by a phrase in French such as:

– '*Sur cognizance de droit, come ceo qu'il ad de son done*': (acknowledegment of the right of the cognizee, as a gift of the cognizor), known as a 'feoffment of record' or a 'come ceo'.
– '*Sur concessit*' (the cognizor acknowledges no precedent right but grants anyway to the consignee an estate *de novo*, usually for life or so many years).
– '*Sur cognizance de droit tantum*' (simple acknowledgment of the right).
– '*Sur done grant et render*' (a 'double fine', including the first and second above and used to convey certain limitations of estate and to other person not named in the writ).

The party making the acknowledgement is called the 'conusor' and may be either the plaintiff or the defendant, and the party whose right is being acknowledged is the 'conusee'.

In most fines there is a 'habendum' clause (from its first word, meaning 'to have') and there will be detail on whether the descent of the property is directed to the heirs of the grantee, whether it descends to the husband's or the wife's heirs, the feudal superior, etc. If the intention was to direct a specific succession (like an entail, Chapter 9) the habendum clause will be particularly complex.

If there is to be a 'consideration' given theoretically by the grantee to the grantor, this may be a single payment or an annual rent: in that case, it was often twenty times the notional annual value or 'extent' of the property.

If a manorial lord wanted to dispose of an interest in land held by a free tenant, the tenant would have to give his agreement, called 'attornment', which would have been recorded; the tenants might also be recorded as present in the court.

As ever, there are variants to all of the above, through time and in different jurisdictions, but it should be possible to navigate a final concord by looking for the clues given here.

Court of Common Pleas fines and recoveries from 1194 to 1875 are held at The National Archives (CP 25/2) but the Palatinate Courts of Durham, Cheshire etc. had their own records

(CHES 31/DURH 12/ PL 17). As noted earlier and in 'Further Reading', calendars (indexes and/or abstracts) have been published by local record societies and also by HMSO.

However, there is a major project underway at the University of Houston, called AALT (Anglo-American Legal Tradition), which is digitising all pre-modern rolls of the Court of Common Pleas held at The National Archives, as well as many other early English legal records. So far (2012) there are over 5 million images, including most Common Plea Rolls to the end of the reign of King Henry VIII and some after that, but with gaps. These can be seen at http://aalt.law.uh.edu/IndexPri.html and then searched by monarch's reign.

Further Reading

Online

Maitland, F.W., *Forms of Action at Common Law* (1909). Available at Medieval Sourcebook: www.fordham.edu/halsall/basis/maitland-formsofaction.asp

Books

Biancalana, Joseph, *The Fee Tail and the Common Recovery in Medieval England 1176–1502* (Cambridge University Press, 2001)

Hastings, M., *The Court of Common Pleas in Fifteenth Century England: A Study of Legal Administration and Procedure* (1947), Cornell University Press, New York

Milsom, S.F.C., *Historical Foundations of the Common Law* (1981 Butterworth-Heinman) pp. 150–3

Some examples of feet of fines abstracts available in printed form by county and reign are:

Abstracts of Feet of Fines Relating to Wiltshire for the Reign of Edward III (Wiltshire Record Society, 1984);

Wiltshire Feet of Fines, Edward I and II, vol. 1 (Wiltshire Archaeological Society, Records Branch);

Huntingdonshire Feet of Fines, vol. 37 (Cambridge Antiquarian Society, octavo series);

Surrey Feet of Fines, 1509–58, vol. 19 (Surrey Record Society);

An Index to Worcestershire Fines, 1649–1714 (Worcestershire Historical Society, 1896).

Many are available for download at www.archive.org, such as *A calendar to the feet of fines for London & Middlesex Richard I to III* (1892) and subsequent volumes for later reigns.

18

England and Wales: Manorial Documents

ORIGINS OF THE MANORIAL SYSTEM

Manors, in the sense of a piece of land held heritably and parts of it tenanted out, possibly existed in pre-Norman England, but it is with the arrival of feudalism that it flowered fully and structured the lives of a great deal of the rural population of England and a fair part of Wales. Tracing the origins of any given manor can be tricky, as manorial names may have changed when the landholder did, the manor may have subdivided into two or more lesser manors at some point, or one manor may have been subsumed into another. This happened particularly in the Middle Ages. The original owner of a manor would have been the tenant (strictly, feudal vassal) of a more wealthy and powerful nobleman holding a large area of land directly of the Crown: a baron, in other words (the term still current in Scotland – see Chapter 13). The baron may have sublet a manor for some form of feudal service, or a payment, but in time some manors were bought out or converted to freehold.

The manorial landlord – often called a 'squire', which betrays its origins as the rank above a mere 'gentleman' and below a 'knight' – would live there and work the land, along with his children and possibly wider extended family. As sons married, grew up and needed land of their own, this could be provided by parcelling out a part of the manor into lesser manorial holdings, all based around the original manor place or manor house. The manor was indeed a physical and geographical place, but in reality it operated more as a social and economic organism, with the landlord, family and tenants in a kind of kinship group, regardless of their familial or genetic links, if any. In that, it closely resembles a Scottish feudal barony and to some extent a Scottish clan or family. John Norden, who published *The Surveyors Dialogue* in 1607 defined a manor as 'little common wealth, whereof the Tenants are the members, the Land the bulke and the Lord the head' and it is the idea of 'common wealth' that rings most true: if everyone pulled together, everyone would be better off.

Minor landlords were called 'yeomen' and were the landed, farming middle class, but usually with a decent education and a firm idea of the relevant genealogical lineage and patrimony. To this day, territorial (volunteer) cavalry units are called yeomanry, harking back to the time when those who owned and could ride a horse were asked to help defend England if invaded.

A manor often consisted of two portions:

– Demesne lands: those parts reserved for the lord's own use, worked by his own family and servants.
– Assised lands: lands let out to tenants, either for monetary rent alone or combination of rent and services (which might include contracted cultivation of the demesne).

The demesne lands would usually be based around the manor house and possibly the parish church, as well as the 'woods and waste' (and, therefore, firewood) of the manor, but the tenants may have had rights of pasture or rights to collect brushwood and so on. The cultivated fields of the demesne were not necessarily physically separated from the assised lands – into a separate 'home farm' within an enclosure, for example – but were often in amongst them.

Fields under cultivation would be divided into strips of 200 yards long shared between the tenants and the lord and called 'selions', which in turn were organised in blocks called 'furrow longs' (hence the measurement 'furlong') separated by 'balks' (ridges). There would be unploughed 'headland' at each end of a furlong for turning the oxen and plough. Any bits of land left over – in an awkward or unploughable corner, for instance – was a 'gore'.

A manor need not be a geographical unit with a single boundary, it could well be a collection of disjointed farmsteads spread amongst land belonging to another manor, not necessarily held by the same lord. Alternatively, a lord might have held several manors, but one would be his principal or capital 'messuage'. In addition there would be common land, used for pasturing tenants' animals etc.

Tenants' services

Manorial tenants were freemen and held their land from the lord for the payment of a rent in cash or kind and usually had the obligation to attend the manor courts for the viewing of their frankpledge (p. 229), to pay an 'entry fine' on admission to a tenancy and to pay a heriot (usually the best beast, see p. 231) on the tenant's death, but otherwise freemen had considerable independence and could, for instance, carry on a craft or trade in their own right.

'Villeins' or 'bondsmen' were vassals: unfreed tenants with the same requirements as freemen but additional other obligations depending upon the 'customs' (p. 235) of the manor, often including services of labour to help in the cultivation of the demesne land and extra 'boon work' when required by the landlord. Villeins also had restrictions on their freedoms and activities – such as not living outwith the manor without permission and probably paying 'chevage' in return; paying a 'merchet' if a daughter was married (which might also require permission); paying a fine called 'leyrwite' on an unmarried woman found not to be chaste; paying 'wood silver' (cash or kind) for the right to collect firewood, 'sheep silver' (payment in lieu of washing the lord's sheep) and so on. They also had to keep their buildings, hedges, gardens, ditches and so on in first-rate condition.

There were generally four types of services required of tenants:

– *Precariae*: work done by special request (*ad precem*) such as ploughing, looking after a hunting dog or a fighting cock for the lord. *Precariae* were required at the seasons of ploughing and harvest. For example, there might be two *precariae carucarum*, at the winter and Lent (spring) ploughings and sowings, and all the tenants who had a team or part of a team would be required to attend. In addition, every tenant might be duty-bound to plough one acre in summer to lie fallow. The harvest *precariae* in autumn were usually three days long, with more bodies required on the second and third days (the *magna precaria*). If the lord provided a harvest-supper after the third *precaria*, the workers were said to be *solemniter depasti*. If a fourth day was required the lord might provide extra food and drink and so it was called a 'hungerbedrip'.

- *Opera Diurna*: so many days' work per week.
- *Averagia*: carrying services (including gathering nuts and firewood).
- Occasional works: such as threshing, mowing, sheep shearing etc. according to need and season, or providing an annual goose, lamb, cheese, coals or other produce.

By the mid-1500s most customary tenants had had their labour service substituted with a cash payment called 'quit rent'.

Tenants' rights

Depending on the customs of the manor, the lord might allow certain rights of common, including:

- Commons of estovers (timber or lime for repairing buildings).
- Commons of pannage (feeding swine).
- Commons of piscary (fishing).
- Commons of turbary (turf-cutting).
- Commons of venary (hunting).
- Commons of vert (taking green wood).
- Commons of vesture or herbage (grazing or taking a crop of hay).
- Botes: rights of common to do with the taking of wood for defined purposes, such as: cartbote (to make or mend carts), firebote (taking wood for fuel) or fencebote (wood for fencing).

Other manorial inhabitants

The next rung down the social ladder was occupied by cottars or bordars who had no land beyond perhaps a small cot-house (cottage) and garden, and who usually worked for the landlord or larger tenants as agricultural labourers.

Then came 'tenants at will' who lived in a mean dwelling built without permission on manorial waste land. The 'at will' refers to the good will of the landlord, of course. There was established custom and practice about settling if a hut with a roof and a chimney could be built overnight (see p. 239) but generally a rent or some labour service was demanded.

Manor and court rolls

When investigating an estate, it is customary to look for deeds of purchase or of mortgage, but the earliest account of an estate is likely to be in its own private records, called court rolls. These can be hard to interpret, because they often contain local words and obsolete terms.

Manor rolls are the most interesting to local and social historians because they provide evidence of the lowest common denominator of local government, and show how good order was kept in the days before more general magisterial authority existed.

The local manor court did what the magistrates, county court judges and, to an extent, county councils did in later times, including looking after roads, highways and rivers. The old court rolls also make for fun reading when they deal with fines and penalties for offences we no longer recognise or would not consider to carry a punishment, but also some that we would, such as: allowing animals to stray, keeping dogs, pigeons or other animals without the lord's permission, fighting, poaching, trespassing in the woods, taking firewood and more.

Only freed men (and therefore not villeins or anyone lower) could marry or give a daughter in marriage without permission or paying a fine, and a villein could not necessarily leave the land and move elsewhere – that, after all, was the essence of being 'free' (see 'Tenants' services' on p. 229).

What it shows is the intimate connection that existed between tenant or vassal and landlord, whose welfares were intimately intertwined: good tenants meant good farm produce and regular rents, while a good landlord meant protection, welfare and, of course, justice when called for. The judicial rule of the lord of the manor and the twelve jurymen of the court could be arbitrary at times (or so it seems to our modern eyes, in the days of human rights and universal suffrage) but also settled what we might think of as petty grievances, such as accusations of 'bearing false witness' (lying, in other words, or slandering by spreading bogus information) against a neighbour, which is, of course, forbidden by the ninth commandment and therefore taken very seriously indeed.

However, this did put the lord of the manor in the enviable position of being both landlord and judge, with police powers.

Court leet and court baron

King Edward I established a distinction between the court baron, (strictly manorial rights), and the franchised court leet (exercising royal jurisdiction by proxy). However, it became efficient and customary in many manors for the two courts to meet at the same time and streamline the proceedings.

The court leet (the word is derived from Anglo-French *litte*, meaning 'list' and survives in the modern phrase 'short leet' or shortlist) was a court of record that some lords holding the king's warrant were entitled to hold. It dealt mainly with offences committed by tenants and with ensuring that freemen kept their oaths or pledges of peaceful behaviour and honest trade practices. As well as enforcing law and order by franchise from the royal courts, it inspected the working of the frankpledge (see p. 232). A court leet was normally held every six months or at least annually, but often alongside the court baron.

The court baron (cf. Baron Court in Scotland, p. 237) was the main type of manorial court and would be held every three or four weeks. Compared with the annual or semi-annual court leet, the court baron was more administrative in function, managing the manor according to its customs. Tenants paid 'suit of court' (in other words, turned up) at specified times in the year to give a report of their activities, agricultural production and so on, which helped the manor keep its business in order. It was the time for giving an account other services due, such as the yearly goose, lamb, cheese, coals or other produce items and how well the tenant was looking after the dog, pig or fighting cock he kept on his landlord's behalf.

It was also an opportunity to tidy up details like surrender and admission to copyhold land (see p. 240), inheritance after the death of a tenant, extensions and changes to a lease, and presentation of heriots. The heriot – known in Scotland as a 'casualty' – was the tribute or service rendered to the feudal lord on the death of a tenant, which originally would have been the right of the lord of the manor to pick the best horse, cow or weapon of the deceased tenant, in later times becoming a monetary payment, as all feudal services have.

Births of children were sometimes noted, as were marriages and deaths, creation of freedmen etc.

Tenants giving up their tenure did so by 'surrender' and new tenants took over by 'admission'. This involved a ceremony in which the tenant would be offered a rod by the steward, hence 'holding customary land by the rod'. In either case, the surrendering or admitting tenant would be given a copy of the enrolment for his own record of title.

Elections or appointments of local officials would also be recorded. There were a number of functions, some of which might be amalgamated under one person, but they would include:

– The steward: the chief official and judge.
– The bailiff, who supervised the court and made arrests if required.
– The mace bearer and/or crier, which might be combined with the role of bailiff (think of Beadle Bumble in *Oliver Twist*).

- An official variously called a bylawman, byrlawman or barleyman (no relation to or responsibility for barley), responsible for enforcement of the customary or bylaw orders of the court.
- The tithingmen, constables or headboroughs (see below), responsible for good order generally.
- The affeerors, who set the level of amercements (fines).
- The reeve, who oversaw the cultivation of demesne land (and is the origin, in a larger capacity within a county, of the office of shire-reeve, or sheriff).
- The ale tasters (probably a much sought-after position), carniters ('flesh-tasters', likewise) and bread weighers, responsible for quality, freshness and accurate measure.
- The hayward or pinder, who looked after the enclosures, pinfolds and fences on common land, and penned any stray animals.
- The surveyor of highways and brook looker, overseeing the condition of roads and watercourses.

Court rolls and frankpledge

When the manor court was held, there was the annual review of the freedmen living on the estate, and the court leet roll starts with the words '*Visus franciplegii*' (view of frankpledge). The term means 'pledge of peace' and refers to the ancient system whereby ten or so households were united by 'tything' or 'tithing' so that each member was responsible for the conduct of the others. The chief pledge, tithing man or headborough was answerable to the manor court for producing anyone from that tithing suspected of a crime, and if the actual miscreant did not turn up, the whole tithing group could be amerced (fined). However, they could swear to the effect that they had no part in the getaway of the person so summoned. It is this examination of the tything's members before the manor court that leads to the phrase 'view of frankpledge'.

This compulsory sharing of accountability worked because the members were connected in a kinship group, or were bound by an oath of fealty to a knight or lord, such as a Scottish clansman would be to his clan chief. The sanctions that were imposed on offenders were not that far from today's fine and 'ASBO' (antisocial behaviour order).

The term 'tything' is of Scandinavian origin: *ti* means 'ten' and *thing* is 'assembly', just as the Parliament of Iceland (the world's oldest parliamentary institution still in existence) is called the Althing. The tithing also operated as an economic unit, which has come down to us in the concept of tithes: paying a tenth of your income or produce.

Manor court rolls, like most classes of document, follow a fairly fixed structure, whether written in Latin or later, like deeds, written in English. (Latin was the formal language of legal documents in England and Wales until Lady Day, 25 March 1733.) Originally these were, as the name suggests, rolls: written on a roll of parchment, and usually in the hand sometimes called 'Minuscule' (Chapter 1).

The court roll starts with the name of the manor at the top or in the margin and will begin '*Visus franciplegii cum curia*'. This is followed by the name of the lord of the manor, the day and month, the name of the sovereign and the regnal year (Chapter 3). Next, in the margin, comes '*Esson.*', an abbreviation for *essonium* or essoine: literally, 'excuse' of any jury members who pleaded absence from the court with good reason (just like taking 'apologies' at a modern business meeting). Any defaulters – those absent without essoine – would be solemnly noted and an amercement (a penalty, usually a monetary fine) would be levied.

Then the names of the jurymen present are listed: there were always freehold tenants or other freedmen, as a bondsman could not give an oath. The homage, as it was called, was as many as the custom of the manor stipulated – sometimes the well-known 'twelve good men and true', but it could be ten, sixteen or more. They were called a jury or *juratores* because they had been sworn in (*jurat*, 'sworn, gave oath').

Earlier rolls will then have 'presentments' (allegations) of offences to be heard and adjudged upon, as 'articles of enquiry' or a list of questions to the jury. It is a pleasure to be able to report that presentments were usually in English, even before 1733, and typically dealt with offences such as letting animals stray, encroachment, unwarranted enclosure of common or waste land, non-payment of rent (which could mean forfeiting the lease), and other matters pertaining to tenancy conditions and leases.

There may be an assize (licensing, effectively) of bread and ale, to check that those baking and brewing had the right to do so and that adulteration was not in evidence. The privilege of making ale was often restricted to ale wives, and illegal brewing carried a penalty of 1d,: it was usually women who were hauled up for this offence.

The court might then deal with any animals that had strayed and been seized to put in the pinfold (we still have the words 'pen' and 'fold' for a place where stock is kept) by the hayward or pinder, the official whose job it was to do so. (Scotland still uses the term 'poinding' pronounced '*pinding*' for seizure of goods by a court.)

Damage that needed to be repaired – to roads, fences or bridges, for example – would be considered, feuds between neighbours settled (or at least heard), offences such as obstruction of highways and fights or assaults ending in bloodshed adjudicated on, and the parties dealt with.

Finally, there would be a *summa* of fines received above the signatures of the two officers of the assize.

The opportunity might also be taken to make or restate the various customs and regulations known as 'pains' or ordinances. Additionally, the court documents might include estreat rolls listing all the amercements (fines) imposed by the court so that the bailiff could go and collect them. The offending tenants will be named in these rolls, along with their offences and the sums levied, such as, in one example from Havering atte Bower in Essex from 1598:

> not attending the court session – amerced 3d each
> causing affray, bloodshed and other antisocial behaviours – amerced 3s 4d
> failure to maintain fences – amerced 5s.

It's clear which was the greatest offence!

If all this sounds a bit like the annual general meeting of a business combined with a local magistrate's court, that's because it actually was. The manor was the functional economic, social and administrative unit for much of England and Wales. However, it was not all 'Merrie Englande' run by a bunch of chinless wonders who had been good at sports and thus went off to battle alongside the king and got land as a consequence. Three factors, a couple of centuries apart, brought a new, business-aware class into the picture:

– Rampant inflation in the thirteenth century meant extra profits from produce.
– A collapse of profitability following the two Black Death epidemics of the 1300s, so that surveys of the fourteenth and fifteenth centuries were much briefer documents giving the rents due from each tenant, known as a rental. These are of great value because they tend to group tenants by tithings, and give a list of residents, possibly including those who lived on the manor but were not tenants as such.
– The Dissolution of the Monasteries in the 1530s, (sometimes called the Suppression) saw the sale of a great deal of ex-monastic land to a whole new class of people with a background in commerce and bursting to exploit their new assets cost-effectively. Manorial surveys become quite detailed at this point, and some have survey maps, drawn up regardless of the considerable expense because of the convenient presentation of manorial information it afforded.

The court roll was usually the work of a professional clerk or scribe (they are typically in one handwriting and would require someone who could read and write, knew Latin and could count) but it is likely that they were copied out from notes made on the spot: there are hardly ever corrections or erasures, and names are usually spelt one way throughout, a rarity at the time!

By the 1400s, frankpledging had been superseded by local constables operating under the auspices of a justice of the peace (often referred to as the JP), but the documents still exist, and are such a valuable source of local, land and family information that they are worth consulting. After the Reformation in Tudor times, court rolls were considered less highly as records of value, so they are well preserved and in their annual series until then, but are neglected afterwards and not found so frequently.

Quarter sessions and sheriff's *tourns*

Quarter sessions were held four times a year (see 'Term days', Chapter 3), and there would also be the sheriff's tourn (the court held by the representative of the Crown in the shire: the shire-reeve or sheriff), which was held twice per year. These looked more at matters of general or public interest and expense, rather the manor court's province of more local or trivial matters. However, manor court and the sheriff's tourn had the same aims: the keeping of the king's (or queen's) peace; and the dispensing of the king's justice.

Example of a court roll

Below there is an example of a court roll. It should be possible to identify the major sections (look for terms like '*Visus Frankplegii*', '*Essonum*' and '*Summa*') and to determine the date and place. Notice also the sums of money written above certain names (e.g. ij*d*).

OTHER MANORIAL RECORDS

Accounts

The steward or bailiff of the manor would keep accounts of the manorial income ('charges') and expenditure ('discharges') annually, running from Michaelmas to Michaelmas (29 September). Charges would come from rents, produce sales, fines levied in the manor court and so on. Discharges would cover purchases, labour charges, wages, building costs, running repairs and the like.

The financial records may also contain the 'corn account' (the amount of corn sown and harvested, or sown), a livestock account (stock born, died, slaughtered or sold), work and tools costs, and a balance.

Rentals

The rental was a list of all tenants of the manor, with a description of the land held and rental paid, whether in cash or in kind (produce), plus, in some cases, heriots and other services due (see p. 229). These rolls or books are not necessarily annual and may only have been created when, for instance, a new lord of the manor arrived or inherited, or there was a major acquisition or disposal of land, changing the size or nature of the manor.

Custumals

The word 'customs' has come to mean two things: an accepted way of behaving and of doing things or a duty paid on goods (for example, at the point of import or export). The word 'duty' also has two meanings: an obligation of some sort and a payment on goods (as in 'duty free').

All of these concepts are found in custumals. These were essentially a survey or inventory of rents, services and other obligations owed by tenants to the lord of the manor, and of the rights and obligations of the lord to the tenants, in other words the 'customs' by which the tenant held his house, lands, stock and produce. An expanded and more common form of a custumal would also summarise the 'customs' of the manor: its customary (there's that word again) agricultural activities and business dealings, a recital of the local code of laws, a synopsis of the oral sworn tradition of the manor, any written legal arrangements between the lord and the tenants, the manorial court rolls etc. It was to all intents and purposes the legal and practical handbook for running the manor. They often start with a standard rubric (literally, red writing: see p. 248 for a discussion of inks) and in French: '*Ces sont les usages, et les custumes …*' (these are the usages and customs of …).

Looking at the custumals of one manor across time shows the balances of rights and duties of both sides of the bargain as they developed, and also how the services and produce due eventually became payments of money, just as the various form of feu in Scotland (p. 173) eventually all became monetary payments rather than teinds (tithes) of produce or military service.

Right and overleaf: Rentals and custumals from the reign of Edward I of two manors: (this page) the Manor of Hoton (Hutton), Essex and (next page) the Manor of Dyngemares (Dengemarsh), Kent. Both are taken from Scargill-Bird, S.R., (ed.), *The Custumals of Battle Abbey* (for the Camden Society, 1887). Battle Abbey controlled, and took revenue from, a number of manors, as did many ecclesiastical establishments up to the Dissolution in the reign of Henry VIII.

		Ad Natale	Pascha	Sancti Johannis	Sancti Michaelis
Heres Willielmi le Wyte		ij s. vj d.	ij s. vj d.	ij s. vj d.	ij s. vj d.
Johannes de Bosco		iij d.	iij d.	iij d.	iij d.
Ricardus de Nywynton', pro via			ob.		ob.
			Summa totalis vj li. iiij s. vij d.		

Memorandum quod Magister Sancti Bartholomæi London' terram de Donton' per cartam nostram tenet, et debet sectam ad Curiam de Hotona, et cuilibet Magistro cedente vel decedente dabit pro herietto et relevio novus adveniens x s., et jurabit feuditatem domino;

Terra Doun est in manu domini, quæ solebat reddere per annum iiij s. et facere alias consuetudines.

	Epiphaniæ	Hockeday	Sancti Johannis Baptistæ	Sancti Michaelis	HERTHELD Sancti Thomæ Apostoli	ROMESCOT Sancti Petri ad Vincula
Ricardus Kynet	ij s. j d.	ij s. j d.	ij s. j d.	ij s. j d.		
Idem et Walterus Kydelman, pro Johanne Skinelcuere	iij d. ob.	iij d. ob. q*	iij d. ob. q*	ij d. ob.		
Idem Ricardus Kynet, pro heredibus Eletem filiæ Ricardi	v d. ob.	v d. q*	v d. q*	v d.		
Item idem Ricardus Kynet et heredes Johannis Willem, pro Martino Sprot	ix d.	ix d.	ix d.	ix d.	j d.	j d. cum uxore et sine
Heredes Thomæ Kynet	ij s. j d.	ij s. j d.	ij s. j d.	ij s. j d.		
Humfridus Roger, pro Willielmo le Heite	ij d.	ij d.	ij d.	ij d.	ob.	ob. }
Ricardus le Lewere, pro heredibus Alani Robert	iij d. ·	iij d.	iij d.	iij d.	ob.	ob. } cum uxore et sine
Hamo Waryn	x d. ob.	x d. ob.	x d.	x d.	ij d.	j d. cum uxore et sine
Adam et Ricardus, filii Willielmi de la Curt	v d. ob.	v d. q*	v d. q*	iiij d. q*		
Heredes Girardi, Johannis, Roberti atte Wyke	xxiij d.	xxiij d.	xxiij d.	xxij d.	ij d. Item q* de grangia	ij d. Item q* cum uxore et sine
Godelena, filia Godefridi atte Wyke, et participes ejus	xvj d.	xvj d.	xvj d.	xiiij d. ob. q*	j d. Item ob. de grangia	j d. cum uxore
Johannes Gilebert	vj d.	vj d.	vj d.	vj d.	ij d.	j d. cum uxore et sine
Hamo Oter, et participes ejus	vij d.	vj d. ob.	vj d. ob.	vj d.	j d.	j d. cum uxore
Thomas Lambert de Dover'	xiiij d. ob. q*	xiiij d. ob. q*	xiiij d. ob. q*	xij d. ob. q*	j d.	j d. cum uxore
Johannes, filius Johannis Thurgar, et participes ejus	xij d.	xj d. ob. q*	xj d. ob. q*	xj d. ob. q*	iij d.	iij d. cum uxore et sine
Idem, pro terra relicta le Milkere	iij d. ob.	iij d. ob. q*	iij d. ob. q*	ij d. ob.		

Notice the references to Hockday (Hokeday) and Epiphany (see p. 89). Other record payments at Natale (Christmas), Pascha (Easter) Sancti Johannis (St John's day, 24 June, Midsummer) and Sancti Michaelis (Michaelmas) or at other times, according to the customs of the manor concerned.

Extents

As well as an accounting of rentals paid and other income, each manor would need a description and valuation – an inventory, in other words – of everything on the manor. This would not be the value if sold, but if leased, rented out or worked to produce income. It is, therefore, equivalent to 'rateable value' in modern terms and the same as a 'stent' in Scotland. Extents date from an earlier time than rentals, which shows the trend away from the lord of the manor and his immediate family farming the demesne lands directly to a system of leases and rentals of assised lands cultivated by tenants.

The accounting of extent usually started with the manor house and its grounds and gardens, mills and mill streams, a report of the demesne land (with separate sections for arable land under crops, meadow or pasture and woods), the particulars of tenants' rents and services and ended with the totalled value of the manor.

The 'Extent of the Manor of Hoton' shows, in addition to the manor house and its accessories:

73 acres of wood.
756½ acres of arable land.
3 acres of pasture.
43 acres of meadow.

The valuation is given as follows:

	L.	s.	d.
The demesne with its appurtenances	27	11	3½
Rents of Assize (of both free and customary tenants)	7	12	0½
Plough rents (8 *vomeres*)		4	8
Customs and services	7	15	7
Rents of tenants at will		7	8
'Tolcester' or Ale-toll		7	2
Fines, amerciaments and other profits	I	0	0
Total	44	18	5

The following is a direct quote from the Hoton extent and gives a flavour of the general services required of the tenants (new translations inserted in square brackets where necessary):

Each of the *nativi* who had a plough-team, or any part thereof, was to plough at the two *Precariae Carucarum*, '*et parum vel nihil prodest arura de parvis tenentibus quia pauca habent animalia*' [and little or no benefit to the field of small tenants, because they have few animals].

Every free tenant who owed a heriot was to give his best animal, but if he had no animal he gave no heriot, and the same with the *nativi*, from all of whom *qui tenementa tenent edificata* [who held buildings], a heriot was due.

The successor of any *nativus* was also to pay a fine on entry; but the widow of a *nativus* was to remain in possession of his tenement during her lifetime. She must not, however, re-marry without the lord's licence.

Each nativus quando braciaverit [when he brews] was to give two lagenas [flagons] of the best ale, which was called Ale-toll or Tolcester.

Nor could any of the said *nativi*, *neque major neque minor* [neither greater or lesser] give his daughter in marriage, nor make his son a priest without the lord's licence, nor cut down timber without licence, and then only for building.

They did, however, have to gather nuts.

The Scottish equivalent

Barony courts existed (and still exist) and many of the details are similar to manor courts. See *The Rentall Buik Off The Barony Off Wrie*, available online.

Further Reading

Online

Manorial Documents Register (MDR), created in 1926 following the abolition of copyhold tenure by the Law of Property Act, 1922. Now partly computerised and searchable at The National Archives: www.nationalarchives.gov.uk/mdr/

Glossary of Manorial Documents, available at The National Archives: www.nationalarchives.gov.uk/mdr/help/mdr/glossary.htm

Nottinghamshire Manorial Records: www.nottingham.ac.uk/ManuscriptsandSpecialCollections/ResearchGuidance/Manorial/Introduction.aspx

Conisbrough Royal Manor Court Rolls (Yorkshire): www.hrionline.ac.uk/conisbrough/find/manor.html

Cumbrian Manorial Records: www.lancs.ac.uk/fass/projects/manorialrecords/index.htm

Books

Bailey, M., *The English Manor, c.1200–1500*, Manchester Medieval Sources series (Manchester University Press, 2002)

19

England and Wales: Indentures, Deeds and Land

Buying and selling a piece of land ought to be a straightforward enough process: I want to sell it, you want to buy it, we've agreed a price so let's sign a contract, you hand over the money and I'll move out. But do I actually own it, and can I prove my title? Do I have the right to sell it, and of whom do I have to ask for permission, if anyone? What if someone else turns up tomorrow and says 'actually, I bought this last week, so please move out' or 'there's a mortgage on this property that is now your responsibility to pay'?

You can see the problems. This is why it was necessary for there to be a whole architecture of law and custom surrounding land sale and purchase, and a bewildering array of legal procedure and documents. Property and property law lay at the heart of English society, and the proper registration and transfer of land occupied a great deal of courts' time and energy, which also meant that many lawyers were involved. This is not for the faint hearted!

INTRODUCTION: LANDHOLDING AND THE FEUDAL SYSTEM

Before looking at documents that convey land, it is important to understand the basis in which land was held. (Refer to Chapter 18 for details of feudalism.)

In feudal society, a man held land from his lord – the feudal superior – on the stipulation of service: usually knight service in the case of free tenure, or labour service if unfree. No one actually owned his own fief, but merely occupied it as long as the service was provided, and if he defaulted, the lord could take back the property and grant it to someone else. The liability for 'services and incidents' passed with the property when it was sold, inherited or otherwise conveyed to another person.

Originally (as was the case in Scotland: see Chapter 12) the only way to transfer land was to physically give possession: the donor handed the donee a clod of earth or a turf from the land in the presence of witnesses. This public act of enfeoffment (see p. 243) was called 'livery of seisin': 'livery' being a shortened form of 'delivery' after which the new owner was 'seized' of the land.

There was no written deed required until 1677, when this was made compulsory by the Statute of Frauds, for a reason that will be obvious. On the other hand, it was usually thought best to have some documentary evidence, even if not legally required, to record the conditions and provisos of the conveyance (transfer of ownership) and the names of the parties and witnesses involved, especially the legal heir of the landholder. At one time a lord could choose whether to accept a tenants' heir or not, but this became compulsory and enforceable by the royal courts, ensuring succession and secure tenure down the generations. By the thirteenth century there was a prevailing form of deed, the charter of enfeoffment, which was usually and more simply called a feoffment (see p. 243) but sometimes known as a deed of gift.

Who had land?

We should also note that not everyone held land because it was formally granted, nor were they large landowners only. Many smallholdings were established by a 'squatter' rigging up a hut of some sort, but with a roof and, crucially, a chimney, as there was a tradition that such a structure erected in one night established that a claim to the land was thereby established. If left alone, the squatter might enlarge the borders and start to farm in a small way (see p. 230). Of course, the local landowner might view this as a mixed blessing: good that the land was being worked, bad that his territory was being encroached upon, but maybe it could be mutually beneficial if the squatter would pay a small rent or service – often demanded by the lord of the manor as an acknowledgement of the intrusion into a formal lease (see Chapter 18).

There was a surprisingly large number of these small 'key holdings' scattered about all over England and Wales, and they occasionally rise up to bite an unsuspecting hand, such as when someone wants to build a roundabout or a car park and finds such a plot right in the middle of it, held by a local resident suddenly delighted that he or she can scupper the plans for the new and largely unpopular retail park, or whatever. Similarly, the John Muir Trust, for example, has a policy of acquiring key holdings within a landscape that can be used 'to safeguard its finest features and [offer] opportunities to influence its overall management' (See www.jmt.org/assets/pdf/policy/acquisitionprinciples.pdf).

Title deeds

As the oldest class of document to survive in any great number, and with examples dating back to the late twelfth century, deeds are the most important sources of local and family history before the parish records.

In order to transfer property and/or rights, the vendor must produce the deed by which the property was acquired. Before the Law of Property Act of (1925 C. 20, 15 and 16 Geo 5) this would be the whole series of deeds by which the property passed through earlier hands, back to the year dot. The 1925 Act restricted proof of title to thirty years back, or to the last owner's deeds, whichever was the earlier. This has now been reduced to fifteen years and if the property has been entered with the Land Registry, no deeds are required at all. There is a similar situation in Scotland. Suddenly, most documents have become legally irrelevant but have acquired antiquarian as well as sentimental value. Indentures and deeds, at one time offered widely for sale at knockdown prices, are therefore becoming scarcer and more expensive.

Since 1986, English lawyers have been requested not to sell these privately or at auction, but to hand them over to The National Archives or a local repository as they are, genuinely, historic documents. A great many have ended up as parchment for making lampshades. Really, there ought to be a law! However, they can still be found on auction websites and from specialist dealers, and increasingly they are being digitised.

Title deeds name the vendor and purchaser, will generally describe the property in detail (with a plan, if after 1840) and may narrate previous transactions from years before, which can be a great help in tracking the chain of ownership. Anyone who has title deeds from the very recent past will be able to see that there are three categories of document included:

- Abstract of title: a lawyer's summary of the position and derivation of title.
- Title deeds: the actual instruments by which the title is conveyed from the seller to the buyer.
- Miscellaneous papers: such as auction catalogues, contracts for sale, estate agents' particulars, previous deeds and charters (if you're lucky), court papers and such like.

Finding title deeds

Not all have been destroyed, fortunately. Some are still in private hands as the landowners may have a series of documents pertaining to their property over generations or centuries and from previous owners (see Muniments, p. 242). Many have been deposited with county record offices, universities or other archives by the owners, lawyers, banks and mortgage providers who no longer needed to keep them, while others may be in a deeds registry (see below).

Catalogues of these can be accessed by searching the National Register of Archives, starting with an advanced search at www.nationalarchives.gov.uk. Once an index is located, it can often be searched by surname, property name and parish but in many cases The National Archives has scanned lists of holdings, which can be downloaded and consulted at leisure.

An early deeds registry covering the Bedford Levels from the seventeenth century is held at the Cambridgeshire County Records Office. There were attempts to set up non-compulsory deeds registries in some counties in the early 1700s, but the only ones actually established were for the three Ridings of Yorkshire, Ireland (one of the most important sources for Irish genealogy) and Middlesex, which included a large part, but not all, of London. Deeds so deposited were then copied into large bound volumes. The Yorkshire registries are at archives in Northallerton (for the North Riding), Wakefield (West Riding) and Beverley (East Riding); Irish deeds dating from 1707 are held at The National Archives in Dublin (see www.landregistry.ie/eng/About_Us/Registry_of_Deeds_Services); Middlesex deeds are held by the London Metropolitan Archive.

When the Land Registry was established in London in 1862, registration was initially voluntary, but was made compulsory in 1897, and coverage was gradually extended over the next century until the whole of England and Wales was achieved (in 1990). Now, when a property changes hands, this is recorded by the Land Registry (which is why title deeds are no longer required for the conveyance). The register is open to the public at the district offices where a land certificate can be issued for any registered piece of land, and there is a registry website at www.landregistry.gov.uk.

See Chapter 12 for Registers of Scotland, the Executive Agency that acts as Scotland's National Land and Property Register and has established a map-based land register system (www.ros.gov.uk) and for searching in the Register of Sasines and the Public Register of Deeds at the National Records of Scotland (NRS).

Land Registers of Northern Ireland can be found at: www.landwebni.gov.uk, which has details of title to about half of properties registered in the province: it is divided into the map-based Land Registry (dealing with properties known as 'registered land', chiefly in rural areas or recent developments in and near towns) and the Registry of Deeds (covering the remaining properties, known as 'unregistered land' and mainly in towns).

For completeness' sake (and because many Scots and English had land in Ireland), information on land registration in the Republic of Ireland is at www.landregistry.ie dating from 1892.

Do not, in any case, expect to get direct access to a look-up online database: there are usually fees, too.

NATURE OF LANDHOLDING: FREEHOLD AND COPYHOLD

There were three types of freehold interest in land: fee simple, fee tail and life estate.

Fee simple

This is freehold, the nearest thing to absolute possession: land so held could be conveyed to anyone by will, sale or donation (gift) without legal restriction and potentially forever. When freehold land was devised (conveyed in a will or deed) the document will say 'to X.Y. and his heirs, executors, administrators and assigns'.

Fee tail

See p. 143ff. for more detail on entails. Land held by fee tail meant there was an interest in the estate as long as there were living male lineal descendants of the person who first had the land granted. Each successive landholder had what was effectively life interest (see below) but heritably, so it could pass to a particular lineal descendant on death from generation to generation, reverting to the original grantee if the line became extinct. This kept the property within a designated family but had the disadvantage that it could not be alienated (sold on or devised in a will), which could become restrictive as time passed and circumstances changed. The key phrase in a deed or will when conveying land held in fee tail was 'to X.Y. and the heirs [or perhaps 'heirs male'] of his body'.

Life estate

Freehold estate could be granted to a person for the duration of his or her life or perhaps three lives (see below) and that grantee could, in turn, convey the land to someone else, but it would revert to the original holder or his heirs or assigns on the death of the grantee's death. The grant could be made '*pour autre vie*' (for the life of another, say, of a wife), but would revert to the original holder or his heirs on that death. Thus property could pass to several individuals before eventually returning to the original landholder. A deed or will conveying land in life estate will say 'to X.Y. for his [or her] life'. An example would be a husband conveying life estate to his widow in a will, and then, on her death, to another family member, but after their deaths, it would revert.

Copyhold or 'villein tenure' land was physically occupied by someone other than the owner. This is the case with a lease or rental, for example, but manors (Chapter 18) had a form of tenure particular to them, copyhold tenure, which became the customary form of landholding of parts of manorial estates. The advantage for the landlord was that copyhold imposed restrictions on tenants as to what they could do with the land, and obligated them to seek permission from the manor courts (p. 230) to sell, sublet, buy, mortgage, inherit or pass on their copyhold property. These transactions are known as 'Surrenders and Admissions' and were recorded in the manorial court roll or court book, with a copy to the tenant as proof of title. Copyhold tenants were also subject to 'incidents' (what Scots land law calls 'casualties') such as the one-off payment of relief to the lord of the manor when a new tenant took over copyhold property.

There were two forms of copyhold: heritable and for lives.

Heritable copyhold

This meant that the land could pass to the copyholder's heir on his or her death and depending on the manor's customary practice, this could be:

– by primogeniture: to the eldest son (the most common custom).
– by ultimogeniture to the youngest son (also known as 'Borough English' and most popular in East Anglia).

– by gavelkind, meaning equally between all sons (as was the practice in Kent, earlier in Wales and, for a different reason, in Ireland, where the British had an interest in seeing large estates held by Catholics broken up).

By the mid-sixteenth century it was also possible for a copyholder to specify a different heir by enrolling a copy of his or her will in the manorial court records, so that the property would be surrendered to the 'use' (see p. 211) of the will, and when the tenant died and his or her will was produced in court the designated heir would come to be admitted to the land. Heritable copyhold land was commonly converted to freehold in the mid-nineteenth century with the overlord receiving financial compensation.

Copyhold for lives

The second form of copyhold could be for one life, but was usually for three lives – commonly the tenant, his wife and their heir – thus ensuring some form of security of tenure for the immediate family. When all three were deceased, the land would revert to the overlord who could then grant it to a new tenant who might, of course, be the next heir in line, and so it could roll on in the same family. If copyhold for lives seems similar to leasehold for lives (see p. 244), it is, and it was often converted to that. It all went away in 1922 anyway, when copyhold tenure was abolished, and all copyhold land was converted to freehold in 1925.

DEEDS

The form of deed, where only one party is involved, is a deed poll, as opposed to an indenture (see p. 224). The term 'poll' refers to the documents being cut straight across. It only involves one party, so there is no need to match up multiple copies. Examples are wills, bonds, trust deeds, mortgages, marriage contracts or settlements and sales or transfers of land.

The intent and nature of the deed – a land sale, a trusteeship, a mortgage and so on – can be hard to determine at first glance, but the trick is to ignore the legal and technical verbiage and get straight to the effective part of the document.

Early deeds and muniments

There are some (not many) deeds from the early Norman period when lands were being distributed among the Norman noblemen who flocked over to England in the aftermath of the Conquest of 1066, occasionally with some notifications of the Saxons that the lands were 'liberated' from. Domesday Book, compiled in the 1080s, is the great record of who owned what and where.

Likewise, there are few private deeds up to the time of Richard I (1179, said to be the start of 'legal memory') but in reality the earliest to be encountered date from the reign of Edward I (1272–1307), who was assiduous in getting Acts of Parliament passed on all sorts of legal issues and tidying up the laws that existed.

That said, in reality there are not many deeds much further back than the 1500s, largely because before this time almost all land was in the possession either of the Crown, the church and monasteries, or large, often noble, landowners, all of whom kept their own charter books or muniments. (The word 'muniment' is interesting in itself. It has come to mean the documentary evidence of title to a property or some other right but it derives from Latin *munimentum* meaning 'defence' or 'protection' and ultimately from *munire* 'to fortify'. We still use the term 'munitions' in that regard. But the connection to documents is that these would be kept in a storage chamber and within a chest, both for safekeeping and to ensure preservation.)

When Henry VIII ordered the dissolution of the monasteries and confiscation of their huge estates, his Augmentation Office, charged with that task, took care to destroy or 'lose' many original documents while the lands were redistributed or sold to new owners regardless of any prior claims. This was, of course, not just King Henry showing the church (and the Pope) who was boss, it generated a great deal of much-needed revenue, and there is no better way to make money than to confiscate someone else's land and sell it to a willing third party. And why land, specifically? Well, as Mark Twain observed: 'They're not making any more of it.'

Incidentally, this was also the origin of what we would now recognise as estate agents, who had a commission to dispose of properties as expeditiously as possible without bothering the Crown.

Feoffment

This is the oldest and in many ways the simplest form of sale, essentially a grant of title by which the grantee was 'infeft' of the land. (Terms like feoff, fee, infeft, feu, infeudation and others are all related (for examples see the Index).

Feoffments always begin '*Sciant presentes et futuri quod ego …*' ('Know those present and future that I …') followed by the name of the donor, then '*dedi concessi et hac presenti carta mea confirmavi*' ('have given granted and by this my present charter confirmed to …') followed by name of the donee, then '*habendum et tenendum*' ('having and holding') followed by a description of the property concerned.

The feoffment was later replaced by the deed of uses, which had its drawbacks, not least that it needed other deeds as a follow-up before anything like a complete purchase was finalised. This was a result of the Statute of Uses of 1535/36, an attempt to prevent the creation of 'uses' (a use is an acknowledgement of the duty of a person, who has acquired for certain purposes, to carry out those purposes, and thus a beneficial interest in land) because this deprived the king and other lords of their fines and escheats.

The earlier Statute of Wills (1540) had allowed land to be devised to named persons on the death of its holder so ownership of land could now be conveyanced without any accompanying livery of seisin (p. 182): a simple deed of bargain and sale (p. 243) would do. Before this, a seller could not dispose of his estate by a will, but to get around this aspect of common law, the practice had arisen of making feoffments to the use of, or in trust for, persons other than the one to whom the seisin or legal possession was delivered. This was considered an abuse and an evasion of the law and got around the principle that the land of a tenant in fee simple would pass on his death to his eldest son or, if there was no heir, it would escheat to his feudal superior. People got around this by conveying the land to a third party, or trustee, who agreed to let the grantor's beneficiaries (*cestuis que use*) have the full benefit and enjoyment of the land after his death. (This practice was effectively the same as the use of trust disposition and settlement in Scotland – see Chapter 11). Also, it avoided the payment of a feudal burden – the dues a tenant owed his overlord on his death – as the tenant was not himself seized of the land at the time of his death. So, the Statute of Uses was passed in 1536.

However it failed to achieve its main purpose of protecting the financial interests of the overlord and (ultimately) the Crown. By this statute, possession of the land passed directly to any person named as the user, instead of to trustees. The Statute of Uses meant that the legal interest would follow automatically. For the first time, freehold land could be conveyed by deed.

Bargain and sale

A deed of bargain and sale can be told apart from an enfeoffment by its action clause, which says: 'This indenture made [date] between [names of the parties concerned] hath granted bargained and sold … to have and to hold [followed by a description of the property concerned]' (see the Buxton indenture of 1806, p. 253).

There were certain legal deficiencies in this, so the deed was tinkered with to include a feoffment, changing the operative phrase from 'hath granted bargained and sold' to 'hath aliened, granted, bargained, sold, enfeoffed and confirmed …'.

Even this did not fully provide a sufficient conveyance in the eyes of the law, so the lease and release was developed.

Lease and release

It helps to think of this form of land sale and purchase as lease and 're-lease', as will become clear. This was invented at the time that Henry VIII was dissolving (and asset-stripping) the monasteries (see Early Deeds, p. 242) and the need was evident for a simple, quick and effective formula that was also a secret but legally valid conveyance. The great advantage was that it got around the Statute of Enrolment because it did not actually pass on a freehold, and as the release was a deed of grant there was no need for livery of seisin (p. 182).

There are two main deeds associated with a lease and release that had to be kept together, and so one was usually smaller and wrapped or enveloped in the larger. The smaller document, the lease, was drawn up between the parties, for a lease for one year by the granter to the (eventual) purchaser, but without any mention of rent or lease payment (as there would be in a real lease) other than 'a peppercorn if legally demanded' or similar, and the action phrase 'hath remised granted bargained and sold'. Then there was the larger parchment, the release, dated one day after the lease and cancelling it (hence 'release') and containing the price paid and a complete guarantee that the buyer holds it forever, so it is actually a deed of sale and the operational phrase is 'hath granted bargained sold remised released quitclaimed and confirmed'.

By the mid-1700s, this was practically the only form of conveyance and was only finally abolished by the Real Property Act of 1845.

Lease

A proper lease is different. Leasehold is not actual ownership, just a right to have tenure of, to use and enjoy for a certain period, and for payment. The parties named in the documents are the actual owners (or the trustees of a marriage settlement) and the tenant. A lease is identified by the phrase 'yielding and paying' and will state a term of years for the leasehold (often three, five, seven or twenty-one), or it could be renewable annually, or its term may be until a certain event such as the death of a tenant (life lease). Three-life leases were common, the three lives usually being the tenant, his wife and his son, and could be extended in some cases for generations or even centuries. Obviously, this was a very secure occupancy for a farmer and his descendants.

The rental would be a fixed yearly, half-yearly or quarterly payment at one or more of the usual feast days (Chapter 3): Lady Day (25 March), St John or Midsummer (24 June), St Michael and All Angels or Michaelmas (29 September), and Nativity or Christmas (25 December). The lease deed will give the day, month and year, the names of the contracting parties, any co-trustees or witnesses (often relatives or neighbours, which genealogists and local historians enjoy) and a precise terrier (description) giving the location, field or farm names and size. The rent and term of years is then recorded, together with any conditions such as rights of access, responsibility for repairs, any services or heriots (pp. 231, 235) due and whether in cash or kind.

Typically, the rental was low, but there were high and adjustable entry fines each time someone new took over.

Sale by recovery

Fines and recoveries (which were indentured) are dealt with in Chapter 17 but it is worthwhile rehearsing the sale by recovery here. This was a law suit, at one time real, but later a convenient (legal) fiction. Say A wants to sell the land called X to B. B would issue a writ, pretending that he had a claim to the land, X. Enter a third party, C (who is not really involved and could be, say, the lawyer's clerk), who testifies as to the good title of the real owner, who in turn comes forward bringing a witness to prove his ownership. This is uncontested by the seller, so indisputable title is proved. The court would issue a deed of recovery narrating the transaction and agreeing that a stated amount of money should be paid by the purchaser to conclude the bargain.

Yes, it was a farce, but a necessary one. Oliver Cromwell was right when he observed that English land law was 'an ungodly and tortuous jumble'.

Deeds of recovery can be quite decorative, written in Court hand on white parchment, with ornamented headings and initial capital letters and an engraved portrait of the monarch. The most florid are from the Stuart period (1603–1707) and monarchs, after which they more or less fade into history. 'Good riddance', you might well think.

Mortgage

A deed of mortgage – a loan raised against the property as security – can be told apart from a sale or lease by the ridiculous term granted (not unusually 1,000 years) and the nominal rent of one peppercorn annually or some similar token payment. The purpose of the mortgage will be stated, as will a date and place where it is to be redeemed – often a public place, or the house of the local clergyman or lawyer, presumably as this came with an inbuilt reliable witness to the repayment.

Mortgage deeds tended to be destroyed when the loan was repaid (why would anyone keep them?) so not many are extant. Those that do exist were often raised by small cottagers for small amounts of money, and were usually loaned by the local landlord who would have an eye to adding the premises to his property in case of default.

INDENTURES

The term 'indentured servant' – where someone binds himself or herself to serve a master or mistress for a period of years under stated conditions – will be familiar to most. Servitude is not the only form of indenture: it is a general word for a contract between two parties or more to some agreed activity, including the deeds (conveyances) concerning the sale, lease, rental, mortgage, feoffment (p. 243) or use of land, assignments, or (as shown later) an apprenticeship. The term 'indenture' refers to the edge of the document having a wavy or indented edge, originally an irregular sawtooth-shaped cut, that provided a precaution against counterfeiting as the uniquely identifiable copies held by all parties could, if needed, be put together and compared for authenticity, changes that may have been made and so on (see p. 224ff for more information). This is sometimes called 'vandyking', a reference to the shape of a 'Van Dyke' beard.

Early on, indentures were written by hand on large sheepskin sheets (parchment) but later, as in the William Henry Cooper apprenticeship example (p. 248), on a standard pre-printed form that could be added to and amended to fit the particular circumstances.

Structure of an indenture

After about 1675 (subsequent to the Stamp Act of 1694), almost all indentures are written in English – after all, the whole point was transparency and clarity of the obligations of both parties, so there was no point in using a language only the lawyers could understand. They usually start with the title 'This Indenture' written (or later, printed) in large capitals or bold Gothic letters with an ornamental flourish and an engraving of the current sovereign's coat of arms within a garter collar.

Up until about 1800 the text would then narrate the name and year of reign plus titles of the monarch, but later this was placed at the end. It is also missing, naturally, from documents of the Commonwealth (Cromwellian) years and after the Glorious Revolution of William and Mary in 1688–89. The AD year is given in addition, for the avoidance of doubt as to the date.

The stamp

Various Stamp Acts dictated the cost and format of a stamp used on these documents, essentially as a revenue-raising tax. This rather ingenious but simple system of levying a duty was dreamed up by the Dutch in 1624 after a competition in which the public was asked to invent a new form of tax. The first Stamp Act was in 1694 (An act for granting to Their Majesties several duties on Vellum, Parchment and Paper for 10 years, towards carrying on the war against France; 5 & 6 Will. & Mar. c. 21) and, as can be seen, was intended as a temporary measure. It exceeded all expectations, even at duty ranging from one penny to several shillings on grants of various kinds, court documents, wills and other documents of executry and probate, letters of administration, newspapers and insurance policies, stamp duty was found to be bringing in around £50,000 annually to the Revenue.

The stamps themselves were on embossed blue stamp paper with a tinfoil tab in the centre, which both attached it to the parchment and ensured it could not be taken off and reused. The back of the stamp sheets had a royal cypher seal, also to prevent illegal reuse.

The stamp duty on indentures was initially 6d, so a single sixpenny stamp was enough, but as the tax doubled and tripled, multiple stamps were used. A strip of the three stamps is common throughout the 1700s, but there was also a 1/6d (one shilling and sixpence) stamp, used from the 1770s.

Incidentally, the American Revenues 1/6d. stamp of 1765 (*Duties in American Colonies Act 1765*; 5 George III, c. 12) imposed on books, farming almanacs, newspapers, land deeds, court documents, commercial papers and so on, was one of the taxes the American rebels were protesting against, not least because the additional revenue was being raised specifically to fund the war against them and pay for troops stationed in North America after the British victory in the Seven Years' War of 1756–63. The British government felt that the American colonies were getting the benefit of the increased military strength, and should therefore pay towards it. The Americans, in the main, tended not to share this view and objected to both the soldiery and the taxes that paid for them. They felt this was unconstitutional, as it effectively bypassed the thirteen colonial assemblies. The British took this as defiance of the law by a bunch of ungrateful colonials who didn't know what was good for them. This offended almost everyone on the North American continent, who responded with 'No Taxation without Representation'. Out of that, America was born.

Back in the UK, these laws were succeeded by the Stamp Duties Management Act and the Stamp Act, both passed in 1891, which still govern stamp duties today. In 1914 the Stamp Office also oversaw the production of the first Treasury notes (banknotes) until 1928 when the Bank of England took over banknote production, and it wasn't until 1963 that postage stamps used to send letters by Royal Mail became the responsibility of the General Post Office (GPO), first established in 1660 but known as the Post Office since 1969, a statutory corporation rather than a department of state.

The stamp of £1 or £1 10s introduced in the later 1800s was a significant tax increase, especially when the average wage was a few shillings per week: £1 could be an indentured servant's 'allowance' (wage) for up to ten weeks.

Signed and sealed

The indenture finishes with the signatures of the contracting parties, or 'The mark + of' when a party was illiterate or otherwise unable to write. But why a cross? Notice that it isn't an 'X'. In the days when neither Saxon nor Norman noblemen could sign their own names (not a situation found as frequently in Scotland), they used the sign of the Christian cross to indicate their good faith, almost like an oath.

Finally, one of the parties, but most usually the lawyer, would then authenticate each signature, including his own, with a wax seal. In this usage, 'sealed' does not mean closed up (as we would 'seal up' a letter today) but impressed with one or more seals. These were eventually made on a threaded ribbon to preserve their integrity (see the Cheesman indenture on p. 251).

The use of seals and sealing wax is ancient, and probably arrived in Britain with the Romans, but progressively came to be used on legal documents from Saxon times. Early deeds have small, rather trivial seals, but they were at least proof that the document was approved by the person or persons concerned. A seal or signet was a precious thing, in that it was the sole possession of one person, and was usually broken up on his death so that it could not be used for fraudulent post-mortem counterfeits.

This is the origin of coats of arms belonging to one person at a time. The use of seals and signets predates heraldry, but in many cases pre-existing sigils found their way into a man's armorial bearings when arms became prevalent after the twelfth century (see Chapter 6). There is evidence on many fourteenth- and fifteenth-century deeds that small private-bearing armorial-like devices had been attached, but these are fragile and few have survived. Although from 1714 (the beginning of the Hanoverian period) large private seals were out of fashion, small private seals may bear the arms and crest of the person signing, so a knowledge of heraldry is a great help if the signature itself is hard to read.

The sealing wax used was either its natural yellowish colour (but could have been white originally and now discoloured by ageing), or red, dark green and black waxes could also have been used. Originally, the wax was made by boiling a mixture of wax and resin in turpentine. Usually this was beeswax and coniferous tree rosin, but shellac (a sixteenth-century import from India made from insects) was used later. Yellow seals used mica, black probably came from bitumen or simple lamp black (soot), red was from vermillion, cochineal (more insects) or sinople, and green from verdigris (oxidised copper compounds).

Officials, and the bodies they represented, had seals. Apart from royal seals (see p. 313), there would be a seal for an abbey but also for the abbot himself (p. 116 has a Scottish example) as there would be for burghs, universities, guilds and so on.

Somewhere – it may be at the foot, or on the *verso* – the document will be docketed by the Revenue tax collectors, using the phrase 'signed, sealed, and delivered' and in later documents a statement warning everyone to make sure the date, names and condition were correctly filled in to comply with the law, or else!

PARCHMENT AND VELLUM

Parchment and vellum are treated animal skins. Vellum is made from the skins of young or even stillborn animals, which is therefore of finer grade and less likely to have the imperfections and blemishes of the skins of mature animals. However, a larger, adult skin would be needed for the larger documents. Skins are far more hard-wearing and likely to resist damage than paper, which is why it was ordered that parish registers were written on parchment (see p. 125).

Dating parchment and vellum is not an exact science without a laboratory and lots of experience, but in general the skins on which very early deeds were written (say, before 1400) tend to be small, dark yellow or light brown with a woolly surface. By the 1500s the preparation methods were better and the skins are larger, a lighter yellow or even near-white and smoother to the touch. Documents vary in the grade, colour and thickness of the skins and there are often small holes naturally present. If anything, these are evidence of a genuine parchment rather than a more modern reproduction.

Parchment and vellum do tend to discolour, especially at the edges, but this does not usually affect readability except where a fold or crease has obliterated some words. It is possible to flatten out a document by refolding backwards along the original folds and allowing it to 'relax', but this should not be done more often than necessary and should never be helped along by heat or moisture. If you must, flatten the document by refolding it then flattening between two sheets of thin wood or rigid plastic with weights on top. This has often been done to framed indentures, which have often been pasted to a mounting card, preventing inspection of the *verso* (the back of the sheet).

INKS

The main ingredients of black ink – often made by the scribe – were oak galls and iron sulphate. If it has oxidised and faded, it is possible to restore it to some extent, usually with ammonium sulphate, but this can stain the skin itself. Generally, it is better to try and enhance an image of the document digitally.

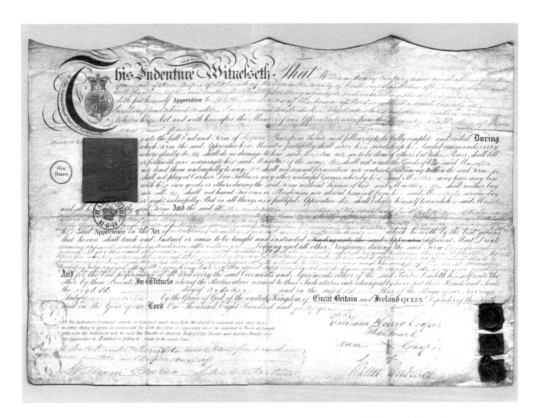

The 1844 apprenticeship indenture of William Henry Cooper. *Kindly provided by Douglas Butle*

The lawyer's seal, 'P' for Pearce, against each signature or mark.

The stamp (One Pound) plus a date – notice that it says 'Hampshire', the modern equivalent of 'County of Southampton'.

Coloured inks were only used for illuminations (the fancy, painted letters, usually completed later by a specialised illuminator) and on certain legal documents, such as the red 'rubric' at the top. In addition to black, it was possible to make blue, red and green from mineral pigments: blue from lapis lazuli stone finely powdered (very expensive) or a copper salt; red from red lead or iron oxide; green from copper salts. It is no coincidence that the standard heraldic tinctures are black (Sable), blue (Azure), red (Gules) and green (Vert) as these were the colours generally available, in addition to the two metals: gold (Or, which would require either gold leaf or a pigment made from ochre) and silver (Argent, usually indicated by leaving the colouration blank, so that it bears the background colour of the paper or parchment).

THE COOPER INDENTURE

Transcription

Words written or printed in large Gothic script have been rendered in upper case; the pre-printed sections are in italic. Bold words are in bold (e.g. **Apprentice**, line 4); and the handwritten sections are in regular type. Notice:

- Spaces left for gender: *h*(is) or *h*(er), *M*(aster) or *M*(istress) etc.
- The ban on drinking, gambling, going to plays and marriage without the apprentice-master's consent (lines 12–14, although this document seems to imply that 'fornication' could be permitted, which probably isn't what the document drafters intended).
- That William's mother is housing, feeding and clothing William (otherwise the phrase 'Finding unto the said Apprentice' in line 23 would not be crossed out) so he is probably living at home, with his allowance going to help his widowed mother.
- The incomplete lines filled in by a pen stroke (transcribed here as ~ ~ ~, as in lines 7 and 29).
- The twelve- to thirteen-hour working day (lines 28–29).
- The mark of Ann Cooper, although the 14-year-old William has rather a good hand, and presumably had some schooling.
- Certain antiquated word forms that nobody actually used in speech by that time (*useth*, line 22 and *bindeth*, line 30).

THIS INDENTURE WITNESSETH THAT William Henry Cooper now aged about fourteen
years, son of Ann Cooper of the Parish of Portsea in the County of Southampton Widow of his own
free will and
with the consent of his said mother testified by her being a party to and executing the presents
doth put himself **Apprentice** to Walter Andrews of the town of Portsea in the said County of
Southampton Cabinet maker, Joiner and Undertaker his executors administrators and assigns
to learn his Art and with him after the Manner of an Apprentice to serve from the twenty sixth day of June
now last past ~ ~ ~
unto the full End and term of Seven Years from thence next following to be fully complete and ended **DURING**
which term the said Apprentice his Master faithfully shall serve his secrets keep his lawful commands every
where gladly do. He shall do no damage to his said Master nor see to be done by others but to his Power shall tell
or forthwith give warning to his said Master of the same. He shall not waste the Goods of the said Master
nor lend them unlawfully to any. He shall not commit fornication nor contract Matrimony within the said term. He
shall not play at Cards or Dice Tables or any other unlawful Games whereby his said Master shall have any loss
with his own goods or others during the said term without Licence of his said Master. He shall neither buy
nor sell. He shall not haunt Taverns or Playhouses nor absent himself from his said Master's service day
or night unlawfully. But in all things as a faithful Apprentice he shall behave himself towards his said Master
and all his during the said term And the said Walter Andrews in consideration of the strict and faithful
services to be done and
performed by the said Apprentice hereby agrees to pay him one shilling every week during the first
[unreadable]
years of the said term Two shillings a week during the fourth year, Three shillings a week during the
fifth year and Four shillings weekly and every week during the sixth and seventh years of the
said term and also
his said **Apprentice** in the **Art** of a cabinet maker, joiner and undertaker which he useth by the best means
that he can shall teach and Instruct or cause to be taught and instructed ~~Finding unto the said Apprentice~~ (Sufficient
Meat Drink
wearing apparel, washing, medicine attendance Lodging and all other Necessaries during the said term being
found and
provided for the said Apprentice by his said mother) And it is hereby agreed by the said parties hereto
that the weekly allowances agreed to be paid by the said Walter Andrews to his said Apprentice as
aforesaid shall be
paid only during such time as the said Apprentice shall attend to the concerns and business of his said
Master
And it is also agreed that the working hours of the said Apprentice shall be from six to seven in the
summer and from
eight to eight in the winter ~ ~ ~
AND for the true Performance of all and every the said Covenants and Agreements either of the said Parties
bindeth himself unto the
other by these Presents IN WITNESS whereof the Parties above named to these Indentures interchangeably have
put their Hands and Seals
the eighth day of October and in the eighth Year of the Reign of our Sovereign
Lady Queen Victoria by the Grace of God of the united Kingdom of Great Britain & Ireland Queen Defender
of the Faith
and in the Year of our Lord One thousand Eight Hundred and forty four

NB. *The Indenture Covenant Article or Contract must bear date the day it is executed and what Money or other thing is given or contracted for with the clerk or Apprentice must be inserted in Words at Length otherwise the indenture will be void the Master or Mistress forfeit Fifty Pounds and another penalty and the Apprentice be disabled to follow h__ trade or be made Free.*	(Sd) William Henry Cooper The mark Ann + Cooper of (Sd) Walter Andrews

Signed Sealed and Delivered (the same being first read over}
by the said parties) in the presence of   }
William Pearce Solicitor Portsea

THE CHEESMAN INDENTURE OF 1888

Transcription

Notice that it is not 'indentured'. It was written in America.

This 1888 indenture concerns Edmund George Cheesman 1860–1929 and his brother Alfred Addison Cheesman (1861–1934) both living in Leavenworth, Kansas, and their mother Amelia Caroline Davies (1835–1915), then widowed and living in Cheltenham, England.

Edmund and Alfred had been born in Tunbridge Wells, Kent, England, to George Cheesman and Amelia (watch out for the confusion over the spellings of Tunbridge and Tonbridge Wells). Their father's will bequeathed 'all of the lands and real estate in the United States of America' that he possessed at death. Edmund left for America when he was about 20 and initially lived with his uncle Charles Davies at Heslington Park, Reno, Kansas. Edmund initially farmed, then ran a store and mill and later worked as a shipping clerk in a furniture business. About 1915, Edmund and his family moved to Sherman, California, which became Hollywood, where he owned a grocery store on Sunset Boulevard.

The indenture was written and 'Remembered' by James H. Brown, Notary Public in Leavenworth, Kansas but naturally lodged with the English court. The import of it was to rationalise what had happened to the money inherited by their mother in England after their father, George Cheesman, died in 1886. Their father's will had stipulated that his property would be placed in trust, sold, and a sufficient amount invested to provide an annuity to his wife Amelia, incomes to his daughters for their 'separate use' (i.e. the husbands couldn't get their hands on it) and to his two sons. It seems from other documents, that most of the bequests turned out to be worthless when the father died and it is said that one of his clerks stole £33,000 of bearer bonds, although he did leave a total estate of about £29,000. By this indenture Edmund and Alfred were paid £350 by their mother, although not provided for very well herself, who bought out their interest in a capital sum of £5,500 specified in George's will. This gave the young men much-needed ready cash while Amelia could collect the interest on the capital if it were ever to reappear. But Edmund and Alfred could buy back their interest in the capital – for a higher sum.

This may seem extreme lengths for a family to go to over what was effectively a present of money from mother to sons, but they were right to do so: with sisters and their children in the picture, and conditions in George's will as to grandchildren, there could be decades of legal wrangling if the whole thing weren't spelled out properly.

For the record, when Amelia died (which was not to happen for another twenty-seven years, but they weren't to know that), she left a total of about £7,600.

The Cheesman Indenture. The document is folded so as to show the salient details on the outside. Notice the back of the threaded ribbon for the seals.

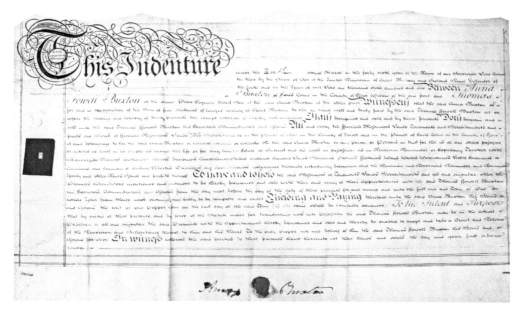

THE BUXTON INDENTURE OF 1806

Transcription

THIS INDENTURE made the tenth day of March in the forty sixth year of the reign of our sovereign Lord George

the third by the grace of God of the United Kingdom of Great Britain and Ireland and King Defender of

the faith and in the Year of our Lord one thousand eight hundred and six **BETWEEN**

ANNA BUXTON of Earls Colne in the County of Essex widow of the one part and Thomas

Fowell Buxton of the same place Esquire Eldest son of the said Anna Buxton of the other part

WITNESSETH that the said Anna Buxton

for and in consideration of the sum of five shillings of lawful money of Great Britain to her in hand well and truly paid by the said Thomas Fowell Buxton at or

before the sealing and delivery of these presents the script Receipt whereof is hereby acknowledged

HATH bargained and sold and by these presents **DOTH** bargain

and sell unto the said Thomas ffowell Buxton his Executors Administrators and Assigns **ALL** and every the ffreehold Messuages Lands Tenements and Hereditaments and

parts and shares of freehold Messuages Lands ^Tenements and Hereditaments in the parish of Wick in the County of Dorset and in the Parish of Earls Colne in the county of Essex

of and belonging to her the said Anna Buxton or whereof wherein or whereto she the said Anna Buxton or any person or persons in trust for her is or are seized possessed

or intitled as well in fee simple as during her life or for any limited Estate or Interest and as well in possession as in Reversion Remainder or Expectancy Together with

all and singular Houses Outhouses Edifices Buildings Coachhouses Stables Orchards Gardens Lands Meadows Pastures Feedings Wards Watercourses Rights Easements

Commons and Common of Pasture Liberties Privileges and Appurtenances whatsoever thereunto respectively belonging and the Reversion and Reversions Remainder and Remainders

yearly and other rents Issues and profits thereof **TO HAVE AND TO HOLD** the said Messuages or Tenements Lands Hereditaments and all and singular other the premises herein before mentioned and intended to be hereby bargained and sold with their and every of their appurtenances unto the said Thomas ffowell Buxton

his Executors Administrators and assigns from the day next before the day of the sale of these presents for and during and unto the full end and Term of one

whole year from thence next ensuing and fully to be complete and ended **YIELDING AND PAYING** therefore unto the said Anna Buxton Heirs

and Assigns the rent of one Pepper Corn on the last day of the said Term (if the same shall be lawfully demanded) **TO THE INTENT** and **PURPOSE**

that by virtue of these presents and by force of the Statute made for transferring uses into possession the said Thomas ffowell Buxton may be in the actual

possession of all and singular the said premises with the appurtenances hereby bargained and sold and thereby be enabled to accept and take a Grant and Release

of the Reversion and Inheritance thereof to him and Heirs To the only proper use and behoof of him the said Thomas ffowell Buxton Heirs and

assigns **IN WITNESS** whereof the said parties to these presents have hereunto set their hands and seals the day and year first above

written. //

(Signature here and a seal) Anne [seal] Buxton

Notes:
– This is a 'bargain and sale' (see p. 243) between Anna Buxton and her son, for five shillings. Essentially she is giving it to him, but there is no bargain without a payment.
– Just to make sure, she also assigns all rights etc. for a rent of 'one Pepper Corn': the original peppercorn rent.

PART III

GLOSSARIES

20

Latin and Scots: Legal and Genealogical Glossary

This is a combined glossary of terms likely to be encountered in the document classes considered in this book. Each entry may be followed by one or more abbreviations in italic: *La* (Latin); *Sc* (Scots); *En* (English); *Fr* (French); *Le* (Legal); *Oc* (Occupations), *Pal* (Palaeography). Gaelic is dealt with separately (Chapter 7).

Included here are some very common Latin words and phrases (given in italic), and some not typically found in Latin dictionaries, for which the *Collins Latin Dictionary and Grammar* is especially recommended. See also The National Archives' *Beginners' Latin: Latin 1086–1733: a practical online tutorial for beginners* (www.nationalarchives.gov.uk/latin/beginners).

Scots is a separate language that developed alongside and at the same time as the current predominant dialect of English spoken in London and the south-east of England (which is by no means the only English dialect) and it is a mere accident of history that Britain, and therefore the world, does not speak Scots and read the Authorised Version of the Bible in Scots. English and Scots are about as similar as German and Dutch or Norwegian and Danish, and there are Scots words routinely used in legal and official documents up to 1710 and beyond, which genealogists and family historians must be able to recognise and understand.

Old documents may throw up terms that are either Scots words, or are particular to the Scottish legal system.

a (ab)	*La*	from, by
ab hoc mense	*La*	from this month on
abaid, baid	*Sc*	delay
abandon	*Le*	giving up, a total desertion, an absolute relinquishment
abandonment	*Le*	leaving behind of property; an indifference as to the fate of a chattel
abavia	*La*	great-great-grandmother, female ancestor in the fourth degree
abavus	*La*	great-great-grandfather, male ancestor in the fourth degree
abbacinare	*Le*	mediaeval corporal punishment, permanently blinding by hot irons
abbacy	*Sc*	the office or position of abbot

abbot	*Sc*	senior monk of an abbey (pre-Reformation, Catholic or Episcopal)
Abbot of Na Rent	*Sc*	same as the Abbot of Unreason and identified with Robin Hood at festivals and pageants
abdjudication (for debt)	*Sc Le*	passing of a debtor's property to his creditors; *see* apprising
abdormitus	*La*	died
abdormivit	*La*	he/she died
aberemurder	*Le*	spontaneous and gratuitous murder
abiit	*La*	he/she died
abinde	*La*	since
abitus est	*La*	he/she died, went away
abjectarius	*La*	cabinetmaker, woodworker
abjuro	*La*	to renounce by oath
ablutus	*La*	baptism, christening
ablutus est	*La*	he was baptised
abnepos	*La*	great-great-grandson, male descendant in the fourth degree
abneptis	*La*	great great granddaughter, female descendant in the fourth degree
aboleist	*Sc*	abolished
abortivus	*La*	premature birth
abs	*La*	from, by
abscessus	*La*	death
absolvitor	*Sc Le*	judgement for the defender in a civil action (when the court assoilzies)
absque	*La*	without, except
abstersus	*La*	baptised
abstract of title	*Le*	statement of the conveyances and charges appearing of record and affecting the title to real property
abuilyements, abulzeaments	*Sc*	habiliments, clothing, garments, equipment
abuo	*La*	I baptise, I wash
ac	*La*	and
ac (conj.)	*La*	and
acatholicus	*La*	non-Catholic, Protestant
acceleration clause	*Le*	clause in a contract that states that if a payment is missed, or some other default occurs (such as the debtor becoming insolvent), then the contract is fully due immediately
accidents	*Sc Le*	payment when becoming a burgess
accipio	*La*	to accept, take, receive, take possession of
accola	*La*	local resident
accomptant	*Sc*	accountant
accretion	*Sc Le*	enlargement of an inheritance when a co-heir fails to prove rights to a share
acicularius	*La*	needle maker
acquiescat	*La*	he/she is content with, reposes, dies

acquiet	*Sc*	guarantee undisturbed possession or use of land
acquietus est	*La*	he died
acra	*La*	acre
Act of C	*Sc Le*	Act of Council
acta and decreta	*Sc*	acts and decreets (decrees), specifically of the Privy Council
actis	*Sc*	acts, legal documents
actorney	*Sc*	attorney, lawyer
actum	*La*	record
ad	*La*	at, to, in, for, towards
ad huc/adhuc	*La*	thus far, as yet, still, in addition, in the future
ad modum (adv.)	*La*	very, quite; fully; + *non.* = at all
ad opus et usus	*La Le*	to the use and behoof
adeill	*Sc*	at all; not adeill = not at all
adhuc	*La*	as yet, still
adjudication (charter of)	*Sc*	charter granted by the Crown to a creditor giving over the estate of a debtor in settlement of the debt
adjudication in implement	*Sc*	decision by a court to implement a faulty title to land
adjuge	*Sc*	sentence to pay a fine
adjutor	*La*	assistant
adjuvenis	*La*	assistant
adminicle	*Sc*	supporting documents and evidence as when proving the existence and details of a lost deed or testament
Adminiculum	*La Le*	evidence to support something else
admittance (or admission)	*Le*	ceremony by which a new tenant gained entry to a customary holding, by paying a fine; usually preceded by a surrender
admitto/ere	*La Le*	to admit
admoneis	*Sc*	admonish
adnepos	*La*	great-great-great-grandson, male descendant in the fifth degree
adnul	*Sc*	annul
adnullit	*Sc*	annulled
adoes, adois	*Sc*	business (e.g. without further ado)
adolescens	*La*	young man, adolescent
adulterium	*La*	adultery
Adv	*Oc Sc*	advocate, equivalent of a barrister
advenit	*La*	he came, appeared
adverse possession	*Le*	possession of land, without legal title, for a period of time sufficient to become recognised as the legal owner
advise	*Sc*	take care of, e.g. advise affairs
Advocate	*Sc Oc Le*	1. (noun) Scottish barrister; 2. (verb) bring a judgement before a higher court or tribunal for review
advocatus	*La*	lawyer

advoke	*Sc*	*see* advocate
advowson or advocation	*Sc*	the right to appoint someone to a church living or benefice
ae	*Sc*	one, only; e.g. ae son = only son
ae coo's meat	*Sc*	sufficient land to raise one cow, or the rent or value of such
ae fur land	*Sc*	sloped or steep land that can only be plowed in one direction
aeger	*La*	sick
aegyptus	*La*	gypsy
aequalis	*La*	equal
aetas (aetatis)	*La*	age
aetate	*La*	(being) in the age of, age
affeerer	*Le*	person chosen to asses the level of a fine
afferator/oris	*La Le*	assessor/affeerer
affines	*La*	relatives by marriage, in-laws
affinitas	*La*	relationship by marriage
affinitas	*La*	relationship by marriage
affirmavit	*La*	he/she affirmed, asserted, confirmed
affray	*Le*	fight between two or more persons in a public place so as to cause terror to the public
afoir	*Sc*	before, in front of, prior to
Ag Lab	*Oc*	agricultural labourer
aganis	*Sc*	against
agent	*Sc*	person acting for another in official, business or financial matters
agentis	*La*	of the official
agnate	*Sc*	related on the father's side
agnatus	*La*	male blood relative
agonia	*La*	cramps
agricola	*La*	farmer
ahenarius	*La*	coppersmith
aide-de-camp	*Sc*	junior officer assistant to a senior officer
aik	*Sc*	oak
air	*Sc*	heir
air by progress	*Sc*	heir by virtue of the usual titles
aire	*Sc*	circuit court
airis	*Sc*	heirs
airmy	*Sc*	army
airschip guidis	*Sc*	moveable goods falling to the heir
airschipe	*Sc*	heirship
airth	*Sc*	direction from which the wind blows, a certain quarter e.g. a house open to every airth
airt and pairt	*Sc*	*see* 'art and part'

airts	*Sc*	arts
aisle	*Sc*	covered burial place in or attached to a church
aits	*Sc*	oats
aitseed	*Sc*	the season for sowing oats
aitsen tyme	*Sc*	the season for sowing oats
aixies	*Sc*	illness, ague, fever
alba firme	*Sc*	Latin for *blench ferme*: lands held for a peppercorn rent
albus	*La*	white
ale	*Sc*	beer fermented in an open vessel using yeasts that rise to the top, but unflavoured by hops
alemannus	*La*	German
aleuin	*Sc*	eleven
alewife	*Oc*	female owner or manager of an alehouse
alhallow, allhallowtide, alhallow day	*Sc*	All Saints Day, 1 November
Alia Enormia	*La Le*	catch-all phrase in trespass pleadings to refer to all such other harms and damages that may have been caused by the alleged trespasser other than those specified
alias	*La*	otherwise, also, or, at, another (called)
alibi	*La*	at another time, elsewhere
aliment	*Sc*	maintenance of children, wife, parent etc. (similar to alimony)
alimenta, alimento	*La*	provision made for younger sons or unmarried daughters
aliquam	*La*	in some degree
aliquando	*La*	at times, sometimes; once, formerly
aliqui/qua/quod	*La*	some, any
aliquis/qua/quid	*La*	someone, something; some, any
aliquotiens	*La*	several times, at different times
aliud (alius)	*La*	other, another
alius, alia, aliud	*La*	other
allegeance	*Sc*	allegations
allekay, allakay	*Sc*	1. bridegroom's attendant (best man); 2. footman or manservant; 3. lackey
allemania	*La*	Germany
allenarly	*Sc*	only or exclusively
allkymist	*Sc*	alchemist
allutarius	*La*	tanner
Allutarius	*Oc*	tanner
allyat	*Sc*	allied
allye	*Sc*	kinship, ally or associate
almeral	*Sc*	admiral
altare	*La*	altar

alter	*La*	the next, the other
alter, altera, alterum	*La*	the other of two
altera die	*La*	on the next day
alutarius	*La*	tanner
amand	*Sc*	1. compensation; 2. fine
amarold	*Sc*	1. emerald; 2. haemmorrhoid (also 'emerod')
ambo	*La*	stranger or foreigner
ambo	*La*	both, two together
amercement	*Le*	penalty, fine
amerciament	*Sc*	literally 'being in mercy', a fine imposed on an offender
amerciamentum/i	*La Le*	amercement
amerciat	*Sc*	1. fined; 2. a fine
amita	*La*	aunt (father's sister)
amita magna	*La*	grandfather's sister, grandaunt
amita uxoris	*La*	wife's father's sister
amitinus	*La*	cousin (child of father's sister)
amrie, aumrie	*Sc*	cupboard (Fr. *armoire*)
ancient lights	*Le*	opening through which light has flowed uninterrupted for twenty years and which can, in some circumstances, support a claim for nuisance if blocked
ancillus/a	*La*	servant
andedictus	*La*	aforesaid
andermess, andersmess	*Sc*	St Andrew's Day (30 November)
ane	*Sc*	one
anent	*Sc*	about, concerning
aneuct	*Sc*	enough
anglia	*La*	England
Anglo-Norman	*En*	Norman who settled in England, or French spoken by such
anima	*La*	soul, spirit
animam reddidit domino suo	*La*	he/she returned the soul to his/her Lord (died)
Animus Furandi	*La Le*	intent to do wrong
anis	*Sc*	once
annals	*Sc En*	history of events year by year
annalzie	*Sc*	transfer of ownership
annat	*Sc*	initial six months' or year's income paid to executors of an estate
annealer	*Oc*	finisher of metal or glass, using furnace and chemicals
annesis	*Sc*	things annexed to land, appurtenances
annex	*Sc*	smaller property subsidiary to a larger or more important one; pendicle
annexation	*Sc*	uniting lands to the Crown (polite term for 'confiscation')

anni proximi elapsi	*La*	of the preceding year
anno	*La*	in the year (of)
anno domini	*La*	in the year of (our) Lord
anno incarnationis	*La*	in the year (since/of) the incarnation (of the Lord)
annual rent	*Sc*	interest on money lent or mortgage, payable yearly from land revenue (but NOT a rent as such)
annuallar	*Sc*	person in receipt of annual rent (interest)
annuatim	*La Le*	annually
annuitant	*Oc*	person with an annual income or pension
annus	*La*	year
annus bissextus	*La*	leap year
anonymus/a	*La*	stillborn son/daughter
ansuer, ansuere, ansueir	*Sc*	answer
ansuert	*Sc*	answered
ante	*La*	before, in front of, prior to
ante meridiem (a m)	*La*	before noon
antecessour, antecestre, antecestor	*Sc*	ancestor, antecedent
anti	*La*	against, opposite
antiant	*Sc*	ancient
anticipet	*Sc*	anticipated
antiquus	*La*	old, senior
apayn of	*Sc*	under penalty of
apoplexia	*La*	stroke
apostacy	*Le*	ancient criminal offence of atheism or not being Christian, or of denying the doctrines of a state religion
apoth	*Oc*	apothecary
apothecary, apothecarie	*Oc*	pharmacist, surgeon
apouse	*Sc*	spouse, husband or wife
app reg		register of apprentices
app. reg.	*Sc*	register of apprentices
apparent	*Sc*	heir to landed property, who has already succeeded
apparent (appeirand air)	*Sc*	where the process of succession of an heir has begun after the death of the predecessor but is not complete (not to be confused with heir-apparent)
apparent heir	*Sc*	'apparent' meaning, in this case, 'obvious' or 'clear', the heir who will succeed to a title or land; *see* heir presumptive
appeirand air (heir)	*Sc*	where the process of succession of an heir has begun after the death of the predecessor but is not complete (not to be confused with heir-apparent)
appell	*Sc*	appeal
appoint	*Sc*	order the destination of property (in court)

appraisal	*Le*	informed and objective inspection and estimation of a thing's worth
apprehend	*Sc*	arrest, seize in the name of the law
apprentice	*Oc*	trainee learning a craft or trade, usually bound to a Master
apprentice, apprent	*Sc*	person working for and with a craftsman attached by formal arrangement to learn the craft
apprise	*Sc*	value and sell the land of a debtor to pay off a debt
apprising, apprysing	*Sc*	sentence of a court whereby a debtor's heritable property is sold to pay the debt, later replaced by adjudication
appurtenance	*Sc*	something hung on to, e.g. a small portion of land
aprilis	*La*	of April
apud	*La*	at the house of, at, by, near
aqua	*La*	water
aqua, aqua vitae	*Sc*	whisky, water of life
aquavite	*Sc*	whisky
aquavitie man	*Sc*	whisky distiller
arage, arrage	*Sc*	feudal service with avers (draught animals)
arand	*Sc*	ploughing
arbiter	*Sc*	1. arbitrator; 2. arbitration
arbor consanguinitatis	*La*	family tree
arch-beddle, archpedell	*Sc*	senior church or university officer, *see* beddle
archbishop	*Sc*	senior clergyman in charge of a province (pre-Reformation, Catholic, Episcopal)
archbp.	*Sc En*	Archbishop
archdeacon	*Sc*	senior clergyman in a diocese (pre-Reformation, Catholic, Episcopal)
archdean	*Sc*	clergyman attached to a cathedral (pre-Reformation, Catholic, Episcopal)
archer	*Sc*	bowman
archicoquus	*La*	head cook
archidiaconus	*La*	archdeacon
archiepiscopus	*La*	archbishop
archivum	*La*	archive
archpedell	*Sc*	arch-beddle, senior church or university officer, *see* beddle
arcularius	*La*	carpenter
arenarius	*La*	sand digger or vender
argentier	*Oc*	controller of finances, comptroller, treasurer
ark, arch	*Sc*	1. chest or trunk for storing grain, etc; 2. mill waterway
arle	*Sc*	take into service on payment of money
arles, arrels	*Sc*	payment to signify completion of the bargain, money given to servants to bind an engagement: there is no contract without payment, but it could be a token payment
arlis-pennie	*Sc*	token payment, *see* arels

arma	*La*	coat of arms
armentarius	*La*	herdsman
armiger	*La*	gentleman, squire
armorum	*La*	of coats of arms
armourer, armorer, armorar	*Sc*	1. maker of armour; 2. officer in charge of arms
Army H P	*Oc*	soldier on half pay
arragia	*La*	customs duties
arreragium/i	*La Le*	arrears
arrest	*Sc*	1. apprehend; 2. seize property of a debtor held by a third party
arrestee	*Sc*	the person from whom a third party's assets are taken or recovered
arrestment	*Sc*	seizure after legal process of a person or property
arrestments	*Sc*	relaxing attachment for debt
art or part, art and part	*Sc*	be 'art and part in', to be involved in or an accessory to
artailzerie	*Sc*	artillery
articles of roup	*Sc*	the conditions under which a property may be auctioned after roup
articles, lords of	*Sc*	a committee of Parliament that selected what would be considered, and therefore a curb on Parliament's powers
as	*Sc*	than, e.g. sma'er as = smaller than
as accords (of law)	*Sc*	agreeable to (law)
as wodinsday, ask wedinsday	*Sc*	Ash Wednesday, the first day of Lent, six and a half weeks before Easter
ascender	*Pal*	the part of a lower case letter projecting above the top, as with b or h; *see* descender
Ash Wednesday	*Sc*	first day of the Lent fast
ashet	*Sc*	large oval or round serving plate; (later) saucer
asiament	*Sc*	1. easement, advantage, convenience; 2. euphemism for lavatory (seat of easement)
askit actis	*Sc*	asked to have it recorded that …
assaillie	*Sc*	attack
assay	*Sc*	attack, assault, trial of endurance
assedat	*Sc*	let or leased for a period
assedation	*Sc*	tack (let) of land for a set period
assig	*Sc Le*	assignation
assignation	*Sc*	deed assigning or conveyance of a person's rights in moveable property, claim for debts, or rights in leased land, to another
assignay	*Sc*	assignee
assisa/ae	*La Le*	assize(s)
assize	*Sc*	sitting of a jury, inquest or court
assize herring	*Sc*	royalty of herring paid to king from herring fishermen

assize of bread and ale	*Le*	system regulating the price and quality of bread and ale
assizor	*Oc*	juror at a trial (assize)
assoilzie	*Sc*	acquit, absolve from the outcome of a legal action, decree not liable (in a civil action)
assume	*Sc*	to tax Church property
Assumpsit	*La Le*	Medieval era action for breach of contract
assurance	*Sc*	guarantee
assyth, assythement	*Sc*	compensation, recompense, indemnification, money paid by the killer of someone to the relatives or friends, similar to *cro* or *wergeld*
astrenze	*Sc*	place under an obligation
astriction	*Sc*	requirement for landholders to have their corn ground at one particular mill, for which they would pay multures and sequels; the lands astricted or thirled are the mill's sucken
at	*La*	but
at (form of *ad* = in addition to)	*La*	but (introducing changes)
atavus	*La*	great-great-great-grandfather, male ascendant in the fifth degree
atentic	*Sc*	authentic
athill	*Sc*	noble
atour	*Sc*	over, beyond
atour	*Sc*	moreover, in addition, often found in a precept of sasine or a charter
atque	*La*	and, as well, even, together with, in all
atque	*La*	and
atque ... atque	*La*	both ... and
atqui	*La*	rather, however, but at any rate, but for all that
attingent	*Sc*	close in age or relationship
attornatus/i	*La Le*	attorney(s)
attorney-at-law	*Sc*	advocate, lawyer appearing in court
attour	*Sc*	besides
aucht	*Sc*	1. eight or eighth; 2. owned; 3. owed; 4. a possession; 5 .anything or everything
Audita Querela	*La Le*	application to a court after judgement seeking to avoid execution of that judgement because of some event intervening between judgement and execution that compromises the judgement creditor's entitlement to execution
auditor	*Sc*	examiner of accounts or goods
auen	*Sc*	own (as in 'my own')
augmentation	*Sc*	1. increase in feu duty; 2. action by a churchman to get an increase in stipend
augusti	*La*	of August
aula	*La*	hall
auld	*Sc*	old
auntie	*Sc*	1. unmarried woman who kept an inn; 2. drink purchased in such a place

aurifaber, aurifex	*La*	goldsmith
auriga	*La*	driver
austral	*Sc*	southern, southerly
aut	*La*	or, at least, or else
aut … aut	*La*	either … or
autem	*La*	but, on the other hand, however
author	*Sc*	original owner, the person from whom a title or ownership originated by sale or gift
autograph manuscript	*Pal*	manuscript that the scribe originally authored
auxentium	*La*	Alsace
ava	*La*	grandmother
availl	*Sc*	worth, monetary value
aventayle	*Sc*	visor of a helmet
aver, avair	*Sc*	1. draught horse, old horse; 2. to swear or assert as fact in legal proceedings
avi	*La*	ancestors, grandparents
avi relicta	*La*	grandfather's widow
avia	*La*	grandmother
aviaticus	*La*	nephew
avunculus	*La*	uncle (mother's brother)
avus	*La*	grandfather
aw (stand aw of)	*Sc*	be greatly afraid of
awand (awin)	*Sc*	owing
award, awat	*Sc*	ground ploughed after the first crop from lea (ley) or fey
awblaster	*Sc*	crossbow
awful	*Sc*	terrible
awner	*Sc*	shipowner
awys	*Sc*	judgement, determined advice
ay, aye	*Sc*	always, ever
aye and while	*Sc*	until
ayr	*Sc*	heir
ayris	*Sc*	heirs
B	*Oc*	burgess (of a burgh)
b (or by) r of	*Sc*	by right of
B R	*Sc*	burgess register
B.	*Sc*	burgess
bacallarius	*La*	bachelor
back up	*Sc*	endorse, support
backman	*Sc*	supporter in wartime
backseats	*Sc*	subleases of land

badgering	*Le*	buying of food products in one place and selling them elsewhere at a profit
baginet, beginet	*Sc*	bayonet
baick bread, balk breddis	*Sc*	kneading or baking board
bailery, bailiery	*Sc*	bailie's area of jurisdiction
bailie	*Oc*	magistrate in a Scottish burgh court
bailie, baillie, bailer, bailze, bailzie	*Sc*	magistrate in a burgh or in a barony, officer employed to give sasine or formal possession of land
bailie clerk	*Sc*	clerk to bailies in a burgh
bailie court	*Sc*	a court presided over by a bailie as magistrate
bailie depute	*Sc*	deputy to a burgh magistrate
bailiff	*Le*	oversaw day-to-day running of a manor
baillie in that pairt (part)	*Sc*	representative appointed for a specific function, such as the giving of sasine
baillivus	*La*	bailiff
baillivus/i	*La Le*	bailiff(s)
bairn, barne	*Sc*	1. young person (as opposed to the modern usage, child or infant); 2. schoolboy or chorister
bairn's pairt (part)	*Sc*	child's share of a parent's estate, patrimony
bairn's pairt of gear	*Sc*	child's share of a parent's moveable property on his death, also called *legitim*
bairntime, bairnteme	*Sc*	offspring, brood of children or animals
bait wricht, bait wright	*Sc*	boat wright, boat builder, shipwright
baith, baitht, bath, batht, bayth	*Sc*	both
bajan	*Sc*	first-year university student
balance	*Sc*	flat dish or plate
bale of fire	*Sc*	beacon fire
ballandis	*Sc*	scales for madder, a dye stuff
balulalow	*Sc*	lullaby
band	*Sc*	bond, contract
bandis	*Sc*	marriage banns
banerman, bannerman, bennerman	*Sc*	bearer of army standard
banis, bannes, baneis	*Sc*	banish
banisment, baneisment	*Sc*	banishment, exile
banket	*Sc*	banquet
banksman	*Oc*	miner at the pithead unloading coal from cages
bannest	*Sc*	banished

banni	La	marriage banns
bannorum, liber	La	register (book) of marriage banns, announcements
bannum	La	bann, marriage proclamation
baptisatus/a	La	baptised
baptisatus/a est	La	he (or she) was baptised
baptisavit	La	he baptised
baptismatis	La	of baptism
baptismi	La	baptism, christening (which are not the same thing)
baptismus/a	La	baptism
baptist	Sc	baptised, named
baptizatorum, liber	La	register of baptisms
baptizatus	La	christening
baptizatus est	La	he was baptised, has been baptised
baptizavi	La	I baptised, have baptised
bar		barony
barber, barbour, barber-chirurgeon	Sc	apart from the usual meaning, barbers also extracted teeth and carried out basic surgery
barbetonsor	La	barber
barbican	Sc	outer gate of a castle
barded, barbed	Sc	horse accoutred with armour
bareman	Sc	a bankrupt, person in debt
bargain, bergan	Sc	dispute
bargan	Sc	struggle, conflict
barker	Sc	tanner
barnman	Sc	thresher
baro	La	baron
baron	Sc	holder of lands (barony) direct from the Crown (*in baroniam*), which had certain privileges (such as the administration of justice) and duties (like military service); a barony may be only a title, with no land or rights
baron (or barony) officer	Oc	early policeman, who enforced the law within the barony
baron bailie, baron bailze	Sc	law officer in a barony
baron court	Sc	barony tribunal presided over by the baron or his deputy (baillie)
baron of exchequer	Sc	senior officer in the Exchequer
baronet	Sc	lowest rank of nobility, essentially a hereditary knighthood, granted by the Crown
barony, free	Sc	an estate of the Crown raised by crown charter into a barony, with power to hold courts, impose penalties, etc.; *see* sheriffdom, regality
barony officer	Sc	baron bailie
barrack master	Sc	non-commissioned officer in charge of an army barracks

barrator	*Le*	person who, on more than one occasion, incites litigation or spreads false rumours
barres	*Sc*	barrier, outworks of castle, enclosure for tournament
barrikin	*Sc*	small barrel
barrister	*Sc*	court lawyer (English)
basar	*Sc*	executioner
base right or base fee	*Sc*	the right of someone holding lands from a former vassal, not from the superior of the lands; the buyer was normally also infeft by the superior
bassing and lawar	*Sc*	basin and laver, washing jug and bowl
bastion, baston	*Sc*	cudgel
batel, battel, batailze	*Sc*	battle
bathe as ane and ane as bathe	*Sc*	jointly and equally
batoun	*Sc*	baton
battard	*Sc*	small cannon
bauchill	*Sc*	to denounce/disgrace publicly
bauchle	*Sc*	small, usually deformed person (term of abuse)
baudkin	*Sc*	embroidered
baxtarie, baxtrey	*Sc*	baking (craft name)
baxter, bagster	*Oc*	baker
baxter, bakester	*Sc*	baker
baytht	*Sc*	both
be	*Sc*	by (e.g., be rights)
be r. of	*Sc*	by right of
be r. of w.	*Sc*	by right of his wife (daughter to a burgess)
beadle	*Oc*	parish or church official who assisted the minister with administrative work and acted as usher
beadle, bedell, beddal, beddell	*Sc*	church or university officer
beadman, bedeman, bedesman, bedeswoman etc.	*Oc*	licensed beggar, *see* beidman
beamer	*Oc*	weaving mill worker who loaded yarn onto the beam of a loom
beand	*Sc*	being
bear, beir, bere	*Sc*	barley, specifically the once common four-rowed variety
bearer	*Sc*	coal carrier, often a girl or woman, who hauled coal in baskets from the face to the shaft
bear-sawing, bear-seed	*Sc*	1. seed barley; 2. barley sowing season
beatus	*La*	blessed, deceased
bedellus/i	*La Le*	hayward(s)

bedhous, bede hous	*Sc*	hospital or almshouse
bee scaifs	*Sc*	beehives
beet	*Sc*	bundle of flax
beetler	*Oc*	fabric embosser in a cloth mill
beetyach, bittoch, bittock	*Sc*	small sword or dagger
beidman, beadman, beadsman	*Sc*	1. person living in an almshouse, pauper; 2. beggar. *See* beadman
beitting	*Sc*	building
beken	*Sc*	admit as possessor
bell penny	*Sc*	money saved up to pay funeral costs
bellman, belman	*Sc*	bell ringer, town cryer
bene	*La*	well
benefice	*Sc*	a church 'living', i.e. the income from rents, produce, collections etc.
benis	*Sc*	beans
bent silver	*Sc*	money paid by children to a school to pay for 'bent grass' to cover the floor
bere fra	*Sc*	to dispossess someone of land or property
Bereans	*Sc*	dissenting Protestant sect
bergarius	*La*	shepherd
beris	*Sc*	place of burial
bern	*Sc*	barn
bers, barse	*Sc*	small cannon
beschop	*Sc*	bishop
besom	*Sc*	1. brush; 2. woman (term of affection or abuse, depending on context)
best aucht	*Sc*	the most valuable animal or other possession claimed by a superior on the death of a tenant
betterment	*Le*	improvement put upon a property that enhances its value more than mere replacement, maintenance, or repairs
betuix	*Sc*	betwixt, between
beuk, buik	*Sc*	book
bibil	*Sc*	bible
bicker	*Sc*	assail
bidie-in	*Sc*	woman cohabiting without marriage
biduum	*La*	two-day period
biennium	*La*	two-year period
big	*Sc*	build
biggen	*Sc*	pregnant
bigget	*Sc*	built
bigging ,biggin	*Sc*	building
biker	*Sc*	beaker, bowl

bilget, billiet	*Sc*	written military order
bill	*Le*	petition, document for the king or Chancery Court requesting legal action
bill chamber	*Sc*	court presided over by judges of Session
Bill of Attainder	*Le*	conviction and sentence to death directly by statute, as opposed to resulting from trial
Bill of Lading	*Sc*	document listing the type and amounts of cargo loaded onto a ship or waggon
bind	*Sc*	standard barrel measure for packing goods
bing	*Sc*	1. funeral pile; 2. spoil tip from coal or other mine workings
bink	*Sc*	bench, ledge, rack or shelf for dishes or at a fireplace
binus, bina, binum	*La*	double, twofold, two at time, two-by-two, two each, twice, in pairs
bird alane	*Sc*	only child
birl quheil	*Sc*	spinning wheel
birlaw court	*Sc*	local court for lesser disputes
birlaw man	*Sc*	person elected as judge in a birlaw court
birlin, birling	*Sc*	rowing boat or galley in the West Highlands
birning	*Sc*	punishment by branding
birny, byrne, byrnie, birnie	*Sc*	coat of chain mail
birth	*Sc*	crop, produce
birthful, berthy, birthy	*Sc*	fertile, usually of animals
bishop	*Sc*	clergyman in charge of a see (diocese) (pre-Reformation, Catholic, Episcopal)
bissextilis	*La*	leap year (*annus bissextus*)
blac	*Sc*	black
blac(k) hous(e)	*Sc*	thatched Highland hut of stone and turf with a central fireplace on an earth floor
black letter Gothic	*Pal*	large, clear, formal book hand
black litster	*Oc*	black dyer
black mail	*Sc*	rent payable in labour, cattle or non-silver coinage
black ward	*Sc*	holding in ward by a subtenant of another tenant who himself is held in ward of his superior
blacker, berlin blacker	*Oc*	varnisher of ironware products
blacksmith	*Sc*	smith, iron-forge worker
blanter	*Sc*	oat-based food (e.g. porridge, bread, meal pudding)
blason	*Sc*	badge of authority of a king's messenger
blaxter	*Oc*	bleacher (of cloth)
bleacher	*Oc*	bleacher of textiles or paper

bleeze silver	*Sc*	gift of money to a schoolteacher at Candlemas (2 February): feast of the Purification of St Mary the Virgin and the Presentation of Christ in the Temple, chosen by the Catholic Church to coincide with the ancient Celtic feast of Imbolc at the start of February
blench ferme, blench-duty, blench holding	*Sc*	land tenure at nominal or peppercorn rent, or only to be paid if asked for (*si tamen petatur*); in theory the seller would remain the granter of the land but in practice have no further rights in them
blench holding	*Sc*	holding of land under *blench ferme*
blew	*Sc*	blue
blockcutter	*Oc*	carver of wooden blocks used for printing
blockmaker	*Oc*	broker, trader
blockprinter	*Oc*	printer (on paper or cloth) using wooden blocks
blok	*Sc*	a bargain
blokit	*Sc*	bargained for
blude roll	*Sc*	list of persons accused of bloodshed
bludewite, bludeweck	*Sc*	guilty of or charged with bloodshed
blue	*Sc*	whisky or other spirit (from the colour of the flame)
blue blanket	*Sc*	craftsmen's guild banner
blunderbush	*Sc*	blunderbuss
boat	*Sc*	butt, barrel, cask, tub
boatman	*Oc*	boat operator at loch or river crossings
boatswain, boatswain-yeaman, bo'sun, bosun	*Sc*	officer in charge of ship's crew
bobbin turner	*Oc*	maker of spools (bobbins) for textile mills
bocht	*Sc*	bought
boday	*Sc*	scarlet dye
boddoch	*Sc*	mutchkin, the liquid measure equivalent to three-quarters of a pint
bodily	*Sc*	personal (e.g. bodily oath, a solemn oath personally given, or bodily harm)
boid	*Sc*	bid
boirdours, bordours	*Sc*	borders
boll	*Sc*	1. dry measure of weight or capacity equal to six bushels (of grain); 2. valuation of land by the number of bolls it produced annually; 3. payment in kind (usually food) to a farm worker
bombardier	*Sc*	corporal in an artillery regiment
bona	*La*	possessions
bona vacantia	*Sc Le*	ownerless goods, usually unclaimed estate
bond	*Sc*	written obligation to pay or do something
bond and disp.	*Sc Le*	bond and disposition in security
bond corrob. and disp.	*Sc Le*	bond of corroboration and disposition

bond of caution	*Sc*	an obligation by one person to provide security, surety or guarantee for another
bond of corroboration	*Sc*	confirmation of a debt (for example to the inheritor of the original bond
bond of disposition in security	*Sc*	the most common type of heritable security in the nineteenth century, where a personal bond by the borrower was secured on land
bond of manrent	*Sc*	an obligation by a free person to become the follower of a protector, in turn undertaking to support the protector (quite unusual)
bond of provision	*Sc*	bond by a father providing for his offspring
bond of relief	*Sc*	an undertaking to relieve a cautioner (*see* bond of caution) from an obligation
bond of taillie	*Sc*	entail
bondage, binage, bonnage	*Sc*	service owed by a farm worker to the farmer
bondelsoure, bonelesew	*Sc*	pasture linked to bond service
bone plewis	*Sc*	unpaid ploughing as part of service
bone silver money	*Sc*	paid in lieu of service
bone wark, bonday wark	*Sc*	service, unpaid work as part of service
bone-setter	*Sc*	surgeon
bonnet laird	*Sc*	small farmer who owns his land
bonnet, bannet	*Sc*	metal helmet
bonnet-maker, bonatmaker, bonnat-maker, bonat-maker	*Sc*	hat maker, milliner
bonus	*La*	good
book hand	*Pal*	script used for transcribing books
book-bosom'd	*Sc*	priests often carried their mass books close to their chests
bookmaker	*Sc*	person who takes or arranges bets and wagers on horse and dog races etc.
books of adjournal	*Sc*	records of the Court of Justiciary
books of discipline	*Sc*	two volumes listing the laws of the Reformed Church, adopted 1560 and 1581
books of sederunt	*Sc*	(literally 'those who were sitting'); records of the acts of the Court of Session
boot clicker	*Oc*	bootlace hole maker
boot closer	*Oc*	stitcher of boots and shoes
boot laster	*Oc*	shoemaker, using a metal 'last'
boot sprigger	*Oc*	shoemaker, using 'sprigs''' (headless nails) to nail soles to uppers
borch, broch, borowis	*Sc*	surety, bail
bordarius	*La*	cottager, tenant, border
bordel, brothe bordeler	*Sc*	brothel keeper, customer of brothels

border warrant	*Sc*	warrant for the arrest of person and effects in England for debts in Scotland
boreaus, borreaus, burriours	*Sc*	executioners, hangmen
boreing	*Sc*	borrowing
borough charter		grant to a town of certain privileges and control over its affairs
borow, borrow	*Sc*	stand surety or bail on behalf of
borussia	*La*	Prussia
bos	*Sc*	leather wine flask
bot, butt	*Sc*	without ('Touch not the cat bot a glove': motto of Clan Chattan)
bote	*Sc*	wine cask
bothyn	*Sc*	lordship (occasionally sheriffdom)
botisman, boitisman, boitman, botman	*Sc*	boatman
bottler	*Oc*	bottle filler, usually in a distillery
bound court	*Sc*	district tribunal or jury
bountie	*Sc*	gratuity or gift in addition to wages in an employment contract
bounty	*Sc*	extra money paid to fishermen at the end of the season
bouster, bowster	*Sc*	bolster, pillow
bouthous	*Sc*	mill building where the flour is sifted
bovata/ae	*La Le*	bovate
bovate	*Le*	measurement of land
bow	*Sc*	1. herd of cattle; 2. church message
bow house	*Sc*	cow shed
Bower	*Oc*	Bowmaker
Bower	*Oc*	bowmaker
bower, bowar, bowyer, bowet-maker	*Sc*	archery bow-maker
bowman	*Oc*	sub-tenant who looked after cows for a season
bowne	*Sc*	prepare, make ready
box master	*Sc*	treasurer, keeper of a cashbox or its keys
box penny	*Sc*	duty paid to be at market
boxmaster	*Oc*	treasurer or deacon of a trade guild
boyart	*Sc*	small, one-masted vessel
boyis	*Sc*	leg irons
Bp	*Oc*	bishop
braboner	*Sc*	weaver (also brabonar, brabaner, brabiner, brabanar, barboner, bradboner)
brae	*Sc*	1. hill; 2. salmon trap
braig	*Sc*	knife
braith	*Sc*	fury, fit of rage
braithly	*Sc*	very angrily

branks	Sc	iron face bridle used in public punishment of abusive language, slander, gossiping etc.
brasener	Oc	brass worker
brasiator	Oc	brewer
brasiator	La	brewer
brasier, brass–smith, brassier	Sc	brass worker
brazier	Oc	brass metalworker
bred	Sc	unit of measurement for hides
breek brothers	Sc	rivals for a girl's affections
breve of inquest	Sc	writ empowering a sheriff (or bailies) to investigate a claimant's title
breve of mortancestry	Sc	writ directing an inquest into a claim that ancestor's land or property is wrongfully held by someone else
breve, brieve	Sc	brief or writ from Chancery in the king's name, often under the privy seal ordering an enquiry or service
brew talloun	Sc	duty paid for rights to brew beer
brewar, browstar, browster, brouster, brewster, brewer's servant	Sc	brewer
brewster	Oc	brewer (of beer)
bridle silver	Sc	small payment to a servant for leading the horse
brieve bauck	Sc	ridge of land unploughed
brigadier	Sc	army officer leading a brigade
brigantine	Sc	1. leather armour with metal scales or plates; 2. two–masted ship
brim	Sc	stream, burn
brocker	Sc	possibly stone dresser, builder's labourer
brodinster, broudster	Oc	embroiderer
broken	Sc	without a feudal chief, outlawed
broken men	Sc	landless men; assumed to be living by spuilzie or stouthrief
brokin	Sc	shipwrecked or stranded
brothers german	Sc	true brothers, children of the same father or parents
brothers uterine	Sc	of the same mother but different fathers
brouster, browster	Oc	brewer
browd, browdinstare, browdstare, browdinster, broudinstar	Sc	embroider
brught	Sc	burgh
brusery	Sc	embroidery
brusher	Oc	coal-mine worker who kept mine roofs and sides in repair

bu (bow, bull)	*Sc*	head farm of a udal estate
buckler	*Sc*	small, round shield
buckram-stiffner	*Sc*	maker of buckram (coarse cloth pasted) for bookbinding
buggis	*Sc*	lamb's wool
buirde	*Sc*	board, lodgings
buit	*Sc*	compensation
bull (Papal)	*Sc*	written grant of some privilege by the pope, incorrectly used to mean any papal document
bulla	*La Pal*	lead seal attached to legal documents from the papal chancery (hence 'papal bull')
bun	*Sc*	small barrel
bunnet	*Sc*	cloth cap, bonnet
bunsucken	*Sc*	thirled (bound in service) to a mill
burcht	*Sc*	burgh
burd cloth	*Sc*	tablecloth
burdiner	*Sc*	1. guarantor to a monetary transaction; 2. someone who takes financial responsibility for another
burding	*Sc*	burden
burgage	*Sc*	1. burgh law; 2. type of tenure under which land in a royal burgh is held by the king; 3. the land itself held under burgage
burgage	*Le*	freehold property
burgage holding	*Sc*	the conditions of holding, owning or occupying property in royal burghs
burgagium/i	*La Le*	burgage
burgensis	*La*	burgess, citizen
burgess air	*Sc*	the heir of a burgess, who might normally inherit burgess status
burgess ticket	*Sc*	document conferring burgess status
burgess, burges, burgs, burgesser	*Sc Oc*	citizen, freeman of a burgh, member of a burgh guild, person with rights to trade freely within a burgh, enrolled as merchant or craftsman in a burgh
burgh clerk	*Sc*	clerk in burgh administration
burgh court	*Sc*	town or burgh tribunal
burgh law	*Sc*	town law, based on the fifteenth-century '*Leges Quatuor Burgorum*', the 'Laws of the Four Burghs'
burgh rudis	*Sc*	cultivated land belonging to the burgh
burn	*Sc*	brook, stream
burn ledar, burneman	*Sc*	water carrier
buroustounis, burroustounis	*Sc*	burgh towns
burryman	*Sc*	ritual scapegoat for all the ills of a community
buschement	*Sc*	ambush
but (bot, butt)	*Sc*	without
butterman	*Sc*	butter seller

button gilder	*Sc*	craftsman who adds gold to metal buttons
by	*Sc*	beside, apart from, e.g. 'be and by the law', according to but apart from the law
by and attour	*Sc*	over and above
bygottin	*Sc*	illegitimate, by-blow
byreman	*Oc*	farm worker in the byre (cow shed)
byronis	*Sc*	arrears
C		council (town or burgh)
CS		commissioner's servant
cabinetmaker	*Oc*	wooden furniture maker
cadaver	*La*	dead body
caddie, cadie, cadet	*Sc Oc*	carrying servant, porter for hire, military cadet, runner of errands or parcel carrier; later, golf club carrier
cadger, cadgear	*Sc Oc*	carrier, carter, travelling dealer or pedlar
cadroun, caudron	*Sc*	cauldron
caduciar	*Sc*	subject to, by means of
caelebs	*La*	bachelor, unmarried man
caelum	*La*	heaven, sky
caementarius	*La*	stonemason
caibe	*Sc*	cabinet maker, joiner
cair	*Sc*	go
caird	*Sc*	tinker, pot mender
cairt	*Sc*	1. cart; 2. ship's chart
cairter	*Sc*	carter
Cait	*Sc*	Pictish kingdom roughly equivalent to modern Caithness
caitchpeller	*Oc*	keeper of a caitchpell or tennis court
caitchpeller	*Oc*	keeper of a caitchpell or tennis court
cal prin	*Oc*	calico printer (on cotton cloth from India)
calcearius	*La*	shoemaker, cordwainer
calciator	*La*	shoemaker, cordwainer
caledonia	*La*	Scotland (specifically the north)
caligator	*La*	shoemaker, cordwainer
callan	*Sc*	girl
callenderer	*Oc*	smoother of cloth or paper using rollers
calligraphy	*Pal*	art of ornamental handwriting
calsay	*Sc*	causeway, street
calsay-maker	*Sc*	road builder
cambria	*La*	Wales
cameranius	*La*	chamberlain, groom, valet
candavaig	*Sc*	salmon

candilmaker	*Sc*	candlemaker
Candlemas	*Sc*	2 February, a Scottish quarter day (with Lammas, Martinmas and Whitsunday), the days on which contracts, leases, tacks and rents began and ended and when bills were settled
candler	*Oc*	candle maker or retailer
cannoner	*Sc*	gunner
canny	*Sc*	1. canvas; 2. careful
canon	*Sc*	clergyman attached to a cathedral (pre-Reformation, Episcopal)
canon law	*Le*	ecclesiastical rules or laws covering matters of faith, morals and discipline
canous	*Sc*	grey-haired
cap seller, cop seller	*Oc*	seller of wooden bowls
cape	*Sc*	privateer
capella	*La*	chapel
capellane	*Sc*	chaplain
capellanus	*La*	chaplain
caper	*Sc*	1. bread or oatcake with butter and cheese; 2. dance, fool about
capercailzie	*Sc*	black grouse
capilliciarius	*La*	periwigmaker
capilliciarius	*Oc*	periwigmaker
caping, capring	*Sc*	privateering
capitanry	*Sc*	captaincy
capitis	*La*	chief, head
capmaker, quaiffmaker	*Sc*	soft hat maker
capo	*La*	caupo, taverner
capper	*Sc*	copper
capt et jurat	*La*	taken and sworn
captain-lieutenant	*Sc*	army lieutenant
captain-tailor	*Sc*	regimental tailor and cloth buyer
caption	*Sc*	arrest
caption, letters of	*Sc*	authority to arrest (capture) a debtor, or someone who has not carried out some undertaking (such as a promise to repay a debt or to marry)
captour	*Sc*	officer appointed by a court to apprehend criminals, and early policeman
caput	*La*	head, chief
carage	*Sc*	carraige, a service on a tenant that bound him to carry for the superior a stated amount of grain, goods, coal etc. or to provide men and horses for a certain number of days per year
carbonarius	*Oc*	charcoal maker
carbonarius	*La*	collier, coal miner
carder	*Oc*	brushed wool ready for spinning using wire 'cards'
cardow	*Sc*	work or trade illegally guild or craft membership or burgh freeman status

cardower	*Sc*	1. unlicenced worker in a craft or trade; 2. travelling tinker, tradesman or tailor
care sonday	*Sc*	Easter Sunday
carecake	*Sc*	cake eaten on Shrove Tuesday, before Lent
carecarius	*La*	carter
carnarius	*La*	butcher
carnifex	*La*	flesher
caroline weaver	*Sc*	loom weaver
carpentarius	*La*	carpenter
carpeter	*Sc*	carpets weaver
carrier, curriour	*Sc*	person who transports goods
carry	*Sc*	weir in a stream
carta	*La*	charter, deed, map
carter	*Oc*	worked with horse and cart, carrying goods
cartow	*Sc*	cannonball weighing a quarter of a hundredweight (28lbs, about 12.7kg)
cartwright	*Oc*	maker and repairer of horse carts
carver	*Sc*	wood patterner
casale	*La*	estate, village
casatus	*La*	cottager
cast	*Sc*	repeal, cancel, annul, nullify
castellaw	*Sc*	measure of cheese or flour
castellward	*Sc*	payment in lieu of feudal service to guard a castle
casting up the heretage	*Sc*	taking up peats on an estate
casualties, feudal	*Sc*	payments that became due to a superior when certain events happened, such as marriage, relief, non-entry or wardship
cataster	*La*	land, property record
catchword	*Pal*	word written in the margin on the last page and again as the first word on the next page
catechist	*Oc*	church teacher of the catechism, instructor in religion
cateran	*Sc*	outlaw, Highland freebooter
catholicus	*La*	Catholic
Caulker	*Oc*	Repaired ships' hulls by sealing with 'caulk' (tar)
caupo (cauponis)	*La*	innkeeper
causa	*La*	cause, sake, because of
causewaymaker	*Oc*	road (causeway) builder using stone setts
causey paiker	*Sc*	prostitute
caution	*Sc*	security, surety, guarantee; bail
cautioner	*Sc Le*	guarantor, one who stands caution (surety) for another (pronounced 'kay-shunner'
caveat	*La Le*	let him beware, formal warning

cavel	*Sc*	share of property by lot
caw, ca'	*Sc*	1. pull, carry; 2. call
Ce	*Sc*	Pictish kingdom roughly equivalent to modern Moray and Buchan
cedent	*Sc*	one who assigns property to another
celator	*La*	turner
celebraverunt	*La*	they celebrated, they were married
cellarius	*La Oc*	vintner, butler
cellarman	*Oc*	keeper of beer, wine and spirits
census	*La*	census
centenarius	*La*	person 100 years old
cerarius	*La*	wax worker or chandler
cerdo (cerdonis)	*La*	handworker
Certificate of Pending Litigation	*Le*	registration of a notice or warning that litigation is ongoing as to ownership of a particular piece of land or other real property
certiorat	*Sc*	certified
cessio bonorum	*Sc*	legal process by which a debtor could avoid prison by surrendering up all his goods to his creditors
cessioner	*Sc*	someone in receipt of property surrendered by another to pay debts
ch.	*Le*	charter
ch. conf.	*Le*	charter of confirmation (from a feudal superior)
ch. conf. and novodamus	*Sc Le*	charter of confirmation and novodamus
ch. resig.	*Sc Le*	charter of resignation (from the feudal superior)
ch. resig .and adjud.	*Sc Le*	charter of resignation (by a superior) on an adjudication
ch. resig. G S	*Sc*	charter of resignation under the Great Seal
chairbearer, chairman	*Sc*	carrier of a sedan chair and passenger
chairman	*Oc*	porter of a (sedan) chair
chairmaster	*Oc*	1. hirer out of sedan chairs; 2. overseer of sedan chair carriers
chaise setter, chaise hirer	*Sc*	arranger of hired passenger vehicles
chaisemaker	*Oc*	carriage maker
chakkeraw	*Sc*	the Exchequer row and by extension a chequered cloth or chess board
chalans	*Sc*	accuse, call to account, challenge
chalder	*Sc*	Scottish unit of grain measure, 16 bolls or 4–6 imperial bushels
chalfe	*Sc*	chaff, used to stuff mattresses
challender	*Sc*	maker of coverlets
challop	*Sc*	shallop, a type of small light boat with a schooner rig often used for fishing
chamber iron chimney	*Sc*	an iron grate for a room
chamberdeacon	*Le*	Irish beggar

chamberlain, chalmerlaine, chamerlane	Sc	1. a principal officer of the Scottish Royal household; 2. circuit court presided over by the chamberlain
chamlet	Sc	light cloak
champart	Sc	the share of produce due to a feudal superior
chancellor	Sc	senior legal official
Chancery	Sc	Royal office that wrote charters, brieves and other documents, kept records etc.
chancery hand	Pal	script used by the Royal Chancery
chandler	Oc	dealer in supplies, usually for ships
chandler, chandlar	Sc	candlestick and candle maker
changekeeper	Sc	innkeeper, ostler
chantour	Sc	choirmaster in church
chaplain	Sc	privately appointed clergyman
chaplainry	Sc	chaplaincy
chapman	Oc	stallholder or travelling salesman
chapman, chepman, chopman, chapman traveller	Sc	pedlar, travelling salesman, shopkeeper, stallholder or trader
chapper, chapper-up	Oc	knocked ('chapped') on doors to wake early-shift workers
chaptane	Sc	captain
charge	Sc	a command in the king's name
charge des affaires, charge d'affaires	Sc	diplomat representing a country's business matters abroad
charger	Sc	plaintiff
charpenteir	Sc	carpenter
chartarius	La	paper miller
charter	Sc	document of title, grant from the Crown or a superior, conveyance of an estate
charter	Le	written grant of rights by monarch or legislature
charter hand	Pal	script used for writing charters and other legal documents
charterour	Sc	Carthusian monk
charwoman	Oc	female domestic cleaner
chaste	Le	person who has never voluntarily had sexual intercourse outside of marriage, such as unmarried virgins
chaumer, chalmirleir	Sc	chambermaid
chaumercheild	Sc	valet
check weighman	Oc	mine official who checked a miner's production so he could be paid
check wheel	Sc	spinning wheel with a check inserted to stop after a certain amount spun
cheesemonger	Sc	cheese seller

cheiffis	*Sc*	chiefs
cheinyie	*Sc*	chain
cheirothecus	*La*	glover
chekker, chakker	*Sc*	official auditor in court cases concerning royal revenues
Chelsea pensioner	*Sc*	retired soldier living at or with a pension from the Royal Hospital Chelsea
chemist	*Sc*	pharmacist, apothecary
chetery	*Sc*	land reverting to the feudal superior if the tenant dies intestate (escheat)
chief supercargo	*Sc*	owner's representative on board ship
childer, childir, cheldyr	*Sc*	1. sailors, deck hands; 2. children; 3. people in general
chimney crewkes	*Sc*	hooks to hang pots over a fire
chimney gallowes	*Sc*	bar projecting from the fireplace on which cooking pots were hung
chimney raxes	*Sc*	*see* raxes
chimney speel	*Sc*	roasting spit
chir	*La Oc*	chirurgeon, surgeon
Chir. apoth.	*Oc*	chirurgeon-apothecary, surgeon who also makes and supplies medicines; *see* chirurgeon
chirograph	*Pal*	legal agreement in which the text is entered twice or more, then the parts are cut in a sawtooth manner and given to each party; *see* indenture
chirotherarus	*La*	glover
chirurgeon, cirurgyen, chirurgian, chirugenair	*Sc*	surgeon
chirurgeon–apothecary	*Sc*	surgeon who also makes and supplies medicines
chirurgia	*La*	surgery
chirurgus	*La*	surgeon
choap keeper	*Sc*	shopkeeper
chopeine, chopin, chappin	*Sc*	1. liquid measure, half a Scots pint, approximately 0.85l; 2. a container of this volume
chopis bak	*Sc*	back shops, where preparation took place
chowder	*Oc*	fishmonger
chramarius	*La*	merchant
christin, cristin, christian chrissenmas, christinmes	*Sc*	Christmas
chymna	*Sc*	chimney
cimeterium	*La*	cemetery
cingarus	*La*	gypsy
cinquefoil	*Sc*	five leaves, a charge in heraldry
circa	*La*	about, around, nearly

Circinn	*Sc*	Pictish kingdom roughly equivalent to modern Angus
circiter	*La*	about, approximately
circuit court	*Sc*	a court that goes round the country trying criminal cases; in Scotland called the Court of Justiciary
cisteus	*Sc*	Cistercian monk
citat	*Sc*	cited
cite	*Sc*	city
citinar, citiner	*Sc*	citizen
civis	*La*	citizen
clag	*Sc*	claim against property
clagger	*Oc*	removed clags (dirt and clumps) clots from wool
clais, clathis	*Sc*	clothes
clait, claith	*Sc*	cloth or clothing
claith drapper	*Sc*	cloth draper
clamant	*Sc*	demand for redress
clap dyke	*Sc*	turf or earth drainage wall
clare constat	*La Le*	clearly appears; a writ or precept (order) granted by a subject superior to an heir, whose right to a property is obvious from documents and which orders the giving of sasine
clark	*Oc*	clerk
clasp maker, clespmaker	*Sc*	maker of clothes fastenings
clause of warrandice	*Sc*	*see* warrandice: provision against a defect in a title, with arrangement for alternative payment
clausit	*La*	he/she finished, closed
claustrarius	*La*	locksmith
clausum	*La*	closed, finished
claviger	*La*	macer
clayth, claith, clath	*Sc*	cloth
clayth-draipper	*Sc*	draper, cloth and thread seller
Clean Hands	*Le*	maxim of the law to the effect that any person, individual or corporate, that wishes to ask or petition a court for judicial action, must be in a position free of fraud or other unfair conduct
clearances	*Sc*	practice of removing tenants from land (mainly Highlands)
cled	*Sc*	provided, clothed
cleme	*Sc*	claim
clepe and call	*Sc*	court summons
clericus	*La*	clerk
clericus	*La*	clergyman
clerk of the bills	*Sc*	official who manages bills of complaint presented to a court
clicker	*Oc*	lace hole maker (boots and shoes)
clogger	*Oc*	maker of wooden clogs

cloot, clout	*Sc*	cloth or clothing
clostrarius	*La*	locksmith
cloth dresser	*Oc*	cloth cutter in a textile mill
cloth lapper	*Oc*	cleaned cotton fibres before carding
clothier, claythman	*Sc*	cloth worker or seller
cloth laper	*Sc*	cloth finisher
clout	*Sc*	1. small piece of land; 2. a cloth, clothes ('Ne'er cast a clout till May be out')
club	*Sc*	apprentice (usually in shoemaking) not yet a freeman
clubmaker	*Sc*	maker of golf clubs
coachman, cotchman	*Sc Oc*	coach driver; the word 'coach' derives from KOCs in Hungary, where the conveyance was first made
coachmaster	*Sc*	overseer of a fleet of coaches
coad (cod)	*Sc*	pillow or cushion
coadwair ,codwair	*Sc*	pillow slip, cushion cover
coal factor, coal grieve	*Sc*	coalmine overseer, manager
coal fauld	*Sc*	coalyard
coal trimmer	*Oc*	balanced coal barges or ships
coalcawer, coilbeirar	*Sc*	coal carrier
coal heuch	*Sc*	coal pit, coalmine working
coalmaster	*Oc*	owner and/or operator of a coal mine
coast waiter	*Sc*	coastguard
cobbler	*Sc*	shoemaker or shoemender
coble and net	*Sc*	symbols used in the transfer of ownership of fishing rights
coble, cobel	*Sc*	1. small fishing boat; 2. malt-steeping vat
cocket, cocquet, coket, coquet (letter of)	*Sc*	certificate or seal that customs have been paid on exported goods
cocquetour	*Oc*	cook
cod, coad	*Sc*	cushion, pillow
codex	*Pal*	manuscript in book form
codicology	*Pal*	study of books
codware	*Sc*	cushion cover, pillowcase
coelebs	*La*	bachelor, single man
coemeterium	*La*	cemetery
cofe, coffing	*Sc*	an exchange
coffee man	*Sc*	coffee-house keeper
coft	*Sc*	bought
cog	*Sc*	container, bowl or pail made of wooden staves
cognati	*La*	maternal relations

cognationis	*La*	blood relationship
cognition	*Sc*	recognising an heir as entitled to a property
cognition and sasine	*Sc*	the process whereby an heir is accepted as having property
cognomen	*La*	name, family name, surname
cognosced	*Sc*	formally recognised (as heir etc.)
cogster	*Sc*	flax dresser
coll	*Sc*	coal
coll bearer	*Sc*	female coal carrier
coll heuch	*Sc*	mine
collar	*Sc*	haysheaf maker
collation	*Sc*	approval given by a bishop to appoint someone to a church living or benefices
collector	*Sc*	revenue gatherer
collegiate church	*Sc*	church founded by a private person, in free alms
collep	*Sc*	drinking vessel
collever	*Sc*	coal-bearing horse
collier	*Oc*	coal miner working at the coalface
collier, colzear, colzeare, coalhewer, coliar, coalhewar, coalheaver, coilheaver	*Sc*	coal miner or coal merchant
collis	*La*	hill
collum	*Sc*	ship
colman	*Sc*	furnisher
colonel	*Oc*	officer in charge of an army regiment
colonus	*La*	colonist, settler, resident (sometimes farmer, peasant)
colophon	*Pal*	inscription added to the end of a manuscript book by the scribe, like a graphic signature
colorator	*La*	dyer
colourmaker	*Sc*	paint maker or seller
colourman	*Oc*	mixer of dyes for textiles
colporteur	*Sc Oc*	travelling seller of religious or political tracts
combmaker	*Oc*	maker of combs for textiles or hair
comburges	*Sc*	fellow burgess
comes	*La*	count
comitas	*La*	county
comitatus	*La*	county
comite of states	*Sc*	committee of estates
comitissa	*La*	countess

com-maker, combmaker	Sc	comb maker
commander	Sc	senior officer on ship
commander-in chief	Sc	senior officer in a large army unit
commater	La	godmother
commendator, commendatar	Sc	one who managed the income from an abbey benefice when vacant or who had grant of a vacant benefice for life (before the Reformation usually the abbot, afterwards usually a layman)
commissar	Sc	civil official of the commissary court; *also* commissary, commisser
commissar clerk	Sc	clerk in a commissary office, mainly recording wills; *also* commisser officer, commissary clerk
commissariot	Sc	1. registry for confirmation or probate of wills etc.; 2. the district covered by the jurisdiction of a commissary court: these had the same geographical boundaries as the pre-Reformation church courts and (more or less) the mediaeval dioceses, but not to the old counties
commissary	Sc	officer making a confirmation or grant in matters of inheritance, confirmation of testaments etc.: originally, this was a bishop's official, but after the Reformation became an official of the commissary court
commissary court	Sc	office administering the estates of deceased persons in cases of intestacy, and confirmed testaments: submitted by parish priests to bishops pre-Reformation and after 1584 a civil office, the first of which was in Edinburgh and a further twenty-one were elsewhere
commissioner	Sc	lawyer qualified to hear and record oaths
commissioners of supply	Sc	people appointed by county to assess land tax due, maintain the roads, raise and provision the militia etc.
commixtion	Sc	joining property of different owners, which affects their rights differently
commodities	Sc	advantages and benefits arising from the ownership, possession or use of property
common area	Le	areas of multi-owner real property that are for the exclusive use of all individual owners
common law	Le	judge-declared law that exists and applies to a group on the basis of customs and legal precedents developed over hundreds of years in Britain
common pleas	Le	court to resolve civil disputes between private citizens and not otherwise involving the Crown
common scold	Le	now extinct offence of an angry woman who, by brawling and wrangling amongst her neighbours, disturbs the public peace
common serjand	Sc	burgh officer, law officer, town officer
commonty	Sc	a common: ground used or owned by more than one person
commorantes	La	living, residing
communis/e	La Le	common
commutation of services	Le	replacement of labour services owed with a money payment
comp.		comprising
comparatio	La	presence, appearance
comparere	La	to appear

comparuit	*La*	he/she appeared, was present
comparuit pro me	*La*	he/she appeared before me
compater	*La*	godfather
compear, compearance	*Sc*	to appear in a legal proceeding
compos	*La*	in possession of
composition	*Sc*	payment to the superior of land by an heir succeeding to it
compositor	*Oc*	setter of type for printing
compositor, componitour	*Sc*	1. arbitrator in legal cases; 2. sum paid in settlement; 3. agreement to settle
compotus/i	*La Le*	account(s)
compromit	*Sc*	settlement, agreement
comprysing	*Sc*	comprehending, but legally similar to apprysing
compt	*Sc*	account
comptroller, controller, comtreller	*Sc*	official in charge of revenue payments on goods
compurgation	*Le*	defence to a crime, or answer to a civil claim, perfected by the relevant oaths of the defendant and a number of supporters
con. excamb.	*Sc Le*	contract of excambion, for the exchange of properties, for example to rationalise boundaries
con. fee and liferent	*Sc Le*	conjunct fee and liferent (joint fee, two or more persons during their lives)
con. of ground annual	*Sc Le*	contract of ground annual (form of heritable security)
conand	*Sc*	covenant
conarius	*La*	tanner
concedo/ere	*La Le*	to grant
concepta est	*La*	she was pregnant
conceptus/a/um	*La*	conceived
concessit	*La*	consented
concurrent estates	*Le*	property owned by two or more persons at the same time
condescend	*Sc*	to state the facts
condescendance	*Sc*	summary of the facts in a trial
condicillus	*La*	codicil, list
conditione, sub	*La*	conditionally
conduce	*Sc*	employ, hire
conduck	*Sc*	conduit, water channel
confectioner	*Sc*	maker or seller of sweetmeats and cakes
confirmation of grant	*Sc*	confirmation of a charter by a superior
coniuges	*La*	married couple
coniunx (coniux)	*La*	husband or wife

conjugatus	*La*	married
conjuges	*La*	married couple
conjugum	*La*	of/from the married couple
conjunct	*Sc*	1. joint e.g. conjunct fiar (joint ownership of land); 2. connected by blood
conjunct fee	*Sc*	title to lands held jointly, by husband and wife, a number of heirs, business partners etc.
conjunct right	*Sc*	a right held jointly
conjuncti	*La*	marriage
conjuncti sunt	*La*	they were joined (in marriage)
conjunctly and severally	*Sc*	two or more individuals having an obligation, duty or empowerment to do something, whether singly or together
conjux	*La*	spouse (wife or husband)
Conjux, uxor	*La*	wife
connex	*Sc*	appurtenance, something connected with an estate
connotar	*Sc*	public notary acting alongside another
conqueish, conquess, consques, conquis	*Sc*	1. to conquer; 2. to acquire property by purchase, donation or exchange rather than inheritance
conquest, heir of	*Sc*	an heir succeeding by ascent, as representing an older line, e.g. if the middle of three brothers dies, the youngest succeeds to his heritable property but the eldest to the conquest property, a distinction ended in 1874
cons.	*Le*	consideration
consanguinean	*Sc*	half-sibling, child of the same father but different mother
consanguinitas	*La*	blood relationship (impediment to marriage if too close)
consanguinitatis	*La*	of blood relationship
conservator	*Oc*	guardian or custodian, often an official of a body corporate or institution
consobrinus	*La*	cousin (mother's side), male or female
consors (consortis)	*La*	wife
constable	*Sc*	law officer
contorar	*Sc*	contrary
contra	*La*	against, opposite
contract	*Le*	agreement between persons that obliges each party to do or not to do a certain thing
contract law	*Le*	body of law that regulates the formation and enforcement of contracts
contracted	*Sc*	betrothed: in Scotland this was legally equivalent to marriage as consent was legally binding and the marriage ceremony was introduced in order to make the contract publicly known, although it was not essential
contracti	*La*	contracted, drawn together
contrahere	*La*	to contract, to draw together
contraxerunt	*La*	they contracted (marriage)
convener	*Sc*	chief official of a craft or trade
conveyance	*Sc*	transfer of property
convulsionis	*La*	of convulsions

cookie	*Sc*	prostitute
cooper	*Oc*	maker of wooden barrels and casks for beer etc.
cooper, cowper, cupper	*Sc*	cask or barrel maker; *see* coupar, couper
cooperta	*La*	married (of a woman)
co-ownership	*Le*	generic legal term for various forms of ownership over one asset by more than one person
cop	*Sc*	cup used as a liquid or grain measure
coparcener	*La*	co-heir
coper guis pan	*Sc*	copper pan for cooking goose
coppersmith	*Sc*	one who works with copper
copseller	*Sc*	cap seller, maker and seller of cups (not cops)
copulati	*La*	marriage
copulati sunt	*La*	they were married, joined
copulatio	*La*	marriage
copulationis	*La*	of marriage
copulatus	*La*	married, joined
copulatus/a	*La*	married man/woman
copulatus/a est	*La*	he/she was married
copulavit	*La*	he married (performed wedding)
copyhold	*Le*	form of holding land, marked by the fact that the tenant would have a copy of the court roll recording his admission
coquet	*Le*	a form of seal
coqueter	*Sc*	clerk of cocquet
coquus	*La Oc*	cook
coram	*La*	in the presence of
coram (adv.) and (prep.)	*La*	in the presence of, before
cordiner	*Oc*	shoemaker; *also* cordwainer, cordonar, cordoner, cordinar, corduner, cordowner, cordoner
coriarius	*La*	leather worker, tanner
cork cutter	*Oc*	cut and prepared imported cork bark
corkcutter	*Sc*	cutter of cork bark
corn chandler	*Sc*	corn merchant
corn couper	*Sc*	corn dealer
cornel, crownell, crowner	*Sc*	1. colonel; 2. coroner
cornet	*Sc*	lowest rank of army commissioned officer, sub-lieutenant, ensign
corody	*Le*	pension in food or such other things as may be required for sustenance
coronell	*Sc*	coroner
coronicles, cornicles, corniclis	*Sc*	chronicles

corporal	*Sc*	non-commissioned army officer
corpus (corporis)	*La*	body
corshous	*Sc*	building standing at right angles to others
corslet	*Sc*	furnished with a corslet (upper-body armour), as when seeking admission as a guild brother and required to be armed
cose, cosse	*Sc*	exchange, usually of land
cosnant	*Sc*	wages without board or lodgings
cost side	*Sc*	coast
costermonger	*Oc*	street seller of fruit and vegetables
cotarius	*La*	cottager
cottar	*Oc*	tenant with a cottage and minimal land
cottar land	*Sc*	land attached to a cothouse
cottar, cottrall, cotter	*Sc*	tenant occupying a farm cottage, sometimes with a small piece of land in exchange for working on the farm
cotton piecer	*Oc*	leant over spinning machines to repair broken threads (often small children)
cotton warper	*Oc*	cotton mill loom operator in weaving
cotton winder	*Oc*	wound the threads onto a weaving looms
Council and Session	*Sc*	the 'Books of Council and Session' are the Register of Deeds
councillor	*Sc*	1. town councillor; 2. counsellor, advocate
count	*Sc*	English or French equivalent of earl
counter	*Sc*	hostile encounter
counter warden, compter warden	*Sc*	keeper of accounts, treasurer
countermaister	*Sc*	ship's mate
countess	*Sc*	wife of an earl or count
coup	*Sc*	1. refuse tip; 2. manure cart; 3. basket used to catch or carry salmon
couper	*Sc*	herring dealer
couper-boit	*Sc*	herring dealer's boat
cours	*Sc*	coarse (of linen)
court baron	*Le*	court held by the lord of the manor for his local tenants to administer the customs of the manor and enforce payment of dues and services
court hand	*Pal*	document hand used by government offices
court leet	*Le*	of the frankpledge and dealt with the administration of local justice for common offences
Court of Justiciary	*Sc*	the main criminal court in Scotland, operating by a number of circuits
Court of Session	*Sc*	supreme civil court in Scotland
court plaint	*Sc*	feudal privilege of dealing with complaints made to a court of justice
court roll	*Le*	parchment-roll record of law court proceedings
courten roads	*Sc*	curtain rods
courtesy	*Sc*	entitlement to income from the heritage of a deceased; *see* liferent

covenant	*Le*	written document in which signatories either commit themselves to do a certain thing, to not do a certain thing or in which they agree on a certain set of facts
cowclink	*Sc*	prostitute
cowfeeder, cow-feeder	*Sc Oc*	dairy farmer
cowper	*Oc*	maker of cups
cow's mail	*Sc*	the rent of sufficient land to graze a cow
coxswain	*Sc*	navigator of a boat or ship
cramer, cremer	*Sc*	stallkeeper, pedlar, occupant of a crame (booth)
cran	*Sc*	barrel, barrelful of unsalted herrings
crannog	*Sc*	old lake dwelling, a wooden house on stilts on an island lake or earth mound standing in water
cras	*La*	tomorrow
creamer	*Oc*	occupant of a cream or kraim (booth)
crear	*Sc*	small merchant vessel
creatura dei	*La*	foundling (creature of God)
credit draper	*Sc*	person who sells linen or clothes door-to-door on credit and collects the money weekly or monthly
creel	*Sc*	wicker fish basket, lobster cage
creelman, creillman, creilman, creelaman, crealman, creilmaker	*Sc Oc*	maker of creels for lobster and crab fishing, carried produce to market in a creel (basket)
creep	*Sc*	crêpe material, used to make hoods etc.
creve	*Sc*	crave, petition for a right to do something
crimpson	*Sc*	crimson, red
crippelt	*Sc*	crippled, with a physical disability
cro	*Sc*	financial recompense for a killing
croft	*Sc*	small piece of land adjoining a house
crofter	*Sc Oc*	smallholder tenant of farm and cottage (croft), usually in the Highlands
cross dwelling	*Sc*	lodging
crowdie-mowdie	*Sc*	oatmeal and water eaten uncooked
crownes of the sun	*Sc*	French coins, named for the minting mark, worth about 14*s*
crue	*Sc*	croy, hovel
cruives	*Sc*	enclosures used in salmon fishing
cruk	*Sc*	circle, hook, shepherd's crook, bishop's crozier
crukit hauche	*Sc*	low ground (hauch of haugh) or water meadow beside a winding river
crummock	*Sc*	an edible tuber or rootplant
cryit fair	*Sc*	fair with advance public proclamation
cubicularius	*La*	valet, 'chamber chyld'

cuch bed	*Sc*	couch bed
cucking stool	*Le*	medieval form of punishment; a chair in which an offender was restrained
cui impositum est nomen	*La*	to whom was given the name
cuik, cuke	*Sc*	cook
cuius	*La*	whose
cuius est solum ejus est usque ad coelum et ad inferos	*La Le*	whoever owns the soil, it is theirs up to the skies and down to the depths below (hell); including minerals
cuiusdam	*La*	of a certain
culina	*La*	kitchen
cullour	*Sc*	colour
cultellar	*Sc*	cutler, knife sharpener
cultellarius	*La*	cutler
cultellarius, cultellar	*La*	cutler
culvering	*Sc*	1. handgun; 2. cannon
culvert	*Sc*	drain, dewer
cum	*La*	with
cummer, kimmer	*Sc*	witch
cumptour	*Sc*	money counter, accountant
cunigar, cuningar	*Sc*	rabbit warren
cunnar, cunstar	*Sc*	ale taster
cuntra, cuntray, cuntre	*Sc*	country
cunyie	*Sc*	corner plot of land
cunzehous	*Sc*	the mint
cunzeour	*Sc*	master of the mint, coiner, minter
cuprifaber	*La*	coppersmith
cur	*La*	why
curate	*Sc*	clergyman not fully ordained, minister's assistant (pre-Reformation, Episcopal)
curator, curat	*Sc Oc*	person appointed by law to act for someone unable to manage his or her own affairs, such as minor or lunatic; a minor was between 14 (12 if female) and 21
curator ad litem	*Sc*	guardian of a minor in a lawsuit or of a wife sueing a husband
curia	*La*	court
curia baronis	*La Le*	court baron
curia leta	*La Le*	court leet
curia magna	*La Le*	court leet
curia parva	*La Le*	court baron
curn, curne	*Sc*	literally, a single grain of corn, but usually appearing as 'the third curn' or with another number, indicating a proportion of the crop; small number of quantity, a few

currach	*Sc*	coracle, small fishing boat
currarius	*La*	carriage builder
currier	*Sc*	tanner of skins, hides and leather
currour	*Sc*	forest warden
cursive	*Pal*	script in which the letters are joined together
curtilage	*Sc*	a courtyard or other piece of ground near or belonging to an occupied building
curtilage	*Le*	piece of ground attached to house
curtilagium /i	*La Le*	curtilage
cussing	*Sc*	cousin
customary tenant	*Le*	tenants holding land according to the customs of the manor
customarye	*Sc*	levying of customs or excise
customer, custumer, customar	*Sc Oc*	receiver of customs or excise, customs officer
custom-house officer	*Sc*	collector of revenues in a customs house
customs of the manor	*Le*	the set of rules by which manors were governed/administered
custos (custodis)	*La*	custodian, guard
custumal	*Le En*	document specifying tenure and the customary law of a manor
custumarius /a /um	*La Le*	customary
cuthill	*Sc*	wood
cutler, cutlar, coilter, cultellar	*Sc*	cutlery maker
cutter	*Oc*	cuts cloth for a tailor
d	*Sc*	1. died ; 2. doughtur
D G	*Sc*	dean of guild
dag maker, dagmaker	*Oc*	pistol maker
dailis	*Sc*	ewes fattened for slaughter, usually because they have not lambed
dairymaid	*Oc*	girl who milked cows and made butter in a dairy
dale, deal	*Sc*	wooden shelf or container, usually for milk
damasker	*Sc*	damask cloth worker
dame	*Sc*	married or widowed lady
dampnum /i	*La Le*	damages
dapifer	*Oc*	steward in a royal or noble household
dative	*Sc*	as in testament dative or tutor dative (granted by the court and containing no will) as opposed to testamentar (done or appointed by the testator and containing a will)
datum	*La*	date, given
davach	*Sc*	measurement of land, about four ploughgates
dawern	*Sc*	day's work

day labourer	Sc	workman paid daily
de	La	of, from, by, concerning, about
de eodem	La	of that ilk (Scot)
de facto	Sc	in fact, something that has actually been done, is a fact
de placito debiti	La Le	in a plea of debt
de placito transgressionis	La Le	in a plea of trespass
de ritu sanctae matris ecclesiae	La	according to the rite of the holy mother church
deacon	Sc	1. official of craft or trade guild; 2. lay official in a church
deacon convener	Sc	chief official of craft or trade guild
deacon warner	Sc	official summoning members to a guild, court, council or church meeting
deall	Sc	board of deal (or pine)
dean	Sc	1. chief official of craft or trade guild; 2. head of a university faculty
dean of gild (guild)	Sc	president of a guildry, judge of the dean of guild's court and usually magistrate in a royal burgh
deathbed law	Sc	an heir could cancel deeds not to his advantage by a terminally ill predecessor within sixty days before the death
debatable	Sc	land and boundaries subject to dispute
debeo/ere	La Le	to owe
debilitas	La	illness, weakness
debitum fundi	Sc	debt of the land, arising out of it, e.g. arrears of rent or feu duty
dec.		deceased
decanatus	La	deanery, section of diocese
decanus	La	deacon
decembris	La	of December
decenna/ae	La Le	tithing(s)
decennarius/i	La Le	tithingman (men)
decerned	Sc	decreed to be
decessit	La	he/she died
decessit sine prole (d.s.p.)	La	died without issue, childless
decessit vitae patre (d.v.p.)	La	died in father's lifetime
decessus	La	died, death
decimae	Sc	tithe or tenth part of annual produce of land due to the church, same as teinds
declarator	Sc	action to have a right or interest declared by law
decr arb	Sc Le	decreet arbitral
decree of locality	Sc	decree of the teind court apportioning how a stipend should be paid by each of the parish heritors
decree of modification	Sc	decree of the teind court altering a churchman's stipend

decree of valuation	*Sc*	decree of the teind court determining a heritor's teinds
decree, decreet, decreit	*Sc*	decree, sentence or final judgement of a court
decreet arbitral	*Sc*	award to parties in a dispute after arbitration
decreet of *cognitionis causa*	*Sc*	decision of a court on the amount of a debt to be paid out of a deceased's estate by the heirs; it may also confirm the creditor as executor of the estate
decreet of removal	*Sc*	judgement ordering defenders to leave lands
decretum	*La*	decree
decubuit	*La*	he/she died, lay down
dede, deid	*Sc*	1. deed; 2. dead; 3. death
dedimus potestatem de attornato faciendo	*La Le*	ancient common law exemption from the requirement to attend any court summons in person allowing, instead, representation by an attorney
dedit	*La*	he/she gave
deed	*Sc*	formal written document in a particular format laying out the terms of an agreement, contract, obligation but not a sasine and not concerned with heritable property and its transfer or assignment
def	*Le*	deforciant
defalta/ae	*La Le*	default
defectus redditum	*La Le*	defect of rent
defence of habitation	*Le*	right to use lethal force to prevent a felony committed within a person's home
defender	*Sc*	Scots law equivalent of defendant in a suit or trial
deflorata	*La*	deflowered, no longer a virgin
deforcement	*Sc*	1. occupying property belonging to someone else; 2. resisting officers of the law
defuit	*La*	he/she departed, died
defunct	*Sc*	deceased person
defunctorum	*La*	of the dead
defunctorum, liber	*La*	register of the deceased
defunctus est	*La*	he died
defunctus/a/um	*La*	dead, death
defungitur	*La*	he/she dies, is discharged
dehinc (adv.)	*La*	while, from here, from now, henceforth; then, next
dei	*La*	of God
deid's part, deid's pairt, dead's part	*Sc*	that part of someone's moveable estate they may dispose of by testament after death; the other parts are the bairn's part and the *jus relictae*
deinde	*La*	then, thereafter, next
deinde (adv.)	*La*	from there; then, afterwards; secondly, next (in order), in second (next) place
delated	*Sc*	accused
deliverance	*Sc*	judgement
demesne	*Le*	land held by a noble under the English feudal system, in absolute ownership
demittit	*Sc*	demitted, dismissed, resigned, given over

dempster, doomster	*Oc*	one who pronounces judgement, a sentencing judge
demum (adv.)	*La*	at last, finally, not till then; precisely, exactly, just, in fact, certainly, to be sure
demurrage	*Sc*	payment made to a shipmaster or shipowner if a ship is held up longer than usual while loading or unloading
denarius	*La*	penny, small coin, money
denatus	*La*	deceased, dead, death
denatus est	*La*	he died, has died
denique (adv.)	*La*	finally
denunciatio	*La*	publication of marriage banns
denuntiationes	*La*	marriage banns
deodand	*Le*	object that has been involved in some personal injury, is forfeit to the government
depone	*Sc*	depose, give evidence, make an oath
deponent	*Sc*	someone who makes a deposition before a court
deposit in security	*Le*	money paid to another to be held as security for the occurrence of a specified event
deposition	*Sc*	testimony of a witness put down in writing
depute	*Sc*	deputy
derfly	*Sc*	boldly
descender	*Pal*	part of a letter extending below baseline, as with p or q; *see* ascender
design	*Sc*	assign, bestow, give, grant
desponsationis	*La*	engagement
desponsatus	*La*	engaged
desponsus/a	*La*	betrothed
destination	*Sc*	nomination of successors to a property in a specific order; *see* entail
Deus	*La*	God
deviding	*Sc*	division of lands or property
devoid and red	*Sc*	vacate land or property
dew service, deservice, do-service	*Sc*	service owed or performed by a tenant on behalf of a superior
dewetie, dewtie	*Sc*	duty, fee
dexter	*Oc*	dyer of textiles
dexter	*La*	right
deyman	*Sc*	1. day labourer; 2. dairyman
dictus	*La*	said, stated, known as
didymus/a	*La*	twin male/female
die	*La*	on the day
die sequenti	*La*	on the following day
die vero	*La*	this very day

diem clausit extremem/um	La Sc Le	he/she finished his last day (died), the name of a royal order sent to a sheriff to enquire into the death of a debtor of the Crown, and to ensure the Crown is satisfied for the debt
dies (diei)	La	day (days)
dight	Sc	prepared, armed, equipped etc.
dignus	La	worthy
diker	Oc	builder of dry stone walls (dykes)
diligence	Sc	1. legal proceedings in the recovery of debts, enforcement of payments etc; 2. court warrant to make witnesses attend a trial or to require the production of documents
dimidius/a/um/	La	half, broken, divided
dimitto/ere	La Le	to demise/lease
diocese	Sc	the extent of a bishop's jurisdiction, which continued to be important after the Reformation as the area determined the boundaries and jurisdiction of the commissary court
diocesis	La	diocese
diploma	Pal	highly formal legal document or charter
diploma hand	Pal	European document hand used for legal or administrative documents
diplomatic	Pal	study of the formal properties of a document, including standardised wordings, clauses and layout
dirrogatione	Sc	derogation, partial repeal of a law
discessit	La	he/she died
disch.	Le	discharge
discharge	Sc	written deed that cancels or extinguishes an obligation, usually one to repay debt
disclamation	Sc	renunciation of obligation by a tenant to the superior
disheris, disherish	Sc	disinherit
disorderly house	Le	place where acts prohibited by statute are habitually indulged in or permitted
disp.	Le	disposition
disp. and assig.	Le	disposition and assignation
disp. of tailzie	Sc Le	disposition of tailzie (an entail)
dispone	Sc	dispose of, convey (land), alienate
disponsationis	La	permission
disposition	Sc	a deed whereby a right to property (either heritable or moveable) is alienated by one person and conveyed to another
disposition in implement	Sc	disposition granted in implement of a previous, imperfect conveyance
dispositive clause	Sc	the clause in a deed which transfers property of any sort
dissasine	Sc	dispossession
dissenting	Sc	Protestant but not part of the 'established' Church of Scotland
distitut	Sc	destitute

distraint	*Le*	right of a landlord to seize the property of a tenant that is in the premises being rented, as collateral against a tenant that has not paid the rent or has otherwise defaulted on the lease, such as wanton disrepair or destruction of the premises
distress	*Le*	common law remedy available to landlords to hold the tenant's belongings while the tenant is behind on rent but continues to occupy the premises
districtio/onis	*La Le*	distraint(s)
distringo/ere	*La Le*	to distrain
ditcher	*Sc*	digger or cleaner of ditches
dittay	*Sc*	the substance of the charge against a person accused of a crime
diuers	*Sc*	divers, various
diuidit	*Sc*	divided
divortium	*La*	divorce
do/dare	*La Le*	to give
doageria	*La*	dowager
dochtir	*Sc*	daughter
docker	*Oc*	docks worker, loading and unloading ship cargo
docquet	*Sc*	docket or statement of authenticity annexed to a document recording a sasine (transfer of property)
doctor	*Sc*	1. medical practitioner; 2. schoolmaster
document hand	*Pal*	script used for transcribing legal or administrative documents
dodum	*La*	formerly, recently
dom. serv.	*Oc*	domestic servant
domestic	*Sc*	household servant
domestic animal	*Le*	pet: dogs, cats or other tame animals or birds that serve some purpose for its owner or others
domi	*La*	at home
domicella	*La*	young lady, servant, nun
domicellus	*La*	young nobleman, servant (usually in a monastery)
domicillis	*Sc*	domiciles, dwellings
domicills	*Sc*	household goods
domina	*La*	lady
dominant tenement	*Le*	used when referring to easements to specify that property (i.e. tenement) or piece of land that benefits from, or has the advantage of, an easement
dominica	*La*	Sunday
dominical lands	*Sc*	the mains or principal farm on an estate, owned by the lord or dominus
dominie	*Sc Oc*	schoolmaster
dominion utile	*La Le*	property rights of a tenant; exclusive right to use a thing
dominium directum	*Sc*	direct lordship: the interest a feudal superior had in property such as the right to feu duties, casualties etc.
dominium utile	*Sc*	lordship by usage: the interest a tenant had in landed property such as the right to direct usage and enjoyment of the income from it

dominium/i	*La Le*	lord
dominus	*La*	clerical title
dominus	*La*	lord, rule, the Lord (Jesus Christ)
dominus, with 'miles'	*La*	Sir (Knight)
dominus/i	*La Le*	lord
domus	*La*	home, house, family
donator	*Sc*	the receiver of a donation, following failure of the rightful succession
donec	*La*	while, as long as, until
donum	*La*	gift
doom	*Sc*	judgement or sentence
doomster	*Sc*	the public executioner, who, at one time, pronounced sentence
dornick, dornyk	*Sc*	work or naperie, from cloth woven at Tournay, France
dorso	*Pal*	left-hand page of an open book, or reverse side of a page or document, often abbreviated as d; *see recto, verso*
dos (dotis)	*La*	dowry
dote	*Sc*	give or grant lands as an endowment
dowager	*Sc*	widow, retaining courtesy title and privileges e.g. dowager queen
Dr	*Sc*	1. daughter; 2. doctor
dr.		daughter
dragmaker	*Sc*	net maker
draper	*Oc*	cloth, fabrics and thread seller; *also* drepper, clayth draipper
draw dykes	*Sc*	ditches for water
drawer	*Oc*	mineworker who pushed or dragged coal carts
drawn and quartered	*Le*	punishment for traitors: partial hanging, disembowelling and cutting of body into quarters
drayman	*Oc*	cart driver of a dray (long flatbed cart)
dresser	*Oc*	1. surgeon's assistant in hospital; 2. stone worker in a quarry cutting rocks to shape; 3. foundry worker cleaning metal after casting
drest	*Sc*	dealt with harshly, maltreated
drover	*Oc*	cattle dealer or mover of cattle to market or between farms
druggist	*Sc*	apothecary, pharmacist, chemist
drysalter	*Oc*	dealer in dried, tinned, pickled or salted foods etc.
dryster	*Sc*	grain drier
duae	*La*	two
ducatus	*La*	duchy
duchess	*Sc*	wife of duke, highest noble title under the sovereign
ducis	*La*	of the duke or leader
ducking stool	*Le*	contraption of medieval English justice comprised of a chair in which a convict was affixed and then immersed repeatedly into a body of water
ductus	*Pal*	order and direction of strokes forming a letter

duke	*Sc*	highest noble title under the sovereign
dum	*La*	while, when, until, as long as
dum (conj.)	*La*	while, now; so long as, provided that, if only; until
duris	*Sc*	harm, injuries
dustman	*Oc*	street and domestic rubbish collector
dutyfeu	*Sc*	service or payment owed to a superior
dux	*La*	duke, leader
dwell	*Sc*	owned or occupied by someone in particular
dyer, dyster, litster	*Sc*	person who makes dyes and colours cloth
dyke	*Sc*	wall
dyker, dykar	*Oc Sc*	builder of dry-stone walls (dykes)
dysenteria	*La*	dysentery
dytements, dyting	*Sc*	poetry, writing
dyvour	*Sc*	bankrupt
e	*La*	out of, from
EIC		East India Company, until 1708 (*see* HEIC)
e, ex	*La*	from
eadem	*La*	the same
eam	*La*	her
earl	*Sc*	nobleman, above viscount and below marquis, equivalent to count; his wife is a countess
earn, erne	*Sc*	Scottish eagle
Eas.		Easter
Easement	*Le*	legal right to the access over or use of another's land or waterway
easement, esement, aisment	*Sc*	1. easement, advantage, convenience; 2. euphemism for lavatory (seat of easement)
eavesdroppers	*Le*	those convicted of the obsolete offence of intentional, covert and direct listening-in to another's conversations, and the subsequent use of the contents thereof to disturb the peace
ebdomada	*La*	week
ecclampsia	*La*	convulsions
ecclesia	*La*	church
econimus	*Sc*	steward, manager, bursar
edh	*Pal*	character in the Old English alphabet derived from a rune, representing 'th', written 'ð'
edict	*Sc*	public proclamation summoning persons to compear (appear) before a court
edict of curatory	*Sc*	edict on family from both sides to act as curators (guardians) to a minor
effeir	*Sc*	fall by right, as in as effeirs, correctly, as appropriate
effeirs, as effeirs, effeiring	*Sc*	correctly relating or corresponding to
ego	*La*	I
eik	*Sc Le*	an addition or supplement to a deed or will

eik, eiking	*Sc*	addition, as to a will
eiked	*Sc*	added
eild	*Sc*	children, issue
eiusdem, ejusdem	*La*	the same
ejustdem die	*La*	of the same day
elapsus	*La*	past, elapsed
eld.	*Sc*	elder, eldest
elder	*Sc*	one of twleve laymen who administer a church along with the minister (post-Reformation)
elder, eldar, eldder, elde, elser, eldest, senior	*Sc*	older or oldest heir; *see* younger
elderman	*Sc*	alderman, burgh magistrate or councillor
elemosinar, elimozinar	*Sc*	almoner
elide	*Sc*	weaken evidence
ell	*Sc*	measure of length, about 1 yard, traditionally the distance between nose and fingertips
embracery	*Le*	improper influence on a juror
eme	*Sc*	uncle or male near relation
emerode	*Sc*	emerald, but also haemorrhoids
emmet	*Sc*	ant
emphiteose	*Sc*	feu duty in perpetuity
emphyteusis	*Le*	civil law: a long-term lease of land or buildings; ninety-nine years or such similar long term, or even in perpetuity
empicus	*La*	lung disease
end	*Sc*	outcome of a legal process
enfranchise	*Le*	convert copyhold land into freehold tenure
engel	*Sc*	angel, a gold coin
engeneret, engendrit	*Sc*	engendered, begotten
engine keeper	*Oc*	operator of an industrial steam-driven engine
Englishry	*Le*	proving to the authorities that a killed person was English
engrossed	*Pal*	hand-written
engrossing	*Le*	buying of products in bulk and the individual resale at profit
enim	*La*	for, namely, truly
enim (conj.)	*La*	namely, indeed, certainly, in fact, for, because
ensign	*Sc*	lowest army commissioned officer rank in foot regiments, sub-lieutenant
entail	*Sc*	or tailzie, a deed that altered the legal succession of lands to another line, or by which the descent of lands can be secured to a specified succession of heirs
enter, inter	*Sc*	1. obtain or take possession of lands, property or an office; 2. to put someone in possession

enticement	*Le*	old common law action against any person who caused a husband to lose the love, services or society of his wife
entres	*Sc*	interest
entress, entry	*Sc*	1. entrance; 2. appointment of an heir as a new vassal with his superior
entrie silver	*Sc*	dues paid when entered as heir in an estate
entry fine	*Le*	payment due when new customary tenant entered land
eo quod	*La*	because
eo tempore	*La*	at this time
eod die	*La*	*eodem die* (on the same day)
eodem	*La*	the same
eodem die	*La*	on the same day
eodem mense	*La*	in the same month
episcopal	*Oc*	pertaining to a bishop
episcopus	*La*	bishop
epitome	*Pal*	extracts or condensations of a written work
epphipiarius	*La*	saddler
epphipiarius	*Oc*	saddler
equalis	*La*	equal
equerry	*Sc*	attendant on a noble or sovereign, especially in connection with his horse
eques (equitis)	*La*	knight, cavalry soldier
equipollent	*Sc*	equivalent, of equal authority or value
erant	*La*	they were
erat	*La*	he/she/it was
erd erthe and stane	*Sc*	earth and stone, figurative expression used in conveyance (transfer of property)
erer	*Sc*	rather
ergo	*La*	therefore, because of
erl	*Sc*	earl
erratum	*La*	error
escheat, eschet, ascheat	*Sc*	forfeit, as in escheat goods or estate forfeited or confiscated on conviction for a crime, non-payment of debt etc.
eschew	*Sc*	accomplish, succeed
esquire	*Sc*	title of gentleman, as opposed to mister or master, which indicated a university graduate
esquire	*Le*	mostly informal title associated with those who practice law
essay master	*Sc*	assay master in the Royal Mint
esse	*La*	to be
essoin	*Le*	valid excuse for not appearing in court when summoned
essonia/ae	*La Le*	essoin(s)
est	*La*	he/she/it is
estaitis	*Sc*	estates (of the Crown)

estin	*Sc*	eastern
estover	*Le*	limited rights granted to a tenant of land to certain product of the land, mostly wood
estreat	*Le*	collective term for fines and amercements imposed in the manorial court
et	*La*	and, even
etenim (conj.)	*La*	and indeed, for, as a matter of fact
etiam	*La*	also, besides; even, actually; (time) still
etiam	*La*	and also, and even
etsi (conj.)	*La*	though, although, and yet
ettlit	*Sc*	aimed (at)
eum	*La*	him
evenar	*Sc*	arbitrator appointed to apportion lands
eviction	*Le*	some permanent act by a landlord, or by person or thing under his control, which deprives a tenant of enjoyment of the rented premises
evidents	*Sc*	title deeds, documents proving ownership
ex	*La*	from, out of (places of origin)
ex causa	*La*	on account of, for the sake of, because of
ex hac mortali ad immortalem vitam	*La*	from this mortality to immortal life (died)
ex illegitimo thoro	*La*	of illegitimate status
examiner	*Sc*	auditor or inspector of business, trade etc.
excamb, excambion	*Sc*	exchange; the exchange of one heritable subject for another, for example, someone may have exchanged a piece of land for some agreed service, and that passes to the heir of the deid (deceased). The Montgomery Act (1770) was aimed at agricultural improvements by allowing 50 acres arable and 100 acres not fit to plough to be excambed. The Rosebery Act of 1836 allowed a quarter of an entailed estate, not including the mansion house, home farm and policies, to be excambed, provided the heirs took no more grassum (entry fee) than £200. The Rutherford Act of 1848 applied it to the whole estate. The necessary consents of substitute heirs are regulated by the Entail (Scotland) Act 1882 and there were more land reforms later. If the umquhile (deceased) had exchanged something or inherited something exchanged then the right to continue this is inherited
exchequer	*Le*	the main financial office of the monarchy or government
excise officer, exciseman	*Oc*	collecter of customs revenues or taxes
excrescens	*La Le*	interest
executor	*Le*	legal administrator of the moveable property of a dead person, nominated either in the deceased's testament (executor nominate) or by the commissary court (executor dative)
executor dative	*Le*	person appointed by a court to effect a warrant
executor nominate	*Le*	person appointed by a testator to effect a warrant, as in the executor of an estate, appointed in a will
executrix	*Le*	female executor
executry	*Le*	moveable property of the deceased, as opposed to heritable (immovable) land, buildings, mineral and fishing rights etc.

exhalavit animam	*La*	he/she breathed out his/her soul (died)
exhorter	*Sc*	preacher, minister (Protestant, post-Reformation)
exitus/us	*La Le*	issue/revenue/profit(s)
exoner	*Sc*	exonerate, free from liability
explicit	*La Pal*	heading indicating the end of a section of text; *see* incipit
expropriation	*Le*	forced purchase of land by a public authority from a private owner
extent	*Le Eng*	manorial document listing holdings and tenants with their obligations in labour services and rent, also known as a terrier
extenta/ae	*La Le*	survey(s)
extents	*Sc*	assessments
extinguishment	*Le*	termination of legal rights
extra	*La*	outside of, beyond
extract sp service	*Sc Le*	extract of special service
extraneus	*La*	stranger, foreign
extremum	*La*	last
extremum munitus	*La*	last rites provided
exulatus	*La*	exile
eyrn	*Sc*	iron
F	*Sc*	freeman
F S	*Oc*	female servant
faber	*La Oc*	craftsman, maker, smith
faber ferrarius	*La Oc*	blacksmith
faber lignarius	*La Oc*	wright, woodworker
faber muriarius	*La Oc*	builder, mason
factis tribus denunciationibus	*La*	three marriage banns having been published
factor	*Oc*	agent appointed by another to conduct affairs on his behalf, business agent, rent collector, attorney
factory	*Sc Le*	power of attorney
factrix	*Oc*	female factor
factus	*La*	made
fader, fadir	*Sc*	father
fadir-in-gode	*Sc*	godfather
fadir-of-lau	*Sc*	father in law
faillie, failzie	*Sc*	failure to comply with something, or non-fulfillment of an obligation
failzand	*Sc*	lacking in e.g. an heir
failzieing	*Sc*	failing
fair market value	*Le*	hypothetical most probable price that could be obtained for a property by average, informed purchasers
falcon and culver	*Sc*	artillery pieces
falconer	*Sc*	falcon and hawk trainer or handler

falsing the doom	*Sc*	making a protest against a doom (judgement) before taking the matter to a higher court
falso	*La*	falsely, incorrectly
familia	*La*	family
familiaris	*La*	relative, slave, friend, follower
famulus	*La*	servant
famyle	*Sc*	family, kindred, lineage, relations
farder	*Sc*	further
farding land	*Sc*	fourth part of a penny land
farm servant	*Oc*	farm worker under contract
farrier	*Oc*	blacksmith who shoes horses
farrier, ferrier	*Sc*	farrier, horse shoer, horse veterinarian
fas (est)	*La*	(it is) right, proper
fastern's night	*Sc*	shrove Tuesday, eve of the Lent fast
father in law	*Sc*	step-father or wife's father (gude father)
fault	*Sc*	need
fayr	*Sc*	father (the *y* is the 'thorn' character, pronounced '*th*')
fayve	*Sc*	five
fealty	*Le*	allegiance or fidelity
fear	*Sc Le*	one to whom property belongs in reversion
feber (febris)	*La*	fever
februarii	*La*	of February
fecit finem pro ingressu	*La Le*	he paid an entry fine
fecunda	*La*	pregnant
fede	*Sc*	feud, blood enmity
fee	*Le*	1. full right of property in heritage, as distinct from liferent; 2. hire oneself out for farm work
feet of fines	*Le En*	third copy of final concords retained by court as a record; *see* chirograph, final concord
feild	*Sc*	field
feill	*Sc*	many
fellis	*Sc*	fells, hills
felonious homicide	*Le*	killing of a human being without justification or excuse
feltmaker	*Sc*	maker of cloth by pressing (felting), without a loom
feme covert	*Fr Le*	married woman
feme sole	*Fr Le*	unmarried woman
femina	*La*	female, wife, woman
fence	*Sc*	1. escape from prison or arrest; 2. seizure of goods or land
fenced court	*Sc*	court opened and held with all due solemnity

fencible	*Oc*	militiaman, soldier recruited for war
fencing master	*Sc*	teacher of fencing and swordplay
feoffment	*Sc*	legal giving of possession of land and the fact of being legally possessed (*see* infeftment)
ferd	*Sc*	fourth
ferd corne	*Sc*	fourth corn, grain for sowing
fere	*Sc*	friend, comrade
fere	*La*	almost, nearly
feria	*La*	day, holiday
ferme, ferm	*Sc*	1. annual rent (*see* blench ferme); 2. firm, steady; 3. farm
fermorar	*La*	farmer
fermorar, fermourer, fermour	*Sc*	farmer
ferrier	*La*	farrier
ferry louper	*Oc*	Orkney name for an arriving mainlander
ferryman	*Sc*	ferry operator
festum	*La*	feast, festival, wedding
fethelar	*Oc*	fiddler, musician
feu ch	*Sc Le*	feu charter
feu con	*Sc Le*	feu contract
feu disp	*Sc Le*	feu disposition
feu, few	*Sc*	holding of property under feudal tenure, i e held of a superior
feuar	*Oc*	landholder who paid a feu (fee) to the superior
feuar, fewer, fiar, fewar, feuer	*Sc*	1. person who holds a feu (land or house) at a rent; 2. agent who collects that rent on behalf of the superior
feudal system	*Le*	social structure that existed throughout much of Europe between 800 and 1400 and that revolved around a multi-level hierarchy between lords (who held land granted under tenure from the king), and their tenants (also called 'vassals')
feu-duty, feu-mails, feu-fermes	*Sc*	amount paid for a feu, usually annually
fiall	*Sc*	feudal tenure
fiar, fear	*Sc*	owner, person holding a property in fee, e.g. an heir who has the fee (ownership) as distinct from the person in possession of the liferent
Fib	*Sc*	Pictish kingdom of Fife
Fidach	*Sc*	Pictish kingdom roughly equivalent to modern Strathspey
fidelis	*La*	faithful
fidlar	*Sc*	fiddler, violinist
fieri facias	*La Le*	that you cause to be made; refers to a writ of judgement enforcement under the old common law of England
figulus	*La*	potter

filia	La	daughter
filia fratris/sororis	La	niece, daughter of brother/sister
filia populae	La	illegitimate daughter
filiaster	La	stepson
filiastra	La	stepdaughter
filiola	La	little daughter
filiolus	La	little son
filius	La	son
filius fratris/sororis	La	nephew, son of brother/sister
filius populi	La	illegitimate son
final concord or fine	En Le	documentary record of the result of a lawsuit in the form of an indenture or chirograph; *see* chirograph, feet of fines, indenture
finis	La	border, end
fireman	Oc	1. tender of a furnace or fire, for cooking, brewing, metal working etc, as on a train or ship; 2. firefighter; 3. placer of explosives in mines
firle	Sc	ferrule, metal ring binding a knife or fork to its handle
firlot	Sc	Scottish measure, which, like the rest, differed from place to place and depended on what it was being used to measure; as far as grain was concerned, it was the fourth part of bol (and therefore anything from about nine-tenths to one and half imperial bushel
firlot mell	Sc	measure of meal or other dry goods; a quarter-boll
firmarius	La	farmer
firmarius/i	La Le	farmer/renter(s)
fischer	Sc	fisherman or fish seller: *also* fischerman, fisher, white fisher, fishman
fishcurer	Oc	drier and salter of fish for transport in barrels
fishmonger	Sc	fish seller
fishwife	Oc	woman selling fresh fish door-to-door
fitter	Oc	installer or assembler of machinery, furnishings etc.
flaggan, flacon	Sc	flagon
flax scutcher	Oc	beat flax fibres before dressing
flaxdresser, flax-raiser	Sc	preparer of flax for spinning to make linen
flaxman	Oc	flax dealer
flegeoure	Sc	fletcher, arrowmaker
flemens-firth	Sc	asylum for outlaws
flesher, fresher, flesches, flescher	Oc	butcher
fletcher	Oc	arrow maker
fleur-de-luce	Sc	fleur-de lys, the stylised iris used in heraldry
flit	Sc	remove, in the sense of leaving land or a house
floater	Sc	plasterer, surface leveller
flockmaster	Oc	shepherd in charge of a flock of sheep

flood waters	Le	waters that escape from a watercourse in great volume and flow over adjoining lands in no regular channel
fluxus	La	dysentery
focus	La	fireplace, hearth, home
foderator	La	cloth worker, fuller (can also mean furrier)
fodiator	La	digger
foir	Sc	fore, front
foir bears	Sc	forebears, predecessors, ancestors
foirfadirs	Sc	forefathers, ancestors
foirgrandscheir	Sc	great-grandfather
foirsaid, foyrsaid	Sc	aforesaid
fold dycks	Sc	dykes or walls for enclosing livestock
folio	Pal	single leaf or page of a manuscript; *see dorso, recto, verso*
folium	La	page
fons (fontis)	La	baptismal font, spring, fountain
fons et origo	La	fount and origin
fool	Le	human in form but destitute of reason from birth
foranent	Sc	up against, adjoining
foreclosure	Le	eliminate a right of redemption on mortgaged real property
foregranddame	Sc	great-grandmother, but occasionally female relative further back
foregrandfather, foregrandsire	Sc	great-grandfather, great-great-grandfather or earlier male ancestor
foreland, foirland	Sc	front tenement or house
foreman	Sc	person in charge of workers at a farm, factory etc.
foremast man	Sc	foremost man, foreman
forespeaker	Oc	advocate, pleader in court
forestalling	Le	purchase of food products before it arrives at, or as it comes to, a food market, with the intent to sell the same again at a higher price
forester	Sc	forest worker, tree tender
forework	Sc	stone facings on the frontage of a building, often ornamental
fore-worker	Sc	stone mason concerned with forework (the frontage of a building)
forfault	Sc	1. forfeit; 2. confiscation of rights or property
forsamekle	Sc	forasmuch
fort major	Sc	army officer in charge of a fort, castle, camp barracks etc.
fortalice	Sc	fortress, tower of a fortified house
Fortriu	Sc	Pictish kingdom roughly equivalent to modern Perthshire, centred on Forteviot
fossor	La	grave digger, miner
fostering	Sc	it was the practice amongst noble and royal families and clan chiefs, to have their heirs brought up elsewhere, partly to reinforce links, partly as hostage against disagreements
fosteris	Sc	children or other dependants

Fotla	*Sc*	Pictish kingdom roughly equivalent to modern Atholl
foullis	*Sc*	fowls, chickens
founder	*Oc*	foundry worker, caster of metal items in an iron or brass foundry
Fr		French
Fr	*Sc*	father
frame smith	*Sc*	maker of shoulder yokes for carrying pails
frankpledge	*Le*	community pledge in medieval England whereby a defined number of people were jointly held responsible for the denunciation of any crime within their group
franktenement	*Sc*	freehold
franktenementar	*Sc*	freeholder
frater	*La*	brother
frater ex materno latere	*La*	half-brother, common mother
frater ex paterno latere	*La*	half-brother, common father
frater germanus	*La*	twin brother
frater naturalis	*La*	brother
fray	*Sc*	scare, frighten
fre lands	*Sc*	free lands (*see* barony)
free forest	*Sc*	forest with hunting rights granted under charter to the owner by the Crown
freeholder	*Le*	tenants who paid a money rent to the lord of the manor
freeman	*Oc*	not feued to a feudal lord, and able to own property and trade in a burgh
free woman	*Sc*	woman with the right to trade in a burgh, female equivalent of freeman
fregerunt assisiam panis et cervisie	*La Le*	they broke the assize of bread and ale
freith	*Sc*	free
french polisher	*Oc*	wood finisher, using sandpaper and oils
Frenchie	*Sc*	person from France, or one who puts on airs to appear sophisticated
freshly	*Sc*	briskly
frething	*Sc*	freeing, unburdening
fructuarius	*La*	fruit seller
fruictman	*Oc*	fruit seller
fruiter	*Sc*	fruit seller
fuerunt	*La*	they were
fui	*La*	I was
fuit	*La*	he/she/it was
full	*Sc*	clean or thicken cloth by treading
fuller	*Sc*	cloth-finisher
fuller, fouller	*Sc Oc*	person who cleans, thickens and finishes cloth by wetting and walking on it
fulling	*Sc*	cleaning and thickening cloth prior to finishing

fullo	La	fuller, waulker
fundlin	Sc	foundling, orphan
furm	Sc	form or bench
furnaceman	Oc	looked after furnace in a metalworks
furnarius	La	baker
furrier	Sc	prepares and seller of furs and fur garments
furth of	Sc	beyond, abroad, outside the borders (of)
furthputting	Sc	eviction from property
futter	Sc	fodder or straw
fyfe	Sc	small flute
Fyfe, Fyffe	Sc	the County and Sheriffdom of Fife (properly, 'Kingdom' of Fife)
fyft, fyift	Sc	fifth
fyftye	Sc	fifty
fyiftein	Sc	fifteen
G.	Oc Sc	guild brother
G fr		grandfather
GR	Sc Le	general register (of sasines)
GS	Sc le	great seal
gabart	Sc	barge, lighter
gabartman, gabertman	Sc	lighterman, bargee
gaberlunzie	Oc Sc	travelling beggar
gairn waird bleads	Sc	garden hedge scissors
gais	Sc	gauze material
gais scarfe	Sc	gauze scarf
gait	Sc	goat
gallearius	La Oc	sailor
gallouaye	Sc	Galloway
gallowes	Sc	swing beam, e.g. on a chimney
gallus	Sc	1. gallows; 2. trouser braces (gallusses); 3. comely (e.g. 'a gallus lassie')
gamekeeper	Oc	keeper and breeder of game on an estate
ganger	Oc	leader of a gang of workmen
gangrel	Oc	vagrant, tramp
gaol	Sc	jail
gaoler	Oc	jail keeper
garcio	La	boy, servant
gardianus	La	church warden
gardiner, gardner, gairdner, gairner	Sc	gardener
garnette	Sc	siege engine used in war

garnison, garnisoun	*Sc*	garrison
gasfitter	*Oc*	fitted pipes for domestic gas supply
gat	*Sc*	begot, gave birth to, sired
gauger	*Oc*	excise officer
gause	*Sc*	fine cloth, gauze
gave in commend	*Sc*	made over as a benefice
gavelkind	*Le*	form of limited land ownership in England pre-Conquest (1066) that vested all sons equally in the heritage
gaynest	*Sc*	most suitable
geir, gear	*Sc*	1. goods e.g. household gear; 2. implements used in a mill e.g. 'lyeing and goeing geir' some of which went to the tenant while others were the property of the superior
gemellae	*La*	twins (female)
gemelli	*La*	twins (male, or one male and one female)
gemellus/a	*La*	twin
geminus/a	*La*	twin
gemmarius	*La*	jeweller
gemmarius	*Oc*	jeweller
gen. lab.	*Oc*	general labourer
genealogia	*La*	genealogy
gener	*La*	son-in-law, cousin
general supervisor	*Sc*	overseer, usually in an office, government department or business
generallity	*Sc*	generality, as in 'among the generallity of our People'
generis	*La*	of the type, sex, etc
generosus	*La*	of noble birth, gentleman
genitor	*La*	father
genitores	*La*	parents
genitour	*Sc Oc*	janitor
genitum	*La*	begotten, born
genitus	*La*	birth
genitus est	*La*	he was born, begotten
genoligie, genolligie, genolygie	*Sc*	genealogy
gens (gentis)	*La*	male line, clan, tribe, lineage
gentleman	*Sc En*	someone with means, above a commoner but below a noble
genuit	*La*	he/she was begotten
genus	*La*	type, kind, birth, descent, sex, origin, class, race
genus (generis)	*La*	sex, type, kind, birth, descent, origin, class, race
german	*Sc*	full, related by blood as opposed to marriage (of a brother or sister, or cousin; *see* brothers german)

germana	*La*	sister german (sister by blood)
Germania	*La*	Germany
germanus	*La*	brother german (brother by blood)
Ghillie	*Oc*	keeper of wild game especially deer on Highland estates
gif, gyf	*Sc*	if, whether
gilder	*Oc*	used gold leaf to adorn furniture, frames etc
gilding	*Sc*	applying a layer of gold to an object (button, picture frame etc.)
gird	*Sc*	1. child's toy, consisting of a metal hoop (gird) pushed by a hooked stick (cleek); 2. iron cartwheel cover; 3. belt
girder	*Sc*	1. maker of hoops for cartwheels (girds); 2. belt maker
girdle	*Sc*	griddle, iron baking plate
girdler, girdlesmith	*Sc*	maker of girdles (iron baking plates)
girds, girdis	*Sc*	horse girths
girnalman	*Oc*	in charge of granary or grain store
glamour	*Sc*	enchantment, magical spell, delusion
glass grinder	*Sc*	window-glass maker
glazier, glassier, glassinwright	*Sc*	maker and fitter of window glass
glebe, glebeland	*Sc*	land attached to a parish church to which the minister had a right in addition to his stipend
glebe house	*Sc*	church manse
gll'allity	*Sc*	contracted form of 'generallity'
gloris	*La*	brother's wife, wife's sister
glos	*La*	husband's sister
gloss	*Pal*	commentary on or translation of a manuscript written between the lines or in the margins of the text
glover	*Oc*	glove maker and seller
glufis, gluiffis	*Sc*	gloves
gnall.	*Sc*	general
godfather, godmother	*Sc*	witness to a baptism
gold drawer	*Sc*	maker of gold wire by drawing it through a die
goldsmith	*Sc*	worker in gold
goodsone, gudesone	*Sc*	grandson or son-in-law
gossip	*Sc*	cousin, friend
governor	*Sc*	castle, prison, hospital or almshouse overseer and manager
gowcher	*Oc*	grandfather
gradus	*La*	degree, grade
graith	*Sc*	wealth
graithit	*Sc*	make ready
gramarye	*Sc*	magic

gramercy	Sc	thank you, from the French *grand merci*
granger	Oc	keeper of grain store (granary)
granter, granger, grinterman	Sc	granary keeper
grantschir, grandscheir	Sc	grandsire, grandfather
grassum, gersum	Sc	entry fee paid by holder of a tack (rent)
gratia	La	grace, sake
gravida	La	pregnant
great seal	Sc Le	most important of royal seals
gren	Sc	green
grewgren silk	Sc	grosgrain silk
grieve	Oc	factor who collected farming rents
grieve, greive, grief	Sc	manager, overseer, factor of a farm or estate, sometimes provost of a burgh
grissillis, grissels	Sc	grilse, immature salmon
grit	Sc	great
groom	Sc	person who tends horses in a stable
ground officer	Oc	manager or factor of an estate, supervisor of tenants
guarantor	Le	person who pledges payment or performance of a contract of another, but separately, as part of an independently contract with the obligee of the original contract
guardianus	La	guardian
gubernium	La	domain
gudame	Sc	grandmother
gude father	Sc	wife's father
gudeman, goodman, guidman	Sc	farm owner or tenant, gentleman; James V used to go about incognito calling himself 'the Gudeman o' Ballengeich', which was land adjacent to Stirling Castle
gudeson	Sc	grandson or sometimes son-in-law
gudewife, goodwife, guidwife	Sc	mistress of a household or farm, wife of a gudeman
gudger	Oc En	grandfather (gudsire)
gudsyr, guidschyr, gudscheir, gudscher	Sc	grandfather
guid, guidis	Sc	good, goods
guids and geir	Sc	possessions (moveable as opposed to heritable)
guild	Sc	band of tradesmen (sometimes craftsmen) with powers to control trade levy duties etc.
guild brother	Sc	guild member
guild officer	Sc	elected position in a guild, such as treasurer or deacon
guis, guys	Sc	goose

guther	Sc	grandfather (see gudsyr)
guyder	Sc	guide, guardian
gyle	Sc	guile
HEIC		Honourable East India Company, formed from a merger in 1708 as the United Company of Merchants of England Trading to the East Indies, commonly called the Honourable East India Company was colloquially known as John Company (see EIC)
HLW	Oc	hand loom weaver, weaver of cloth at home
habeas corpus	La Le	court petition that orders that a person being detained be produced before a judge for a hearing to decide whether the detention is lawful
habent	La	they have
haberdasher	Oc	seller of threads, buttons, ribbons, small clothing wares etc.
habere	La	to have, to hold
habet	La	he/she has
habile	Sc	1. manageable, easy to use; 2. with the capacity or power (to do something)
habit and repute	Sc	reputation (often criminal)
habitans	La	resident, inhabitant
habitantes	La	residents
habitare	La	to reside
habitatio	La	residence
habitavit	La	he/she resided, dwelt
habuit	La	he/she had, held
hackbut, harquebus	Sc	short musket, arquebus, early match-lock field gun (too heavy to be shoulder-fired but used throughout Europe from 1450–1550)
hackbuteer, hackbutter	Sc	musketeer, soldier armed with a hackbut (harquebus)
hackler	Oc	lint dresser who separated coarse flax with a toothed hackle
hackney coachman	Sc	driver of a coach for hire
haec (hac)	La	this, the latter
haereticus	La	heretic
hag	Sc	firm ground in a bog, moss or swamp
hagbuit		armed with a hagbut or arquebus (see corselet)
hagbut	Sc	type of musket
haiffand	Sc	having
haill	Sc	whole
hair merchant	Sc	dealer in hair, such as horsehair for stuffing chairs
halket kyne	Sc	spotted cows
hals	Sc	neck
hames, haimes	Sc	leather traces for a horse, cart, plough etc.
hamesucken	Sc	1. crime committed on a person in his or her own home; 2. fine or penalty for such a crime
hammerman	Oc	metal worker, smith

hand	*Pal*	distinctive features of handwriting
handsell	*Sc*	the first payment for goods etc.
handseynzie	*Sc*	banner, hand-sign
hardiment	*Sc*	boldness
harnessmaker	*Sc*	maker of leather harnesses and traces for horses, oxen, ploughs, carts etc.
hatter	*Oc*	hat maker, milliner
haud	*La*	not
haundy	*Sc*	handy
havand	*Sc*	having
haver	*Sc*	possessor or custodian of a document needed as evidence
hawker	*Oc*	pedlar, door-to-door seller of small items
hayward	*Le*	oversaw the making of hay and harvesting
heatherer	*Oc*	thatcher, roofer using heather divots or stems
hebdomada	*La*	week
hech	*Sc*	promise
hecht	*Sc*	promised
hecklemaker, heckilmaker	*Oc Sc*	maker of flax combs for the hackler/heckler
heckler	*Oc*	*see* hackler
heddler	*Oc*	weaving loom operator in a textile mill
hedger	*Oc*	laid and repaired hedges around fields
heelmaker, heilmaker, pantoun–heilmaker	*Sc*	maker of shoe heels
heiche	*Sc*	high
heid	*Sc*	head
heilsome	*Sc*	wholesome
heims, hemmyngs	*Sc*	shoes of untanned leather
heir general	*Sc Le*	one who succeeds to both the heritable and moveable property of a deceased person, who also happens to be that person's heir at law and heir by normal course of succession (his heir of line)
heir in heritage	*Sc Le*	(normally) the eldest son
heir male	*Sc Le*	heir descending through the male line
heir of provision	*Sc Le*	heir of tailzie, heir by virtue of a deed of entail or provision
heir of tailzie, heir of provision	*Sc Le*	heir by virtue of a deed of entail or provision
heir portioner	*Sc Le*	one of several heirs taking equal parts, often in the case of daughters
heir presumptive	*Sc Le*	one who expects to succeed to an estate but whose right may be defeated by a birth nearer in blood to the ancestor; *see* heir apparent
heir special	*Sc Le*	heir to a particular subject or thing
heirs	*Sc Le*	heirs were of various forms: heir general, the heir of provision, heir special, heir portioner, apparent heir

heirship moveables	*Sc*	certain moveable goods (usually the best or most valuable) belonging to the deceased, to which the heir in heritage was entitled by law
hekil	*Sc*	heckling comb
Helvetia	*La*	Switzerland
herald	*Sc*	royal messenger, senior official of an heraldic court
herald painter	*Sc*	coat of arms painter
herd	*Oc*	shepherd
herd, hird	*Sc Oc*	shepherd, stockman
hereditatio/onis	*La Le*	inheritance
heres (heredis)	*La*	heir
heres masculus	*La*	male heir
heresy	*Le*	historic criminal offence comprised of the act of public denial of Christian doctrines
heretage	*Sc*	immoveable property (land etc.) devolved on the heir at law as opposed to an executor
herezeld or herit	*Sc*	form of death tax: tribute due to the feu superior on the death of the fiar or occupier and if not expressly stipulated in money, was usually the best horse, ox, cow etc.
heri	*La*	yesterday
heriot	*Le*	right in ancient common law of a land lord, upon the death of his tenant, to pick any beast belonging to the estate of the deceased tenant
herit, heriot	*Sc*	*see* herezeld
heritable	*Sc*	capable of being inherited; pertaining to land and houses, i.e. the property that went by inheritance to the heir-at-law as opposed to moveable property; 'heritable right' meant right by inheritance
heritable proprietor	*Sc*	owner of heritable property
heritably	*Sc*	by heritage
heritage	*Sc*	inheritance, heritable estate, property in the form of land and houses which descended to the heir-at-law on the death of the proprietor
heritage	*Le Sc*	Scots law: real property
heritier	*Sc*	heir, inheritor
heritor	*Sc*	local property or land owner with financial responsibilities for parish burdens, e.g. poor relief, schools, church buildings, almshouse
hesp	*Sc*	hasp, brooch clasp, hinge
hetheleder	*Oc*	person who cut and sold heather for fuel
heuch	*Sc*	glen with steep sides, crag
hew	*Sc*	hue
hewer	*Oc*	miner cutting coal at the coalface
Hibernia	*La*	Ireland
hic	*La*	here
hic, haec, hoc	*La*	this
Hil	*Le*	Hilary (term)

hinc	*La*	from here
hind, hyne, hynder	*Sc*	farm servant
hint	*Sc*	gripped
hird, hyrd	*Sc*	shepherd, cattle herd, keeper of livestock
hirer	*Sc*	arranger of labourers, servants, animals, carts, coaches etc. for a fee
his	*La*	this, the latter
hisband	*Sc*	husband
Hispania	*La*	Spain
hissing	*Le*	common-law right given to the audiences of public performances to openly express their opinion of the performance
hoc	*La*	this, the latter
hoc die/mense/anno	*La*	on this day/month/year
hodie	*La*	today
hog, hogg	*Sc*	pig (or 1-year-old sheep)
hogstone	*Sc*	worsted jacket
holder-on	*Oc*	rivetter's assistant in ship building etc.
holograph	*Sc*	testament written by the hand of the testator and therefore valid in law
homage	*Le*	the tenants who attended a manor court
homagium/i	*La Le*	homage
homo (hominis)	*La*	man, human being
homologate	*Sc*	indirectly approve of, agree with, confirm, prove, ratify
honestus	*La*	respectable, honorable
honor/oris	*La*	honour
hookmaker	*Sc*	maker of buttonhooks
hooper	*Oc*	made hoops for barrels
hora	*La*	hour
horn (at the)	*Sc Le*	denounced as a criminal, debtor or outlaw
horner	*Sc*	maker of horn items, e.g. combs, spoons, drinking cups
horning (letters of)	*Sc Le*	writ obtained by a creditor ordering a debtor to pay or be 'at the horn'
horning (relaxed from)	*Sc Le*	released from the effects of letters of horning
horse, master of	*Sc*	stable overseer
horse-cuper, horse-cooper	*Sc*	horse merchant
horsesetter, horse-setter	*Sc*	horse hirer, owner of horses for hire
hortulanus	*La Oc*	gardener
hosier	*Oc*	maker or seller of wool or silk stockings (hose)
hospes (hospitis)	*La*	innkeeper
hospital	*Sc*	almshouse
hospital-master	*Sc*	almshouse keeper

hostler	Sc	ostler, innkeeper
household master	Sc	butler, chamberlain in charge of a household
housekeeper	Sc	senior household servant, usually female
house-maills, house-meals	Sc	house rent
house-steward	Sc	senior household manservant, butler
houshald	Sc	household
hoviss	Sc	house
howdywife	Oc	midwife
howff, hough	Sc	1. inn, tavern; 2. burial ground; 3. place of resort
hr appt	Sc	heir apparent
huc	La	here, to this place; so far, for this purpose
huckster	Sc	pedlar, hawker
hue and cry	Le	community fugitive-containment strategy of medieval England where a yell went up denouncing a crime, and all within earshot took up the chase
huius	La	of this, of the latter
hulster cairds	Sc	holster cards
humantio	La	burial
humantus	La	burial
humatio, humationis	La	burial
humatus/a	La	buried
humest	Sc	uppermost
humilis	La	humble, lowly
Hungaricus	La	Hungarian
husband land	Sc	26 acres ploughed by two oxen
husbandman	Oc	tenant of a homestead on an estate, keeper of farm animals
hydropsis	La	dropsy, oedema
hypodidasculus	La	schoolmaster, usher
hypothec	Le	charge on property upon which an unpaid creditor may enforce payment of the debt
hypothecate	Sc Le	mortgage to secure a debt
hyrd	Sc	*see* hird
iam	La	already
ibi	La	there, then, therein, on that occassion
ibidem (ib, ibid)	La	in the same place
idcirco	La	for that reason, on that account, therefore
idem, eadem, iden	La	the same
ideo	La	therefore, for this reason
ides	La	13th or 15th of Roman month; *see* Chapter 3
ifans	La	child
igitur	La	therefore

ignotus/a	*La*	unknown
ihone	*Sc*	John
iit	*La*	he/she went
ilius	*La*	of that
ilk (of that)	*Sc*	of that place or race, but meaning *de eodem*, where the name of the family and estates are the same granted by royal charter e.g. Durie of Durie or Durie of that ilk: the right to be so called survives if the estate is lost but purchasing a property does not automatically guarantee a title, unless the barony is also purchased
ilke, ilkane	*Sc*	each, every one
ille, illa illud	*La*	that
illegitimus/a	*La*	illegitimate
illius	*La*	of that, of the former
illuc (adv.)	*La*	(to) there, to that, to him/her
imbrodinster	*La*	embroiderer
immo (adv.)	*La*	or rather; indeed; no, yes (emphasis)
immovable	*Le*	land and fixture, *see* moveable
imp	*Le*	impedient
impedimentum	*La*	hindrance, impediment (often to a marriage)
impedimentum consanguinitas	*La*	impediment of too close a blood relationship
imperium	*La*	empire
implement	*Sc*	completion, fulfillment
imponere	*La*	to place upon, to impose
imponit	*La*	he imposes, places upon
impositus/a/um	*La*	imposed, placed upon, given
imposui	*La*	I placed upon
impraegnavit	*La*	he impregnated
impregnata	*La*	pregnant
in facie ecclesiae	*La*	in front of the church
in manus domini	*La*	into the hands of the lord
in plena curia	*La Le*	in open court
in propria persona sua	*La Le*	in his own person
in quantum	*La*	to what extent
in r of	*Le*	in or by right of
in respectu ad proximam curiam	*La Le*	adjourned until the next court
in sinum maternum conditus	*La*	given unto the maternal breast (buried)
in twyn	*Sc*	apart, asunder
incarnationis	*La*	of the incarnation (of the Lord)

incipit	La	heading indicating the beginning of a section of text; *see* explicit
incola	La	inhabitant, resident
incontinent after our deceiss	Sc	without delay after my death
incorporeal hereditament	Le	intangible right that is attached to property and which is inheritable , such as a Scottish barony
incunabulum, a	La	book printed before 1500
inde	La	from there, from that source, then, after; from then
indenture	Le	*see* chirograph
index (indicis)	La	index
indite	Sc	indictment
indweller, indwellar, induellar	Sc	inhabitant, resident (in a burgh)
inerunt	La	they entered into (marriage)
infans/infanta (infantis)	La	child, infant
infeft	Sc	1. to seize or give formal possession; 2. to be in possession of
infeftment	Sc	1. giving a new owner legal possession of land or heritage; 2. action or deed recording formal possession
infeftment in security	Sc	temporary infeftment in heritable property as security against loan, debt or other obligation
inferior	La	lower
infirmus	La	weak
infra	La	below, under, later
infrascriptus	La	written below, undersigned
Ingland	Sc	England
Inglis	Sc	English
ingraver	Sc	engraver, patterner on metal or glass
ingressus/us	La Le	entry(ies)
inhibition	Sc Le	writ forbidding a debtor to part with, burden, mortgage etc. his heritage, so securing it for the next heir or a creditor
iniit	La	he/she entered, began
initiatus est	La	he was baptised
injuria	La	injury, worry
inquest, inquisition	Sc	inquiry before a jury into a person's right to succeed as heir
inquisitio/onis	La Le	inquiry
inscription	Le	part of a charter which identifies the grantor of the rights stated
insicht	Sc	furniture, or household goods, *see* outsicht
inspeximus	La Le	copy of an earlier document, confirmed by an authority, such as a legal copy or extract
instant, inst	La	this month
institor	La	pedlar, cramer

instrument	*Sc*	legal document, often testifying to completion of act of e.g. sasine, putting in possession of land
intendent	*Sc*	person in charge, keeper, superintendent
inter	*La*	between
interdict	*Sc*	inquisition
interdum	*La*	occasionally, sometimes, now and then
interlocutor	*Sc*	strictly speaking, a judgement or order of a court or of the lords ordinary pronounced in the course of a lawsuit short of the final judgement and not finally settling the case
intermeddle	*Sc*	interfere without right
interrogatory	*Sc*	formal question requiring a reply under oath
interruption	*Sc*	legal action to extend the length of a period of prescription (*see* prescription)
intertainer	*Sc*	entertainer, in the sense of a guardian looking after and housing a minor
intra	*La*	within, during
intres thairto	*Sc*	interest in
intrometter	*Sc Le*	person concerned in the affairs of another e.g. a trustee or executor
intromission	*Sc Le*	1. being concerned in the affairs of another; 2. possession and management of property belonging to someone else: legal, when someone is designated as an 'intromettor with the goods and gear' or illegal, when it is called 'vicious intromission'
intronizati	*La*	marriage
intronizati sunt	*La*	they were married, have been married
intronizaverunt	*La*	they married, have married
intrusit	*Sc*	intruded
inuptus/a	*La*	unmarried
invenit	*La*	he/she found, discovered
inventar	*Sc*	inventory of moveable possessions, debts etc.
inventar judicial	*Sc*	inventory made by order of the court
Ionnais, Ioannes	*Sc*	John
ipse/a/um	*La*	himself/herself/itself
iron bak	*Sc*	ash pan, iron basket
iron dresser	*Oc*	foundry worker who cleaned sand etc. from cast metal after moulding
iron miner	*Oc*	miner of ironstone rock
iron moulder	*Oc*	foundry worker who poured molten iron into moulds
iron planer	*Oc*	planed flat surfaces onto cast iron
iron shingler	*Oc*	operated a steam hammer on wrought iron
iron weigher	*Oc*	weighed iron products in foundry for sale by the ton
ironmonger	*Sc*	seller of iron goods and hardware, tools etc.
irritancy (clause of)	*Sc Le*	clause in a legal document specifying a condition to some right such as changing one's name on marriage as a condition of ensuring succession for heirs
ischear	*Sc*	1. usher, official who kept order in a church or court; 2. assistant teacher

ita	La	thus, so, in this way
ita	La	so, thus
ita vero	La	it is so, yes
ita … quomodo	La	just as
ita … ut	La	just as, so … that
itaque	La	therefore
item	La	also, likewise
iuge	Sc	judge
iugit	Sc	judged
iunior	La	younger
iurare	La	to swear, take an oath
iure	La	legally
iuris-consultours	Sc Le	legal counsel
ius, iures	La	law, laws
iuvenis	La	young person
iuxta (adv)	La	near by, alike, equally
iuxta (prep.)	La	close to, right after, near to, beside, according to
iuxta aliquid	La	to some extent
ivit	La	he/she went
JP	Oc	justice of the peace, local magistrate
jack, jak	Sc	coat of mail
jackman	Oc	attendant or man-at-arms to a nobleman or landowner
jactitation	Le	false boast designed to increase standing at the expense of another
jailer	Sc	jail keeper
jak of bane deer	Sc	bag or coat of deerskin
janitor	Sc	caretaker, doorkeeper
januarii	La	of January
japanner	Oc	applied black gloss lacquer to furniture
javelor	La	jailor
jobbing man	Oc	carried out a variety of small jobs e.g. minor carpentry
jocktaleg	Sc	large clasp knive
joiner	Oc	wood worker, carpenter, wright
joint tenancy	Le	when two or more persons are equally owners of some property
jointure	Sc	provision for a widow, usually in her marriage contract, of an annual payment during her lifetime and giving her first claim if her husband died a debtor or bankrupt
journee	Sc	a day's battle
journeyman	Oc	qualified craftsman working for someone else after serving apprenticeship
jovis, dies	La	Thursday
judaicus	La	Jewish

judicium	*La*	court, judgement
julii	*La*	of July
juncti sunt	*La*	they were joined (married)
junii	*La*	of June
junior	*Sc*	younger, in the sense of heir to a title or land
Jura Regalia	*Le*	rights which belong to the Crown or to the government
jurare	*La*	to swear, take an oath
jurator/oris	*La Le*	juror
juravit	*La*	he/she swore, took an oath
jure	*La*	legally, lawfully
juro	*La*	I swear, I testify
jus mariti	*La Le*	husband's right to his wife's moveables
jus relictae	*La Le*	right of the relict (widow), the third share of the moveable goods of a marriage to which a widow was entitled on the death of her husband: one-third would go to any children as the bairns' pairt or *legitim*, one-third would be the dead's pairt, which the deceased can direct by a will
jus spatiandi et manendi	*La Le*	right to travel and remain
jus, jures	*La*	law, laws
justiciar	*Le*	obsolete judicial position of English nobility; that of Chief Justice of the realm
justi-coat	*Sc*	vest with sleeves
juvenis	*La*	young person
juxta	*La*	near, beside
kaichpeller	*Sc*	tennis-court attendant
kain	*Sc*	1. rent paid in kind (animals, grain etc); 2. when paid along with money, the value of the payment in kind
kalens (or kalends)	*La*	first day of a Roman month; *see* Chapter 3
kamys	*Sc*	1. combs; 2. ridged ground
keill, kill	*Sc*	kiln
keilman	*Sc*	furnaceman, kiln worker
kemmyng-stok	*Sc*	combing stock for wool
ken, kend, kent	*Sc*	know, known
ker	*Sc*	cart or sledge for moving transport hay
kerfull	*Sc*	cartload
kertar, cairter	*Sc*	carter, maker or driver of carts
kill	*Sc*	kiln, oven for drying malt etc.
King's Bench	*Le*	originally, the common criminal court of the common law; later, the general superior court
King's Remembrancer	*Sc*	Crown debt collector
King's Weigher	*Sc*	officer appointed by the court to keep official weights and measures and to weigh and measure dry and liquid goods

kippage	*Sc*	disorder
kirkmaster, kirk–master	*Sc Oc*	paid official in charge of church buildings and responsible for their upkeep; deacon in a church
kirk officer	*Sc*	church officer, beadle, church warden
kish maker	*Oc*	willow basket weaver
kist	*Sc*	chest, trunk
kithes	*Sc*	appears, shows
knag	*Sc*	cask (of wine, vinegar etc.)
knapscall	*Sc*	headpiece of armour
Knight Marischall, Knight Marischal	*Sc*	title granted to Sir John Keith, third son of the 6th Earl Marischal, in 1660 for saving the royal honours from capture by Oliver Cromwell; the title was later held by others as part of the ceremonial office of Hereditary Lord High Constable and Knight Marischal
knock	*Sc*	mallet for beating linen
knock	*Sc*	clock
knycht	*Sc*	knight
knychthed	*Sc*	knighthood
kou, coo	*Sc*	cow
ky and followers	*Sc*	cow with calves
ky, kyne	*Sc*	plural of kou, cows
kyrk	*Sc*	kirk, church
LoS	*Sc Le*	Lords of Session
laborius	*La*	labourer, worker
laceman, lace weaver	*Sc*	cord maker
lache volt	*Sc*	low–vaulted room
ladie	*Sc*	lady, woman of high birth, wife of a nobleman
ladill	*Sc*	ladle, large spoon
laird	*Oc*	landowner of a rural estate
laird, lard	*Sc*	holder of land directly from the king, landowner, landlord, chief
lammas	*Sc*	1 August: one of the quarter, or term, days (with Candlemas, Martinmas and Whitsunday) on which contracts, leases, tacks and rents began and ended and when bills were settled
lamplighter	*Oc*	lighter of the gas street lamps in towns
lanarius	*La*	wool worker
lanatus	*La*	clothed in wool
land surveyor	*Sc*	estimator of land area
landlord	*Le*	land or building owner who has leased the land, the building or a part of the land or building, to another person
land waiter	*Sc*	customs officer, especially concerned with the landing and taxing of goods at a port
lang syne	*Sc*	long since, log ago ('For auld lang syne')
laniarius (or laniator)	*La*	butcher

lanifex (lanificis)	*La*	weaver
lanio	*La*	flesher
lantrone, lanthorn	*Sc*	lantern
lapper	*Sc*	person who folds and wraps linen
larceny	*Le*	criminal offence now more commonly referred to as theft, covering the unlawful or fraudulent removal of another's property without the owner's consent
last maker	*Sc*	maker of cobbler's lasts for shoemaking
laterarius	*La*	brick maker
lathamus, lathomus, latomus	*La Oc*	quarryman, mason
lathsplitter	*Oc*	made thins strips of wood (laths) for nailing to walls and ceilings as a base for plastering
laubeir, laubir, laubyr	*Sc*	labour
lauberar	*Sc*	labourer
lauds	*Sc*	midnight service of the Catholic Church
lau'll	*Sc*	abbreviation of 'lawful'
laundress	*Oc*	washerwoman
lautus	*La*	baptism, christening
lautus/a est	*La*	he/she was baptised
lavacrum	*La*	font
lavare	*La*	to wash, to baptise
lavatus est	*La*	he was baptised, washed
lave	*Sc*	rest
lavo	*La*	I baptise, wash
Law French	*Le*	original language of the English courts after the Norman Conquest
Law Merchant	*Le*	international commercial law; the law as it relates to merchant
law burrows	*Sc*	legal security, bound over to keep the peace
lawful (daughter or son)	*Sc*	legitimate, born in wedlock
lawman	*Oc*	officer with magisterial powers
lawn	*Sc*	fine linen, used to make sleeves etc.
lawrightman	*Oc*	controlled local weights and measures and land tax
laxfisher, laxfischer	*Sc*	salmon fisherman
lay by the heels	*Le*	commit to prison
leaf	*Pal*	single page of a book
lease	*Le*	special kind of contract between a property owner and a person wanting temporary enjoyment and exclusive use of the property, in exchange for rent paid to the property owner
leasehold	*Le*	real property held under a lease
leat	*Sc*	late

leather dresser	Sc	person who prepares leather for cutting
lecens	Sc	licence
lecturer	Sc	university teacher, instructor in a church
leerie	Oc	lamplighter (gas lamps)
leet	Sc	list of candidates for election
legator	Sc	the person to whom a legacy is left
legatour	Sc	only legatee
legged dollar	Sc	dollar of Liege; a Dutch coin, in which an armed man seems to have one leg, the other being hidden by his shield (about 1689–94)
legio	La	legion
legitim	Sc La Le	bairn's pairt of gear, child's share of a parent's moveable property on his death: one-third if there was a surviving spouse, otherwise half, but only applied after satisfaction of any other prior rights
legitimatus	La	legitimate
leid	Sc	folk
leillie & treullie	Sc	legally and honestly (in later testaments the word used was 'faithfully')
leispund	Sc	unit of weight for butter, oil, wool equal to 18 Scottish pounds
lengthsman	Oc	rail worker who maintained a length of track
lenth	Sc	length
lessee	Le	tenant, the person to whom exclusive possession of a thing is granted under the terms of a lease
lessor	Le	landlord; a person who grants a lease, usually the owner of the thing being leased
let	Sc	hindrance
letter carrier	Sc Oc	delivered letters by hand (later, postman)
letters	Sc	writ or warrant
letters close	Le	sealed or private letters
letters patent	Le	royal letters containing instructions or starting legal action, sent open and certified by a seal
lettrone	Sc	lectern, reading desk
levabat	La	he was holding, raising, lifting up
levans (levantes)	La	godparent(s)
levantibus	La	by the godparents
levare ex fonte	La	to raise from the baptismal font, to act as a godparent
levir	La	husband's brother, brother-in-law
lex non scripta	La Le	unwritten law; the common or custom law
lex situs	Le	conflict of law rule that selects the applicable law based on the venue or location of something
ley	Sc	lea, pasture land, unploughed land
liber	La	book, register, free
liber baptizatorum	La	baptismal register
liber defunctorum	La	death register

liber matrimoniorm	*La*	marriage register
liberi	*La*	children
libra	*La*	pound (weight); scales
libraire	*Sc*	bookseller
libri	*La*	books
license	*Le*	special permission to do something on, or with, somebody else's property, which, were it not for the license, could be legally prevented or give rise to legal action in tort or trespass
licentiat	*Sc*	licensed e.g. to practise medicine or law
licet	*La*	all right; (with dative + infinitive) it is right to
licet (conj.)	*La*	although, even if
lichnopeus	*La*	candle maker
lie	*Sc*	word used to introduce local names or any Scots word or phrase used in a Latin document
lieutenant	*Oc*	army or navy officer, below captain
lieutenant colonel	*Oc*	army rank below colonel
lieutenant general	*Oc*	army rank below major-general
lieutenant governor	*Oc*	deputy governor e.g. of a province, jail, castle etc.
liferent	*Sc*	ownership for life only, as opposed to fee (full ownership) and not to be passed on: it might be a sum of money paid yearly, or the income from a piece of land, or use of the land
liferenter	*Sc Le*	person who has the liferent, the right to live in and/or receive revenue from a property for life, but not to sell or dispose of it
ligati	*La*	marriage
ligati sunt	*La*	they were married, have been married
ligature	*Pal*	method of writing certain letter combinations in which two separate letters are joined into a new form, such as Æ
ligatus	*La*	married, joined, married person
ligatus/a est	*La*	he/she was joined or married
ligavi	*La*	I joined (in marriage)
lighterman	*Sc*	boatman, operator of a harbour lighter or barge
lignarius	*La*	cabinetmaker, joiner, woodworker
lignicidus	*La*	woodcutter
lime merchant	*Sc*	dealer in lime for use in fertiliser, cement, paint etc.
limmer	*Oc*	thief, scoundrel
limner	*Sc Oc*	portrait painter, artist who decorates (limns) manuscripts
lineator	*Oc*	surveyor, measurer
linen draper	*Sc*	linen seller
linen lapper, linen stamper	*Sc*	linen printer
linifex (linificis)	*La*	linen weaver

lint dresser, lint heckler	*Sc*	flax dresser
lintdresser	*Sc*	*see* flaxdresser
lint-wheel wright	*Sc*	maker of spinning wheels for flax spinning
liquidat	*Sc Le*	debts or other due payments fixed in advance at a definite sum, or having a monetary equivalent by decreet of court
lis pendens	*La*	dispute or matter that is the subject of ongoing or pending litigation
litherlie	*Sc*	idle
lithographer	*Oc*	made printing plates from typeset paper or film
litster	*Oc*	cloth dyer
litster, litstar, litser, lister	*Sc*	dyer
litster, littister	*Oc*	dyer
littet, littit	*Sc*	dyed
indweller	*Sc*	resident in Edinburgh, unless otherwise stated
lockit buik	*Sc*	locked book in which the names of burgesses were recorded on appointment
locksmith	*Sc*	maker and repairer of locks and keys
loco tutoris	*La*	in the role of a tutor (custodian or a minor)
locus	*La*	place
locus sigilli	*La*	where a person's seal is placed (on a document)
long tempore	*La*	for a long time
longum morbum	*La*	after a long illness
loon, loun	*Oc*	boy or young man (north-east Scotland); *see* quine
loosing arrestment	*Sc*	release from arrestment for debt when security is found
lord	*Sc*	1. title of a noble (peer); 2. honorific title given to a senior judge or administrator
Lord Clerk Register	*Sc*	senior judge
Lord Lyon King of Arms	*Sc*	chief officer of heraldry in Scotland
Lords of Council	*Sc*	king's council sitting as a court of law, before the Court of Session was instituted
lorimer	*Oc*	maker of metal parts for horse and ox harnesses etc.
lotter	*Oc*	1. one who batched odd lots of wool for sale; 2. croft or small farm divided into lots, usually worked by the crofter's sons
lous	*Sc*	loose
loused	*Sc*	closed (because when a shop, for instance, was 'loused' the workers were 'loosed'
lozenge cutter	*Oc*	cut and prepared sweets or preserves
lucre	*Le*	financial advantage taken in bad faith
ludgeing, ludgen, ludgin, ludgins	*Sc*	lodging, often the town house of a landed family as in Argyll's Ludgins, Stirling

ludimagister	La	schoolmaster, teacher
ludus	La	game, training school, jest
luggs	Sc	1. ears; 2. handles of a jug; 3. hinges
lugyng	Sc	temporary lodging
lunae, dies	La	Monday
lustratio	La	baptism, christening
lustrationis	La	of the baptism
lybel	Sc	1. libel; 2. indictment; 3. list e.g. 'these lybelled', items specified in a document
lyfrent	Sc	see liferent
lymeman, lymemaker	Sc	lime worker, lime mixer
M	Le	ancient common law: the symbol branded on the thumb of persons convicted of manslaughter
MS	Oc	1. male servant; 2. merchant service (seaman); 3. maiden surname
M.B.	Sc	merchant burgess; see 8 December 1500
MTC	Sc	minutes of town council
macellator	La	butcher
macer, messer, messor	Sc	mace bearer, usher in court or parliament
madder	Sc	dyestuff
magis	La	more
magister	Sc	Master (indicating a university graduate, a master of arts)
magister/i	La Le	master(s)
magistrate	Sc	local judge
magnus, magna	La	great, large
maii	La	of May
mail, maills and duties	Sc	mail is the Scots word for rent; maills and duties were the yearly rents of an estate due in money or grain
Maill	Le Sc	rent
maill, meall, meill	Sc	meal
maills	Sc	rent or payment (see house-maills)
mails (males)	Sc	feu duties, rents
mainprize	Le	taking of a person into friendly custody
mains, mayns	Sc	chief or home farm of an estate
maintenance	Le	obligation of one person to contribute, in part or in whole, to the cost of living of another person
mair	Sc	1. mare; 2. more
maister	Sc	master
major	Sc	army rank between captain and colonel, in charge of a battalion
major	La	greater, older
majorennis	La	of legal age

majores	*La*	ancestors
major general	*Sc*	army rank above lieutenant general
majoritatatis	*La*	of legal age, majority
make menyng	*Sc*	lament
male	*La*	badly
malis, mailings	*Sc*	small farms (rented)
malthouse	*Sc*	brewery
maltman, maltster	*Sc*	brewer
maltmill-maker	*Sc*	maker of mills for preparing malt
maltster, maltman, malter, maltmaker	*Sc Oc*	person who malts barley etc. for brewing or distilling
malus	*La*	bad, evil
man of weir	*Sc*	fighting man, soldier, warrior (weir = war)
mandate	*Le*	letter from an authority giving instructions or permission
mane	*La*	in the morning
manerium/i	*La*	manor(s)
manf.	*Oc*	manufacturer
mangler	*Oc*	washerwoman who wrung out clothes through a mangle
manor place	*Sc*	main mansion of an estate
mantua maker	*Oc*	bonnet maker
manu propria	*La*	by one's own hand (signed)
manumission	*Le*	act of freeing a slave
manus/us	*La*	hand(s)
manuscript	*Pal*	document or book transcribed by hand
mar. con.	*Le*	marriage contract
marable, marbole, marboll	*Sc*	marble
marasmus	*La*	weakness
marcat, mercat	*Sc*	market
marchand, marchant, merchan, mechant, merchand	*Sc Oc*	merchant, buyer and seller of goods
marchioness	*Sc*	wife of a marquis
mareit	*Sc*	married
marikin maker, marikin-maker	*Oc Sc*	maker of dressed goat's skin or Spanish (Moroccan) leather, called maroquin or marikin
mariner	*Sc*	sailor
maris	*La*	of a male, man
marita	*La*	married, wife
mariti	*La*	marriage, married couple
maritus	*La*	married, husband

mark or merk	Sc	1. silver coin worth 13s. 4d. (or two-thirds of a pound) Scots and therefore just over 1s. sterling at the time of the Union; 2. unit of valuation of land
marquis, marquess	Sc	rank of nobility between earl and duke
marriage contract	Sc	contract made between the husband or promised husband and the male relatives of the wife, made either before marriage ('ante-nuptial') or after ('post-nuptial')
marshall, marischall, marischal	Sc	officer of state or burgh official
martii	La	of March
martimonium	La	marriage
Martinmas, Mertinmas	Sc	11 November: one of the quarter, or term, days (with Lammas, Candlemas and Whitsunday), when contracts, leases, tacks and rents began and ended and when bills were settled
martis, dies	La	Tuesday
mas	La	male, man
mason masoun	Oc	stone cutter and layer
masser	La	macer
master	Oc	1. graduate (MA); 2. head schoolteacher; 3. qualified, self-employed craftsman or tradesman
master mariner	Oc	ship's captain
mater (matris)	La	mother
mater meretrix	La	mother of illegitimate child
matertera	La	maternal aunt, mother's sister
matrica	La	register, record book
matrimonium	La	marriage
matrimonium contraxerunt	La	they contracted marriage
matrina	La	godmother
matruelis	La	cousin on mother's side
mayhem	Le	violently depriving another person of a body part to render less effective that person's defence of self
me	La	me
mealmaker	Sc	oatmeal seller: also mailmaker, maillmaker, mealman, meilman, meilmane, mealmonger
mealwright	Sc	mill wright
measour	Sc	measure
measurer	Sc	official who weighs and measures goods for market, often taking a tithe in duty
mecum	La	with me
mediciner, medicinar	Sc	physician, apothecary
medicus	La	doctor
meeting house	Sc	dissenting place of worship (not Church of Scotland)

meil, meill, meall	*Sc*	measure of grain weight in the Northern Isles, equal to between 120–210lb
meinie	*Sc*	company
mell	*Sc*	associate with, or have dealings with
memell	*Sc*	fork handles
mendicant	*Oc*	beggar living on alms e.g. mendicant monks
mendicus	*La*	beggar
mense	*La*	in the month (of)
mensis	*La*	month
mercat	*Sc*	market
mercat cross	*Sc*	usually the main market square of a town, with a cross or pedestal to indicate this
mercator	*La*	merchant
mercatrix	*La*	female merchant
mercenarius	*La*	day labourer
merchet	*Le Sc*	payment made for obtaining permission for a daughter to marry
merchetum/i	*La Le*	merchet(s)
mercurii, dies	*La*	Wednesday
meretrix (meretricis)	*La*	harlot, prostitute
meridies	*La*	noon
merinell, marinell	*Sc*	mariner, sailor
merk	*Sc*	mark Scots, worth 3s 4d Scots; also measure of weight in Northern Isles = 18oz, 24 merks = 1 lispund *see* mark
merk land	*Sc*	land valued at 1 mark sterling
messinger, messanger	*Sc*	messenger
messor/oris	*La Le*	hayward(s)
messr	*Sc*	messenger
met and measour	*Sc*	mete (meter) and measure
metstar, metster	*Sc*	official measurer of goods or land for sale
meus/a/um	*La*	my, mine
meydvyf	*Sc*	midwife
Mic	*Le*	Michaelmas
mickle, meikle	*Sc*	small amount ('many a mickle mak's a muckle')
Middle English		English as spoken and written from around the fourteenth century
Middle Irish		Gaelic as used between 900 and 1200
Middle Scots		Scots as spoken and written from around the fourteenth century
midshipman	*Sc*	senior sailor
midwife	*Sc*	childbirth assistant, usually an older woman
miles (militis)	*La*	knight, soldier
millar, milner, mylner	*Sc*	miller

millar knaife, miln–knaif	*Sc*	undermiller
miller	*Oc*	in charge of a meal or grain mill
milliner	*Oc*	hat maker
millwright	*Oc*	mill builder or repairer
miln, milne, myl	*Sc*	mill
milnwright, miln–wright, mylne–wright	*Sc*	mill wright, mill builder
min., minr.	*Oc*	minister (or miner)
minchak, minschok	*Sc*	young nanny (female) goat
miner	*Oc*	worker at a mineral mine, usually coal, ironstone or shale
minim	*Pal*	vertical strokes of lower case letters in Gothic script: *n* has two minims and *m* has three
minimus/a natu	*La*	youngest
minister	*Sc*	ordained cleric (post Reformation)
minor	*Sc*	below the age of majority, child older than 12 if female or 14 if male, but still under the age of 21, although 'minority' also referred to the whole period from birth until 21: minors often had curators appointed to look after their affairs when young
minorennis	*La*	not of legal age
minoritatis	*La*	below legal age, minority
minstrall, menstraler	*Sc*	minstrel, musician
minus	*La*	less
mis	*Sc*	misadventure
miscegenation	*Le*	interracial cohabitation or marriage
misercordia/ae	*La Le*	amercement(s)
misprision	*Le*	offence of the most seriously punished crimes in the ancient common law of England
misprison, mispreson, misperson	*Sc*	1. slander; 2. conceal a crime as in 'misprision of murder'
modir	*Sc*	mother
modo	*La*	lately, now, presently
modo demum	*La*	only now, just now.
modus	*La*	manner, way
mola	*La*	mill
molitor	*La*	miller
moneta	*La*	money
moneyer	*Oc*	mintmaster, maker of coins
monger	*Oc*	seller of goods, e.g. fishmonger, ironmonger
monk	*Sc*	member of pre-Reformation Celtic, Catholic or Episcopalian religious order

mons (montis)	La	mountain
morbus	La	disease
more novo	La	(according to) the new style (of calendar)
more vetere	La	(according to) the old style (of calendar)
moritur	La	he/she died
mors, mortis	La	death
morsing horns	Sc	gunpowder flasks
mortcloth dues	Sc	money paid for the use of the public pall (death shroud) at a funeral
mortgage	Le	interest given on a piece of land, in writing, to guarantee the payment of a debt or the execution of some action
mortgagor	Le	person who borrows money secured by conceding a mortgage against his interest in real property
mortifyed money	Sc	money left by deceased persons for mortification (charity)
Mortmain Statutes	Le	statutes of ancient English law that prevented the transfer of real property to or from corporations in general, or to or from religious corporations in particular
mortuus, mortutuus	La	death
mortuus/a est	La	he/she died
mortuus/a/um	La	dead, deceased
mos (moris)	La	custom, manner
moss trooper	Sc	border marauder who regularly pillaged the English
moulder	Oc	poured molten metal into moulds
mouterer	Oc	fee received by miller for grinding corn etc.
movable	Le	civil law: things not attached to land and that may be carried from place to place
moveable property	Sc	as opposed to heritable, every type of property not land or connected with land
moyr	Sc	mother
Mr, Mgr	Oc	magister: a teacher or employer, or one with a university degree equivalent to an M.A.
mt	Oc	merchant
muck	Sc	dung, manure
muckle	Sc	large amount ('many a mickle mak's a muckle')
muir	Sc	moor
muis	Sc	bushels, measures
muked	Sc	mucked, manured
mulier	La	woman, wife
muller	Sc	moulded work such as a picture frame
multure, multour dewetie (=duty)	Sc	payment in grain and/or money to a mill owner for grinding; see astriction
multurer	Sc	collector of multure duty in a mill – also multerer, moulterer, moulturer, moulterer
multus	La	many

munitus	*La*	fortified, provided
music–seller	*Sc*	seller of sheet music and printed songs
musitiane, musicianer	*Sc*	musician
muskitt	*Sc*	armed with a musket, the rule being that 'anyone being made burgess must be sufficiently airmit with ane furnisht muskitt'
muslin singer	*Sc*	person employed in singeing the nap off muslin
mutchkin	*Sc*	¼ pint (Scots) equal to 1 pint English measure
mutuo consensu	*La*	by mutual consent
mutuus	*La*	common, mutual
myle	*Sc*	mile
mylne	*Sc*	mill
myre	*Sc*	marsh
myster	*Sc*	need, emergency
nb (*nota bene*)	*La*	note well, notice
nn (*nomen nescio*)	*La*	name unknown (I do not know the name)
nacket	*Sc*	1. scorer or marker at tennis, billiards etc.; 2. stone used in playing shinty; 3. pinch of snuff or tobacco
nackety	*Sc*	conceited, well dressed
nag, naig	*Sc*	horse
naigis	*Sc*	nags, small horses or ponies
nailer	*Oc*	blacksmith who made nails
napery, naperie, naprie	*Sc*	table linen, napkins
Na-Rent	*Sc*	*see* Abbot of Na-Rent
nascit	*La*	he/she is born
nat.	*Sc En*	natural
natales	*La*	birth
natalis	*La*	natal
nati	*La*	birth
nativitas	*La*	birth
natural fool	*Le*	human being in form but destitute of reason from birth
naturalis	*La*	natural, illegitimate
natus	*La*	birth
natus est	*La*	he was born
natus/a	*La*	born (adj.), son/daughter (noun)
natus/a est	*La*	he/she was born
nauta	*La*	sailor
navvie	*Oc*	navigator; canal and road digger
nec	*La*	neither, nor
necessitate baptismo	*La*	by emergency baptism

necessitatis	*La*	of necessity
neck verse	*Sc*	first verse of Psalm 51, which if read by a criminal on the scaffold, entitled him to have his life spared but be exiled
necnon	*La*	also, moreover, certainly, besides
need-fire	*Sc*	signal beacon
negotiator	*La*	merchant (commerce)
nemo (neminis)	*La*	no one
nempe	*La*	to be sure, of course
neosponsus/a	*La*	newlywed
nepos (nepotis)	*La*	nephew, grandson
nepos ex fil	*La*	grandson
nepos ex fratre	*La*	brother's son
nepos ex sorore	*La*	sister's son
neptis	*La*	niece, granddaughter
neque	*La*	and not
nescit	*La*	he doesn't know
neuo	*Sc*	nephew
niger	*La*	black
night soil carrier	*Oc*	remover of toilet waste
nihil	*La*	nothing
nisi	*La*	if not
nobilis	*La*	noble
nobilitatis	*La*	of nobility
nobmaker	*Sc*	maker of hard shoe tips
nocte	*La*	at night
Nolle Prosequi	*La Le*	no prosecution
nolt driver	*Sc*	cattle drover
noltherd, nolthird	*Sc*	cattleherd
nolts' tongues	*Sc*	cow tongues
nomen	*La*	name, given name
nomen nescio (nn)	*La*	name not known
nominatus est	*La*	he was named
nomine	*La*	by/with the name (of)
non	*La*	not, no
non numquam	*La*	sometimes
nonagenarius	*La*	person in his/her 90s
nondum	*La*	not yet
nonentry maills (gift of)	*Sc*	rents of lands in the possession of the superior until the heir can take possession
nones	*La*	fifth or seventh day of month; *see* Chapter 3

nonnullus/a/um	*La*	some, several
Norman French	*En*	form of French spoken by the Normans; *see* Anglo-Norman
northt, northin	*Sc*	northern
northtest	*Sc*	northeast, northeasterly
nortuest	*Sc*	northwest, northwesterly
nos	*La*	we, us
noster	*La*	our
not adeill	*Sc*	not at all
not instrument	*Le*	notarial instrument, drawn up by a notary
nota bene (nb)	*La*	note well, notice, take heed
notar, noter, notary	*Sc Le*	notary, notary public, someone licensed to record legal transactions
notarial docket	*Sc Le*	notary's certificate at the foot of a document
notarial instrument	*Sc Le*	deed drawn up by a notary
notarial symbol	*Sc Le*	sign or seal used by a notary
notarius	*La Le*	notary
notary	*Oc Le*	lawyer, solicitor able to notarise documents, official qualified to draw up legal documents and certify them by signature and colophon
nothus	*La*	illegitimate child
novembris	*La*	of November
noverca	*La*	stepmother
novodamus	*La Le*	new grant of land, renewal of a feudal grant by charter, often with some amendments or additions (eiks)
nox	*La*	night
nudius	*La*	earlier
nudius terius	*La*	three days earlier
nudius tertius	*La*	three days earlier
nuisance	*Le*	excessive or unlawful use of one's property to the extent of unreasonable annoyance or inconvenience to a neighbour or to the public
nulloque detecto impedimento matrimonio	*La*	and no hindrance to the marriage having been discovered
nullus/a/um	*La*	no, none
numerus	*La*	number
nunc	*La*	now, at this time
nunc dies tertius	*La*	three days earlier
nunc temporis	*La*	of the present time
nunquam	*La*	never
nuntius	*La*	messenger
nuper	*La*	recently, lately (sometimes of a deceased person)
nupserunt	*La*	they married
nupta	*La*	married woman, bride

nupti	*La*	marriage
nuptias	*La*	wedding
nuptus/a	*La*	married
nurseryman	*Sc*	worker in a plant nursery
nurus/a	*La*	son's wife, daughter-in-law
nusquam	*La*	nowhere
nutritor	*La*	foster father
nutrius	*La*	foster child
nutrix (nutricis)	*La*	foster mother
nux	*La*	nut
nychtbour	*Sc*	neighbour
oakum worker	*Oc*	took old ropes apart for the hemp fibre (oakum) to be used for caulking
oastlair	*Sc Oc*	ostler, innkeeper
ob	*La*	on account of, for, according to
ob (prep.)	*La*	before, in front of; on account of, because of; for the sake of; instead of; in proportion to
ob imminens mortis periculum	*La*	on account of imminent danger of death (as with emergency baptism)
ob rem	*La*	to the purpose, usefully
obdormitus est	*La*	he fell asleep, died
obierunt	*La*	they died, have died
obiit	*La*	he/she died, went away, departed
obiit sine prole	*La*	died without issue
obitus	*La*	death, died
oblig.	*Le*	obligation
obligement	*Sc*	bond, obligation
obolus/i	*La Le*	halfpenny(ies)
obstetrix (obstetricis)	*La*	midwife
occupation	*Oc*	description
oct.	*Sc En*	octave (day a week later)
octobris	*La*	of October
octogenarius	*La*	person in his/her 80s
odal	*Sc*	udal, having no fuedal superior
oeconimus	*Sc*	steward, manager, bursar
officialis	*La*	official
oil leather-dresser	*Sc*	preparer of leather
Old English		English as spoken and written before and just after 1066
Old Irish		form of the Gaelic language as it was used between AD 600 and 900
Old Scots		Scots as spoken and written up to the mid-1500s, overlapping with Early Scots (qv)
olim	*La*	once; of old; one day

olim	*La*	formerly, once (sometimes of a deceased person)
omissa	*Sc Le*	items that had been originally omitted from the deceased's estate
omnia bene	*La Le*	all is well
omnibus sacramentis provisis	*La*	(he/she) was given all the last rites
omnis	*La*	all, every
on life	*Sc*	still alive, e.g. only bairn on life (only surviving child)
on-delyverit	*Sc*	undelivered
onleful	*Sc*	unlawful
onus/eris	*La Le*	charge(s) (in accounts)
operarius	*La*	day labourer
oppidum	*La*	city, town
orbus/a	*La*	orphan
ordinans, ordinance	*Sc*	order
ordinar, cordiner	*Sc Oc*	cordwainer; shoemaker
originis	*La*	of the birth
origo (originis)	*La*	origin, birth
oriundus	*La*	birth, originating (from), born
orphanus	*La*	orphan
orraman	*Oc*	odd-job man
orris weaver	*Oc*	maker of gold or silver lace
orthography	*Pal*	form of a document, art or study of correct spelling and established usage
ortus	*La*	origin, birth
oslair	*Sc*	ostler, innkeeper
ost	*Sc*	host
ostler	*Oc*	one who looks after horses at an inn; *see* hostler, oastler
oukis	*Sc*	weeks
oure	*Sc*	over
our-gilt	*Sc*	overgilt, gilded over, gilt-edged
ourman	*Oc*	overseer
outbrecks	*Sc*	barren land not worth cultivating
outfeild	*Sc*	outlying and less fertile part of a farm, where the ground was hardly or never cultivated (before enclosure and crop rotation in the eighteenth century)
outred	*Sc*	finish off, complete
outreddar	*Sc*	person who fits out a ship ready for a voyage or unloads it of cargo in port
outsicht or outsight plenishing	*Sc*	moveable property kept or lying out of doors: livestock and implements such as ploughs, but not corn or hay; *see* insicht
outworker	*Oc*	employed at outdoor work
overman	*Oc*	colliery supervisor

overman, oversman, oursman	Sc	overseer
ovilius	La	shepherd
ovis	La	sheep
ower	Sc	over
oxengate of land	Sc	13 acres
oxgang	Sc	measure of land generally about 13 acres
oy, oye, oe	Sc	grandson, granddaughter, sometimes niece, nephew or other descendant
P	Sc Oc	prentice (apprentice)
PLW	Oc	power-loom weaver in a textile mill
PR	Sc Le	particular register (of sasines)
pacatio	La	payment
packman	Sc	pedlar, chapman, travelling merchant
paenarium	La	pantry
paene	La	almost, nearly
pagina	La	page
pagus	La	district, village
pain	Le	rule/regulation of the manor
pairt	Sc	part, portion, share of an estate
pairts and pertinents	Sc	what a piece of land was always granted with, everything connected with the land whether specified or not
paitlet, paytellat	Sc	woman's ruff
palaeography	Pal	study of the form of older handwriting
palatium	La	palatinate
palfurniour, palfurner	Sc	groom, person with care of horses
palimpsest	Pal	manuscript which has been reused by scraping off the original text and overwriting it
pand, pane	Sc	draperies for a bed, e.g. counterpane
panifex	La	baker
panter	Sc	painter
Panton heel maker, pantoun-heilmaker	Sc	maker of heels for soft shoes, slippers etc.
papa	La	pope
papal bull	Le	legal document issued under the authority of the Pope; *see* bulla
paper stainer	Sc	paper colourer
par.	Sc En	parish
parapris	Sc	paraphrase
parchment	Pal	writing membrane made of animal skin; *see* vellum
parchment maker	Sc	preparer of skins for parchment
parentes	La	parents

pariochialis	*La*	parochial, parish
pariter	*La*	equally, also
park	*Le*	area of land set aside for passive common use, where certain types of activities are restricted, to permit individuals to escape the intensity of urban life
paroch, parochin	*Sc*	parish
parochia	*La*	parish
parochiner, parochinar	*Sc*	parishioner
parochus	*La*	parish priest
pars (partis)	*La*	area, region
parson, person, farson	*Sc*	parish clergyman (pre-Reformation)
partibus	*La*	part, share, portion, piece; region, direction, role, party, faction, side
partus	*La*	birth, childbirth
parvulus	*La*	very little, small
parvus	*La*	little
pasment	*Sc*	passement, decorative border on cloth or lace
pasment–weifar	*Sc*	weaver of passement, decorative border on cloth or lace
passenger	*Sc*	1. traveller; 2. ferryman
pastor	*La*	pastor, shepherd
patent rolls	*Le*	rolls in the Chancery (England) where copies of letters patent were recorded
pater (patris)	*La*	father
pater familias	*La*	head of family or household
paticer, pothisar	*Sc*	pastry cook
patres	*La*	ancestors, forefathers
patria	*La*	fatherland, native land
patrinus/a/i	*La*	godfather/godmother/godparents
patris familias	*La*	head of family or household
patruelis	*La*	cousin on father's side
patruerlis	*La*	paternal nephew
patrui relicta	*La*	paternal uncle's widow
patruus	*La*	paternal uncle
pattern maker	*Oc*	maker of metal patterns and moulds for iron casting
pattesier	*Oc*	pastry cook
patton (or panton) heel maker	*Oc*	maker of heels for slippers
pauper	*La Oc*	without money or means of livelihood, reliant on poor relief
pavier, pavior	*Sc Oc*	street paver, layer of pavement slabs and flagstones
pax (pace)	*La*	peace
pease	*Sc*	peas, a porridge or broth made of peas

peces	*Sc*	1. pieces, title deeds; 2. any article considered alone
pedagog	*Sc*	teacher
pedall, peddel, beddal	*Sc*	beadle, a church or university officer
pedegogus	*La*	teacher
pedlar	*Oc*	door-to-door seller of small goods
pekis	*Sc*	pecks (measure)
pellio	*La*	bonnet maker
pelliparius	*La*	furrier
pena/ae	*La Le*	pain/penalty
pendicle	*Sc*	appurtenance, often a small portion of land added to a larger
pendicler	*Sc*	tenant of a pendicle, smallholder with some grass and arable land
penny land	*Sc*	unit of land value for taxation purposes
penny-pie baker	*Sc*	maker and street seller of small pies
pensioner	*Oc*	person in receipt of a pension, originally after army service
penult	*La*	the last but one, next to last
peper	*Sc*	paper
per	*La*	through, by means of
per infortunium	*La Le*	by misadventure
per subsequens matrimonium legitimatus	*La*	legitimised by subsequent marriage
per tout et non my	*Fr Le*	as to the whole and not just a part
peregrinus	*La*	foreign, strange
perendi (or perendie)	*La*	day after tomorrow
perfecit	*La*	he/she completed, did
periit	*La*	he/she perished, died
peritus	*La*	death, deceased, dead
peritus est	*La*	he died
periwig, peir-weik, pirivick, peruke	*Sc*	gentleman's wig
periwig maker	*Oc*	gentleman's wig maker; *also* peir-weik maker, pirivick-maker, peruke-maker
perquisitum/i	*La Le*	profit(s)
personalty	*Le*	personal property, chattels, goods, property other than real property
pertaining in heritage	*Sc*	belonging to someone as heir
pertinentia/ae	*La Le*	appurtenance(s)
peste, pestelens	*Sc*	pestilence, plague
pestis	*La*	plague
petar	*Sc*	petard, explosive charge in a box, firework
petition	*Le*	document directed to an authority initiating legal action to arbitrate a complaint against another, also called a bill

petitioner	Sc	someone who brings an action in court
petivit admitti tenens	La Le	he petitioned to be admitted tenant
peto/ere	La Le	to claim
peuterer	Oc	worker in pewter, also pewterer, pewder-man, pewderer, pewdirer, peutherer, peuterer, peutrar, pewtherer, putherer
philosophical instrument maker	Oc	maker of scientific and astronomical instruments
phthisis	La	consumption, tuberculosis
pictor	La	painter
pie	La	piously
piece, the piece	Sc	each
piecer	Oc	mill worker who joined threads broken by spinning
pieman	Sc	pie street seller
pier master	Sc	harbour master
pigator	La	dyer
pikar	Oc	petty thief
pikman	Sc	miner who uses a pick
pilearius, pileator	La	hat maker
pilgit	Sc	argument, fight, quarrel
pillory	Le	medieval punishment and restraining device made of moveable and adjustable boards through which a prisoner's head or limbs were pinned
pilot	Sc	boatman who guides vessels into or out of harbour
pinder	Le	kept the manorial pound/pinfold
pinut	Sc	pint
pipemaker	Sc	maker of water or drainage pipes
piper, pyper	Sc	bagpipe player
pirn winder	Oc	mill worker who threaded yarn onto bobbins (pirns)
piscarius	La	fishmonger
piscator	La	fisherman
pisces	La	fish
pissanis	Sc	pisane, armour for chest and neck (from Pisa)
pistolat	Sc	1. small pistol; 2. coin (pistole)
pistor	La	baxter, baker (Sc)
pit brusher	Oc	repaired coal mine roofs and sides
pit roadman	Oc	preparing and repaired coal mine passageways
pitheadman	Oc	coal mine (pit) worker above ground
pius	La	pious
pl.	Le	plaintiff
plag	Sc	plague
plain	Sc	open, flat country or field of battle

plantation of kirks	Sc	farmland, orchards etc. providing goods and revenue for one or more parish churches; *see* Glebe
planter	Sc	plantation worker (tobacco, sugar or tea in the West Indies)
plat	Le	subdivision map prepared for approval by a governmental authority
platelayer	Oc	railway worker who laid and repaired rails
plea rolls	Le Eng	transcription of the proceedings of the courts of common law
plegius	La	surety, cautioner
plenishing insight	Sc	furniture in a house
plenishing outsight	Sc	farm or estate stock, implements etc. but not sown crops
plenishings	Sc	furniture and other moveable goods
plet slevis	Sc	pleated sleeves
pleugh	Sc	plough
plewman	Oc	ploughman
pley	Sc	plea, complaint in law
ploughgate	Sc	measure of land, 8 oxgangs or about 100 acres
ploughwright	Sc	plough maker
plumber	Oc	worked with lead on roofs, water pipes etc.
plutus	La	baptism, christening; baptised, sprinkled
pm'es, promes	Sc	promise, oath
pnt.	Sc	present
pntlie	Sc	presently
pnts	Sc	presents (meaning documents and evidence presented)
pocing iron	Sc	poker
pocket book	Sc	wallet
pointsman	Oc	railway worker who operated points
pok	Sc	pocket
polentarius	Oc	malt maker
policy, policies	Sc	lands, gardens and pleasure grounds surrounding a mansion or farmhouse
pomerid (post meridiem)	La	afternoon (p.m.)
pons (pontis)	La	bridge
pony driver	Oc	led ponies pulling coal hutches underground
pookman	Sc	porter
popula	La	people
por, port	Sc Le	portioner, *qv*
port	Sc	martial musc played on the bagpipes
porter	Sc	1. carrier, servant, caddie, gate keeper; 2. stout ale
porter dealer	Sc	buyer and seller of porter stout (a beer)
portion natural	Sc	share a child has in the estate of an intestate father
portioner, portiner	Sc Le	inheritor of a share of land jointly (usually daughters or their heirs)

post	La	after
post boy	Oc	guard travelling on a mail coach
post meridiem, (p.m.)	La	after noon (p.m.)
post-nupt. mar. con.	Le	post-nuptial marriage contract
post partum	La	after childbirth
post, toun post	Sc	letter deliverer
postea	La	afterwards
posterus	La	following
posthumus	La	born after death of father
postman	Oc	deliverer of mail (letters and parcels)
postmodum	La	afterwards; presently
postridie	La	on the day after, a day later
pot iron	Sc	iron pot stand
potter	Sc	maker of clay or earthenware pots, jugs etc.
potticar, pottefar	Sc	apothecary
potuit	La	could
poultrie-man, pultriman	Sc	poultryman, person who takes care of hens, ducks, geese and other domestic birds and fowls
poynding, poinding	Sc	(pronounced 'pinding') seizing (attaching) lands or goods to discharge a debt
pr. chan.	Sc Le	precept furth of chancery (similar to clare constat but where the Crown was the superior)
pr. cl. con.	Sc Le	precept of clare constat
praemunire	Le	offence initially to prefer the pope or his authority as against the King of England or Parliament, but later included a wide assortment of offenses against the king and always leading to serious penalties
praeterea	La	besides, moreover; hereafter
pranter	Sc	printer
preacher	Sc	religious exhorter
prebend	Sc	1. churchman's stipend; 2. land, tithe or other source of a stipend, cathedral benefice, usually the revenue from one manor of the cathedral estates to provide a living for one cathedral canon; see prebendary
prebendary, prebenter	Oc	cathedral canon maintained by a prebend, canon or member of the chapter of a cathedral or collegiate church who holds a stipend (pre-Reformation or Episcopal)
precentor, precenter, presenter	Sc	leader of singing in church
precept	Le	order issued to the bailiff of the manor for the holding of a court
preceptor, praeceptor	La	teacher, instructor
predefunctus	La	previously deceased (e.g. before the birth of a child)
predictus	La	aforesaid
prefatus	La	aforesaid

prefectus	*La*	magistrate
pregnata	*La*	pregnant
premises liability	*Le*	liability of an occupier of real property towards injury to others
premissus	*La*	published previously (e.g. marriage banns)
prenobilis	*La*	esteemed, honorable, respected
prentice	*Sc*	apprentice
prentice master	*Sc*	qualified craftsman looking after an apprentice
prepositus/i	*La Le*	reeve(s)
presbytery, presbetrie	*Sc*	court of the ministers and elders of a district overseeing several parishes
presens (presentis)	*La*	present, in attendance
presentatio/onis	*La Le*	presentment(s)
presenter of signatures	*Sc*	official in the Court of Exchequer
presentment	*Le*	statement by the jury of matters to be dealt with by the manorial court
presents	*Sc*	things, usually documents, presented to make a case, as in 'by these presents'
preter	*La*	besides, also, past, beyond
pretor	*La*	village mayor
pretorium	*La Le*	tolbooth
pridie	*La*	(on) the day before
pridie	*La*	the day before
priest	*Sc*	ordained churchman (pre-Reformation, Catholic or Episcopalian)
primare, primer	*Sc*	principal of college or university
primary source	*Pal*	writings of a contemporary author or first-hand witness, or an original document
primme	*Sc*	first, main, prime
primus, primum	*La*	first or firstly
princeps	*La*	prince
principal	*Sc*	academic in charge of school, college or university
principatus	*La*	principality
prinll	*Sc*	abbreviation of principal
print compositor	*Oc*	set up type for printing
print cutter	*Oc*	maker of printing blocks
printfield worker	*Oc*	mill worker who printed cloth with dyes and inks
prior	*Oc*	head of a priory for men
priores	*La*	ancestors
prioress	*Sc*	head of a priory for women
priory	*Sc*	religious house, monastery, nunnery
prisar	*Sc*	apprisor, appraiser, one who apprises and puts goods etc. up for sale to pay a creditor
prisit	*Sc*	apprised

private charter	*Le*	legal document or grant of rights raised by an individual rather than by an authority
privateer	*Sc*	private fighting ship with a commission from the government
privignus/a	*La*	stepson/stepdaughter
privy seal	*Sc Le*	one of the royal secretariats to forward instructions to the Chancery; a lesser or private seal; *see* great seal
pro	*La*	for, on behalf of, as far as
pro indiviso	*La*	undivided
pro tempore	*La*	for (at) the time
proavus/a	*La*	great grandfather/great grandmother
probationer	*Sc*	Church of Scotland minister not yet ordained
proc. resig.	*Sc Le*	procuratory of resignation
proces	*Sc*	legal proceedings
proclamatio	*La*	bann, decree
proclamationis/es	*La*	decree(s), marriage bann(s)
procr	*Sc Le*	procurator (legal official)
procreat	*Sc*	begotten
procul	*La*	far off
procurator	*Sc La Oc*	1. lawyer in lower courts; 2. person authorised to act on behalf of another to manage his affairs, so a solicitor or law agent
procurator-fiscal	*Sc Le Oc*	originally a solicitor with responsibility for the 'fiscal' or treasury; now the main law offer in a burgh or sheriffdom, public prosecuter in criminal cases and also the equivalent of coroner
professor	*Sc*	senior academic in a college or university
profit à prendre	*Fr Le*	servitude that resembles an easement and that allows the holder to enter the land of another and to take some natural produce such as mineral deposits, fish or game, timber, crops or pasture
progenitus	*La*	firstborn
proinde (adv.)	*La*	consequently, therefore; just as
proles	*La*	child
proles	*La*	child, issue, offspring (gender not stated)
proles spuria	*La*	illegitimate child
promulgationis	*La*	decree, bann
proneptus	*La*	grand niece
prope	*La*	near, close to
property	*Le*	comprehensive collection of legal rights over a thing
propinqui	*La*	relations, relatives
proport	*Sc*	purport, intend, convey
propriis manibus	*La*	by his (or her) own hand
propter	*La*	because of, near
propterea	*La*	for that reason, therefore
propyn	*Sc*	gift or present

prorsus/um (adv.)	*La*	forwards; absolutely; in short
prosecution of signatures	*Sc*	following or obtaining a signature (*see* signature)
prosocrus	*La*	wife's grandmother
protocol	*Sc*	first copy of an instrument, written by a notary in a protocol book
protomedicus	*Sc*	main doctor
prout	*La*	as, accordingly, according as
prove	*Sc*	attempt
provincia	*La*	province
provisus	*La*	provided (with)
provost	*Sc Oc*	elected head and chief magistrate of a town or burgh council, equivalent to (English) mayor
proximo, prox.	*La*	of the next month
proximus	*La*	previous, preceding
proximus consanguineus	*La*	nearest relation
prydit, provydit	*Sc*	provided
publican	*Oc*	keeper of a public house (pub) selling ales, wines and spirits
puddler	*Oc*	iron worker operating a puddling or ball furnace to turn cast iron into wrought iron
pudicus/a	*La*	chaste, upright, virginal
puella	*La*	girl
puer	*La*	boy, child
puera	*La*	girl
puerperium	*La*	childbirth
pultreman	*Sc Oc*	poultryman
puncheons	*Sc*	tunnel props in mining
pund	*Sc*	pound Scots, worth one-fifth of an English pound sterling from 1560 and one-twelfth (1s 8d) from 1603
pundis	*Sc*	pounds (monetary)
pundler	*Sc*	weighing machine using weights and a lever
punzoun	*Sc*	small company
pupil	*Sc*	1. minor (under 14 if male, 12 if female) whose affairs were managed by a tutor; 2. schoolchild
pupilarity	*Sc*	being a pupil (a minor under 14 years old if male, 12 if female)
purgatus	*La*	baptism, christening
purgatus/a	*La*	baptised, cleansed, purged
purring iron	*Sc*	poker
purs	*Sc*	purse
purser	*Sc*	administrative officer and money keeper on a ship
pursue, persew	*Sc*	prosecute a lawsuit
pursuer	*Sc*	plaintiff, complainer in a court case

pursuivant	*Sc*	member of an heraldic court of the rank below herald
puta	*La*	reputed, supposed
pynour	*Sc*	labourer, porter, caddie
q	*Sc*	abbreviation for con; e.g. qsents = consents
qrof	*Sc*	whereof
qua (adv.)	*La*	where, as far as, how; qua … qua
quaestor	*La*	treasurer, paymaster
quaiffmaker, queffmaker	*Sc*	cap or soft-hat maker
quair	*Sc*	quire, book
qualibit	*La*	anywhere, any way, as you please
quails/ -e	*La*	what sort of, what kind of, such as, as
qualiter (adv.)	*La*	how, as, just as
quam	*La*	how, as much as
quam (adv.)	*La*	how, how much; as, very
quam ob rem	*La*	wherefore, accordingly
quamdiu	*La*	as long as; while; inasmuch as
quamquam	*La*	although
quamvis (adv.)	*La*	however
quamvis (conj.)	*La*	although
quando	*La*	when, (after *nisi, ne*) ever
quando (conj.)	*La*	when, since, because
quandoque (adv.)	*La*	at some time
quandoque (conj.)	*La*	whenever, as often as, since
quanto	*La*	for how much
quantum (adv.)	*La*	as much as, as far as, so much as, to what extent
quantum ad	*La*	in terms of; as far as x is concerned; with respect to
quantus	*La*	how great, how much
quapropter	*La*	wherefore
quare	*La*	by what means, how; why, wherefore
quarrier	*Oc*	worker in stone quarry
quariour, quarriour, querrior	*Sc*	quarry worker, quarrier
quarter day	*Sc*	Candlemas, Lammas, Martinmas and Whitsunday, the days on which contracts, leases, tacks and rents began and ended and when bills were settled
quartermaster	*Sc*	person in charge of supplies in the army, a guild etc.
quartis	*La*	fourth
quasi	*La*	as if, as though
quasi	*La*	almost, as if
quatenus (adv.)	*La*	(*interrog.*) how far, how long? (*rel.*) as far as, in so far as, since
que	*La*	and (as a suffix, e.g. paterque, and the father)

Queen's Bench	*Le*	Originally, the common criminal court of the common law; later, the general superior court
quemadmodum (adv.)	*La*	in what way, how
quemadmodum (conj.)	*La*	as, just as
quey, quoy, coy	*Sc*	heifer
quh	*Sc*	read as 'wh', e.g. Cuneoquhy = Kennoway; quhar = where
quha	*Sc*	who
quhair, quhar	*Sc*	where
quhairbe	*Sc*	whereby
quhairin	*Sc*	wherein
quhais	*Sc*	whose
quham	*Sc*	whom
quhar	*Sc*	where
quharfor	*Sc*	wherefore
quhatsomevir	*Sc*	whatever, whatsoever
quheill	*Sc*	while
quheilwright	*Sc Oc*	wheelwright
quheit	*Sc*	white
quhen	*Sc*	when
quherin	*Sc*	wherein
quhiddir	*Sc*	whether
quhil	*Sc*	while (in the sense of 'until')
quhilk, whilk	*Sc*	which
quhome	*Sc*	whom
quhou	*Sc*	how
quhoubeit	*Sc*	howbeit, howsoever
quhy	*Sc*	why
quhyle	*Sc*	while
qui, quae, quod	*La*	who, which, what
Quia Emptores	*Le*	1290 English statute that held that notwithstanding the subdivision (subinfeudation) of a feeholding, the new tenant owed feudal rights and obligations not to the seller but to the landlord; this more or less ended subinfeudation in England
quick	*Sc*	alive
quick take	*Le*	formal process of the exercise of eminent domain in which the government takes possession before the adjudication of compensation
quicquam	*La*	anything
quicquid plantatur solo, solo cedit	*La Le*	whatever is planted in the ground, belongs to the ground
quicumque/quae-/ quod-	*La*	whoever, whatever; all that, any whatever

quidam, quaedam, quodam (or quoddam)	*La*	a certain person (male/female) or thing
quidam/quae-/quid-	*La*	a certain one, someone, a kind of
quidem	*La*	indeed, in fact
quiet enjoyment	*Le*	landlord's obligation to provide the tenant with reasonable privacy and freedom from any interference with the tenant's exclusive use and enjoyment of the rented premises
quin, quindene	*La*	a day two weeks later
quine	*Sc*	young woman (queen) (north-east Scotland) *see* loon
quippe (adv.)	*La*	certainly, of course
quippe (conj.)	*La*	(*explaining*) for in fact, because, since
quisquam quid-	*La*	anyone, anything
quisque quidque	*La*	each, each one, every
quisquis/quisquid	*La*	whoever, whatever; all
quo	*La*	where, what for, to what end
quoad	*La*	as to, with respect to
quocumque	*La*	how so ever; wither so ever
quod	*Sc*	quoth, said
quod	*La*	because
quod (conj.)	*La*	because, as far as, in so far as, as for the fact that, in that, that
quod si	*La*	but if
quodamodo	*La*	in a way
quomodo	*La*	how, in what way; (*rel.*) as, just as
quondam	*La*	once, sometimes, formerly
quondam	*La*	former or deceased
quoniam	*La*	because, since, seeing that, now that
quoque	*La*	also, too
quot	*La*	how many; (*conj.*) as many
quot	*Sc*	twentieth part of the moveable estate of a deceased person, originally due to the local bishop but paid to the commissaries after the Reformation
quotiens	*La*	how often; (*rel.*) as often as
quoy, quoyland	*Sc*	1. enclosure; 2. piece of land brought into cultivation from outside a hill dyke
quyt of entry	*Sc*	quit of entry, having paid fees due to a superior on inheriting lands
RCC	*Oc*	Roman Catholic Clergyman
RN	*Oc*	Royal Navy
r.	*Sc*	right (eg. be r. of = by right of)
rabut	*Sc*	repulse, rebate
rack	*Le*	medieval form of punishment or confession extractor in which the subject was affixed to a wooden platform and separate ropes were attached to each of his four limbs, which were then pulled apart by a system of pulleys
racken	*Sc*	reckon

raising letters	Sc	taking out legal summons
ranking, process of	Sc	system for arranging creditors in order of precedence for payment
ranselman	Oc	empowered by a court to search houses for stolen property
rapina	La Le	to take away forcefully
rase	Sc	rash, uncouth
ratif	Le	ratification
ratsche	Sc	lock (powder tray) of a gun
raxes	Sc	chain on which a roasting spit is turned over a fire
reader	Oc	teacher of law, medicine, classics etc.
reader, reider	Sc	1. reader in church; 2. member of university ranked between senior lecturer and professor
real estate	Le	same as real property; land and rights attached to land
real obligation	Le	legal obligation associated with real property
real property	Le	property interest in land
rear–admiral	Sc	admiral's deputy in charge of a fleet
receiver general	Sc	senior customs official
recepta/ae	La Le	money(ies) received
recognito	La	examination, inquest by jury
record	Sc	repute, account
recorder	Le	ancient judicial position in the legal history of England and Wales, now mostly a part-time judicial appointment given to practising barristers or solicitors in England and Wales
recte	La	rightly, correctly
recto	Pal	right–hand side of a double page, or front of a folio, in a book, abbreviated as 'r'; *see dorso, verso*
rector	Sc	1. head schoolmaster; 2. senior clergyman in charge of a college, religious house, or congregation (Catholic) and in receipt of tithes (Episcopal); 3. member of university court elected by the students
rectus	La	right, direct
red leader	Oc	painter of red lead-oxide paint onto metal surfaces
reddendo	Sc	(literally) returning: what the feu superior could expect from the vassal in exchange for the grant of land and protection, in the form of military service, provision of men and equipment, payment of rent in cash or kind (feu duty) etc. Changes in the law of feudal tenure after the 1745 Jacobite Rebellion restricted this to the annual payment of feu duty
reddendum, reddendo	La Le	part of a lease setting out the amount of rent and when it is payable
rede	Sc	counsel, advice
reedmaker, reidmaker, redemaker	Sc Oc	1. maker of reeds for musical instruments; 2. arrow maker
reeler	Oc	mill worker who put yarns onto reels for weaving
reeve	Le	'foreman' of the manor
reft	Sc	bereft

refut	*Sc*	defence, stronghold
regality	*Sc*	territorial jurisdiction granted by the Crown, whereupon the holder is styled lord of the regality with powers to hold courts, impose sentences etc.; (*see* barony, sheriffdom)
regeneratus est	*La*	he was baptised
regent	*Sc Oc*	1. ruler or administrator of a country during the minority, or incapacity of the sovereign; 2. senior teacher or administrator in certain schools or universities
Regiam Majestatem	*La Le*	ancient compendium of Scottish law; *c.* 1320
regimine pedestre	*La*	infantry regiment
regina	*La*	queen
registrar, register	*Sc*	official who keeps registers of births, marriages, deaths, wills and other documents
registrum	*La*	index, list
regius	*La*	royal
regnum	*La*	kingdom
regrating	*Le*	buying of food products at a market not for demonstrable personal need, but for the purposes of resale at the same market, or one nearby
reidare	*Oc*	reader, lesser clergyman in early church
relict	*Sc Le*	widow or widower
relictus/a	*La*	widower/ widow
religio (religionis)	*La*	religion
relinquit	*La*	he/she left behind, abandoned
remanent	*Sc*	remaining
ren	*Le*	renunciation
renanus	*La*	of the Rhine
renatus	*La*	baptism, christening
renatus/a est	*La*	he/she was baptised
rent	*Le*	money or other consideration paid by a tenant to a landlord in exchange for the exclusive use and enjoyment of land, a building or a part of a building
rental	*Le En*	list of manorial tenants with acreages and rents to be paid
renunciation	*Sc*	1. renouncing a right or a title to property, redeeming a debt etc.; 2. deed by which this is enacted
repertorium	*La*	index, list
replevin	*Le*	legal action taken to reclaim goods that have been distrained
reponit reponed	*Sc*	replaced
requiescat in pace	*La*	may he/she rest in peace
resetter	*Oc*	receiver, concealer or 'fence' of stolen goods
resiant	*Le*	resident of a manor
residenter	*Sc*	inhabitant (of somewhere)
residenter, resinder, resider	*Sc*	resident, inhabitant
residential tenancy	*Le*	lease of residential premises for residential purposes

resig. ad. rem.	*La*	*resignation ad remanentiam*
resignation	*Sc*	return of a feu by a vassal to the superior, either permanently, or *in favorem*, where the intention was that the superior should make a new grant, as when land was sold
ressaver	*Sc*	receiver
resting	*Sc*	remaining due, owing
restio	*La*	rope maker
restrictive covenant	*Le*	contract in which a party agrees to be restricted in some regards as to future conduct
rests	*Sc*	arrears
ret. gen. serv.	*Le Sc*	retour of general service
retour	*Sc*	extract from Chancery of the service of an heir to his progenitor in which the heir is proven to succeed or inherit
retour of inquest	*Sc*	report of a jury called to decide if an heir is entitled to inherit
retraxit	*La Le*	withdrawal of a legal action
reustrie, revestry	*Sc*	vestry of a church
reverse mortgage	*Le*	loan made by the homeowner on which the home stands as collateral, and which payment is not required until the homeowner sells, moves out or dies, and the loan amount and interest is then paid out of the proceeds of sale
reversionary interest	*Le*	any interest, vested or contingent, the enjoyment of which is postponed
rex (regis)	*La*	king
rex dollar	*Sc*	German silver coin valued from; 2*s* 6*d* to 4*s* 6*d* at different times
riddle	*Sc*	large seive for stones etc.
riddler	*Oc*	maker or user of coarse sieves (riddles) for grain, soil etc.
riever	*Oc*	robber, originally of cattle (esp. in Scottish Borders)
rig and rendell	*Sc*	*see* runrig
risp	*Sc*	creak
ritus	*La*	rite, ceremony
rive	*Sc*	rip, rend, tear
river	*Le*	watercourse of capacity to be navigated
rivetter	*Oc*	joiner of metal plates with hammered rivets
road contractor	*Sc*	person who oversees road building
roda/ae	*La Le*	rood(s) (measure of land)
roll	*Pal*	long, narrow document stored rolled
rondle, roundall, rowndall	*Sc*	basically anything round, such as a shield, a table a tower, a song (rondel, rondellay)
rood	*Le*	measurement of land
room	*Sc*	space
rooming house	*Le*	rented residential premises where an individual shares a kitchen and bathroom with others
room-setter	*Sc*	renter-out of rooms
rope spinner	*Oc*	maker of rope by braiding yarns

rotulus	La	roll
round sheets	Sc	sheets around a mattress
rounder bed plaids	Sc	woollen bedcovers
roup	Sc	sale by auction, governed by conditions called 'articles of Roup'
rout	Sc	company
rubric	Pal	heading in red letters, often instructions, using a red lead or iron-oxide ink
rufus	La	red
running stationer	Oc	caddie (qv) stationed to run errands
runrig, rig and rendell	Sc	system of cultivation in which separate strips of a field were cultivated by different people
rursum	La	again
rursus	La	again, in turn
rusticus	La	peasant, farmer
rys	Sc	twigs, small branches
s and h, s. and h.	Le Sc	son and heir
sabbatinus, dies	La	Saturday
sabbatum	La	Saturday
sacellanus	La	chaplain
sacer, sacra, sacrum	La	sacred
sacerdos (sacerdotis)	La	priest
sacramentis totiis munitiis	La	fortified by all the last rites
sacramentum	La	sacrament, ordinance, rite
sacrist	Sc	head porter and mace bearer (especially at Aberdeen University)
sacro fonte baptismi	La	in the sacred font of baptism
saddle tree, sadle-trie	Sc	wooden frame of a saddle
saddler	Oc	maker and repairer of horse saddles and leathers
saddler, sadler	Sc	maker and and seller of saddles
sadill of aik	Sc	seat of oak
saeculum	La	generation, century, age, eternity, world
saepe	La	often
saidis	Sc	aforesaid
saidle	Sc	1. saddle; 2. wooden seat
saifand	Sc	saving, excepting
salarium	La	salary
salbe	Sc	shall be
salinator	Oc	preserver who used salt e.g. for fish
salmond	Sc	salmon
salt backet	Sc	salt tub

salt officer, salt grieve	Sc	overseer of saltworks or salt pans
saltare	La	salter, maker of salt
salter	Sc	salt manufacturer or merchant
saltfat, saltfoot	Sc	pewter saltcellar
saltpans	Sc	pits for boiling salt from seawater
salt watchman	Sc	person who guards saltpans
salutation	Pal	formal greeting to whom a charter is addressed
samekle	Sc	so much
samen	Sc	same
sanctuary	Le	special criminal law option available in medieval times to persons who had just committed a crime, allowing them to seek refuge in a church or monastery
sanctus/a/um	La	holy, sacred, a saint
sandpaperer	Oc	see french polisher
sane	La	reasonably, sensibly; certainly, doubtless, truly; of course
sang	Sc	song
sanus	La	healthy
sarcinator	La	patcher, sackmaker
sarcinator	Oc	cobbler, patcher, sackmaker
sartor	La	tailor
sasine	Sc	act giving legal possession of property and the deed recording this
sasine register	Sc Le	list of property sasines (land conveyances)
satis	La	enough
saturni, dies	La	Saturday
sauld	Sc	sold
sawbones	Oc	surgeon
sawer, sawar, sawyer	Sc Oc	timber cutter
say master	Sc	person in charge of assay (at the mint)
scabinus	La	judge, lay assessor
scaccarium	La Le	chess game, but in English law, the exchequer, usually in reference to the Court of Exchequer
scallag	Oc	poor farm servant of a tacksman
scarlatina	La	scarlet fever
scaur	Sc	steep embankment
scavenger ('scaffie')	Oc	1. dustman, street sweeper or refuse collector; 2. worker in a jute mill who picked up loose material from the floor
schade	Sc	shadow
scheigrinder	Sc	scissors sharpener
scheip	Sc	sheep
scheipcottis	Sc	sheep cotes

scheiphirdis	*Sc*	shepherds
scheirsmith	*Sc*	scissors maker
scheise	*Sc*	cheese
schepherd, schiphird	*Sc*	shepherd
scho	*Sc*	she
schola	*La*	school
scholar	*Oc*	child at school
schoolmaster	*Oc*	head schoolteacher
schryne, scrine	*Sc*	shrine, desk, screen
scilicet (adv.)	*La*	evidently, naturally, of course
scilicet (as explanatory)	*La*	namely, that is to say, in other words
scissor	*La*	tailor
sclaitter	*Sc*	slater
sclater	*Oc*	slater, roof tiler
scold	*Le*	troublesome and angry woman who breaks the public peace, and becomes a public nuisance
scolding	*Le*	medieval offense; women who were verbally disputative
scorbutus	*La*	scurvy
scorifex (scorificis)	*La*	tanner
scorta	*La*	unmarried mother, whore
scotia	*La*	Scotland
scourer	*Oc*	washer of raw wool with soap or in urine before processing
scribe	*Sc Pal*	clerk, secretary, writer, one who transcribes documents or takes dictation by hand
scribo	*La*	I write
scripsit	*La*	he/she wrote
script	*Pal*	generic form of handwriting
scriptorium	*La*	room in a monastery where documents were written and copied
scriptus/a/um	*La*	written
scrivener	*Oc Pal*	scribe employed to draft contracts, accounts etc.; loosely applied to any writer
scruittore	*Sc*	escritoire, writing table
scule	*Sc*	school
scullery maid	*Oc*	kitchen servant (female)
scutifer	*Sc*	shield bearer
se defendendo	*La Le*	self-defence
seafarer	*Oc*	seaman, sailor, mariner
seal	*Pal*	piece of wax with the impression of a symbol indicating its source or authority
se'all	*Sc*	abbreviation of 'severall' (several)

seaman	Sc	sailor
seamstress, semstress	Oc	woman who made, sewed and mended clothes
seceder	Oc	member of Secession Church (after 1733)
secretary hand	Pal	French document hand used widely as a book hand from the fourteenth century
secundum consuetudinem manerii	La Le	according to the custom of the manor
secundus	La	second
sed	La	but
sedition	Le	speaking or publishing to excite public disorder or in defiance of lawful authority
seedman, seedsman	Sc	seed merchant
seisin	Le	legal possession of property; historically, possession under claim of freehold
seisina/ae	La Le	possession
selch	Sc	seal (the marine mammal)
selch's skin	Sc	sealskin
selffis	Sc	selves
sellarius	La	saddler
semel	La	once, a single time
semi	La	half
semper	La	always, forever
Sen. Coll. Just.	Sc Le Oc	Senator of the College of Justice (Judge of the Court of Session)
senescallus/i	La Le	steward
senex (senicis)	La	old man
senilis	La	weak from age
senior	Sc	elder of two (brothers, heirs etc.)
senior	La	older, elder
senium	La	old age
sensyne	Sc	since that time
sepelire	La	to bury
sepelivi	La	I buried
septagenarius	La	person in his/her 70s
septembris	La	of September
septemtrional, septentrional	Sc	northern (usually on maps, e.g. *Terres Arctiques Septemtrional et Boreales*)
septimana	La	week
sepulti	La	burial
sepultorum, liber	La	burial register
sepulture	Sc	grave, burialplace

sepultus	*La*	burial
sepultus/a/um	*La*	buried
seq.	*Le*	sequestrated
sequel	*Sc*	*see* astriction
sequens (sequentis)	*La*	following
serdo (serdonis)	*La*	tanner
sergeant, serjeant	*Sc*	1. senior non-commissioned officer; 2. town or court law officer
seriand	*Oc*	constable or bailiff
servant bailie	*Sc*	legal representative; *see* servitor
servator	*Sc*	napkin, serviette
servicium/i	*La Le*	service(s)
servient tenement	*Le*	land that suffers or has the burden of an easement
servitor, servitour, servitrix	*La Oc*	1. agent, custodian, secretary, clerk; 2. apprentice; 3. domestic servant
servitude	*Le*	equivalent to common law easement: access rights over, under or on the property of another
servus	*La*	servant
session clerk	*Sc*	senior elder in a Kirk (post-Reformation)
sett	*Sc*	let to
setting	*Sc*	unit of weight for grain = 24 marks or ⅙ meil, equivalent to 1 leispund
settmaker	*Oc*	cutter of stones for cobbled streets
seu	*La*	and (as *et*); or
sevine, sewln, seuyn	*Sc*	seven
sewster	*Sc*	seamstress, needlewoman
sex	*Sc*	six
sext	*Sc*	sixth
sexten	*Sc*	sixteen
sexton	*Oc*	layman guarding a church and vestments
sexus	*La*	sex
seye	*Sc*	sea
shadow half	*Sc*	north side of land
shag lyning	*Sc*	cloth with rough nap
shambo dresser	*Sc*	chamois leather-dresser
sheds of land	*Sc*	portions or fields of land
sheeling, shieling	*Sc*	shepherd's hut
sheerman	*Sc*	scissors maker
sheirs, sheers, shears	*Sc*	scissors
sheriff	*Oc*	Chief officer of the Crown in a county; in Scotland, the equivalent of a magistrate

sheriff clerk, sheriff-clerk	*Sc*	clerk to the sheriff court and keeper of the court records
sheriff depute	*Sc*	deputy sheriff appointed by the Crown to a county or district
sheriff in that part	*Sc*	someone appointed by the Crown to take the place of a sheriff for a particular purpose
sheriff officer	*Sc*	bailiff, law officer representing and carrying out order of a sheriff
sheriffdom	*Sc*	district under jurisdiction of sheriff, county (*see* barony, regality)
sheriff substitute	*Sc*	assistant (usually part-time) sheriff
shilling-a-week man	*Sc*	person who sells goods on credit and collects the payments weekly
shingler	*Oc*	roof tiler using wooden shingles (cf. slater) (*see* iron shingler)
ship master	*Oc*	owner or captain of a ship
ship stager	*Oc*	builder of the wooden scaffolding and platforms around a ship that was being constructed
shipmaster	*Sc*	captain of a merchant ship
ship's mate	*Sc*	second in command on board a ship
shipwright	*Oc*	maker and repairer of ships, ship's carpenter
sho.	*Oc*	shopman, i.e. employed in retail
shod, shode, shot	*Sc*	separate from others
shop	*Sc*	originally a workshop, but later a place for selling goods
shore man	*Sc*	harbour worker
shore master	*Sc*	harbour master
shuttles	*Sc*	small internal drawers in a cabinet
si	*La*	if
sic	*La*	thus, so, yes
sicklike, siclyk, sicklyk	*Sc*	suchlike, like, likewise, in the same manner
sieve wright,	*Sc*	maker of sieves and riddles
sigillum	*La*	seal
signalman	*Sc*	1. operator of railway or road signals; 2. signaller, person who sends and receives signals (military)
signature	*Sc*	warrant subscribed by the king to grant a charter
signet	*Le*	personal seal of the monarch, developed into a separate royal secretariat in the fourteenth century, or a small personal seal; *see* writer to the signet
signum	*La*	sign, mark
signum fecit	*La*	he/she made a mark, signed
silkman	*Sc*	silk dealer
siller	*Sc*	money, silver
sillis, syllis	*Sc*	sills, strong horizontal timbers
silva	*La*	woods, forest
simony	*Le*	selling of miracles or the promise of some other alleged form of divine service in exchange for money

simul	*La*	at the same time; together; likewise
sin	*La*	but if
sine	*La*	without
sinister	*La*	left
sinus	*La*	bosom, breast
siquidem	*La*	if in fact; if only, if indeed; since indeed, since that
sivi (conj.)	*La*	or, or if, whether … or
SJB		St John the Baptist (birth of)
skaith	*Sc*	hurt, damage, injury
skaithless	*Sc*	undamaged, uninjured
skat	*Sc*	land tax of Viking origin of various types, e.g. salt skat, malt skat, butter skat
skimmer	*Sc*	1. flat, perforated spoon for skimming fat; 2. person who skims milk etc.
skinner	*Oc*	flayer of animal skins for leather, furs etc.
skinner, skyner	*Sc*	preparer and seller of animal skins
skipper	*Sc*	captain of a boat or ship
sklaiter	*Oc*	slater
slander of title	*Le*	intentionally casting aspersion on someone's property including real property, a business or goods (the latter might also be called slander of goods)
slater, slatter, sclater, sklaiter	*Sc Oc*	roof slate preparer and fitter
slavery	*Le*	when a person (called master) has absolute power over another (called slave) including life and liberty
sledder	*Oc*	driver of a sled or sledge, used over soft ground rather than a wheeled cart
sleist, sluther	*Sc*	vagabond, lazy individual
sloop	*Sc*	single-masted sailing vessel rigged fore and aft
sloppis	*Sc*	bands
smigator	*La*	soap maker
smith	*Oc*	metal worker, usually a blacksmith
smith, smyth, smythe	*Sc*	metal worker, especially of iron
soam	*Sc*	rope or chain pulling a plough
soap boiler	*Sc*	soap maker
socage	*Le*	term of the feudal land ownership system that referred to the tenure exchanged for certain goods or services that were not military in nature
socer (*socris*)	*La*	father-in-law
socius	*La*	apprentice, comrade, associate
socrinus	*La*	brother-in-law
socrus	*La*	mother-in-law
socrus magna	*La*	maternal grandmother
sol (*solis*)	*La*	the sun
solemnicatio, solemnicationis	*La*	marriage

solicitor	Oc En	lawyer, usually not appearing in court (cf. advocate)
solidus/i	La Le	shilling(s)
solis, dies	La	Sunday
solutus/a/um	La	unmarried, free from debt
solvo/ere	La Le	to pay
somler	Sc	butler, sommelier
sommance	Sc	summons
sone, soune	Sc	1. son; 2. the sun
soney	Sc	sunny
sonyeit	Sc	hesitate, delay
soror	La	sister
sororius	La	brother-in-law
souertie	Sc	surety or cautioner
soumes	Sc	sums
souter	Oc	shoemaker
southt	Sc	south
southyn	Sc	southern
spargener	Oc	plasterer
special service	Sc Le	serving as heir to a special subject (property etc.)
spectioner	Oc	third mate on a whaling ship, responsible for correct stowage in the hold
speet, speit	Sc	1. roasting spit; 2. spite
sphaeristerium	La	bowling green
spices and wine	Sc	in very early days instead of paying in money for admission, a new burgess furnished 'spices and wine' as a treat to those admitting him
spinster	Oc	1. woman who spun textiles; 2. unmarried woman
spirit dealer	Sc	buyer and seller of alcohol, vinegar etc.
spirit merchant	Oc	dealer in spirits, but also vinegar
spirituales, parentes	La	godparents
spiritualities	Sc	teinds due to the Church
spite fence	Le	fence built not to any beneficial purpose but, rather, to annoy a neighbour
spleuchis	Sc	splints
sponsalia	La	marriage banns
sponsalis	La	betrothed
sponsati	La	marriage
sponsatus	La	married
sponsor	La	godparent
sponsus/a	La	groom/bride, husband/wife, spouse, betrothed
spoue	Sc	spouse, husband or wife
spounge	Sc	sponge
spouse	Sc	husband or wife

sprigger	*Oc*	embroiderer of lace and muslin; *see* boot sprigger
springzie rapper	*Sc*	springy rapier
spuilzie	*Sc*	robbery, stealing moveable goods ('spoils'); *see* broken men
spuilzied	*Sc*	despoiled, robbed, stolen
spurius/a	*La*	illegitimate
squarewright	*Oc Se*	carpenter of fine furniture, cabinet maker
St Barnabright	*Sc*	St Barnaby's day, 11 June, usually bright and sunny
stabler, stabular	*Sc*	owner or operator of stables for horses
staff and baton	*Sc*	symbols used when a tenant resigns lands to the superior
staig	*Sc*	young horse
staithless, scaithless	*Sc*	skaithless, undamaged, uninjured
stallarius	*La*	stabler
stamper	*Sc*	stamping machine operator
stampmaster	*Oc*	quality controller, especially of linen; official inspector with powers to fine for faulty or fraudulent maunufacture
stand aw of	*Sc*	be greatly afraid of
staner	*Sc*	dye maker
stapis, stoups	*Sc*	large pitchers or jugs
Star Chamber	*Le*	elitist, secretive and abusive court convened from time to time by British kings from at least King Henry VII (1457–1509) to 1640
stark	*Sc*	strong
starr	*Le*	medieval English law term for legal transactions involving a Jewish person
statim	*La*	immediately
station master	*Oc*	railway employee in charge of a station
stationer	*Sc*	dealer in paper, pencils, ink, printer material etc.
statuary	*Sc*	1. sculptor, carver; 2. sculpture
status	*La*	condition, status
Statute of Frauds	*Le*	statute that set a minimum standard for enforceable contracts, usually something in writing or the actual exchange of obligations, at least in part
stays	*Sc*	corsets
stead	*Sc*	place
steall	*Sc*	stale
steddyngis, stedings	*Sc*	farmhouse and outbuildings
stemma (gentile)	*La*	pedigree
stent	*Sc*	extent, value and thus assessed tax
stentar	*Sc*	tax collector
steward	*Oc*	1. manager of an estate; 2. chief servant of royal, noble ot memorial household; 3. officer on a ship responsible for food etc.
steward clerk	*Sc*	clerk to a steward
stewart depute	*Sc*	assistant to steward of an estate

stifing	*Sc*	starch
stinarius	*La*	ploughman
stirk	*Sc*	weaned heifer (2 or 3 years old)
stirps	*La*	origin, source
stob and staik	*Sc Le*	permanent residence
stoker	*Oc*	stoked fuel into a furnace or boiler, e.g. on a ship
stone hewer	*Oc*	sculptor or stonemason
stot, stottikin	*Sc*	bullock
stoup	*Sc*	water pail
stour	*Sc*	conflict
stouthrief	*Sc*	robbery from a dwelling house; *see* broken men
straight condemnation	*Le*	formal process for the exercise of eminent domain in which a price is adjudicated and then the property bought by the government
stravaiger	*Oc*	wanderer, vagrant
stream	*Le*	watercourse having banks and channel through which waters flow, at least periodically
stribs, stirroubis	*Sc*	stirrups
stuiver	*Sc*	Dutch coin
stuprata	*La*	pregnant out of wedlock
stuprator	*La*	father of illegitimate child
stylus	*Pal*	pointed instrument for writing on a wax tablet
sub	*La*	under, beneath, below
sub tutela	*La*	under guardianship
subdean	*Sc*	assistant to a dean in a guild, university etc.
subfile order	*Le*	declaration of rights as regards waterways for the interim regulation of those rights pending a final determination of those rights either by contract or judicially
subinfeudation	*Le*	under the feudal system of tenure, a person receiving a grant of land from a lord could himself become a landlord by subdividing and subletting that land to others heritably
sublease	*Le*	subsequent lease of property that is itself leased; with the primary tenant retaining an interest in the original lease
submission	*Sc*	*see* decreet arbitral
subscripsit	*La*	he/she signed
subscriptus	*La*	undersigned
subsequentis	*La*	following, subsequent
subsignatum	*La*	marked (signed) below
subsignavit	*La*	he/she signed with a mark below
sub-tenant	*Sc*	person who sub-rents property from a tenant
sucken	*Sc*	*see* astriction
suevia	*La*	Sweden
suffragant	*Sc*	assistant to a clergyman

sugar baker	Oc	refiner in a sugar factory
sugar boiler	Sc	sugar refiner, one who prepares sugar for processing
suit	Sc	pursuit
suit of court	Le	attendance at a manor or baronial court
suit service	Le	service rendered by attendance at the manor court
sum	La	I am
sumlier	Oc	butler (sommelier)
summa	Sc	Latin for all, sum or total, usually found at the end of an inventory totalling the value of the deceased's estate
summa totalis	La	sum of the total
sunny half	Sc	south-facing part of land
sunt	La	they are/were
superior	La	upper
superstes	La	surviving, still living
supervisor	Sc	overseer
supra	La	before, above, beyond
supradictum	La	above written
surdus	La	deaf
surface waters	Le	waters falling on the land by precipitation or rising from springs
surfaceman	Oc	Laid and repaired surfaces of roads, railways or mine passage
surg. apoth.	Oc	surgeon apothecary
surgeon, chirurgeon, chirurgean,	Sc	one who carries out medical operations, amputations, bleedings etc.
surgeon major, surgeon general	Sc	military medical ranks
surrender	Le	ceremony by which an existing tenant gave up a customary holding; usually followed by an admission
surrender (decreet of)	Sc	ordering tithes or teinds to be surrendered to the Crown
surrogate	Sc	1. to appoint as a substitute; 2. proxy or substitute in connection with a right or claim
survey	Le En	document listing the holdings and obligations of manorial tenants, later with detailed topographical descriptions and/or maps; see extent, terrier
surveyor	Sc	estimator of quantities and values of land, buildings and goods for reasons of valuation, construction or revenue
susceptor/orix/ores	La	godparent (male/female) godparents
suspension (letters of)	Sc Le	order that charges on bills, decrees be suspended until pleas are heard
sutor	La	cordiner, cobbler, shoemaker
suus/a/um	La	his/her/its/their own
swar	Sc	snare
Swerde-slipper	Oc	sword sharpener and mender

swerde–slipper, sword slipper	*Oc*	sword sharpener and sheath maker
swippit	*Sc*	supped
swith	*Sc*	instantly, now, without delay
swmes	*Sc*	sums
swyr	*Sc*	sword
syd	*Sc*	side
sylebob	*Sc*	syllabub, drink made of milk mixed with spirits or cider, spiced, sweetened and served hot
symblair	*Sc*	butler, sommelier
syne	*Sc*	since; *see* lang syne
synergus	*La*	apprentice
taberna	*La*	inn, tavern
tack	*Sc*	lease by formal written contract between landlord and tenant, renewable every nineteen years in Scotland; usually renewable every three in Shetland
tack of lands	*Sc*	customs, lease
tacksman	*Sc*	lease holder, tenant of land who sub-lets or rents (tacks)
tailor, talor, tallor, tailzeour, tailor burges	*Sc*	tailor of men's clothes
tailzie	*Sc*	entail, a deed which fixed the legal succession to lands
tailzier	*Sc*	entailer, someone in receipt of a deed which fixed the legal succession to lands
take lugyng	*Sc*	to camp, lodge in a temporary place
tales	*Le*	act of supplementing a jury otherwise incomplete
tales de circumstantibus	*La Le*	order to the local sheriff to round up as many new jurors as may be required to complete a jury on which one or more jurors are missing or have been successfully challenged
talis/ -e (adj.)	*La*	such, of such a kind, the following
taliter	*La*	in such a manner, so
tam	*La*	so, so greatly
tam … quam	*La*	so … as, much … as, as well as
tambour	*Sc En*	hoop used to hold embroidery fabric
tambourer	*Oc*	embroiderer
tamen	*La*	yet, nevertheless, still
tamen	*La*	however
tamquam	*La*	as, just as; *(conj.)* as if, just as if
tandem	*La*	at last, finally
tandem	*La*	at first, finally
tannator	*La*	tanner
tanner	*Oc*	hide or leather curer
tantum (adv.)	*La*	so much, so greatly; to such a degree; so far; only

tantus/-a/-um (adj.)	*La*	of such (a size); so great, so much
tapestrier	*Sc*	tapestry weaver
tapsman	*Oc*	chief servant
tapster	*Oc*	barman, server of beer
tarn	*Sc*	mountain lake
tas, tassie	*Sc*	cup
tasker	*Oc*	pieceworker
tavernor	*Oc*	innkeeper, ostler
taxt-ward	*Sc Le*	casualty of a superior for lands in non-entry; *see* casualty
tayngis	*Sc*	tongs
tearer	*Oc*	assistant to a cloth printer in a print mill
tegularius	*La*	tiler, slater
tegularius	*La*	brick maker
teick, tick	*Sc*	ticking of a bed, mattress, pillow etc
teind sheaves	*Sc*	tithe of grain
teinds, teindsheaves	*Sc*	one-tenth part of annual produce of land, due to the church
teleonarius	*La*	tax collector
teller	*Sc*	bank clerk, money counter
temple lands	*Sc*	lands that once belonged to the Knights Templar, possibly first invited into Scotland by Robert Bruce when both were excommunicated
tempus (temporis)	*La*	time
tenancy	*Le*	contract by which the owner of real property (the landlord), grants exclusive possession of that real property to another person (tenant), in exchange for the tenant's periodic payment of some sum of money (rent)
tenancy by the entireties	*Le*	form of common law co-ownership where, when real property was transferred to a husband and a wife, the property could not be seized or sold unless both spouses agreed or by ending the marriage
tenant	*Le*	renter, inhabiter of rented property, land etc. to whom a landlord grants temporary and exclusive use of land or a part of a building, usually in exchange for rent
tenant at will	*Le*	tenants who paid a rent and whose tenure was entirely dependent on the good will of the lord
tenants in common	*Le*	share a specified proportion of ownership rights in real property and upon the death of a tenant in common, that share is transferred to the estate of the deceased tenant
tenement	*Sc Le*	(literally) a holding, but meaning a house, flat or piece of land; property that could be subject to easements
tenementer	*Sc*	1. holder of a tenement; 2. tenant of a tenement dwelling
tenendum	*La Le*	to be held in law, that part of a contract in which an interest in real property is created that sets out the extent or limitations of that interest
tenens/entis	*La Le*	tenant
teneo/ere	*La Le*	to hold
tennent	*Sc*	tenant

tenter	*Oc*	mechanic who maintained power looms
tenura/ae	*La Le*	tenure(s)
terce	*Sc*	the third share of heritable (immovable) property due to the relict (widow) if no other provision has been made for her, the other two shares being for the children, if any, and the rest for the deceased to bequeath at will
terce-pryour	*Sc*	prior, head of a priory
term	*Sc*	date when interest or rent is due
terra	*La*	land, earth
terrier	*Le En*	manorial document listing tenants and their obligations to provide labour or payment; *see* extent
terris et baronia	*La*	land and barony (of)
tertia parte quartae partis	*La*	third part of a one-quarter part (i.e. one-twelfth)
tertius/a	*La*	one-third
testament	*Sc*	grant of administration of an estate by the authorities – not the same as a will (in Scotland)
testament dative	*Sc*	grant of administration by court of will, as opposed to probate
testamentar	*Sc*	done or appointed by the testator (as opposed to dative, ordered by a court) and containing a will; *see* dative
testamentum	*La*	will, testament
testes	*La*	witnesses
testibus	*La*	by witnesses
testimentum	*La*	will, testament
testis	*La*	witness
textor	*La*	weaver
thatcher	*Oc*	thatch roofer, worker with reeds or straw for roofing
theats	*Sc*	horse traces on plough, cart, carriage etc.
theicker, theikar, theiker	*Sc Oc*	*see* thatcher
thesaurer	*Sc*	treasurer
thir	*Sc*	these
thirl	*Sc*	bind in service, obligate; *see* astriction, multure, thirlage
thirlage	*Sc*	obligation on owner or tenants of land to grind their grain at a particular mill; *see* Multure
thomie	*Sc*	thumb
thorus	*La*	status of legitimacy, bed
thrid	*Sc*	third
throng of	*Sc*	full of, crowded with
throuster	*Sc*	trusser, hay baler
throw	*Sc*	through
thwarter	*Sc*	athwart, crossing
tick maker	*Oc*	upholsterer, weaver of fabrics (ticking)

tide surveyor, tidesman, tide officer, tide-waiter	*Sc*	senior customs officer who checks cargo being loaded onto ships and duties payable from merchant ships coming into harbour
tidy or tydie ky	*Sc*	pregnant or lactating cow
tignarius	*La*	carpenter
timber merchant	*Sc*	dealer in rough (uncut) wood
timberman, timmerman	*Sc*	tree feller and preparer of rough wood
time of the essence	*Le*	contractual term requiring performance within a specified time
tinctor	*La*	litster, dyer
tinker	*Oc*	travelling tinsmith, seller of pots and pans
tinplate worker	*Sc*	maker of tinplate goods
tinsel, tynseil	*La*	loss
tinsmith	*Sc*	worker with tin
titellis	*Sc*	titles
tithingman	*Le*	one of a group of ten men with a mutual responsibility for their good behaviour
tobacco spinner	*Sc*	preparer of tobacco for sale
tobacconist, tobaconnist	*Sc*	seller of tobacco, pipes, matches and other smoking products
tocher	*Sc*	dowry brought by a wife to her husband at their marriage
tocher guid	*Sc*	goods or money making up the dowry
tod, todd	*Sc*	fox
todman	*Oc*	one employed to kill foxes (tods) on an estate
toft	*Sc*	land attached to a house; *see* messuage
tolbooth	*Sc*	building in a burgh that was toll collection office, courtroom and prison
tolerance	*Sc*	deed granting a privilege
toll-gatherer	*Sc*	tollgate guard and duty collector
tomus	*La*	volume
tonsor	*La*	barber
tornator	*La*	turner, lathe worker
Torrens Land Registration System	*Le*	land registration system invented by Robert Torrens and in which the government is the keeper of the master record of all land and their owners
tot	*La*	as many, so many
totus	*La*	all, entire
toun post	*Sc*	town letter deliverer, postman, messenger
toun, toune, town	*Sc*	town; steading plus houses of cotters ('ferme-toun')
town clerk	*Sc*	legal officer and secretary in town council
town major	*Sc*	town's law and ceremonial officer
town officer, toun officer	*Sc*	town law officer, common serjand

towsman	Oc	in charge of the halyards on a fishing boat
tractatus de legibus et consuetudinibus regni Angliae	La Le	1188 statement of English common law
trader	Sc En	buyer and seller of goods
trafficker	Sc	trader, buyer and and seller of goods
trans	La	across
transcript	Pal	handwritten copy of a document
transfer	Le	delivery from one person to another of property
transferee	Le	person who receives property being transferred
transferor	Le	person from whom title or ownership to property moves
transitus est	La	he died
translation	Sc	document transferring a bond from one holder to another
transumpt	Sc	official copy of a deed
traveller, travellour, traveler, chapman	Sc	travelling salesman or dealer, door-to-door or dealing with businesses
treason	Le	aid or enlist with a state enemy or to attempt or conspire to harm the head of state
treasurer	Sc	senio financial manager in a burgh, department, organisation etc.
treasurer clerk	Sc	clerk in the office of treasurer or treasury
tred and handling	Sc	trade and business
trencherman	Oc	cook
trespass	Le	unlawful interference with another's person, property or rights
tressure	Sc	narrow border around a coin, token or shield
trial by battle	Le	ancient dispute resolution method where those in dispute would fight one another until submission or death
trial by ordeal	Le	trial of a criminal or civil action, in medieval England, by torture or drowning
tribus	La	clan, lineage, tribe
triduum	La	space of three days, three-day period
trigemini	La	triplets
Trin.		Trinity (term)
Trinoda Necessitas	La Le	three necessities owed all common law landowners to the kingdom
tron	Sc	beam and scales for weighing goods
tronman	Oc	chimney sweep
trover	Le	old English and common law legal proceeding against a person who had found someone else's property and has converted that property to their own purposes
trowblance	Sc	molestation
trumpeter	Sc	trumpet player (usually military)
trumpmaker	Sc	maker of trumpets and other brass instruments
trunkmaker	Sc	maker of travelling trunks, chests etc.

tubinnator	*La*	trumpeter
tuffell cloath, taffill cloth	*Sc*	table cloth
tum	*La*	then
tumulatus	*La*	buried
tunc	*La*	then, at that time, immediately
tunc (adv.)	*La*	then, just the; thereupon, accordingly, consequently
tunc temporis	*La*	of former time
turkey red	*Oc*	turkey red (from madder root) was used to dye cotton
turner, turnour	*Sc Oc*	lathe operator, shaping wood or metal
turssyt	*Sc*	carry, truss
tussis	*La*	cough
tutela	*La*	guardianship, tutelage
tutelage	*Sc*	state of being under a tutor, under the age of majority
tutor	*Sc Le La*	1. legal representative, guardian or adminstrator of a pupil (minor); 2. private teacher
tutory	*Sc*	appointment of a tutor
tuus	*La*	your
twidlen	*Sc*	twill cloth
tymous	*Sc*	betimes, timeous, timely
tyne and wine	*Sc*	lose and win
tyne, tynt	*Sc*	lose, lost
type founder	*Oc*	printer who set out individual letters on printing blocks
typhus	*La*	typhoid fever, typhus (note, these are not the same disease)
ubi	*La*	where
ubicumque	*La*	wherever, everywhere
udal, uthell, odal	*Sc*	having no fuedal superior, freehold, allodial
ult, ultima, ulttimo	*La*	of the preceding month
ultimus/a/um	*La*	last, final
umq, umqle, umquhile, umquhyle	*Sc Le*	late, deceased, erstwhile
unctio	*La*	annointing, unction
unctio extrema	*La*	extreme unction, last rites
unde	*La*	whence, from where; wherefore; this being the case; whereupon, whence
under–miller	*Sc*	assistant worker in a mill
uneath	*Sc*	scarcely, hardly
ungaricus	*La*	Hungarian
unigenus/a	*La*	only begotten son/daughter, unique
unitis	*La*	combined into
unlaws	*Sc*	fines

unus	*La*	one, only, together
upholsterer	*Sc*	cloth or leather furniture finisher
upset	*Sc Le*	fee for entering, as 'prentice'
urbs (urbis)	*La*	city
usher, ischear	*Sc*	1. court or church official who kept order; 2. assistant teacher
usque	*La*	as far as, all the way, continually, straight on, up to; until
usquebaugh, usquebea, uisge beatha	*Sc*	water of life, whisky
usufruct	*Le*	rights to the product of another's property
usufructuar, usufructuary	*Sc*	trustee who enjoys the produce or income from property he holds in trust for somebody else e.g. an abbey
ut	*La*	how, as, so that, therewith, in order that
ut infra	*La*	as below
ut supra	*La*	as above
ut … ita	*La*	while … nevertheless
utencilis & domiceillis	*Sc*	household goods
uterine	*Sc En*	children of same mother
uterinus	*La*	on mother's side (of family), of the same mother
uterque/-raque/-rumque	*La*	both, each (of two)
uthairis	*Sc*	others
utinam	*La*	would that, if only
utique	*La*	anyhow, at least, at any rate
utpote	*La*	as, in as much as
utrum (conj.)	*La*	either, whether
uxor	*La*	wife
uxoratis	*La*	married
vagabundus	*La*	wanderer, vagabond
vagus	*La*	tramp
vaik (of a tack)	*Sc*	vacancy of a tenancy
valent	*Sc*	upheld, valorised
Vandyked	*Pal En*	indentured, a reference to the shape of a 'Van Dyke' beard
vanman	*Oc*	driver of a light commercial vehicle
variola	*La*	smallpox
vassal	*Sc*	person to whom land is conveyed by a superior for the payment of a yearly rent or feu-duty or the performance of some regular service such as military aid
vassus	*La*	servant, vassal
vel (vel … vel)	*La*	or (either … or)
velle	*La*	will, testament

vellum	*Pal*	writing membrane made from animal skin, of better quality than parchment
velut	*La*	as, just as, as it were, as though
vendico/are	*La Le*	to claim
vendo/ire	*La Le*	to sell
venerabilis	*La*	venerable, worthy
veneris, dies	*La*	Friday
venia	*La*	permission, indulgence
vennel	*Sc*	narrow street or passage
verdour bed	*Sc*	bed with landscape or sylvan tapestry design
veredictum/i	*La Le*	verdict(s)
vernacular	*Pal*	writer's native or customary language
vero (conj.)	*La*	but, truly
vero, die	*La*	on this very day
verso	*Pal*	left hand of a double page in a book, or reverse of a folio, abbreviated as 'v'; *see dorso, recto*
verumtamen	*La*	but yet, nevertheless
vespere	*La*	in the evening
vester	*La*	your
vestiarus	*La Oc*	keeper of the wardrobe, clothier
vetula	*La*	old woman
vetus (veteris)	*La*	old
via	*La*	road, way
vicar, viccar	*Sc*	parish clergyman (pre-Reformation, Episcopal)
vicarius	*La*	vicar
vicar pensioner	*Sc*	ordained clergyman who received a living, house, land and/or salary from the income of a parish or abbey
vicecomes	*La*	sheriff, reeve
vicinus	*La*	nearby, neighbourhood
victricus	*La*	stepfather
victual, victuelis	*Sc*	1. grain; 2. food of any kind; 3. goods in kind
victualler	*Oc*	grocer, supplier of food and provisions
vicus	*La*	village
vide	*La*	see
videlicet (viz.)	*La*	clearly, evidently; namely
viduus/vidua	*La*	widower/widow
view of frankpledge	*Le En*	system of mutual responsibility for the maintenance of law and order, usually consisting of around ten households
vill	*Sc*	village, buildings round a castle
villa	*La*	farm, country home, estate , large country residence or seat, villa, village
villanus/i	*La Le*	villein(s)

villein	Le	tenant who occupied lands on condition of performing services for the lord of the manor
villeinage	Le	form of slavery under the English feudal land system; the lord owned a villein outright, as a chattel
villicanus	La	reeve, steward
vintner, vinther, vintiner, wintner	Sc	wine merchant, innkeeper
violer, vialer	Sc	fiddler, violin player, viol player
vir	La	man, male, husband
virgata/ae	La Le	virgate(s)
virgate	Le	measurement of land
virgo (virginis)	La	virgin, female, girl
virtuosus/a/um	La	virtuous, honorable
viscount	Sc	noble title below earl or count but above baron
viscountess	Sc	wife of viscount, the rank below earl or count
visitor	Sc	inspector of a university, a business etc.
visus franciplegii	La Le En	view of frankpledge
vita	La	life
vitam cessit	La	he/she departed from life (died)
vitri compositor	La Oc	glassinwright, glazier
vitriarius	La	glassmaker
vitricus	La	stepfather
vivens (vivus)	La	living
viz (videlicet)	La	namely
volt	Sc	1. vault; 2. channel in which a mill stone grinds
vos	La	you
vphaldyn	Sc	upheld
vrak (wreck) of salmon	Sc	salmon lying ashore
vulcanite comb maker	Oc	made hard (vulcanite rubber) combs for the textile industry
vulgo	La	generally, commonly
vxor (uxor)	La	wife
WS	Oc	writer to the signet (solicitor)
w.	Sc	wife
wabster	Oc	weaver
wad	Sc	1. dye; 2. stuffing
wadset	Sc Le	deed giving the rent of a debtor's lands etc. to a creditor in payment of the debt; mortgage
wadsetter	Sc Le	creditor, holder of a wadset (property mortgage)
wadwife	Sc	female wad maker (wad: dye or stuffing)

wage	*Sc*	reward, pledge, wage
waggoner	*Sc*	driver of heavy-goods wagons
wagon maker	*Sc*	maker of heavy-goods wagons
waillyt	*Sc*	chosen, chose
wainwright	*Oc*	wagon maker
wair and bestow	*Sc*	spend
waiter	*Sc*	watchman or guard
waled men	*Sc*	chosen men
walkaris craft	*Sc*	fuller's trade or guild; *see* fuller, walker
walker, waulker, waker, walkster, wacker etc.	*Sc Oc*	cloth fuller, who cleaned and thickened cloth, often by walking on it in water
wanes	*Sc*	dwellings
wappinschaw	*Sc*	*see* weapn schaw
ward lands	*Sc*	lands held in ward
ward superior	*Sc*	person entitled to take rent from the lands of a deceased vassal while the heir is not infeft or is a minor and thus cannot give military service
ward vassal	*Sc*	wardater, person holding lands in ward (i.e. in exchange for military service)
ward, waird	*Sc*	feudal land tenure rights in exchange for military service by a tenant
wardater	*Sc*	ward vassal, person receiving lands held in ward from the ward superior
warden	*Sc*	person in charge of a hospital, almshouse, poorhouse etc.
warit	*Sc*	expended
warnstore	*Sc*	magazine, store for provisions
warrand	*Sc*	warrant
warrandice	*Sc*	assurance against any wrong arising from a defect in a title or otherwise
warrandice land	*Sc*	lands conveyed provisionally as a guarantee in case a purchaser should be evicted from the lands bought
warrant	*Le*	internal document passed between secretariats initiating legal process or action
warrison	*Sc*	order to attack, blown on horns
waryt	*Sc*	cursed, spent
wast	*Sc*	west
watchmaker	*Sc*	maker and repairer of clocks and watches
watchman	*Sc*	night guard
watercourse	*Le*	stream usually flowing in a particular direction, in a definite channel, having a bed or banks, though it need not flow continually
waterman	*Sc*	person who works near a river or harbour, possibly a boatman
waverand	*Sc*	having doubtful title
wax chandler	*Sc*	wax seller, candle maker
wax maker	*Sc*	preparer of wax for candles, etc
weapon schaw	*Sc*	massed soldiery of a clan or county

webster, wabster, wobstar, wobster	Sc	loom weaver
wecht	Sc	weight
wed	Sc	mortgage
weigher	Oc	weighed goods before sale; see iron weigher
weighhouseman	Sc	operator of a weigh house for weighing goods before market
weivar, weifar, weiffar	Sc	loom weaver
wellar	Sc	well sinker, well builder, well borer
wen or wyn	Pal	character in the Old English alphabet derived from a rune, like a narrow p, later replaced by w
wenschoat, wainscoat	Sc	wainscot, oak furniture
werrament	Sc	really, verily
wesy	Sc	go to see, look at closely
weyhouse	Sc	building where standard weights and measures were held
weying	Sc	weighing
Weyver, wobster	Oc	weaver
weyverr	Oc	weaver
wharffinger	Sc	owner or operator of a wharf
wheelwright	Sc	maker, repairer and fitter of cart and coach wheels
whinger	Sc	large knife
white fisher	Sc	catcher of white fish, e g cod, haddock
white iron	Sc	cast iron containing a small amount of graphite
white-iron smith, whitesmith	Oc	worker in light metals (cf. blacksmith)
white-ironman	Sc	seller of white iron (cast iron) goods
Whitsunday	Sc	15 May: one of the term, or quarter, days (with Lammas, Martinmas and Candlemas) when contracts, leases, tacks and rents began and ended and when bills were settled
whoip	Sc	whip
wight	Sc	strong
will	Sc	express wishes of someone as to the disposal of their property when they die, but not the same as a testament; see testament
win	Sc	dry (peats)
wincey weaver	Oc	weaver using string cotton thread
winder	Oc	textile worker who wound the thread on looms
wine cooper	Sc	wine barrel maker
witenagemote	Le	assembly of local elders in medieval England
with	Sc	in ownership or possession of
wmbeset	Sc	surrounded
wobster	Oc	weaver; see wabster

woolcomber	*Sc Oc*	preparer of wool yarn for use
woolfyner	*Sc Oc*	*see* woolcomber
woollen draper	*Sc*	woollen cloth seller
wool stapler	*Sc*	person who weighs wool for selling at market
words of limitation	*Le*	words in a conveyance or in a will that set the duration of an estate
workman	*Oc*	porter, chiefly at weighhouse
worset	*Sc*	worsted, woollen cloth
worset–man	*Sc*	worsted dealer
worthis	*Sc*	needs
wowman	*Sc*	woolman, wool dealer
wrack and wair	*Sc*	wreckage, driftwood, seaweed on the seashore, and the right to collect it
wraith	*Sc En*	ghost
wrangis	*Sc*	wrongs, injuries, harm
wrecker	*Oc*	plunderer of a shipwreck: some lured ships to destruction for the purpose
wright, wricht, wrigth	*Sc Oc*	craftsman; maker, joiner or carpenter
writ	*Le*	legal document or writing; document from royal authority conferring a privilege or issuing a command
writer	*Sc Oc*	1. clerk or scribe; 2. attorney, notary, solicitor
writer to the signet	*Sc*	highest order of writers (essentially solicitors) with authority to prepare writs for the royal signet
writing master	*Sc*	1. teacher of writing; 2. writer of documents for others
wroken	*Sc*	avenged
wryt	*Oc*	writer (to the signet), solicitor
wuip	*Sc*	whip
wynd	*Sc*	narrow street or passage
wys	*Sc*	wise, advice
wyssie, wissie	*Sc*	inspect
Y	*Oc*	yeoman (sometimes 'of the guard')
yarn bleacher	*Oc*	bleached textile fibres e.g. flax
yarn boiler	*Sc*	person who prepares yarn
yarn dresser	*Oc*	prepared flax fibres; *see* hackler
yarn merchant	*Sc*	buyer and seller of thread
yarn twister	*Oc*	twisted silk into threads or yarn
yauger	*Oc*	pedlar of local fish and produce (Shetlands)
year book	*Le*	summary of court cases during the year
yeartak	*Sc*	one year's lease
yerk	*Sc*	twitch, as shoemakers and leather workers do in fixing stitches
yoak	*Sc*	yoke
yor, yr	*Sc*	younger

younger	*Sc*	title given to the heir-apparent of someone with a geographical designation as part of the surname or a Scottish chief, such as George Hay, Younger of Yester to distinguish him from his father, George Hay of Yester
ypor	*Oc*	apothecary
z	*Sc*	the letter *y* was often written like a *z* in Scots documents: thus the name Menzies is actually pronounced '*Mingiss*', *z*-words make sense when pronounced with a *y* (as they were)
zaird, zeard	*Sc*	yard
zeirs	*Sc*	years
Zetland	*Sc*	Shetland
zingarius	*La*	gypsy
zit	*Sc*	yet
zoungair	*Sc*	younger

21

Latin: Glossary of Forms of First Names and Surnames

Please do not get the impression that many of these are names the Romans would have used. In some cases, that will be so (such as Æneas), but mostly these are back-inventions of names to use in Latin documents. It's extremely unlikely, for example, that the Bridgewater was originally named 'Aqua pontanus Ancariis': that's merely some scribe's attempt to find a Latin equivalent. Nor is Durie any sort of derivative of the Latin adjective *durus/dura* meaning hard: it probably derives from a Gaelic place name meaning 'black water', but there had to be a Latinised equivalent, Duraeus for use in papers. Likewise, Caradoc is a fine old Welsh or British name, but the Romans may well have come across it and given it their equivalent – Caradocus. Some are obvious (Alice/Alicia) but others might require some head-scratching: Guildford becomes 'de Aureo vado' or 'de Aureo bado' or similar , as in the case of John of Guildford, Johannes de Bado Aureo, the noted late-fourteenth-century heraldic writer, based on the old Roman name for the town. But in that case, anyone with the surname Bath should have it Latinised to 'de Aquae Sulis' rather than 'de Bada'.

Aba	Abbot
de Abbacia	Abbess
Abbas	Abbott
de Abrincia	D'Avranches
Acutus	Hawkwood
Ademarus	Aymer
Adhelina	Adeline
de Adurni portu	Etherington
Ægidius	Giles
Æneas	Enoch
de Agnellis	Agnew, Daguall
Agnes (Agnetis)	Agnes

de Agnis	Aignes, Ains
Ailbertus	Albert
de Aillio	D'Aile, Alley
Ailmaricus	Emery
Ailmerus	Aylmer
Ala campi	Wingfield
Alanus	Aleyn, Alan
de Alba marla	Albemarle
Alberedus	Alfred
Albericus	Aubrey
Albericus, Albrea, Albraeus	Aubrey, Awbrey
de Albineio	D'Aubeney, Albiney
Albinus	Aubyn
de Albo monalserio	Whitchurch
de Alditheleia	Audley
Alecia	Alice
Alemannicus	Allman
Alicia	Alice
Alionora	Eleanor
de Alneto	Dawnny, Dannoy, Dennett
Aloysius	Lewis
Alselinus	*see* Ascelinus
de Alta ripa	Dawtrey, Daltry, Hawtrey
de Alta villa	De Hauteville
Aluredus	Alfred
Amabilla	Mabcl
de Amblia	De Amblie, Hamley
Amicia	Amice
Anastasius	Anstis
de Ancariis	Dancer
Andreas	Andrew
Anglicus	Inglis
Angnes	Agnes
de Angulis	Angell
Anicia	Annis
Anna	Anne
de Ansa	Daunee
Apparitor	Sumner
de Aqua frisca	Freshwater

Aqua pontanus	Bridgewater
de Aquila	Eagle, D'Eagles, Diggles
Arbalistarius	Arblaster, Alabaster
Archidiaconus	Archdeacon
de Archis	Arch
de Arcla	Argles
de Arcubus	Bowes
de Arenis	Dareus
de Arida villa	Dryton, Drydon
Artorius	Arthur
Arundelius	Arundel
Ascelinus	Ansell
Asculphus	Ayscough, Askow
de Asneriis	Daniers, Denyer
Aubericus	Awbrey
de Auco	Owe
Audoinus	Owen
Audomarus	Omer
de Augo	D'Eu, Ange, Agg, Dagg
Augustinus	Austin
Augustinus	Austin
de Aula	Hall
de Aurea valle	Dorival, Dorvell, Darvall
de Aureo vado (or bado)	Goldford, Guldeford, Guildford
Avicia	Avis
Avonius	Of Northampton
de Aynecuria	Daincourt
de Ba, Baa	Baugh
de Bada	Bath
de Baha	*see* de Ba
de Bajocil	de Bayeux, Bews
Bardulphul	Bardolph
Bartholomaeus	Bartholomew
de Batonia	Bath
Beatrix	Beatrice
de Beevilla	Beville, Beavill
de Belesmo	de Belesme
de Bella aqua	Bellew
de Bella fide	Beaufoy

de Bella villa	Belville
de Bello alneto	Bellany
de Bello campo	Beauchamp
de Bello fago	Beaufoe
de Bello foco	Beaufeu
de Bello loco	Beaulieu, Bowley
de Bello marisco	Beaumarsh
de Bello monte	Beaumont
de Bello prato	Beaupre
de Bello situ	Bellasise
Benedictus	Bennott
Benedictus	Bennet
de Benefactis	Benfield
Benevolus	Benlows
Berengarius	Barringer
de Berevilla	de Berville, Burfield, Berowell
Beroarius	Barker
de Beverlaco	Beverley
Bituricensis	de Bourges
Blancpain, Blaupain	Whitbread
Blasius	Blaise
de Blostevilla	Blovile, Blofield
de Bloys	Blew, Bligh
de Blundevilla	Blundeville, Blomfield
Blundus	Blount
de Boevilla	*see* de Bovis villa
Bononius	Boleyn
de Borgeis	Burges
Borlasius	Borlaco
de Bortano, de Burtana	Burton
de Bosco	Boys, Boyce
de Bosco Roardi	Borhard
de Boularia	de Bollers, Buller
de Bovis villa	Bovill
de Braiosa	de Braose, Brewis, Brewhouse
Bricius	Brice
Brigitta	Bridget
de Broillelo	de Bruilly, Briley
de Bruera	Bryer, Briewer, Brewer

Brunus	Le Brun, Brown
de Bucca	Buck
de Bucca uncta	de Bouchaine, Budgen
de Bucla	de Buces, Bouche, Bush
Budellus	de Buelles, Boyle
de Buesvilla	Bouville, Bousville, Bousfield
de Buliaco	Buisly, Builly
Burgensis	Burges
de Burgo	de Burgh, Burke, Bourke
de Burgo charo	Bourchier
Burgundiensis	de Bourgogne, Bourgoyne, Burgon
de Burnavilla	Bernwell, Barnwell
de Burtana	Burton
de Cadomo	de Caen, Caine
de Cadurcis	Chaworth
Caecilius	Cecil
Calcearius	Le Chaucier, Chaucer
Calixtus	Killick
de Calleio	de Cailly, Cayley
Calvinus	Caffyn, Chaffyn
de Calvo monte	Chaumond
Calvus	Baud, Cafe, Calf
de Camera	Chambers
Camerarius	Chamberlayne
de Campania	Champneys
Camparnulphus, de Campo Arnulphi	Champernoun
de Campis	Descamps, Kemp
de Campo fiorido	Champfleui
de Camvilla	Camvil
de Canceio	Chauncey
de Caneto	Cheney
Canonicus	Le Chanoin, Cannon
de Cantilupo	Cantlow, Cantello
Cantor	Le Chaunter, Singer
de Capella	Capel
Capellanus	Caplin, Chaplin
de Capis	de Chappes, Cope, Capes
de Capra	de la Chievre, Cheevers, Chivers
de Capreolocuria, de Capricuria	Chevercourt

Caradocus	Caradock, Cradock
Caretarius	Carter
Carnotensis	de Chartres
de Caro loco	Carelieu
Carolus	Charles
de Casa Dei	Godshall
de Casineto	Chedney, Cheney
Castellanus	Catlin
de Castello	Castle, Castell
de Castello magno	Castlemain
de Castro	Castell
de Catherege	Catherick, Cartwright
Cecus	Cheke
Cedde	Chad
Cenomannicus	Maine
de Cerasio, de Cericio	de Cerisy, Cherry
de Cestria	Chester
de Chaisneto	Cheney
de Chalvennio	de Clavigny, Clabone
de Chauris	Chaworth
Cheligrevus	Killigrew
de Chesneto	Chesney, Cheney
de Cheveriis	de Chevrieres, Chaffers
Chirchebeius	Kirby
Christiana	Christian
Christina	Christine
Christophorus	Christopher
Cinomannicus	Maine
de Clanso	Close, Class
Claranus	Clare
de Clarifagio	Clerfay
de Claris vallibus	Clereville
de Claro fageto	*see* Clarifagio
de Claro monte	Clermont
de Clintona	Clinton
de Clivo forti	Clifford
de Coarda	de Cowert, Coward
Cocus	Cook, Coke, Cocks
de Colavilla	Colville

de Coldreto	de Coudray
Collinus	Knollys
de Columbariis	Columbers
de Conductu	Chenduit
de Conneris	de Coignieres, Conyers
Constantia	Constance
Corbaldus	Corbould
de Corcella	Churchill
de Cormeliis	de Connayles, Cormie
de Cornubia	Cornwayle
Corvesarius	Corveser, Corsar
de Corvo spinae	Crowthorn
de Cramavilla	Cranwell
Crassus	*see* Grassus
Crecilius	Cecil
Crecilla	Cecily
de Crepito corde	Crevecoeur, Crawcour
de Criwa	Crewe
Crocus	Croke
de Crotis	Croot, Grote
de Cuillio	Colley
de Cuminis	Comyn
Cunetius	Kennett
de Curceo, Curci	de Courcy
de Curia	Delacour, Cure
de Cusancia	Cussans
Dacus	Daneis, Dennis
Daincuriensis, de Aynecuria	Daincourt
Dalenrigius	Dalegrig
Daniscus	Dennis
de David villa	D'Aiville, D'Eyville
Decanus	Dean
deSakenvilla	Sackville
deSandwico	Sandwich
Desiderius	Didier
Diabolus	Deeble, Dibble
Dionysius	Denis
Dispensarius, Dispensator	Le Despencer, Spencer
de Diva	Dive, Dives

de Doite	Dwight
de Dovera	de Douvres, Dover
Draco	Drake, Drage
de Drocis	de Dreux, Drew
Droco, Drogo	Drue, Drew
Drogo	Drew
de Dumovilla	Domville, Dunville
de Duna	Don, Down
Dunestanvilla	Dunstavill
Duraeus	Durie
Durandus	Durrant
Dutentius	Doughty
Eadmundus	Edmund
Eadwardus	Edward
Easterlingus	Stradling
de Ebroicis, de Ebrois	D'Evreux
Elena	Ellen
Elianora	Eleanor
Elias	Ellis
Elisabetha	Elizabeth, Isabella
Elyas	Ellis
Elyota	Elliott
de Ericeto	Briewer
de Ermenolda villa	d'Ermenonville
Ernaldus	Ernaut, Arnold
de Erolitto	Erliehe
de Eschovilia	Escoville, Schofield
de Essartis	Essart, Sart
de Esseleia	Ashley
de Estlega, Estleia	Astley, Estley
Etheldreda	Audrey
Eudo	Eade, Eades
Eudo	Eudes
Eustachius	Eustace
Eva	Eva, Eve
Extraneus	L'Estrange
Facetus	Le Facet
de Fago	Beech, Beecher; Fagge
de Faia	de Fai, Fay

Falcho	Falk
Falterellus	Futerel, Fewtrell
Felicia	Felise
Ferdinandus	Farrant
de Ferrariis	Ferrars
Fides	Faith
de Fiervilla	Fierville, Fairfield
de Filiceto	Fernham
Filine Adelini	FitzAdelin, Edlin
Filins Guidonis	Fitzwith
Filins Gulielmi	FitzWilliam, Williamson
Filins Hardingi	FitzHardinge
Filiul Briani	FitzBrian
Filiul Reginaldi	FitzRaynold, Reynolds
Filius Alani	FitzAlan
Filius Aluredi	FitzAlard, Fitz Allred
Filius Amandi	FitzAmand
Filius Andrem	FitzAndrew
Filius Bernardi	FitzBarnard
Filius Comltis	FitzCount
Filius Eustaehii	FitzEustaco
Filius Fulconia	FitzFulk
Filius Galfredi	FitzGeoffry
Filius Gerrardi	FitzGerrard
Filius Gilberti	FitzGilbert
Filius Guarini	FitzWarren
Filius Hamonis	FitzHamon
Filius Henrici	FitzHenry, Henrison, Harrison
Filius Herberti	FitzHerbcrt
Filius Hugenis	FitzHugh
Filius Humfredi	FitzHumphry
Filius Jacobi	FitzJames, Jameson
Filius Joahannis	FitzJohn, Johnson
Filius Lucae	FitzLucas
Filius Mauricii	FitzMaurice
Filius Michaelis	FitzMichael
Filius Nicholai	FitzNichol, Nicholson
Filius Oamondi	FitzOsmond
Filius Odenis	FitzOtes

Filius Oliveri	FitzOliver
Filius Osburni	FitzOsburn
Filius Pagani	FitzPain
Filius Patricii	FitzPatrick
Filius Petri	FitzPeter, Peterson
Filius Radulphi	FitzRalph
Filius Ricardi	FitzRichard, Richardson
Filius Roberti	FitzRobert, Roberts
Filius Rogeri	FitzRoger, Rogers
Filius Simonis	FitzSimon, Simonds
Filius Stephani	FitzStephen, Stephenson
Filius Thomae	FitzThomas, Thomson
Filius Walteri	FitzWalter, Walters
Filius Warini	FitzWarin, FitzWarren
de Firmitate	de la Ferte
Flandrensis	Flemyng
Flavus	Blund, Blount
Flecharius	Le Flechier, Fletcher
de Fluctibus	Flood
de Folia	Folev
de Foliis	Foulls
de Fonte	Font, Fannt
de Fonte Ebraldi	Fonteverard
de Fonte limpide	Sherburn
de Fontibus	Wells
de Forda	Ford
de Fornellis	de Furnel
de Forti scuto	Fortesce
de Fortibus	de Forz, Force
de Fossa nova	Newdike
de Fote australi	Southwell
Francisca	Frances
Franciscus	Francis
Francus	Frank
de Fraxineto	de Fraine, de Fresne
de Fraxino	Frenn, Aaho
Fresceburnus	Freshburne
Frevilla	Frevil, Fretchville
Fridericus	Frederick

de Frigida monte	de Fremond, Fremont
de Frisca villa	Frevile, Fretchville
de Frisco marisco	Freshmarsh
Fulco	Fulk
de Fulgeriis	de Fougeres, de Filgeres
de Furnellis	Furneaux, Furness
de Gaio	Gai, Gay
Galfridus, Gaufridus	Geoffrey
de Gandavo, Gandavensis	Gaunt
de Gardinis	Garden
Garnerus	Guarnier , Warner
de Gasconia	Gascoyne
de Geneva	Genevile
de Genisteto	Bromfield
de Gerardi villa	Greville, Graville
Gerardus	Gerard
Geroldus	Gerald
Gervasius	Gerveis, Jarvis
Gervasius	Gervase
de Gianeto	de Gisney, Gynney
Gilebertus	Gilbert
Ginevra	Guenever, Wenhovcr
Giovanus	Young
Gislebertus	Gilbert
de Gisortio	de Gisors
de Glanvilla	Glanvil, Glanville
Godefridus	Godfrey
Godelacius	Guthlac
de Gorniaco	Gorney, Gurney
Goscelinus	Jocelin
de Granavilla, Greenvilla	Greenvil, Grenvile
de Grandavilla	Granvile
Grandis, or Magnus venator	Grosvenor
Grassus	Le Gras, Grace
Gratia	Grace
de Grava	de la Grave, Graves
de Grendona	Greendon, Grendon
de Grente	Grente, Grinde
Griffinus	Griffin, Griffith

de Griperia	Gripper
de Grossa venatore	Grosvenor
de Grosso	de Gruce, Gross
de Grosso monte	Grismond
de Grue	Crane
Gualterus	Walter
Guarinus	Warin
Guido	Guy, Gee
Guido	Guy
de Guidovilla	Wydville, Wyville
Gulielmus	William
de Gundevilla	Gonville
de Guntheri sylva	Gunter
de Haia	Hay
Hamo	Hamon, Hamlet
de Hantona	Hanton
Haraldus	Harold
de Harcia	Harkley
de Haula	de la Hale, Hill, Hawley
Havardus	Howard
de Haya	de la Haye, Hay
Helena	Helen
Helewisa	Helowis, Eloise
Helyas	Ellis
Henricus	Henry
Heremita	Armit
Heres	Le Hare, Eyre
Hervaeus	Harvey
Hervicius	Harvey
Hieremias	Jeremiah
Hieronymus	Jerome
de Hirundine	Arundel
de Hoga	de la Hoge, Hogg
Honoria	Honor, Honour
de Hosata, de Hosa	de la Hose, de la Huse, Hussey
Howardus	Howard
Hugo	Hugh
Humfredus	Humphrey
de Illeriis	de St Hellier, Hillier

Infans	L'Enfant, Child
Ingelramus, Ingeramus	Ingram
de Insula	Lisle
de Insula bona	Lislebone •
de Insula fontis	Lilburne
Iohannes	John
de Ipra	de Ipres
Isabella	Isabel
Isolda	Iseult, Isoude
de Ispania	Spain
Jacobus	James
de Joannis villa	de Jehanville, Geneville, Ganville
Joceus	Joice
Jodoca	Joice
Jodocus	Joice
Johanna	Joan, Jane
Joneta	Jonet, Janet
Josias	Josiah
Judal	Jude
Judocus	Jesse
Juvenis	Lejeune, Young
de Kaineto, de Kaisneto	Chesney, Cheney
de Keyneto	Keynes
de la Mara	Delamare
de Lacu	de Lake, Lake
Laetitia	Lettice
de Laeto loeo	Lettley
de Laga	Lee, Lea, Leigh
Lambardus	Lambard, Lambert
de Landa	de la Lande, Land
Landebertus	Lambert
de Langdona, Landa	Langdon
Larderarins	Lardenier, Lardner
de Largo	Large
Latinarius	Latimer
de Lato campo	Bradfield
de Lato pede	Braidfoot
de Lato vado	Bradford
Laucilottus	Lancelot

Lauremarins	Lorimer
Laurentii filius	Lawson
Laurentius	Lawrence
de Lega	Leigh
de Leica, Lecha	Leke
de Leicestria	Lester
Leodegarius	Ledger
Leuchenorius	Lewkin
Levelinus	Llewellyn
de Lexintuua	Lexington
de Limesi	Limsie
de Linna	Linne
Lionhardus	Leonard
de Lisoriis	Lizurs, Lisors
de Longa spatha	Longespee
de Longa villa	Longueville, Longville
de Longa villa	Longville
de Longo campo	Longchamp
de Longo prato	Longmede
Lucas	Luke
de Luceio	Luey, Lewaey
Lucia	Luey
Ludovicus	Lewis, Louis
de Luera	Lower
de Lunda	Lund
Lupellus	Lovel
Lupus	Le Loup, Love, Loo, Woolf
de Luxa	de Los
lvo	Ives
Mabilla	Mabel
Macer	Le Meyre
de Magna villa	Mandeville
de Magno monte	Grosmount, Groumount
Magnus venator	Grosvenor
de Mala herba	Malherbe
de Mala platea	Malpas
de Mala terra	Mauland
de Mala villa	Melville
Male conductus, de Malo conduetu	Malduit

Maledoetus	Malduit, Mauduit
de Malehenceio	Munehensy
de Malis manibus	Malmains
de Malo laeu	Mauley
de Malo leone	Mauleon
de Malo visu	Malvoisin
de Malpassu	Malpas
Malus catulus	Malcael, Mulchein, Machel
Malus leporarius	Maleverer, Mallieure or Mallyvery
Malus lupellus	Maulovel, Mallovel
Malus vicinus	Malveisin, Malvoisin
de Mandavilla	Mandeville
de Maneriis	Manners
de Mara	Mare
de Marchia	de la Marche, March
de Marci vallibus	Martival
de Marco	Mark
Marcus	Mark
Marescallus	Marshal, Le Marshal
Margareta	Margaret
Margeria	Margery
Maria	Mary
Mariana	Marion
de Marisco	Marsh
Marruglarius	Le Marler
de Masura	Le Massor, Measor
Matilda, Matildia	Matilda, Maud
Matthaeus	Matthew
Matthias	Matthew
Maurenciaeus	de Montmoreney
Maurieius	Morris
de Mauritania	de Morteine
de Media villa	Middleton
Medicus	Leech
de Meduana	Maine
de Melsa	de Meaulx, Meux, Mews
de Mercato	de Marche, March
Mercator	Mercer
de Mesleriis, de Meuloriis	Mellers

de Micenis	Meschines
Michaelis	Michael
Milo	Miles
de Mineriis	Miners, Minours
Misericordia	Mercy
de Moelis	Moolles
Molendinarius	Miller
de Molendinis	Molines
de Molis	de Moels, Mills
Monachus	Le Moigne, Monk
de Monasteriis	Musters, Masters
de Moncellis	Monceaux, Monson
de Monemutha	Monmouth
de Monte acuto	Montacute
de Monte alto	Montalt, Muhaut, Moald, Maude
de Monte aquilae	Mounteagle
de Monte Begonis	Montbegon
de Monte Canesio, Canisto	Montchensey, Munchensi
de Monte fixo	Montfitchet
de Monte Gaii, de Monte Gaudii	Montjoy
de Monte Gomerico	Montgomery
de Monte Hermerii	Monthermer
de Monte Jovis	Montjoy
de Monte Kanesi	Munchensi
de Monte Marisco, Moraci, Morentio	Montmorcney
de Monte Pessono, de Monte Pessulano, Monte Pissonis, de Monte Pissoris	Montpesson, Mompessou
de Monteforti	Montfort
de Morisco	Moore
de Mortuo mari	Mortimer
de Mowbraia	Mowbray
Moyses	Moses
ad Murum	Walton
de Musca	Mus, Mosse
de Musco campo	Muschamp
Nappator	Le Naper, Napier
de Naso	de Nes, Ness
Nepos	Le Neve
de Nevilla	Nevl
Nicholas	Nichola

Nicholaus	Nicholas
Nigellus	Niele, Neal
Nigellus	Nigel, Niel
de Nodariis, Nodoriis	Newres
Norensis	Nereis
Normandus	Normand
Norrisius	Nerris
de Norwico	Norwich
de Nova terra	Newland
de Nova villa	Neufville, Neville
de Novo burgo	Newburgh
de Novo castello	Newcastle
de Novo loco	Newark
de Novo mercato	Newmarch
Nutricius	Nurse
de Oileio, Oili, Oilius	D'Oyly
Olaus	Olaf, Olave
de Omnibus Sanctis	Toussaint
de Oughtia	Doughty
Owinus	Owen
de Paceio	de Pasci, Pacy
Paceus	Pace
Paganellus	Pagnell, or Painel
Paganus	Payne
Paganus	Paiu
Palmarius	Le Paumier, Palmer
de Palude	Puddle, Marsh
Pancratius	Pancras
de Parco	Park
Parmentarius	Tayler, Parmenter
de Parva turri	Torel, Tyrrel
de Parva villa	Littleton
Parvus	Le Petit, Petty
de Pascuo lapidoso	Stanley
Patricius	Patrick
de Pauliaeo, de Pavilliaco	Paveley
de Peccato, Peccatus	Peche, Pecke
Peitonus	Peyton
Pelliparius	Skinner

de Pede planco	Pauncefoot
Perfectus	Parfey
Pero	Piers
de Perrariis	Perrers
de Petra	Petre
de Petraponte	Pierrepout, Perpoint
Petronilla	Parnel
Petrus	Peter, Piers
Pictaviensis	Poytevin, Peto
Pincerna	Butler
Piperellus	Peverell
de Pisce, de Piscis	Fish
de Planca	de la Planche
de Plantagenista	Plantagenet
de Plessetis	Plaiz, Place
de Pola	de la Pele
de Poleio	Poley
Polus	Pole, Poole
de Ponte	Bridge
ad Pontem	Atte Brigge, Brigge, Pauntou
de Pontibus	Bridgeman, Bridges
Porcarius	Le Porcher
de Porcellis	Purcell
le Poure	Power
de Praelliis	*see* de Praeriis
Praepositus	Prevot
de Praeriis	Praers, Prahers
de Pratellis	des Pres, Despreaux, Diprose, Meadows
de Pratis	Praty, Prettie
de Prato	Dupre, Mead, Pratt
de Puilleta	l'aulet
de Pulchro capellitio	Fairfax
de Purcellis	Purcell
de Puteaco	Pudsey, Pusey
de Querceto	Cheney
de Quercu	Quirk, Kirk, Oake
de Quincito	Quincey, de Quincey
de Radeneio	de Reyney, Rodney
de Radeona	Rodney

de Radio	Raye
Radulphus	Radulf, Ralph
Ragotus	Le Raggide, Raggett
de Ralega	Raleigh
Randolphus	Randolf Randal
Ranulphus	Ranulf, Ralph, Rafe
de Rea	de Ree, Ray
de Redveriis	Rivers
Reginaldus	Reynelds
Reginaldus	Reginald, Reynold
Regulus	Rule
Reinardus	Rayner, Reyner
Reinerus	Rayner
Renoldus	Reynold
Rex	King, Reeks
de Ria	de Rie, Rye
Ricardus	Richard
de Rico monte	Richmond
Rigidius	Rivers
de Riperia, Ripariis, Riveria, Riveriis	Rivers, Driver
de Rnpe	Roche, Droope, Drape, Rock
de Roca	Rock
Rodericus	Rothiery
de Rodollo	de Roel, Rolle
Rohelendus	Roland
de Roillio	de Roilli, Reuilly, Rowley
de Roka	Rock
de Romeliolo	de Romilli, Romilly, Rumley
Rosa, Rosia	Rose
Rotarius	Wheeler
de Rotis	Rote, Rootes, Roots
de Rotundo	Round
de Rua	Rue
de Rubeo monte	Rougemont
de Rubra manu	Redmayne
de Rubra spatha	Rouxcarrier, Roussir, Rooper, Roper
de Rubro clivo	Radcliffe
de Ruda	Routh
de Ruella	Ruel, Rule

Rufus	Le Roux, Rous
de Rupe forti	Rochefort
de Rupe scissa	Cutcliffe
de Rupella	Roupell
de Ruperia	*see* Rupetra
de Rupetra	de Rupierre, Rooper, Roper
de Rupibus, Rupinus	Roche, Rock
de Sabaudia	Savoy
de Sacca villa	Sackville
de Saceio	de Sace, de Sauce
de Sacra fago	Hollebech, Holbeach
de Sacra quercu	Holyoak
de Sacro bosco	Holywood
de Sacro fonte	Holybrook
Sagittarius	Archer
de Saio	Say
de Salceto	Saucey
de Salchavilla	Salfeld
de Salicosa mara	Wilmore
de Salicosa vena	Salvein
de Salso marisco	Saltmarsh
de Saltu capellre	Sacheverel
Salvagius	Savage
Sancho	Sankey
de Sancta Barbara	Senbarb, Simberb
de Sancta Clara	St Clare, Ste Claire, Sinclair
de Sancta Cruce	St Croix, Cross
de Sancta Ermina	Armine
de Sancta Fide	St Faith, Faith, Fiddes
de Sancta Terra	Holyland
de Sancto Albano	St Alban
de Sancto Albino	Seyntabyn, St Aubyn
de Sancto Alemondo	Salmou
de Sancto Amando	St Amand, Samand
de Sancto Audemaro	St Omer
de Sancto Audoeno	St Owen
de Sancto Bricio	Brice
de Sancto Cinerino	Chinnery
de Sancto Dionysio	Dennis

de Sancto Edmondo	Edmunds
de Sancto Edolpho	Stydolph
de Sancto Edwardo	Edwards
de Sancto Gelasio	Singlis
de Sancto Germano	Germain
de Sancto Johanne	St John, Singen
de Sancto Laudo	St Laud, Sentlo, Senlo
de Sancto Leodegario	St Leger, Sallenger
de Sancto Lizio	St Lys, Senliz
de Sancto Lupo	Sentlow
de Sancto Martino	Samarton, Martin
de Sancto Mauricio	St Morris
de Sancto Mauro	St Maur, Seymour
de Sancto Medardo	Semark
de Sancto Olavo	Toly
de Sancto Paulo	Sampol, Semple
de Sancto Petro	Sampier
de Sancto Quintino	St Quintin
de Sancto Remigio	de St Remy, Remy
de Sancto Seremio	*see* de Sancto Cinerino
de Sancto Vedasto	Foster
Sapiens	Le Sage
Saracenus	Sarazin, Sarson
Sarra	Sarah
Savaricus	Savory
de Saviniaco	de Savigny, Saveney
de Saxo ferrato	Ironston, Ironzon
de Scalariis	Scales
de Sella	de Salle, Sale
Serlo	Scarle
de Sevecurda	Seacourt
Sewallus	Sewell
Sibella	Sybil
de Sicca villa	de Sacheville, Satchwell
de Sidevilla	Sidwell
Silvanus	Silvain, Salvin
Siwardus	Seward
de Smalavilla	Sec Malavilla
de Solariis	Solers

de Spada	Speed
de Spineto	Spine, Spinney
de Stagno	Stanhow, Poole, Pond
de Stampis	d'Estampes, Stamp
de Stella	Stol, Steele
Stephanus	Stephen, Steven
Stigandus	Stiggins
de Stipite sicco	de la Zouche
de Stotevilla	d'Estoteville, Stutfield
de Stratavilla	d'Estreville, Streatfield
de Stratona	Stretton
de Sudburia	Sudbury
de Suilleio	de Suilli, Sully
Super Tysam	Surteys, Surtees
de Surevilla	Surville, Sherville
de Suthleia, Sutleia	Suthley, Sudley
de Sylva	Weld
Sylvanectensis	Senliz, Seyton
Symon	Simon
de Taberna	Taverner
Talliator	Taylor
de Tanaia	Taney
de Taneo	de Tani, Tawney
de Tankardi villa	Tankerville
Tannator	Tanur, Tanner
Taxo	Tesson, Tyson
Telarius	Taylor
de Tertia manu	Tremayne
Teutonicus	Tyes, Teys
de Thaneto	Thanet, Tanet, Tent
Theobaldua	Theobald, Tybalt
Theobaldus	Tipple
Theodoricus	Terry
Timotheus	Timothy
Tobias	Toby
de Toleta	Tollitt, Tullet
de Torto	Turt
de Tribus minetie	Treminet
de Troublevilla	Troubleville, Turberville

de Tulka	Tuke, Toke, Took
de Turbida villa	Turberville
Turchetillus	Turchill
de Turpi vado	Fulford
de Turri	Towers, Torry
Turstanus	Thurstan
de Tylia	Tille, Tyiey
de Umbrosa quercu	Dimoak, Dimock
Umfridus	Humphrey
de Urtiaco	de Lorty, Lort, Hort
de Usseio	Ducie
de Vaaceio	de Vanccy, Vaizoy
Vaca	de la Wac, Wake
Vacarius	Vacher
de Vado	Wade
de Vado boum	Oxford
de Vado saxi	Stanford
Valchelinus	Wakelin
de Valeia	de Valle, Wall
de Valencia	Valence
de Valle	Wale, Wall
de Valle torta	Valetor, Vautort
de Vallibul	Vaux
de Vallo	Wail
de Valuinis	Wauwain, Walwyn
de Vannarlo	Le Vanner
de Verincio	de Verigny, Verney
de Vernaco	de Vernai, Ferney
de Vesci	Vesey
de Vetere aula	Oldhail, Oldham
de Vetere ponte	Vieuxpont, Vipont, Vipond
de Vetula	Viel, Vyel
de Vetulis	de Vielles
Vetulus	Viel
de Vicariis	Viccars, Vickers
Vicinus	Le Veysin
de Vico	de Vicques, Vick
Vidulator	Le Vielur
de Vigneio	de Vigny, de Wignai

de Vilariis	Villiers
Vilfredus	Wilfrid
de Villa magna	Mandeville
de Villa mota, mouta	Wllmot
de Villa torta	Croketon
Vincentiua	Vinccnt
de Vino salvo	Vinesau
Vitulus	*see* Vetulus
Vulpis	Renard, Rainer
Vulsaeus	Wolsey
Vulstanus	Wulfstan
de Wacellis	Wasel, Vassall
Walchelinus	Wkelin
Wallensis	Le Walleis, Wallace
de Walprla	de Guaspre, de Waspre, Vosper
de Wanceio	Wansey
Warenna	Warren
de Warnevilla	Warneville
de Wartevilla	*see* de Watevilla
de Wasa	Wace
de Watelega	Wateley, Wheatley
de Watevilla	Wateville, Waterfield
de Wellebo	de Wellebof, Welbore
Wilhelmus	William
Willelmus	William
Wiscardus	Wishart
Wollaeus	Wolley
Wolsaeus, Wolvesaesus	Wolsey
Yvo	Ives

22

Latin: Glossary of Place Names

As with personal names (p. 382) please do not assume the modern names are in every case derivatives of the Latin ones here. In many cases the Latinised version was invented much later to use in documents. For example, the Romans certainly knew about Londinium (London) but would never have heard of Edimburgo (Edinburgh) as it wasn't called that in those days. Likewise, Aberistyvium is a neo-Latin rendition of the Welsh place name Aberystwyth. Also notice the multiple examples of Latin renditions for Bath (Acemanni Civitas, Akemancester, Aquae Calidae, Aqure Solis, Aquae Sulis, Armis, Ba, Baa, Bada, Badiza, Badunum, Balnea, Baleneodunum, Batha, Bathonia, Mons Solis, Thermae, Thermal) and Berwick-upon-Tweed (Abreuicum, Abrevicum, Barneua, Baruicus, Barwickus, Beruicium, Berwicus) to take just two examples.

LATIN PLACE NAMES

Aballaba, Aballiaba: Appleby, Westmoreland; Watchcross, or Papcastle, Cumberland

Abbandonia, Abbandunum: Abingdon, Berks

Abbas aestuarium: River Humber, Yorks

Abbendonia: Abingdon

Abbotesbiria: Abbotsbury, Dorset

Abbus: Humber

Abedesberia: Abbotsbury, Dorset

Abenduna: Abingdon, Berks

Aberconouium: Aberconway; *also* the River Conway; *see* Conouium

Aberdeia: Aberdona, Aberdonia: Aberdeen, Scotland

Aberdora: Aberdura: Aberdore, and Aberdour, Scotland

Abergennium: Abergavenny, Monmouthshire

Aberistyuium: Aberystwyth, Cardiganshire

Abernaethum: Abernethy, Scotland

Aberuanus: Aberruanus; *see* Abrauannus

Abindonia: Abingdon

Ablatum Bulgium: Cardunnock, or Bowness, Cumberland; or Middleby, Dumfries

Abomina: Bodmin, Cornwall

Abona Flu: River Avon, Hants

Abone, Abonis: Sea Mills, on the Avon; Alvington-on-the-Severn, Abstone, or Aunsbury, Gloucestershire

Aboya: Athboy, Meath, Ireland

Abrauannus, Abrauanus Flu: the estuary at Ravenglass, Cumberland; or Glenluce Bay, Wigtownshire

Abreconium: Abercorn, Linlithgow

Abredea: River Dee, Aberdeen

Abredesega Insula: Bardesey Island, Carnarvonshire

Abrenethaeum: Abernethy, Scotland

Abretaum: Swansea, Glamorganshire

Abreuicum: Berwick-upon-Tweed

Abrinca: Abernethy

Abundena: Abingdon

Abus aestuarium: Humber

Acantium promontorium: North Foreland

Acastra: Acaster, Yorks

Accara: Castle Acre, Norfolk
Acemanni Civitas: Bath
Achada: Achonry, Sligo
Achadia: Aghadoe, Kerry, Ireland
Achathkonrensis, Achathronensis: of Achonry, Ireland
Achelandia: Bishop's Auckland, Durham
Achilia: Achill Isles, Connaught, Ireland
Achinctona: Ripe, Sussex
Aclea: Oakley, or Ocley, Surrey; Aycliffe or Auckland, Durham
Acmodae Insulae: Seven Islands, mentioned by Pomponius Mela and Pliny; the name is used both for the Scilly and the Shetland Islands
Acra: Acre, Norfolk
Ad Ansam: Ithanceaster, Witham Barklow, Tolshunt Knights, or Halstead, Essex; Wratting or Stratford St Mary, Suffolk
Ad Candidam Casam: Catwade Bridge near Brantham, Suffolk
Adcouecin: *see* Comberetonium
Adelingia, Adelona: Athelny, Somerset
Ad-Lapidem: Stoneham, Hampshire
Ad-Latus Bouium: Boverton, Glamorganshire; *see* Bonium
Ad-Murum: Walbottle, or Walton, Northumberland
Ad-Pontem: Paunton, Lincs.; Southwell or Farndon, Notts., or Zouch Bridge, over the Trent
Ad-Portum Dubris: Dover, Kent
Ad-Portum Lemanis: Lympne, Kent
Ad-Portum Rutupas: *see* Rutupae
Adron Flu: River Adder, Berwickshire, or River Wear, Durham; *see* Ouedra
Adros: Bardsey Island, Caernarvonshire; or Lambay, Dublin
Adtanatos Insula: Isle of Thanet
Ad-Taum: Tasburgh, Norfolk, or Norwich
Ad-Tisam: Piersbridge, Durham
Adtropam: Thrup, Abingdon
Adurni Portus: Porchester, Hants; Aldrington, or Old Shoreham, Sussex
Aebudae: Hebrides, west of Scotland
Aedulfiberga: Ellesborough, Bucks
Aegelesbyri, Aeglesburgus: Aylesbury, Bucks
Aeiglea: Iley Mead, near Melksham, Wilts.
Aeilecuriana: Vale of Aylesbury, Bucks
Aelfete: Adlingfleet, Yorks
Aelfinensis: of Elphin, Ireland
Aelia: Ely; *see* Elia
Aelia Castra: Alcester, Warwickshire
Aeliani Porta: a town near Hadrian's Wall
Aemonia: Inchcolme, on the River Forth
Aera: River Ayr, Scotland

Aesycha, Aesica: Netherby, Cumberland; Great Chesters, Northumberland
Aetona, Aetonia: Eton, Bucks
Afena: Littleborough, Notts
Afena Flu: River Avon
Agamerium: Aghamore, Co. Mayo, Ireland
Agelocum: Littleborough, Notts
Agmundishamum: Agmundisham or Amersham, Bucks
Agneda: Edinburgh
Ailenetona: Aylton, Herefordshire
Ailesberia: Aylesbury, Bucks
Ailesmera: Ellesmere, Shropshire
Aiscaranus: of Aysgarth, Yorks
Aissoura: Ashover
Aiwella: Ewell, Surrey
Aka: Rock, Worcestershire
Akelea: Ockley, Surrey
Akemancester: Bath
Ala Campi: Wingfield; Winkfield
Alachda: Killalla, bishopric in Connaught
Alaenus Flu: River Axe, Devon; River Stour, Dorset; River Alne, Warwickshire
Alana: Alloway, Ayrshire
Alannius: River Avon, Wilts.
Alata Castra, Alatum Castrum: Tain, Ross; Edinburgh; or Burghead, Moray
Alauna Civitas: Alnwick, Northumberland; Alcester, Warwickshire; Allchester, Oxon; Camelon, Stirling; a place near Poole, Dorset
Alauna Flu: River Stour, Dorset; Alna, Northumberland
Alauna Silua: borders of Hampshire and Dorset, or perhaps Stourhead, Dorset
Alauni fluuii ostia: Alnmouth; Tweedmouth
Alaunicastrum: Alcester, Warwickshire
Alaunicus Pons: Maidenhead, Berks
Alaunicus Portus: Milford Haven, Pembrokeshire
Alauniuadum: Aylesford, Kent
Alaunodunum: Maidenhead
Alaunouicus: Alnwick, Northumberland; *see* Alauna
Alaunus: Maidenhead
Alaunus Flu: River Alne or River Tweed, Northumberland
Alba Domus: Whiteland, Caermarthenshire
Alba Lundy: Blanchland, Northumberland
Albalanda: Whiteland, or Ty Gwyn ar Taf, Caermarthenshire; Blanchland, Northumberland
Albana: Scotland
Albania: Scotland, or Britain north of Humber
Albi Equi Mons: White Horse Hill, Berks
Albinunno Civitas: Caer Nonou or Whitewalls, Monmouthshire

Albion: Britain

Album Castrum: Whitchester, Northumberland; Oswestry, Shropshire

Album Monasterium: Whitchurch, the seat of the Stranges; Oswestry, Shropshire, of the FitzAlans

Alcheseia: Alchester, Dorset

Alcluith: Dunbritton, on the Clyde

Alcmundeberia: Almondbury, Yorks

Aldeburia: Oldbury or Woldbury, Warwickshire

Aldedelega: Audley, Staffordshire

Aldithelega: Audley, Staffordshire

Aldud: Dumbarton

Alecana: Ilkley, Yorkshire

Alectum: Dundee

Alencestria: Alcester, Warwickshire

Alenus Flu: *see* Alaenus

Alexodunum: *see* Axelodunum

Alicincia: Ilkley; *see* Olicana and Alecana

Aliennia: Athelney, Somerset

Alincestria: Alcester, Warwickshire

Alione, Alionis: Whitley Castle, Northumberland; Ambleside, Westmoreland; Kirkbride or Allonby, Cumberland

Alitacenon Civitas: Elgin, Scotland

Alkesia: Halsway, Somerset

Allectum: Dundee

Alna: Alne, Yorks; River Alne, Northumberland

Alnetum: Llangerniw on the Elwey, Denbighshire; Dodnash Priory, Suffolk

Alneuicum: Alnwick, Northumberland

Alone: Bowness, Cumberland; Whitley Castle, Northumberland; Ambleside, Westmoreland

Alone Flu: River Alne, Northumberland

Alongium, Alouergium Civitas: Carnbrea, Cornwall

Alpes Peneni Montes: Pendle Hill, Lancashire

Alre: Aller, near Bridgwater, Somerset

Alrene: Alderney

Alta Clera: Highclere, Hants

Alta Prisa: Haltemprice or Howdenprice, Yorks

Altum Peccum: the Peak, Derbyshire

Aluerodunum Brigantum: North Allerton, Yorks

Aluertonia: North Allerton, Yorks

Aluestana: Olveston, Gloucestershire

Aluion: *see* Albion

Alunna: Castleshaw, Yorks

Alunus: River Alan, Wales

Ambegianna: *see* Amboglanna

Ambesbiria: Amesbury, Wilts

Amboglanna: Ambleside, Westmoreland; Burdoswald, Cumberland

Ambresbiria: Amesbury, Wilts

Ambreslega: Ombersley, Worcestershire

Ambrosia, Ambrosii Burgus, Ambrosii Mons: Amesbury, Wilts

Ammera: Anmere, Norfolk

Anachoreticus Vicus: Ankerwick, Bucks

Anandia Vallis: Annandale, Scotland

Ancalites: a tribe near Henley, Oxfordshire

Anchoreticus Sinus: Ankerwick, Bucks

Anderelio: *see* Anderida

Anderida: Newenden, Kent; Pevensey, Eastbourne, or Arundel, Sussex

Andeuera, Andouera: Andover, Hants

Andium: *see* Adros

Andreapolis: St Andrew's, Scotland; *see* Fanum Reguli

Andresega: an old monastery on the site of Burton Abbey, Staffordshire

Andrium, Andros: Bardsey Island, Caernarvonshire; *see* Adros

Anecastrum: Ancaster, Lincolnshire

Anegus: Angus, Scotland

Angelocum: Ancaster, Lincolnshire

Anglesega: Anglesey

Anglia: England

Angra, Angria: Ongar, Essex

Anguillaria Insula: Isle of Ely

Anguillarianus: of Ely

Angulia: Flintshire

Angusia: Angus, Scotland

Anicetis Civitas: in Dorset

Ansoba: River Galway, Ireland

Antiuestaeum promontorium: Land's End, Cornwall

Antona: River Avon, Northants; River Anton, Hants

Antona Australis: Southampton

Antona Borealis: Northampton

Antrum Flu: the Erme, Devonshire

Apaunaris Civitas: in Devonshire

Apelbia: Appleby, Westmoreland

Apiacum: Hexham, Northumberland; Papcastle, Cumberland

Apletrea: Appledore, Kent

Applebeia, Applebera: Appleby, Westmoreland

Apultrea: Appledore, Devon

Aqua Rubra: Redbourn, Herts; Redbourne, Lincolnshire

Aquae Calidae: Bath, Somerset

Aquae Solis, Sulis: Bath

Aquaedonum: Eton, Bucks; Aikton, Cumberland

Aquaedunensis Saltus: Waterden, Norfolk

Aquaedunum: Waldron, Sussex; Waterden, Norfolk

Aquaeuadensis Pons: Eye Bridge, Dorset

Aquapontanus: Bridgwater, Somerset

Aquelmum: Ewelme, Oxfordshire

Aquila: Eagle, Lincolnshire

Aquilodunum: Hoxne, Suffolk

Aquis Civitas: *see* Aquae Calidae

Aramis, Aranus Civitas: in Dorset

Arbeia: Moresby or Ireby, Cumberland; Armley or Castleford, Yorks

Archfordensis: of Ardfert, Co. Kerry

Archmachia: Armagh

Arclouium: Arklow, co Wicklow, Ireland

Arcmacensis: of Armagh

Arcmorensis: of Ardmore, Waterford

Arcubus, Curia de: Court of Arches

Ardacha: Ardagh, Co. Longford

Ardahachdensis: of Ardagh, Ireland

Ardaoneon Civitas: Old Sarum; Silchester, Hants

Ardatum: Ardat or Ardathen, Co. Kerry

Ardefertensis: of Ardfert, Co. Kerry

Ardgathelia: Argyll, Scotland

Ardmacha: Armagh

Ardmoria: Ardmore, co Waterford

Ardraeum: Ardee, Co. Louth; Ardree, Co. Kildare, Ireland

Ardraicum: Ardagh, Co. Longford

Ardua: Lostwithiel, Cornwall

Arewa: River Orwell, Suffolk

Argadia, Argathelia: Argyle, Scotland

Argistillum: in Gloucestershire, or perhaps Arwystli, Powys

Argita: Lough Foil, Londonderry; Camden applies this name to Lough Swilley

Ariconium: Kenchester, Ross, or Penyard Castle, Herefordshire

Armaca: Armagh, Ireland

Armanothia: Ardmeanach, Scotland

Armethua: Armathwaite, Cumberland

Armis: Bath

Armone: Caernarvon

Arnemega: Willoughby-on-the-Wolds, Notts; *see* Verometum

Arrania: Isle of Arran, Scotland

Arregaidela: Argyll

Arthferdensis, Arthfertensis: of Ardfert, Co. Kerry

Arthmorensis: of Ardmore, Co. Waterford

Arundelia, Arundellum: Arundel, Sussex

Arundinis Vadum: Redbridge, Hants.

Aruntina Vallis: Arundel, Sussex

Arunus Flu: River Arun, Sussex

Aruone: Caernarvon

Aruonia: Caernarvonshire

Arus: River Aire, Yorks

Asaphopolis: St Asaph, Flintshire

Ascaranus: *see* Aiscaranus

Ascdala: Eskdale

Athanaton, Athanatos: Isle of Thanet; *see* Tanathos

Athesis Flu: River Tees; *see* Tesa

Atholia: Athol, Scotland

Athra: Athenry, Co. Galway

Atina Insula: Thanet; *see* Adtanatos

Atrebati: People of Berks

Atrium Dei: Hinton, Somerset

Attacotti: conquered tribes north of the Roman wall

Aualana: Watchcross; *see* Aballaba

Aualonia: Glastonbury, Somerset

Auchelandia: Bishops Auckland, Durham

Aue: River Avon, or Avin, Scotland

Auena Flu: River Avon, Wilts

Auenina, Auenna Flu: River Afan, or Avon, Glamorganshire

Auenmorus: Blackwater River, Cork

Auennus: River Avon, a tributary of the Clyde, Scotland

Aufona: River Avon, Northants.

Augusta: Aust, Gloucestershire

Augusta Trinobantum, Augusta: London

Augustaldia: Hexham, Northumberland

Auinus: River Avon, or Avin, Scotland

Aula Cervina: Hart Hall, Oxford

Aula, vel Villa Antiqua: Aldbury, Herts

Aumodishamum: Amersham, Bucks

Auna: Awn, bishopric in Ireland

Aunest': Elstow, Beds

Auona: Bungay, Suffolk

Auona: River Avon; River Nen, Northants

Auona Littoralis, sive Australis: Southampton

Auona Mediterranea, sive Borealis: Northampton

Auona, Auondunum: Hampton Court, according to Leland

Auonae Vallis: Oundle, Northants

Auondunum Limenorum: Southampton

Auonii palatium: Winchester House, Southwark

Aura: Awre, Gloucestershire

Aurauanus: *see* Abrauannus

Aurea Vallis: Golden Vale, Herts

Aurenium: Alderney, or Herm Island

Aureum Vadum: Guildford, Surrey

Ausoba: *see* Ansoba

Ausona: River Avon, Northants

Auteri, Auterii: people of Galway and Roscommon, Ireland

Autona: Avon, Northants

Aventio Flu: River Aun, or Avon, Devon

Axelodunum: Hexham, Northumberland; Burgh-by-Sands, or Bowness, Cumberland

Axeministra: Axminster, Devon

Axiholma: Axholme, Lincolnshire

Axium Flu: River Axe, Devon

Ba, Baa: Bath

Babaglanda: Burdoswald; *see* Amboglanna

Babbegraua: Baggrave, Leicestershire

Bachelagana: Bacheleia Sylva: Bagley Wood, Berks

Bada: Bath, Somerset

Baddanbyrig: Badbury, Dorset

Badecanwella: Bakewell, Derbyshire

Badiza: Bath; *see* Aquae Calidae

Badonicus Mons: Badon Hill, or Bannesdown, a hill near Bath

Badunum: Bath

Baenburgus: Bamborough, Northumberland

Bagilogana Sylva: Bagley Wood, Berks

Bainardi Castellum: Baynard's Castle, London

Bainus Pons: Bainbridge, Yorks

Bala: Bala, Merionethshire

Balingium: Bowes-upon-Stanmore, Yorks

Balmuraeum: Balmerinach, Fife

Balnea, Baleneodunum: Bath

Baltifordia: Waterford, Ireland

Bamfum: Banff, Scotland

Bana Insula: an island opposite the mouth of the River Taff, Glamorganshire

Banatia: Bean Castle, Murray; Comrie, Perthshire; or near Inverness

Bancornensis: of Bangor

Banesinga Villa: Bensington, Oxfordshire

Banna: Cambeck, or Castlesteeds, Cumberland

Banna: River Ban, Ulster

Bannauenna, Bannauentum: Borough Hill, near Daventry; or Weedon, Northants; or Banbury, Oxfordshire

Banneberia: Banbury, Oxfordshire

Bannio: Abergavenny; *see* Gobannium

Bannochorus, Bangorium: Bangor, North Wales

Bannouallum: *see* Bannauenna

Banua: Bannow, Ireland

Banus Flu: River Bain, Lincolnshire

Bara: Dunbar, Scotland

Barangae: *see* Brangonia

Barcsciria: Berkshire

Bardeneia: Bardney, Lincolnshire

Bardunus: River Bure, Norfolk

Barnastapula: Barnstable, Devon

Baromaci: *see* Caesaromagus

Baruicus, Barwickus: Berwick-upon-Tweed

Basenga, Basingum: Basing, Basingstoke, Hants

Basselawa: Baslow, Derbyshire

Batalia: Battle Abbey, Sussex

Batersega: Battersea, Surrey

Batha, Bathonia: Bath

Batilfordia: Waterford, Ireland

Batonicus: of Bath

Bdora: River Dore, Herefordshire

Beanflota: Bamfleet, Essex

Bearrocscira: Berkshire

Beatitudine, Abbatia de: Bectiffe Abbey, Co. Meath

Bebba, Bebbanbyrig: Bamborough, Northumberland

Bechewrda: Badgworth, Somerset

Bechlanda: Byland, Yorks

Bedeforda: Bedford

Bedericia, Bedericum: St Edmundsbury, Suffolk

Bedfordia: Bedford

Begesse: a town on the Wall of Antonine

Beggewurda: Badgworth, Somerset

Belaisena: Ballinasloe, Co. Galway

Belerium promontorium: Land's End

Belgae: inhabitants of Somerset, Wilts., and Hants., occupying the South Coast in Roman times

Belgae: Wells, Somerset

Belinus Sinus: Billingsgate

Belisama: River Ribble, or Mersey, Lancashire

Bella Vallis: Beauvale, in Gresley Park, Notts

Bellalanda: Byland, Yorks

Bellesitum: Oxford

Bellisama: *see* Belisama

Bellocliuum, Bellodesertum: Bedesert, or Beaudesert, Warwickshire

Bellomariscus: Beaumaris, Isle of Anglesey

Bellositum: City of Oxford

Bellum: Battle, Sussex

Bellum Beccum: Beau Bec, Co. Meath

Bellum Caput: Beauchief, Derbyshire

Bellum Verum: Belvoir, Leicestershire

Bellus Campus: Bulcamps, Suffolk

Bellus Locus: Beaulieu, Hants; Beaulieu, Moddry or Mylbrook, Beds; Beauly, Inverness; Beaudesert, Warwickshire; Killagh, Kerry, Ireland

Bellus Locus Regis: Beaulieu Abbey, Hants

Bellus Portus: Kilclehin, Co. Kilkenny

Beluerum: Belvoir, Leicestershire

Benethleya: Bentley, Middlesex

Bennauenna: *see* Bannauenna

Bennones: *see* Venonae

Bentensis: for Ventensis; *see* Venta

Beohrtforda: Burford, Oxon.

Bera: Bere Forest, Hants; Beer, Dorset

Berca: Barcombe, Sussex

Berceia, Berceria: Berkshire

Bercheleia: Berkeley, Gloucestershire

Bercheria: Berkshire

Bercheya: Barraway, Cambridgeshire

Berclea: Berkeley, Gloucestershire

Berdeniga: Bardney, Lincolnshire

Berdeseia: Bardsey Island, or Ynys Enlli, Caernarvonshire

Berdestapla: Barnstaple, Devon; Barnstable, Essex

Berechingum: Barking, Essex

Bereda: *see* Voreda

Berekingum: Barking, Essex

Berga: Bridgnorth, Shropshire

Bergefelda: Burghfield, Berks

Bergonium: a vitrified fort, opposite Connell Ferry, at the mouth of Loch Etive, Lorne

Berkeria: Berkshire

Berkleia: Berkeley, Gloucestershire

Bermundesaia, Bermundsheia, Bermundi Insula: Bermondsey, Surrey

Bernardi Castellum: Barnard Castle, Durham

Bernia: *see* Hibernia

Bernicia: province reaching from the River Tees to the Frith of Forth

Berogomum: a castle in Lorn, West Dumbartonshire, Scotland

Bersetelawawapentagium: Bassetlaw Wapentake, Notts

Berua: River Barrow, Ireland

Berubium promontorium: Duncansby Head, or more probably Noss Head, Caithness, Scotland

Beruchensis: of Berkshire

Beruicium, Berwicus: Berwick

Betesdenna: Bediston, Devon

Beuerlacum, Beuerlea: Beverley, Yorks

Bibrocassi, Bibroci: a tribe near Bray, Berks

Bimonium: Binchester, Durham; *see* Vinnouium

Bindogladia: *see* Vindocladia

Binonium, Binouia, Binouium: Binchester, Durham; *see* Vinnouium

Birgus: River Barrow, Waterford

Biria: Berryn Arbor, Devon

Birila Insula: Burril Island, Co. Down, Ireland

Birwda: Burnham Wood

Bishamum: Bustlesham, or Bisham, Berks

Bistaghnensis: of Glendalough, Co. Wicklow

Blacamora: Blackmore, North Riding of Yorks

Blacinctona: Blatchington, Sussex

Blacna: Blakeney

Bladinae Montes: Sliabh Bladhma, now called Slieve Bloom Mountains, in the barony of Ossory, Queen's County, Ireland

Bladunum: Malmesbury; *see* Maidulphi Curia

Blakingraua: a hundred of Wiltshire, in the time of Henry II

Blancaforda: Blandford, Dorset

Blancalanda: Blanch Land, Northumberland; Whiteland, Caermarthenshire

Blancum Castrum: White Castle, or Blane Castle, Monmouthshire

Blanii: a tribe about Dublin

Blatum Bulgium, Ablatum Bulgium: Middleby, Dumfries; or Bowness, or Cardunnock, Cumberland

Bledewurda: Blidworth, Notts

Blengata hundredum: Blackheath hundred, Kent

Blestium: Monmouth; Oldtown, Herefordshire

Blia, Blida: Blythe, Notts

Blidberia, Blieberia: Blewbury, Berks

Blithodunum: Blyton, Lincs.

Blokelega: Blockley, Worcestershire

Blya: Blythe, Notts

Boanda, Boandus: River Boyne, Ireland

Bobium: *see* Bomium

Boccania, Boccinia, Boccinum: Buckingham; Buckenham, Norfolk

Bodenna: Bodmin, Cornwall

Boderia: *see* Bodotria

Bodianum: Bodiam, Sussex

Bodotria: Firth of Forth

Boduni: *see* Dobuni

Boena: a town in the west of Scotland

Boghania: Buchan, Aberdeenshire, Scotland

Boisgraua: Boxgrove, Sussex

Bolbenda: River Beaumont, Durham

Bolerium: the Land's End

Boleshouera, Bolesoura: Bolsover, Derbyshire

Boluelaunio: Poole, Dorset

Bomina: Bodmin, Cornwall

Bomium: Cowbridge, Boverton, or Bridgend, Glamorganshire; or Axbridge, Somerset

Bonium, Bonuium: Stretton, Bangor, or Queenhope, Flintshire; Bunbury, Cheshire; or Whitchurch, Shropshire

Bonno: *see* Bomium

Boraeum promontorium: Malin Head, Ireland

Borcouicum, Borcouitium, Borcouium: Housesteads, Northumberland; Berwick

Bosco, Domus St Egidii in: Flamsted, Herts.

Boscus Arsus: Brentwood, Essex (Fr. *Boisars*)

Boselawa: Baslow, Derbyshire

Bosmanacha: Bodmin, Cornwall

Bosphorus Picticus: Pentland Firth, Scotland

Bosuenna: Bodmin, Cornwall

Botelega: Botley, Hants; Bolney, Oxfordshire

Bothmenia: Bodmin, Cornwall

Botis: Bute Island, west coast of Scotland

Bouenia: Boveney, Berks

Bouium: *see* Bomium, Bonium

Boxelega, Boxeleia: Boxley, Kent

Boxora: Boxford, Berks

Braboniacum: *see* Bremetonacum, Bremeturacum, Brouonacis

Bracchium: Burgh, or Bainbridge, Yorks

Brachilega: Brackley, Northants

Bradeweya: Broadway, Worcestershire

Brage: *see* Brige

Braitha: River Brathay, Lancashire

Bramenium: *see* Bremenium
Bramptonia: Brampton, near Huntingdon
Branconium: *see* Branoricum
Brangonia, Brannogenium: Bangor: *see also* Branoricum
Brangoria: Bangor
Branodunum: Brancaster, Norfolk
Branoricum, Branouium, Brauinium, Brauonium: Worcester; Ludlow, Leintwardine, or Onibury, Shropshire
Brechinia: Brecknock
Brechinium: Brechin, Scotland
Bredenestreta: Broadways, Worcestershire
Brehinium: *see* Brechinium
Breinensis: of Brechin, Scotland
Brembra: Bramber, Sussex
Bremenium: Newcastle or High Rochester, Northumberland; Brampton, Northants
Bremesgraua: Bromsgrove, Worcestershire
Bremetonacum: Overborough, Lancaster, or Clitheroe, Lancashire
Bremeturacum: either Bremetonacum Old Penrith or Bromfield, Cumberland; or Ribchester, Lancashire
Brendanici Montes: Knock Brandon, Kerry
Brendanicum Mare: the Atlantic
Brenna: Breubege or Brynabege, Glamorgan
Brentae Vadum: Brentford, Middlesex
Bresnetenati Veteranorum: *see* Bremeturacum and Bremetonacum
Brexarum: Burgh, Lincolnshire
Bribra: perhaps the same as Bremeturacum
Brigantes: inhabitants of Yorkshire, Lancashire, Durham, Westmoreland and Cumberland; also of Waterford and Kilkenny, Ireland, and Galloway, Scotland
Brigantium: York
Brige: Bridgnorth, Shropshire; Broughton, or Titchfield Bay, Harris; Ryde
Brigewatera: Bridgwater, Somerset
Brigomono: Bargeny, Wigtown
Brigus: Barrow River, Ireland
Brillendunun: Bridlington, Yorks
Brimesgraua: Bromsgrove, Worcestershire
Brincaburga: Brinkburn, Northumberland
Brinchelawa: Brinklow, Warwickshire
Briodunum: Bredon, Worcestershire
Bristelmestuna: Brighton, Sussex
Bristoldum: Bristol
Bristolia, Bristolium, Bristollum, Bristowa: Bristol
Britanni: people of Britain
Britannia Prima: Britain south of the Thames
Britannia Secunda: Britain west of the Severn; or from Bristol Channel to Mersey, and from Thames to Humber
Britannicus Oceanus: English Channel
Britannodunum: Dumbarton, Scotland
Brithania: *see* Britannia
Britones: people of Britain
Britonum Castrum: Dunbritton, or Dumbarton, Scotland
Brocara, Brocavo: Brough or Brougham-on-the-Eamont, Westmoreland
Broconiacum: Brougham, Westmoreland
Brodenestreta: Broadways, Worcestershire
Bromfelda: Bromfield, Denbighshire
Brouonacis: Aldstone Moor, Brough, Brougham, or Kirkbythure, Westmoreland
Brueria: Bruerne Abbey, Oxon
Bruga: Bridgnorth, Shropshire
Bruga Walteri: Bridgewater, Somerset
Brugia: Bridge, Devon
Bruhella: Brill, Bucks
Brutannia: *see* Britannia
Brycstowa: Bristol
Brygiona: Boxgrove, Sussex
Bubris: *see* Dubris
Buccinghania: Buckingham
Buchania: Buchan, Scotland
Bucostenum: Buxton, Derbyshire
Budeforda: Bedford
Buellium: Boyle, Ireland
Buffestra: Buckfastleigh, Devon
Buksiria: Buckinghamshire
Bulgium: Bowness, Cumberland
Bullaeum: Builth, Brecknock; or Usk, Monmouth
Bumsteda: Bumpstead, Essex
Bungehia: Bungay, Suffolk
Burgamera: Bolmer, Sussex
Burgensis Pons: Boroughbridge, Yorks
Burgodunum: Burton, Staffordshire
Burgus: Brough, Westmoreland; Peterborough; Burgh, Norfolk; Bridgnorth, Shropshire
Burgus Regine: Queenborough, Kent
Burgus super Zabulum: Burgh-by-Sands, Cumberland
Burhella: *see* Bruhella
Buroauerus: *see* Durouernum
Buroleuo: *see* Durolenum
Burrio: Usk, Monmouthshire; Ledbury, Herefordshire
Burwardescota: Buscot, Berks
Busenia: Binsey, Oxon.
Bustelli Domus: Bustlesham or Bisham, Berks
Buuenia: Boveney, Berks
Buuinda: River Boyne, Ireland
Byligesleaga: Billingsley, Shropshire

Byrdena: Burdon, Durham
Cacaria: Tadcaster or Aberford, Yorks
Caerdiffa: Cardiff, Glamorganshire
Caerdigania: Cardigan
Caer-Lincoit: Lincoln; *see* Lincolnium
Caermardinia: Caermarthen, Wales
Caerperis: Porchester, Hants
Caerseuerus: Salisbury, Wilts
Caesarea, Caesaria: Jersey
Caesaris Burgus: Searbyrig, Old Sarum
Caesaromagus: Chelmsford, Writtle, Widford, Burntwood, Canvey Island, or Billericay, Essex
Calacum: *see* Galacum
Calaterium: River Calder, Yorks
Calaterium Nemus: Forest of Galtress, Yorks
Calatum: *see* Galacum
Calcaria: Tadcaster or Aberford, Yorks
Calcetum: a monastery near Lewes
Calcoensis, Calchouensis: of Kelso, Scotland
Calcua, Naleua: *see* Calleua and Galleua
Caldei Insula: Ynys Pyr, or Caldey Island, Pembrokeshire
Calderus Flu: River Calder, Yorks
Caledonia: Callander, Perthshire; also used for the whole of Scotland
Caledonia Sylva: Argyle, Lochaber and Moray
Caledonii: Inhabitants of north-west Scotland
Caledonium Castrum: Dunkeld
Calgachi Roboretum: Doire Chalgaich, Derry, Ireland
Calidoniae Sylvae: Florus applies this name to the interior of England
Calkoensis: of Kelso
Calleua: Basingstoke, Hants
Calleua Attrebatum: *see* Galleua Atrebatum
Calna: Calne, Wilts
Calonia: Coldingham, Berwick
Calunio: same as Galacum; or Wakefield, Yorks
Camaldunum: Camalodunum: Maldon, Colchester, or Lexden, Essex
Camaletum: Camel, Somerset
Cambium Regale: Royal Exchange, London
Cambodunum: Almondbury, Greetland, or Elland, West Riding of Yorkshire
Camboricum, Camborium: Icklingham, Suffolk; or Cambridge
Cambretonium: *see* Comberetonium
Cambria: Wales
Cambula: River Camel, Cornwall
Camelodunum: Doncaster, Yorks
Camerum: Castell Cwm Aram, Denbighshire
Camestrum: Campsterne, Dorset
Camolodunum: *see* Camaldunum
Campodunum: *see* Cambodunum

Campus Altus: Hatfield, or Hautfield, Herts
Campus Fabrum: Smithfield, London
Campus Nouo-Forensis: Newmarket Heath, Cambridgeshire
Camudolanum: *see* Cambodunum
Camulodunum: *see* Camaldunum and Cambodunum
Cana Insula: Sheppy; *see* Counos
Canachina Silva: Cannock Chase, Staffordshire
Canani Terra: Merioneth
Cancani: people living in Carnarvonshire
Cancanum: *see* Canganorum
Cancia: Kent
Candalia: Kendal, Westmoreland
Candida Casa: Whitehorn, Whithern, Wigtonshire
Candida Ecclesia: Whitchurch, Salop
Canewella: Canwell, Staffordshire, a Benedictine Priory
Canganorum promontorium: Braichy Pwll Point, Carnarvonshire: the same as Ganganum
Cangi: a tribe in Somerset, or perhaps the same as Cancani
Caninga: Bishop's Canning, Wilts
Canonium: Canewdon, or Fambridge; or near Kelvedon, Essex
Canouaci: people in Argyll, Lorn, and Lennox
Cantabrigia: Cambridge
Cantae: a tribe in Sutherland
Cantebrigia: Cambridge
Cantia, Cantium: Kent
Cantiuenti: a tribe probably in Westmoreland
Cantium promontorium: the North Foreland, Kent
Cantuaria: Canterbury
Cantuaritae: Kentish Saxons
Canubio: *see* Conouium
Caprae Caput, Caprocephalia: Gateshead, Durham: *see* Gabrocentum
Capreolum: Cheverell, Wilts.; some place in Brecon
Carbantium: Caerlaverock, Dumfriesshire
Carbantorigum: Drummore, Dumfries; Caerlaverock
Carbonarius Collis: Coleshill, Flintshire
Carcaria: *see* Calcaria
Cardelum: Carlisle
Cardigania: Cardigan, Wales
Careni: inhabitants of Caithness
Carleolium: Carleolum: Carlisle
Carmarthinia: Caermarthen
Carnaruonia: Caernarvon
Carnetum: Carnedon Prior, Cornwall
Carnonacae: people of Ross, Scotland
Carphillis: a castle, supposed to have been built by the Romans, Glamorganshire

Carricta: Carrick, Scotland

Carrum: Charmouth, Dorset; Carham, Northumberland

Carsuilla: Kerswell, Devon

Cartusia: Witham Charterhouse, Somerset

Carugia: Kerry, Ireland

Casa Candida: *see* Candida Casa

Casella: Cashel, Ireland

Cassaceastre: Chichester, Sussex

Cassi, Cassii: a tribe in Hertfordshire

Cassilia: Cashel, Ireland

Cassiterides: Scilly Islands

Cassiuelauni oppidum: St Albans; *see* Verolamium

Casta Silua: Kilcreunata, co Galway

Castellum Haroldi: Haroldeston, in the deanery of Ross

Castra: Caistor, Lincolnshire

Castra Alata: *see* Alata Castra

Castra Exploratorum: Burgh by Sands, Netherby, Old Castle, or Bowness, Cumberland

Castrodunum: Chesterton, Cambridgeshire

Castrum Britonum: Dunbritton, Scotland

Castrum Caledonium: Dunkeld

Castrum Cubii: Holyhead

Castrum de Aruon: Caernarvon Castle

Castrum de Vies: Devizes, Wilts

Castrum Dei: Fermoy Abbey, Ireland

Castrum Episcopi: Bishop's Castle, Shropshire

Castrum Godrici: Goodrich, Herefordshire

Castrum Legionis, Leonis: Holt Castle, Denbighshire

Castrum Matildis: Paincastle, Herefordshire

Castrum Oscae: Usk, Monmouthshire

Castrum Puellarum: Edinburgh

Cataracta Flu: River Swale, Yorks

Cataracta, Cataractonium: Thornburgh, near Thirsk, Allerton, or Catterick Bridge, Yorks

Catenessa: Caithness

Cateracta: Catterick, Yorks

Cateuchlani: *see* Catuellani

Catguilia: Kidwelly, Carmarthenshire

Cathania: Caithness, Scotland

Cathinensis: of Caithness

Catini: people of Caithness

Catteleia: Catley, Lincolnshire

Catuellani, Catyeuchlani: people of Buckingham, Bedford, and Hertfordshire

Caua: Cave, Yorks

Cauae Dirae: Holderness, Yorks

Cauci: tribe living in Wicklow, Ireland

Cauda: River Calder, Cumberland

Cauda Alicii: La Quealiz, a wood in Brill Forest, Bucks

Cauerna Viperina: Aspeden, Herts

Cauna: *see* Counos

Caunonio: *see* Canonium

Cauoda: Cawood, Yorks

Causennae, Causennis: Boston, Ancaster, Brig Casterton, or Swineshead, Lincolnshire

Cawda: *see* Cauoda

Cealchithe: Chalk, Kent; Chelsea

Cealtide: Chelsea

Ceangi: *see* Cangi

Ceastra: Chester; Chester-le-Street, Durham

Celerion: Callender Castle, Perthshire

Cella Canici: Kilkenny

Cella Reguli: Kilreule, St Andrews

Cella S Brigittae: Kilbride

Celnius Flu: River Findhorn, or River Spey, Elgin

Celouion: *see* Celerion

Celunno: *see* Cilurnum

Celurca: Montrose, Forfar

Cenenensis: of Kells, Ireland

Cenimagni: the same as the Iceni, a tribe in the east of Britain

Cenion Flu: River Falle, Cornwall

Centum fontes: Hundredskelde, or Hinderwell, Yorks

Ceolesega: Selsey, Sussex

Ceolesegia: Cholsey, Berks

Cerda: Chard, Somerset

Cerda Selgouarum: Dumfries

Cerdici Vadum: Chardford, Hants

Ceretica: Ceredigion, a province of South Wales; Cardiganshire

Cerneia: Charney, Berks

Cernelium: Cerne, Dorset

Cernualia, Curnualia: Cornwall

Cerones, Ceronii: inhabitants of Lochaber and Ross

Cerota Insula: Chertsey, Surrey

Cerqueyum: Sark

Cerringa: Charing, Kent

Certesia: Chertsey, Surrey

Cerui Insula: Chertsey; *also* Hartlepool, Durham

Cesarea, Cesaria: Jersey

Cesaris Tumulus: Carn Ceasra, Connaught

Cestratona: Chesterton

Cestre: is used for York, Chester, and Chester-le-Street

Cestrescira: Cheshire

Cestria: Chester; Cheshire; Chester-le-Street, Durham; Castle Knock, Dublin

Cestrisiria: Cheshire

Chaluelea: Cheveley, Cambridgeshire

Chanani Terra: Merioneth

Chanrea, Chanoricum: Chanonry, Ross-shire

Chardum: Chard, Somerset

Chathania: *see* Cathania

Chauci: *see* Cauci

Chausega: Cheausey, or Cholsey, Berks

Cheleswurda: Chelworth, Wilts

Chelmerium: Chelmsford, Essex

Chemesinga: Kemsing, Kent

Chentenses: Kentish men

Chepstouium: Chepstow, Monmouthshire

Chesterfelda: Chesterfield, Derbyshire

Chestria, Chestrum: *see* Cestria

Cheua: Kew, Surrey

Chibii Castrum: Holyhead, Anglesey

Chicum: St Osith, Essex

Chienfernensis: of Clonfert, Ireland

Chimela: Keymer, Sussex

Chineglissi Castrum: Kenilworth Castle, Warwickshire

Chingesordia: King's Worthy, Hants

Chingestona: Kingston

Chingeswuda: Kingswood

Chingeswurtha: King's Worthy, Hants

Chirca: Chirk, Denbighshire

Chirchbeia: Kirkby, Kirby

Chiringecestra: Cirencester, Gloucestershire

Chonderensis: of Coonor, Co. Antrim

Chorfa: Corfe, Dorset

Choro Benedicti, Abbatia de: Chore or Middleton Abbey, Cork

Chridiantune: Crediton, Devon

Cibra: a town on or near the Antonine Wall

Cica: Chich St Osyth, Essex

Ciceastria, Cicestria (Cissaceastre): Chichester, Sussex

Cilurnum, Cilurinum: Walwick Chesters, or Collerton, Northumberland

Cindocellum: a town in Scotland, north of Antonine's Wall

Cirecestria, Cirencestria, Cirinium: Cirencester, Glouc

Cirnea: Charney, Gloucestershire

Ciuella: Cheveley

Ciuitas Legionum: Caerleon, Monmouthshire; Chester

Clandensis: Glendalough, Wicklow

Clanouenta: Lanchester, Durham; Cokermouth or Ellenberough, Cumberland

Clara: County of Clare, Ireland

Clarentia: Clare, Suffolk

Claria: Clare County, Ireland

Clarofontanus, Clarus Fons: Sherbourne, Dorset; Moycoscain, Co. Derry

Claudiana provincia: Gloucestershire

Claudiocestria: Gloucester

Clauinio: a town probably in Dorset

Clausentum: Bishop's Waltham; Southampton; Bittern, Hants.; Chichester, Sussex

Clawurda: Clayworth, Notts.

Cledhea Flu: River Cleddy, Pembrokeshire

Cleituna: Clayton, Sussex

Cleocestria: Gloucester

Clera Regis: Kingsclere, Hants

Cletlinga: Cleatlam, Durham

Cleuum: Gloucester; *see* Claudia

Clidum: Ardoch, Perthshire; *see* Lindum

Cliua: King's Cliff, Northants

Cliuelanda: Cleveland

Clocheria, Clocherium: Clogher, Ireland

Cloenensis: Clonmacnois, King's County, Ireland

Clokorna: Clogher, Tyrone

Clona: Clone or Cloone, Ireland

Clonfertum: Clonfert, Cork

Clota: River Clyde

Clouesho: Cliffe at Hoo, Kent

Cluainfertensis: Clonfert, Cork

Cluainvanea, Cluanania, Cluanum: Cloyne, Co. Cork, Ireland

Cluanumensis: of Cloyne, Co. Cork

Cluda: River Clyde

Cluenerardensis: of Clonard, Co. Meath

Cluida, Cluta: River Clwyd, Denbighshire

Clunererardensis: of Clonard, Co. Meath

Clutina Vallis: Diffryncloyd, Wales

Cnapa: Knepp, Surrey

Cnaresburgus: Knaresborough, Yorks

Cnobheriburgus: Burgh Castle, Suffolk

Coantia: River Kent, Westmoreland

Cocarus: River Coke, Yorks; Cocker, Lancashire

Coccium: Blackrode, or Ribchester, Lancashire

Cocuneda Civitas: on the River Coquet, Northumberland

Cocwuda: River Coquet

Cognacta: Connaught, Ireland

Coguuensuron Flu: River Soar, Leicestershire

Coila: Kyle, west of Scotland

Cokarus: *see* Cocarus

Colania: Carstairs, or Crawford, Lanarkshire; Coldingham, Berwickshire

Colanica: Coldingham, or Colchester

Colcestria: Colchester, Essex

Coldania: Coldingham

Coleceastra, Colecestra: Colchester, Essex

Collis Magnus: Crug Mawr, Pembrokeshire

Collis Victoriae: Knockmoy, a Cistercian Abbey, Co. Galway

Colmonora: *see* Cumanora

Colnia Flu: River Colne

Colonia: Colchester, Maldon, or Mersea Strood, Essex

Colonia Victricensis: Maldon, Essex

Coludum: Coldingham, Berwickshire

Colunum: Colnbrook, Bucks

Comberetonium: Brettenham; Stratford St Andrew; or Hadleigh, Suffolk

Combretouium: *see* Comberetonium

Comparcus: Combe Park, Surrey

Conacta: Province of Connaught, Ireland

Conallea: Tirconnell, Ireland

Concangios: Watercrook, near Kendal; or Chseter-le-Street, Durham; or Burgh, near Woodbridge, Suffolk

Concani: people of Munster, Ireland

Condate: Congleton, Northwich, Kinderton, or Arley Hall, Great Budworth, Cheshire

Condercum: Chester-le-Street, Durham; Benwell, Northumberland

Congauata: Stanwix, or Drumburgh, Cumberland

Congericuria: Congersbury, Somerset

Connaccia, Connachtia: Connaught, Ireland

Connacta: Connaught

Connaria: Connor, Co. Antrim, Ireland

Connatium: Connaught

Conneria, Connertum: *see* Connaria

Cononium: Chelmsford, Essex

Conouium: Caer Rhyn, or Caerhen, on the Conway, Caernarvonshire

Conouium, Conouius: River Conway, North Wales; also used for the town of Conway

Contaracta: River Swale, Yorks

Conuennon, Conuennos Insula: *see* Counos

Conuetoni: *see* Comberetonium

Conventria: Coventry, Warwickshire

Coqueda Insula: the Isle of Coquet, on the coast of Northumberland

Coqueda, Coquedus: Coquet River, in Northumberland

Corcagia: Cork, Ireland

Corcensis: of Cork

Corda: Cumnock, Ayrshire; Lynekirk, Peebles, or some town near Loughcure, Scotland

Coria: Corbridge, Northumberland

Coria Damniorum: Carstairs, Lanark; or Kirkurd, Peebles

Coria, Curia Ottadinorum: Jedburgh, Roxburghshire; or Currie, Edinburghshire

Corie: Patrington, Yorks

Coriendi: a tribe in Wexford, Ireland

Corinea: Cornwall

Corinium, Corinium Dobunorum: Cirencester, Gloucestershire

Corinus Flu: the River Churne, Gloucestershire

Coriondi: folk in South Ireland

Coritani, Coritaui: people of Northampton, Leicester, Rutland, Derby, and Nottingham shires

Cornabii: tribe in Strathnavern, Scotland

Cornauii, Cornabii: Inhabitants of Warwick, Worcester, Stafford, Shropshire, and Cheshire

Corneliensis: of Cerne, Dorset

Cornualia, Cornuallia: Cornwall

Cornubia: Cornwall

Cornutum Monasterium: Hornchurch, Essex

Corragia: Cork

Corstopilum, Corstopitum: Corbridge, Morpeth, Gorbet, or Corchester, Northumberland

Corsula Insula: perhaps Holyhead

Coruesgeata: Corfe, Dorset

Coterinus Mons: Cotterdale, North Riding of Yorkshire

Cotteswoldia: Cotswold, Gloucestershire

Cottona: Cotham, near Yarm, Durham

Coualia: Kyle, Ayrshire

Couentria: Coventry, Warwickshire

Couesgraua: Cosgrove, Northants

Couiburchelega: Coverly, Gloucestershire

Couintrea: Coventry, Warwickshire

Counos: Isle of Sheppey, Kent; or Canvey Island, Essex

Cranburna, Craneburgus: Cranborne, Dorset

Crativallis: Cratundene, Cambridgeshire

Craua, Crauena: Craven, Yorks

Creccanforda: Cricklade, Wilts

Crecolada: Cricklade, Wilts

Credigone: Caerriden, on the Wall of Antonine

Credio: Crediton, Devon

Crenodunum: Crendon, Bucks

Creones: tribe living in Ross; *see* Cerones

Cricgealada: Cricklade, Wilts

Cridea, Cridia, Cridiatunum, Cridiodunum: Crediton, or Kirton, Devonshire

Crococalana, Crocolana: Ancaster, Lincolnshire; Brough, near Collingham; or Car-Colston, Notts

Croucingo: Crosby

Crowlandia, Croylandia, Cruilandia: Crowland, Lincolnshire

Croyreys: Royston

Crucelandia: Crowland

Crukeri Castrum: Pey-y-Crug, Radnor

Crulandia: Crowland, Lincolnshire

Crux Chariniana: Charing Cross

Crux Oswaldi: Oswestry, Shropshire

Crux Roesiae: Royston

Cubii Castrum: Holyhead, Anglesey

Cucufelda: Cuckfield, Sussex

Culenum: Cullen, Banff

Culerna: Colerne, Wilts

Cumanora: Cumnor, Berks

Cumberlandia: Cumberland

Cumbremara: Combermere, Cheshire

Cumbri: people of Cumberland

Cumbria: Cumberland
Cunacia: Connaught
Cunctona: Compton, Sussex
Cunecacestre: Chester-le-Street, Durham
Cunetio: Marlborough, Mildenhall, or Ramsbury, Wilts
Cunetio Flu: River Kennet
Cunga: Cong, Ireland
Cunia: River Conway
Cunio: Mull of Cantire
Cuprum: Coupar in Angus
Cuprum Fifae: Cupar Fife
Curia Edmundi: Bury St Edmunds, Suffolk
Curia: *see* Coria
Curnualia: Corwall
Cuuichelmeslawa: Cuckhamsley, Berks
Cyneta: River Kennet
Dabrona: River Avonmore, Cork, Ireland
Dacorum clades: Danes-end, Herts
Dacorum hundredum: Hundred of Upper and Lower Deans, Herts., de Aneis or de Daneis, twelfth century
Dammucensis: of Dunwich, Suffolk
Damnii: People of Clydesdale and Stirling
Damnium, Damnonium promontorium: Lizard, or Dodman Point
Damnonia, Domnania: Devon
Damnonii: People of Devon and Cornwall
Danacastra: Doncaster, Yorks
Danecastria: Doncaster, Yorks
Daneia: Denny, Cambridgeshire
Danica Sylva: Andredswald Forest, Sussex; also the Forest of Dean, Gloucestershire
Danmonii: *see* Damnonii
Danubiae Sylva: Forest of Dean
Danum: Doncaster, Yorks
Danus Flu: the Dane, Lincolnshire; Dan, or Daven, Cheshire; Don, or Dun, Yorks
Darbia: Derby
Darensis: of Kildare
Darentiuadum: Dartford, Kent
Darentus Flu: Darenth, or Dart River, Kent
Darinum: Estanford, Strangford, Ulster
Darnii: a tribe in Ulster
Darotenses: people of Dorset
Daruentia: River Derwent, Derbyshire
Daruernum: Canterbury; Rochester
Daumuicensis: of Dunwich, Suffolk
Daurona: *see* Dabrona
De Fontibus: Wells, Somerset
Dea: River Dee, Cheshire
Debba: *see* Bebba
Decha: a town in Scotland, north of the Forth
Decuaria: *see* Petuaria

Deia: River Dee
Deidonum: Dundee
Deilocum: Godstow, Oxfordshire
Deira: Abbey of Deer, in Buchan
Deira: the part of the kingdom of the Northumbrians on the south side of the Tyne
Deira Sylva: Deerhurst, Gloucestershire
Deirorum Sylva: Derewald, or Beverley, Yorks
Dela: Deal, Kent
Delgouitia: Goddmanham, Fimber, Millington, or Market Weighton, East Riding of Yorks
Deluinia: Delvin, Westmeath, Ireland
Demerosesa: Dumfries
Demetae, Dimetae: people of South Wales
Demetia, Demetica: Dyved, a province in South Wales, Pembrokeshire, and a part of Caermarthenshire
Dena Victrix: Chester; *see* Deua
Dena, Foresta de: Forest of Dean
Denaea Sylva: Forest of Dean
Denbighia: Denbigh, Denbighshire
Deomedum: South Wales
Deorbeia: Derby
Derae: Derry, Ulster
Derbentione: Little Chester, near Derby
Derebisciria: Derbyshire
Derelega: Darley, Derbyshire
Derentiuadum: Dartford, Kent
Dereta: River Dee or Derwent
Derewenta: River Derwent
Derstemuta: Dartmouth, Devon
Derte Ostium, Dertmuta: Dartmouth, Devon
Deruentione: Holtby, Kexby, or Stamford Bridge, on the Derwent, Yorkshire; Pap Castle, Cumberland
Desmonia, Dessemonia: Desmond, Ireland
Dessia: Decies, co Waterford, Ireland
Deua: Dundee; Chester
Deua Flu: River Dee, Cheshire
Deuana: Aberdeen; Chester; Doncaster
Deuania: Cheshire
Deucaledonii: the Scots
Deucaledonius oceanus: the sea on the west of Scotland
Deuenescira: Devonshire
Deui Flu: River Dovey, Wales
Deuionisso: Devonport
Deuna: Chester; *see* Deua
Deunana: Doncaster
Deuonia: Devonshire
Deuouicia: *see* Delgouitia
Deuus Flu: River Dovey
Dewi: St David's
Dextralis Cambria: Deheubarth, i.e. South Wales

Deya: River Dee
Dicelinga: Ditchling, Sussex
Dicetum: Diss, Norfolk
Dicia: Diss, Norfolk
Dictis: Ambleside, Westmoreland
Dictum: Diganwy, Caernarvonshire
Dimetae: people of South Wales
Dineuour: South Wales
Diona: River Dee, Scotland
Dirtouicum: Droitwich, Worcestershire
Diuana: *see* Deuana
Diuilena, Diuilina: Dubh-lein (the Black Pool), now called Dublin
Diuisae, Diuisio: Devizes, Wiltshire; *see* Castrum de Vies
Dixio: *see* Dictis
Dobaria: Dover
Dobuni, Boduni: people of Gloucestershire and Oxfordshire
Docestria: Dorset
Doffra: Dofris: Dover
Dolocindo: a town in Dorset
Domnania: *see* Damnonia
Domnia: Dunwich, Suffolk
Domus Sanctae Crucis: Holyrood House, Edinburgh
Donalmum: Durham
Donewicum: Dunwich, Suffolk
Donus: River Done, Durham
Dorbeia: Derby
Dorcadae: the Orkneys
Dorcestria: Dorchester, Dorset
Dorcinia: Dorchester, Oxfordshire
Dorcinni Civitas: Dorchester, Oxfordshire
Doresetesciria: Dorset
Dorfris: Dover, Kent
Doris Cantiorum: Dover
Dorkcestria, Dorkecestra: Dorchester, Dorset
Dornaceaster: Dorchester
Dornocum: Dornock, Dumfriesshire, Scotland
Dornsetta: Dorchester, Dorset
Dorobellum: *see* Daruernum
Dorobernia: Canterbury; Dover
Dorobreuum: *see* Durobriuis
Dorobrina: Dover
Dorocina: Dorchester
Dorouernum: Canterbury; Dover
Doroventio: *see* Deruentione
Dorpendunum: Orpington, Kent
Dorseta, Dorsetania, Dorsetia: Dorset
Doruantium, Doruatium: River Dart, Darenth, or Derwent
Dorubernia: Canterbury; Dover
Doruenta: River Derwent or Darenth

Doruentani: people of Derbyshire
Doruernum: *see* Daruernum
Dorus Flu: the Dor, Herts
Doruuernia: *see* Dorubernia
Douaria, Douera, Douerha, Doueria, Douoria: Dover
Doura: Dover
Dourus: Dingle Bay
Douus Flu: River Dove, Derbyshire
Dromoria: Dromore, Co. Down, Ulster
Duablisis, Duabsisis: Dupplin, Perthshire
Duacum: Kilmacduagh, Galway, Ireland
Dublicensis: of Dublin
Dublinia, Dublinium, Dublinum: Dublin: *see* Diuilena
Dubris: Dover, Kent
Dufelda: Duffield, Derbyshire
Duflinum: Dublin
Duglassus Flu: River Douglas, Clydesdale
Dulce Cor, Suauicordium: Sweetheart, or New Abbey, Kirkcudbrightshire
Dulma: *see* Magiouinium
Dulmanum: Durham
Dumbarum: Dunbar, Haddingtonshire
Dumbinensis: of Dunblane
Dumblanum: Dunblane, Perthshire
Dumbrosa: Bundroose, or Bundoram, Leitrim
Dumbum promontorium: Bengore Head, or Fair Head, Antrim
Dumera: Dummer, Hants
Dumna: Fair Island, one of the Orkneys
Dumnonia: Devonshire; *see* Damnonia
Dumnonii: *see* Damnonii
Dumwicus: Dunwich, Suffolk
Duna: Down, Downpatrick
Dunamum: Downham, Cambridgeshire
Dunamutha: Tynemouth, Northumberland
Duncheldinum: Dunkeld; *see* Caledonium Castrum
Duncheranum: Dunkerrin, King's County, Ireland
Dundalcum: Dundalk, Louth, Ireland
Dunedinum: Edinburgh
Dunelmia, Dunelmum, Dunelmus: Durham
Dunestaplia: Dunstable, Beds
Dunestor: Dunster, Somerset
Duneuetum: Launceston, Cornwall
Dunfreia: Dumfries, Scotland
Dungallum: Donegal, Ulster
Dunholmum, Dunholmus: Durham
Dunistabulum: Dunstable, Bedfordshire
Dunium: Dorchester, Dorset; *see* Moridunum
Dunmonii: *see* Damnonii
Dunolmum: Durham
Dunouicum: Dunwich, Suffolk
Dunrodunum: Dornoch, Sutherland

Dunuicus: Dunwich, Suffolk

Dunum: Down, Downpatrick, Ulster; Doncaster, Yorks.; Dundalk, Co. Louth; Salisbury; Waterford, Ireland

Dunum Sinus: Scarborough Bay, Yorks, or Teesmouth

Dunus Flu: River Doon, Ayrshire

Dunus Sinus: *see* Dunum Sinus

Dunwicus: Dunwich, Suffolk

Dura: Derry, Ireland

Duracastrum: Dorchester, Oxfordshire

Durbis: River Dour, Kent

Durcinate: *see* Durolipons

Durelmum: Durham

Duri, Duris: 'That part of the Bay of Dingle where is the mouth of the River Maing' Co. Kerry

Duria: Dorset

Duris: Dover

Durius: River Stour

Durnium: Dorchester

Durnonouaria: Dorchester, Dorset

Duroauerni: Canterbury

Durobrabis, Durobrena: *see* Durobriuis

Durobriuas: Caistor, Lincolnshire; or West Lynne; or Wiggenhall St Germain's, Norfolk

Durobriuis: Rochester, Strood, or Cuxton, Kent

Durobrouae: *see* Durobriuis

Durobrus: *see* Durobriuis

Durocastrum: Dorchester, Oxon.

Durocobriuis: Dunstable, Beds; Hertford, Great Berkhampstead, or Redbourne, Herts

Durocornouium: Cirencester

Durolani Flu: River Len, Kent

Durolenum, Duroleuum: Newington, Lenham, or Westwell, Kent

Durolipons: Cambridge, Godmanchester, or Ramsey, Hunts

Durolitum: Old Ford, Leyton, Romsey, or Purfleet, Essex

Duronouaria: Dorchester, Dorset

Duroprouis: *see* Durobriuis

Durosipons: *see* Durolipons

Durotriges: men of Dorsetshire

Durouernum: Canterbury

Durus Flu: River Stour

Dusceleberga, Dusteleberga: Desborough hundred, Bucks

Duthena: River Duddon, Lancashire

Duuelescense Castrum: Duleek, Meath

Duuelina: Dublin

Duuere: Dover

Dwthena: *see* Duthena

Dyrwenta: River Derwent

Eadmodum: Emmet, Yorks

Earipolensis: Jerpont, co Kilkenny

East-Sexena: Essex

Eathelingiana Via: Watling St

Eaxanceastra: Exeter

Ebbecastrum: Bamborough Castle, Northumberland

Eblana: Dublin; *see* Diuilena

Ebodia: the Isle of Alderney

Eboracum: York

Ebuda Insula: two islands are thus named by Ptolemy, of which one is Skye or Islay, the other Lewis or Jura

Ebudae: used for the Western Isles of Scotland generally

Eburacum: York

Eburocastrum: near Rochester, Northumberland

Edenburgus: Edinburgh

Ederosum Monasterium: Ivychurch, Wilts

Edmundi Burgus: Bury St Edmunds, Suffolk

Edra: River Whitadder

Edros Insula: Bardsey Island, Caernarvonshire, or Ireland's Eye

Edulfesberga: Ellesborough, Bucks

Edwella: Ewell, Surrey

Edwiniburgus: Edwinstow, Notts

Efenewuda: Evenwood, Durham

Egelesforda: Aylesford, Kent

Eia: Eye, Suffolk; Eye, near Westminster

Eidumania Flu: Blackwater River, or mouth of the Stour and Orwell, Essex

Eilecuriana Vallis: Vale of Aylesbury, Bucks

Eilecurium: Aylesbury

Eiluius, Eluius: St Asaph's

Eiudensca: Jedburgh, Roxburghshire

Eladunum: Eildon, Roxburghshire

Elauiana: Islay

Elconium: a town in Cornwall

Eldunum: the Eildon Hills

Eleueinia: *see* Eluemia

Elginum, Elgis: Elgin, Scotland

Elgotii, Elgouae: inhabitants of Liddisdale, Ensdale, Eskdale, Nidisdale, and Annandale, in Scotland

Elia: Ely, Cambridgeshire

Eliensis Insula: the Isle of Ely

Ellandunum: Allington, near Amesbury, or Wilton, Wilts

Ellebri: people in Kerry, Ireland

Ellesmara: Ellesmere, Shropshire

Elmelega: Elmley, Worcestershire

Elnicestria: Alceter, Warwickshire

Eltabo: *see* Voluba

Elteshamum: Eltham, Kent

Eltherburna: Halterburn, Roxburghshire

Eluadunum: Elphin, Roscommon

Eluemia: Elvael, a cantref in Powys, Radnorshire

Eluium, Elwa: St Asaph's

Elys: Ely, Cambridgeshire

Embesea: Embsay or Emshaw, Yorks

Emelia: Emly, Co. Tipperary

Emonia: May Isle, in the Firth of Forth

Enachdunensis: Annadown, Co. Clare, Ireland

Enchegallia: Inisgall, i.e. Iona, Tiree, Coll, Canna, and Rum

Engleschyria: England

Englewria: England

Ennabrensis: of Kilfenora, Co. Clare

Eouercon: Abercorn, Scotland

Eouerwicum: York

Eouesum: Evesham, Worcestershire

Eoyrus: River Nore, Ireland

Epeiacum, Epiacum: Hexham, or Papcastle: *see* Apiacum

Epidii: Tribe living in Cantire

Epidium Insula: Islay

Epidium promonotorium: Mull of Cantire

Epocessa: perhaps Upper Stanton, Herefordshire

Erchenefelda: Irchingfield, Herefordshire

Erdingeleya: Ardingley, Sussex

Erdini: people of Fermanagh, Ireland

Ergadia: Argyll

Eripolensis: of Jerpont, Ossory

Ermonia: Ormond, Tipperary

Ernulphi Curia: Eynesbury, Hunts

Erpeditani: *see* Erdini

Esca: River Esk, Dumfries

Esica: *see* Aesycha

Esse Insula: Stourmouth, Kent

Esselega: Ashley

Essendona: Ashdon, Essex

Essexa: Essex

Estantona: Stanton

Estlega: Astley, Worcestershire

Estratona: Stratton, Bedfordshire

Estreia: Eastry, Keny

Estrindia: East Riding

Estsexia: Essex

Esturministra: Sturminster, Dorset

Ethandunum: Hedddington, Wilts.

Ethelingia: Athelney, Somerset

Ethona: Nuneaton, Warwickshire

Etlingeleia: Athelney, Somerset

Etocetum: Kingsbury, Warwickshire; or Wall, Staffordshire

Etona: Nuneaton, Warwickshire

Euania: *see* Meuania

Eubonia: Isle of Man; *see* Mania

Euenlodus Flu: River Evenlode, in Oxfordshire

Euerwica, Euerwika: York

Eufania: Isle of Man

Euonium: Dunstaffnage, Argyle

Eura: River Ure or Yore, Yorks

Exa Flu: River Exe, Devonshire

Exancestria: Exeter

Excambium Regium: the Royal Exchange, London

Excestra: Exeter

Exexa: Essex

Exoche: Gunfleet, Essex; or Wintertonness, Norfolk

Exonia: Exeter

Exosades: islands off Norfolk or Essex

Exploratorum Castra: Burgh by Sands, Cumberland

Extensio: *see* Exoche

Eya: Eye, Norfolk

Fagrovella: Fairwell, Staffordshire

Fala Flu: River Fal, Cornwall

Falensis Portus: Falmouth

Fanocodi: A town in Cumberland

Fanum ad Taffum: Llandaff, Glamorganshire

Fanum Andreae: St Andrews, Scotland

Fanum Canici: Kilkenny

Fanum Christi: Christchurch, Hants

Fanum Germani: Llanarmon, Denbigh

Fanum Iltuti: Llantwit, Glamorganshire

Fanum Iuonis Persiae: St Ives, Hunts

Fanum Leonis: Leominster, Herefordshire

Fanum Neoti: St Neots's, Hunts

Fanum Oswaldi: Nostal, Yorks

Fanum Reguli: St Andrews, Scotland, also called Kirkrule and Kilrule

Fanum S Albani: St Albans, Herts

Fanum S Asaphi: St Asaph's, Flintshire

Fanum S Botolphi: Boston, Lincolnshire

Fanum S Edmundi: Bury St Edmund's, Suffolk

Fanum S Johannis: St John's, Roscommon, Ireland

Fanum S Mauditi: St Mawe's, Cornwall

Fanum Stephani: Kirkby-Stephen, Westmoreland

Fanum Teclae: Llandegla, Denbigh; St Tecla's Chapel, an island at the mouth of the Wye

Farina: Fearn, Ross

Farlega: Farley or Farleigh Monkton, Wilts; a cell to Lewes Priory

Fauoria: Faure, Meath, Ireland

Faustini Villa: *see* Villa Faustini

Fawenses: inhabitants of Fowey, Cornwall

Felicia: Felixstow, Suffolk

Felicis Oppidum: Flixton, Suffolk

Ferberga: Farnborough

Ferlega: *see* Farlega

Ferleia: *see* Farlega

Fermedona: Farringdon, Hants

Fernae: Ferns, Wexford, Ireland

Fernlega: *see* Farlega

Fernum: *see* Fernae

Ferulega: Hereford

Fibrilega, Fibrolega: Beverley, Yorks

Fifburgensis: of the Five Boroughs: Lincoln, Nottingham, Derby, Leicester, and Stamford

Finnabrensis: of Kilfenora, *alias* Edumabrach, *alias* Fenabore, Co. Clare, Ireland

Fisela: Fishlake, Yorks

Flagaflora, Flauflor: Sparsholt, Berks

Flaua Caesariensis: province of Roman Britain between the Thames, Humber and Mersey; or between Humber, Mersey and Great Wall

Flexelega, Flexlega: Flaxley, Gloucestershire

Flintia: Flint

Fluentanus Carcer: Fleet Prison, London

Flumen Dei: Kilbegain, Co. Meath

Fons Amnensis: Amwell, Herts

Fons Brigidae: Bridewell, London

Fons Clarus: Sherbourne, Dorset

Fons Clericorum: Clerkenwell, London

Fons Interfraxinus: Ashwell, Herts

Fons Limpidus: Fairwell, Staffordshire

Fons S Patricii: Ballintobber, Co. Mayo

Fons Sacer: Holywell

Fons Scotiae; Scotland-well, Kinross

Fons Vivus: Maur, Co. Cork

Fontanae: Fountains Abbey, Yorks

Fontanetum, Fontanensis Ecclesia: Wells, Somerset

Fontes: Wells; Fountains Abbey, Yorks

Fonticuli: Wells

Fontis, Villa: Holywell, Flintshire

Fordunum: Fordoun, Co. Kincardine, Scotland

Forenna: part of the City of Wells

Forgium: Kilmoney Abbey, Co. Clare

Forneseta: Forcett, Yorks

Fors (Fons?) de Caritate: a Cistercian house in Wensleydale, Yorks

Forthae aestuarium, Fortheia: Firth of Forth

Forum: Cheap, London,

Forum Jouis: Marazion, Cornwall

Fouera, Fouria: Fore, Westmeath

Fraxula Flu: in Derbyshire

Freskewattera: Freshwater, Isle of Wight

Fretum Britannicum, Fretum Gallicum, Fretum Morinorum: the Straits of Dover

Frigidum Mantellum: Freemantle, Hants

Frigmareventus: Winchelsea, Sussex

Friscodunense coenobium: Freston Abbey, Lincolnshire

Frodrenela: Fotharta, Leinster, Ireland

Fromus, Froma: River Frome

Frumentarius Mons: Cornhill, London

Gabaglanda: *see* Amboglanna

Gabrantonicorum, Gabrantouicorum Sinus: Bridlington or Filey Bay, Yorkshire

Gabrocentum, Gabrosentis: Gateshead, Durham; Black Dyke or Drumburgh, Cumberland

Gadeni: inhabitants of Fife, Tweeddale, March and Lothian in Scotland

Gadiua: Aberffraw, on the Isle of Anglesey

Gaelwallia: Galloway, Scotland

Gaidingtona: Geddington, Northants

Gaingtona: Geddington

Gaini: people of Lincolnshire

Gainiburgus: Gainsborough, Lincolnshire

Galacum: Appleby, Kendal, or Whallop Castle, Westmoreland

Galaua: Old Town, Keswick, or Wythburn, Cumberland; or Walwick, Northumberland

Galensis: a Welshman

Galetum: Langley Gale, Sussex

Galewegia: Galloway

Galienses: men of Galloway

Gallaua: *see* Galaua

Galleua Atrebatum: Guildford, Silchester, Henley, Reading, Wallingford, Calve Pit Farm, near Reading, or Haslemere, Surrey

Galliua: Galway, Ireland

Gallouidia: Galloway, Scotland

Gallunio: Aldborough; *see* Isurium

Gallutum: *see* Galacum

Galueia: Galloway

Galuia: Galway

Galwalenses: people of Galloway

Galwedia, Galwegia: Galloway

Galweia: Galloway

Gangani: people of Connaught, Ireland

Ganganum promontorium: Braichy Pwll Point, Caernarvonshire

Garbantorigum: Caerlaverock, Scotland

Gareotha: Gaury or Gowrie, Scotland

Gariannonum: Yarmouth, or Burgh Castle, Norfolk

Garmundi Via: Garmondsway, Durham

Garrienis, Garyenus, Flu: Yare River, Norfolk

Garryeni Fluvii ostium: Yarmouth

Gauelforda: Camelford, Cornwall

Gauinga: Wenge, Bucks

Gaurouicum: Warwick; *see* Verouicum

Gausennae, Gausennis: *see* Causennae

Gedewurda: Jedburgh, Roxburghshire

Gegenforda: Gainford, Durham

Geldeforda: Guildford, Surrey

Genesborwia: Gainsborough, Lincolnshire

Genunii: people living on the border of Scotland

Gereseya: Jersey

Gerewedona: Garendon, Leicestershire

Gernemua, Gernemutha: Yarmouth, Norfolk
Gerneria: Guernsey
Geroldona: Garendon, Leicestershire
Gersuium: Jersey
Geuentonae: Chevington, Suffolk
Geuini: a river in Wales that runs into the River Usk
Geuissi: West Saxons
Gipeswica, Gippeuicum: Ipswich, Suffolk
Girouicum: Jarrow, Durham
Giruii: inhabitants of the Fens
Giruum, Girwa: Jarrow, Durham
Giuela: Yeovil, Somerset
Glamorgania, Glamorgantia: Glamorganshire
Glandelacum: Glendalough, Wicklow, Ireland
Glannibanta, Glanouenta: *see* Clanouenta
Glasbiria: Glasbury, Brecknock
Glasconia: Glastonbury, Somerset
Glascouium: Glasgow
Glascua: Glasgow
Glascum: Glascwm, Radnorshire
Glasquum: Glasgow
Glastincbiria: Glastonbury, Somerset
Glastonia: Glastonbury
Glaudiocestra: Gloucester
Glauorna, Glaworna: Gloucester
Gleastonia: Glastonbury
Glenus: River Glen, Northumberland
Glessoburgus: Glastonbury
Glestingia, Glestonia: Glastonbury
Gleuum: Gloucester
Glocestria, Gloecestra: Gloucester
Glota: Isle of Arran
Glota, Glottiana: River Clyde, Scotland
Glouceastria, Glouernia, Glowecestria: Gloucester
Gobannium: Abergavenny, Monmouthshire
Goccium: *see* Coccium
Goderici Castrum: Goodrich Castle, Herefordshire
Godestoua: Godstow, Oxfordshire
Godritona: Codrington, Gloucestershire
Gouheria: Gower, Glamorganshire
Graecolada: Cricklade, Wilts
Grampius Mons: the Grampians
Grangia: Gransha, Down, Ireland
Granta: River Cam, Cambridgeshire
Granta, Grantanus Pons: Cambridge
Grantebreggia: Cambridge, sometimes Cambridgeshire
Graua: Grovebury, Beds
Grauesenda: Gravesend, Kent
Greglada: Cricklade, Wilts
Grenewicum: Greenwich, Kent
Grenouicus, Grenouicum: Greenwich, Kent
Grenteburga: Cambridge

Greua: Gravesend
Greuanus: River Girvan, Ayrshire
Grimboldesessa: Grombold Ash, Gloucestershire
Grinuicum: Greenwich
Grossus Mons: Grosmont, Monmouthshire
Grubba: Gubeon, Northumberland (near Bedlington)
Guala, Guallia: Wales
Guarae, Guarus: Ware, Herts
Guella: Wells, Norfolk
Guerfa Flu: the River Wharfe, Yorkshire
Guidonicus Cliuus: Guy's Cliff, Warwickshire
Guildhalda Teutonicorum: The Steel Yard, London
Guilon Flu: River Will, or Wiley, Wilts
Guincestria: Winchester
Guinethia: Wales
Guinta: Gwent, a province in South Wales, between Usk and Wye
Guinuga: Wenge, Bucks
Guiramutha: Wearmouth, Durham
Guiunga: Wenge, Bucks
Guldeforda: Guildford, Surrey
Gumicastrum: Godmanchester, Hunts
Gwallia: Wales
Gwirchia: Chirk, Denbigh
Gyruum: Jarrow, Durham
Habenduna: Abingdon, Berks
Habitancum: Risingham, Northumberland
Habus: the Humber
Hadriani Murus: Picts' Wall, or Wall of Hadrian
Haebuda: *see* Ebuda
Haemodae: *see* Acmodae
Hafren Flu: the Severn
Haga: the Hay, or Hasely, in Brecknockshire
Hagulstada: Hexham, Northumberland; Alston, Cumberland
Hagustaldunum: Hexham, Northumberland
Haia: Eye, Suffolk; Hay, Brecknockshire
Halaenus: River Avon, Hants
Hamonis Portus: Southampton
Hamptonia, Hamtona: Southampton; Northampton; Hampton
Hancstesia: Hinksey, Oxfordshire
Hansus Flu: River Hans, Staffordshire
Hantonia: Hampshire
Haraia: Harris, one of the Hebrides
Harefordia: Hereford
Harlecum: Harlech, Merionethshire
Harlepolis: Hartlepool, Durham
Haroldi Crux: Harold's Cross, near Dublin
Haruicum: Harwich, Essex
Hastinga: Hastings, Sussex
Hauerberga: Harborough, Warwickshire

Hauerfordia: Haverfordwest, Pembrokeshire

Haugustaldium: *see* Hagustaldunum

Hauma: Hamme, Berks

Hauteuorta: Highworth, Wilts

Hauxoniensis: Of Hawkshead, Lancashire

Haya: Hay, Brecknockshire

Heastinga: Hastings, Sussex

Hebrides: a cluster of islands on the west coast of Scotland

Hebuda: *see* Ebuda

Hederosum Monasterium: Ivychurch, Wilts

Hedros: *see* Edros

Hedwa: Hythe, Kent

Hegdunensis: of Annaghdown, Co. Clare, Ireland

Heia: Hythe, Kent

Heisa: Hayes, Kent

Helaturnum: Ellerton, Yorkshire

Helenum promontorium: Land's End

Helia: Ely, Cambridgeshire

Helma: Helmington, Durham

Helmanensis: Of Elmham, Suffolk

Helmelum: Elmley

Hengestesdunum: Hengston Hill, Cornwall

Henlega: Henliy-upon-Thames, Oxfordshire

Henoforthum: Hereford

Heortforda: Hertford

Heoueshamnensis: of Evesham, Worcestershire

Heppa: Shap, Westmoreland

Herboldona: Harbledown, Kent

Herculis promontorium: Hartland Point, Devonshire

Herdingheleia: Ardingly, Sussex

Herefordia: Hereford, formerly Ariconium

Herkeloua: Arklow, Connaught

Herlaua: Harlow, Essex

Hernleia: Hurley, Berks

Hertfordia: Hertford

Hesperides: Scilly Isles

Hestelega: Astley, Warwickshire

Hestinga: Hastings, Sussex

Hestingi: East Angles

Hetha Pratorum: Maidenhead, Berks

Hetha Regine: Queenhithe

Heya: Eye, Suffolk

Hibernia: Ireland

Hichelendunum: Ickleton, Cambridgeshire

Hichena: River Itchen, Hants

Hichia coenobium: Newbiggin, or Hitchin, Herts

Hichteslapa: Islip, Oxon

Hictredeberia: Heytesbury, Wilts

Hida: Hyde, near Winchester

Hieron Promontorium: Greenore Point, or Carnsore Point, Wexford

Hildesleia: Ilsley, Berks

Himba: one of the Acmodae Islands

Hinchisega: Hinksey, near Oxford

Hirtha: one of the Hebrides

Histesleapa: Islip, Oxfordwhire

Hitha Regine: Queenhithe

Hithinus portus: Hythe, Kent

Hlediae: Leeds, Kent

Hludense Monasterium: Lough Park Abbey, Lincolnshire

Hodneius Flu: Honddhu River, Brecknockshire

Hoilandia, Hollandia: Holland, a part of Lincolnshire

Holgoti, Castrum de: Castle Holdgate, Herefordshire

Holmus: Hulme, or St Bennet's-in-the-Holme, Norfolk

Homdeleia: Hundsley, Yorks

Homelea Flu: River Hamble, opposite the Isle of Wight, Hants

Horesti: people living north of the Firth of Forth

Horka: Dunnet Head, Caithness

Hornecastra: Horncastle, Lincolnshire

Horspada: Horspath, Oxon

Hospitium Leonis: Lyon's Inn, London

Hothenia: rivers Hodni or Honddu, in Brecknockshire and Monmouthshire

Houendena: Hoveden, Yorks

Houlandia: *see* Hoilandia

Hripum: Ripon, Yorks

Hrofi, Hrosi Civitas: Rochester

Hulla, Hullus: Kingston-upon-Hull, Yorkshire

Hultonia: Ulster, Ireland

Humbra Flu: River Humber

Hundesdena: Hunsdon, Herts

Hundredeskelda: Hunderthwaite, Yorks

Hunegetona: Honington or Hunnington, Staffordshire

Hungreforda: Hungerford, Berks

Hunnum: Sevenshale, or Halton Chesters, Northumberland

Hunsdona: Hunsdon, Herts

Huntendonia, Huntundona: Huntingdon

Hurstanum Castellum: Hurst Castle, Hants

Hurstelega: Hurley, Berks

Husseburna: Hurstbourne, Hants

Huya: Holy Island

Hwerwella: Wherwell, Hants

Hwiccii: people of Worcestershire, and about the Severn

Hydropolis: Dorchester, Oxon

Hymalia: Achad-Fobhair, Co. Mayo

Hymbrionenses, Hymbronenses: People of Northumberland

Hyrebothla: Harbottle, Northumberland

Hyrtha: one of the Hebrides
Hyta: Hythe, Kent
Iberni: people of Desmond, Ireland
Ibernia: Ireland
Ibernio: Bere Regis, or Iwerne, Dorset
Ibernis: Dunkerrin, King's Co., Ireland
Ibernium: Iwerne, Dorset
Iberran: a town in Scotland, north of the Forth
Icannum: Boston, Lincolnshire
Iceni: people of Suffolk, Norfolk, Cambridge, and Huntingdon shires
Iciani, Icinos: Chesterford, Essex; Thetford or Igborough, Norfolk; or Southwold, Suffolk
Icini: *see* Iceni
Ictis Insula: St Michael's Mount, Cornwall; or, perhaps, the Isle of Wight (Vectis)
Idumanus: Blackwater River, or the mouth of the Stour and Orwell, Essex
Iena aestuarium: Wigton Bay, Galloway
Ierne, Iernis: Ireland
Iernus: River Erne, or Kenmare Bay, Ireland
Igenia: Part of Flintshire
Ihona: *see* Iona
Ila Flu: River Wick, Scotland
Ila Insula: Islay, west of Scotland
Illega Combusta: Brent Eleigh or Illegh, Suffolk
Illega Monachorum: Monk's Eleigh, Suffolk
Imelaca: Emly, Co. Tipperary
Imelensis: of Emly
Imensa aestuarium: mouth of the Thames
Imlaca: Emly
Immemera: Mere, Wilts
Incuneningum: Cunningham, Scotland
Inderauuda: Beverley, Yorks
Ingetlingus: Gilling, Yorks
Ingiruum: Jarrow, Durham
Ingoluesmera: Ingoldmells, Lincolnshire
Inmeleccensis: of Emly, Tipperary
Innerlothea: Inverlochy, Inverness
Insula: Eynesham, or Ensham, Oxfordshire; Axholm, Lincolnshire; Isle, near Stockton, Durham; Little Island, Waterford Harbour
Insula Cervi: Hartlepool, Durham
Insula Missarum: Inchaffray, Perthshire
Insula Sacra: Ireland; also Holy Island, Northumberland
Insula Sancti Columbae: Columbkill, Iona
Insula Sanctorum: Ynis Enlly, Bardsey, Caernarvon
Insula Vectis: Isle of Wight
Insularis Villa: Islington
Interamna, Interamnium: Christ Church, Hants
Inuernessus: Inverness, Scotland
Iona: Iona, or Icolmkill Isle, west coast of Scotland
Iphletha: Evelith, Shropshire

Ircenefelda: Archenfield, or Irchingfield, Herefordshire
Iris: Ireland
Isaca: River Exe, Devonshire; also River Esk, Scotland
Isamnium: St John's Foreland, or Point, Co. Down, Ireland
Isannauantia, Isannauaria, Isannauatia: Stony Stratford, Northants, or the same as Bannauenna; Allchester, Oxon, between Wendlebury and Bicester
Isannium: *see* Isamnium
Isca: Liskeard, Cornwall
Isca: River Exe; River Usk
Isca Dumnoriorum: Chiselborough, Somerset; or Exeter
Isca Legio II Augusta, Isvelegua Augusti, Isca Silurum, Iscamum: Caerleon, Monmouthshire
Iscalis: Ivelchester, now Ilchester, Somerset
Iscamum: Caerleon
Ischalis: *see* Iscalis
Isiacum: Oxford
Isiburna: Woburn, Bedfordshire
Isidis Insula: Ousney, or Oseney, near Oxford
Isidis Vadum: Oxford
Isis Flu: River Isis, Oxford; the Ouse, Buckinghamshire; and the Ouse, Yorkshire
Istelhorda: Isleworth, Middlesex
Isubrigantum: *see* Isurium
Isuria: Yorkshire
Isurium: Aldborough, or Boroughbridge, Yorkshire
Isurouicum: York
Ittingaforda: Hitchin, Herts
Itucadon: a town between Tyne and Forth
Ituma, Ituna: River Eden, Cumberland; or Solway Firth
Itys: Loch Eu, Torridon, or Duich, Scotland
Iuecestra: Ilchester, Somerset
Iuerianus Pons: Iford Bridge, Hants
Iuernia: Ireland
Iuernis: Dunkerrin, King's Co., Ireland
Iuorus: Newry, Co. Armagh
Jaciodulma: *see* Magiouinium
Jamesa, Jamissa: River Thames
Jano: a town in Caithness
Jarum: Yarm, Yorks
Jernmuthia: Yarmouth, Norfolk
Jerouallae: Jervaulx, Yorks
Joriuallis: Jervaulx, Yorks
Judaismus: Old Jewry, London
Jugantes: *see* Brigantes
Jugo Dei, de: Jude or Gray: a Cistercian Abbey, co Meath, a cell of Holme Coltram
Jugum Fraxinetum: Ashridge, Bucks

Julia Strata: a Roman road in South Wales, from Newport to Caerleon, Caerwent, and the Wye

Julianus Pons: Julian Bridge, Wimborne Minster

Juliocenon: *see* Tunnocelum

Jumanius: *see* Eidumania

Juuerna: Ireland

Kaerperis: Porchester, Hants

Kanna: Calne, Wilts

Kanus Flu: River Ken, or Kent, Westmoreland

Karintona: Catherington, Hants

Karlegion: Chester

Karlenefordia: Carlingford, Louth, Ireland

Katenessa, Kathenessia: Caithness, Scotland

Katinensis: of Caithness

Kauna: Calne, Wilts

Kenceleia: Hykinselagh, a district in Leinster

Kenelcunillia: Tirconnel, Ulster

Keneleonia: Cinel-Eoghain, Ulster

Keneta Flu: River Kennet, Berkshire

Kenintona: Kennington, Kempton

Keresburga: Carisbrook, Isle of Wight

Keretica: Ceredigion, a province of South Wales; Cardiganshire

Kermelum: Cartmel, Lancashire

Kerriensis Comitatus: Co. Kerry, Ireland

Kerrigia: Kerry

Kesteuena: Kesteven, a division of Lincolnshire

Kiemela: Keymer, Sussex

Kilchennia, Kilchennium: Kilkenny, Leinster, Ireland

Kildabewensis: of Killaloe, Ireland

Kildareuensis: of Killaloe

Kildaria: Kildare, Ireland

Killathensis: of Killalla, Ireland

Kilmalochum: Killmallock, Limerick

Kilmora: Kilmore, Co. Cavan, Ireland

Kinardeferia: Kinardferry, Axholm

Kinebantum Castrum: Kimbolton Castle, Hunts

Kinetus fluvius: River Kennet

Kirchuallum: Kirkwall, Orkney Islands

Kirketona: Kirton, Lincolnshire

Koila: *see* Coualia

Korcensis: of Cork

Kubii Castrum: Holyhead

Kyenfernensis: of Clonfert

Kyma: Kyme, Yorks

Kynemeresforda: Kempsford, Wilts

Kynlathensis: of Killalla

Kyrieleyson: Odorney Abbey, Kerry

Kyuela: Keevil, Wilts

La Hyda: Hyde, Hants

Laberus: Killare Castle, Westmeath, Ireland

Lacra: Castle Acre, Norfolk

Lactodorum, Lactorodum: Towcester, Northants; Stony Stratford, Bucks; Bicester, Oxfordshire; Bedford; or Loughborough or Lutterworth, Leicestershire

Ladeni: *see* Gadeni

Ladensis Episcopatus: the bishopric of Killalla, Co. Mayo, Ireland

Laentonia: Lanthony

Laetus Locus: Netley, Hants

Lagecium: Castleford, near Pontefract, Yorks

Lagenia: *see* Laginia

Lagentium: *see* Lagecium

Laghlinum: Leighlin, Co. Carlow, Ireland

Laginia: Leinster, Ireland

Lagubalium: *see* Luguvallum

Lamea, Lamheya, Lamitha, Lamithus, Lampheia: Lambeth, Surrey

Lamyrii Montes: Lammermuir Hill, Scotland

Lancastra, Lancastria: Lancaster

Landa: Launde, Leicestershire

Landava: Llandaff, Glamorganshire

Landinium: London

Lanelvensis: of Llanelwy, i.e. St Asaph, Wales

Langanum promontorium: *see* Canganorum

Langeleia: Langley

Lanhondenum: Lanthony, Monmouthshire

Lanhondenum Claudianum: Lanthony, Gloucestershire

Lania: Lancashire

Lanicolae: Lancashire men

Lannotaua: Llandaff, Glamorganshire

Lanstuphadonia, Lanstauentum: Launceston, Cornwall

Lantodhenia: Llanthony, Monmouthshire

Lantonia: Llanthony, Monmouthshire

Laodonia: Lothian

Laonia: Killaloe, Co. Tipperary

Lapis Tituli: Stonor, on the Isle of Thanet, Kent

Lathelada: Lechlade, Gloucestershire

Latisaquensis: Lewes, Sussex

Latum Bulgium: *see* Blatum Bulgium

Lauatres, Lauatris, Lauaris: Bowes, North Riding of Yorkshire; or Barnard Castle, Durham

Laudenia, Laudonia: Lauden, or Lothian, Scotland

Lawedra: Lauder, Berwickshire

Lecefelda: Lichfield, Staffordshire

Lechenlada, Lechelada: Lechlade, Gloucestershire

Lechlinia: Leighlin, Co. Carlow, Ireland

Lectoceto: *see* Etocetum

Ledanum Castrum: Leeds Castle, Kent

Ledesia: Leeds, Yorkshire

Ledone: Dunbar

Legacestra: Chester

Legacestria, Legecestria: Leicester

Lege Dei, B V M de: Leix Abbey, Queen's Co.

Legeolium: Pontefract, Castleford, Goole, or Ferrybridge, Yorks; *see* Lagecium

Legercestria: Leicester

Leghelensis, Leghglensis: of Leighlin

Legio VI Victrix: York

Legio XX Victrix: Chester

Legionum Urbs: Chester; Caerleon

Legoria: Leicester

Legra: River Soar, Leicestershire

Legrecastrum: Leicester

Legrecestria: Leicester; Chester

Lehecestria: Leicester

Leicestria: Leicester

Leis: Leix, Leixlip, co Kildare, Ireland

Lelannonius, Lelamnonius Sinus: Loch Fyne

Lelienus Flu: River Rother, Kent

Lemana Flu: the Rother, Kent; the Loman, Devon

Lemanis portus, Lemauio: Lympne, Kent

Lemaus: Lympne, Kent; Lynn, Norfolk

Lena: Monkland, Hereford

Lenes: Lessness, Kent

Leofense Coenobium: Leominster, Herefordshire

Leofrici Villa: Leverington, Cambridgeshire

Leogereceastria: Leicester

Leogoria: Leicester

Leogus: Lewis, one of the Hebrides

Leonense Coenobium: Leominster

Leonis: Lothian

Leonis Castrum: Lyons, *alias* Holt Castle, Denbighshire

Leonis Monasterium: Leominster, Herefordshire

Leouechenora: Lewknor, Oxfordshire

Leouense Coenobium: Leominster

Lesinae: Lesnes or Lessness, Kent

Lesmoria: Lismore, co Waterford

Lestinga: Lastingham, Yorks

Lesua: Lewes, Sussex

Letha: Leith, Co. Edinburgh

Lethglensis: of Leighlin, Co. Carlow

Leuarum: *see* Leucarum

Leuca: River Low

Leucarum: Glastonbury, Somerset; Loughor, Glamorganshire; or Llandybi, Caermarthenshire

Leucobibia: *see* Lucopibia

Leucomago: *see* Verlucio

Leuena: River Leven, Lancashire

Leugosena: River Loughor, South Wales

Leuinia: Lennox, Stirlingshire

Leuinus: River Leven, Scotland

Leuiodanum: Livingstone, Linlithgow

Leuioxana: Lennox

Leuissa: Lewis Island, Hebrides

Leuisum: Lewes, Sussex

Lewae: Lewes

Lewensis: of Lewes

Leya: Canon Leigh, Burlescombe, Devon

Liar Flu: River Liver, Lancashire

Libaeus: Sligo Bay

Libnius: River Liffey, Ireland

Licestria: Leicester

Licetfelda, Lichfeldia: Lichfield, Staffordshire

Lichia: Leach, Gloucestershire

Lichinus Campus: Lichfield

Liddenus Flu: River Leadon, Herefordshire

Lideforda: Lydford, Devon

Lidocollina: Lincoln

Ligea: River Lea

Ligeria: Leicester

Ligrecastrum: Leicester

Limenus: River Rother, Kent

Limericum: Limerick, Ireland

Limes Praetorius: Gravesend, Kent

Limnos, Limnus: Dalkey Isle, or Lambay Isle, Dublin

Limodomus: Limehouse, near London

Limonius Mons: Plinlimmon, Cardiganshire

Limpida Sylva: Sherwood Forest, Notts

Lincolinum, Lincolnia, Lindecolina: Lincoln

Lindeseia: Lindsey, Lincolnshire

Lindicolinum: Lincoln

Lindis: River Witham, Lincolnshire

Lindisfari: Lindsey

Lindisfarnea, Lindisfarnum: Holy Island, or Farn Isle, on the coast of Northumberland

Lindisgia, Lindisi: Lindsey, Lincolnshire

Lindisseia: Lindsey

Lindocollinum: Lincoln

Lindonium: Lincoln; London

Lindum Damniorum: Linlithgow, or Ardoch, Perth

Lindum, Lindum Colonia: Lincoln: *see* Lincolinum

Linia: Bardsey Island, Caernarvonshire

Liniennus: River Rother, Kent

Linum Regis: King's Lynn, Norfolk

Linus: River Lin, Notts

Liserpalus: Liverpool, Lancashire

Lisia: *see* Lissia

Lismora: Lismore, Co. Waterford

Lismoria: Lismore, Argyleshire; Lismore, Co. Waterford

Lissia: the Wolf Rock, or the Seven Stones, between the Scilly Islands and the Cornish coast

Litana: Linlithgow

Litecota: Littlecote, Wilts

Litinomago: Linlithgow

Littus Altum: Roxburgh

Littus Saxonicum: Eastern and southern coasts of Britain

Llanlienis: Leominster, Herefordshire

Locherinum stagnum: Lough Owel, Westmeath

Locus Benedictus: Stanlawe, Cheshire

Locus Dei: Hethorp, Gloucestershire; Hinton Charterhouse, Somerset

Lodanum Castrum: Leeds Castle, Kent

Lodeneium, Lodoneium, Lodonis (dat): the Lothians, Scotland

Loegria: England between Humber and Severn

Loennais: Lothian

Logi: a tribe in Sutherland and Strathnairn

Logia Flu: River Bann, which flows north from Lough Neagh Camden applies the name to Lough Foyle

Logus: River Llugwy, Wales

Loidis: Lothian

Lokerleia: Lockerley, Hants

Lomandus: *see* Lomundus

Lombormora: Lammermoor, Midlothian

Lomea: the Goodwin Sands

Lomithis: Lambeth

Lomulla: Lemallyon, Cornwall

Lomundus: Loch Lomond

Lonais: Lothian

Loncastria: Lancaster

Londa: Launde, Leicestershire

Londinia, Londinium, Londinia Augusta: London

Londino–Deria: Londonderry, Ireland

Londinum, Londonia, Londoniae: London

Longa Leta: Longleat, Wilts

Longouicariorum, Longouico: Launchester, or Chester-le-Street, Durham; or Lancaster

Longum Aestuarium: Loch Linnhe, Argyllshire

Longus Pons: Longbridge, Gloucestershire

Loonia: Lothian

Louentinum: Powysland, in Wales; *see also* Luentinum

Lounecastra: Lancaster

Loxa: River Lossie, Elgin; or the Loth, Sutherland

Loxa Civitas: Inverlochy, Scotland

Luceni: the people of West Munster

Lucga: River Lugg, Herefordshire

Lucopibia: Whitherne, Galloway; *see* Candida Casa

Lucus Benedictus: Stanlawe Abbey, Cheshire

Luda: Louth, Ireland, Louth, Lincs; Ludlow

Luddolocus, Ludelawa: Ludlow, Shropshire

Luentinum: Llanddewybrefy, Cardiganshire

Lugas: River Lug, Herefordshire

Lugdunum: Louth, Ireland

Lugensis: of Louth, Ireland

Lughbelunensis: of Louth, Ireland

Lugi: people in the north of Scotland

Luguballia, Luguballium: Carlisle, or Plumpton Wall, Cumberland

Lugundinum: Lanchester, Durham

Luguuallum: Carlisle, Cumberland; *see* Luguballia

Luia: Louth

Luia: River Lea, Herts

Lumbricus: Limerick

Lummalea: Lumley, Durham

Lumniacum, Lumpniacum: Limerick

Luna: Lynn, Norfolk

Lunda: Monk Bretton, Yorks

Lundinium, Lundonia: London

Lunia: Lancashire

Lutudarum: Tapton, near Chesterfield, Derbyshire

Lutum: Louth, Ireland

Luua: Louth County, Ireland

Luueth: Louth, Ireland

Luuius: River Lee, Cork

Lychefeldia: Lichfield, Staffordshire

Lyssa: Liss, Hants

Macatonion: the same as Ariconium

Machui: Mayo, Ireland

Macolicum: Mallow, Co. Cork, Ireland

Madus: Maidstone, Kent, or Strood; *see* Vagniacae

Maeatae: people living near the Wall of Antonine

Magesetae: the people of Radnorshire, or Herefordshire

Magiouinium, Magiouintum: Dunstable or Ashwell, Beds; or Fenny Stratford, or Aylesbury, Bucks

Magis: Pierce Bridge, Durham, or Lonsdale Hundred, Lancs

Magium: Nenay, Co. Cork

Maglonae, Maglouae: Machynlleth, Montgomeryshire; Greta Bridge, Yorks; or Lancaster

Magnis: Bowness, Cumberland; Caervoran or Chester-in-the-Wall, near Haltwhistle, Northumberland; Kenchester, or Old Radnor, Herefordshire

Magnitum: *see* Magiouinium

Magnus Portus: Portsmouth

Maia: May Island, on the Firth of Forth

Maidulphi Curia, Maidulphi Urbs: Malmesbury, Wilts

Maigonensis: of Mayo, Ireland

Mailenia: Maelienydd, a province in Powys, North Wales

Mailoria Wallica: Maylor, Flintshire

Maina Flu: the Mintern, Dorset

Maionensis: of Mayo

Mala Platea: near Wenlock, Shropshire

Malaca: Isle of Mull

Malbanus Vicus, Vicus Malbus: Wyz Mauban, Nantwich, Cheshire

Malcolicum: Mallow, Co. Cork

Maldunense Coenobium: Malmesbury Abbey, Wilts

Malea Platea: Ill Street, Cheshire

Maleos: Isle of Mull, west of Scotland

Malesbergia: Marlborough, Wilts

Malmesbiria: Malmesbury

Maluerna, Maluernia, Maluernum: Malvern, Worcestershire

Malum Oppidum: Yeovil, Somerset

Malus Passus: Malpas, Cheshire

Mamceastra: Manchester, Lancashire

Mamucium: Manchester

Manapia: Wicklow, or Wexford, Ireland

Manaui: *see* Meneuia

Mancunium: Manchester

Manduessedum: Mancetter, or Kenilworth, Warwickshire

Mania, Manna, Mannia: the Isle of Man

Mannechestria: Mancetter, Warwickshire

Mantauis: St Davids, Pembrokeshire

Mantio: Manchester

Manucium: Manchester

Mara, Foresta de: Delamere Forest, Cheshire

Marawuda: Marwood, Durham

Marchenium: Roxburgh

Marchia: March, or Mers, Scotland

Marchia Walliae: the Marches or borders of Wales

Marchidunum: Roxburgh

Marcotaxon: a town north of the Wall of Antonine

Mare Britannicum: the English Channel

Mare Caledonium: the Scotch Sea

Mare Hibernicum: the Irish Channel

Mare Sabrinianum: the Severn Sea

Mare Virginium, Verginium: the sea on the south of Ireland

Margaberga: Marlborough, Wilts

Margidunum, Margitudum: East Bridgeford, Notts; or Mount Sorrel, Leicestershire

Maridunum: Caermarthen

Mariscallia: the Marshalsea, London

Marlebrigia: Marlborough

Marnia: Mearns, Kincardine, Scotland

Marria: Marr, Aberdeen, Scotland

Martona: Merton, Surrey

Masona: a town probably in Devonshire

Massamensis Pons: Masham Bridge, Yorks

Matillis Castellum: Painscastle, Herefordshire

Matouion: a town north of the Wall of Antonine

Mauditi Castrum: St Mawe's Castle, Cornwall

Mauia: River Maw, Merionethshire

Maulion: a town north of the Wall of Antonine

Mauordina: Marden, Herefordshire

Mauritanea: probably Llanbadarn Vaur, Cardiganshire

Mauthia: Meath, Ireland

Maxima Caesariensis: province of Britain, north of the Humber and Ribble, and south of Tyne; or the Scottish Highlands, north of the Wall of Severus

Mealdunum: Maldon, Essex

Mealmesbiria: Malmesbury

Mealtuna: Malton, Yorks

Meandari: *see* Meanuari

Meanuari: a tribe living in Hampshire, whose name remains in Estmeon and Westmeon hundreds

Mearlsberga: Marlborough, Wilts

Meatae: people of Lothian

Meaudunum: Maldon, Essex

Mecelnia, Michennia, Michlania: Muchelney, Somerset

Meddercota: Nethercote, Oxfordshire

Medeguaia: River Medway

Medena: Newport, Isle of Wight

Medeshamstundensis: of Peterborough, Northants

Media: County of Meath, Ireland

Mediamnis: Medmenham, Bucks

Medimna: Christchurch, Hants

Mediolanium: Middleham, Yorks

Mediolanum: Llanvyllin or Meifod, Montgomery; or Nantwich, Cheshire; Drayton, Whitchurch, or Bearstone, Shropshire; or Chesterton, Warwickshire

Mediomanum: the same as Mediolanum, or Maentwrog, Merionethshire

Medionemeton: on the Wall of Antonine

Mediterranei Angli: people of the Midland Counties

Medius Vicus: Middlewich, Cheshire

Meduaga, Medweacus: River Medway

Mela: Isle of Mull

Melamon: in Devonshire

Melanclani, Melanchlani: people of the Scilly Islands

Melduna: Maldon, Essex

Meldunum: Malmesbury, Wiltshire

Melesburia: Melbury, Dorset

Melezo: in Dorset

Mella monasterium: Meaux Abbey, Yorks

Mellifons: Mellifont, Louth

Melsa: Meaux, Yorks

Memanturum: a town north of the Wall of Antonine

Menan: Meneg, Cornwall

Menapii: tribe inhabiting Wexford

Menauia: Isle of Man

Menes: Meon, Hants

Meneuia: St Davids, Pembrokeshire

Menna: Meneg, Cornwall

Menstra: Minster, Kent

Mentae: people on the Scotch Border; *see* Meatae

Meodewega: River Medway

Mercia: middle part of England

Mercii: inhabitants of Mercia

Merionithia: Merionethshire

Merleberga: Marlborough, Wilts

Merleberia, Merlebrigia: Marlborough

Merscum: Marske, Yorks

Mersia: River Mersey, Cheshire

Mertae: tribe inhabiting Sutherland

Meruinia: Merionethshire

Metaris Aestuarium: the Wash, Norfolk

Meuania: Isle of Man; Anglesey

Miba: Midhurst, Sussex

Mictis: *see* Ictis

Mida: Meath, Ireland

Midcelania: Muchelney, Somerset

Middlesexia: Middlesex

Midia: Meath

Mildeshala: Mildenhall, Suffolk

Mildetunensis: of Middleton, Dorset

Milfordiensis Portus: Milford Haven

Milidunum: in Devonshire

Milidunum: same as Meldunum

Milleferda: Milford, Pembrokeshire

Miluerdicus Portus: Milford Haven

Minarii Montes: Mendip Hills, Somerset

Mincheneleya: Canonleigh, Burlescombe, Devon

Mineruae Insula: Peninsula of Morvern, Argyllshire

Mira Vallis: Merevale, Warwickshire

Mirmanton: according to Nennius the same as *Cair Segeint*, which Henry of Huntingdon says is Silchester; but one MS of Nennius adds, '*Id est urbs Eboraca*'

Mitfordia: Mitford, Northumberland

Mochinga: Mucking, Essex

Modanus: River Liffey, Ireland

Modarnus: River Mourne; once applied to the Foyle

Moina: man

Molis Flu: the Mole, Surrey

Momonia: province of Munster, Ireland

Mona: Anglesey

Mona Ulterior: Isle of Man

Monaaeda, Monapia: the Isle of Man

Monachodunum: Monkton, Yorks

Monachopolis: Newcastle-on-Tyne (Munekeceastre)

Monasterium Cornutum: Hornchurch, Essex

Monasterium Hederosum: Ivychurch, Wilts

Monega: Anglesey

Monemuta: Monmouth

Monia: Anglesey; Man

Monmuthia: Monmouth

Monocotona: Monkton, Kent

Monomia: *see* Momonia

Monouaga: Monmouth

Mons Acutus: Montacute, Somerset

Mons Altus: Mold, Flintshire

Mons Arenosus: Sandon, Herts

Mons Dives: Richmond, Surrey

Mons Dolorus: Stirling

Mons Draconis: Mount Drake, Devon

Mons Gaudius: *see* Mons Jouis

Mons Gomericus: Montgomery

Mons Grampius: Grampian Hills

Mons Jouis: Mountjoy, or Monge, Norfolk

Mons Michaelis: St Michael's Mount, Cornwall

Mons Rosarum: Montrose, Forfarshire

Mons S Andreae: Sallay, or Sawley, Yorks

Mons Solis: Bath

Mont Dolerus, Chastel de: Montrose

Montaccola: near Caermarthen

Monte Gilberti, Foresta de: the Wrekin, Shropshire

Montgomeria: Montgomery

Monumethia: Monmouth

Mora: More, Shropshire

Moravia: Moray or Murray, Scotland

Morbium: Moresby, Cumberland; Hornsea, or Temple Brough, Yorkshire

Morda: River Meole, which joins the Severn near Shrewsbury

Moricamba, Moricambe Aestuarium: Morecambe Bay, Lancashire

Moridunum: Seaton, or Honiton, Devon; Eggerton, Dorset

Morpitium: Morpeth, Northumberland

Morsiburgus: Bridgenorth, Shropshire

Mortuus Lacus: Mortlake, Surrey

Mucletona: Mickleton

Mula: Isle of Mull, west coast of Scotland

Munekacastra: Newcastle-on-Tyne, Northumberland

Munemuta: Monmouth

Munus: River Monnow, which divides Herefordshire from Monmouthshire

Murevia: Moray, Scotland

Muridunum: Caermarthen

Muridunum: *see* Moridunum

Murimintum, Muriuindum: Silchester, Hants

Murionio: in Dorset

Murotriges: *see* Durotriges

Murrevia: Moray, Scotland

Murthlacum: Murtley, Aberdeen

Murus: River Vere, Herts

Murus Picticus: the Picts' Wall; *see* Hadriani Murus

Muscomaria: Mossdale Moor, Yorks

Mussalburgum: Musselburgh, Edinburgh
Mutuantonis: Lewes, Sussex; Whitewalls, Wilts
Mygensis: of Mayo, Ireland
Nabaeus: *see* Navaeus
Naeomagus: *see* Neomagus; Nouiomagus
Naesbeia: Naseby, Northants
Nagnata: Sligo, or Limerick
Nalcua: the same as Galleua
Nanaeus: *see* Nauaeus
Nantouicum: Nantwich, Cheshire
Nasense Castrum: Naas, Kildare
Nasi Enei Collegium: Brasenose College, Oxford
Nauaeus: River Naver, Scotland
Nauesbia: Naseby, Northants
Naurum: the Nadder, Wilts; the Naver, Sutherland
Nautgallum: Walbrook, London
Nauticus Sinus: Rotherhithe
Neagora: Newmarket
Nemedus: Barrymore, near Cork
Nemetotacio: a town in Cornwall
Nemus Aquilinum: Elstree, Herts
Nemus Boreale: North-hall, Herts
Neomagus: Buckingham; *see also* Nouiomagus
Neoportus: Newport, Isle of Wight; Newport, Essex
Neoportus Paganellicus: Newport Pagnell, Bucks
Neorus: Lagan Water, Ulster
Nerigon Insula: Isle of Lewes
Neslandia: west of Scotland
Neuarca, Newerca: Newark, Notts
Nicholia, Nicole: Lincoln
Nicolesciria: Lincolnshire
Nidum: Portbury, Somerset; Neath, Glamorganshire
Nidus: River Nid, Yorks
Nigera: Blakeney, Norfolk
Nincolia: Lincoln
Niomagus: *see* Nouiomagus
Nithia: Nidisdale, Scotland
Niuburia: Newbury, Berks
Niuicollini: Snowdon Mountain, Caernarvonshire
Niwebota: Newbottle, Durham
Niweburia: Newbury, Berks
Nobius: *see* Nouius
Nocteleia: Nutley, Bucks
Nordhumbra, Nordhumbria: Northumberland
Nordoricum: Norton Hall, Yorks
Nordouicum: Norwich
Nordouolca: Norfolk
Norflita: Northfleet, Kent
Norhamtuna: Northampton
Norhantescira: Northamptonshire
Norhumbria: Northumberland
Northaluertonia: Northallerton, Yorks
Northamptonia, Northamtuna: Northampton: *see* Bannavenna

Northanimbria: Northumberland
Northantonia: Northampton
Northimbria: Northumberland
Northumbria: Northumberland
Northwicum: Norwich
Northymbria: Northumberland
Nortmannabia: Normanby, Yorks
Nortobricum: Norton Hall, Yorks
Nortouicum: Northwich, Cheshire
Noruicum: Norwich
Norwallia: North Wales
Norwicia, Norwicus: Norwich
Notium Promontorium: Mizen Head, Wicklow, Ireland
Nottingamia: Nottingham
Noua Aula: Newhall, Essex
Noua Porta: Newgate, London
Noua Terra: Newland, Gloucestershire
Noua Villa: Newton, Co. Down
Nouantii, Nouantae, Nouantes: the inhabitants of Galloway, Carrick, and Arran
Nouantum Promontorium, Nouantum Chersonesus: Mull of Galloway; Cockermouth
Nouia: River Rother, Sussex
Nouiodunum: Newenden, Kent
Nouiomagus, Nouiomagnus: Woodcote, Surrey; Chichester; Holwood Hill, Keston, or near Plumstead, Kent
Nouius Flu: River Nid, Scotland; *see also* Conouium
Nouum Castellum, Nouum Castrum: Newcastle-upon-Tyne, Northumberland; Newcastle-under-Lyme, Staffordshire
Nouum Forum, Nouum Mercatum: Newmarket, Cambridgeshire
Nouum Oppidum sub Lima: Newcastle-under-Lyme
Nouum Oppidum super Tinam: Newcastle-on-Tyne
Nouus Burgus: Newport, Isle of Wight; Newport, Monmouthshire; Newhaven or Rye, Sussex; Newbury, Berks; Newburgh, Yorks; a Benedictine convent near Llandaff
Nouus Locus: Newark, or New Place, near Guildford; Newstead, Notts
Nouus Portus: Newport; Newhaven, Kent; Rye, Sussex
Nuba: Midhurst, Sussex; *see* Miba
Nubiria, Nuburia: Newbury, Berks
Nulla Ejusmodi, Nulli Par, Nulli Secunda: Nonsuch, Surrey
Oboca Flu: River Avoca, Ireland
Occidua Wallia: Cornwall
Oceanus Verginius: the Irish Ocean

Ocellum Promontorium: Spurnhead, Holderness, Yorks

Ocetis: Shetland, Pentland, Skerries

Ochthe Hupsele: Ord of Caithness

Ocite: Baz Island on the West of Ireland (Bear Isle, Bantry Bay)

Ockhamptonia: Okehampton, Devon

Ockus: River Okement, Devon

Ocrinum, Ocrium Promontorium: Lizard Point, Cornwall

Octapitarum Promontorium: St David's Head, Pembrokeshire

Odrona: Idrone, Co. Carlow

Oestrymnicus Sinus: Mount's Bay, Cornwall

Oestrymnides Insulae: Scilly Island

Offalaia: Offaly, Co. Kildare

Offedena: Howden, Yorks

Offelana: Offaly

Offelawa: Offlow, Staffordshire

Oissereia: Ossory, Ireland

Okesseta: Oxshot, Surrey

Olanega: Olney, Bucks

Oleiclauis: Ogle Castle, Northumberland

Olenacum: Old Carlisle, or Ellenborough, Cumberland; Ilkley, Yorks

Olerica: Ilkirk, Cumberland

Olfinum: Elphin, co Roscommon, Ireland

Olicana: Ilkley, or Halifax, Yorks

Omire: Southampton

Omnium Sanctorum ad Foenum Parochia: Allhallows the Great, London

Omnium Sanctorum de Barking: Allhallows, Barking, London

Omnium Sanctorum Garscherch: Allhallows, Lombard Street

Omnium Sanctorum in Mellis Viculo: Allhallows, Honey Lane, London

Omnium Sanctorum in Vico Longobardico: Allhallows, Lombard Street, London

Omnium Sanctorum in Vico Pistorum: Allhallows, Bread Street, London

Omnium Sanctorum Pictorum Delibuentium: Allhallows Staining, London

Omnium Sanctorum super (or ad) Celarium: Allhallows the Less, London

Omnium Sanctorum supra Murum: Allhallows-the-Wall, London

Onna: Andover, or Alton, Hants

Onno: *see* Hunnum

Ophelania: Offaly, Leinster

Ora: Ore, Sussex

Orcades Insulae: the Orkney Islands

Orcaneia: Orkney

Orcas Promontorium: Dunnet Head, Caithness

Orchadia: *see* Orcades

Ordeuices, Ordolucae: people of North Wales

Ordouicae: tribe near Berwick

Ordouicum: Norwich; *see* Nordouicum

Orkeneia: Orkney Islands

Ormondia: Ormond, Ireland

Orrhea: Orrock, Fifeshire

Orsteda: Horsted Keynes, Sussex

Orus Flu: River Ore, Suffolk

Osca: River Usk, Wales

Oseneia: Oseney, Oxfordshire

Osseria, Ossoria: Ossory, Ireland

Ossonia: Oxford

Ostium Sturae: Stourmouth, Kent

Ostuthus: River Ystwith, South Wales

Oswaldeslawa: Osbaldstow, Worcestershire

Oswaldi Arbor: Oswestry, Shropshire

Oswaldi Crux: Oswestry

Oteleia: Otley, Yorks

Othona: Ithanchester, or Bradwell-juxta-Mare, Essex

Otreuum: Up Ottery, Devon

Ottadeni, Ottadini, Ottalini: people on the coast from Tyne to Forth

Ottanforda: Otford, Kent

Otthea: Otham, Kent

Ottodani: *see* Ottadeni

Ouedra: River Adder, Berwickshire

Ouinia Insula: Isle of Sheppey, Kent

Ousa: River Ouse, Yorks, and Bucks

Outerini: people of Desmond, Ireland

Oxebea: Christchurch, Hants

Oxefordia, Oxenforda: Oxford

Oxeneia: Oxney, Lincolnshire

Oxenhala: Oxenhall, Durham

Oxeria: Ossory, Ireland

Oxinega: Oxney Isle, Kent

Oxonia, Oxonium: Oxford

Oza: River Ouse

Pagula, Pagula Fleta: Paules Flete, now Paghill or Paull, Yorks

Palus Argita: Lough Derg, Ireland

Palus Salsa: Pwllheli, Caernarvonshire

Palustris Vicus: Fenchurch Street, London

Pampocalia: the same as Calcaria

Pangorensis: of Bangor

Panhovius: Penhow, Monmouthshire

Panteneia: Pentney, Norfolk

Parathalassia: Walsingham, Norfolk

Parcus Ludus: Louth Park, Lincolnshire

Parisi: people of Holderness, Yorks

Parva Cella: a monastery in Ireland

Parvus Burgus: Littleborough, Notts, and Lancs

Pascia: Pacey, Leicestershire

Pasletum, Passeletum: Paisley, Renfrewshire

Paterni Magni Ecclesia: Llanbadarn Vawr, Cardiganshire

Patricii Purgatorium: Ellanu Frugadory, on an island in Lough Derg, Donegal

Pecchum: the Peak, Derbyshire

Pedreda: Penenden Heath, Kent

Pedridon Flu: River Parret, Somerset

Pegelandia: Peakirk, Northants

Pembrochia, Penbrochia: Pembroke, Wales

Pencricum: Penkridge, Staffordshire

Pendinas: Pendennis Castle, Cornwall

Penguernum: Shrewsbury

Penlinnia: a place in Merionethshire, the source of the River Dee

Penmona: Priestholme, Anglesey

Penna: Penselwood, Somerset; or Stourhead, Wilts

Pennocrucium: Penkridge, or Lichfield, Staffordshire

Pennorinum: Penrhyn, Merionethshire; Penryn, Cornwall

Pente Flu: River Pant, Essex

Peonnum: Pen, Somerset; *see* Penna

Perscora, Persora: Pershore, Worcestershire

Perthum: St Johnstone, or Perth, Scotland

Peterillus, Peterus Flu: the Peterill, Cumberland

Petra Duacensis: Kilmacduagh, Co. Clare

Petra Fertilis: Corcumroe, Clare

Petriana: Castle Steeds, Plumpton Wall, or Cambeck Fort, Cumberland; Walton House; Lanercost

Petriburgus, Petroburgum, Petropolis: Peterborough, Northants

Petuaria: Beverley, or Brough Ferry on the Humber, Yorks

Peuenesea: Pevensey, Sussex

Pexa: a town near Dumbarton

Picalia: Pickhill, Yorks

Pictauia, Pictandia: the country of the Picts

Picti: the Picts, a people living north of the Antonine Wall

Pilais: a town in Cornwall or Devon

Pilla: Pille, a Benedictine Priory in Stainton, Pembrokeshire

Pincanhale: Finchale Priory, Durham

Pinnatis Civitas: *see* Alata Castra

Piona Canonicorum: Canon Pyon, or Pewen, Herefordshire

Piona Regis: King's Pyon

Pirri, Insula: Ynys Pyr, or Caldey Island, Pembrokeshire

Piscaria: Fish Street, London

Piscaria Vetus, Piscenaria: Old Fish Street, London

Placentia: a palace at Greenwich, built by Humphrey, Duke of Gloucester

Placeto, Castellum de: Pleshy, Essex

Plimmuta, Plymutha: Plymouth, Devon

Pohanlech: Poughley, Berks

Pohhela: Poughley, Berks

Pola: *see* Strata Marcella

Poleslawa: Polleshoe, Devon

Poletria: the Poultry, London

Pomona: Mainland, one of the Orkney Isles

Pons Aelii: Ponteland, or Newcastle, Northumberland

Pons Belli: Stamford Bridge, Yorks

Pons Burgensis, Pons Burgi: Boroughbridge, Yorks

Pons de Burc: Boroughbirdge

Pons Episcopi: Bishopsbridge, Lincolnshire

Pons Ferie: Ferrybridge, Yorks

Pons Fractus: Pontefract, or Pomfret, Yorks

Pons Fractus Super Tamisiam: Pomfret, near Stepney Marsh

Pons Stephani: Lampeter, Cardiganshire

Pons Vianus: Cowbridge, Glamorgan

Pontaquinum: Bridgwater, Somerset

Ponte, de: a house of Dominican firars in Armagh dioc, perhaps at Drogheda

Pontes: Colnbrook, Old Windsor, Staines, Reading, or Byfleet

Pontuobici: Cowbridge, Glamorganshire

Pontus Flu: the Point, Northumberland

Populorum Lapis: Folkestone, Kent

Porcestra: Porchester, Hants

Poreoclassis: Orrock, Fife; Forfar; or Barry

Porteseia: Portsca, Hants

Portesmua, Portesmuda: Portsmouth, Hants

Portesmutha, Portesmuta: Portsmouth

Portesoka: the Portsoken, London

Portlandia: Portland, Dorset

Portlargium: Waterford, Ireland

Portlocon: Porlock Bay, Somerset

Portunia Insula: Isle of Portland, Dorset

Portuosus Sinus: Sewerby, Yorks

Portus Adurni: Porchester, Hants; Aldrington, or Old Shoreham, Sussex

Portus Ammonis: Sandwich, Kent

Portus Britanniarum: Portsmouth; or Richborough, Kent

Portus Ecgfridi: Jarrow Slake, Durham

Portus Lemanis: Lympne, Kent

Portus Magnus: Portsmouth

Portus Novus: Rye, Sussex (in the Roman period); Newhaven, Sussex

Portus Ostium: Portsmouth

Portus Patrum: Abbey at Enachdune, Co. Galway

Portus Salutis: Cromarty, Scotland

Portus Sistuntiorum: *see* Setantiorum Portus

Pouisia, Powisa, Powisia: Powys, Wales

Praesidium: the same as Praetorium

Praesidium Civitas: Camelon, Co. Stirling

Praetorium: Patrington, Broughton, Flamborough, or Hedon, Yorks

Prata Domini Regis: Kingsmead, Derbyshire

Pratis, S Maria de: S Mary de Pré or de la Pré, or S Mary of Prees

Prestona, Prestonium: Preston, Lancashire

Pridania: for Britannia

Princiduelo: Prittlewell, Essex

Pritannia: for Britannia

Priuotes Flu: River Privet, Hants

Procolitia: Prudhoe Castle, or Carrawburgh, Northumberland

Profundum Vadum: Deptford

Pteroton Stratopedon: Edinburgh; *see* Alata Castra

Puellarum Castrum: Edinburgh

Pulchra Vallis: Beauvale, Notts

Pulchrum Vadum: Fairford, Gloucestershire

Pulchrum Visu: Belvoir, Leicestershire

Pulla: *see* Pilla

Punctuobice: Cowbridge, Glamorganshire

Purocoranauis: a town in Cornwall or Devon

Putewurtha: Petworth, Sussex

Puttenega: Putney, Surrey

Pyonia: *see* Piona

Quadraria, Quarrera, Quarera: Quarre, Wight

Quentona: Quinton, Northants

Radecotanus Pons: Radcot Bridge, Oxon

Rademora: Radmore, Staffordshire

Radenawra, Radenoura: Radnor

Radinge: Reading, Berks

Radnoria: Radnor

Raedinga: Reading

Raga, Ragae: Leicester; Retford

Raganeia: Rayleigh, Essex

Ramense: of Ramsey

Ramesburia: Ramsbury, Wilts

Ramesia, Rameseya: Ramsey, Hunts

Ranatonium: *see* Rhetigonium

Randuaria: Renfrew

Rapa, Rapotum: Raphoe, Donegal, Ireland

Ratae: Leicester; Ratby, or Brinklow, Warwickshire

Ratecorion: *see* Ratae

Rathpotensis, Rathpothesis: of Raphoe, Donegal, Ireland

Ratostabius: *see* Rhatostathybius

Ratupis: *see* Rutupae

Rauenatone: a town in Cornwall or Devon

Rauendala: Ravensworth, Durham

Rauimagum: *see* Nouiomagus

Rauius: River Erne, Connaught

Rauonia: a town probably in Cumberland

Rebodunum: Ribchester, Lancashire

Reculsum: Reculver, Kent

Redingum: Reading, Berks

Redmella: Rodmell, Sussex

Regaina Insula: Isle of Arran

Regalis Locus: Riallieu, Rewley, Oxon

Regata: Reigate, Surrey

Regentium: *see* Regnum

Reginae Burgus: Queenborough, Kent

Regiodunum Hullinum: Kingston-upon-Hull, Yorks

Regiodunum Thamesinum: Kingston-upon-Thames

Regis Burgus: Queenborough, Kent

Regis Comitatus: King's County, Ireland

Regni: People of Surrey, Sussex, and the sea coast of Hampshire

Regni Sylva: Ringwood, Hants

Regnum: Ringwood, Hants; Chichester, or Steyning, Sussex

Regulbium: Reculver, Kent

Reguli Fanum: St Andrews, also called Kirkrule and Kilrule

Reodburna: Rodburne, Wilts

Reofhoppa: Ryhope, Durham

Reopadunum: Repton, Derbyshire

Repandunum: Repton

Retha: Ryde, Isle of Wight

Reuedala: *see* Rauendala

Rhaeba: Rheban or Rheib, Queen's County, Ireland

Rhage: Leicester

Rhatostathybius Flu: River Taff, Glamorganshire, Wye, or Ogmoor

Rhauius: *see* Rauius

Rhedus Flu: River Read, Northumberland

Rhemnius: River Remny, Glamorganshire

Rherigonius Sinus: Loch Ryan, or Luce Bay

Rhesi Civitas: Rochester, Kent

Rhetigonium: Barlan or Stranraer, Galloway

Rhibellus Flu: the Ribble, Lancashire

Rhicina: Isle of Rum, or Rathlin; *see* Richina

Rhigia: Limerick, Ireland; Railstown, Tipperary

Rhigodunum: Ribchester, Warrington, or Manchester

Rhitubi Portus, Rhitupis Portus: Richborough or Sandwich, Kent; *see* Rutupae

Rhius: River Rye, Yorkshire

Rhobodunum: *see* Rhigodunum

Rhobogdii: people of Donegal, Ireland

Rhobogdium Promontorium: Fair Foreland, now called Malin Head, Co. Donegal

Rhofi Civitas: Rochester, Kent

Rhutubi, Rhutupiae: *see* Rutupae
Richala: Riccal, Yorks
Richemundia, Richmondia: Richmond, Yorks; also Richmond, Surrey
Richina, Ricina, Ricinia, Ricnea: Rathlin Isle, Co. Antrim; or Rum, one of the Hebrides
Ridumo: *see* Moridunum
Riduna: *see* Richina
Rievallensis: of Rievaulx, Yorkshire
Rigia: *see* Rhigia
Rigmundia: St Andrews *see* Fanum Reguli
Rigodunum: Richmond, Yorks; Ripon, Yorks; Ribchester, Lancashire
Ripa: River Ribble
Ripa Alta: Ordhill, near Findhorn
Ripa Regine: Queenhithe
Ripadium, Ripandunum: Repton, Derbyshire
Riparia Regine: Queenhithe
Ripensis: of Ripon
Ripodunum, Ripodum: Ripon, Yorks
Ritupis Portus: *see* Rutupae
Rius: Rye, Sussex
Roberti Pons, Robertinus Pons: Robert's Bridge, Sussex
Roboretum, Campus Roborum: Derry, Ireland
Rochesburga: Roxburgh
Roctomessa: River Racon
Rodecotanus Pons: Radcot Bridge, Oxfordshire
Rodolanum: Rhuddlan, Flintshire
Roesperra: Rusper, Sussex
Roffa: Rochester, Kent
Roibus: *see* Roffa
Roisiae Oppidum, Villa de Cruce Roesiae: Royston, Cambridgeshire
Rokesburga: Roxburgh
Rosae Castellum: Rose Castle, Cumberland
Roscomia: Roscommon
Rosea Vallis: Monaster-evin, Ireland (Ware 1455); Ross Glass, Co. Kildare
Rosenensis: of Ross, Scotland
Rosensis: of Ross, Ireland; of Rhos, Pembrokeshire
Rossa, Roscrea: Ross, Wexford County, Ireland
Rossia: Rosse Land, Cornwall; Ross, Herefordshire; Ross, Scotland; Rhos, Pembrokeshire
Rotelandia: Rutland
Rothelanum: Rhuddlan, Flintshire
Rothesia: Rothesay, Isle of Bute, west coast of Scotland
Rotibis: Rochester or Maidstone, Kent
Rouecestria: Rochester
Rouensis: of Rochester
Rouia: River Rother, Sussex
Rowleia: Rothley Temple, Leicestershire
Ruber Cliuus: Redcliffe, or Ratcliffe, near London

Ruda: Routh, Yorks
Ruelega: Rowley Regis, Staffordshire
Rugnitunia, Ruitonia: Ryton-upon-Dunsmoor, Warwickshire
Rumabo Civitas: Drumburgh Castle, Cumberland
Rumeseia: Romsey, Hants
Rupa: Roch, Pembrokeshire
Rupe, de: Roche, an abbey in Yorks
Rupes Fergusii: Carrickfergus, Ireland
Rupis Aurea: Goldcliffe, Monmouthshire
Ruscomia: Roscommon, Ireland
Ruthunia: Ruthin, Denbighshire
Rutlandia: Rutland
Rutunia; *see* Rugnitunia; Rutunium
Rutunium: Wem, Shropshire; Chesterton, Staffordshire; Rowton, Shropshire
Rutupae, Rutupi, Rutupiae, Ritupis Portus: Richborough, Kent; or Sandwich
Rutupinum littus: the coast between the North and South Forelands, Kent
Ruturugum Stagnum: Bay of Dundrum, Co. Down
S Albanus: St Albanus
S Albanus in Vico Ligneo: St Alban's Wood Street, London
S Andreas: St Andrew's, Scotland
S Andreas ad Vestiarium: St Andrew's by the Wardrobe, London
S Andreas sub Malo Cereali: St Andrew's Undershaft, London
S Anna Nigrorum Monachorum: St Anne's, Blackfriars, London
S Asaf: St Asaph, Flintshire
S Bartholomaeus pone Peristylium: St Bartholomew's near the Exchange, London
S Benedictus in Graminoso Vico: St Benet's Gracechurch Street, London
S Benedictus Shorhog: St Bennet's Sherehog, London
S Boscus: Holywood, Belfast Bay
S Botolphus ad Episcopi Portam: St Botolph's Bishopsgate, London
S Botolphus ad Portam Bellini: St Botolph's Billingsgate, London
S Botolphus ad Veterem Portam: St Botolph's without Aldgate, London
S Botolphus Alneae Portae: St Botolph's without Aldersgate, London
S Clari Castellum: St Clear's, Caermarthenshire
S Clemens Dacorum: St Clement Danes, Strand
S Columbae Insula: Icolmkill, Iona
S Crux: Holyrood, Edinburgh
S Davidis Oppidum: St David's, Pembrokeshire
S Edmundus: Bury St Edmund's, Suffolk

S Edmundus in Vico Longobardico: St Edmund's, Lombard Street, London

S Edwardi Abbatia: Shaftesbury, Dorset

S Edwardi Villa: Shaftesbury; Corfe Castle, Dorset

S Egidii in Bosco, domus: Flamsted, Herts

S Gabriel in Vico Palustri: St Gabriel's Fenchurch Street, London

S Genovefa: Fornham St Genevieve, Suffolk

S Jacobus ad Clericorum Fontem: St James' Clerkenwell, London

S Jacobus ad Ducis Hospitium: St James', Duke Place, London

S Jacobus ad Montem Allii: St James' Garlickhithe, or Hill, London

S Joannes Zakarie: St John Zachary, in Adersgate Ward

S Johannes Baptista super Walbroc: St John Baptist's, Walbrook, London

S Katarina de Colmancherche: St Catharine Colman, London

S Katarina Trinitatis: St Catharine Cree Church

S Laurentius in Judaismo: St Lawrence Jewry, London

S Laurentius Pountneus: St Lawrence Pountney, London

S Margareta a Caligarum Venditione: St Margaret Pattens, London

S Margareta extra Fossam: St Margaret Outditch, Rochester

S Margareta juxta Pontem: St Margaret, Bridge Street, or St Margaret, New Fish Street, London

S Margareta Moysi: Mt Margaret Moses, London

S Maria a Lintris Statione: St Mary Bothaw, London

S Maria Abbatis Ecclesiae, or de Abbecherch: St Mary Abchurch, London

S Maria ad Collem: St Mary-at-Hill, London

S Maria ad Lanae Trutinam: St Mary Woolchurch, London

S Maria ad Villam Insularem: St Mary, Islington

S Maria ad Villam Novam: St Mary Newington, London

S Maria de Alba Capella: St Mary Whitechapel, London

S Maria de Arcubus: St Mary-le-Bow, London

S Maria de Insula: Alceter, Warwickshire

S Maria de Monte Alto: St Mary Mounthaw, London

S Maria de Newcherche: St Mary Woolchurch, London

S Maria de Rupe: Kirkheugh, St Andrews

S Maria de Sabaudia: St Mary Savoy, London

S Maria de Wlchershawe: St Mary Woolchurch, London

S Maria in Aldermannorum Burgoparochia: St Mary's Aldermanbury, London

S Maria in Campis: St Mary in the Fields, Edinburgh

S Maria Magdalena de Bermendi Insula: St Mary Magdalen, Bermondsey, London

S Maria Magdalena in Veteri Piscario Foro: St Mary Magdalen, Old Fish Street, London

S Maria Magdalena in Vico Lacteo: St Mary Magdalen, Milk Street, London

S Maria Salvatoris in Australi Opere: St Mary's Southwark

S Maria Senioris Mariae: St Mary Aldermary, London

S Maria Wolnothi: St Mary Woolnoth, London

S Martinus ad Luddi Portam: St Martin's Ludgate, London

S Martinus de Pomerio: St Martin's Pomeroy, London

S Martinus in Ferrariorum Viculo: St Martin's Ironmonger Lane, London

S Martinus in Vinariis, or de Vinetria: St Martin's Vintry, London

S Martinus juxta Charinge Crosse: St Martin's-in-the-Fields, London

S Martinus Ogari: St Martin's Ogars, London

S Martinus Outwichi, or Ottewish: St Martin's Outwich, London

S Michael ad Blada: St Michael's at the Quern, London

S Michael ad Ripam Reginalem: St Michael's, Queenhithe, London

S Michael de Woudestrete: St Michael's, Wood Street

S Michael extra S Trinitatis: St Michael's without the Holy Trinity

S Michael in Curuo Viculo: St Michael's Crooked Lane, London

S Michael in Foro ad Bladum: St Michael's-atte-Corn, or le Quern

S Michael in Hordeaceum Collem: St Michael's Cornhill, London

S Michael Paternoster Cherch in Riola: St Michael's Royal

S Mundus: Kilmund, Argyleshire

S Neothus: St Neot, Cornwall; St Neots, Hunts

S Nicholaus ad Macella: St Nicholas' Fleshambles, London

S Nicholaus Aldrethegate ad Macella: St Nicholas' Fleshambles, London

S Nicholaus Aureae Abbatiae: St Nichols' Cole Abbey, London

S Nicholaus Hakun: St Nicholas Acon, London

S Nicholaus Olof: St Nicholas Olave's, London

S Olauus in Argenteo Vico: St Olave's, Silver Street, London

S Olauus in Australi Opere: St Olave's, Southwark

S Olauus in Ceruina Platea: St Olave's, Hart Street, London

S Olauus juxta Turrim: St Olave's, Hart Street

S Ositha: St Osyth's, Essex

S Oswaldus de Nostellis: Nostal, Yorkshire

S Pancratius in Vico Smegmatico: St Pancras Soper's Lane, London

S Paternus: Llanbadarn, Cardiganshire

S Paulus in Conuentuali Horto: St Paul's Covent Garden, London

S Petrocus: Petrockstow, Devon

S Petrus de Grano Piaco: St Peter's Cornhill

S Petrus in Foro: St Peter's Cheap, London

S Petrus super Tamisiam: St Peter's Pauls Wharf, London

S Stephanus in Vico Colmanni: St Stephen's Coleman Street, London

S Vinini Ecclesia: Kilwinning, Ayrshire

Sabaudia: the Savoy, London

Sabriana, Sabrina: River Severn

Sabulovicum: Sandwich, Kent

Sacana: River Shannon, Ireland

Sacra Capilla: Halifax, Yorks

Sacra Insula: Holy Isle, Northumberland

Sacra Sylva: Halifax, Yorks

Sacrum Nemus: Halywood Monastery, Galloway

Sacrum Promontorium: Greenore Point, or Carnsore Point, Wexford

Sadberga: Sadberge, Durham

Safteberia: Shaftesbury, Dorset

Salebeia: Selby, Yorks

Salenae: Chesterton, nead Sandy, Beds

Salesburia: Salisbury, Wilts

Salicetum, foresta de: Salcey Forest, Northants

Salimnos Insula: Sulmey Isle, near Milford Haven

Salinae: Droitwich, Worcestershire; Nantwich, Cheshire; Slaughter, Gloucestershire; *see also* Salenae

Salisbiria: Salisbury; Shrewsbury

Salopesburia: Shrewsbury, Shropshire

Salopescira, Salopesiria: Shropshire

Salopia: Shrewsbury

Saltria: Sawtry, Hunts

Saltus Andreda: the Weald of Sussex

Saltus Salmonis: Leixlip, Co. Dublin

Salutaris Portus: Sewerby, Yorks

Salwarpus: Salwarpe River, Worcestershire

Samairus: River Erne, Ireland

Samothea: Britain

Sancta Anna intra Portum Alneani: St Anne's, Aldersgate, London

Sancti Botolphi Oppidum: Boston, Lincolnshire

Sancto Johanne, Ville de: Perth, Scotland

Sanctus Aegidius ad Portam Membris-captorum: St Giles Cripplegate, London

Sandicum: Sandwich, Kent

Sandouicum, Sanwicius: Sandwich

Sareberia: Salisbury, Wilts

Saresburia, Sarisbiria: Salisbury, Wilts

Sarnia: Guernsey

Sartis, de: Wardon Abbey, Beds

Sarua: River Severn

Sauerennus: River Bandon or River Lee, Cork

Sauerna: River Severn

Sauranus Flu: River Avonmore, Cork

Saxonicum Littus: the eastern and southern coast of Britain

Scadum Namorum: *see* Isca Dumnoniorum

Scala Celi: St Wolstan's Abbey, Co. Kildare

Scandia: Sanday Island, one of the Orkneys

Scapeia: Sheppey, Kent

Scardeburgum, Scardus Burgus: Scarborough, Yorks

Scartheburga: Scarborough, Yorks

Sceaftesbiria: Shaftesbury, Dorset

Sceargeta: Sarratt, Herts; Shearsby, Leicestershire

Sceftonia: Shaftesbury, Dorset

Scena: River Shannon

Sceptonia: Shaftesbury, Dorset

Scetis: Isle of Skye

Schafbera: Shebbear, Devon

Schaftesbiria: Shaftesbury, Dorset

Schellus Flu: River Skell, Yorks

Schelsega: Chelsea, near London

Schepeia: Sheppey

Scireburna: Sherborne

Scona: Scone, Perthshire

Scorberia, Scorbesberia: Shrewsbury

Scornae: Shorne, Kent

Scoti: the Scots

Scotia: Ireland; Scotland

Scrobesberia, Scropesbyria: Shrewsbury

Searesbiria: Salisbury

Sebasta Altera Legio: Liskeard, Cornwall

Secandunum: Seckington, Warwickshire

Sedes Animarum: Soulseat, Galloway

Seftesberia, Seftonia: Shaftesbury, Dorset

Segedunum: Sedghill; Cousinshouse, or Wallsend, Northumberland

Segelocum: Ollerton, or Littleborough, Notts

Segeswalda: Seckington, Warwickshire

Seggesfelda: Sedgefield, Durham

Segontiaci: a tribe living near Silchester

Segontium, Seguntium: Cairseint, Caernarvon; Silchester

Selburgi Tumulus: Silbury Hill, Wilts

Selebia: Selby, Yorks

Seletuna: Monk Hesleton, Durham; Silton, Yorks

Selgouae: people of Nithsdale and Annandale

Sellinae Insulae: Scilly Islands

Seluestuna: Selston, Notts

Sena: River Shannon

Senna: River Senni, or River Usk, Brecknockshire

Senus: River Shannon

Seolesia: Selsea, Sussex

Sepes Inscisa: Hay Castle, Brecknock

Serberia, Serbyria: Salisbury

Serduno: *see* Segedunum

Seresberia: Salisbury

Setantiorum Portus: Windermere, or the mouth of the Ribble, Lancashire

Seteia Aestuarium: the mouth of the Dee, Cheshire

Seueria: Salisbury

Sewardeslega: Sewesley near Towcester, Northants

Shaftonia: Shaftesbury, Dorset

Shaga: Shaw, Berks

Sharpenora: Sconce Point, Isle of Wight

Shenum: Shene, or Richmond, Surrey

Siambis: River Shannon

Sibbetonum: Sibton, Suffolk

Sienus: River Shannon

Sigdeles: the Scilly Isles

Silamesteda: Sulhamstead, Berks

Silesia: Selsea, Sussex

Silionnus: *see* Limnos

Sillinae Insulae: Scilly Islands

Silura Insula: Scilly Islands

Silures: people of South Wales

Simeni: a tribe in Norfolk and Suffolk

Sineius Flu: River Shannon, Ireland

Sinnenus: River Shannon

Sinnodunum: Sinodum Hill, near Wallingford, Berks

Sinomagus: *see* Sitomagus

Sinus Felix: Bridlington or Filey Bay, Yorks

Siresburna: Sherborne, Dorset

Siriolis: St Cyriol, Bangor

Sirwuda: Sherwood, Notts

Sitomagus: Thetford, Norfolk; Woolpit, Stowmarket, Dunwich, or Eye, Suffolk

Slana: River Slaine, Wexford

Slepa: St Ives, Hunts

Slicheius: River Gitley, *olim* Sligo

Slopesberia: Shrewsbury; Shropshire

Smedefelda: Smithfield

Snaudonia: Snowdon Forest, Caernarvonshire

Sobrica: Ardnamurchan, Argyleshire

Socinus: River Shannon

Sodera: Sodor, islands on the west coast of Scotland

Soltra, hospitale de: Soutra, between Ediburgh and Kelso

Soluathianum Aestuarium, Soluaeum Flumen: Solway Firth

Somaridunum: Somerton, Lincolnshire

Somersata, Somerseta, Somersetania, Somersetensis, Somertunensis Comitatus: Somerset

Sorbiodunum, Soruiodunum: Old Sarum; Carisbrooke; also Shrewsbury

Southamptonia: Southampton

Southeria: Surrey

Southerlandia: Sutherland, Scotland

Southriana: Surrey

Southsexena, Southsexia: Sussex

Southwella: Southwell, Notts

Spea: River Spey, Elgin, Scotland

Spinae: Speen, near Newbury, Berks

Spinarum Insula: Thorney Isle, the site of Westminster Abbey

Spinetum: Spinney, Cambridgeshire

Spinodunum: Thornton, Lincolnshire

Staffordia: Stafford

Stanfordia, Stanforda: Stamford, Lincolnshire

Starkelea: Startley, Wilts

Starus: River Stour

Statiarius Lapis: Clough, Co. Antrim

Statio Deventia: in Devonshire, Totness

Steafordensis: of Stafford

Stellata, Camera: the Star Chamber

Stenum: Stean, Northants

Steofordensis: of Stafford

Stinsiarius: River Stinchar, Ayrshire

Stiuentona: Staunton, Gloucestershire

Stokeporta, Stokeportus: Stockport, Cheshire

Stourus: River Stour

Strata Florea, Strata Florida: Ystrad Flur, or Stratflower, now Mynachlogfur, or Caron-llwch-Clawdd, Cardiganshire

Strata Marcella: Strat Margel, or Ystrad Marchel, Montgomeryshire

Stratcluttenses: Britons of Strathclyde

Streoneshalf: ancient name of Whitby Abbey

Stretgledwali: *see* Stratcluttenses

Stretlea: Streatlam, Durham

Strigulense Castrum: Striguil Castle, Monmouthshire

Strigulia, Stringulia: Chepstow, Monmouthshire

Striuellina, Striuilingum: Stirling, Scotland

Stroda: Strood, Kent

Stubeheda, Stubhutha: Stepney

Stuccia, Stucia Flu: River Ysthwith, or Dovey, Cardiganshire

Stura: River Stour

Sturodunum: Stourton, and Stourminster, Dorset

Sturus Flu: River Stour

Sualua: River Swale, Yorks

Suauicordium, Dulce Cor: Sweetheart, or New Abbey, Kirkcudbrightshire

Subdobiadon: a town on the Wall of Antonine

Sudereia: Surrey

Sudesexia: Sussex

Sudhamtonia: Hampshire

Sudouerca: Southwark

Sudouolca, Sudouolgia: Suffolk

Sudria: Surrey

Sudsexa: Sussex

Sudwallia: South Wales

Sudwercha: Southwark

Suella: Southwell, Notts

Suelloniaca: Brockley Hill, near Ellstree, or Chipping Barnet, Herts

Suffolicia: Suffolk

Suiftus: River Swift, Leicestershire

Suina: Swinhey, Yorks

Suirus: Suir River, near Waterford, Ireland

Sukius: River Suck, Connaught

Sulcalua Flu: River Swale, Yorks

Sulloniaca, Sullonica: *see* Suelloniaca

Sumersetanea, Sumertunensis, Summurtunensis Paga: Somerset

Sunningum: Sonning, near Reading, Berks

Surium: Inislaunagh, Co. Tipperary

Surra, Surria, Surreia: Surrey

Sussexia: Sussex

Susura: Isle of Jura

Suthamtonia: Southampton

Suthamtunensis Provincia: Hampshire

Suthburia: Sudbury, Suffolk

Sutheria: Surrey

Suthesexia: Sussex

Suthimbria: England south of the Humber

Suthregia, Suthreia: Surrey

Suthriona: Surrey

Suthsaxonia: Sussex

Suthsexia: Sussex

Suthumbria: *see* Suthimbria

Suthwalonia: South Wales

Suthwella: Southwell, Notts

Suthweorca: Southwark

Suwallia: South Wales

Suwella: Southwell, Notts

Sweynesia: Swansea, Glamorganshire

Swina: Swinhey, Yorkshire

Swthwella: Southwell, Notts

Syli: people of S Wales

Syllina, Sylina: Scilly Isles

Syreburna: Sherborne, Dorset

Taba: Teignmouth, Devon

Tadecastrum: Tadcaster; *see* Calcaria

Tadoriton: a town between the Walls of Hadrian and Antonine

Taffus Flu: River Taff, Glamorganshire

Tagea: Monteith, Perthshire

Taisa: River Tees

Taizali: the people of Buchan, Scotland

Taizalum Promontorium: Buchanness, or Kinnaird Head, east coast of Scotland

Tama: Thame, Oxfordshire

Tama Flu: River Tame, Oxfordshire; River Teme, Worcestershire

Tamara: Tamerton-Foliott, Devon; or Saltash, Cornwall

Tamara Flu: River Tamar, Cornwall

Tamare: Tavistock, Devon

Tamaris Fluvii Ostia: Plymouth

Tamaris: *see* Tamara

Tamarus: River Tamar

Tamawordina: Tamworth, Staffordshire

Tambra: River Tamar

Tameia: Dunkeld, Perthshire

Tamensis: River Thames

Tamese: Kingston, Surrey, or Streatley, Berks

Tamesia, Tamesis: rivers Thames and Medway

Tamewrda: Tamworth, Staffordshire

Tamion: River Tavy

Tamisa, Tamisis: River Thames

Tamworthia: Tamworth, Staffordshire

Tanarus: River Tamar

Tanathos Insula: Isle of Thanet, Kent

Tanaus: the Firth of Forth

Tanetos: *see* Tanathos

Tanfelda: Tanfield, Yorks

Taniatidae: *see* Tanathos

Tanodunum: Taunton, Somerset

Taodunum: Dundee

Tarensis: of Derry, Ireland

Tarenteforda: Dartford, Kent

Taruedum, Taruisium: Duncansby Head, Caithness

Tarxa: Torksey, Lincolnshire

Tatecastra: Tadcaster, Yorks

Taua: River Tay, Scotland

Taua: Teignmouth, Devon

Tauistokia: Tavistock, Devon

Taus: River Tay

Tawus: River Taw, Devon

Teauus: River Tavy, Devon

Techelesberia: Tewkesbury, Gloucestershire

Tedfordia: Thetford, Norfolk

Tegoeus Lacus: Lake Tegid, or Bala, Merionethshire, Wales

Teisa, Teisis: River Tees, Durham
Temdus: River Teme
Temesforda: Tempsford, Beds
Templum Florum: Kynloss, or Kilfloss, Moray
Tenos: Isle of Thanet
Teodforda: Thetford, Norfolk
Terdebigga: Tardebigg, Worcestershire
Terentus Flu: River Trent
Terna: River Tern, Shropshire
Tesa: River Tees, Durham
Tesedala: Teesdale
Tesobius: River Conway
Tethfordum: Thetford, Norfolk
Tetocuria: Tetbury, Gloucestershire
Teuidalia: Teviotdale, Scotland
Tewiensis fluvius: River Tywi, Caermarthenshire
Texali: people of Buchan, Aberdeenshire; *see* Taizali
Teysa: River Tees
Thamesis, Thamisia: Thames
Thanatos, Thanathos: Thanet
Theisa: River Tees
Themis: River Teme, Worcestershire
Thenodunum: Taunton, Somerset
Theobaldenses Aedes: Theobalds, Herts
Theoci Curia: Tewkesbury, Gloucestershire
Theodforda: Thetford, Norfolk
Theodorodunum: Wells, Somerset
Theokebiria, Theokesberia: Tewkesbury
Theorodunum: *see* Theodorodunum
Theostrota: Toccotes, Yorks
Thermae: Bath
Theta: Little Ouse River, Norfolk
Thetfordia: Thetford, Norfolk
Thewda: River Tweed
Thiletheya: Tiltey, Essex
Thinemutha: Tynemouth, Northumberland
Thinus Flu: River Tyne, Northumberland
Thongum: Thong, Yorkshire
Thonodunum: Taunton, Somerset
Thonus: River Tone, Somerset
Thorncia: Thorney, Cambridgeshire
Thornega: Thorney Isle, the site of Westminster Abbey
Thorp Comitisse: Countessthorpe, Leicestershire
Thuemia: Tuam, Galway
Thuenensis: of Down, Ireland
Thuetmonia: Thomond, Ireland
Thule: Shetland Isles, or Iceland
Thweda: River Tweed
Tibius, Tybius Flu: River Teify, Cardiganshire
Tibraccia: Tibraghny, Kilkenny; perhaps sometimes Tipperary
Ticcelea: Thickley, Durham
Tichehella, Tichehulla: Tickhill, Yorks

Tichfelda: Titchfield, Hants
Tietforda: Thetford, Norfolk
Tignea: Teign Canon, Devon
Tikehilla: Tickhill, Yorks
Tilae: *see* Thule
Tileburgum: Tilbury, Essex
Tiliapis: *see* Tolapia
Tina Flu: River Tyne, Northumberland; or the Eden, Fifeshire
Tindolana: Winchester in the Wall, Northumberland
Tinea Flu: River Teign, Devon
Tinemutha: Tynemouth, Northumberland
Tinna: *see* Tina
Tinomoutum: Tynemouth
Tintagium: Tintagell, Cornwall
Tinus: *see* Tina
Tiretia: Tiltey, Essex
Tisa: River Tees
Tisis, Tisobis Flu: River Conway, North Wales
Tistonia: Tisted, Hants
Tiueteshala: Titshall, Norfolk
Tiwa Magna: Great Tew, Oxfordshire
Tobius Flu: River Towy, Caermarthenshire
Toesobis: *see* Tisis
Tolapia, Toliapis, Toliatis: Sheppey, or Thanet
Toller Porcorum: Swinetoller, Dorset
Tomewordina: Tamworth, Staffordshire
Tomondia: Thomond, Ireland
Tonbrigium: Tonbridge, Kent
Tonellum: the Tun, a prison in Cornhill
Torcestria: Towcester, Northamptonshire
Torkesega: Torksey or Torsey, Lincolnshire
Tornai, Torneia: Thorney, Cambridgeshire
Tornetuna: Thornton, Yorks
Torteoda: Tortworth, Gloucestershire
Tortuna: Thornton-le-Street, Yorks
Totonesium Littus: coast of Hampshire, opposite Totland's Bay, Totness
Trajectus: Henbury, Hanham, or Bitton, near Bristol
Trajectus Augustae: Austcliff, or Henbury, Gloucestershire
Treanta: River Trent
Trecastellum: Beaumaris, Anglesey
Trefontana: Three Fountains, Lammermuir
Trehenta: River Trent
Trellinum: Welshpool, Montgomery
Trenovantum: London
Trenta: River Trent
Trepelawa: Triplow, Cambridgeshire
Treska: Thirsk, Yorks
Triburna: Kilmore
Trimontium, Trimuntium: Annand, Dumfriesshire, or Eildon

Trinoantes, Trinobantes, Trinouantes:the people of Middlesex and Essex

Tripontium:Towcester, or Lilbourne, Northants; Rugby, Cave's Inn, or Kineton, Warwickshire

Trisanton: River Test, Hants; River Ouse, Sussex

Trisanton, Trisantonis Portus: Southampton; *see* Clausentum

Triuerium:Truro, Cornwall

Trumense castrum:Trim, Meath

Trutulensis Portus: probably an error for *Rutupensis*, or the Humber

Tuai Aestuarium: mouth of the Spey, Scotland

Tuama, Tuaima:Tuam, Galway, Ireland

Tueda: River Tweed

Tuemia:Tuam, Galway,

Tueoxbea, Tueoxnea: Christchurch, Hants

Tuerobis Flu: River Teify

Tuesis: River Tees, Berwick

Tweda, Tweodum: River Tweed

Twomondia:Thomond, Ireland

Tybius: River Teify, Cardiganshire

Tykeilla:Tickhill, Yorks

Ubbanforda: Norham, Northumberland

Udiae: people about Cork

Uffintona: Ufton, Berks

Ugrulentum: a town north of the Wall of Antonine

Ugueste: a town north of the Wall of Antonine

Ulidia: the province of Ulster, Ireland

Ullerwuda: Ollerton, Cheshire

Ulmetum: Elmley, or Emley, Yorks; North Elmham, Norfolk

Ultonia, Uluestera: Ulster, Ireland

Umalia:Achad Fobhair, co Mayo, Ireland

Umber: River Humber

Undalium, Undola: Oundle, Northants

Uniuallis: *see* Ureuallis

Urbs Legionum: Chester

Ureuallis: Jervaulx, Yorks

Urgalia: Louth, Ireland

Uriconia:Wrottesley, Staffordshire

Uriconium: *see* Virioconium

Uriponium: Ripon, Yorks

Urithlesia:Wrexham, North Wales

Uriuallis: Jervaulx, Yorks

Uroconium: *see* Virioconium

Urolanium: *see* Verolamium

Urosullum:Wressell, Yorks

Urouicum:York

Urus: River Ure, or Yore, Yorks

Usa: River Ouse

Usocona, Usoconna: Sheriff Hales, Oeaken Gates, Shropshire; or Bednall, Staffordshire

Uterni: a trive living in South Desmond

Utriconion: *see* Virioconium

Uxacona: *see* Usocona

Uxela: Exeter, Bridgewater, or Lostwithiel

Uxelis: Lostwithiel, or Launceston, Cornwall

Uxelludamum: Hexham, Northumberland

Uxelum: Caerlaverock, or Wardlaw, Dumfriesshire

Uxena: Crockherne Well, Devon

Uxinus Pons: Uxbridge, Middlesex

Uzela Aestuarium: *see* Vexala

Uzelium: *see* Uxelum

Uzella: *see* Uxela

Vacomagi: people of Murray and Athol, Scotland

Vadum Boum: Oxford

Vadum Ceruinum: Hertford

Vadum Pulchrum: Fairford, Gloucestershire

Vadum Rubrum: Hertford

Vadum Salicis:Wilford; Walford, Herefordshire

Vadum Saxi: Stanford

Vaga Flu: River Wye, Herefordshire

Vagniacae, Vagniacum: Maidstone, Wrotham, Northfleet, or Strood, Kent

Valeia:Whalley, Lancashire

Valentia: province of Britain between the walls of Hadrian and Antonine, i.e. the Forth and the Tyne; or between the walls of Hadrian and Severus

Vallidena: Saffron Walden, Essex; Walden, Lincolnshire

Vallis Anangia:Annandale, Scotland

Vallis Aurea: Golden Vale, Herefordshire

Vallis Crucis: an abbey at Llan Egwestl or Egwast, Denbighshire

Vallis Dei:Vaudey, or Walden, Lincolnshire; Killenny, Co. Kilkenny

Vallis Doloris:Wedale, Scotland

Vallis Longa: Combehire, or Cumhil, Radnorshire

Vallis Lucis: Glenluce, Galloway, Scotland

Vallis Regalis:Vale Royal, Cheshire

Vallis S Andreae: Pluscardin, Moray

Vallis S Mariae in Snaudonia: Beddgelert, Caernarvonshire

Vallis Salutis: Baltinglass, Co Wicklow

Vallis Virtutis: Charterhouse at Perth

Vallum: the Picts' Wall; *see* Hadriani Murus

Valteris: *see* Verterae

Vanantinga:Wantage, Berks

Vandalis Flu: River Wandle, Surrey

Vandelbiria:Vandlebury, or Wandlesborough, a hill near Cambridge

Vanduaria: Paisley

Vara Flu: Murray Firth

Varae Castrum: Dunbar

Varia Flu: River Frome, Dorset

Varingtonium:Warrington, Lancashire

Varis: Bodvari, Flintshire; Llanfair, Denbighshire

Varuicum: Warwick

Vecta, Vectesis: Isle of Wight

Vectis Insula: Whitehorn Island, Galloway; Isle of Wight

Vecturiones: Picts

Vedra, Vedrus: River Wear, Durham, or the Tyne

Velabri: People of Munster

Velox Flu: River Ivel, Somerset

Velunia: a town in Scotland

Veluntium: Arless, Queen's Co., Ireland

Venantodunia: Huntingdonshire

Venantodunum, Venatorum Mons: Huntingdon

Venedotia: Gwynedd, North Wales

Veneris: *see* Verterae

Venicnium, Vennicuium: Ram's Head, or Horn Head, Donegal

Venicontes: people in Fife

Vennicnii: people of Tyrconnel, Ireland

Venonae, Vennones: Claybrooke, near Bensford Bridge, Leicestershire; or Southam, Warwickshire

Venta Belgarum: Winchester or Havant, Hants

Venta Icenorum, Simenorum, Cenomum: Caistor or Norwich, Norfolk

Venta Silurum: Caer-went, Monmouthshire

Ventanum: Winchester

Ventolacensis: of Wensleydale, Yorks

Ventus Morbidus: Windsor, Berks

Ventusfrigetmare: Winchelsea, Sussex

Venutio: the same as Banatia

Veratinum: Cressage, Shropshire; Warrington; or the same as Verometum

Verbeia: River Wharfe, Yorks

Vergiuius, Verginius Oceanus: The sea to the south of Ireland

Verlucio: Warminster, Leckham, Spy Park, or Sandy Lane, Wilts

Vernalis: a town in Cornwall or Devon

Vernemetum: *see* Verometum

Vernicones: the Picts

Verolamium: Verulam, now St Albans, Herts

Verometum: Burrow Hill, or Cosby, Leicestershire; or Willoughby, Notts

Veromum: a town north of the Forth

Verouicum: Warwick

Verregraua: Wargrave, Berks

Verterae, Verteris: Brough-upon-Stainmore, Westmoreland; Watgarth, Durham; or Bowes, Yorks

Verteuia: a town in Cornwall or Devon

Vertis: Bourton-on-the-Water, Gloucestershire

Veruedrum Promontorium: Strathy, or Duncansby Head, Scotland

Veruicum: Warwick

Verulamium: Verulam, or St Albans, Herts

Verus: River Wear, Durham

Veruuium: *see* Berubium

Vetadunum: Watton, Yorks

Vetelegans Pons: Wheatley Bridge, near Oxford

Vetilingiana Via: Watling St

Vetta Insula: Isle of Wight

Vetus Burgus: Elvet, Durham; Aldborough, Yorks

Vetus Piscaria: Old Fish St, London

Vexala, Uzela Aestuarium: the mouth of the Yeo or Ivel, or of the Brent, Somerset

Vexfordia: Wexford, Ireland

Via Cava: Holloway, Middlesex

Via Noua: Monastery of Gormorgan, Co. Clare

Vicanum: Etchingham, Sussex

Viconia: *see* Vinnouium

Victesis: Isle of Wight

Victoria: Wigton; Abernethy, Perthshire; Inchkeith; or Dealgin Ros, Strathern

Victuarii, Vectuarii: Men of the Isle of Wight

Vicumba: Wycombe, Bucks

Vicus Albanus, Malbus, or Malbanus: Nantwich, Cheshire

Vicus Orientalis: Eastwick, Herts

Vicus Saxeus: Staindrop, or Stainthorp, Durham

Vidogara, Vidotara, Aestuarium: Mouth of the River Ayr or River Irvine, Ayrshire

Vidua: River Crodagh, Donegal

Vieruedrum: *see* Veruedrum

Vigornia: Worcester

Villa Albani: St Albans

Villa de Cruce Roesiae: Royston, Herts

Villa de S Johanne: Perth

Villa Faustini: Dunmow, Woolpit, Bury St Edmunds, or Orford in Suffolk

Villa Noua: Newnham, Herts; Newtownards, Co Down

Villa Novi Castri super Tinam: Newcastle-upon-Tyne

Villa Regia: Kingston-upon-Hull; St Edmundsbury, Suffolk

Vilsedonum: Willesden, where there was a celebrated image of the Virgin Mary

Vilugiana Provincia: Wiltshire

Vimutium: Weymouth, Dorset

Vinchelsega: Winchelsea, Sussex

Vindagora: Windsor

Vindediuii: Drogheda, Ireland

Vindelis: Winchelsea

Vindelisora: Windsor, Berks

Vindelocomum: Winchcombe, Gloucestershire

Vinderius: Bay of Carrickfergus, or Loch Strangford

Vindesorium: Windsor

Vindobala: Rutchester, or Rouchester, Northumberland

Vindocladia, Vindogladia: Cranbourne, Wimborne, or Blandford, Dorset; or Alum Bay, Isle of Wight

Vindolana, Vindolanda: Little Chesters, or Chesterholm, in Northumberland

Vindomara: Ebchester, Durham; Dod's End, Northumberland; or Killhope Cross, Durham

Vindomus, Vindonum: Silchester; Farnham; near Whitchurch; or Winchester

Vindouala: *see* Vindobala

Vindugladia: *see* Vindocladia

Vinduglessus: River Gaunless, Durham

Vinetria: the Vintry, London

Vinnouium, Vinouia: Binchester, or Egglestone, Durham

Virdogladia: *see* Vindocladia

Virecinum, Virecium: *see* Virioconium

Viride Lignum: Newry, Ireland

Viridis Sinus: Greenwich

Viridis Stagni Monasterium: Soulseat, Galloway

Virioconium, Viroconium: Wroxeter, Shropshire; or Stone, Staffordshire

Virolamium: *see* Verolamium

Virosidum: Ellenborough, Old Carlisle, or Workington, Cumberland

Viruedrum: *see* Veruedrum

Visimonasterium: Westminster

Visi-Saxones: West Saxons

Vitrea Insula: Glastonbury

Vituli Insula: Selsea, Sussex

Viuidin: River Fowey, Cornwall

Viurus: River Wear

Vodiae: People about Cork

Volantium: *see* Olenacum

Voldia: Cotswold, Gloucestershire

Voliba: *see* Voluba

Volitanium: probably on the Wall of Antonine

Volsas Sinus: Loch Broom, Ross-shire, or Loch Assynt

Voluba: Lostwithiel, Tregony, Falmouth, Bodmin, or Grampound, Cornwall

Volucrum Domus: Fulham, Middlesex

Voluicum: Woolwich

Voluntii: people of Ulster, Ireland

Voluntium: Ardglass, Down, Ireland

Volurtion: *see* Borcouicum

Voran: Caervoran, Northumberland, or Warran, Forfar

Voreda: Old Penrith, Plumpton Wall, or Kirk Oswald, Cumberland; or Whelp Castle, Westmoreland

Vosargia: Herm Island in the Channel

Vusa: River Ouse

Wabruna: Weybourne, Norfolk

Wachefelda: Wakefield, Yorks

Waga, Waia: River Wye; River Wey

Walalega: Whalley, Lancashire

Walani: Welshmen

Waldena: Saffron Walden, Essex

Waldintona: Waldington, Yorks

Walenesteda: Godstone, Surrey

Walensis: Welshman

Walia: Wales

Walingforda: Wallingford, Berks

Waliscus, Wallanus: a Welshman

Walla Londoniarum: London Wall

Wallia: Wales

Walonicus: Welsh

Waltifordia: Waterford, Ireland

Wanlokensis: of Wenlock, Shropshire

Wanneforda: Wangford, Suffolk

Wara: Ware, Herts

Warengeforda: Wallingford, Berks

Warewella: Wherwell, Hants

Warle Septem Molarum: Warley, Essex

Warsopa: Worksop, Notts

Waruicus: Warwick

Wasfordia: Wexford, Ireland

Watafordia: Waterford, Ireland

Watelega: Wheatley

Waterfordia: Waterford, Ireland

Watria: Wavertree, Lancashire

Wauerlega: Waverley, Hants

Waya: River Wye; River Wey

Wdestochia, Wdestoka: Woodstock, Oxfordshire

Weableia: Weobley, Herefordshire

Weda: River Tweed

Wekefeldia: Wakefield, Yorks

Welandus: Welland River, Northants

Welcomestowa: Walthamstow, Essex

Wella, Welliae: Wells, Somerset

Wendoura: Wendover, Bucks

Wennescoita: Coedowen, Brecon

Wenta: Winchester; *see also* Winta

Wenti: people of Monmouth

Wera: Weare, Somerset

Werkewurda: Warkworth, Northumberland

Werregraua: Wargrave, Berks

Werreministra: Warminster, Wilts

Wertemora: Stainmore, Westmoreland

Werwella: Wherwell, Hants

Wesefordia: Wexford

Weskus: Esk River, Yorks

Wessefordia: Wexford, Ireland

Westberia: Westbury

Westmaria: Westmoreland

Westmonasterium: Westminster

Westmoria, Westmorlandia: Westmoreland

Westmulna: Westmill, Herts
West-Walani: Cornish men
Wetha: Isle of Wight; *see* Vecta
Weuerus: River Wever, Cheshire
Weum: Wem, Shropshire
Wherfus: River Wharfe, Yorks
Wheta: Isle of Wight
Wiableia: Weobley, Herefordshire
Wibigginum: Wigan, Lancashire
Wiburti Villa: Wiveton, Norfolk
Wiccia: Worcestershire
Wiccii: people living in Worcestershire
Wichcombia: Wycombe, Bucks
Wichia: Droitwich
Wichium: Northwich, Cheshire
Wichum: Wick, Gloucestershire
Wictona: Witton, Durham
Wicumba: Wycombe, Bucks
Wicus: *see* Vicus
Wienornis: Wimborne, Dorset
Wigornia: Worcester
Wika Hamonis: Wyke Hamon, Northants
Wilda Sussexiae: The Weald of Sussex
Willensis: of Wells
Wilsates: inhabitants of Wilts
Wiltenses: inhabitants of Wilts
Wiltesciria: Wiltshire
Wiltonia: Wilton; Wilts
Wimundhamia: Wymondharm, Norfolk
Winburna: Wimborne, Dorset
Wincelcumba: Winchcombe, Gloucestershire
Wincestria: Winchester
Winchelcumba: Winchcombe
Winchelsega: Winchelsea
Windesora, Windleshora, Windresora: Windsor, Berks

Winta: Gwent, a province in South Wales, between Usk and Wye
Winternia: Whithern, Wigtonshire, Scotland
Wintonia: Winchester
Wira: River Wear, Durham
Wiramutha: Wearmouth, Durham
Wirecestrescira: Worcestershire
Wirecestria: Worcester
Wiremunda: Wearmouth, Durham
Wirus: River Wear, Durham
Wistendena: Withdean, Sussex
Witebia: Whitby, Yorks
Witerna, Witernia: Whithern, Wigtonshire
Witlesia: Whittlesey, Cambridgeshire
Witteneia: Witney, Oxon
Witternensis: of Whithern, Wigtonshire
Wluestera: Ulster
Wodnesberia: Wednesbury, Staffordshire
Wodneslega: Wendesley or Wensley, Derbyshire
Wotha: Isle of Wight
Wrekus: River Wreke, Leicestershire
Wudestocha: Woodstock, Oxon
Wulfrunehantona: Wolverhampton, Staffordshire
Wychium: Northwich, Cheshire
Yarienis: River Yare, Norfolk
Yarmuthia: Yarmouth, Norfolk
Yarum: Yarm, Yorkshire
Yeogerieceastria: Worcester
Yetzhamsteda: Easthampstead, Berks
Ylvernis: Inverness, Scotland
Ymiliacum: Emly, Tipperary
Ypocessa: Lower Stanton, Herefordshire
Ysteleswurda: Isleworth, Middlesex
Yuelcestria: Ilchester, Somerset
Yxninga: Exning, Suffolk
Zeviota: The Cheviots

BISHOPRICS IN SCOTLAND

Aberdonensis: Aberdeen
Argadire: Orkneys
Argatheliae: Argyle
Brechinensis: Brcchin
Caledoniensis: Dunkeld
Candidae Casae: Whithorn, Galloway
Cathanenais: Caithness
Dunblanensis, Dunblivensis: Dunblane
Dunkeldensia: Dunkeld
Dunroduni: Domoch, Sutherland
Gallovidiensis: Galloway

Glascuensis, Glascensis: Glasgow (Archbishopric)
Hebridensia: the Isles, or Sodor
Lismorensis: Lismore
Moraviensis: Moray
Murthlaci: Mortlach
Orcadiensis: Orkneys
Rossansia: Ross
S Andreae, Sanctandreanus: St Andrews (Archbishopric)
Sodorensia: the Isles, or Sodor
Whitternensis: Whitherne

BISHOPRICS IN ENGLAND

Asaphensis, Assauensis: St Asaph's

Bagarensis, Bangorensis, Bannochorensis: Bangor

Bathoniensis, or Bathoniensis et Wellensis: Bath and Wells

Bristoliensis: Bristol

de Burgo Sancti Petri: Peterborough

Cantuariensis: Canterbury (Archbishopric)

Carleolensis: Carlisle

Cestrensis: Chester

Cicestrensis: Chichester

Couentrensis: Coventry and Lichfield

Dunelmensis: Durham

Eboracensis, Eburacensis: York (Archbishopric)

Eliensis: Ely

Exoniensis: Exeter

Glocestrensis: Gloucester

Heliensis: Ely

Herefordensis, Herfordiensis: Hereford

Landavensis: Llandaff

Lichfeldensis: Coventry and Lichfield

Lincolniensis: Lincoln

Londiniensis, Lundoniensis: London

Meneuensis: St David's

Noruicensis, Norwicensis: Norwich

Oxoniensis: Oxford

Pangorensis: Bangor

Petriburgensis: Peterborough

Roffensis, Rouecestrensis: Rochester

Sarisburiensis: Salisbury

Sodorensis: Sodor and Man

Vigorniensis: Worcester

Westmonasteriensis: Westminster

Wigorniensis: Worcester

Wintoniensis: Winchester

BISHOPRICS IN IRELAND

Acadensis, Achadensis: Achonry

Achadiensis, Achatensis: Aghadoe

Achathkonrensis: Achonry

Aelfinensis: Elphin

Airthermuighensis: Armoy

Akadensis: Achonry

Alachdensis, Aladensis: Killala

Alfinensis: Elphin

Anachdunensis: Annaghdown

Aondruimensis: Nendrum

Aras-Celtair: Down

Archfordensis: Ardfert

Archmorensis: Ardmore

Arcmacensis: Armagh (Archbishopric)

Arcmorensis: Ardmore

Ardacensis, Ardachadensis, Ardahachtensis: Ardagh

Ardartensis: Ardfert

Ardbrekensis: Ardbracchan, Meath

Ardcarnia: Ardcarne

Ardecadensis: Ardagh

Ardefertensis: Ardfert

Ardmacanus: Armagh

Ardmorensis: Ardmore

Ardsrathensis: Ardstraw, Ardrath

Armacanus, Armakensis: Armagh (Archbishopric)

Arthferdensis, Artfertensis: Ardfert

Artmorensis: Ardmore

Athrumensis: Trim

Aunensis: Awn

Baltifordia, Batilfordia: Waterford

Bangorensis: Bangor

Bistagniensis: Glendelough

Brefiniensis: Brefiny, or Kilmore

Campulus Bovis: Aghavoe, or Achadboe, in Ossory

Canic: Kilkenny

Carkagensis: Cork

Cashelensis: Cashel, Munster; Cassiol Irra, Connaught

Casselensis, Cassiliensis: Cashel, Munster (Archbishopric)

Cellaiaro: Cellaiar, in the province of Tuam

Cellumabrath: Kilfenoragh

Cenanus, Cenenensis: Kells

Charensis: Derry

Chienfernensis: Clonfert (?)

Chonderensis: Connor

Cinana: Error for Cluana: *see* Cluainensis

Clochorensis, Clogharensis: Clogher

Cluainensis, Cluanensis: Clonmacnois, or Seven Churches, King's County

Cluanumensis: Cloyne

Cluanuama: Cloyne

Cluenerardensis: Clonard

Coigners: Connor

Conactensis: Connaught

Conamy: Cinani, or Clonmacnois

Conga: Cong

Connerensis, Conorensis: Connor

Corcagiensis, Corcensis: Cork

Corcumrothensis: Corcumroe, afterwards at Kilfenora

Cuilectrannensis: Culfeightrin

Cuilrathensis: Coleraine

Dalnliguirensis, Damhliagensis: Duleek
Darensis: Kildare
Dearrhiensis, Derensis: Derry
Diuilensis: Dublin (Archbishopric)
Domnachmor: Donoghmore
Donnaclsacheling: Dunshaughlin, Meath
Doune: Down, or Dundalethglas
Droncliuensis: Drumclive
Drumorensis: Dromore
Drunimorensis: Dromore
Duacum, Duatum: Kilmacduagh, Galway
Dublinensis: Dublin (Archbishopric)
Dulicensis: Duleeek, Meath
Dundalcensis: Dundalk
Dundalethglas, Dunensis: Down
Dunkerrensis: South Kerry, i.e. Ardfert
Edumabragh: Kilfenoragh
Elnamirand: error for Cluanard, or Clonard
Elphinensis: Elphin
Emiliensis: Emly
Enabrensis: error for Fennabrensis, Kilfenoragh (?)
Enachdunensis: Annaghdown, or Enaghdune
Ergallia: Clogher
Eripolensis: Jerpont
Favoria: Fore, Meath
Fernensis: Ferns
Finnabrensis: Fenabore, or Kilfenoragh
Furensis: Fore, Foure
Fynnaborensis: Fenabore, or Kilfenoragh
Gathay, Insula de: Inniscathay, or Inniscattery
Glandelacensis: Glendelough, or Glendalach
Hymlacensis: Imelaco: Ibhair, or Emly
Iarmuanensis: of West Munster
Imelacensis: Imelaca: Ibair, Emly
Inmelettensis: Emly
Iniscathrensis: Inis: scattery
Kenanusensis, Kenlis: Kells, Meath
Kildabewensis: error for Killdalua (?)
Kendaluam: Killaloe
Kildarensis: Kildare
Kildareuensis: Killaloe (?)
Kildelo: Killaloe
Kilfenorensis: Kilfenoragh
Kilkenensis: Kilkenny
Kill: Aladh, Killaleth: Killala, Co. Mayo
Killdalua: Killaloe
Killmunduach: Kilmaceduagh, or Kilmacough
Killruaidhensis: Kilroot
Kilmorensis: Kilmore, Kilmore Moy
Kyenfernensis: Clonfert (?)
Kynlathensis: Killala
Kyry: Kerry
Ladensis: Killala, Co. Mayo
Laginiensis: Leinster

Laonacensis: Killaloe
Laoniensis: Killaloe
Leclinensis, Leghelensis, Leghglensis: Leighlin
Lessemore: Lismore
Lethlegensis: Leighlin
Limricensis: Limerick
Lismorensis: Lismore
Lugdunensis: Louth, united to Clogher
Lugundunensis: Louth
Lumbricensis, Lumniacensis, Lumpniacensis: Limerick
de Mageo, Maigonensis: Mayo
Maghbilensis: Moville, Co. Down
Medensis: Meath
Melicensis: Emly
Middensis, Midiensis: Meath
Ofiachramuy: afterwards at Killala
Omanensis: Omaine, Clonfert
Osseriensis: Ossory
Rapotensis, Rathbocensis, Rathbotensis: Raphoe
Rathasithensis: Rashee
Rathaspicensis: Ratehaspuicinnic
Rathbothensis: Raphoe
Rathlucensis, Rathlurensis: Rathluraigh
Rathmurbhulgensis: Rathmurbholg
Rechrannensis: Rathlin
Rosalither: Rosscarbery, united to Cork
Roscomon: Roscommon
Roscreensis: Roscrea
Rosensis: Ross
Rossiensis: Roscrea
Ruscomia: Roscommon
Saigerensis: Saiger, Seirkeran, translated to Aghavoe, in Ossory
Skrynensis: Skreene
Slanensis: Slane, Meath
Tarensis, Tharensis: Derry
Thuenensis: Down
Tighbonensis: Tighbohin
Tiramalgaid: Tirawley
Triburnensis: another name for the See of Brefiny, or Kilmore
Trimensis: Trim, Meath
Tuaimensis, Tuenensis: Tuam (Archbishopric)
Tullagensis: Tulach
Tume: Tuam
Ulagensis: Down
Umalia: Achadfobhair, Mayo
Wasefordensis: Wexford
Waterfordensis: Waterford
Wexfordensis: Wexford
Ymlagh: Emly

Index